# GIACOMO CASANOVA

*Chevalier de Seingalt*

# HISTORY OF MY LIFE

FIRST TRANSLATED INTO ENGLISH IN ACCORDANCE
WITH THE ORIGINAL FRENCH MANUSCRIPT

*by Willard R. Trask*

VOLUMES 5 AND 6

THE JOHNS HOPKINS UNIVERSITY PRESS
*Baltimore and London*

Originally published as *Histoire de Ma Vie,* Edition intégrale, by
Jacques Casanova de Seingalt, Vénitien, by F. A. Brockhaus,
Wiesbaden, Librairie Plon, Paris, 1960. © F. A. Brockhaus,
Wiesbaden, 1960.

This edition originally published in the United States as a Helen
and Kurt Wolff book by Harcourt, Brace & World, Inc.
Johns Hopkins Paperbacks edition, 1997
9 8 7 6 5 4 3


The Johns Hopkins University Press
2715 North Charles Street
Baltimore, Maryland 21218-4363
www.press.jhu.edu

Library of Congress Catalog Card Number 97-70304

A catalog record for this book is available from the British
Library.

ISBN 0-8018-5664-7 (pbk.: Vols. 5 and 6)

# HISTORY OF MY LIFE
## *Volume 5*

# CONTENTS

## *Volume 5*

# LIST OF PLATES

## *Volume 5*

# VOLUME 5

## CHAPTER I

*I go to lodge in the house of the chief of the* sbirri. *I spend a delicious night there and completely recover my strength and health. I go to mass; untoward meeting. Violent means I am forced to employ to obtain six zecchini. I am out of danger. My arrival in Munich. What happens to Balbi. I leave for Paris. My arrival in that city; attempt on the life of Louis XV.*

ON A hill some fifty paces away I noticed a shepherd driving a flock of ten or twelve sheep, and I went to him for the information I needed. I asked him what the village was called, and he answered that I was in Valdobbiádene,[1] which surprised me because of the distance I had covered. I asked him the names of the owners of five or six houses I saw in the distance and nearby, and I found that all those whom he named were known to me but were people to whom I must not bring trouble by appearing at their houses. I saw a palace belonging to the Grimanis, in which the head of the family, then a State Inquisitor,[2] was no doubt residing, so I must not show my face there.

I asked the shepherd who was the owner of a red house I saw at some distance, and I was very much surprised when I learned that it belonged to the so-called Capitano della Campagna, who is the chief of the *sbirri*. I said good-by to the peasant and mechanically walked down the hill. It is inconceivable that I went to that terrible house, which both reason and nature told me to shun. I went straight to it, and I know for a fact that I did not go to it on purpose. If it is true that we all have a beneficent invisible being who guides us aright,* as happened, though rarely, to Socrates, I must believe that what made me go there was such a being. I admit that in all my life I never took so daring a step.

I enter the house with no hesitation and even with no sign of embarrassment. In the courtyard I see a little boy playing with a top; I ask him where his father is; and instead of answering he goes for his mother. In a moment I see a very pretty pregnant woman, who asks me most politely what I want with her husband, who is not there.

"I am as sorry that *my fellow sponsor* is not at home as I am glad to make the acquaintance of his beautiful wife."

"*Your fellow sponsor?* Then am I not speaking to His Excellency Vitturi? [4] He told me that you have been so good as to promise him you would stand sponsor to the chiid which you see I am carrying. I am most happy to make your acquaintance, and my husband will be very much disappointed that he was not at home."

"I hope he will not be long in coming, since I want to ask him to favor me with a bed for tonight. I dare not go anywhere in the condition you see me in."

"You shall have a bed even so, and a decent supper, and my husband will call on you when he gets back, to thank you for the honor you have done us. He left an hour ago on horseback with all his men, I do not expect him home again for three or four days."

---

* *Saepe revocans raro impellens.* (C.'s note in the margin.)[3]

"Why will he stay away so long?"

"Haven't you heard that two prisoners have escaped from the Leads? One is a patrician and the other a person named Casanova. He received a letter from Messer Grande ordering him to search for them; if he finds them he will take them to Venice, and if he doesn't he will come home; but he will look for them for at least three days."

"I am very sorry to hear it, *my dear fellow sponsor;* but I would not wish to put you to any trouble, and the more so since I want to go to bed at once."

"You shall do so, and my mother will wait on you. What is the matter with your knees?"

"I had a fall hunting on the mountain; they are bad scrapes, and I have lost blood."

"Poor gentleman! But my mother will look after you."

She called her, and after telling her everything I needed she left. The pretty constable's wife had not learned much of the trade, for nothing could seem more like a fairy tale than the story I told her. Hunting in a taffeta coat! On horseback in white stockings! Without a cloak or a servant! When her husband came back he would laugh at her. Her mother looked after me with all the courtesy I could have expected among people of the greatest distinction. She treated me like a mother and always addressed me as "son" while she was dressing my wounds. If my soul had been at peace I should have given her unmistakable proof of my own courtesy and my gratitude; but the place where I was and the dangerous role I was playing preoccupied me too gravely.

After examining my knees and my thighs she said I would have to bear a little pain but that in the morning I would be cured; I had only to see that the wet napkins she put on my wounds stayed there all night and to sleep without moving. I ate a good supper and then surrendered to her ministrations; I fell asleep while she was working on me, for I do not remember having seen her leave; she must have undressed me as if I were a child; I said nothing and thought nothing. I ate to supply my want of food, and I fell asleep yielding to a need which I could not resist. I had no consciousness of anything which required the exercise of reason. It was the first hour of night when I fell asleep, and when I woke in the morning to hear the clock striking thirteen[5] I thought I was under a spell, for I felt as if I had only just fallen asleep. It took me more than five minutes to return to my senses, to summon my mind back to its proper functions, to convince myself that my situation was real, and, in a word, to pass from sleep to real waking; but as soon as I came to myself I quickly got rid of the napkins, amazed to see that my wounds were perfectly dry. I dressed in less than four minutes, I put my hair in a bag without help, and I left my room, which was wide open; I went down the stairs, crossed the courtyard, and walked away from the house, paying no attention to two men who were standing there and who could be nothing but *sbirri*. I left a place where I had found courtesy, good food, health, and the complete recovery of my strength, with a feeling of horror which made me tremble, for I saw that I had most imprudently exposed myself to the most obvious of dangers. I was amazed that I had entered the house and even more amazed that I had been able to leave it, and I thought it impossible that I was not being followed. I walked for five hours on end through woods and over mountains, meeting no one but a few peasants and never looking back.

It was not yet noon when, still walking on, I heard a bell ringing. Looking down from the height on which I was, I saw the little church from which the sound came, and, seeing people going in, I thought it must be a mass; and I suddenly wanted to hear it. When a man is in distress, whatever comes into his mind seems an inspi-

ration. It was All Souls' Day. I go down, I enter the
church, and I am surprised to see Signor Marcantonio
Grimani,[6] the nephew of the State Inquisitor, with his
wife Signora Maria Pisani. I saw that they were astonished. I bowed to them and I heard the mass. When
I left the church the Signore followed me, the Signora
remained inside. He approaches me and says:

"What are you doing here? Where is your companion?"

"I gave him seventeen lire[7] I had so that he could get
away in another direction which is easier, while I am
making for the border this way, which is more difficult,
and I haven't a soldo. If Your Excellency would be so
good as to give me some assistance, I could manage
better."

"I cannot give you anything; but you will find some
monks who will not let you die of hunger. But tell me
how you succeeded in breaking through the Leads."

"It is an interesting story, but a very long one; and
*meanwhile the hermits may have eaten everything up.*"

So saying, I bowed to him. Despite my extreme need
his refusal to give me anything pleased me. I felt I was
much more of a gentleman than the Signore. I learned
in Paris that when his wife heard of it she reproached
him in strong terms. There is no doubt that right feelings
are found in women more often than in men.

I walked until sunset, when, tired and starving, I
stopped at a solitary house which looked promising. I
asked to speak to the owner, and the caretaker's wife told
me he had gone to a wedding on the other side of the
river[8] and would spend the night there, but that she had
orders to welcome his friends. So she gave me an excellent
supper and a very good bed. I discovered from the
addresses on a number of letters that I was in the
house of Signor Rombenchi,[9] consul of I forget what
country. I wrote to him, and I left my sealed letter

there. After a good sleep I dressed quickly, I crossed the river by promising to pay on my return, and after walking for five hours I dined at a Capuchin[10] monastery. After dinner I walked on until twenty-two o'clock[11] to reach a house the owner of which was a friend of mine. I had learned this from a peasant. I go in, I ask if the master is at home, and I am shown to the door of a room in which he was sitting alone, busily writing. I run to embrace him; but as soon as he sees me he draws back and tells me to leave instantly, giving all sorts of shallow and insulting reasons. I explain my situation to him and my need, and I ask him for sixty zecchini[12] against my note, assuring him that Signor Bragadin will send them to him, and he answers that he cannot help me or even offer me a glass of water, since the sight of me in his house set him shaking with fear that he would incur the displeasure of the Tribunal. He was a man of sixty, a broker on the Exchange, and under obligations to me. His heartless refusal had a different effect on me from Signor Grimani's. Whether from anger or indignation or prompted by the claims of reason or the law of nature, I took him by the collar, advancing my pike toward him and threatening him with death if he raised his voice. Shaking all over, he took a key from his pocket and, pointing to a desk, said that there was money in it and that I had only to take what I wanted, but I told him to open it himself. He did so and opened a drawer in which were gold pieces; I told him to count me out six zecchini.

"You asked for sixty."

"Yes, when I asked them from friendship; but from violence I accept only six, and I will not write you a note. They will be returned to you in Venice, to which I will send an account tomorrow of what you have forced me to do, you coward too base to live."

"Forgive me, I implore you; take it all."

"No. I am going, and I advise you to let me go quietly, or expect that I will come back and set your house on fire."

I walked for two hours and, seeing night falling, I stopped at a peasant's house, where, after eating a wretched supper, I slept on straw. In the morning I bought an old redingote, and I mounted a donkey after buying a pair of boots near Feltre. It was in this style that I passed the shanty known as "La Scala." [13] A guard who was there did not even ask my name. I took a two-horse cart and arrived early at Borgo di Valsugana, [14] where I found the inn for which I had given Father Balbi directions. If he had not come up to me I should not have recognized him. A green redingote and a hat worn with the brim turned down over a cotton cap disguised him completely. He told me that a farmer had given them to him in exchange for his cloak, with a zecchino to boot, and that he had arrived there that morning and had been well treated. He ended his story most generously by saying that he was not expecting me *because he had not supposed I had intended to keep my promise to him.* I spent the whole of the following day at the inn, never leaving my bed and writing more than twenty letters to Venice, ten or twelve of them circular letters in which I told what I had had to do to obtain six zecchini. The monk wrote impertinent letters to Father Barbarigo, his Superior, and to his patrician brothers, and love letters to the servant girls who had caused his ruin. I took the lace off my coat and sold my hat, for their richness made me too conspicuous.

The next day I slept at Pergine, [15] where a young Count d'Alberg [16] came to see me, having learned—though I never found out how—that we were escaping from the State of Venice. I went on to Trento and from there to Bolzano, where, needing money for a change of clothes and some shirts, I called on an old banker named

Mench,[17] who gave me a reliable man whom I sent to
Venice with a letter to Signor Bragadin, who accredited
it. The banker Mench put me up at an inn where I
spent all the six days which the man took to go and come
back. He came back with a bill of exchange for a hundred
zecchini, drawn on Mench. With the money I bought
a change of clothes; but first I did the same for my
accomplice, who every day gave me some new reason to
find his company intolerable. He said that without him
I would never have escaped and that by virtue of my
promise I owed him half of whatever wealth I might
come to possess. He was in love with all the servant girls,
and since he had neither the figure nor the face to make
them kind and submissive, they received his approaches
by giving him hearty slaps, which he received with
exemplary patience. It was my only amusement.

We had taken the post, and on the third day we
arrived in Munich.[18] I went to lodge at the "Stag," [19]
where I immediately learned that two young Venetian
friars, of the Contarini family, had been there for some
time with Count Pompei of Verona; but not having the
honor of their acquaintance and no longer needing to
find monks in order to live, I did not trouble to make
my bow to them. I went and made it to Countess Coronini,[20] whom I had met in Venice at the Convent of
Santa Giustina[21] and who was highly regarded at Court.

The illustrious lady, who was then seventy, received
me very well and promised that she would immediately
apply to the Elector[22] to have me granted asylum. The
next morning, after keeping her promise, she told me
that the sovereign had no reservations about me and that
I could consider myself safe in Munich and anywhere in
Bavaria, but that there was no safety for Father Balbi,
who, as a Somaschian and a fugitive, could be claimed
by the Somaschians[23] of Munich, and that the Elector
did not want to have any difficulties with monks. So the

Countess advised me to get him out of the city as soon
as possible to rehabilitate himself elsewhere and thus
avoid any trouble which his fellow monks might be preparing for him.

Feeling that both conscience and honor obliged me to
look after the wretch, I went to the Elector's confessor[24]
and asked him for a letter of recommendation for the
monk to some town in Swabia. The confessor, who was
a Jesuit, received me as badly as possible. He said in
passing that my reputation was well known in Munich.
I asked him firmly if he was telling me this as good news
or bad, and he did not answer. He simply walked away,
and a priest told me that he had gone to verify a miracle
of which all Munich was talking.

"The Empress," [25] he said, "the widow of Charles
VII, whose body is still exposed to public view, has warm
feet though she is dead."

He said that I could go and see the wonder for myself.
Most eager to be able to boast at last that I had witnessed
a miracle, and one which was of the greatest interest to
me since my feet were always icy, I go to see the illustrious corpse, which did indeed have warm feet, but
it was because of a hot stove[26] which stood very near
her defunct Imperial Majesty. A dancer who was there
and who knew me quite well came up and congratulated
me on my good fortune, which was already being talked
of throughout the city. The dancer invited me to dinner
and I accepted; his name was Michele dall'Agata,[27] and
his wife was the same Gardela[28] whom, sixteen years
earlier, I had known in the house of old Malipiero[29] who
had hit me with his cane because I was fooling with
Teresa.[30] La Gardela, who had become a celebrated
dancer and was still very pretty, was delighted to see
me and to hear the whole story of my escape from my
own lips. She wanted to do something for the monk,
and she offered me a letter of recommendation for

Augsburg addressed to Canon Bassi, of Bologna, her friend and Dean of the Chapter of St. Moritz.[31] She wrote the letter then and there and, as she handed it to me, assured me I need no longer be concerned for the monk, for she was certain that the Dean would take care of him and even patch things up for him in Venice.

Delighted to get rid of him in such an honorable way, I run to the inn, I tell him the story, and I hand him the letter, and I promise not to abandon him if the Dean does not give him a good reception. I sent him off at daybreak the next morning in a good carriage.

He wrote me four days later that the Dean could not have received him more cordially, had put him up in his own house, had outfitted him as an abbé, had presented him to the Prince-Bishop, who was a Darmstadt,[32] and had persuaded the city to grant him asylum. In addition the Dean had promised to keep him in his house until he had obtained his secularization into the priesthood from Rome, together with freedom to return to Venice, for as soon as he was no longer a monk he ceased to be guilty before the Tribunal of the State Inquisitors. Father Balbi ended his letter by asking me to send him a few zecchini for pocket money, for he was too much of a gentleman, he said, to ask money from the Dean, who was not gentleman enough to offer him any. I did not answer him.

Left alone and in peace, I turned to recovering my health, for the fatigue and the sufferings I had undergone had given me nervous spasms, which might become very serious. In less than three weeks a good diet restored me to perfect health. During these days Madame Rivière[33] came from Dresden with her son and her two daughters, the elder[34] of whom she was taking to Paris to be married. Her son had finished his studies and was highly accomplished in every way, and her elder daughter, whom she was going to marry to an actor, combined the prettiest

figure possible with a talent for dancing; she played the
harpsichord perfectly and she possessed the social graces
together with all the charms of youth. The whole family
was delighted to see me, and I thought myself most
fortunate when, anticipating my wish, Madame Rivière
gave me to understand that she would welcome my company as far as Paris. There was no question of asking
me to pay my share, and I had to accept the gift as it
was given. Since my plan was to establish myself in
Paris, I took this intervention of Fortune as a prophecy
that success awaited me in the career of adventurer on
which I was about to embark in the only city in the universe in which the Blind Goddess dispensed her favors
to those who trusted in her completely. I was not mistaken, as the reader will see at the proper time and
place; but Fortune's bounty was of no use to me, I
spoiled everything by my thoughtless behavior. Fifteen
months of the Leads gave me time to learn all the defects
of my character; but I should have had to stay there
longer to adopt principles which would remedy them.

Madame Rivière very much wanted me to go with her,
but she could not put off her departure, and I had to
wait for an answer from Venice and for money, which,
however, could not be long in coming. Having made sure
that she would spend a week in Strassburg, I felt con-
fident that I would catch up with her, and I saw her
leave Munich on December 18th.

I received the bill of exchange I was expecting from
Venice two days after her departure, I paid my small
debts, and I at once set out for Augsburg, not so much
to see Father Balbi as to meet the worthy Dean Bassi,
whose treatment of him had been princely. Reaching
Augsburg seven hours from the time I left Munich, I
went at once to call on the Dean. He was not at home;
I found Father Balbi, dressed as an abbé, bareheaded,
and with hair powdered, which made his skin look even

darker. Not yet forty, the man was not only ugly but had a cast of countenance which indicated baseness, cowardice, insolence, and stupid malice. I saw that he was well lodged and well served and had books and all the requisites for writing; I congratulated him, I told him he was fortunate and I no less fortunate in having been able to procure him all these advantages together with the expectation of soon becoming a secular priest. Far from thanking me, he said I had got rid of him, and when he learned that I was going to Paris he said he would much rather go with me, since in Augsburg he was bored to death.

"What do you expect to do in Paris?"

"What will you do there yourself?"

"I will turn my talents to account."

"So will I mine."

"Then you have no need of me. Go there yourself. The people who are taking me there might not want my company if I had you with me."

"You promised not to abandon me."

"Do you call it abandoning someone to leave him with everything he needs?"

"Everything? I haven't a soldo."

"You don't need money. And if you think you need some for your pleasures, ask your brothers[35] for it."

"They haven't any."

"Your friends, then."

"I have no friends."

"So much the worse for you; it is proof that you have never been a friend to anyone."

"You will let me have a few zecchini."

"I have none left."

"Wait for the Dean; he will be back tomorrow. Talk to him, persuade him to lend me money. Tell him I will return it to him."

"I will not wait, for I am leaving at once and I should

never be so imprudent as to tell him to give you money.''

After this acid dialogue I left him; I went to the post, and I set out, very ill pleased to have brought such good luck to a man who did not deserve it. At the end of March in Paris I received a letter from the generous and honorable Dean Bassi in which he told me that Father Balbi had absconded from his house with one of his maidservants, taking a sum of money, a gold watch, and twelve silver table services; he did not know where he had gone.

Toward the end of the year I learned that he had gone with the Dean's maid to Coire, the capital of Grisons, where he asked to be accepted into the Calvinist church and to be recognized as the legal husband of the lady who accompanied him, but when it was discovered that he was incapable of earning his living he was turned away. When he came to the end of his money the maid whom he had deceived left him after giving him several beatings. Not knowing where to turn or how to earn money, Father Balbi then decided to go to Brescia, a city belonging to the Republic,[36] where he went to the Governor, informed him of his name, his escape, and his repentance, and asked him to take him under his protection and secure his pardon. The Governor's protection began by clapping the stupid petitioner into jail, then he wrote to the Tribunal, asking what to do with him; pursuant to the orders he received he sent him in chains to Messer Grande,[37] who delivered him to the Tribunal, who sent him back to the Leads, where he did not find Count Asquin, who, in pity for his age, had been sent to ''the Four''[38] three months after my escape. I learned five or six years later that the Tribunal, after keeping Father Balbi under the Leads for two years, had sent him to his monastery, where his Superior had packed him off to the monastery of the Order near Feltre, which was built on a hill; but Father Balbi re-

mained there only six months. He escaped, went to Rome,
and threw himself at the feet of the Rezzonico[39] who
was then Pope, who absolved him from his monastic vows,
and he then went back to his native country as a priest,
where he led a miserable life because he could never behave himself. He died in poverty in the year 1785.

At the "Spirit"[40] in Strassburg I rejoined Madame
Rivière and her charming family; she received me with
tokens of unfeigned pleasure. We spent several days
there and left for Paris in a good berlin, in which I
thought I should do my share by keeping the company
in perpetual high spirits. Mademoiselle Rivière's charms
ravished my soul, but I was in a humiliating position
and I should have considered that I was failing in respect
to her mother and in what I owed to my situation if I
had shown the least sign of any amorous inclination.
Although too young for it, I enjoyed playing the role of
father and attending to all the things which must be
done if a party is to travel comfortably and spend its
nights in good beds.

So we reached Paris on the morning of January 5,
1757, which was a Wednesday, and I got out at the
house of my friend Balletti,[41] who welcomed me with
open arms, assuring me that though I had not written
to him he was expecting me, for since my escape necessarily entailed my leaving Venice and even being exiled,
he could not imagine that I would choose any other place
to stay in than a city in which I had spent two years enjoying all the pleasures of life. Joy reigned in the house
as soon as my arrival was known; and I embraced his
father and mother, whom I found treating me just as
they had done when I left in 1752. But what struck me
was Mademoiselle Balletti, my friend's sister. She was
fifteen years old [42] and had become very pretty; her
mother's teaching had given her everything that a fond
and highly intelligent mother can give her daughter in

the way of talents, graces, good behavior, and knowledge of society. After renting a room in the same street,[43]
I set off for the Hôtel de Bourbon[44] to call on the Abbé
de Bernis, who was the head[45] of the Ministry of Foreign
Affairs, and I had good reason to hope that he would
put me on the road to fortune. I go there, I am told that
he is at Versailles; impatient to see him, I go to the
Pont Royal,[46] I take the kind of carriage called a "chamber pot,"[47] and I reach Versailles at half past six.
Learning that he had gone back to Paris with the Count
of Cantillana,[48] the Neapolitan Ambassador, I had no
choice but to do likewise. So I go back in the same carriage; but scarcely have I reached the gate before I see
a great crowd running in all directions in the utmost
confusion, and I hear people crying to right and left:

*"The King has been assassinated, His Majesty has just
been killed."*

My terrified coachman thinks only of going on; but
my carriage is stopped, I am ordered out of it and put
in the guardhouse, where in three or four minutes I see
more than a score of people arrested, all just as astonished and just as guilty as I am. I did not know what
to think, and since I do not believe in witchcraft I believed I was dreaming. There we were, looking at each
other and not daring to speak; surprise overpowered
us, and every one of us, though innocent, was afraid.

But four or five minutes later an officer came in and,
after begging our pardons most politely, said that we
could leave.

"The King," he said, "is wounded and has been carried to his apartment. The assassin,[49] whom no one knows,
has been arrested. Monsieur de la Martinière[50] is being
looked for everywhere."

No sooner was I back in my carriage, and very glad to
be there, than a well-dressed young man with a face
which speaks eloquently in his favor asks me to take

him with me, on condition that he pay his half; but despite the laws of politeness I refuse to do him the service. There are moments when one must not be polite.

During the three hours it took me to get back to Paris, for "chamber pots" travel very slowly, at least two hundred couriers passed me at full gallop. I saw another every minute, and each courier was shouting the news he carried to the four winds. The first few said what I knew; a quarter of an hour later I learned that the King had been bled, then I learned that the wound was not mortal, and an hour later that the wound was so slight that His Majesty could even go to Trianon if he wished.

Bearing this interesting news I went to Silvia's, where I found the whole family at table, for it was not yet eleven o'clock. I enter, and I find everyone in consternation.

"I have just this moment come," I said, "from Versailles."

"The King has been assassinated."

"Not at all; he could go to Trianon if he wished. Monsieur de la Martinière has bled him, the assassin has been arrested, and he will be burned after being drawn and quartered alive."

At the news, which Silvia's servants immediately spread, all the neighbors came in to hear me tell the story, and it was to me that the whole neighborhood owed sleeping well that night. In those days the French imagined that they loved their King, and they went through all the motions of it; today we have come to know them somewhat better. But at bottom the French are always the same. By its very nature their nation is always in a state of eruption; there is no reality among them, everything is mere appearance. It is a vessel which only asks to move and which demands wind, and whatever wind may be blowing is good. And in fact the arms of Paris display a ship.

## CHAPTER II

*The Minister of Foreign Affairs. Monsieur de*
*Boulogne, the Comptroller-General. The Duke*
*of Choiseul. The Abbé de Laville. Monsieur*
*Pâris-Duverney. Establishment of the lottery.*
*My brother comes to Paris from Dresden; he*
*is received into the Academy of Painting.*

ONCE MORE I am in the great city of Paris and,
since I can no longer count on my own country, obliged
to make my fortune there. I had spent two years in
Paris; but since at that time my only object was to enjoy
life I had not studied the city. This second time I had
to pay my court to those with whom the Blind Goddess
made her abode. I saw that to accomplish anything I
must bring all my physical and moral faculties into
play, make the acquaintance of the great and the powerful, exercise strict self-control, and play the chameleon
to all those whom I should see it was my interest to
please. To follow these principles I saw that I must
scrupulously avoid what is known in Paris as "dubious
company" and renounce all my old ways and any pretensions which could make me enemies who could easily
give me the reputation of being a man not fit to be
trusted with important business. As the result of these

meditations I decided to practice a systematic reserve in both act and word which would lead to my being considered even more fit for affairs of consequence than I had any reason to suppose I was. As for living expenses, I could count on the hundred écus[1] a month which Signor Bragadin would never have failed to send me. It was enough. I had only to see that I was well dressed and decently lodged; but to begin with I needed a sum of money, for I had neither suits nor shirts.

So the next day I went back to the Palais Bourbon. Being sure that the porter would tell me the Minister was engaged, I went there with a note which I left for him. I announced my arrival and told him where I was lodging. To say more would have been to say too much. Meanwhile I found that wherever I went I had to tell the story of my escape; it was a task, for it took two hours; but I felt I must oblige those who were eager to hear it, for their eagerness could arise only from their lively interest in myself.

At supper at Silvia's I found all the evidence of friendship I could wish for, but in a calmer atmosphere than on the previous evening; and I was greatly impressed by the merits of her daughter. At the age of fifteen she had all the qualities which captivate. I congratulated her mother who had fostered them in her, and at the time I did not think of defending myself from her charms: I was not yet at ease enough to suppose that they could assail me. I left early, impatient to see what the Minister would say in reply to my note.

I received his answer at eight o'clock. He said that I would find him alone at two o'clock in the afternoon. He received me as I expected he would. He conveyed to me not only his pleasure over my triumph but all the joy which he felt in having an opportunity to be of use to me. He at once told me that as soon as he had learned of my escape by a letter from M. M. he had felt certain I would go nowhere but to Paris and that my first visit would be to him. He showed me the letter in which she[2] informed him of my arrest, and her last letter, in which she told him the story of my escape as she had heard it. She said that since she could no longer hope to see either of the two men on whom alone she could count, her life had become a burden to her. She lamented that she did not have the resource of devotion. She said that C. C. often came to see her and that she was not happy with the man who had married her.

Having looked through what M. M. wrote him about my escape and finding that all the details were wrong, I promised to send him the true story of it. He took me at my word, promising that he would send it on to our unfortunate friend and giving me a roll of a hundred louis[3] with the most perfect tact. He promised to keep me in mind and to let me know when he would need to speak to me. With the money I outfitted myself; and a week later I sent him the story of my escape, giving him permission to have it copied and to use it as he thought best to interest anyone who could be helpful to me. Three weeks later he sent for me and told me that he had spoken about me to Signor Erizzo,[4] the Venetian Ambassador, who had found nothing to say against me; but that, not wanting to compromise himself with the State Inquisitors, he would not receive me. I did not need him. He said that he had given my story to Madame la Marquise,[5] who knew me and with whom he would try to obtain me an interview, and in closing he said that when I went to see Monsieur de Choiseul,[6] I would be well received, as I would be by the Comptroller-General Monsieur de Boulogne,[7] with whom, if I used my head, I should be able to work out something substantial.

"He will himself," he said, "give you hints, and you will see that 'the man who is listened to is the man who obtains.' Try to think up some project profitable to the royal exchequer, avoiding anything complicated or chimerical, and if what you write is not too long I will give you my opinion on it.''

I left him full of gratitude, but at a loss to find a way to increase the King's revenues. Having not the faintest notion of finances, no matter how I racked my brains all the ideas which came to me were only for new taxes, and since they all struck me as odious or absurd I rejected them all.

My first visit[8] was to Monsieur de Choiseul, as soon as I learned that he was in Paris. He received me at his toilet table, where he was writing while his hair was being dressed. The courtesy he showed me was to interrupt his letter at short intervals, asking me questions, which I answered, but to no purpose, for instead of listening he went on writing. Now and again he looked at me; but that meant nothing, for the eyes see, they do not hear. Nevertheless the Duke was a man of great intelligence.

After finishing his letter he said to me in Italian that the Abbé de Bernis had told him part of the story of my escape.

''Tell me how you managed to bring it off.''

''The story, Monseigneur, takes two hours, and I have the impression that Your Excellency is in a hurry.''

''Tell it to me briefly.''

''It is the very shortest version of it which takes two hours.''

''You can tell me the details another time.''

''Without the details the story is not interesting.''

''Of course. But one can abbreviate anything as much as one wishes.''

''Very well. I will tell Your Excellency that the State Inquisitors had me imprisoned under the Leads.[9] At the end of fifteen months and five days I made a hole in the roof; I entered the Chancellery[10] through a dormer and broke open the door to it; I went down to the Piazza; I took a gondola which carried me to the mainland, whence I went to Munich. From there I came to Paris, where I have the honor to pay you my respects."

"But—what are the Leads?"

"That, Monseigneur, takes a quarter of an hour."

"How did you manage to make a hole in the roof?"

"That takes half an hour."

"Why were you imprisoned up there?"

"Another half hour."

"I think you are right. The interest of the thing is in the details. I have to go to Versailles. I should be glad to have you call on me from time to time. Meanwhile, think of how I can be of use to you."

On leaving him I went to call on Monsieur de Boulogne. I saw a man entirely different from the Duke in appearance, dress, and manner. He at once congratulated me on the interest which the Abbé de Bernis showed in me and on my financial abilities. I very nearly burst out laughing. He was with an octogenarian whose face bore the stamp of genius.

"Let me have your ideas, either by word of mouth or in writing; you will find me a good pupil and ready to grasp them. This is Monsieur Pâris-Duverney,[11] who needs twenty millions for his Military School.[12] The thing is to find them without burdening the State or embarrassing the royal treasury."

"There is only one God, Monsieur, who has the power of creation."

"I am not God," Monsieur Duverney replied, "yet I have sometimes created, but everything has changed."

"Everything," I answered, "has become more difficult, I know; nevertheless, I have a plan in mind which would yield the King the return on a hundred millions."

"And how much would such a yield cost the King?"

"Only the expense of collecting it."

"Then it is the nation which would supply the revenue?"

"Yes, but voluntarily."

"I know what you have in mind."

"I should be surprised, Monsieur, for I have imparted my idea to no one."

"If you are not otherwise engaged, come to dinner with me tomorrow, and I will show you your project, which is admirable but which is beset with almost insurmountable difficulties. Nevertheless, we will discuss it. Will you come?"

"I will do myself the honor."

"Then I will expect you. I am at Plaisance." [13]

After he left, the Comptroller-General praised his talent and his probity. He was the brother of Pâris de Montmartel,[14] whom secret history made the father of Madame de Pompadour, for he was Madame Poisson's lover at the same time as Monsieur Le Normand.[15]

I went to walk in the Tuileries, reflecting on the fantastic piece of luck which Fortune seemed to be offering me. I am told that twenty millions are needed, I boast that I can furnish a hundred millions without having any idea how to do it, and a famous man, thoroughly experienced in business, invites me to dinner to convince me that he already knows my plan. If he thinks he can worm it out of me I defy him to do it; when he has imparted his own plan to me I shall be at liberty to tell him whether he has guessed mine or not, and if the thing is within my comprehension I will perhaps say something new; if I don't understand a word of it, I will maintain a mysterious silence.

The Abbé de Bernis had described me as a financier only to get me a hearing. Otherwise, I should not have been admitted. I was sorry I did not at least know the jargon of the department. The next morning I took a hackney coach and, in low spirits, told the driver to take me to Monsieur Duverney's at Plaisance. It was a little way beyond Vincennes.

So here I am at the door of the famous man who had

saved France after the crashes brought on by Law's[16] system forty years earlier. I find him with seven or eight gentlemen before a great fire. He announces me by my name, adding that I am a friend of the Minister of Foreign Affairs[17] and of the Comptroller-General. He then introduces me to his guests, giving three or four of them the title of Intendant of Finances.[18] I bow, and instantly fall to worshiping Harpocrates.[19]

After touching on the Seine, which was frozen more than a foot deep, on Monsieur de Fontenelle,[20] who had just died, on Damiens, who refused to confess anything, and on the five millions which his trial would cost the King, the conversation turned to the war and then to praise of Monsieur de Soubise,[21] whom the King had chosen as commander. This subject led to the cost of the war and to the resources for maintaining it and the country. I spent an hour and a half in boredom, for all their discussions were so stuffed with the technical terms of their profession that I understood nothing. After an hour and a half at table, where I opened my mouth only to eat, we went into a drawing room, where Monsieur Duverney left the company and took me to his study with a good-looking man of about fifty years of age whom he had presented to me by the name of Calzabigi.[22] A moment later two Intendants of Finances came in too. Smiling, Monsieur Duverney put in my hands a folio notebook, saying:

"There is your plan."

I see on the title page: "Lottery[23] of ninety lots, of which the winning lots, drawn each month at random, can only fall on five numbers," etc., etc. I hand it back to him and I do not hesitate an instant before telling him that it is my plan.

"Monsieur," he said, "you have been forestalled; the scheme is Monsieur de Calzabigi's."

"I am delighted to find that Monsieur and I think

alike: but if you have not adopted it, may I ask you the reason?''

"Several very plausible arguments have been raised against the plan, and the answers to them have been indecisive.''

"I know only one argument in the whole of nature,'' I answered coldly, ''against which I could say nothing. That would be if the King would not allow his subjects to gamble.''

"That argument has no bearing, the King will permit his subjects to gamble. But will they gamble?''

"I am astonished that there should be any doubt of it, if people are sure that they will be paid if they win.''

"Then let us suppose that they will gamble if they are certain that there is money with which to pay. How is the money to be raised?''

"The royal treasury. A decree of the Council. It is enough if the King is believed able to pay a hundred millions.''

"A hundred millions?''

"Yes, Monsieur. The thing is to dazzle.''

"Then you think the King could lose them?''

"I suppose it possible; but after taking in a hundred and fifty millions. If you know the value of a political calculation, you can only start from there.''

"Monsieur, I am not the only one. Will you not admit that at the very first drawing the King can lose an immense sum?''

"Between possibility and reality there is infinity; but I admit it. If the King loses a great sum at the first drawing, the success of the lottery is assured. It is a misfortune to be desired. Moral forces are calculated like probabilities. You know that all insurance companies[24] are rich. I will prove to you before all the mathematicians in Europe that, granted God is neutral, it is impossible that the King will not make a profit of one in five by this lottery. That is the secret. Will you admit that reason must yield to a mathematical proof?"

"I admit it. But tell me: why cannot the *castelletto*[25] guarantee the King an unfailing profit?"

"There is no *castelletto* in the world which can make it patently and absolutely certain that the King will always profit. The *castelletto* serves only to maintain a temporary balance on one number or two or three, which, being unusually overloaded, could if they came out cause the backer of the lottery a great loss. In such a case the *castelletto* declares the number closed. The *castelletto* could only make you sure of profiting by putting off the drawing until all the chances carried an equal load, and then there would be no lottery, for the drawing might not take place for ten years; and, besides that, I will tell you that under those circumstances the lottery would become a sheer fraud. What saves it from that dishonorable name is the scheduled drawing every month, for then the public is sure that the backer can lose."

"Will you be good enough to speak before the full Council?"[26]

"With pleasure."

"Will you answer all objections?"

"Every one."

"Will you bring me your scheme?"

"I will not communicate my scheme, Monsieur, until its theory is accepted and I am certain that it will be adopted and that I will receive the benefits for which I shall ask."

"But your plan can only be the same as this one."

"I doubt it. In my plan I set forth approximately how much the King will profit each year, and I prove it."

"Then it could be sold to a company which would pay the King a fixed sum."

"I beg your pardon. The lottery can prosper only under a precondition whose effect is absolutely necessary.

I would not go into it to serve a committee which, to augment the profit, would set about increasing the operations, and thereby diminish the eagerness to participate. I am sure of that. The lottery, if I am to have anything to do with it, must be royal or nothing."

"Monsieur de Calzabigi is of the same opinion."

"Nothing could please me better."

"Have you capable people for the *castelletto*?"

"All I need is intelligent machines, of which there must be plenty in France."

"What do you estimate the profit will be?"

"Twenty per cent at each drawing. Whoever brings the King six francs will receive five, and the crush will be so great that, *caeteris paribus* ['other things being equal'], the whole nation will pay the monarch at least five hundred thousand francs a month. I will prove it to the Council on condition that its members are men who, once they have recognized a truth which follows from either a scientific or a political calculation, will no longer hesitate."

Delighted that I could keep my word in everything I had undertaken to do, I got up to go somewhere. When I came back I found them still standing discussing the matter among themselves. Calzabigi came to me and asked in a friendly tone if I included the *quaterna* in my plan. I answered that the public should be free to play the *cinquina*[27] too, but that in my plan I made the stake higher, because the player could not stake on the *quaterna* or the *cinquina* without also playing them as a *terno*.[28] He answered that in his plan he admitted the simple *quaterna* with a profit of fifty thousand for one. I mildly replied that there were very good mathematicians in France, who, when they found that all the chances did not yield equal gains, would profit from collusion. He then clasped my hand, saying that he hoped we could speak further. After giving my address to Monsieur Duverney I left at nightfall satisfied, and certain that I had left a good impression on the old man's mind.

Three or four days later Calzabigi appeared at my lodging, and I received him with the assurance that if I had not presented myself at his door it was because I had not dared. He said straightforwardly that the way I had spoken to the gentlemen had impressed them and that he felt certain that if I would apply to the Comptroller-General we would establish the lottery, which would be most profitable to us.

"I believe it," I answered; "but the profit they would draw from it themselves would be even greater; despite that, they are in no hurry; they have not sent for me, and in any case it is no longer my chief interest."

"You will hear something today. I know that Monsieur de Boulogne has spoken of you to Monsieur de Courteuil." [29]

"I assure you that I made no application to him."

He asked me most cordially to come and dine with him, and I accepted. Just as we were leaving I received a note from the Abbé de Bernis, who wrote me that if I could be at Versailles the next day he would arrange for me to speak with Madame la Marquise, and that I would find Monsieur de Boulogne there at the same time.

It was not vanity but policy which prompted me to give the note to Calzabigi to read. He said that I was in possession of everything I needed to force Duverney himself to start the lottery.

"And your fortune," he said, "is made, if you are not rich enough not to care. We have been moving heaven and earth for two years to get this project accepted, and we have never had anything for our pains but stupid objections, which you demolished last week. Your project must be very much the same as mine. We should join forces, believe me. Remember that, by yourself, you will encounter insurmountable difficulties, and that the 'intelligent machines' you need are not to be found in Paris. My brother[30] will take all the work on himself; use your powers of persuasion, and then be content to enjoy half the emoluments of the directorship while you amuse yourself.''

''Then it is your brother who originated the plan.''

''It is my brother. He is ill, but his mind is perfectly active. We will call on him.''

I saw a man in bed covered with scab; but that did not keep him from eating with appetite, writing, conversing, and performing all the functions of a man in health. He did not appear in public because, in addition to the disfiguring scab, he had constantly to scratch some part of his body, which in Paris is an abomination which is never forgiven, whether the scratching is due to a disease or is simply a bad habit. So Calzabigi told me that he stayed where he was and saw no one because he itched all over and his only relief was to scratch.

''God,'' he said, ''can have given me fingernails for no other purpose.''

''Then you believe in final causes, and I congratulate you. Nevertheless I believe you would scratch even if God had forgotten to give you fingernails.''

I saw him smile, and we discussed our business. In less than an hour I found that he was very intelligent. He was the elder brother and a bachelor. A great arithmetician, thoroughly acquainted with theoretical and practical finance, familiar with the commerce of all nations, versed in history, a wit, a worshiper of the fair sex, and a poet. He was a native of Leghorn; he had worked at Naples in the Ministry, and had come to Paris with Monsieur de l'Hôpital.[31] His brother was also very clever, but inferior to him in every respect.

He showed me a great pile of papers in which he had worked out all the details of the lottery.

''If you think,'' he said, ''that you can do it all with-

out needing me, I congratulate you; but you would be
deluding yourself; for if you have had no practical experience and if you are without trained assistants who
know what they are doing, your theory will get you nowhere. What will you do when you have obtained the
decree? When you speak to the Council you would do
well to set a date after which you will wash your hands
of the matter. Otherwise they will keep putting you off
till the Greek Kalends.[32] I can assure you that Monsieur
Duverney will be very glad to see us join forces. As for
the analytical relations between equal winnings from all
chances, I will convince you that they should not be
taken into account for the *quaterna.*"

Thoroughly persuaded that I should join forces with
them but without letting them know that I considered I
should need their help, I went downstairs with his
brother, who was to introduce me to his wife before dinner. I saw an old woman well known in Paris as La
Générale La Mothe[33] and famous for her former beauty
and her drops, another superannuated lady, known in
Paris as Baroness Blanche,[34] who was still Monsieur de
Vaux's[35] mistress, another who was called La Présidente,[36] and still another, pretty as an angel, who was
called Madame Razzetti,[37] from Piedmont, the wife of a
violinist at the Opéra and then on the best of terms not
only with Monsieur de Fondpertuis,[38] Master of the
Revels,[39] but also with several other gentlemen. I did not
shine at dinner. It was the first I had attended with serious business on my mind. I never once spoke. That evening at Silvia's the company also thought me preoccupied, despite the love which the young daughter of
the house increasingly inspired in me.

Two hours before dawn the next day I set off for Versailles, where Minister de Bernis received me banteringly,
saying he would wager that, but for him, I should never
have discovered that I was an expert in finance.

"Monsieur de Boulogne told me that you amazed Monsieur Duverney, who is one of the greatest men in France. Go to him at once, and pay court to him in Paris. The lottery will be established, and it is for you to profit by it. As soon as the King has gone hunting, be in the private apartments,[40] and when I see the opportunity I will 'show you off' to Madame la Marquise. After that you will go to the Foreign Affairs office and introduce yourself to the Abbé de Laville;[41] he is first secretary, he will give you a good reception.''

Monsieur de Boulogne promised me that as soon as Monsieur Duverney informed him that the Council of the Military School had agreed, he would have the decree establishing the lottery issued, and he encouraged me to inform him of any other ideas which I might have.

At noon Madame de Pompadour came to the private apartments with the Prince of Soubise and my patron, who immediately pointed me out to the great lady. After curtsying to me, as was the custom, she said that she had read the story of my escape and had found it most interesting.

''Those gentlemen *up there*,'' [42] she said with a smile, ''are greatly to be feared. Do you visit the Ambassador?''

''I cannot better show him my respect than by not going there.''

''I hope that you are now thinking of settling among us.''

''Nothing could make me happier; but I need patronage, and I have learned that in this country it is accorded only to talent. That discourages me.''

''I think that you need set no limit to your hopes, for you have good friends. I shall be glad to do what I can for you if I have an opportunity.''

The Abbé de Laville received me very well and did not leave until he had assured me that he would have me in mind as soon as an opportunity arose. I went to dine at an inn, where a good-looking abbé came up and asked me if we might dine together. Politeness did not permit

me to refuse. As we sat down at table, he congratulated
me on the excellent reception which the Abbé de Laville
had accorded me.

"I was there," he said, "writing a letter; but I heard
almost all the kind things he said to you. May I ask you
to whom you owe your introduction to the worthy
Abbé?"

"If you are extremely curious to know, Monsieur
l'Abbé, I will be glad to tell you."

"Oh, no, no! Pray excuse me."

After this indiscretion he spoke only of indifferent and
amusing things. We left together in a "chamber pot"
and reached Paris at eight o'clock, where, after promising
to exchange visits and telling each other our names, we
parted. He got out in the Rue des Bons Enfants and I
went to supper at Silvia's in the Rue du Petit Lion. That
woman among women congratulated me on my new acquaintances and advised me to cultivate them.

At home I found a note from Monsieur Duverney asking me to be at the Military School the next morning at
eleven o'clock. At nine o'clock in came Calzabigi, whom
his brother had sent to me with a large sheet of paper
containing the arithmetical table of the entire lottery,
which I could explain to the Council. It was a calculation
of the probabilities which, set over against the certainties,
proved what I had only stated. In substance it showed
that the lottery would have come out exactly even so far
as paying the winning tickets was concerned if instead
of five numbers six should be drawn. Only five were to
be drawn, and this made it scientifically certain that the
advantage would always be one in five, which came to
eighteen in ninety, which was the total number of lots in
the lottery. This demonstration had the corollary that the
lottery could not be maintained with drawings of six
numbers, since the operating expenses amounted to a
hundred thousand écus.

Thus instructed, and thoroughly persuaded that I

ought to follow this plan, I proceeded to the Military
School, where we at once went into conference. Monsieur
d'Alembert[43] had been asked to be present as the great
master of universal arithmetic. His presence would not
have been considered necessary if Monsieur Duverney had
been by himself; but there were some who, in order to
avoid accepting the result of a political calculation, stub-
bornly denied its validity. The conference lasted three
hours.

After my argument, which took only half an hour,
Monsieur de Courteuil summarized all that I had said,
and an hour was spent in nugatory objections which I
easily refuted. I said that if the art of calculation in
general was properly the art of finding the expression
of a single relation arising from the combination of
several relations, the same definition applied to moral
calculation, which was as certain as mathematical calculation. I convinced them that without that certainty the
world would never have had insurance companies, which,
all of them rich and flourishing, laugh at Fortune and at
the weak minds which fear her. I ended by saying that
there was not a man at once learned and honorable in the
world who could offer to be at the head of this lottery
on the understanding that it would win at every drawing,
and that if a man should appear with the temerity to give
them that assurance they should turn him out, because
either he would not keep his promise or, if he kept it, he
would be a scoundrel.

Monsieur Duverney rose and said that in any case
they could always abolish the lottery. After signing a
paper which Monsieur Duverney presented to them, all
the gentlemen left. Calzabigi came the next morning to
tell me that the thing was settled and that it was now
only a matter of waiting for the decree to be issued. I
promised him I would call on Monsieur de Boulogne
every day and that I would have him made a director

as soon as I learned from Monsieur Duverney what my emoluments were to be.

The proposal made to me, which I accepted at once, was six collector's offices and an income of four thousand francs[44] a year secured by the lottery itself. It was the return on a capital of a hundred thousand francs, which I was at liberty to withdraw if I relinquished the offices, since the capital represented my guarantee.

The decree of the Council was issued a week later. The direction was given to Calzabigi, with emoluments of three thousand francs per drawing and a yearly income of four thousand francs—the same as mine—and the main office of the enterprise in the Hôtel de la Loterie in the Rue Montmartre. Of my six offices I at once sold five for two thousand francs each, and I opened the sixth[45] in luxurious quarters in the Rue Saint-Denis, putting my valet there as chief clerk. He was a young and highly intelligent Italian who had formerly served as valet to the Prince of La Cattolica,[46] the Neapolitan Ambassador. The day for the first drawing was set, and it was announced that all winning tickets would be paid a week after the drawing at the main office of the lottery.

Within twenty-four hours I had bills out to the effect that all winning tickets signed by me would be paid at my office in the Rue Saint-Denis twenty-four hours after the drawing. The result was that everyone came to my office for tickets. My profit consisted in the six percent on receipts. Fifty or sixty clerks from the other offices were stupid enough to complain of my move to Calzabigi. He could only answer them that they were free to catch up with me by doing the same thing, but that they had to have the money.

My receipts at the first drawing[47] were forty thousand livres. An hour after the drawing my clerk brought me the register and showed me that we had to pay out seven-

teen or eighteen thousand livres, all on *ambi*,[48] and I
gave him the money. It was very profitable for my
clerk, who though he asked for nothing always accepted
the tips he was given, and from whom I did not demand
any accounting. The lottery made a profit of six hundred
thousand francs on the total receipts, which amounted
to two millions. Paris alone contributed four hundred
thousand francs. I dined at Monsieur Duverney's the
next day with Calzabigi. We had the pleasure of hearing
him complain that he had made too much. In Paris only
eighteen or twenty *terne* won; though they were small,
they gave the lottery a brilliant reputation. The rage
being on, we expected that the receipts at the next drawing would be twice as large. The good-natured banter
to which I was subjected at table over my scheme delighted me. Calzabigi demonstrated that my inspiration
had assured me of an income of one hundred and twenty
thousand francs a year, which ruined all the other collectors. Monsieur Duverney replied that he had often
acted on similar inspirations and that, in any case, the
collectors were all free to do the same thing, for it could
only make the lottery more highly thought of. The
second time, a *terna* of forty thousand francs forced me
to borrow money. My receipts had been sixty thousand,
but I had to turn them over to the financial agent the day
before the drawing. In all the great houses to which I
went and in theater lobbies, as soon as people saw me
they gave me money, asking me to stake for them as I
chose and to give them the tickets, for they knew nothing
about it. I carried tickets for large and small amounts in
my pockets, from which I let people choose, and I returned home with my pockets full of money. The other
collectors did not have this privilege. They were not of
a sort to be accepted in society. Only I went about in a
carriage of my own; it gave me a reputation and unlimited credit. Paris was, and still is, a city where people

judge everything by appearances; there is not a country in the world where it is easier to make an impression. But now that I have given my reader a full account of the lottery I will mention it only as it comes up.

A month after my arrival in Paris my brother Francesco, the painter, with whom I had left Paris in 1752, arrived from Dresden with Madame Silvestre.[49] He had spent four years there copying all the finest battle paintings in the celebrated gallery.[50] We were very glad to see each other again; but when I offered him the support of all my highly placed acquaintances to get him into the Academy, he answered that he did not need influence. He painted a picture representing a battle, he exhibited it at the Louvre, and he was received [51] by acclamation. The Academy paid him twelve thousand francs for his picture. After his reception my brother became famous, and in twenty-six years he earned nearly a million; however, extravagance and two bad marriages ruined him.

## CHAPTER III

*Count Tiretta, of Treviso. The Abbé de La-
coste. La Lambertini, pretended niece of the
Pope. The name she gives Tiretta. Aunt and
niece. Conversation at the fireside. Execution
of Damiens. Tiretta's mistake. Anger of Madame XXX; reconciliation. I am happy with
Mademoiselle de la M—re. Silvia's daughter.
Mademoiselle de la M—re marries; my jealousy and desperate resolve. Change for the
better.*

---

*AT THE* beginning of March a handsome young man
with an easy manner betokening high birth appeared
before me wearing a redingote and carrying a letter. Yet
something in the way he hands it to me makes me decide
that he is a Venetian. I open it and am delighted. It
was from my dear and worthy friend Signora Manzoni.[1]
She asked my good offices for the bearer, Count Tiretta,[2]
of Treviso, adding that he would tell me his sad story
himself. She was sending me a small chest in which she
said I would find all my manuscripts, for she was sure
she would never see me again.

I at once rose and told him that if he wanted me to
serve him in any way he could not have a stronger
recommendation.

"So tell me, Count, how I can be of use to you."

"I need your friendship. A year ago the Council of
my country chose me to fill a dangerous post. I was

made a director of the pawn office[3] with two other noblemen of my age. The pleasures of the Carnival having left
us in want of money, we used some of what we had in
the till, hoping to return it before we should have to
account for it. Our hope proved vain. The fathers of
my two colleagues, who were richer than mine,[4] saved
them by paying at once, and I, having no means of paying, decided to flee. Signora Manzoni advised me to
entrust myself to you, at the same time asking me to
bring you a small chest, which you shall have today.
I arrived yesterday by the diligence from Lyons; I have
only two louis left; I have shirts, but no suit except the
one I am wearing. I am twenty-five years old, with an
iron constitution and an absolute determination to do
anything to earn an honest living; but I have no train-
ing and no talents; I only play the flute to amuse myself;
I neither speak nor write any language but my own,
and I am not a man of letters. What do you think
you can do with me? I must also tell you that I have
no hope of receiving the slightest help from anybody, least
of all from my father, who to save the honor of the
family will dispose of my inheritance, which I shall have
to renounce for the rest of my life.''

His brief account surprised me, but his sincerity
pleased me. I told him to go at once and bring his baggage
to a room next to mine which was for rent and to order
something to eat in his room.

"All that, my dear Count, will cost you nothing, and
in the meanwhile I will consider your situation. We will
talk tomorrow. I never eat at home. Leave me now, for
I have work to do; and if you go out for a walk beware
of bad company and above all tell no one your business.
You are fond of gambling, I suppose?''

"I loathe it, for it is the cause of half my ruin.''

"And the other half?''

"Women.''

"Women? They are more likely to pay you."

"God grant that I find some who will. At home we have nothing but trollops."

"If you are not too scrupulous in the matter of women you will do very well in Paris."

"What do you mean by scrupulous? I could never be a pimp."

"You are right. By scrupulous I mean a man who can only be loving if he is in love, who cannot bear holding some old harridan in his arms."

"If you mean no more than that, I am not scrupulous. I suspect that a rich woman would find me loving enough even if she were an utter horror."

"Bravo! You will do. Shall you call on the Ambassador?"

"God forbid!"

"At the moment all Paris is in mourning.[5] Go up to the third floor; you will find a tailor. Have him make you a black suit, and tell him from me that you must have it tomorrow morning. Good-by."

When I came back at midnight I found in my room the chest containing all my correspondence and the miniature portraits which were of concern to me. I have never in my life pawned a snuffbox without removing the portrait it contained. In the morning I saw Tiretta dressed in solid black.

"You see," I said, "how quickly things get done in Paris."

Just then the Abbé de Lacoste[6] is announced. I did not remember the name, but I have him shown in. I see the same Abbé who had seen me with the Abbé de Laville. I ask him to excuse me for not having had time to call on him. He congratulates me on my lottery. He says he has heard that I distributed over two thousand écus' worth of tickets at the Hôtel de Koelen.[7]

"Yes, I always carry eight or ten thousand francs' worth in my pocket."

"I will take a thousand écus' worth too."

"Whenever you please. At my office you can choose the numbers."

"I don't care about that. Just give me what you have."

"Gladly. Here they are. Choose."

After choosing he asks for paper and pen to write me a receipt.

"There is no need of that," I said, smiling and taking back my tickets; "I only give them out for cash."

"I will bring it to you tomorrow."

"And you shall have the tickets tomorrow; they are recorded at the office, and I cannot do otherwise."

"Give me some which are not recorded."

"I do not issue any such, for if they won I should have to pay them out of my own pocket."

"I think you could take that risk."

"And I think not."

He then speaks to Tiretta in Italian and offers to introduce him to Madame Lambertini,[8] the widow of a nephew of the Pope's. I say that I will go too, and we are driven there.

We get out at her door in the Rue Christine. I see a woman whose age, despite her youthful appearance, I put at forty years—thin, with black eyes, lively, scatter-brained, given to laughter, and in short a woman capable of inspiring a passing fancy. I set her talking and I find that she is neither a widow nor a niece of the Pope's; she was from Modena and an out-and-out adventuress. I see Tiretta becoming interested in her. She tries to keep us for dinner, but we excuse ourselves. Only Tiretta remains. I let the Abbé out at the Quai de la Ferraille and go to dine at Calzabigi's.

After dinner he takes me aside and says that Monsieur Duverney had told him to warn me that I was not allowed to distribute tickets on my own account.

"Then he considers me either a fool or a rogue. I shall complain to Monsieur de Boulogne."

"You will be making a mistake, for a warning is not an insult."

"You insult me yourself by giving me the warning. But no one shall give me another of the kind."

He calms me and persuades me to go with him to talk with Monsieur Duverney. The worthy old man, seeing that I am angry, begs my pardon and says that a self-styled Abbé de Lacoste had told him I was making so free. I did not see the Abbé anywhere again; he was the same man who three years later was sentenced to the galleys, where he ended his days, for having gone about Paris selling tickets for a lottery in Trévoux[9] which did not exist.

The day after the Abbé's visit I saw Tiretta in my room, just getting back. He said he had spent the night with the Pope's niece and that he thought she had found him satisfactory, since she proposed to put him up and keep him in funds if he would tell Monsieur Lenoir,[10] her lover, that he was her cousin.

"She claims," he said, "that Monsieur Lenoir will give me a post in the tax farming administration.[11] I replied that, since you were my intimate friend, I could not decide anything without first consulting you. She begged me to persuade you to dine with her on Sunday."

"I will do so with pleasure."

I found the woman madly in love with my friend, whom she dubbed "Count of Six Times," a name by which he was known in Paris as long as he remained there. She had recognized him as lord of that fief, which is thought to be fabulous in France, and she wanted to become its lady. After telling me of his nocturnal exploits as if I had been her oldest friend, she said that she wanted to give him room and board, that she had already obtained the consent of Monsieur Lenoir, who in fact was delighted to have her cousin stay with her.

She expected him after dinner, and she could not wait to introduce them to each other.

Reverting after dinner to the subject of my fellow countryman's powers, she excited him to the point where, wanting to convince me of his stamina, he confirmed her testimony in my presence. The sight had not the slightest effect on me; but observing my friend's extraordinary build I admitted that he could expect to make a fortune wherever he could find women with money.

At three o'clock two old women arrived. They were gamblers. La Lambertini introduced the "Count of Six Times," her cousin. By that imposing name he became an object of intense scrutiny, and the more so when his gibberish proved to be unintelligible. The heroine did not fail to whisper the explanation of his grandiose name into her friends' ears and to boast of the incredible wealth of the lord of the fief. "It is unbelievable," said the matrons, looking him up and down; and Tiretta seemed to answer: "Mesdames, have no doubt of it."

A hackney coach arrives. I see a stout woman,[12] well beyond middle age, a niece[13] pretty enough to eat, and a pale man wearing black and a round wig. After the embraces La Lambertini introduces her cousin Six Times; the name arouses surprise, but the explanation passes without comment; the only point dwelt upon was the strangeness of a man who dared to be in Paris without knowing a word of French and nevertheless jabbered away to the entire company, who, understanding not a word, did nothing but laugh. La Lambertini got up a game of brelan[14] and did not make me play; but she insisted that her dear cousin play beside her and on half shares. He did not know one card from another, but that didn't matter, he would learn; she would teach him. Since the charming young lady knows no card games I offer to keep her company in front of the fire. Her aunt says with a laugh that I shall be hard put to it to find subjects interesting enough to persuade her to talk; but that I must excuse her, for she had only been out of the convent for a month.

So as soon as I see the game started I go and sit down with her in front of the fire. It was she who broke the silence by asking me who the handsome man who could not talk was.

"He is a nobleman from my country who has left it because of an affair of honor. He will speak French when he has learned it, and then no one will laugh at him. I am sorry I brought him here, for in less than twenty-four hours he has been spoiled."

"How?"

"I do not dare tell you, for your aunt might not like it."

"I have no intention of making a report; but perhaps my curiosity deserves a rebuke."

"Mademoiselle, it is I who am in the wrong; but I will make amends by telling you everything. Madame Lambertini made him sleep with her and has given him the absurd name of 'Six Times.' That is all. I am sorry, because he was not a libertine before this happened."

Could I have supposed that I was talking to a well-born girl, a decent girl and a novice, in La Lambertini's house? I was surprised to see her face fiery red from shame. I refused to believe it. Two minutes later she astonishes me with a question I should never have expected.

"What is there in common," she asked, "between 'Six Times' and having slept with Madame Lambertini?"

"He did to her six times running what a decent husband does to his wife only once a week."

"And you think I am fool enough to tell my aunt what you have just told me?"

"But I am sorry for another thing too."

"I will come back in a moment."

After taking the little excursion which my charming

story apparently made her feel she needed, she re-entered the room and stood behind her aunt's chair examining the hero's face; then she came back to her seat, blushing furiously.

"What is the other thing you said you were sorry for?"

"Dare I tell you all?"

"You have told me so much that I think you can have no scruples left."

"Then I will tell you that after dinner today she made him do it to her in my presence."

"If that offended you, obviously you were jealous."

"No. I felt humiliated because of something which I don't dare mention to you."

"I think you are mocking me with your 'don't dare.'"

"God forfend, Mademoiselle! She showed me that my friend outmeasured me by two inches."

"On the contrary, I think you are two inches taller than he is."

"It is not a question of height, but of another dimension, which you can imagine and in which my friend is a monster."

"A monster! But why should you mind that? Isn't it better not to be a monster?"

"That is very true; but in this respect certain women, who are not like you, prefer monstrosity."

"I haven't a clear enough idea of the matter to imagine what dimension can be called monstrous. I still consider it strange that you should have felt humiliated."

"Would you have thought it of me when you saw me?"

"When I came into the room and saw you I did not think about it. You appear to be a well-proportioned man, but if you know you are not I feel sorry for you."

"Please look."

"I think it is you who are the monster, for you frighten me."

She went and stood behind her aunt's chair; but I

had no doubt that she would come back, for I was far
from thinking her either stupid or innocent. I thought
she wanted to pretend that she was; and not caring
whether she had played the role well or badly I was
delighted to have turned it to profit. I had punished her
for wanting to impose on me, and as I thought her
charming I was delighted that my punishment could
certainly not have displeased her. Could I doubt her
intelligence? It was she who had kept our entire dialogue
from breaking off, and all that I had said and done had
only been in consequence of her specious objections.

Four or five minutes later her stout aunt, having lost
a game, told her niece she was bringing her bad luck and
that it was bad manners to leave me alone. She did not
answer her, and she came back to me smiling.

"If my aunt," she said, "knew what you have done
she would not have accused me of being impolite."

"If you knew how mortified I am by it now! The
only proof of my repentance I can give you is to leave.
But will you not be offended if I do?"

"If you go my aunt will say that I am stupid and
have bored you."

"In that case I will stay. So until now you had no
idea of what I thought you would not mind my showing
you?"

"Only a vague idea. It is no more than a month since
my aunt had me come here from Melun[15] where I had
been in a convent since I was eight years old, and now
I am seventeen. They tried to make me take the veil,
but I did not let them talk me into it."

"Are you angry at what I did? If I acted wrongly,
I meant well."

"I have no right to be angry with you, for it was
my fault. I only beg you to be discreet."

"Have no doubt that I will be; for I shall be the first
to suffer if I am not."

"You have given me a lesson which will be useful to me in future. But you are going on with it. Stop, or I will leave you and not come back."

"Stay, it is finished. On this handkerchief you see the proof of my pleasure."

"What is that?"

"It is the substance which, placed in the proper retort, emerges nine months later male or female."

"I understand. You are an excellent tutor. You deliver yourself like a professor. Should I thank you for your zeal?"

"No. You should forgive me, for I would never have done what I did if I had not fallen in love with you the first moment I saw you."

"Then am I to take it as a declaration of love?"

"Yes, my angel. It is a daring one, but it is not to be doubted. If it did not come from a very strong love I should be a scoundrel who deserved death. May I hope that you will love me?"

"I have no idea. All I know is that I ought to loathe you. In less than an hour you have taken me on a journey which I thought I could not finish until after I married. You have left me with nothing to learn of a subject on which I never dared allow my mind to linger, and I feel guilty because I have let you seduce me. But how is it that you have now become calm and decent?"

"Because we are talking rationally. Because after the height of pleasure, love rests. Look!"

"What, again! Is this the end of the lesson? As I see you now, you do not frighten me any more. The fire is going out."

She puts on a log and, to poke up the fire, goes down on her knees. As she bends forward in this posture I put a determined hand under her dress, and I instantly find a completely closed door which could only lead me to happiness by being broken open. But at the same moment she rises, sits down, and says gently but with feeling that she is a well-born girl and believes she has the right to demand respect. At that I ask her pardon profusely, and the end of my speech calms her. I said that my daring hand had made me certain she had not yet enjoyed happiness with any man. She replied that the man who would make her happy could only be the man who would marry her, and she showed her forgiveness by letting me cover her hand with kisses. I would have gone further if someone had not arrived. It was Monsieur Lenoir, who had come in response to Madame Lambertini's note to hear what she had to tell him.

I see a man of mature years, simple and modest, who very politely asks everyone not to get up and not to interrupt the game. La Lambertini introduced me, and on hearing my name he asked if I was the artist. When he learned that I was his elder brother he congratulated me on the lottery and on Monsieur Duverney's high opinion of me; but what interested him more was the "cousin," whom she at once introduced to him as Count Tiretta. It was I who said that he had been recommended to me and had been forced to leave his country because of an affair of honor. La Lambertini then added that she wanted to put him up, but had not wished to do so until she learned if he would approve. He answered that she was sole mistress in her own house, and that he would be delighted to have him one of her circle. As he spoke Italian very well, Tiretta breathed again. He left the game and the four of us sat by the fire, where, when her turn came, the pretty young lady conversed very sensibly with Monsieur Lenoir. He led her to talk of her convent, and when she told him her name he spoke of her father, whom he had known. He was a Councilor in the Parlement of Rouen.[16] The charming girl was tall, a natural blonde, with regular features and a countenance marked by candor and modesty. Large and prominent blue eyes whose expression was of the tenderest bore witness to the ardent desires of her soul. Her close-fitting buttoned dress displayed the elegance of her waist, leaving the beauty of her bosom to be divined. I saw that Monsieur Lenoir, though he did not tell her so, was as sensible of her merits as I had been. But he was not in a position to show it as I had done. At eight o'clock he left. A half hour later Madame XXX also left, accompanied by her niece, whom she called De la M—re, and by the pale man who had come with them. I then left with Tiretta, who promised he would come to stay with her the next day; he kept his word.

Three or four days after this arrangement was made, my clerk sent me a letter which had been addressed to me at my office. The letter was from Mademoiselle de la M—re. Here is a copy of it:

"My aunt Madame XXX, sister of my late mother, is sanctimonious, fond of gambling, rich, stingy, and unjust. She does not love me and, not having succeeded in making me take the veil, she wants to marry me to a merchant of Dunkirk whom I do not know. Note that she does not know him either. The marriage broker speaks highly of him. He asks only that she guarantee him twelve thousand francs a year as long as she lives, since he is certain that on her death I will inherit fifty thousand écus. But note that, in accordance with the terms of my mother's will, she ought to give me twenty-five thousand when I marry. If what has happened between you and me has not made me contemptible in your eyes, I offer you my hand with twenty-five thousand écus and another twenty-five thousand on the death of my aunt. Do not answer me, for I do not know how or through whom or where to receive a letter from you. You shall answer me by word of mouth Sunday at Madame Lambertini's. Thus you have four days before you in which to think it over. I do not know if I love you; but I know that I must prefer you to

any other man if I am to love myself. It is for me to win
your esteem, and to give you the opportunity to win mine.
Then, too, I feel sure that you will make life pleasant
for me. If you consider that the happiness to which I
aspire can contribute to yours, I warn you that you
will need an attorney, for my aunt is stingy and may
well go to law. As soon as you have made up your mind,
you will have to find a convent for me, to which I can
go before I take the slightest step, otherwise I should be
terribly ill-treated and I cannot bear the thought of that.
If the proposal I make to you does not suit you, I ask you
for one favor which I hope you will grant me and for
which I will be grateful to you. You will make an effort
not to see me again, taking care to avoid any places
where you think I might be. You will thus help me to forget you. Do you not understand that I cannot be happy
unless I marry you or forget you? Good-by. I am sure I
shall see you on Sunday.''

Her letter touched me. I saw that it was dictated by
virtue, honor, and good sense. I found that Mademoiselle
de la M.'s mind deserved even more praise than her body.
I felt ashamed that I had seduced her and worthy of the
worst punishment if I refused the hand which she
offered me with such dignity, and at the same time I
saw that she offered me a fortune far larger than any
for which I could reasonably hope; but the idea of
marriage made me shudder; I knew myself too well not
to foresee that in a settled way of life I should become
unhappy and hence my wife would be unhappy too.
My vacillation in coming to a decision during the four
days she gave me to think it over convinced me that I
was not in love with her; nevertheless, I could never
make up my mind to reject her proposal, still less to
tell her so. I spent the whole four days thinking of her,
feeling that I esteemed her, repenting that I had wronged
her, but never having the firmness to decide to repair my

wrongdoing. When I thought that, if I did not, she would hate me, I could not tolerate that idea either; and such is always the unhappy predicament of a man who must make a decision and cannot make it.

Fearing that some demon would lead me to fail in my duty to Mademoiselle de la M—re by compelling me to go to the theater or the opera, I went to dine at La Lambertini's with my mind still not made up. She was at mass. Tiretta was in his room playing the flute; as soon as he saw me he came out to pay me what his black clothes had cost him.

"So you are in funds now—I congratulate you."

"Better condole with me, for it is stolen money, though I am only an accomplice. There is cheating here, and I have been taught to lend a hand; and I take my share so they won't call me a fool. My hostess and three or four other women shear the sheep. It revolts me, I cannot put up with it. One day or another I shall be killed or I will kill, and either way it will cost me my life; so I am planning to get out of this den of thieves as soon as I can."

"That would be my advice to you, my friend, and I urge you to follow it. Better leave today than tomorrow."

"I do not want to precipitate anything, for Monsieur Lenoir, who is a gentleman and my friend, and who thinks I am the trollop's cousin and knows nothing of her infamous proceedings, would suspect something and might leave her when he learned what had driven me away. In five or six days I will find some excuse and come back to you."

La Lambertini said she was delighted that I had dropped in to take potluck; she told me that Mademoiselle de la M—re and her aunt would be of the company. I asked her if she was satisfied with "Six Times" and she answered that he did not always lodge in his fief but that she loved him none the less. Madame XXX arrived with her niece, who concealed her pleasure at seeing me. She was in half-mourning, and so beautiful that I was amazed at my indecision. Tiretta came down and as there was no reason why I should not show that I felt attracted by Mademoiselle de la M—re, I paid her every attention. I told her aunt that I would renounce my bachelorhood if I could find a wife like her.

"My niece, Monsieur, is virtuous and sweet-tempered, but she has neither intelligence nor piety."

"As for my intelligence, my dear aunt, I have nothing to say, but no one at the convent ever reproached me with lack of piety."

"I can well believe it. They are female Jesuits. Grace is what matters, my dear niece, grace; but let us change the subject. All I ask is that you please the man who will be your husband."

"Is Mademoiselle about to be married?"

"Her intended will arrive at the beginning of next month."

"I suppose he belongs to the legal profession?"

"He is an extremely well-to-do merchant."

"Since Monsieur Lenoir has told me that Mademoiselle is the daughter of a Councilor, I did not expect a misalliance."

"It does not signify. He is noble[17] if he is honest, and it will be her own fault if he does not make her happy."

Since this sort of talk could only be painful to the charming girl, who was listening and saying nothing, I changed the subject to the great crowd which would be at La Grève[18] to watch Damiens's execution; and seeing that they were all curious about the horrible spectacle I offered them a large window from which all five of us could see it. They accepted on the spot.[19] I promised to call for them; but since I had no window, when we rose from table I pretended I had some important business and hurried in a hackney coach to La

*Venetian in Traveling Cloak*

*Assassination Attempt on Louis XV*

Grève, where within a quarter of an hour I rented a good
window one flight up between two staircases for three
louis. I paid and was given a receipt with a forfeit of
six hundred francs. The window faced the front of the
scaffold. Returning to La Lambertini's, I found her playing *piquet à écrire*[20] with Tiretta, while Madame XXX
kept score.

As Mademoiselle de la M—re knew only "Comet," [21]
I offered her my company, and, since we had something
to say to each other, we retired to the other end of the
room. I told her that the receipt of her letter brought
me to realize that I was the most fortunate of men and
at the same time to realize that her mind and her
character were such as to make her adored by any man
endowed with common sense.

"You shall be my wife," I said, "and until my last
breath I will bless the fortunate boldness with which
I surprised your innocence, for without it you would
never have come to prefer me to a hundred other men of
your own rank, none of whom would ever have refused
you even without the bait of fifty thousand écus, which are
nothing in comparison with the charms of your person
and your good sense. Now that you know what my feelings are, let us not be precipitate; trust me. Give me
time to take a house, furnish it, and put myself in a
position to be considered worthy to marry a girl of your
condition. Consider that I am still living in a furnished
room, that you have relatives, and that I should be
ashamed to look like an adventurer in a matter of such
moment."

"You heard that my supposed future husband is to
arrive; and when he arrives they will move quickly."

"Not so quickly but that in twenty-four hours I can
free you from all constraint without your aunt's even
knowing that it will be I who deal her the blow. Know,
my angel, that I have only to ask it and the Minister of

Foreign Affairs, certain that you want no other husband than myself, will secure a refuge for you in one of the best convents in Paris; that it is he who will supply you with a lawyer, and he who, if the language of the will is clear, will within a few days force your aunt to give you your dowry and furnish security for the rest of your inheritance. Keep calm, take no action, and wait for the merchant from Dunkirk. Be sure that I will not leave you in difficulties. You will no longer be in your aunt's house on whatever day they set to sign the contract.''

''You have convinced me, and I put myself entirely in your hands; but I beg you to give no weight to one circumstance which pains my delicacy in the highest degree. You said that I would never have proposed to you that you either marry me or cease to see me if you had not taken such liberties as you took last Sunday. It is true in one respect, for without an overpowering reason I should have been mad to offer you my hand point-blank; but our marriage could equally well have come about in a different way, for I can truly tell you that in any case I should have given you the preference over all men.''

On hearing this magnanimous confidence, I kissed her hand again and again and with such a fervor of feeling that I should not have waited a quarter of an hour to marry her if a notary and a priest empowered to give us the nuptial blessing had been present. Entirely absorbed in our own concerns, we paid no attention to the terrible racket the company was making at the other end of the room; but I thought I ought to look into it, at least in order to calm Tiretta.

I saw an open casket, filled with jewels ranging from mere trumpery to articles of value, and two men arguing with Tiretta, who had a book in his hand. I immediately thought it was a lottery; but why the quarrel? Tiretta said that they were scoundrels, who had won thirty or forty louis from them by means of the book, which he handed me. One of the men told me that the book contained a lottery than which nothing could be more honest.

"This book," he said, "contains twelve hundred leaves, two hundred of which represent prizes and the others are blanks. Each winning leaf, then, is followed by five losing ones. The person who wants to play pays a petit écu and puts the point of a pin at random between the leaves of the closed book. The book is opened at the place where the pin went in, and the leaf is examined. If it is blank the person who paid the petit écu loses it, and if it indicates a prize he is given the prize written on the leaf or its value in money, as stated on the same leaf. Observe that the smallest prize is worth twelve francs and that there are prizes which run up to six hundred and one to twelve hundred. In the hour during which these ladies and this gentleman have been playing they have already won several prizes, and Madame here has won a ring worth six louis, which she would still have if she had not preferred to take the money, which, continuing to play, she has lost."

"In short," said Madame XXX, who had won the ring, "there are six of us here, and these gentlemen have won our money with their accursed book. You can see that we were taken unawares."

Tiretta called them scoundrels, and one of them replied that in that case the collectors for the Military School lottery were scoundrels too. At that Tiretta gave him a sound slap; whereupon I stepped between them, demanded silence, and proceeded to end the matter.

"All lotteries," I said, "are advantageous to the backers; but the backer of the Military School lottery is the King himself, and I am the chief collector. As such, I confiscate this casket, and I give you your choice. Either you will give these persons back the money you have won and I will let you leave with your casket, or I will send for a police officer, who on my demand will put you in prison until tomorrow, when Monsieur Berryer[22] himself will judge the case. I will take this book to him tomorrow morning. We shall see if, because you are scoundrels, we have to admit that we are the same.''

Seeing that they were in a poor position they decided to give back the money. They were made to give back forty louis in all, though they swore they had won only twenty. I was convinced of it; but *vae victis* (''woe to the vanquished'')[23]; I was angry with them and was determined that they should pay. They asked for their book, but I would not give it to them. They thought they were lucky they could leave with their casket of jewels. The ladies were touched and after they were gone said that I might at least have let the poor wretches have their conjuring book.

They came to see me at eight o'clock the next morning, and they made me relent by presenting me with a large case containing twenty-four eight-inch Saxon porcelain[24] statues. At that I gave them back the book, threatening that I would have them arrested if they went about Paris any longer with their lottery. The same day I took all twenty-four of the pretty figures to Mademoiselle de la M—re. It was a sumptuous present, and her aunt thanked me profusely.

A few days later—it was March 28th[25]—I went very early to call for the ladies, who were breakfasting at Madame Lambertini's with Tiretta, and took them in my carriage to La Grève, holding Mademoiselle de la M—re on my lap. All three of the ladies crowded into the front of the window, leaning forward with their elbows on the sill so as not to prevent us from seeing. The window had two steps, they had got up on the second, and, since we were behind them, we had to be on it too, for if we had stood on the first we could have seen nothing. I have reasons for acquainting my reader with this particular.

We had the firmness to remain present at the horrible spectacle[26] for four hours. I shall say nothing about it, for it would take too long and in any case everyone knows the details. Damiens was a fanatic who had tried to kill Louis XV in the belief that he was doing a good deed. He had only just pierced the King's skin; but that made no difference. The populace at his execution called him a monster spewed up from Hell to assassinate "the best" of kings, whom they believed they adored and whom they had named "the Well-Beloved." Yet it was the same populace which massacred[27] the whole royal family, all the noblemen of France, and all those who gave the nation the fair character which made it esteemed, loved, and even taken as a model by all other nations. The people of France, said Monsieur de Voltaire himself, is the most abominable of all peoples. It is a chameleon which takes on all colors and is ready to do whatever a leader wants it to do, whether for good or for evil.

While Damiens was being tortured I had to turn away my eyes when I heard him shriek with only half his body left; but La Lambertini and Madame XXX did not look away; and it was not because they were hardhearted. They told me, and I had to pretend to believe them, that they could not feel the least pity for such a monster because they loved Louis XV so well. It is true, however, that Tiretta kept Madame XXX so strangely occupied during the whole execution that it may have been only on his account that she never dared to stir or look around.

Being behind her and very close to her, he had raised her dress so as not to step on it, and that was all very well. But later, looking toward them, I saw that he had raised it a little too high; whereupon, determining neither to interrupt my friend's enterprise nor to embarrass Madame XXX, I took up a position behind my beloved which assured her aunt that what Tiretta did to her could be seen neither by myself nor by her niece. I heard the rustling of a dress for two whole hours, and finding the whole thing most amusing I never swerved from the resolve I had taken. I admired Tiretta's appetite even more than his boldness, for in that respect I had often been as daring as he.

When at the end of the execution I saw Madame XXX straighten up, I turned too. I saw my friend as lively, fresh, and calm as if nothing had happened; but I thought the lady looked pensive and more serious than usual. Between keeping La Lambertini from laughing at her and preventing her niece from discovering mysteries of which she should still be ignorant, she had been under the dire necessity of having to dissimulate and patiently put up with all that the brute had done.

I dropped La Lambertini at her door, asking her to leave Tiretta with me, since I needed him. Then I dropped Madame XXX at her house in the Rue Saint-André-des-Arts,[28] where she asked me to call on her the next day as she had something to say to me. I noticed that she did not curtsy to my friend. I took him to dinner at Landel's, who had a wineshop in the Hôtel de Buci[29] and furnished excellent meals, even on fast days, for six francs a head.

"What were you doing," I asked him, "behind Madame XXX?"

"I am sure neither you nor the others saw anything."

"That may well be; but having seen the beginning of the performance and guessing what you were going to do, I took up a position which prevented Mademoiselle de la M—re and La Lambertini from seeing you. I can imagine what you did, and I admire your hearty appetite; but Madame XXX is angry."

"Then she is pretending to be, for since she stayed still

for two whole hours, I cannot believe anything but that I gave her pleasure."

"I believe it too; but her self-esteem leaves her no choice except to claim that you affronted her—as indeed you did! You see that she is vexed with you and that she wants to talk with me tomorrow."

"But I cannot imagine she will talk to you about anything so trifling. She would be out of her mind."

"Why not? You don't know these pious women. They are delighted to have an opportunity to weep and confess such things to a third person, especially if they are ugly. It is quite possible that Madame XXX will demand reparation; and I shall be delighted to take a hand in it."

"I do not see what kind of reparation she can demand. If she hadn't been willing she could have given me a kick which would have knocked me off the step backward."

"La Lambertini is vexed with you too, I noticed. She may have seen what happened and feel that you have cheated her."

"La Lambertini is vexed with me for another reason. Last night I raised a row and I shall move from there before evening."

"Really?"

"Really. Here is the story. Last evening a young man in the tax farming administration, whom an old Genoese harridan brought to supper with us, after losing forty louis at *petits-paquets*[30] threw the cards in my hostess's face and called her a thief. I picked up the candlestick and put the candle out on his face, at the risk, I confess, of blinding him, but it did not go into his eyes. He ran for his sword, shouting, and if his Genoese friend had not held him round the waist there would have been a murder, for I had already unsheathed. When the poor fellow saw his wound in the mirror he became so furious

that the only way they could quiet him was to give him
back his money. They did so despite my protests; for
giving it back was tantamount to admitting that they had
cheated him. This led to a bitter quarrel between myself
and La Lambertini after the young man had gone. She
said that nothing would have happened and we should
still have the forty louis if I had stayed out of it; that it
was she and not I whom he had insulted; to which the
Genoese added that if we had kept our heads we should
have fleeced him for a long time, but God knew what
he would do now with the scar on his face from the burning candle. Disgusted with their trollops' morality, I
told them to go . . . . . themselves; on which my dear
hostess said that I was a tramp. But for Monsieur
Lenoir's arrival I would have given her a beating. They
told me to keep still, but I was too angry. I told the
worthy man that his mistress had called me a tramp, that
she was a whore, that she was not my cousin, and that I
would move out today. So saying I went up to my room
and locked myself in. I shall go back there in two hours
for my clothes, and I will drink coffee with you tomorrow
morning.''

Tiretta was right. The more I learned of his character,
the more I saw that he was not born for the trade of
fancy man.

The next day about noon I went on foot to call on
Madame XXX, whom I found with her niece. A quarter
of an hour later she told her to leave us alone, then
spoke to me as follows:

''You will be surprised, Monsieur, by what I have
to say to you. It is a complaint of an unimaginable
nature, which I have determined to lay before you without making any long reflections, for the situation is both
painful and urgent. To come to the decision I had only
to remind myself of the impression you made on me the
first time I saw you. I believe you to be intelligent,

discreet, a man of honor and decent behavior, and, what is more, of true religious feeling; if I am mistaken it will be most unfortunate, for insulted as I feel that I have been, and not lacking in resources, I will find a way to avenge myself; and, as his friend, you will regret it."

"Are you complaining of Tiretta?"

"None other. He is a villain and he has insulted me in an unheard-of manner."

"I should never have believed him capable of it. What, Madame, is the nature of the insult? You may count on me."

"Monsieur, I will not tell you; but I hope you can guess it. For two whole hours yesterday at the execution of that monster Damiens he took the strangest advantage of his position behind me."

"I understand, and you need tell me no more. You are justified; and I condemn him, for it was a low trick; but permit me to tell you that the thing is not unheard-of, or indeed unusual; I even consider that it can be forgiven either to love or to the situation at the moment, to the extreme proximity of the fiendish temptation, to the extreme youth of the offender. It is a crime for which reparation can be made in a number of ways, with the full consent of the parties. Tiretta is a bachelor, a gentleman with the best connections, and a marriage can easily be arranged; and if a marriage does not accord with your ideas, he can make reparation by a most constant friendship, of a nature to give you the clearest evidence of his repentance and worthy of your indulgence. Consider, Madame, that he is a man and hence subject to all the weaknesses of humanity. Consider, too, that your charms must have played no small part in exciting his senses beyond measure. In short, I believe he may hope to obtain your forgiveness."

"Forgiveness? All that you have just said flows from the wisdom of a Christian soul; but your whole argument is founded on a false supposition. You do not know what took place. But alas! how could anyone guess it?''

Madame XXX then shed a few tears, which baffled me. I did not know what to think. ''Can he have stolen her purse?'' I wondered. After drying her tears she went on as follows:

''You imagine a crime which, by an effort, one could reconcile with reason and hence, I admit, discover some proper reparation for it; but what the brute did to me is so infamous that I must not even think of it, for it is of a nature to drive me mad.''

''Good God! What are you saying? I tremble. Tell me, I beg you, if I have guessed.''

''I think so, for I do not believe it possible to imagine anything worse. I see that you are upset. Yet such is the case. Forgive my tears, and seek their source, I beg you, only in resentment and shame.''

''And in religion.''

''That too. Indeed it is their chief source. I did not mention it because I do not know if you are as attached to it as I am.''

''I am so to the extent of my powers, thank God!''

''Then be prepared to let me damn myself, for I demand vengeance.''

''Renounce it, Madame; I could never be your accomplice in seeking vengeance, and if you will not renounce it, at least keep it from my knowledge. I promise to tell him nothing, even though, since he is staying with me, the laws of hospitality demand that I warn him.''

''I thought he was staying with La Lambertini.''

''He left her house yesterday. It was a den of iniquity. I got him out of there.''

''What are you saying? You astonish and edify me. I do not seek his death, Monsieur; but admit that he owes me reparation.''

''I admit it; but I know of none commensurate with

the insult. I can think of only one, and I will undertake
to procure it for you."

"Tell me what it is."

"I will trick him into coming here, I will hand him
over to you and leave him alone with you to face all your
righteous anger—but on condition that, without his knowing it, I shall remain in the room next to the one in
which you will have him at your mercy, for I hold myself
responsible for his life."

"I consent. You shall be in this room, and you shall
leave him with me in the room in which I will receive you
both; but he must not know."

"He will not even know that I am bringing him to
your house. I do not want him to be aware that I know
anything about his abominable crime. I will find some
excuse for leaving him with you."

"When will you bring him? I can hardly wait to abash
him. I will make him tremble. I cannot imagine what
excuses he will jabber out to justify his insolence."

She made me stay for dinner with her and the Abbé
Desforges,[31] who arrived at one o'clock. The Abbé was a
pupil of the famous Bishop of Auxerre,[32] who was still
alive. At table I talked so eloquently of grace and quoted
St. Augustine to such good purpose that the Abbé and
his sanctimonious disciple took me for a most zealous
Jansenist,[33] which was against all probability. Mademoiselle de la M—re never once looked at me, and assuming that she had her reasons I never spoke to her.

After dinner I promised Madame XXX that I would
bring her the culprit the next day when we were walking home from the Comédie Française,[34] for I was certain
that at night he would not recognize her house.

But Tiretta only laughed when I told him the whole
story, reproaching him in serio-comic vein with the horrible act he had dared to perpetrate on a woman in every
way respectable.

"I should never have believed," he replied, "that she would bring herself to complain of it to anyone."

"Then you do not deny having done this horrible thing to her ?"

"If she says I did, I will not contradict her; but may I die if I believe I can swear to it. In the position in which I was placed, I apparently could do nothing else. But I will calm her, and I will try to make short work of it so as not to keep you waiting."

"No, no. On the contrary, your interest and mine demand that you take a long time over it, for I am sure I shall not be bored. You must not know that I am in the house; and even if you stay with her only an hour, take a hackney coach and leave. There is a hack stand in the street. You must realize that the least Madame XXX owes me in the way of politeness is not to leave me alone and without a fire. Remember that she is well born, rich, and pious. Try to gain her friendship—not front to back but *de faciem ad faciem* ['face to face'], as the King of Prussia said.* [35] You may find it very profitable. If she asks you why you are no longer living with La Lambertini, do not tell her the reason. Your discretion will please her. In short, try your best to expiate your execrable crime."

"I need only tell her the truth. I didn't know where I was going in."

"It's an excuse in a million, and a Frenchwoman may very well consider it legitimate."

When we left the Comédie I dismissed my carriage, and I ushered the culprit into the presence of the matron, who received us most politely, saying that she never supped but that if we had let her know beforehand she

---

* D'Alembert dared to correct him. I would have done the same. Why should a king insist on speaking Latin when he has not learned it ? (C.'s note.)

would have had something for us. After telling her all
the news I had heard in the foyer, I asked her to allow
me to leave my friend with her, since I had to call on a
foreigner at the Spanish Embassy.[36]

"If I am not back within a quarter of an hour," I said
to Tiretta, "do not wait for me. You will find hackney
coaches in the street. We will meet tomorrow."

Instead of going downstairs I entered the adjoining
room by the door from the hall. Two or three minutes
later I saw Mademoiselle de la M——re, who, carrying a
candle, said with a smile that she did not know if she
was dreaming.

"My aunt," she said, "ordered me not to leave you
alone and to tell the chambermaid not to come up until
she rang. You have left 'Six Times' alone with her, and
she told me to speak softly because he is not to know you
are here. May I ask what this strange business is? I admit
it makes me very curious."

"You shall know all, my angel, but I am cold."

"She also told me to make a good fire. She has become
generous. As you see, there are candles."

As soon as we were seated in front of the fire I told her
the whole story, to which she listened with the utmost
attention but which she found it difficult to understand
when it came to explaining the nature of Tiretta's crime.
I was not sorry that I had to explain it to her in clear
terms, accompanying them with gestures, which made her
laugh and blush together. I told her that when I had
made myself responsible for her aunt's receiving reparation, I had arranged the thing in a way to make it
certain that she and I would be together and perfectly
free during all the time that her aunt was occupied; and
thereupon I for the first time covered her lovely face
with kisses, which, as they were not accompanied by any
other liberties, she candidly received as indubitable proof
of my love.

"There are two things," she said, "which I do not understand. The first is how Tiretta managed to commit a crime on my aunt which I can see is possible if the party assaulted consents but which must be impossible if she does not—which leads me to conclude that, since the crime was committed, my good aunt must have consented to it."

"Certainly, for she could have changed her position."

"Even without that—for it seems to me she could simply have made it impossible for him to enter."

"In that, my angel, you are mistaken. A well-equipped man asks only for no change in position; granted that, he breaks through the barrier easily enough. Besides, I do not believe that achieving entrance in the case of your aunt is the same as it would be in, let us say, yours."

"That I defy a hundred Tirettas to do. The other thing I do not understand is how she can have told you about the affront, which, as she should have known if she had any intelligence, could only make you laugh, for it makes me laugh too. Nor do I understand what kind of reparation she can expect from a wild brute who probably considers the whole thing completely unimportant. I believe he would have tried to play the same trick on anyone behind whom he happened to be standing at that frenzied moment."

"You are right, for he told me himself that he had entered but really did not know where."

"Your friend is a strange sort of creature."

"As for the kind of reparation your aunt may demand, and which she perhaps hopes to obtain, she told me nothing; but I believe it will consist in a formal declaration of love on his part and that he will expiate the crime he unwittingly committed by becoming her devoted lover and spending this very night with her just as if he had married her this morning."

"Come now—that would be too amusing. I don't be-

lieve it. She is too much in love with her saintly soul;
then, too, how can you suppose our young man can play
the role of lover to her when he has her face before his
eyes? He didn't see her when he did what he did to her
at La Grève. Have you ever seen as repulsive a face as
my aunt's? Her skin is freckled, her eyes are rheumy,
her teeth rotten, and her breath unbearable. She is hideous.''

"Those are trifles, dear heart, for a man like my friend,
who, being twenty-five, is always ready. It is I who can
only be a man when I am stimulated by charms like yours,
which I cannot wait to possess completely and legitimately.''

"You will find me the fondest of wives, and I am sure
I shall conquer your heart so that nothing can take it
from me until I die.''

As an hour had already passed, and her aunt's conversation with Tiretta still continued, I saw that the thing
had become serious.

"Let us eat something,'' I said.

"I can't give you anything but bread, cheese, and ham,
and some wine which my aunt thinks very good.''

"Bring them all, for my stomach is perishing.''

No sooner have I spoken than she lays two places on a
small table and brings everything she has. The cheese
was Roquefort and the ham delicious. There was enough
for ten people, but since there was nothing else we ate it
all with ravenous appetites and emptied the two bottles.
Pleasure shone in the charming girl's beautiful eyes;
even so, we spent an hour over our frugal repast.

"Are you not curious,'' I asked her, "to know what
your aunt has been doing with 'Six Times' during the
two hours and a half they have been together?''

"They may be playing cards; but there's a hole. All I
see is the two candles, with wicks an inch long.''

"Didn't I tell you? Give me a coverlet, and I will lie

down on this sofa; and you be off to sleep. Let us go see your bed.''

She took me into her little room, where I saw a pretty bed, a prayer stool, and a large crucifix. I said her bed was too small, but she said it wasn't, and she showed me that she was perfectly comfortable in it stretched out full length. What a charming wife I was to have!

''Oh, I beg you, don't move, and let me unbutton this dress which hides things unknown I am dying to devour.''

''My dear, I cannot defend myself; but afterward you will no longer love me.''

The unbuttoned dress showing me only half of her, she could not resist my insistence. She had to let my eyes enjoy all her bared beauties and my mouth devour them; and at last, burning with desires equal to mine, she opened her arms to me, making me promise to spare her in the one crucial point. What does one not promise in such moments? But where is the woman, if she really loves, who calls on her lover to keep his promise when love has taken the place vacated by his reason? After spending an hour in amorous toying which inflamed her and of which until that moment she had known nothing, I showed my mortification at having to leave her without paying her charms the chief homage they deserved. I saw her sigh.

As I had to resign myself to sleeping on the couch, and the fire having gone out, I asked her for a coverlet, since it was very cold. If I stayed in bed with her and abstained as I had promised I would, I should only too easily fall asleep. She told me to stay in bed while she went to light a faggot. Wanting to hurry, she did not think of dressing, and in a minute I saw a fine fire; but it was less strong than the one kindled in my mind and body by her charms, whose power, in the position she assumed to light the faggot, became overwhelming. I ran to her, determined to break my promise and certain that she would not have the firmness to resist me. Clasping her in my arms, I said that I would be too wretched unless, at least from pity if not from love, she would consent to make me happy.

"Then let us be happy," she answered, "and be sure that on my side pity has nothing to do with it."

We then lay down on the couch, and we did not leave each other until daybreak. After lighting the fire for me again, she went off to bed in her own room, locking the door behind her, and I fell asleep.

It was Madame XXX who waked me in the morning, dressed in a fetching dishabille.

"Good morning, Madame. What has become of my friend?"

"And mine. I have forgiven him. He gave me the clearest proof that he made a mistake. He has gone home. You must not tell him that you spent the night here, for he might think you had spent it with my niece. I am obliged to you. I am in need of your indulgence and especially of your discretion."

"You may count on that, Madame; it is enough for me to know that you have forgiven him."

"How could I help it? He is really something more than mortal. If you knew how he loves me! I am grateful to him. I am taking him to board with me for a year, and he will be well lodged and even better fed. So we shall leave today for La Villette,[37] where I have a charming little house. Just at the beginning I have to do this to silence spiteful tongues. At La Villette there will be a good room for you whenever you wish to come for supper. You will find a good bed in it. I am only sorry that you will be bored, for my niece is sulky."

"Your niece is very pleasant, she gave me a tasty supper and kept me excellent company until three o'clock in the morning."

"I congratulate her. How did she manage it when there was nothing in the house?"

"We ate all there was, and afterward she went off to bed and I slept very well here."

"I didn't think the girl had that much intelligence. Let us go see her. She has locked her door. Open up, will you! Why did you lock your door, you prude? Monsieur is a man of honor."

She opened her door, excusing herself for appearing in such undress, but she was dazzling.

"There she is," said her aunt. "As you see, she's not bad-looking. It's a pity she's so stupid. You were right to give Monsieur Casanova supper. I gambled all night; and when one gambles, one forgets everything else. I quite forgot that you were here, and not knowing that Count Tiretta would eat supper, I did not order anything. But in future we will sup. I have taken him to board. He is a young man of character and intelligence. You'll see how quickly he will learn to speak French. Get dressed, niece, for we must pack. After dinner we shall go to spend the whole spring at La Villette. And listen, niece, there's no need for you to tell my sister anything about all this."

"Never fear, my dear Aunt. Did I tell her anything *the other times?*"

"You see how stupid she is! Her 'the other times' would make one suppose the thing had happened to me before."

"I meant that I never tell her anything at all."

"We will dine at two o'clock, you shall dine with us, and we will leave immediately afterward. Tiretta promised me he would be here with his portmanteau. We will put everything in a hackney coach."

I promised her that I would not fail to come. I hurried home, very curious to hear the whole story from Tiretta himself. As he got out of bed he told me that he had sold himself for a year for twenty-five louis a month and board and lodging.

"I congratulate you. She tells me that you are something more than mortal."

"I worked all night for that; but I am sure you didn't waste your time either."

"Get dressed, for I am to dine there with you, and I mean to see you off for La Villette, where I shall go sometimes too, for your little darling has told me I have a room there."

We arrived at two o'clock. Madame XXX, dressed in clothes suitable for a girl, was a laughable sight, and Mademoiselle de la M——re was as beautiful as a star. At four o'clock they set out with Tiretta, and I went to the Comédie Italienne.[38]

I was in love with Mademoiselle de la M——re; but Silvia's daughter, with whom I had only the pleasure of supping at the family table, weakened a love which now left me nothing to desire. We complain of women who, though they love us and are sure that they are loved, refuse us their favors; and we are wrong. If they love us they must fear to lose us and hence must do all that they can to keep alive our desire to attain possession of them. If we attain it, nothing is surer than that we will no longer desire them, for one does not desire what one possesses; so women are right in refusing to yield to our desires. But if the desires of the two sexes are equal, why is it that a man never refuses a woman whom he loves and who urges him on? The reason can only be this: The man who loves and knows that he is loved rates the pleasure he is sure he will give the loved object more highly than the pleasure which that object can give him in fruition. Hence he is eager to satisfy her. Woman, whose great preoccupation is her own interest, cannot but rate the pleasure she will herself feel more highly than the pleasure she will give; hence she procrastinates as long as she can because she fears that in giving herself she will lose what concerns her most—her own pleasure. This feeling is bound up with the nature of the female sex, and it is the sole cause of coquetry, which reason forgives in women and which it can never forgive in a man. And in fact coquetry in a man is very seldom seen.

Silvia's daughter loved me, and she knew that I loved her even though I had never made her a declaration; but she took great care not to let me know it. She feared she would encourage me to demand favors of her, and not feeling sure that she would have the firmness to refuse, she felt afraid that she would lose me afterward. Her mother and father planned to marry her to Clément,[39] who had been her harpsichord teacher for the past three years; she knew it, and she could do nothing but consent, for though she was not in love with him she did not dislike him. Knowing that he was to be her husband, she could not but see him with pleasure. Most well-brought-up girls enter marriage without love having played any part in it, and they are content to do so. They seem to know that their husbands are one thing and their lovers another. Men commonly take the same attitude, especially in Paris. Frenchmen are jealous of their mistresses, never of their wives; but Clément the harpsichordist was visibly in love with his pupil, and she was delighted that I noticed it. She knew that, once I was certain of it, I should be led to make a declaration, and she was not mistaken. I resolved on it after Mademoiselle de la M——re left, and I had reason to repent. After my declaration Clément was dismissed; but I found myself in a worse position. The man who declares that he is in love with a woman except by the language of gesture needs to go to school.

Three days after Tiretta left, I took his few belongings to him at La Villette, and Madame XXX was pleased to see me. Just as we were sitting down at table the Abbé Desforges arrived. The stern rigorist, who had been most friendly to me in Paris, ate his dinner without ever giving me a look and did the same to Tiretta. But the latter finally lost his patience at dessert. He rose from the table

first, asking Madame XXX to let him know in advance
when she again entertained the gentleman, with whom
she immediately withdrew. Tiretta took me to see his
room which, as might be expected, was next to Madame's.
While he was putting away his clothes Mademoiselle took
me to see my room. It was a very attractive one on the
ground floor; hers was across from it. I pointed out how
easily I could go into hers when everyone was in bed,
but she replied that, as her bed was too small, she would
come to me.

She then told me all the extravagant things her aunt
was doing for Tiretta.

"She thinks," she said, "that we do not know he
sleeps with her. She rang this morning at eleven o'clock
and told me to go and ask him if he had had a good
night. Seeing that his bed had not been unmade, I asked
him if he had spent the night writing. He said that he
had and asked me to say nothing about it to Madame."

"Does he make eyes at you?"

"No. But even if he did—stupid as he is, he must
know that he is contemptible."

"Why?"

"Because my aunt pays him."

"You pay me too."

"Yes, but in the same coin as you give me."

Her aunt said that she was stupid, and she believed it.
Not only was she not stupid, she was both intelligent and
virtuous, and I should never have seduced her if she had
not been brought up in a convent of Béguines.[40]

I went back to Tiretta's room, where I spent more than
an hour. I asked him if he liked his work.

"I don't enjoy it; but since it costs me nothing I don't
think I am badly off. I don't have to look at her face,
and she is extremely clean."

"Does she take good care of you?"

"She is full of consideration. This morning she refused
my morning greeting. She said she was sure her refusal

would pain me, but that I ought to put my health above pleasure.''

The Abbé Desforges having gone, leaving Madame alone, we went to her room. She treated me like an old crony, cuddling up to Tiretta in the most revolting fashion. But my dauntless friend returned her caresses so heartily that I was amazed. She assured him he would not see the Abbé Desforges again. After telling her that she was damned in this world and the next, he had threatened to abandon her and she had taken him at his word.

An actress known as La Quinault,[41] who had retired from the stage and who was a neighbor, came to call on Madame XXX, and a quarter of an hour later I saw Madame Favart[42] with the Abbé de Voisenon;[43] in another quarter of an hour Mademoiselle Amelin[44] arrived with a handsome youth whom she called her nephew and whose name was Chalabre; he looked like her, but she did not think it reason enough to admit that she was his mother. Monsieur Paton,[45] a Piedmontese who was with her, finally let himself be persuaded to make a bank at faro, and in less than two hours won everybody's money except mine, for I did not play. My attention was all for Mademoiselle de la M—re. In addition, the banker was obviously a swindler, but Tiretta did not realize it until he had lost all his money and a hundred louis on his word. The banker then laid down the cards, and Tiretta told him in good Italian that he was a scoundrel. The Piedmontese replied with the utmost coolness that he was a liar. At that I said Tiretta had been joking, and I made him admit it, though he laughed as he spoke. He went off to his room. The affair had no consequences, and Tiretta would have been in the wrong.*

---

* Eight years later I saw Monsieur Paton in Petersburg, and in 1767 he was murdered in Poland. (C.'s note.)

That evening I preached him a most forceful sermon. I showed him that as soon as he played he laid himself open to the skill of the banker, who might be a scoundrel but at the same time a brave man, and hence, by daring to tell him so, he risked his life.

"Then am I to let myself be robbed?"

"Yes, for the choice is yours. You are at liberty not to play."

"By God, I won't pay the hundred louis."

"I advise you to pay even before he asks you for them."

Three quarters of an hour after I had gone to bed Mademoiselle de la M——re came to my arms, and we spent a much sweeter night than the first.

The next morning after breakfasting with Madame XXX and her lover I went back to Paris. Three or four days later Tiretta came to tell me that the merchant from Dunkirk had arrived, that he was to dine at Madame XXX's, and that she wanted me to be of the company. I dressed with anguish in my heart. I could neither consent to the marriage nor do what I could have done to prevent it. I found Mademoiselle de la M——re dressed more elaborately than usual.

"Your suitor," I said, "will not need all that to find you charming."

"My aunt does not think so. I am curious to see him, even though, since I trust you, I am sure he will never be my husband."

A moment later he arrived with the banker Kornmann,[46] who had arranged the marriage. I see a man of about forty with a handsome face expressing perfect frankness, very well dressed though unostentatiously, who presents himself to Madame XXX simply and politely and does not look at his future wife until Madame XXX introduces her to him. When he saw her his manner became less formal, and, eschewing any attempt at

fine phrases, he said no more to her than that he hoped
the impression she made on him might bear at least some
resemblance to the impression he trusted he might make
on her. She answered only with a graceful curtsy, continuing all the while to study him with grave attention.

Dinner is announced, the company sits down at table,
all sorts of things are discussed, but never the marriage.
The eyes of the couple met only by accident, and they
never addressed each other. After dinner Mademoiselle
withdrew to her room, and Madame went to her study
with Monsieur Kornmann and the suitor, where she spent
two hours. When they came out, since the gentlemen
had to go back to Paris, she sent for her and in her
presence told the suitor that she expected him the next
day and that she was sure her niece would be glad to see
him again.

"Will you not, my dear niece?"

"Yes, my dear Aunt. I shall be glad to see Monsieur
again tomorrow."

But for that answer he would have left without having
heard her voice.

"Well, what do you think of your husband?"

"Permit me, Aunt, not to talk of him until tomorrow;
and at table please be so good as to talk to me; for it is
possible that my looks may not have repelled him, but he
cannot yet know if I am capable of thought."

"I am afraid you will say something stupid and spoil
the good impression you have made on him."

"So much the better for him if the truth disabuses
him, and so much the worse for him and for me if we
decide to marry without first knowing at least something
of each other's views and opinions."

"How do you like him?"

"I think he is agreeable; but let us wait until tomorrow. It may be he who will want no more of me tomorrow,
for I am so stupid."

"I know perfectly well that you think you are bright; but that is exactly why you are stupid, despite Monsieur Casanova's saying that you have brains. He is laughing at you, my dear niece."

"I am certain he is not, my dear Aunt."

"There you are! No one could say anything more stupid."

"I beg your pardon," I said. "Mademoiselle is right in thinking that I am far from laughing at her, and I am also certain that tomorrow she will shine on whatever subjects we bring up for her."

"Then you will stay here; I am delighted. We will have a game of piquet and I will sit it out. My niece shall play with you, for she ought to learn."

Tiretta asked his little darling's permission to go to the theater. No visitors arrived, we played until suppertime; and after listening to Tiretta's attempts to tell us what the play was about we went off to bed.

I was surprised to see Mademoiselle de la M—re before me fully dressed.

"I will go and undress," she said, "after we have talked. Tell me frankly if I should consent to this marriage."

"How do you like Monsieur X?"

"I have nothing against him."

"Then consent."

"That is enough. Good-by. At this moment our love affair ends and our friendship begins. I am going to my own bed."

"Let our friendship begin tomorrow."

"No—not if it should kill me, and you too. It is hard, but I have made up my mind. If I am to become the man's wife, I must first assure myself that I am worthy of it. I may even be happy. Do not hold me, let me go. You know how much I love you."

"Let us at least kiss."

"Alas, no."

"You are weeping."

"No. In God's name, let me go!"

"Dear heart, you will go and weep in your room. I am in despair. Stay here. I will be your husband."

"No, I can no longer consent to it."

As she spoke these last words she tore her hands from mine and went, leaving me sunk in shame. I loathed myself. I did not know whether I was more guilty for having seduced her or for abandoning her to another.

At dinner the next day she shone. She conversed with her future husband so intelligently that I saw he was delighted with the treasure he was about to possess. As usual, I pretended to have a toothache as an excuse for saying nothing. Sad, thoughtful, and indeed ill from the painful night I had spent, I realized that I was in love, jealous, and in despair. Mademoiselle de la M—re never spoke to me or looked at me; she was right, but I would not admit it.

After dinner Madame went to her room with her niece and Monsieur X, and an hour later she came out and told us to congratulate her as she was to be married to Monsieur in a week and would leave with him for Dunkirk the same day.

"Tomorrow," she added, "we are all invited to dine at Monsieur Kornmann's, where the contract will be signed."

I am incapable of conveying to my reader the wretchedness which I felt.

They decided to go to the Comédie Française, and since there were four of them I excused myself. I went to Paris, where, thinking I had a fever, I immediately got into bed; but instead of my finding the rest I needed, the torments of my bitter repentance kept me in Hell. I believed that I must either stop the marriage or resign myself to dying. Being certain that Mademoiselle de la

M—re loved me, I could not believe that she would resist me when I made her understand that her refusal would cost me my life. With this idea in mind I got up and I wrote her a letter than which tumultuous passion could dictate nothing stronger. After thus soothing my grief I slept, and very early in the morning I sent my letter to Tiretta, asking him to convey it to the young lady secretly and saying that I would not leave my room until I had received an answer. I received it four hours later. This is what I read, trembling:

"My dear friend, it is too late. Leave your room. Come and dine at Monsieur Kornmann's, and be sure that in a few weeks we will both feel that we have won a great victory. Our love will no longer exist except in our memory. I beg you not to write to me again."

It was too much. Her refusal, with her more than cruel order not to write to her again, made me furious. I felt certain that her inconstant soul had fallen in love with the merchant. This supposition decided me to go and kill him. A hundred foul means of carrying out my infamous purpose crowded into a mind which, already in love and jealous, was now beside itself with anger, shame, and spite. Angel though she was, I saw her as a monster to be hated or a jilt to be punished. I thought of a method which could not fail, and though I considered it base I did not hesitate to embrace it. I determined to go to the future husband at Kornmann's where he was lodging and reveal to him all that had taken place between the young lady and myself, and, if that should not be enough to make him give up marrying her, to inform him that one of us must die, and finally, to murder him if he refused my challenge.

Thoroughly resolved to execute my horrible plan, the mere recollection of which today fills me with shame, I eat with a ravenous appetite, I go to bed, and I sleep soundly all night. When I wake I find no change in me.

I dress; I put a pair of excellent pistols in my pockets, and I go to Kornmann's in the Rue des Greniers-Saint-Lazare.[47] My rival was asleep; I wait. A quarter of an hour later I see him coming toward me with open arms. He embraces me; he says that he has been looking forward to my visit, for he could not but divine the feeling which he must also have inspired in one who was a friend of his future wife's and that he would always share in whatever feeling she entertained toward me.

His honest countenance, his frank manner, the conviction with which he spoke instantly make it impossible for me to talk to him as I had resolved to do. I am at a loss; I do not know what to say to him. Fortunately he gives me all the time I need to recover myself. He talked to me for a good quarter of an hour until Monsieur Kornmann came and coffee was brought. When I had to speak to him, what I said was unexceptionable.

Leaving the house a different man from the one who had entered it, I was amazed; not only was I glad that I had not carried out my purpose, I felt ashamed and humiliated that it was only to chance that I owed not being a base scoundrel. I ran into my brother, and after spending the morning with him I took him to dine at Silvia's, where I remained until midnight. I saw that it was her daughter who would make me forget Mademoiselle de la M—re, whom I felt that I must not see again before her marriage.

The next morning I packed my few traveling things in a hatbox and went to Versailles to pay my court to the ministers.

## CHAPTER IV

*The Abbé de Laville. The Abbé Galiani. Character of the Neapolitan dialect. I go to Dunkirk on a secret mission. I am completely successful. I return to Paris by way of Amiens. My comical escapades. Monsieur de la Bretonnière. My report gives satisfaction. I receive five hundred louis. Reflections.*

THE MINISTER of Foreign Affairs asked me if I would be interested in undertaking secret missions and if I thought I had any aptitude in that way. I replied that I would be interested in anything which I considered honest and by which I could be sure of earning money, and that so far as aptitude was concerned I left it to him. He told me to go and talk with the Abbé de Laville.

The Abbé, the First Secretary, was a man of cold temperament, a profound politician, the soul of his department, and very highly esteemed. He had served the State well as Chargé d'Affaires at The Hague;[1] in gratitude, the King gave him a bishopric on the very day that he died. It was a little too late. The heir to all he possessed was Garnier,[2] a self-made man who had been cook to Monsieur d'Argenson[3] and who had become rich by profiting from the friendship which the Abbé de Laville had always felt for him. The two friends, who were about the same age, had named each other residuary legatee in wills which they had deposited with a notary. The survivor was Garnier.

The Abbé, then, after treating me to a short discourse on the nature of secret missions and on the prudence necessary in those who undertook them, said that he would inform me as soon as anything suitable for me turned up, and he kept me for dinner. At table I met the Abbé Galiani,[4] the Neapolitan Embassy Secretary. He was a brother of the Marchese Galiani, of whom I will speak when we come to my journey to the Kingdom of Naples. The Abbé was very witty. He had an extraordinary knack for giving his most serious remarks a tinge of humor, and always with a straight face, speaking French very well with the incorrigible Neapolitan accent, which made him a favorite in all circles. The Abbé de Laville told him that Monsieur Voltaire complained that his *Henriade*[5] had been translated into Neapolitan verse in a way which made readers laugh. He replied that Voltaire was in the wrong, for the nature of the Neapolitan language was such that it was impossible to handle it in verse except in a way which aroused laughter.

"If you can imagine it," he said, "we have translations of the Bible and the *Iliad* both of which are funny."

"I can believe it of the Bible, but I find it surprising in the case of the *Iliad*."

Having returned to Paris the day before Mademoiselle de la M—re, now Madame P., was to leave, I could not avoid going to Madame XXX's to congratulate her and wish her a good journey. I was more pleased than vexed by her easy and happy manner—a sure sign that I was cured. We talked to each other without the least constraint. I thought her husband a very worthy man. In response to his solicitations I promised him that I would visit them in Dunkirk, not intending to keep my word; but I did keep it. So Tiretta was left alone with his little darling, whom his fidelity made more madly in love with him every day.

My soul being now at peace, I began an Arcadian courtship of Manon Balletti, who every day gave me some new testimony to the progress which I was making in her heart. The friendship and esteem which I felt for her family kept me from harboring any idea of seducing her; but falling more in love with her every day and not intending to ask for her hand in marriage, I had no clear idea at what I was aiming.

At the beginning of May[6] the Abbé de Bernis wrote me that I should go to Versailles to talk with the Abbé de Laville. The Abbé asked me if I thought I was capable of paying a visit to ten or twelve warships which were anchored at Dunkirk and becoming well enough acquainted with their commanding officers to give him a detailed report on how well they were provisioned in all respects, especially as to their supplies in general, the numbers of their crews, their stock of munitions of all kinds, their administration, and their discipline. I answered that I could try, that when I returned I would give him my report in writing, and that it would be for him to tell me if I had done well.

"Since it is a secret mission," he said, "I cannot give you any letters. I can only wish you a successful journey and give you some money."

"I do not want any money. When I return you may give me what you consider I have deserved; as for my making a successful journey, I shall need at least three days before starting, for I must get some sort of letter."

"Then try to be back before the end of the month. That is all I have to say."

On the same day I had a half hour's conversation at

the Palais Bourbon with my patron, who, unable to resist praising me for my delicacy in refusing to take any money in advance, gave me another roll of a hundred louis with his usual magnanimity. From then on I never again needed to make use of the generous man's purse, not even at Rome fourteen years later.

"Since the mission is secret," he said, "I am sorry that I cannot give you a passport; but through Silvia you can obtain one on some pretext from the First Gentleman of the Bedchamber[7] now serving. You must be extremely prudent in your behavior, and above all keep clear of anything *in munere* ['in the way of bribery'],[8] for you know, I believe, that if you get into any difficulty appealing to your principal will avail you nothing. You will be disowned. The only acknowledged spies are the ambassadors. So you need to be even more reserved and circumspect than they are. If when you come back you will let me see your report before you take it to the Abbé de Laville, I will give you my advice regarding what I think you should omit from it."

Full of this business, in which I was a complete novice, I told Silvia that, as I wanted to accompany some English friends to Calais and return to Paris, she would do me a great favor if she would obtain a passport for me from the Duke of Gesvres.[9] Glad to oblige me, she wrote to the Duke, telling me that I must deliver the letter to him personally, since passports of this kind could not be issued unless they contained a description of the bearer. They were valid only in the so-called Île de France,[10] but they procured respect in all the northern part of the kingdom. So I went to him with her husband. The Duke was at his estate in Saint-Ouen.[11] No sooner had he seen me and read Silvia's letter than he had a passport issued for me; and after leaving Mario I went to La Villette to ask Madame XXX if she wanted me to take any message from her to her niece. She said that I could take her

*Joseph de Pâris-Duverney*

*Fulfillment*

the box of porcelain figures if Monsieur Kornmann had
not yet sent it. So I went to see the banker, who delivered
it to me and to whom I gave a hundred louis, asking him
for the same amount in a letter of credit on a reliable
house in Dunkirk together with a personal recommendation, since I was going there for pleasure. Kornmann
gladly did both, and I set out toward evening of the same
day.

Three days later I put up at the Conciergerie[12] in
Dunkirk. An hour after my arrival I gave the charming
Madame P. the most pleasant surprise by delivering her
box and conveying her aunt's compliments to her. Just
as she was praising her husband to me and saying that
he made her happy, he arrived and, delighted to see me,
at once offered me a room without even asking if my
stay in Dunkirk was to be long or short. After duly
thanking him and promising that I would come and take
potluck for dinner at his house from time to time, I
asked him to show me the way to the banker to whom
Monsieur Kornmann had recommended me.

Scarcely had the banker read the letter before he gave
me a hundred louis and asked me to expect him at my
inn toward evening, when he would introduce me to the
Commandant. The latter was Monsieur du Bareil.[13] With
the politeness of all Frenchmen in high office, the Commandant, after asking me the usual questions, invited
me to sup with his wife, who was still at the theater. She
received me as cordially as her husband had done, and
having excused myself from cards, I began making the
acquaintance of the company, especially of the army and
navy officers. Making a point of talking about all the
European navies and giving myself out to be an expert
on the subject from having served in the fleet of my
Republic, it took me no more than three days not only to
pick up an acquaintance of all the naval captains but
to become good friends with them. I rattled away about

shipbuilding and the Venetian system of maneuvers, and I observed that the worthy sailors who listened to me were even more attentive when I talked nonsense than they were when I said anything sensible. On the fourth day one of the captains invited me on board his ship for dinner; whereupon all the others invited me either to breakfast or to a between-meals repast. I devoted the entire day to each of the captains who thus honored me. I showed interest in everything, I went down into the hold, I asked countless questions, and everywhere I found young officers eager to show their importance, whom I had no difficulty in pumping. I got them to confide to me whatever I needed to know for my detailed report. Before going to bed I wrote down everything good or bad I had learned during the day about the ship on which I had been. I slept only four or five hours. In two weeks I considered that I had learned enough.

During this journey neither women nor any other pleasure turned me from my course; my mission was always the sole thing in my mind and the sole object of all my efforts. I dined once at the banker Kornmann's and once at Monsieur P.'s in the city and a second time in a small country house he owned a league away. Madame P. took me there in her carriage, and when she was alone with me I saw that she was delighted with my behavior. I showed her nothing but the fondest friendship. Seeing that she was charming, and my love affair with her having ended only five or six weeks earlier, I was surprised at my coldness. I knew myself too well to attribute my behavior to my virtue. Then what accounted for it? An Italian proverb, which speaks for human nature, gives the real reason: *C. . . non vuol pensieri* ("The p[rick] does not want to think").[14]

My mission being accomplished, I took leave of everyone and got into my post chaise to return to Paris, giving myself the pleasure of taking a different route from that by which I had come. Arriving about midnight at I forget what post station, I order horses to go on to the next. The postilion says that the next post is at Aire,[15] a fortified town which could not be entered at night. I answer that I will get the gate opened for me and I repeat my order to put two horses to my chaise. I come to Aire. The postilion cracks his whip and says, "Courier." After an hour's wait the gate is opened and I am told that I must go to see the Commandant.[16] I go there, cursing, and am shown into an alcove in which a man in an elegant nightcap was in bed with a woman whose pretty face I could see.

"Whose courier are you?"

"Nobody's, but since I am in a hurry——"

"That will do. We will talk tomorrow. Meanwhile you will stay in the guardhouse. Let me sleep. Be off."

I was taken to the guardhouse, where I spent the rest of the night sitting on the ground. Day breaks, I shout, I swear, I say that I must go. No one answers. Ten o'clock strikes; raising my voice, I tell the officer on duty that the Commandant has it in his power to have me murdered but that I cannot be refused writing materials or a courier for Paris. He asks my name; I show it to him on my passport; he says he will take it to the Commandant to read; I snatch it from him; he tells me to go with him and speak to the Commandant, and I consent.

We go. The officer enters first and comes out four minutes later to show me in too. I hand the Commandant my passport, he reads it, looking at me to see if I am the person named in it, then hands it back to me, saying that I am free. He orders the officer to let me take post horses.

"By now," I said, "I am no longer in a hurry. I have to send a courier to someone and wait for him to come back. By delaying my journey you have broken the law of nations."

"It is you who broke it by saying that you were a courier."

"On the contrary, I told you that I was not."

"You told the postilion you were, and that is enough."

"The postilion lied. All I said to him was that I would get the gate opened for me."

"Why didn't you show me your passport?"

"Why didn't you give me time enough?"

"In three or four days we shall know which of us is in the wrong."

"Do whatever you please."

I was taken to the post station, which was also the inn, and a moment later I see my post chaise at the door. I ask the post master for an express messenger ready to leave at my demand, a room with a good bed, paper, pens, and ink, a broth at once and a good dinner at two o'clock. I have my trunk and everything I had in my chaise carried upstairs, I undress, I wash, and I sit down to write, not knowing to whom, for when all was said and done I was in the wrong; but I had undertaken to show my importance and I felt I must continue to play the role I had assumed. However, I was sorry I had made it necessary for me to stay in Aire until the messenger for whom I had asked should return. I had decided to spend the night there, at least I should get some rest. I had nothing on but my shirt and I was drinking the broth I had ordered when the Commandant appeared before me unattended.

"I am sorry," he said most politely, "that you think you have reason to complain, whereas I have only done my duty, for I had to believe what your postilion would never have said unless you had ordered him to do so."

"That is possible, but your duty did not extend to turning me out of your room."

"I needed sleep."

"And I need it now, but politeness keeps me from imitating you."

"May I make bold to ask you if you have ever served ?"

"I have served on land and sea, and I resigned at the age when many others are beginning."

"If you have served you must know that the gate of a fortified town is never opened at night except to royal couriers and to the supreme military command."

"But once it has been opened politeness might be observed."

"Are you disposed to dress and take a walk with me ?"

I am as pleased by his proposal as I am nettled by his haughtiness. The thought of a sword thrust given or received comes to me instantly as a most attractive prospect. I answer calmly and respectfully that the honor of taking a walk with him is enough to make me put off all other business. I asked him to sit down while I hastened to dress. I put on my breeches, throwing the pistols which were in their pockets onto the bed, I send down for a hairdresser who does my hair in two minutes, and I draw my sword from an oilcloth sheath and hang it at my side. After locking my room I leave the key with the innkeeper, and we go out.

After walking along two or three streets we go through a porte-cochere into a courtyard through which I expect we will pass; but he stops at the end of it in front of an open door and I see a numerous gathering of men and women. It did not occur to me to turn back.

"This is my wife," said the Commandant, and, in the same breath, "this," he said to her, "is Monsieur de Casanova who has come to dine with us."

"I am very glad," said the beautiful woman, rising after laying down her cards; "otherwise, Monsieur, I should never have forgiven you for the distress you caused us by having us waked last night."

"Yet it is a fault for which I have paid rather dearly, Madame. After such a Purgatory permit me to say that I deserve the Paradise in which I find myself."

At that she laughed, made me sit down beside her, and returned to the game. I instantly realized that I had been outwitted in masterly fashion; but there was nothing I could do but put a good face on it, and the more so since the pretty trick got me out of a very ugly situation at no cost to my honor and gave me a very plausible excuse for leaving without sending the courier I had ordered to I knew not whom. The Commandant, whose pleasure in his victory put him in high spirits, spoke of the war,[17] the court, the news of the day, often addressing his remarks to me as imperturbably as if there had never been any quarrel between us. He was enjoying himself thoroughly in his role of hero of the play; but on my side I maintained the attitude of a young man who has obliged an old officer to accord him a reparation, for such it was and one which did me all the honor I could ask.

Dinner was served, and since success in my role depended entirely on how well I played it, I have seldom been more wide awake than I was at the table, where the only remarks addressed to me simply provided pretty opportunities for Madame to shine. She was at least thirty years younger than her husband, and the misunderstanding which had condemned me to six hours in the guardhouse was not once mentioned; but at dessert the Commandant himself almost brought things to a head by a sly joke which was not worth making.

"It was very kind of you," he said to me, "to believe that I was going to fight you. I fooled you."

"I don't know if I believed it," I answered, "but I know that I was instantly curious to see what the walk on which you invited me would turn out to be, and I admire your cleverness. But far from considering myself fooled, I consider that you have made me reparation, and I am very grateful to you."

He did not answer, and we rose from the table. Madame invited me to make a third at ombre, then we went for a walk, and toward nightfall I took my leave; but I did not resume my journey until the next morning, after making a fair copy of my report.

At five o'clock in the morning I was sleeping in my chaise when I was waked. I was at the gate of the city of Amiens, and the person who waked me was a clerk of the office at which the duties levied on merchandise in transit are paid. The clerk asked me if I had anything forbidden by the King's orders. In a bad humor, like any man whom some brute deprives of sweet sleep to ask him a tiresome question, I reply that by G.. I had nothing and that he could f...... well have let me go on sleeping.

"Since you see fit to be rude, we shall see."

He orders the postilion to bring my chaise in, has my bags taken off, tells me to get out, demands my keys, and keeps me waiting while everything has been examined.

I at once realized the mistake I had made, and I could no longer set it right. As I had nothing, there was nothing to fear, but my petulance was to cost me two hours of boredom while I raged in silence and let the villains use the right they had. I saw their pleasure in their revenge portrayed on their insolent faces. The clerks who in those days were stationed at the gates of French cities to examine travelers were the scum of the earth; but when they were politely treated by people of distinction they prided themselves on becoming tractable. A twenty-four-sou piece[18] graciously proffered made them human; they bowed to the traveler, they wished him a good journey and gave him no trouble. I knew all this; but there are moments when a man gives in to bad temper and forgets, or disregards, what he knows.

The brutes emptied my bags and even unfolded my shirts, among which, they said, I might have English laces. After going through everything they gave me back my keys; but that was not the end of it. My chaise had to be searched. The scoundrel who searches it exults when he finds the remains of a pound of snuff which I had bought at Saint-Omer[19] on my way to Dunkirk. The head of the gang triumphantly orders my chaise impounded and tells me I must pay a fine of twelve hundred francs.

This time I really lost my patience, and I leave my reader to guess all that I said to the cutthroats. I told them to take me to the Intendant;[20] but they answered that I was free to find my own way there. Surrounded by a growing mob, I enter the city, striding along like a madman. I go into the first open shop I see and ask the proprietor to take me to the Intendant; I tell my story, and a respectable-looking man who happened to be there says that he will show me the way himself but that I shall not find him since he must already be informed of the affair. He says that unless I pay or give security I will not easily escape from my difficulty. I ask him to show me the way and leave the rest to me. He says that I must first get rid of the mob by sending a louis to a distant tavern and telling them to go there for breakfast. I give him a louis and ask him to do me the favor. He executed the maneuver most successfully, and the whole mob disappeared with joyous shouts. Such is the people which today believes itself to be the King of France. The man who was to take me to the Intendant tells me that he is a prosecutor[21] by profession.

We arrive at the Intendant's house; but the porter tells us that he has gone out alone, that he will not come home until evening, and that he does not know where he will dine.

"There's the whole day gone," said the Prosecutor.

"Let us look for him where he is likely to be, he must have friends, habits. I will pay you a louis for your time."

"I am at your orders."

We spent four hours vainly looking for him at ten or twelve houses. In all of them I had talked to the master or the mistress, always exaggerating the indignity to which I had been subjected. They listened, they condoled with me, but the only comfort they offered me was to say that he would certainly come home to sleep and that then he would have to hear me out.

At half past one the Prosecutor took me to the house of an old lady who had great influence in the city. She was at table alone. After listening attentively to my story, she said with the greatest composure that she did not think it would be indiscreet in her to tell a stranger where to find a man whose office forbade him ever to be inaccessible.

"And so, Monsieur, I can reveal to you what is no secret. My daughter told me last evening that she was invited to Madame XX's and that the Intendant was to dine there too. So go there now, and you will find him at table with the best society in Amiens. I advise you," she said with a smile, "to go in without being announced. The servants taking dishes from the kitchen to the dining-room will show you the way without your asking them. Once there, you can speak to him whether he likes it or not and despite your not knowing him; he will hear all the horrors you have told me in your justifiable indignation. I am sorry I cannot be present when you stage your surprise."

I bowed to her hurriedly and ran to the house she had named, accompanied by the exhausted Prosecutor. I had no difficulty finding my way with the servants and my guide to a room in which I saw twenty people at table in high spirits.

"Pray excuse me, ladies and gentlemen," I said, addressing the company, "if in the terrible state in which you see me I am obliged to come here to trouble the peace and festivity of your repast."

At this compliment, uttered in thunderous tones, everyone rises. My hair was in disorder and I was dripping with sweat; my face was that of a fiend; the reader can imagine the surprise of a company made up entirely of elegant women and of men entitled to pay court to them.

"For the last seven hours," I went on, "I have been searching every house in this city for His Honor the Intendant, whom at last I find here because I know that here he is and that, if he has ears, he now hears me. I have come, then, to tell him to order his henchmen, who have impounded my conveyance, to release it to me instantly so that I can continue my journey. If Catalan laws[22] decree that, for seven ounces of snuff, which are for my own personal use, I must pay twelve hundred francs, I repudiate them and I inform him that I will not pay a sou. I will remain here, I will send a courier to my Ambassador, who will complain to the King that the law of nations has been violated upon my person in the Île de France, and I will have satisfaction. Louis XV is great enough to refuse to make himself an accomplice in these extraordinary and murderous proceedings. Moreover, if reparation is denied me this affair will become a great affair of State, for what my Republic will do in reprisal will not be to have every Frenchman traveling in her States murdered but to order every one of them to leave her territories. This is who I am. Read."

Foaming with rage, I throw my passport in the middle of the table. A man picks it up and reads it, and I infer that he is the Intendant. While the paper passed from hand to hand among the startled guests he haughtily said to me that he was in Amiens for no purpose but to enforce the ordinances and that consequently I should not leave unless I paid or furnished security.

"If that is your duty, you should consider my passport an ordinance. Be my security yourself, if you are a gentleman."

"Does the nobility in your country stand security for lawbreakers?"

"The nobility in my country does not lower itself by accepting dishonorable employments."

"In the King's service no employment is dishonorable."

"The hangman uses the same language."

"Take care what you say."

"Take care what you do. Know, Monsieur, that I am a free man and a man of nice honor who has been outraged and that I am afraid of nothing. I defy you to have me thrown out of the window."

"Monsieur," a lady said to me imperiously, "in my house no one is thrown out of the window."

"Anger, Madame, often makes a man lose his head. I am at your feet craving your forgiveness. Be so good as to consider that this is the first time in my life that I am the victim of fraudulent proceedings in a kingdom in which I believed I need only be on guard against the attacks of highway robbers; for them I have pistols; for these gentlemen I have a passport, but I find that it is worthless. For seven ounces of snuff which I bought at Saint-Omer three weeks ago this gentleman despoils me and interrupts my journey, when the King himself is my surety that no one will dare to interrupt it; I am ordered to pay fifty louis, I am consigned to the fury of a raging mob, from which that worthy man there delivered me for a price; I am treated like a criminal, and the man who should defend me sneaks away and hides. His cutthroats at the gate of this city have rumpled my coats and shirts to avenge themselves on me for not having given them twenty-four sous. What has happened to me will be the talk of the diplomatic corps at Versailles and Paris tomorrow, and in a very few days it will be read in numerous gazettes. I will not pay one sou. Speak, sir," I said to the Intendant. "Shall I send a courier to the Duke of Gesvres?"

"Pay. And if you refuse to pay, do whatever you please."

"Then good-by, ladies and gentlemen."

Just as I am leaving the room like a madman, I hear a voice telling me in Italian to wait a moment. I see an elderly man, who addresses the Intendant in these words:

"Give orders at once that the gentleman may leave. I will stand security for him. Do you hear me, Intendant? You do not know the Italian spirit. I served through the whole of the last war in Italy, and I had several opportunities to learn what it is. I consider that this gentleman is in the right."

"Very well, then," the Intendant said to me. "Simply pay thirty or forty francs to the office, for the matter has already been recorded."

"I repeat that I will pay nothing. But who are you, worthy sir, who stand surety for me without knowing me?"

"I am a commissary of war,[23] my name is La Bretonnière,[24] I live in Paris at the Hôtel de Saxe[25] in the Rue du Colombier; I shall be there day after tomorrow. Do me the honor of calling on me and we will go to Monsieur de Britard,[26] who, when he has been apprised of the matter, will release me from my suretyship, which I assume on your behalf with great pleasure."

After expressing all my gratitude to him and assuring him that he would see me at his lodging very soon, I made my excuses to the entire company and went to dine at an inn, inviting my worthy Prosecutor, who was beside himself, to accompany me. As we rose from the table I gave him two louis. But for this man and the stalwart Commissary, I should have been in a great quandary, for though I was not short of money I would never have made up my mind to leave fifty louis there.

My chaise being ready at the door of the inn, just as I was getting into it one of the clerks who had gone through my belongings came up and said that I should find everything in it that I had left there.

"That would surprise me," I answered; "shall I find my snuff too?"

"The snuff, my Prince, has been confiscated."

"That is too bad. I would have given you a louis."

"I'll go for it now."

"I haven't time to wait. Whip up, postilion."

I arrived in Paris the next day. Four days later I went to see La Bretonnière, who took me to the Farmer-General Britard, who released him from his suretyship. He was a young and very agreeable man, who blushed for all that I had been made to suffer.

I at once took my report to the Minister, at the Hôtel de Bourbon; he spent two hours with me making me delete whatever he considered unnecessary. I spent the night making a fair copy of it, and the next day I took it to Versailles to the Abbé de Laville, who after coldly reading it said he would let me know the outcome at his convenience. A month later I received five hundred louis, and I had the pleasure to learn that Monsieur de Crémille,[27] the Minister of Marine, found my whole report not only accurate but informative. A number of well-founded apprehensions made me decline the honor of making myself known to him, though my patron wished to procure it for me.

When I related my two adventures to him one at Aire and the other at Amiens, he was amused; but he told me that the true courage of a man on a secret mission should consist in his never getting into difficulties, for even if he was able to get out of them with no help but his cleverness they were bound to make him talked about and that was precisely what he should avoid.

My mission cost the Department of Marine twelve

thousand francs. The Minister could easily have found out everything I told him in my report without spending a sou. Any young officer could have served his turn, and any intelligent young officer would have served it well in order to gain his good opinion. But such were all the departments of the French ministry under the monarchical government. They squandered money which cost them nothing on their henchmen and on anyone they liked; they were despots, the people was downtrodden, the State in debt, and the finances in such bad condition that the inevitable bankruptcy would have overthrown it: *a revolution was necessary*. This is the language of the representatives who today reign in France, pretending to be the faithful ministers of the master of the Republic, the people. Poor people! Stupid people, which dies of hunger and poverty or goes to be massacred all over Europe to enrich those who have deceived it.

Silvia found my adventures at Aire and Amiens very amusing, and her daughter condoled with me over the wretched night I had been forced to spend in the guardhouse at Aire. I replied that I should have been in despair if I had had a wife with me, and she retorted that if she was a good wife it would have been her duty to go to the guardhouse with her husband.

"On the contrary, my dear daughter," said Silvia in her wisdom; "in such cases a wife who deserves the name, after seeing to the safety of their carriage, goes to the person in charge to plead for her husband's release."

## CHAPTER V

*The Count of La Tour d'Auvergne and Madame d'Urfé. Camilla. My passion for the Count's mistress; ridiculous incident which cures me. The Count of Saint-Germain.*

DESPITE THIS budding love I did not lose my taste for the mercenary beauties who brightened the haunts of pleasure and got themselves talked about; but those who most interested me were the kept women and the ones who claimed to belong to the public only because they sang or danced or acted. Considering themselves free women in all other respects, they enjoyed their privilege by surrendering now to love, now to money, and sometimes to both at once. I had very easily managed to make the acquaintance of them all. The lobbies of the theaters are the noble mart to which men so inclined repair to exercise their talent for entering on intrigues. I had profited well from this pleasant school; I began by making friends with their official lovers, and I succeeded by never asserting any pretensions and especially by appearing to be not ingenuous but innocuous. It was always necessary to have my purse ready when the occasion demanded, but since the sums were not large the pain was not as great as the pleasure. I was sure that in one way or another it would be made worth my while.

Camilla,[1] actress and dancer at the Comédie Italienne, whom I had begun to love at Fontainebleau seven years earlier, was the woman of this kind on whom I especially fastened because of the pleasures I enjoyed in her small house at the Barrière Blanche,[2] where she lived with her lover the Count of Égreville,[3] who made much of me among their guests. The brother of the Marquis de Gamaches[4] and of the Countess du Rumain,[5] he was a handsome young man, very amiable and reasonably rich. He was never so happy as when he saw a great deal of company in his mistress's house. She loved only him; but, full of intelligence and tact, she drove none of her admirers to despair; neither miserly nor prodigal in granting her favors, she made all the members of her circle adore her without having to fear either a blabbing tongue or the mortification of being cast off.

After her lover the man whom she honored with her attention above all the rest was the Count of La Tour d'Auvergne.[6] He was a nobleman of ancient lineage who adored her and who, not being rich enough to have her entirely to himself, had to be content with the share in her which she granted him. She was said to love him second best. She allowed him a modest sum for the expenses of a young girl whom she had, in a manner of speaking, given him as a present on seeing that he had fallen in love with her when she was in her service. La Tour d'Auvergne kept her at Paris with him in furnished rooms in the Rue Taranne;[7] he said that he loved her because she was a present his dear Camilla had given him; and he often took her to sup with her at the Barrière Blanche. She was fifteen years old, simple, ingenuous, without a grain of ambition; she told her lover she would never forgive him an infidelity except with Camilla, to whom she thought she

must yield him because she owed her happiness to her.
I fell so much in love with the girl that I often went to
sup at Camilla's only in the hope of finding her there
and enjoying the artless remarks with which she enchanted the entire company. I tried my best not to
betray myself, but I was so mad about her that by the
time supper was over I would often have become very
gloomy because I saw that my passion could not be
cured in the usual way. Allowing my condition to be
suspected would have made me ridiculous, and Camilla
would have railed at me mercilessly. But now for what
happened to cure me of my passion.

As Camilla's little house was at the Barrière Blanche I
sent my lackey for a hackney coach to take me home when
everyone was ready to leave after supper. Since we had
remained at table until an hour after midnight he told me
that no coaches were to be found. La Tour d'Auvergne
said that it would be no inconvenience to him to take me
home, though his carriage was only for two.

"My little girl," he said, "will sit on our laps."

I accept, of course, and here I am in the carriage, with
the Count at my left and Babet sitting on our thighs. Full
of desire, I determine to seize the opportunity, and, wasting no time, for the coachman was driving fast, I take her
hand, squeeze it, she squeezes mine, I gratefully raise it
to my lips, covering it with silent kisses, and, impatient
to convince her of my ardor, I proceed as my state of bliss
demands that I do; but just at the moment of crisis I
hear La Tour d'Auvergne saying:

"I am obliged to you, my dear friend, for a piece of
your country's politeness of which I thought I was no
longer worthy; I hope it is not a mistake."

At these horrifying words I put out my hand, I feel the
sleeve of his coat; there is no such thing as presence of
mind at such a moment, and the more so since the words
were followed by a laugh which would have confounded

the most hardened of men. I let go, unable either to laugh at the thing or deny it. Babet asked her lover why he was laughing so hard, and when he tried to tell her the reason laughter overcame him again, I said nothing, and I felt an utter fool. Fortunately the carriage soon stopped at my lodging, and, my lackey opening the door for me, I went in, wishing them a good night, which La Tour d'Auvergne reciprocated still laughing uproariously. As for me, I did not begin to laugh at the episode until half an hour later, for, after all, it was funny; nevertheless it depressed and vexed me, for I saw that I must expect to be the butt of many jokes.

Three or four days later I decided to go at nine in the morning and ask the obliging nobleman to give me breakfast, for Camilla had sent to inquire after my health. I did not mean to let the incident stop my visits to her, but I wanted first to know how the thing had been taken.

As soon as the charming La Tour saw me he exploded into laughter and after laughing his fill came and embraced me, mincing like a girl. I begged him, half humorously, half seriously, to forget my silly blunder, for I really did not know how to defend myself.

"Why try to defend yourself?" he answered. "We all like you, it is a very funny story, which has delighted us and delights us every evening."

"Then everyone knows of it?"

"Can you doubt that? Camilla is dying of laughter, and you must come this evening, I'll bring Babet, and she will set you laughing too, for she maintains that you made no mistake."

"She is right."

"What! she is right? Tell that to someone else. You do me too much honor, and I do not believe a word of it; but you are taking the right stand."

And it was the stand I took at table, pretending to be amazed at La Tour's indiscretion and saying that I was

cured of my passion for him. Babet called me a dirty
swine and refused to believe I was cured. For unfathom-
able reasons the episode turned me against her and attached me to La Tour d'Auvergne, who had every quality
to make everyone like him. But my friendship for him
very nearly had a disastrous consequence.

It was on a Monday in the foyer of the Comédie Italienne that the charming Count asked me to lend him a
hundred louis, promising to return them on Saturday.

"I haven't that much. But here is my purse at your
service," I said, "with ten or twelve louis."

"I need a hundred, and immediately, for I lost them
last night on my word at the Princess of Anhalt's." * 8

"I haven't that much."

"A collector of the lottery must have over a thousand."

"Of course, but my cash box is sacred; I have to turn
it over to the fiscal agent a week from today."

"It won't keep you from turning it over, for I will
return them to you on Saturday. Take a hundred louis
from your cash box, and put my word of honor in their
place. Do you think it worth a hundred louis?"

At that I turn my back on him, telling him to wait for
me, I go to my office in the Rue Saint-Denis, I take a
hundred louis, and I bring them to him. Saturday arrives, I do not see him, and on Sunday morning I pawn
my ring and put the same amount in my cash box, which
I turn over to the fiscal agent the next day. Three or four
days later in the amphitheater of the Comédie Française, up comes La Tour d'Auvergne and apologizes. I
reply by showing him my hand and saying that I had
pawned my ring to save my honor. He answers gloomily
that someone has failed him but that he is sure he can
return the amount to me on the following Saturday:

---

* She was the mother of Empress Catherine of Russia. (C.'s
note.)

"And I give you," he said, "my word of honor for it."

"Your word of honor is in my cash box, so you will permit me not to count on it further; you may return the hundred louis to me when you please."

At these words I saw the gallant nobleman turn as pale as a corpse.

"My word of honor, my dear Casanova," he said, "is dearer to me than life, and I will give you the hundred louis tomorrow morning at nine o'clock a hundred paces from the coffeehouse at the end of the Champs Élysées. I will give them to you privately, no one will see us, I hope that you will not fail to be there and that you will have your sword, as I shall have mine."

"I find it very regrettable, sir, that you insist on my paying so dearly for a jest. You do me infinite honor, but I would rather apologize to you, if that can prevent this unfortunate matter from going further."

"No, I am far more in the wrong than you, and the wrong can only be undone by the blood of one of us. Will you come?"

"Yes."

I supped at Silvia's in great depression, for I loved the gallant man, and I loved myself no less. I felt I was in the wrong, for my jest had really been too cutting, but it did not enter my mind not to keep the appointment.

I arrived at the coffeehouse a moment after he did; we breakfasted, he paid, and we left and walked in the direction of the Étoile. When we were sure we were not observed he handed me a roll of a hundred louis with the greatest courtesy; and, saying that one thrust should suffice on either side, he unsheathed after stepping back four paces. My only answer was to unsheathe too, and as soon as I saw that I was in measure I gave him my straight lunge, and, certain that I had wounded him in the chest, I jumped back, calling upon him to keep his

word. Mild as a lamb, he lowered his sword, put his hand
to his chest, and, showing it to me stained with blood, said
that he was satisfied. I spoke to him with all the civility
of which I was capable and which the occasion demanded,
while he applied a handerchief to his chest. I was very
glad when, looking at the point of my sword, I saw that
only one line[9] of it showed blood. I offered to see him
home and he refused. He asked me to be discreet and to
be his friend thenceforward. After embracing him in
tears, I went home very sad and considerably wiser in the
ways of the world. Our meeting never became known. A
week later we supped together at Camilla's.

About this same time I received twelve thousand francs
from the Abbé de Laville as the honorarium for the mission I had accomplished in Dunkirk. Camilla told me that
La Tour d'Auvergne was in bed because of his sciatica,
adding that if I liked we would pay him a visit the next
day. I accepted, we went, and after breakfasting I told
him gravely that if he would let me do what I wished to
his thigh I would cure it, for his trouble was not what
was called "sciatica" but a damp humor which I would
dispel with the Talisman of Solomon[10] and five words.
He laughed but told me to do whatever I pleased.

"Then I will go and buy a brush."

"I will send a servant."

"No, for I must be sure that it is bought without
haggling, and I have to get some drugs too."

I went for niter, flowers of sulphur, mercury, and a
small brush, and I told him I needed a small quantity of
his urine, which must be fresh. His laughter and Camilla's did not impair my gravity; I handed him a glass, I
drew his curtains, and he obeyed me. After making a
little amalgam with it, I told Camilla to rub his thigh
with her hands while I murmured a spell, but that all
would be lost if she laughed. After spending a good
quarter of an hour laughing, they finally prevailed on

themselves to behave as I was behaving. La Tour exposed his thigh to Camilla, who, pretending she was acting a role in a play, began massaging the patient while I mumbled words which they could not possibly understand since I did not myself know what I was saying. I almost spoiled the performance myself when I saw the faces Camilla was making to keep from laughing. Nothing could be funnier. After telling them at last that there had been enough massage I dipped the brush in the amalgam and, making one continuous stroke, drew the Sign of Solomon on him—the five-pointed star composed of five lines, thus ⛤. After that I wrapped his thigh in three napkins and told him that if he could stay in bed and not unwrap it for twenty-four hours I guaranteed that he would be cured. What pleased me was that I heard no more laughter from them. They were astonished.

After this comedy, which I made up and acted with neither purpose nor premeditation, we left, and in the hackney coach on the way I told Camilla a quantity of wonderful tales, to which she listened so attentively that when I left her I saw that she was vastly impressed.

At eight o'clock in the morning four or five days later, when I had almost forgotten what I had done to Monsieur de La Tour d'Auvergne, I hear horses stopping at my door. I look out of my window, I see him dismount and come in.

"You were sure of the result," he said, embracing me, "since you did not come to see how I was getting on the morning after your amazing treatment."

"Certainly I was sure, but if I had had time you would have seen me nevertheless."

"Tell me if I am allowed to take a bath."

"No bath until you feel you are cured."

"I will obey you. Everyone is amazed, for I could not help telling all my acquaintances about your miracle. I find skeptics who laugh at me, but I let them say what they please."

"You should have kept the secret, I think, for you know Paris. Everyone will say I am a quack."

"Not everyone is so narrow-minded, and I have come to ask you to do me a favor."

"What is your pleasure?"

"I have an aunt who is not only well known but famous for her knowledge of all the abstruse sciences, a great chemist, a woman of intelligence, extremely rich, sole mistress of her fortune, and whose acquaintance can only be useful to you. She is dying to meet you, for she claims that she knows you and that you are not the man Paris believes you to be. She begged me to bring you to dinner at her house, and I hope that you will have no objection. My aunt is the Marquise d'Urfé." [11]

I did not know her, but the name d'Urfé impressed me at once, for I knew the story of the famous Anne d'Urfé,[12] who had flourished at the end of the sixteenth century. The lady was the widow of his great-grandson; and I saw that, having entered the family, she might well have become versed in all the sublime doctrines of a science which greatly interested me though I considered it chimerical. I therefore answered Monsieur de La Tour d'Auvergne that I would go to his aunt's house with him whenever he pleased, but not for dinner unless there would be only the three of us.

"She has twelve people to dinner every day, and you will eat at her house with the best of Parisian society."

"That is exactly what I do not want, for I loathe the reputation of magician, which, in the kindness of your heart, you must have given me."

"Not at all; you are known and you are highly regarded. The Duchess of Lauraguais[13] told me that you went to the Palais-Royal four or five years ago and spent whole days with the Duchess of Orléans,[14] and Madame de Boufflers,[15] Madame du Blot,[16] and even Melfort[17] have spoken to me about you. You are wrong not to cultivate your old acquaintances. What you have done for me convinces me that you could have a brilliant and lucrative career. I know any number of the best people in Paris, both men and women, who have the same malady as mine and who would give you half of their possessions if you cured them."

La Tour's reasoning was sound; but since I knew that what I had done to him was only a prank which had happened to succeed I had no wish to incur publicity. I told him that I absolutely declined to make a spectacle of myself, and that he had only to tell his aunt that I would wait on her privately and not otherwise and that I left it to her to indicate the day and the hour. When I got home about midnight of the same day I found a note from the Count telling me to be at the Terrasse des Capucins at the Tuileries the next day at noon, where he would meet me to take me to dinner at his aunt's, and assuring me that we should find her door open only to us.

Meeting punctually at the appointed place and hour, we went to the lady's house the next day. She lived on the Quai des Théatins[18] next door to the Hôtel de Bouillon. Beautiful despite her age, Madame d'Urfé received me most courteously with all the easy grace of the old court in the days of the Regency.[19] We spent an hour and a half in desultory conversation, but all the while, though of course we did not confess to it, she was studying me as closely as I was studying her. Each of us was trying to trap the other into admissions. I had no difficulty in pretending to be ignorant, for I really was so. Madame d'Urfé displayed nothing except curiosity, but I clearly saw that she could not wait to parade her lore. At two o'clock the three of us were served the same dinner which was served every day for twelve. After dinner La Tour d'Auvergne left us to go and see Prince Turenne,[20] whom he had left that morning with a high fever, and then Madame d'Urfé began talking to me of chemistry, alchemy, magic, and all the things with which she was infatuated. When we came to the subject of the Great Work[21] and I guilelessly asked her if she was acquainted with the primordial substance, she did not burst out laughing, for that would have been impolite, but with a gracious smile she told me that she already possessed what was called the philosopher's stone and that she was versed in all the great operations. She showed me her library,[22] which had belonged to the great D'Urfé[23] and his wife Renée of Savoy[24] and to which she had added manuscripts which had cost her more than a hundred thousand francs. Her favorite author was Paracelsus,[25] who, according to her, had been neither man nor woman and had had the misfortune to poison himself with too strong a dose of the universal medicine.[26] She showed me a small manuscript which set forth the great operation in French in very clear terms. She said she did not keep it under a hundred locks because it was written in a cipher of which she alone had the key.

"Then, Madame, you do not believe in steganography?"[27]

"No, Monsieur; and if you will accept it I make you a present of this copy."

I took it and put it in my pocket.

From the library we went to her laboratory, which really astonished me; she showed me a substance which she had kept on the fire for fifteen years and which needed to remain there four or five years more. It was a powder of projection[28] which was to perform the transmutation of all metals into gold in one minute. She showed me a tube through which coal to keep the fire in her furnace always at the same heat came down of its own weight, so that she often went three months without entering her laboratory at no risk of finding her fire out. A small conduit underneath carried off the ashes. The calcination of mercury was child's play for her; she showed me some already calcined and said that she would demonstrate the procedure to me whenever I pleased. She showed me the tree of Diana[29] of the famous Talliamed,[30] whose pupil she was. As everyone knows, Talliamed was the learned Maillet, who, according to Madame d'Urfé, had not died at Marseilles, as the Abbé Le Maserier[31] had led everyone to believe, but was alive, and, she added with a slight smile, she often received letters from him. If the Regent[32] of France had heeded his advice he would still be among the living. She said that the Regent had been her first friend, that it was he who had nicknamed her Égérie[33] and had himself arranged her marriage to Monsieur d'Urfé. She had a commentary by Raymond Lully,[34] which made clear everything that Arnold of Villanova[35] had written following Roger Bacon[36] and Geber,[37] who, according to her, were not dead. This precious manuscript was in an ivory casket, to which she had the key, and in any case her laboratory was closed to everyone. She showed me a cask filled with *patina del Pinto*,[38] which she could turn into pure gold whenever she pleased. It was Mr. Wood[39] himself who had given it to her in 1743. She showed me the same platinum in four different vessels, three of which contained it intact in sulphuric, nitric, and hydrochloric acid, but in the fourth, in which she had used *aqua regia*,[40] the platinum had been unable to resist. She melted it by the burning glass[41] and said that without some admixture it could be melted in no other way, which in her opinion proved that it was superior to gold. She showed me some of it precipitated by sal ammoniac, which was never able to precipitate gold.

She had an athanor[42] which had been kept burning for fifteen years. I saw that the tower of it was filled with black coals, from which I concluded that she had visited it two or three days before. When we went back to her tree of Diana I respectfully asked her if she agreed with me that it was only a toy to amuse children. She answered with dignity that she had in fact only made it to amuse herself, using silver, mercury, and spirits of niter and crystallizing them together, and that she considered her tree only a metallic vegetation which showed in little what nature could do on a great scale; but she said that she could make a tree of Diana which would be a true tree of the sun, producing golden fruits which would be gathered and continuing to produce them until the exhaustion of an ingredient which she would mix with the six "lepers" [43] in proportion to their quantity. I modestly replied that I did not believe it was possible without the powder of projection. Madame d'Urfé answered only with a gracious smile. She then showed me a porcelain bowl, in which I saw niter, mercury, and sulphur, and a plate on which was a fixed salt.[44]

"I imagine," the Marquise said, "that you know these ingredients."

"I know them," I answered, "if the fixed salt is the salt of urine."

"You are right."

"I admire your sagacity, Madame. You have analyzed the amalgam with which I painted the pentacle[45] on your nephew's thigh; but there is no tartar which can show you the words which give the pentacle its efficacy."

"What is needed for that is not tartar but a manuscript by an adept which I have in my room and which I will show you, in which the words are set forth."

I made no answer, and we left the laboratory.

We had scarcely entered her room before she took from a casket a black book, which she placed on her table, then she began looking for a piece of phosphorus; while she was searching I opened the book, which was behind her, and I saw that it was full of pentacles, and luckily I saw the very talisman which I had painted on her nephew's thigh, encircled by the names of the Planetary Geniuses[46] except for two—those of Saturn and Mars—and I quickly closed the book. The Geniuses were the same as Agrippa's,[47] which I knew, but betraying nothing, I returned to her, and a moment later she found the phosphorus, which really surprised me; but I will speak of it elsewhere.

Madame sat down on her sofa, made me sit beside her, and asked me if I knew the Count of Trèves's[48] talismans.

"I never heard of them, but I know Polyphilus's." [49]

"They are said to be the same."

"I do not believe it."

"We shall find out if you will write down the words you spoke when you painted the pentacle on my nephew's thigh. It will be the same book if I find you those words around the same talisman in this one."

"That would be proof, I admit. I will go and write them."

I wrote the names of the Geniuses; Madame found the pentacle, read out the names to me, and, pretending astonishment, I gave her my paper, where with great satisfaction she read the same names.

"You see," she said, "that Polyphilus and the Count of Trèves were masters of the same science."

"I will admit it, Madame, if your book shows the way to utter the ineffable names.[50] Do you know the theory of the planetary hours?" [51]

"I believe I do, but it is not necessary in this operation."

"I beg your pardon. I painted the pentacle of Solomon on Monsieur de La Tour d'Auvergne's thigh at the hour of Venus, and if I had not begun with Anael,[52] who is the Genius of that planet, my operation would have had no effect."

"I did not know that. And after Anael?"

"One must go on to Mercury, from Mercury to the Moon, from the Moon to Jupiter, from Jupiter to the Sun. You see that it is the magical cycle according to the system of Zoroaster,[53] in which I skip Saturn and Mars, which science excludes in this operation."

"And if you had operated during the hour of the Moon, for example?"

"In that case I should have gone to Jupiter, then to the Sun, then to Anael, that is, Venus, and I should have ended with Mercury."

"I see, Monsieur, that you employ the hours with remarkable facility."

"Without that, Madame, one can do nothing in magic, for one does not have time to calculate; but it is not difficult. A month's study will accustom any beginner to it. What is more difficult is the rites, for they are complicated; but one can learn them in due time. I never go out in the morning without knowing how many minutes compose the hour of that particular day, and I take care that my watch is perfectly regulated, for a minute is decisive."

"Would you be so kind as to instruct me in the theory?"

"You have it in Artephius[54] and more clearly in Sandivonius." [55]

"I have them, but they are in Latin."

"I will translate them for you."

"Will you be so obliging?"

"You have shown me things, Madame, which compel me to oblige you, for reasons which I will perhaps tell you tomorrow."

"Why not today?"

"Because I must first know the name of your Genius."

"You know that I have a Genius."

"You must have one, if it is true that you have the powder of projection."

"I have it."

"Give me the oath of the Order."

"I dare not, and you know why."

"Tomorrow I shall perhaps do away with your fears."

The oath was that of the Brothers of the Rosy Cross,[56] which is never exchanged unless the parties first know each other; so Madame d'Urfé was afraid, and rightly so, that she might be indiscreet, and on my side I had to pretend that I felt the same fear. I thought I ought to gain time, but I knew what the oath was. It can be exchanged between men without indecency, but a woman like Madame d'Urfé must hesitate to give it to a man whom she was seeing for the first time that day.

"When we find the oath announced in our Sacred Scriptures," she said, "it is masked. 'He swore,' says the Holy Bible, 'putting his hand on his thigh.'[57] But it is not the thigh. So we never find a man taking an oath to a woman in that manner, for woman has no word."[58]

At nine in the evening the Count of La Tour d'Auvergne arrived at his aunt's and was surprised to find me still with her. He said that his cousin Prince Turenne's fever had increased greatly and that smallpox had broken out. He told her that he had come to take leave of her for at least a month, since he was going to shut himself up with the patient. Madame d'Urfé praised his zeal, and she gave him a sachet, making him promise that he would return it to her after the Prince was cured. She told him to hang it around the Prince's neck and to be certain of a harmless eruption and a sure cure. He promised, took the sachet, and left.

I then said to the Marquise that I did not know what her sachet contained, but that if it was magic I had no faith in it, for she had given him no instructions concerning the hour. She answered that it was an electrum;[59] and, that being the case, I asked her pardon.

She said that she admired my reserve, but that she thought I would not be disappointed in her circle if I would consent to make their acquaintance. She said that she would introduce me to all her friends by having me to dinner with them one at a time and that afterward I would enjoy their company together. In consequence of this arrangement I dined the next day with a Monsieur Gerin[60] and his niece, neither of whom I liked. Another day it was with an Irishman named Macartney, a physician of the old school, who bored me extremely. Another day she ordered her porter to admit a monk, who, talking of literature, said countless inane things against Voltaire, of whom I was fond in those days, and against the *Esprit des Lois,*[61] which he nevertheless refused to credit to its celebrated author, Montesquieu. He attributed it to the malice of some monk. Another day she had me to dinner with the Chevalier d'Arzigny,[62] a man of ninety, who was known as the "dean of the fops" and who, having figured at the Court of Louis XIV, displayed all its courtesy and knew its gossip. He amused me vastly; he wore rouge; his coats were adorned with the pompons of his century; he professed to be tenderly attached to his mistress, who did the honors of a small house for him where he supped every night in company with his friends, all of them charming young girls who forsook other company for his; nevertheless he was not tempted to be unfaithful to her, for he slept with her every night. This amiable though decrepit and shaky old man had such sweetness of character and such unusual manners that I believed everything he said. His cleanliness was extreme. A large posy of tuberoses and jonquils in the top buttonhole of his coat, together with a strong smell of ambergris from the pomade which kept his false hair and eyebrows attached to his head—even with these, his teeth gave off an extremely strong smell, which Madame d'Urfé did not mind but which I found intolerable. Except for that, I would have sought his society as often as I could. Monsieur d'Arzigny was a professed Epicurean, with a serenity which was amazing; he said that he would undertake to receive a drubbing of twenty-four blows every morning if that could assure him that he would not die within twenty-four hours, and that the older he grew the more of a drubbing he would accept.

On another day I dined with Monsieur Charon,[63] Councilor of the Great Chamber,[64] who was her referee in a suit she was prosecuting against Madame du Châtelet,[65] her daughter, whom she hated. The old Councilor had been her accepted lover forty years earlier, and for that reason he felt it incumbent on him to find in her favor. The French magistrates made justice go by favors and they considered they were at liberty to favor their friends because their right to judge was theirs by virtue of the money with which they had bought it.[66] The Councilor bored me.

But on another day I greatly enjoyed the company of Monsieur de Viarmes,[67] Madame d'Urfé's nephew, a young councilor, who came to dinner at her house with his wife. The couple were likable, and the nephew was extremely witty, as all Paris knew from reading the *Remonstrances au Roi*,[68] of which he was the author. He told me that the business of a councilor was to oppose everything the King might do even if it was good. The reasons he alleged for the soundness of this maxim were those put forth by all minorities in collective bodies. I shall not bore my reader by repeating them.

The dinner which I found most entertaining was the one to which she invited Madame de Gergy,[69] who came with the famous adventurer, the Count of Saint-Germain.[70] Instead of eating he talked from the beginning to the end of dinner; and I listened with the greatest attention, for no one was a better talker. He made himself out to be a prodigy in everything, he aimed to amaze, and he really amazed. His tone was peremptory, but no one took it amiss, for he was learned, speaking all languages well, a great musician, a great chemist, with an attractive face and the ability to win the friendship of all women, for at the same time that he gave them paints

*Young Woman with Fan*

*Seduced Seductress*

which beautified their complexions he persuaded them to believe, not that he could make them younger—for that, he said, was impossible—but that he could keep them in their present condition by means of a water which cost him a great deal but which he gave them as a present. This very strange man, who was born to be the most arrant of impostors, would say, without being challenged and as if in passing, that he was three hundred years old, that he possessed the universal medicine, that he could do whatever he pleased with nature, that he melted diamonds and out of ten or twelve small ones made a big one no less in weight and of the finest water. These things were trifles for him. Despite his egregious boasting, his eccentricities, and his obvious lies, I could not bring myself to consider him insolent, but I did not consider him worthy of respect; I found him astonishing despite myself, because he astonished me. I shall speak of him again when the time comes.

After Madame d'Urfé had introduced me to all these people I told her that I would dine with her whenever she wished, but always with no one else present except her relatives and Saint-Germain, whose eloquence and extravagant boasting amused me. When he dined, as he often did, at the best houses in Paris he never ate anything. He said that his life depended on his diet, and people willingly put up with him, for his tales were the spice of the dinner.

I had come to know Madame d'Urfé thoroughly, while she, on her side, believed that I was a genuine adept under the mask of a man of no consequence; but she was confirmed in this chimerical opinion five or six weeks later when she asked me if I had decoded the manuscript which contained the procedure for the Great Work. I told her that I had and hence had read it and that I would return it to her, giving her my word of honor that I had not copied it.

"I found nothing new in it," I said.

"You will excuse me, Monsieur, but without the key I consider the thing impossible."

"Shall I name your key to you, Madame?"

"Please do so."

I thereupon give her the word, which belonged to no language, and I see that she is surprised. She said that it was too much, for she believed that she alone possessed the word, which she kept in her memory and had never written down.

I could have told her the truth, which was that the same calculation by which I had managed to decode the manuscript had taught me the word, but I took it into my head to tell her that a Genius had revealed it to me. It was this false confidence which put Madame d'Urfé in my power. On that day I became the arbiter of her soul, and I abused my ascendancy. Every time I recollect it I feel sorry and ashamed, and I am doing penance for it now through the obligation I have assumed to tell the truth in writing my memoirs.

Madame d'Urfé's great chimera was believing in the possibility of conversing with what are called "elemental spirits." [71] She would have given everything she possessed to acquire the art; and she had known impostors who had swindled her by making her believe they could set her on the right road. Confronted with me, who had given her such a clear proof of my knowledge, she thought she had reached her goal.

"I did not know," she said, "that your Genius had the power to force mine to reveal his secrets."

"He did not have to use force, for he knows everything by virtue of his own nature."

"Then does he know what secret I lock in my soul?"

"Certainly, and he must tell it to me if I question him."

"Can you question him whenever you please?"

"Whenever I have paper and ink; and I can even let

you question him yourself by telling you his name. My Genius is named Paralis.[72] Write a question addressed to him, as if you were putting it to a mortal; ask him how I was able to decode your manuscript and you shall see how I will make him answer you."

Trembling with joy, Madame d'Urfé writes her question; I put it into figures, then into a pyramid as always, and I make her obtain the answer, which she herself puts into letters. She finds only consonants, but by a second operation I make her obtain the vowels, which she combines with the consonants, and she has a perfectly clear answer which surprises her. She sees before her eyes the word which was required to decode her manuscript. I left her, taking with me her soul, her heart, her mind, and all her remaining common sense.

## CHAPTER VI

*Madame d'Urfé's mistaken and contradictory
notions as to my power. My brother marries;
plan conceived on his wedding day. I go to
Holland on a financial mission for the government. I am given a lesson by the Jew Boas.
Monsieur d'Affry. Esther. Another Casanova.
I meet Teresa Imer again.*

---

PRINCE TURENNE having recovered from the
smallpox, the Count of La Tour d'Auvergne had left him,
and, aware of his aunt's interest in the abstruse sciences,
he was not surprised to find that I had become her only
friend. I enjoyed his presence at our dinners, as I did
that of all her relatives, whose courteous manner toward
me delighted me. They were her brothers Monsieur de
Pontcarré and Monsieur de Viarmes,[1] who had just been
elected Provost of the Merchants,[2] and his son, whom I
believe I have mentioned.[3] Madame du Châtelet was her
daughter; but since a suit made them irreconcilable
enemies she was never present.[4]

  La Tour d'Auvergne having had to rejoin his Boulo-
gnese regiment in Brittany at this time, we[5] dined together, with no other company, nearly every day. Madame's servants considered me her husband; they said
that I must be, thinking it the explanation for the long

hours we spent together. Believing that I was rich, Madame d'Urfé supposed that I had taken a post in the Military School lottery only as a mask.

According to her, I not only possessed the stone but could converse with all the elemental spirits. Hence she believed that I had the power to turn the world upside down and determine the fortunes of France for good or evil, and she attributed my need to remain unknown only to my justified fear of being arrested and imprisoned, for that, she insisted, would necessarily follow as soon as the Ministry managed to learn who I was. These wild ideas came from the revelations which her Genius made to her at night and which her heated imagination made her believe were real. Setting them forth to me in perfect good faith one day, she said her Genius had convinced her that, since she was a woman, I could not give her the power to converse with the Geniuses, but that, by an operation which I must certainly know, I could make her soul pass into the body of a male child born from a philosophical union between an immortal and a woman or between a man and a female being of divine nature.

In lending my support to the lady's crazy notions I did not feel that I was deceiving her; for that was already done, and I could not possibly disabuse her. If in strict honesty I had told her that all her notions were ridiculous, she would not have believed me; so I took the course of drifting with the tide. I could not but enjoy letting myself be considered the greatest of all Rosicrucians and the most powerful of all men by a lady who was allied to the greatest houses in France and who, in addition, was even richer from her investments than from a yearly income of eighty thousand livres which she received from an estate[6] and from the houses she owned in Paris. I clearly saw that, if the need arose, she could refuse me nothing, and though I had laid no plan to gain possession of her wealth either in whole or in part, I did not have the strength of mind to renounce my power over her.

Madame d'Urfé was a miser. She spent barely thirty thousand livres[7] a year, and she invested her savings on the Exchange and doubled them. A broker brought her royal securities when they were at their lowest price and sold them for her when they went up. In this way she had greatly augmented her portfolio. She told me several times that she was ready to give all that she had to become a man and that she knew it depended on me.

I told her one day that it was true I could perform the operation, but that I could never bring myself to do it because I would have to take her life.

"I know that," she answered, "and I even know the kind of death to which I must submit, and I am ready."

"And what kind of death, Madame, are you pleased to believe it may be?"

"It is," she answered eagerly, "the same poison which killed Paracelsus."

"And do you believe that Paracelsus attained hypostasis?"[8]

"No. But I know the reason. He was neither man nor woman, and it is necessary to be completely one or the other."

"That is true; but do you know how the poison is made? And do you know that it cannot be made without the help of a salamander?"[9]

"That may be so, but I did not know it. I beg you to ask the cabala if there is anyone in Paris who possesses the poison."

I immediately thought that she believed she possessed it herself; and, not having hesitated to say so in my answer, I pretended to be astonished. It was she who was not astonished, and I saw her triumph.

"You see," she said, "that all I need is the child containing the male word [10] drawn from an immortal crea-

ture. I have been informed that it depends on you, and
I do not believe you can lack the necessary courage because of a mistaken pity you may feel for my old carcass.''

At these words I rose and I went to the window of
her room, which gave onto the quay, and remained there
for a quarter of an hour reflecting on her idiocies. When
I returned to the table at which she was sitting she looked
at me closely and said with deep feeling:

''Is it possible, my dear friend? I see you have been
weeping.''

I let her believe it, I sighed, I took my sword, and I
left. Her carriage, which was at my disposal every day,
was at the door, awaiting my orders.

My brother had been received into the Academy[11] by
acclamation after exhibiting a painting he had made in
which he depicted a battle and which gained the ap-
probation of all the connoisseurs. The Academy itself
wanted to own it and gave him the five hundred louis
he asked for it. He had fallen in love with Corallina and
would have married her if she had not been guilty of an
infidelity which offended him so greatly that, to end any
hope she might have of making it up, within less than
a week he married a dancer[12] who appeared in the ballets
at the Comédie Italienne. The wedding party was given
by Monsieur de Saincy, bursar in charge of vacant ecclesiastical benefices,[13] who was very fond of the girl and
who in gratitude for my brother's chivalry in marrying
her got all his friends to order paintings from him, which
paved the way to the considerable fortune he made and
the great fame which he came to enjoy.

It was at my brother's wedding that Monsieur Kornmann, discoursing to me at length about the great scarcity of money, urged me to speak with the Comptroller-
General concerning a way to remedy the situation. He
said that by giving royal securities at a reasonable price

to a company of brokers in Amsterdam it would be possible in exchange to acquire some other power's notes, which, not being discredited as France's were, could easily be realized. I asked him not to mention it to anybody, promising him that I would act.

No later than the next day I mentioned it to my patron the Abbé, who, considering it an excellent speculation, advised me to go to Holland [14] myself with a letter of recommendation from the Duke of Choiseul [15] to Monsieur d'Affry,[16] who could be sent several millions in royal paper to discount as I saw best. He told me to go at once and discuss the matter with Monsieur de Boulogne, and above all not to appear to be feeling my way. He assured me that, as soon as it became clear that I was not asking for any money in advance, I would be given all the letters of recommendation I wanted.

I was instantly enthusiastic. That same day I saw the Comptroller-General, who, considering my idea excellent, told me that the Duke of Choiseul would be at the Invalides[17] the next day and that I should lose no time before going to him to discuss the matter and give him the note he would write to him. He promised me he would have the Ambassador supplied with twenty millions in securities, which in any case could always return to France. I said somberly that I hoped not, if no more than a reasonable price was asked. He replied that peace was about to be made,[18] and in consequence I must dispose of them only at a very small loss and in that respect I should depend on the Ambassador, who would have all the necessary instructions.

I felt so flattered by a mission of this nature that I did not sleep all that night. The Duke of Choiseul, who was famous for moving rapidly, had no sooner read Monsieur de Boulogne's note and listened to me for five minutes than he had a clerk write a letter to Monsieur d'Affry in my behalf, which he read over and signed without reading it to me; after having it given to me sealed, he wished me a good journey. On the same day I obtained a passport from Monsieur de Berkenrode,[19] took leave of Manon Balletti and all my friends except Madame d'Urfé, with whom I was to spend the whole of the next day, and authorized my faithful clerk to sign the tickets at my office.

A month earlier a very pretty and decent girl, a native of Brussels, had been married under my auspices to an Italian named Gaetano, a dealer in secondhand goods. I had been her sponsor. The brute ill-treating her in his jealous rages, and the unhappy beauty constantly coming to me with her complaints, I had several times made peace between them. They came expecting me to give them dinner on the very day I was packing to leave for Holland. My brother and Tiretta were with me, and as I was still living in a furnished room I took them all to dinner with me at Landelle's,[20] where the food was excellent. Tiretta was in his carriage; he was ruining the ex-Jansenist,[21] who was still in love with him.

At dinner Tiretta, who was handsome and loved to clown and who had never seen the beautiful Fleming, began flirting with her outrageously. She was delighted, and we would have laughed and all would have gone well if her husband had been reasonable and polite; but, jealous as a tiger, the wretch was sweating blood. He did not eat, he kept turning white, he looked daggers at his wife, and he refused to take it as a joke. Tiretta made fun of him. Foreseeing unpleasant scenes, I tried to moderate his excessive high spirits, but in vain. An oyster dropped onto Madame Gaetano's beautiful bosom, and Tiretta, who was sitting beside her, quickly put his lips to it and sucked it in. Gaetano rose in a fury and slapped his wife so vindictively that his hand bounced back from her face to her neighbor's. Roused to rage, Tiretta seized him by the waist and stretched him out on the floor, and since, being unarmed, he took his vengeance only with his fists, we let him continue; but the waiter came up, whereupon the jealous husband left. His wife, her face disfigured by tears and blood—for she was bleeding from the nose, as was Tiretta—asked me to take her somewhere, for she thought her life would be in danger if she went home. I quickly got her into a hackney coach, leaving Tiretta with my brother. She asked me to take her to an old attorney, a relative of hers, who lived on the fourth floor of a six-story house on the Quai de Gesvres.[22] After hearing the whole unhappy story he said to me that, being poor, he could do nothing for the unfortunate girl, but that he would do everything if he had only a hundred écus. I gave them to him, and he assured me that he would set about ruining her husband, who would never be able to find out where she was. She told me she was sure he would do all that he had promised, and after expressing all her gratitude she let me go. On my return from Holland my reader will learn what became of her.

After I assured Madame d'Urfé that I was going to Holland for the good of France and that I would be back at the beginning of February, she asked me to sell some shares in the East India Company of Gothenburg[23] for her. She had sixty thousand francs' worth of them, and she could not sell them on the Paris Exchange because there was no money there; in addition she could not obtain the interest on them, which amounted to a considerable sum since it had been three years since any dividends had been declared. When I consented to do her the service she had to make me the owner of the shares through a bill of sale, which she did in due form on the same day, the transaction being certified by Tourton & Baur,[24] Place des Victoires. Back at her house I offered to give her an undertaking in writing to pay her the value of her shares on my return, but she refused. I left her, gratified to see not the slightest sign of suspicion on her face.

After obtaining a bill of exchange for three thousand florins[25] on the Jew Boas,[26] the court banker at The Hague, from Monsieur Kornmann, I set out; in two days I reached Antwerp, where I took a *jacht*,[27] which the next day brought me to Rotterdam, where I slept. On the day after I went to The Hague, where I put up at Jacquet's inn, the "English Parliament." [28] On the same day, which was Christmas Eve, I called on Monsieur d'Affry just when he was reading the letter from the Duke of Choiseul informing him about me and the business in hand. He made me stay for dinner with Monsieur Kauderbach,[29] Resident for the King of Poland and Elector of Saxony, and he encouraged me to do my best, saying, however, that he doubted if I would succeed because the Dutch had good reason to believe that peace would not be made very soon.

On leaving the Embassy I took a carriage to the house of the banker Boas, whom I found at table with all his ugly and numerous family. After looking at my bill of exchange he said that only that day he had received a letter from Kornmann praising me. He asked me why, since it was Christmas Eve, I was not going to rock the Infant Jesus to sleep; I answered that I had come to celebrate the Feast of the Maccabees[30] with him. He and his whole family applauded my answer, and he begged me to accept a room in his house. Accepting his offer, I at once sent word to my valet to come to the house with my luggage, and when I took leave of Boas after supper I asked him to find me some good piece of business by which I could make eighteen or twenty thousand florins during the short time I intended to stay in Holland. He answered seriously that he would think it over.

The next morning after I had breakfasted with him and his family he said that he had found what I wanted and took me to his study, where, giving me three thousand florins in gold and notes, he said that there was nothing to stop me from making twenty thousand florins in a week, as I had told him I wanted to do the evening before. Greatly surprised, for I had only been joking, at how easy it was to make money in that country, I thank him for his kind interest and I hear him out.

"Here," he says, "is a note which I received day before yesterday from the Mint. It informs me that four hundred thousand ducats[31] have just been struck and that the Mint is prepared to sell them at the current price of gold, which, fortunately, is not very high at the moment. Each ducat is worth five florins, two and three-fifths stüivers.[32] Here is the rate of exchange at Frankfort on the Main. Buy the four hundred thousand ducats, take or send them to Frankfort, obtaining bills of exchange on the Bank of Amsterdam,[33] and there you have just what you asked for. You make one and one-ninth stuiver per ducat, which yields you twenty-two thousand two hundred and twenty-two of our florins. Obtain possession of the gold today, and in a week your profit will be liquid. There you are."

"But," I answered, "will the directors of the Mint not demur at entrusting me with such a sum, which comes to over four million livres tournois?" [34]

"Certainly they will, if you do not buy the ducats for cash or give an equal amount in good paper."

"My dear Monsieur Boas, I have neither that much money nor that much credit."

"Then you will never make twenty thousand florins in a week. Judging from the proposal you made me yesterday evening, I thought you were a millionaire. I will have one of my sons make the transaction today or tomorrow."

After giving me this sound lesson Boas went to his office and I went to dress. Monsieur d'Affry went to the "English Parliament" to return my visit and, not finding me there, wrote me a note asking me to call on him to hear what he had to tell me. I went there, I dined with him, and I learned directly from the letter he had

just received from Monsieur de Boulogne that he was not
to let me dispose of the twenty millions he was to receive
except at a loss of eight percent, for peace was on the
verge of being made. He laughed at the idea and I did
likewise. He advised me not to discuss my business with
Jews, the most honest of whom was only the least dis-
honest, and he offered me a letter of recommendation in
his own hand to Pels,[35] of Amsterdam, which I gratefully
accepted; and to assist me in the matter of my Gothenburg shares he introduced me to the Swedish Ambassador.[36] He, in turn, sent me to Monsieur D. O.[37] I left
on the day after St. John's Day[38] because of the convo-
cation of the most zealous Masons in Holland. The person
who invited me to attend it was Count de Tott,[39] brother
of the Baron who failed to make his fortune in Constantinople. Monsieur d'Affry presented me to Her Highness the Regent, mother[40] of the Stathouder,[41] whom I
thought too serious for his age, which was then only
twelve. She kept dozing off. She died not long afterward,
and her brain was found to be swimming in water. There
I also saw Count Philipp of Sinzendorf,[42] who was looking for five millions for the Empress and who easily obtained them at five percent interest. At the theater I
met a Minister of the Porte[43] who had been a friend of
Monsieur de Bonneval's,[44] and I thought I should see
him die from laughing before my eyes. Here is the rather
comical incident:

The play being given was the tragedy *Iphigenia*.[45] The
statue of Diana was in the center of the stage. At the end
of one act Iphigenia entered followed by all her priest-
esses, who as they passed the statue all bowed low to the
goddess. The candle-snuffer, a good Dutch Christian,
comes out and makes the same bow to the statue. The
parterre and the boxes burst out laughing, and so do I,
but not hard enough to die of it. When, as in duty bound,
I explained the joke to the Turk he fell into such a fit of

laughter that he had to be carried to his inn, the "Prince of Orange." [46] Not to laugh at the thing at all would have proved one stupid, I admit; but one had to have a Turkish sense of humor to laugh at it so hard. Yet it was a great Greek philosopher[47] who died laughing when he saw a toothless old woman eating figs. Those who laugh much are better off than those who laugh little, for gaiety unloads the spleen and generates good blood.

Two hours before reaching Amsterdam in my two-wheeled post chaise with my servant sitting behind, I meet a four-wheeled carriage, drawn by two horses like mine and also carrying a master and servant. The driver of the four-wheeled carriage wanted my driver to make way for him, mine protested that if he did he would upset me in the ditch, but the other insisted. I address the master, a handsome young man, and ask him to order his driver to make way for me.

"I am posting, Monsieur," I say, "and furthermore I am a foreigner."

"Monsieur, here in Holland the post has no special rights,[48] and if you are a foreigner you must admit that you have no greater claim than mine, since I am in my own country."

At that I get out in snow halfway up my boots, and holding my drawn sword I tell the Dutchman to get out or to make way for me. He replied, with a smile, that he had no sword and that in any case he would not fight for such a silly reason. He told me to get back in my chaise, and he made way for me. I arrived at Amsterdam about nightfall and put up at the "Star of the East." [49]

The next day I went to the Exchange and found Monsieur Pels, who said that he would give thought to my chief business, and a quarter of an hour later I found Monsieur D. O., who at once arranged for me to speak with a broker from Gothenburg, who wanted to discount my sixteen shares on the spot, giving me twelve percent

interest. Monsieur Pels told me to wait and assured me
that he would get me fifteen percent. He gave me dinner,
and seeing me delighted with the excellence of his red
Cape wine,[50] he laughed and said that he made it himself
by mixing Burgundy with Malaga. The next day I dined
at the house of Monsieur D. O., who was a widower of
forty and whose only daughter, Esther,[51] was fourteen.
She was a beauty except that her teeth were not good. She
was the heir to all the wealth of her amiable father, who
adored her. With her white complexion, her black hair,
which she wore unpowdered, and her eloquent, very large
black eyes, she made a great impression on me. She spoke
French very well; she played the harpsichord with great
delicacy, and was passionately fond of reading. After
dinner Monsieur D. O. showed me his house, which was
not occupied, for after his wife's death he had chosen
an apartment on the ground floor in which he was very
comfortable. The apartment he showed me was a suite
of six or seven rooms which contained a treasure in
antique porcelain; the walls and the casements were entirely covered with marble plaques, each room in a different color and with floors of the same under magnificent Turkish carpets made to order for the particular
rooms. The large dining room was entirely covered with
alabaster, and the tables and buffets were of cedarwood.
The house was entirely covered with marble plaques
on the outside too. One Saturday I saw four or five
housemaids washing those splendid walls; what made me
laugh was that the maids all had very wide panniers,
which obliged them to wear breeches, otherwise they
would have afforded too interesting a sight to passers-by.
After seeing the house we went downstairs, and Monsieur
D. O. left me alone with his daughter in the anteroom in
which he worked with his clerks; but that day there was
no one there. It was New Year's Day.

After playing a sonata for harpsichord, Mademoiselle

O. asked me if I was going to the concert. I replied that nothing could persuade me to go to it since I was with her.

"Are you thinking of going to it, Mademoiselle?"

"I should like nothing better than to go to the concert, but I cannot go all by myself."

"I should be very happy to escort you, but I dare not hope as much."

"You would be doing me a great favor, and I am certain that if you make the offer to my father he will not refuse you."

"Are you certain?"

"Perfectly certain; since he knows you, he would be guilty of rudeness; I am amazed that you could fear it; my father is most polite; I see that you do not know Dutch customs. In this country unmarried girls enjoy a decent freedom; they lose it only when they marry; go to him, go to him."

I go in to Monsieur D. O., who was writing, and ask him if he will do me the honor of letting me escort his daughter to the concert.

"Have you a carriage?"

"Yes, Monsieur."

"Then I need not order mine. Esther?"

"Yes, Father."

"You may get dressed. Monsieur Casanova is kind enough to take you to the concert."

"Thank you, dear Papa."

After kissing him she goes to dress, and an hour later she appears with joy on her countenance. I could only have wished she had used a little powder; but Esther was proud of the color of her hair, which made her complexion look even whiter. A transparent black fichu covered her bosom, which it revealed as just beginning to develop and too firm.

We go downstairs, I offer her my hand to help her into the carriage, and I wait, supposing that a maid or a governess will attend her; but seeing no one I get in, very much surprised. Her lackey, after closing the door, gets up behind. I thought it impossible. Such a girl alone with me! I was struck dumb. I asked myself if I should remember that I was a great libertine or if I should forget it. Esther, all animation, said we were to hear an Italian singer with the voice of a nightingale, and seeing me speechless she asked me why. I beat about the bush, but finally said that I thought her a treasure of which I did not deserve to be the guardian.

"I know," she said, "that in the rest of Europe girls are not allowed to go out alone with men, but here we are taught to behave ourselves, and we are certain that if we do not we will contrive our own unhappiness."

"Happy the man who will be your husband, and happier still if you have already chosen him!"

"Oh, it is not for me to choose him, that lies with my father."

"And if the man he chooses is not the man you love?"

"We are not allowed to love a man before we know he is to be our husband."

"Then you love no one."

"No one, and what is more I have not yet felt tempted to."

"Then may I kiss your hand?"

"Why my hand?"

She drew it away, she gave me her lips, and modestly returned my kiss with one which went to my heart, but I stopped at that when she told me she would do the same in her father's presence whenever I wished.

We arrived at the concert, where Esther found a quantity of young ladies who were friends of hers, all daughters of wealthy businessmen, some of them pretty, some ugly, and all eagerly asking her who I was. All she could tell them was my name, but she became animated when she saw a beautiful blonde nearby; she asked me if I

thought her attractive; I answered, of course, that I was
not attracted by blondes.

"Even so, I shall introduce her to you, for she may be
a relative of yours; her name is the same, and here is her
father. Monsieur Casanova," she said to him, "I beg to
introduce Monsieur Casanova, a friend of my father's."

"Is it possible? I hope," he said, "I may be your friend
too, but perhaps we are relatives. I am of the Naples
family."

"Then we are relatives, though very distant ones, for
my father was from Parma. Have you your genealogy?"

"I must have it somewhere; but to tell the truth I set
little store by it, for in this country no one considers such
trifles."

"Nevertheless, we can amuse ourselves with it for a
quarter of an hour, and then laugh at it and keep it to
ourselves. Tomorrow I shall have the honor of calling on
you, and I will bring you a tree of my ancestors. Would
it displease you to find the founder of your line among
them?"

"I should be delighted, Monsieur, and I shall have the
honor of calling on you myself at your lodging tomorrow.
May I ask if you have a business establishment at home?"

"No, I am in finance and at present in the service of
the French ministry. I am on a mission to Monsieur
Pels."

Monsieur Casanova then beckoned to his daughter, who
came at once and whom he introduced to me. She was
Esther's intimate friend; I sat down between the two
of them, and the concert began. After a fine symphony, a
concerto for violin, and another for oboe, the Italian
singer who was so highly praised under the name of
Trenti appeared, taking her place behind the musician
at the harpsichord. Great was my surprise when in this
so-called Madame Trenti I saw Teresa Imer,[52] wife of
the dancer Pompeati, whom the reader may remember.

I had known her eighteen years earlier, when old Senator Malipiero had given me a caning when he caught me in some childish naughtiness with her, and I had seen her again at Venice in 1753, where we had made love once or twice, not as children but as real lovers. She had left for Bayreuth, where she was mistress to the Margrave;[53] I had promised to visit her there; but C. C. and the nun M. M.[54] had not left me time for it. Then I was confined under the Leads, and I had heard no more of her. My surprise was great to see her now at a concert in Amsterdam. I said nothing, listening to an aria which she sang with the voice of an angel, preceded by a recitative which began: *Eccoti giunta al fin, donna infelice* ("You have come at last, unhappy woman").[55]

The applause would not end. Esther told me that no one knew who the woman was, that there were countless stories about her, that she was very badly off, and that she lived by traveling to every city in Holland and singing at public concerts, the only payment she received being what the audience put into a silver plate which she carried through all the rows at the end of the concert.

"Does she find her plate well filled?"

"Not at all, for everyone here has already paid for his ticket. So she does well if she takes in thirty or forty florins. Tomorrow she will be at the concert at Leiden and the next day at The Hague and the day after that at Rotterdam, then she comes back here; she has been leading this life for more than six months now, and people are always delighted to hear her."

"Has she no lover?"

"They say she has young men in every city, but that instead of their giving her money she spends it on them, for they haven't a sou. She never wears anything but black, not only because she is a widow[56] but because of some great blow she says she has suffered. You will see her going through our row in half an hour."

Keeping my hands in my muff, I counted out twelve ducats, wrapped them in paper, and waited with my heart beating in a way which made me smile, since I could see no good reason for it.

As she went through the row in front of mine I saw that she was very much surprised when she caught sight of me; but I at once looked away and began talking with Esther. When she stopped in front of me I put the little roll on her plate without looking at her, and she moved on. But I looked closely at a little girl of four or five years who was following her and who, when she reached the end of the row, came back and kissed my hand. I was extremely surprised when I saw that the child had precisely my features. I managed to hide it, but the little girl stood there staring at me.

"Would you like some bonbons, pretty child?" I said. "Take the box too."

So saying I gave her the full box, which was only tortoise shell, but I would have given it to her if it had been gold. At that she left, and Esther laughed and said the child was the image of me.

"A striking likeness," added Mademoiselle Casanova.

"Chance," I said, "often produces resemblances for no reason at all."

After the concert I left Mademoiselle Esther O. with her father, whom we had met there, and I went to the "Eastern Star," where I was lodging. I had ordered a dish of oysters and I was about to eat them before going to bed when I saw Teresa and the little girl appear in my room. I rose to give her the ecstatic embrace which the occasion demanded, whereupon she saw fit to sink into a chair in a faint, perhaps real, perhaps feigned. As it might be genuine, I was willing to play the expected part in the scene, and I revived her with cold water and making her smell eau de Luz.[57] Restored to her senses, she began staring at me without a word. I asked her if she wanted supper, and she answered yes. I quickly ordered three places set, and we were served the usual sort of supper except that it kept us at table until seven o'clock in the morning doing nothing but tell each other our good and bad fortunes. She was acquainted with most of my recent vicissitudes, and I knew nothing of hers. So it was she who talked for five or six hours on end. Sophie[58] (for such was the name of her daughter) slept soundly on my bed until daylight. Teresa kept the most important of her disclosures, and the one which was of greatest concern to me, for the end. She said that Sophie was my daughter, and she took from her pocket the baptismal certificate which showed the date of her birth. We had been lovers in Venice at the beginning of the Fair of the Ascension in 1753, and Sophie was born at Bayreuth the end of that year; she had now just turned six. I said that I was convinced of it, and that since I was in a position to provide her with the best education I was ready to take care of her; but she replied that she was her jewel and that I would tear her soul from her body if I took her away; instead, she offered me her son, who was twelve years old and whom she did not have the means to bring up properly.

"Where is he?"

"He is boarding at Rotterdam, or I had better say in pawn there, for the man with whom he is staying will never give him to me unless I pay him all I owe him."

"How much do you owe?"

"Eighty florins. You have given me sixty-two, give me four more ducats, and my son is yours and I shall be the happiest of mothers. I will bring him to you at The Hague next week, since you say you have to go back there."

"Yes, my dear Teresa. Instead of four ducats, here are twenty. We will meet again at The Hague."

The transports of her gratitude and the joy which

flooded her soul were excessive; but they did not have the power to reawaken my old fondness, or, rather, the old hankering I had had for her, for I had never loved her passionately. She embraced me for more than a quarter of an hour, with increasing demonstrations of the most ardent desire, but in vain; I returned her caresses without ever giving her the proof she sought that they came from the same source as that to which Sophie owed her birth. Teresa melted into tears, then she sighed, took her daughter, and left, after reminding me that we were to meet again at The Hague and that she would leave at noon.

Teresa was two years older than I, she was pretty, blonde, full of intelligence and talent; but her charms were no longer the same, for I should have felt their power. The story of all that had happened to her during the six years after she left Venice for Bayreuth would be worthy of my reader's attention, and I should be glad to write it if I remembered all its details. Convicted of infidelity by the amorous Margrave because of a Monsieur de Montperny,[59] she had been turned out; she had separated from her husband Pompeati and had gone to Brussels with a lover, where for a few days she had taken the fancy of Prince Charles of Lorraine,[60] who gave her a special patent granting her the direction of all theatrical performances throughout the Austrian Netherlands. With this patent she had embarked on the most extensive enterprises which had led her to spend enormous sums, so that in less than three years, after selling all her diamonds, her laces, her wardrobe, and everything she owned, she had been obliged to go to Holland to avoid being sent to prison. Her husband had killed himself in Vienna[61] during a fit of madness brought on by intestinal pains; he had opened his abdomen with a razor and had died tearing out his entrails.

The business I had in hand did not allow me to go

to bed. Monsieur Casanova came to drink coffee with me and invited me to dinner, arranging to meet me at the Amsterdam Exchange,[62] which is an amazing institution to any thinking foreigner. Millionaires who look like yokels are very numerous there. A man who has only a hundred thousand florins is so poor that he does not dare do business under his own name. Monsieur D. O. invited me to dine next day at a small house he had on the Amstel; and Monsieur Casanova treated me very well. After reading my genealogy, which had stood me in such good stead at Naples, he went for his, which he found to be exactly the same, but, completely unimpressed by the fact, he only laughed—quite unlike Don Antonio in Naples, who took it with the utmost seriousness and gave me such excellent proof that he did so. However, he offered me his services and his advice in anything to do with business if I needed them. I thought his daughter pretty, but I was not struck either by her charms or her intelligence; my mind was occupied with Esther, whom I mentioned several times at table, until finally I forced Mademoiselle Casanova to tell me she was not pretty. A girl who knows she is pretty triumphs when she can silence a man who speaks in favor of one of her contemporaries who has indubitable defects. Nevertheless, the girl was Esther's intimate friend.

After dinner Monsieur D. O. told me that if I would sell my shares at fifteen percent above par, he would take them himself and I would be under no expense for either a broker or a notary. I agreed, and after turning them over to him I asked him for payment in a bill of exchange on Tourton & Baur in livres tournois and to my order. After calculating the daler[63] of the Bank of Sweden at eight livres ten sous in accordance with the rate at Hamburg, he gave me a sight bill of exchange for seventy-two thousand francs, whereas at five percent[64] I expected to receive only sixty-nine thousand. It was six percent, which won me great esteem from Madame d'Urfé, who perhaps did not expect such honesty from me. Toward evening I went with Monsieur Pels to Zaandam[65] in a boat set on a sledge with sails. I found the journey extraordinary and most entertaining. We got there surprisingly fast with a wind which took us along at fifteen English miles an hour. It is impossible to imagine a conveyance more comfortable or steadier or freer from danger. There is no one who would not be glad to take a trip around the world in such a carriage over a frozen sea, but with a stern wind, for that is the only possible course, the rudder having no effect. What greatly pleased me was the perfect timing with which two sailors lowered two sails when, having come close to the island, they had to stop the ship. This is the only moment when one may feel afraid, for the ship continued on its way for over a hundred paces even after the sails were lowered, and if there had been a delay of only a second the violence of its collision with the shore would have smashed it to pieces. We ate perch and could not take a walk because of the high wind; but I went there once again, and I say nothing about it because everyone knows the wonders of Zaandam, the hotbed of all the rich merchants who, in time, become millionaires at Amsterdam. We went back to Monsieur Pels's house in a two-horse sleigh which belonged to him. He kept me for supper, and I did not leave him until midnight. He said, with the honesty which was displayed on his countenance, that since I had become his friend and Monsieur D. O.'s I would not need the services of the Jews in my principal business but should apply directly to them.

The next morning, with the snow falling in great flakes, I went early to Monsieur D. O.'s, where I found his daughter in a very good humor. In her father's presence she began by rallying me on having spent the night at my inn with Madame Trenti.

Monsieur D. O., after saying that I need not defend myself because anyone was entitled to love talent, asked me to tell him who the woman was. I said she was a Venetian whose husband had recently killed himself, and that it was almost six years since we had last seen each other.

"The sight of your daughter," said Esther, "must have surprised you."

I replied that the child could not be mine, since her mother's husband was still alive at the time; but she continued to discuss the resemblance and to joke about my having fallen asleep the evening before when I supped at Monsieur Pels's.

"I envy anyone," she said slyly, "who has the secret of getting a good sleep, for of late I never fall asleep until I have courted it for a long time yet dreaded it, for when I wake, instead of finding my mind freer, I find it stupefied and weighed down by the indifference which comes from fatigue."

"Try, Mademoiselle, spending the night listening to the long story of some man in whom you are interested, but from his own lips. You will fall happily asleep the night after."

"Such a person does not exist. I think I need books, and the help of someone who knows them to find me interesting ones. I like history and travels, but I have to be sure that what I read is not invented. If anything makes me suspect it, I stop reading at once."

I promised to bring her some books the next day before I left for The Hague; she accepted my offer, congratulating me on the prospect I had of seeing Madame Trenti again at The Hague.

Esther's frankness set me on fire, and Monsieur D. O. laughed heartily at the way his daughter was calling me to account. At eleven o'clock we got into a sleigh and went to the small house, to which she had told me that

Mademoiselle Casanova would also come with her fiancé. I saw her look pleased when I assured her that nothing could interest me more than herself.

We saw the two of them coming to meet us covered with snow. We get out; we enter a room to take off our furs; and I notice that the fiancé, after looking at me for a moment, whispers to his intended. She laughs, she goes and says something to Esther, who goes and tells her father, who laughs even more. They were looking at me, I was sure that it was about me they were talking; I pretended indifference, but that was no reason for me not to join them. Indeed, good manners demanded it.

"There may be some mistake," said Monsieur D. O.; "we really must look into it. Did anything out of the ordinary," he said, addressing me, "happen to you on your journey from The Hague to Amsterdam?"

At this question I looked at the fiancé, and I at once guessed what it was all about.

"Nothing out of the ordinary," I replied, "except meeting a fine fellow who wanted to see my carriage overturned, and I believe I see him here."

The laughter redoubled, and we embraced; but after he told the whole story in all its details Mademoiselle Casanova told him sharply that he should have fought. Esther disagreed, saying that he had shown more courage by listening to reason, and Monsieur D. O. declared that he was strongly of her opinion; but the refractory girl, after airing some romantic notions, became deliberately sulky with her lover. I chided her for it, which pleased Esther.

"Come, come," said the charming Esther gaily, "let us put on skates and lose no time amusing ourselves on the Amstel, for I fear the ice will melt."

I did not want to ask her to excuse me. Monsieur D. O. leaves us. Mademoiselle Casanova's fiancé puts skates on me, and the young ladies are ready, wearing short skirts

and armed with black velvet drawers to guard against
mishaps. We go down to the Amstel, and, since I was a
complete novice at the sport, the reader can imagine that,
having fallen abruptly on the hard ice at least twenty
times, I thought I would end by breaking my back; but
not a bit of it, I felt ashamed to leave off, and I stopped
only when we were called in to dinner. When we got up
from table I felt as if I were paralyzed in every limb.
Esther gave me a jar of ointment and assured me that
if I had myself rubbed when I went to bed I would feel
perfectly well in the morning. She was right. Everyone
laughed; I let them laugh; I realized that the whole
skating party had been got up only to make me a laughingstock, and I saw nothing wrong in that. I wanted to
bring Esther to love me, and I was sure that so much
submission and obligingness on my part could not but
set me on the road. I spent the afternoon with Monsieur
D. O., letting the young people go back to the Amstel
again, where they enjoyed themselves hugely until twi-
light.

We talked of my twenty millions, and I learned from
him that I should never succeed in discounting them except with a mercantile company which would give me
other papers in exchange, and that even by such a transaction I must be prepared to lose heavily. When I told
him that I would like to make the transaction with the
East India Company of Gothenburg he said that he would
speak to a broker and that Monsieur Pels could be very
useful to me.

When I woke in the morning I thought I was done for.
My last vertebra, which is called the *os sacrum,* seemed
to be in a thousand pieces. Yet I had had myself rubbed
with almost all the ointment Esther had given me. I did
not forget her wishes. I had myself driven to a bookseller's, where I bought all the books I thought might
entertain her. I sent them to her, asking her to send me

back all the ones she had read. She did so promptly, and, thanking me profusely, asked me to come and kiss her before leaving Amsterdam if I wanted to receive a nice present.

I went there very early, leaving my post chaise at her door. Her governess took me to her bed, where I found her in a merry mood, with a complexion of lilies and roses.

"I am certain," she said, "that you would not have come if I had not used the word 'kiss.' "

So saying, she surrendered all the charms of her face to my eager lips. Glimpsing the pink buds of her young breasts, I was about to lay hold of them, but as soon as she saw it she stopped laughing and defended herself. She said that I was well advised to go and amuse myself at The Hague with Madame Trenti, in whose care I had left a most precious pledge of my affection. I assured her that I was going to The Hague only to talk business with the Ambassador, and that she would see me again five or six days later, in love only with her. She answered that she relied on my word, and when I left her she granted me such a sweet kiss that I felt certain she would grant me everything on my return. I left very much in love and reached Boas's house at suppertime.

## CHAPTER VII

*My luck in Holland. I return to Paris with*
*young Pompeati.*

AMONG THE letters I received at the post I found
one from the Comptroller-General which told me that
twenty millions in royal securities were in the hands of
Monsieur d'Affry, who would not deliver them at more
than an eight percent loss; and another from my patron
the Abbé de Bernis which advised me to make the most
advantageous deal I could with them and to be sure that
when the Ambassador communicated it to the Minister
he would be ordered to consent to the transaction, provided that not less was offered than could be obtained on
the Exchange at Paris.

Boas, astonished by the profitable sale I had made of
my sixteen Gothenburg shares, told me he would undertake to get the twenty millions discounted for me in
shares of the Swedish East India Company if I would
persuade the Ambassador to sign an agreement in which
I would undertake to deliver the French royal securities

at a ten percent loss, taking the Swedish shares at fifteen percent above par, as I had sold my own sixteen. I would have consented if he had not stipulated that I give him three months and that my contract could be changed if peace was made. I saw at once that I would do well to go back to Amsterdam, and I would have gone if I had not given La Trenti my word that I would wait for her in The Hague. She arrived from Rotterdam the next day and wrote me that she expected me for supper. I received her letter at the theater. The servant who brought it said that he would take me to her lodging as soon as the play was over. After sending my lackey back to Boas's house, I went.

I found this most unusual woman on the fifth floor of a dilapidated house with her daughter and her son. In the middle of the room there was a table covered with a black cloth on which stood two candles. Since The Hague was a court city I was richly dressed. The woman, clad in black with her two children, made me think of Medea.[1] Nothing could be prettier than the two young creatures. I fondly embraced the boy, calling him my son. His mother told him that from that moment on he was to consider me his father. He recognized me as the man he had seen at Venice in May 1753, in Signora Manzoni's house, and I was very much pleased. His stature was short, he seemed to have an excellent constitution, he was well built, and his delicate features bespoke intelligence. He was thirteen years old.

His sister stood there motionless, seemingly waiting for her turn to come. Having taken her on my lap, I could not have enough of covering her with kisses. For all her silence, she enjoyed seeing that she interested me more than her brother did. She had on only a very light petticoat. I kissed every part of her pretty body, delighted to be the man to whom the little creature owed her existence.

"Isn't this the same gentleman, dear Mother, whom

we saw at Amsterdam and who people thought was my father because I look like him? But that's not possible, because my father is dead.''

"True," I said, "but I can be your fond friend. Do you want me?"

"Oh, my dear friend! Let's give each other a good hug!"

After the laughter which was to be expected, we sat down at table. The heroine gave me a choice supper and excellent wine. She had not, she said, treated the Margrave better at the suppers for two with which she entertained him. Wanting to know the character of her son, whom I had decided to take with me, I talked only with him. I discovered that he was false, secretive, always on his guard, always preparing his answers in advance, and hence never giving such answers as would have come from his heart if he had followed its bidding. All this, however, was accompanied by a show of politeness and reserve which he thought was bound to please me. I told him quietly that his calculated manner might be all very well at the proper time and place, but that there were moments when a man could not be happy unless he was unconstrained and that it was only then that he would be seen to have a lovable nature, if indeed it was such. At that his mother, thinking to praise him, said that his principal quality was discretion; that she had taught him to be discreet always and in everything, and hence she was not hurt by his habit of being as reserved with her as he was with everyone else. I told her to her face that it was abominable, and that I could not imagine how a father could have any fondness—let alone a predilection—for a son who never spoke out.

"Tell me," I said to the boy, "if you feel able to promise me that you will have complete confidence in me and will under no circumstances keep any secrets from me or leave anything unspoken between us."

"I promise you," he answered, "that I will die sooner than tell you a lie."

"That is his character," his mother interrupted; "such is the horror of lying that I have inculcated in him."

"That is all very well," I answered, "but you could teach your son a different road to happiness. Instead of showing him the ugliness of falsehood, you could show him the beauty of truth. It is the only way to make oneself lovable, and in this world to be happy one must be loved."

"But," he answered, with a sly smile which I did not like and which enchanted his mother, "aren't not lying and telling the truth the same thing?"

"Certainly not, for you would only have to tell me nothing at all. The thing is to disclose your soul, to tell me everything that goes on within you and around you, and to reveal to me even what might make you blush. I will help you to blush, my dear son, and before very long you will find yourself in no danger of it; but when we know each other better we shall soon see if we suit each other, for I could never consider you my son without loving you tenderly, and I will never permit you to call me father unless I see that you love me as you might love your closest friend; as for knowing you, I will undertake to do that, for you will never be able to hide the least of your thoughts from me; but if I find it out despite you, I shall love you no longer and you will be the loser. You shall come to Paris with me as soon as I finish my business in Amsterdam, where I am going tomorrow. When I return I hope I shall find that your mother has taught you the rudiments of a new system of conduct."

I was amazed to see my daughter, who, having listened to everything I had said to her brother without batting an eye, was making vain efforts to hold back her tears.

"*Why are you crying?*" said her mother; "*it's stupid.*"

*Palace of Versailles*

*Small* Nécessaire *Suspended from Belt*

At that the child burst out laughing, threw herself on her neck, and kissed her. I saw beyond doubt that her laughter had been as false as her feeling tears had been natural.

"Do you want to come to Paris with me too?" I asked her.

"Yes, my dear friend, but with Mamma, for without me she would die."

"What if I ordered you to go?" said her mother.

"I would obey, but away from you how could I live?"

Thereupon my dear daughter pretended to cry. That she was pretending was obvious. Even Teresa must have known it, and I took her aside and told her that if she had brought up her children to be actors she had succeeded, but that in polite society they were monsters in embryo. I stopped reproaching her when I saw her crying, but real tears. She asked me to stay at The Hague a day longer; I told her I could not, and I left the room to go somewhere; but I was very much surprised on my return to hear Sophie say to me that if she was to believe I was her friend she must have a proof of it.

"What proof, my little darling?"

"Coming to supper with me tomorrow."

"I cannot, for since I have just refused the same thing to your mother she would be offended if I granted it to you."

"Oh no—for it was she who just told me to ask you."

We laughed; but when her mother called her a little fool and her brother added that he would not have committed such an indiscretion, I clearly saw the distress of her soul in the little girl's face. I hastened to reassure her, not caring if I displeased her mother by giving her a taste of new moral principles, to which she listened with wonder. I ended by promising her I would come to supper with her the next day, but on condition that she would give me only one bottle of Burgundy and three dishes.

"For you are not rich," I said.

"I know it, my dear friend, but Mamma said that you would pay for everything."

At this answer I had to hold my sides, and her mother, despite her annoyance, had to do the same. The poor woman, artful though she was, took Sophie's ingenuousness for stupidity. It was intelligence, it was a diamond of the first water which only needed someone to polish it. She said that the wine cost her nothing, that a certain V. D. R.,[2] a young man who was the son of a burgomaster of Rotterdam, provided her with it, and that he would sup with us the next evening if I had no objection. I answered, with a laugh, that I would even be glad to see him. I left after devouring my daughter with kisses. I wished that her mother would give her to me, but it was no use my asking, for I saw that she regarded her as a resource for her old age. This is the usual attitude among adventuresses, and Teresa was nothing else. I gave the mother twenty ducats to spend on dressing my adopted son and Sophie, who, in an outburst of gratitude, flung herself on my neck. Joseph wanted to kiss my hand, but I warned him that in future he was not to show his gratitude to me only by kisses. When I started to go downstairs she showed me a little room in which her children slept. I saw her meaning, but I was far from having any of my old hankering for her. Esther completely occupied me.

The next day at Teresa's I found young V. D. R. A handsome youth of twenty-two, simply dressed, neither cold nor warm, neither polite nor impolite, with no social grace. He had every right to be Teresa's lover, but none to treat me cavalierly. When she saw that he wanted to play the "man in possession" and that he offended me she took a high tone with him. After criticizing the poorness of the dishes and praising the excellence of the wines he sent her, he departed, leaving us at dessert. I, in turn, left her at eleven o'clock, assuring her that I would see her again before I set out. A Princess Galitzin,[3] née Kantemir, had invited me to dinner.

The next day I received a letter from Madame d'Urfé, who sent me twelve thousand francs in the form of a bill of exchange on Boas, saying very generously that since her shares had cost her only sixty thousand francs she did not want to profit from them. This present of five hundred louis[4] pleased me. All the rest of her letter was filled with fantasies. She said that her Genius had told her that I would come back to Paris with a boy born from philosophical intercourse and that she hoped I would take pity on her. Strange coincidence! I laughed in anticipation of the effect which the appearance of Teresa's son would have on her soul. Boas thanked me for my willingness to let him pay me my bill of exchange in ducats. Gold in Holland is a commodity. Payments are made in paper or in silver. At the moment no one wanted ducats because the agio[5] had gone up to five stuivers.

After dining with Princess Galitzin I went for my redingote and then went to the coffeehouse to read the gazettes. I saw V. D. R., who, about to begin a game of billiards, whispered to me that I might well bet on him.

This friendly advance pleased me. I thought he was sure of his skill, and I began betting; but after he lost the third game I bet against him without his knowledge. Three hours later he stopped, having lost thirty or forty games, and, thinking that I had always bet on his side, he expressed his regret. I saw that he was surprised when, showing him thirty or forty ducats, I said that, being a little doubtful of his confidence in his own skill, I had won them by betting against him. All the players laughed; he could not stand a joke; he took great offense at my jibes; he left in a rage; and a moment later I went to Teresa's because I had promised her I would. I

was to leave for Amsterdam the next day. She was expecting V. D. R., but she stopped expecting him when I told
her how and why he had left the billiard room in a rage.
After spending an hour with Sophie in my arms, I left
her, assuring her that we would meet again in three or
four weeks. On my way back to Boas's alone, with my
sword under my arm, I am suddenly attacked in the
brightest moonlight by V. D. R. He says he is curious
to see if my sword is as sharp as my tongue. I try vainly
to calm him by talking reasonably, I do not unsheathe
though he has his bare sword in his hand, I say that he
should not take mere jests so hard, I beg his pardon, I
offer to put off my departure and beg his pardon at the
coffeehouse. Not a bit of it—he is determined to kill me,
and to persuade me to draw my sword he gives me a
blow with the flat of his. It is the only blow I have
received in my entire life. I finally draw my sword, and,
still hoping to make him listen to reason, I fence with
him, giving ground. He takes it for fear, and he gives a
lunge which makes my hair stand on end. He pierced my
cravat on the left, his sword veering off—four lines
farther in, and he would have cut my throat. In my terror I jumped to one side, and, determined to kill him,
I wounded him in the chest and, being sure of it, I
invited him to stop. Saying that he was not yet dead, he
came after me like a madman; I touched him three or
four times in succession. At my last thrust he jumped
back, saying that he had had enough and only begged me
to leave.

I was glad when, starting to wipe off my sword, I saw
that the point of it was very little stained. Boas had not
yet gone to bed. When he had heard the whole story he
advised me to leave for Amsterdam at once, despite my
assuring him that the wounds were not mortal. My chaise
being at the harness-maker's, I set off in a carriage belonging to Boas, leaving my servant orders to start the next

day and bring my baggage to Amsterdam, at the "Second Bible," [6] where I put up. I arrived there at noon, and my servant at nightfall. He had no news to tell me; but what pleased me was that nothing was heard of the matter at Amsterdam until a week later. Though simple enough, the thing could have done me harm, for the reputation of being a brawler is no way to please financiers with whom one is about to conclude profitable business.

As far as appearances went my first visit was to Monsieur D. O., but in reality it was Esther who received the homage of it. The way I had parted from her had set me on fire. Her father was not there; I found her writing at a table; she was entertaining herself with a problem in arithmetic; to divert her I made two magic squares; they delighted her; in return she showed me some trifles which I already knew and in which I pretended to be interested. My good Genius put it into my mind to perform the cabala for her. I told her to write a question asking something she did not know and was curious about, assuring her that by means of a certain calculation she would receive a satisfactory answer. She laughed, and she asked why I had come back to Amsterdam so soon. I show her how to construct pyramids with numbers drawn from words, and all the other ceremonies; then I have her extract a numerical answer herself, which I have her translate into the French alphabet, and she is astonished to read that what has brought me back to Amsterdam so quickly is love. All wonder, she says it is astonishing even if the answer is untrue, and she wants me to tell her what masters can teach such a wonderful calculation. I say that those who know it can teach it to no one.

"Then how do you know it?"

"I learned it by myself from a manuscript which my father left me."

"Sell me the manuscript."

"I have burned it. I am at liberty to teach it to only one person, but not until I reach the age of fifty. If I teach it before then I risk losing it. An elemental spirit who is attached to the oracle would leave it. I learned all this from the same manuscript."

"Then you can find out all the greatest secrets in the world?"

"I should have that privilege if the answers weren't in most cases very obscure."

"As it doesn't take long, would you have the kindness to extract the answer to another question for me?"

She then asked what her destiny was to be, and the oracle answered that she had not yet taken the first step on the road to it. All wonder, Esther calls her governess and thinks she will amaze her by showing her the two oracles; but the good Swiss woman sees nothing extraordinary in it. In her impatience she calls her a fool. She begs me to let her put another question, and I encourage her. She asks what person in Amsterdam loves her most, and, using the same method, she finds the answer that no one loves her more than the person to whom she owes her existence. The poor, intelligent girl then tells me with the utmost seriousness that I have made her miserable, for she will die of grief if she cannot learn the calculation. I do not answer, and she sees me downcast. She writes a question, hiding the paper with her beautiful hand. I get up to leave her free; but while she is constructing the pyramid I glance at the paper as I walk by, and I read her question. After doing everything I had taught her to do, she says that I can extract the answer without having to read her question. I agree, and she blushes and asks me to do her the favor. I consent, but on condition that she will not ask me to do her the same favor again. She promises. Since, having read her question, I know that she asked the oracle's

permission to show her father all the questions she put,
I produce the answer that ''she will be happy if she
never keeps anything which is important to her a secret
from her father.'' At that she oh'd and ah'd, finding no
words strong enough to show me her gratitude. I left
her to go to the Exchange, where I talked at length with
Monsieur Pels about my chief business.

The next morning a handsome and very gentlemanly
man came bringing me a letter from Teresa in which
she introduced him to me, assuring me that if I had
any business to transact he could be useful to me. His
name was Rigerboos.[7] She said that V. D. R.'s five wounds
were all slight, that I had nothing to fear, that no one
knew anything of the affair, and that there was nothing
to stop me if I needed to go back to The Hague. She said
that Sophie talked about me from morning to night, and
that when I came back I would be much better pleased
with her son. I asked Monsieur Rigerboos to give me his
address, assuring him that if the occasion arose I should
have perfect confidence in his probity. A moment after
he left I received a note from Esther in which she asked
me, in her father's name, to come and spend the whole
day with her, unless some important business prevented
me. I answered that except for a transaction of which
her father knew, my only important business in the world
would be whatever I could do to conquer her heart. I
promised to go.

I went there at dinnertime. Esther and her father were
busily examining the calculation which drew rational
answers from the pyramid. Her father embraced me, with
joy painted on his noble countenance, saying that he was
fortunate to have a daughter who had deserved my attention. When I answered that I adored her he encouraged me to kiss her, and Esther gave a cry and
literally sprang into my arms.

''I have attended to everything,'' said Monsieur D. O.,

"and I have the whole day to myself. I have known from childhood, my dear friend, that the science of which you are in possession exists in the world, and I was acquainted with a Jew who made a great fortune by it. He said, as you do, that he could impart it only to one person, upon pain of losing it himself. But he put it off so long that he died without being able to impart it to me. It was a high fever which deprived him of the power. Permit me to tell you that if you do not know how to profit by your skill, you do not know what you possess. It is a treasure."

"My oracle, Monsieur, answers very obscurely."

"The answers my daughter has shown me are perfectly clear."

"It seems she is fortunate in her questions, for the answers depend upon that."

"We shall see after dinner if I have the same good fortune, if you will be so good as to work with me."

At table we talked of other things entirely, for there were some employees present, and among them his head manager, an ugly, coarse fellow, who I thought had notions about Esther. After dinner we withdrew, and, with only Esther present, Monsieur D. O. took two very long questions from his pocket. In one he wanted to know how he should go about obtaining a favorable decision from the States-General [8] in a business matter which was of great consequence to him and of which he gave the details. I answered this question very obscurely and very quickly, leaving it for Esther to put it into words; when he asked his second question I took a notion to answer it clearly. He asked what had been the fate of a ship which was known to have sailed from the East Indies on a certain date, but what had become of it was not. It should have arrived two months since; he wanted to know if it was still in existence or if it had perished, and where and how. No one had ever had any news of it. The company which owned it would be satisfied with an insurer who would give them ten percent, but they found no one. What made it almost certain that the ship was lost was a letter from an English captain who testified that he had seen it go down.

The gist of my answer, which I was stupid enough to give without apprehending any ill consequences, was that the ship still existed and had suffered no damage, and that trustworthy news of it would arrive within a week. So it was that, wanting to raise my oracle's reputation sky-high, I risked its losing it entirely. But I should have done none of this if I had guessed what Monsieur D. O. would do in consequence of my oracle. He went pale for joy. He told us that it was of the utmost importance to speak of the matter to no one, for he was planning to go and insure the vessel at the best rate possible. Aghast, I told him that I did not answer for the truth of the oracle and that I should die of mortification if I were the cause of his losing a large sum. He asked me if the oracle sometimes deceived me, and I answered that it often led to mistakes by being equivocal. Esther, seeing my uneasiness, begged her father to take no steps in the matter.

Monsieur D. O. remained lost in thought, then spoke at length, reasoning erroneously on the so-called power of numbers, and told his daughter to read him all the questions she had asked. There were six or seven of them, all short and all of a nature to be answered plainly or equivocally or humorously. Esther, who had constructed all the pyramids, shone by extracting the answers with my all-powerful help. Her father, in ecstasies at seeing her so clever, thought that she would succeed in mastering the oracle, and Esther herself made bold to believe it. After spending seven hours discussing all the answers, which were acclaimed as divine, we supped. Monsieur D. O. invited me to dine at his house on the

Amstel, which I already knew. I accepted with pleasure.

Returning to my lodging, I passed a house where there was dancing, and, seeing people going in and out, I wanted to see what was doing. It was a *musicau*[9]—a dark orgy in a place which was a veritable sewer of vice, a disgrace to even the most repellent debauchery. The very sound of the two or three instruments which made up the orchestra plunged the soul in sadness. A room reeking with the smoke of bad tobacco, with the stench of garlic which came from the belches emitted by the men who were dancing or sitting with a bottle or a pot of beer to their right and a hideous slattern to their left, presented my eyes and my thoughts with a distressing image which showed me the miseries of life and the level of degradation to which brutishness could reduce pleasures. The crowd which gave life to the place was composed entirely of sailors and others of the common people, to whom it seemed a paradise which made up to them for all that they had suffered on long and painful voyages. Among the prostitutes I saw there I found not one with whom I could possibly have diverted myself for a moment. A shady-looking man who might be a tinsmith and who had the manners of a boor came and asked me in broken Italian if I wanted to dance for a sou. I declined. He pointed out a Venetian woman who was sitting there, saying that I could take her to a room upstairs and drink with her.

I approach, I think I recognize her, but the gloomy light of four unsnuffed candles does not let me make out her features. Impelled by curiosity, I sit down beside her and ask her if it is true that she is a Venetian and if it has been long since she left her native country. She answers that it has been about eighteen years. I am brought a bottle, I ask her if she wants to drink, she says yes, adding that I can go upstairs with her. I answer that I haven't time, I hand over a ducat in payment,

I am given the change, which I put into the hand of the
poor devil of a creature, who offers me a kiss which I
refuse.

"Do you like Amsterdam better than Venice?" I ask
her.

"In my own country I didn't follow this accursed
trade. I was only fourteen, and I lived with my father
and mother."

"Who seduced you?"

"A courier."

"In what *contrada*[10] of Venice did you live?"

"I didn't live in Venice but on an estate in Friuli
not far from there."

An estate in Friuli, eighteen years, a courier—I am
moved, I look at her closely, and I recognize Lucia[11] of
Pasiano, but I am careful not to change my attitude of
indifference. Far more than age, debauchery had withered
her face and all its appurtenances. Lucia, fond, pretty,
ingenuous Lucia, whom I had loved so much and whom
I had spared out of delicacy, in such a state, ugly,
repellent, in a brothel in Amsterdam! She drank without
looking at me and without caring to know who I was.
I did not feel curious to learn her story, I even thought
I knew it. She said that she lived in the *musicau* and
would give me pretty girls if I came to see her. I gave
her two ducats and quickly left. I went to bed overwhelmed with sorrow. I thought I had spent a day of
ill omen, remembering Monsieur D. O. too, who because
of my silly cabala might be going to lose three hundred
thousand florins. The thought, which made me despise
myself, boded ill for the affection which Esther inspired
in me. I foresaw her becoming my implacable enemy together with her father. A man cannot love except with
the hope of being loved. The sight of Lucia in the *musicau*
left an impression on me which brought me the most
ominous dreams. I considered myself the cause of her

misfortune. She was only thirty-two, and I foresaw a horrible future for her.

After tormenting myself and not sleeping, I get up, I order a carriage, and I put on a fine suit to go and make my bow to Princess Galitzin, who was lodging at the "Star of the East." She had gone to the Admiralty. I go there and find her in the company of Monsieur de Reischach[12] and Count de Tott, who had just received news of my friend Pesselier,[13] at whose house I had met him. I had left him very ill when I departed from Paris.

Leaving the Admiralty, I dismiss my carriage and my lackey, ordering him to be at Monsieur D. O.'s house on the Amstel at eleven o'clock. I go there on foot, and, dressed as I am, I find some of the Dutch populace hooting and whistling at me. Esther sees me from the window, a cord is pulled on the second floor, the door opens, I go in, close it behind me, and at the fourth or fifth step on my way up a wooden staircase my foot strikes against something yielding. I look, and seeing a green portfolio I stoop to pick it up, but I awkwardly give it a push, and it drops under the staircase through an opening which had been made in the front of the next step, apparently to give light to the place under the stairs. I do not stop but go on up. I am received as usual, and I explain the reason for my elaborate dress. Esther laughs at my looking like a different person, but I have the impression that they are gloomy. Esther's governess comes in and speaks to them in Dutch. I see Esther look distressed, then go and give her father a hundred caresses.

"I see," I say to him, "that some misfortune has befallen you; if my presence incommodes you, permit me to withdraw at once."

He answers that the misfortune is not great and that he has resigned himself to it, since he is rich enough to bear it with equanimity.

"I have lost," he said, "a quite well-furnished portfolio, which, if I had used my common sense, I would have left at home, for I had no need for it until tomorrow. I can only have lost it in the street—how, I don't know. It contains some sizable bills of exchange, on which I can stop payment, but also some English bank notes, of which the bearers can make what use they please. Let us thank God for all things, my dear Esther, and pray to him to keep us in health and to preserve us from still greater misfortunes. I have suffered worse blows in my life, and I have borne up. So let us say no more of this incident, which I will regard as a small bankruptcy."

I remained silent, with joy in my soul. I was sure that the portfolio was the one I had pushed through the opening, so it was not lost; but I at once thought that I would not let them recover it without some cabalistic trappings. The chance was too good a one for me to fail to use it and give my hosts a great example of the infallibility of my oracle. The idea having put me in a good humor, I said countless things which made Esther laugh and told her stories which ridiculed the French, whom she detested.

We dined very choicely and drank of the best. After coffee I said that if they liked cards I would play; but Esther said it would be a pity to waste time at that.

"I can't get enough of pyramids," she said. "May I ask who has found my father's portfolio?"

"Why not?" I said. "It's a simple question."

She framed it very briefly and the answer which came out, equally brief, told her that no one had found her father's portfolio. She ran and embraced her father, whom the answer had made sure that his portfolio would come back to him; but she was first surprised, then laughed a great deal, when I told her that any hope she had that I would go on working was vain unless she gave me at least as many caresses as she had given her dear father. At that she gave me a quantity of kisses, and she

extracted the pyramid from the question which asked
where the portfolio was. I elicited the words: ''The portfolio dropped through the opening in the fifth step of the
staircase.''

D. O. and his daughter rise, greatly relieved, they go
down, and I follow them. He himself shows us the opening through which the portfolio must have passed. He
lights a candle, then enters a storeroom, goes down an
underground staircase, and with his own hands picks up
the portfolio, which was lying in water exactly under the
opening in the stair. We go back up and spend an hour
in the most serious discussion of the divinity of the oracle
and its ability to make its possessor the happiest of men.
Opening the portfolio, he showed us forty Exchequer bills
for a thousand pounds sterling[14] each, of which he presented two to his daughter and two to me; taking them
with one hand, I gave them to the beautiful Esther with
the other, telling her to keep them for me. She would
not consent until I threatened not to work with the cabala
for her again. To Monsieur D. O. I said that I wanted
nothing from him but his friendship. He embraced me
and promised I should have it to the last day of his life.

By making Esther the custodian of twenty-two thousand florins, I was certain to bind her to me. The girl had
a witchery in her eyes which intoxicated me. I said to her
father that the business I had most at heart was to
negotiate the twenty millions at little loss. He answered
that he hoped to satisfy me, but that since he would
often need me with him, I should come to lodge in his
house. Esther added her solicitations to his, and I accepted, taking great care to conceal all the satisfaction
I felt but at the same time showing them all the
gratitude I owed them.

He then went to his study to write, and, left alone
with Esther, I said that I felt ready to do anything for
her which lay in my power but that first of all she must

give me her heart. She said that the moment when I could ask her father for her hand would come when I was staying in their house. I assured her that she would have me there the next day.

Coming back, Monsieur D. O. said that the next day we would hear a great piece of news on the Exchange. He said that he would himself take over the supposedly lost ship for three hundred thousand florins—and let them call him a fool!

"I should really be a fool," he added, "if, after all that I have seen of the divinity of the oracle, I had doubts. I will make three millions; and if I lose it will not ruin me."

Esther, dazzled by the recovered portfolio, told her father that he must act at once, and for my part I could no longer retreat. Seeing me gloomy, Monsieur D. O. assured me that he would be no less my friend if the oracle proved to be fallacious. I asked him to let me question the oracle again before he risked such a large loss, and I saw that they were both delighted by my zeal for the good of their house.

But here is yet another incident which will make some of my readers incredulous or incline them to condemn me as a thoughtless and even dangerous person. I did everything myself—the question, the pyramid, and all the rest—refusing to let Esther take any part in it. I was delighted to be in time to prevent such a slaughter and determined that I would prevent it. A double meaning, which I could bring from my pen, would have discouraged them both, and since I had it in my head I thought I had expressed it perfectly in numbers on the paper which lay before me. Esther, who had the alphabet by heart, quickly translated it into words and amazed me when she read my answer. She read these words: "In such a case as this, there is nothing to *fear*. Your regret would be too painful." Nothing more was needed. Father

and daughter together ran to embrace me, and Monsieur
D. O. said that when the ship appeared he would owe me
a tenth of his profit. Surprise prevented me from answering him and expressing my gratitude, for I felt certain
that I had written "believe" [*croire*], not "fear"
[*craindre*]. I could no longer draw back.

The next day I went to stay with them in a charming
suite of rooms, and on the day after that I took Esther
to a concert, where she rallied me on La Trenti's not
appearing at it. The girl possessed me entirely, but since
she constantly refused to yield to the essential purpose
of my caresses she kept me languishing.

Four or five days later Monsieur D. O. communicated
to me the decision reached at a conference he had held
with Pels and the heads of six other banking houses
concerning my twenty millions. They offered ten millions
in cash and seven in obligations yielding five and six
percent, with a deduction of one percent for brokerage
fees. In addition they waived all claim to the twelve hundred thousand florins which the French East India Company[15] owed to the Dutch East India Company. I sent
copies of the decision to Monsieur de Boulogne and Monsieur d'Affry, demanding a prompt answer. The answer
I received a week later from Monsieur de Courteuil by
order of Monsieur de Boulogne was that such terms were
unacceptable and that I had only to return to Paris if I
could not do better, and I was again told that peace was
imminent. But Monsieur D. O.'s confidence had increased
extraordinarily some days before this answer arrived. The
Exchange itself had received trustworthy news that
the ship in question was at Madeira. Four days earlier
Monsieur D. O. had bought it with all its cargo for
three hundred thousand florins. What a pleasure it was
when we saw him come into our room with a look of
triumph which confirmed the news! He said that he had
already insured it from Madeira to Texel [16] for a trifle,

and that a tenth of the profit was at my disposition. But what astonished me was these exact words, with which he ended his discourse:

"You are now rich enough to establish yourself in our country with the assurance of becoming immensely wealthy in a few years simply by using your cabala. I will be your agent. Let us make one household, and if you love my daughter I give her to you if she wants you."

Joy shone in Esther's eyes, but in mine she could see only my surprise, which was so beyond measure that it left me dumb and as if stupefied. After a long silence I entered upon a wiredrawn analysis of the feelings appropriate to the situation, ending by saying that though I adored Esther I must go back to Paris before coming to a resolve; I said I was sure that I would be able to decide my fate when I returned to Amsterdam. My answer won their approval and we spent the day in high spirits. The next day Monsieur D. O. gave a splendid dinner for his friends, who only said, amid good-natured laughter, that he had learned before anyone else that the ship was at Madeira, though no one could imagine how he had come to know it.

A week after this lucky incident he gave me an ultimatum on the business of the twenty millions, the upshot of which was that France would lose only nine percent on the sale of the twenty millions, on condition that I could not demand any brokerage fees from the purchasers. I sent accurate copies of this proposal to Monsieur d'Affry by express messenger, asking him to transmit them at my expense to the Comptroller-General together with a letter in which I warned him that the transaction would fall through if he let a single day pass before giving Monsieur d'Affry whatever powers he needed in order to give me the authority to contract. I appealed with no less urgency to Monsieur de Courteuil and the Duke, informing them all that I was to be given

nothing but that I would conclude the transaction nevertheless, being certain that I would be reimbursed for my
expenses and that what was due me as broker would not
be refused me at Versailles.

As it was Carnival,[17] Monsieur D. O. saw fit to give a
ball. He invited all the most distinguished men and women in the city. I will tell my reader only that the ball
was sumptuous, as was the supper. Esther danced all the
contradances with me with every possible grace, and
shone arrayed in the diamonds of her late mother.

We were spending the whole of every day together, in
love and unhappy because abstinence tormented us.
Esther would only go so far as to permit me some little
theft when I went to breakfast with her. She was generous
only with her kisses, which, instead of calming me, made
me frantic. She told me, like all the supposedly decent
girls in the universe, that she was sure I would never
marry her if she let me do whatever I wanted to her.
She did not think I was married, for I had assured her
too often that I was a bachelor, but she had no doubt
that I had some strong attachment in Paris. I admitted
it, and I assured her that I was going to free myself
completely so that I could be bound to her until death
by the most solemn of ties. Alas! I was lying, for she
could not be separated from her father, who was only
forty, and I could not imagine it possible that I should
settle permanently in such a country.

Ten or twelve days after sending the ultimatum I
received a letter from Monsieur de Boulogne in which
he said that the Ambassador had received all the necessary instructions to enable me to conclude the business,
and the Ambassador told me the same. He warned me
to look to my arrangements, for he would not deliver the
royal securities except upon receiving 18,200,000 francs
in currency.

The sad moment of parting having thus come, we did
not try to restrain our tears. Esther gave me the equiv-

alent of the two thousand pounds sterling I had left
with her on the day the portfolio was found, and her
father, in accordance with my instructions, gave me one
hundred thousand florins[18] in bills of exchange on Tourton & Baur and on Pâris de Montmartel [19] and a receipt
for two hundred thousand florins which authorized me to
draw on him until the entire amount was exhausted.
When I left, Esther presented me with fifty shirts of
the finest linen and fifty Masulipatam[20] handkerchiefs.

It was not love of Manon Balletti but a stupid vanity,
a wish to cut a figure in Paris, which made me leave
Holland. The fifteen months I spent under the Leads were
not enough to cure the defects of my character. "Destiny" is a word without meaning; it is we who make our
destiny, despite the maxim of the Stoics: *Volentem ducit,
nolentem trahit* ("[Fate] leads the willing, drags the
unwilling").[21] I am too self-indulgent if I apply it to
myself.

After vowing to Esther that I would see her before
the end of the year I left with a commissioner of the
company which had bought the French securities and,
reaching The Hague, went to stay with Boas, who received me with mingled astonishment and admiration. He
said I had performed a miracle and that I should hurry
on to Paris, if only to enjoy the incense of congratulations. He said, however, that he was sure I could not
have done what I had done unless I had convinced the
company beyond doubt that peace was on the verge of
being made. I replied that I had not convinced them,
but that peace would certainly be concluded. He said
that if I could obtain for him a positive written assurance from the Ambassador that peace would be made
he would present me with fifty thousand florins in
diamonds. I replied that the Ambassador's certainty on
the subject could not be greater than mine but that, even
so, I considered it still only a moral certainty.

The next day I concluded everything with the Ambassador; and the commissioner returned to Amsterdam.

I went to supper at Teresa's, who showed me her children very nicely dressed. I told her to go to Rotterdam the next day and wait for my arrival there to entrust her son to me, for to avoid talk I did not want to take charge of him in The Hague.

From one of Boas's sons I bought a pair of diamond earrings and several fine stones for forty thousand florins. I had to promise him that I would stay with him when I came back to The Hague, but I did not keep my word.

At Rotterdam Teresa bluntly told me that she knew for certain I had made half a million in Amsterdam and that her fortune would be assured if she could leave Holland and set herself up in London. She got Sophie to tell me that my good fortune had been the result of her prayers to God. All this made me laugh. I gave her a hundred ducats and told her that I would arrange to have her paid another hundred when she wrote to me from London. I saw that she thought the amount small, but I did not let that persuade me to give her more. She waited until I had got into my chaise to ask me for another hundred ducats, and I whispered to her that I would give her a thousand on the spot if she would let me have Sophie. After thinking for a moment she said no. I left after giving my daughter a watch. I reached Paris on the 10th of February,[22] and I took a fine apartment in Rue Comtesse-d'Artois near the Rue Montorgueil.[23]

*Flattering reception from my patron. Madame d'Urfé's delusions. Madame* XCV *and her family. Madame du Rumain.*

---

DURING THE short journey I came to the conclusion that my newly adopted son's soul was not as attractive as his person. What his mother had chiefly instilled by the education she had given him was discretion. This quality in her son was the one which her own interest demanded that he should possess above all others; but the unschooled boy carried it too far; he combined it with dissimulation, suspicion, and false confidences. Not only did he not say what he knew, he pretended to know what he did not know; to be successful, he felt that he must be impenetrable, and to that end he had acquired the habit of imposing silence on his heart and never saying anything which he had not framed in his mind beforehand. He thought he was being prudent when he gave a false impression. Incapable of friendship, he became unworthy to win friends.

Foreseeing that Madame d'Urfé would count on the

boy for the accomplishment of her chimerical hypostasis
and that the more I made his birth a mystery, the more
her Genius would lead her to invent wild fantasies, I
ordered him to conceal nothing about himself if a lady to
whom I would present him showed any curiosity about his
circumstances when she was alone with him. He promised
to obey me. He had not been expecting that I would
order him to be sincere.

My first visit was to my patron,[1] whom I found entertaining a large company; among them I saw the Venetian
Ambassador,[2] who pretended not to know me.

"How long have you been in Paris?" asked the Minister, taking my hand.

"No time at all. I have just got out of my post chaise."

"Then go to Versailles, you will find the Duke of
Choiseul and the Comptroller-General there. You have
performed miracles, go and be adored. Come to see me
afterward. Tell the Duke that I have sent Voltaire a
passport in which the King appoints him a gentleman-in-
ordinary."[3]

One does not go to Versailles at noon, but this was
the way Ministers talked when they were in Paris. It
was as if Versailles were at the other end of the street.
I went to Madame d'Urfé's.

The first thing she said to me was that her Genius had
told her she would see me that very day.

"Kornmann," she said, "told me yesterday that what
you have done is incredible. I am sure it was you who
discounted the twenty millions. Securities have gone up,
and within the week there will be a circulation of at
least a hundred millions. Forgive me for having ven-
tured to make you a present of twelve thousand francs.
It is nothing."

I saw no need to tell her that she was wrong. She sent
word to the porter to close the door to everyone, and we
began talking. I saw her tremble with joy when I coolly

told her that I had brought a twelve-year-old boy with me, whom I meant to bring up in the best boarding school in Paris.

"I will put him in Viar's,"[4] she said, "where my nephews are. What is his name? Where is he? I know what the boy is. I cannot wait to see him. Why did you not come straight here?"

"I will present him to you day after tomorrow, for tomorrow I shall be at Versailles."

"Does he speak French? Until I have made all the arrangements for his schooling, you simply must leave him with me."

"We will discuss it day after tomorrow."

After stopping at my office, where I found everything in order, I went to the Comédie Italienne, where Silvia was playing.[5] I found her in her dressing room with her daughter. She said she knew I had done very well with my business in Holland, and I saw that she was surprised when I said that I had worked for her daughter. The girl blushed. After saying that I would go to supper with them I took a place in the amphitheater. What a surprise! In one of the first-tier boxes I see Madame *XCV* [6] with all her family. Here is the story.

Madame *XCV*, of Greek origin, was the widow of an Englishman to whom she had given six children, four girls[7] and two boys. On his deathbed, unable to resist his wife's tears, he declared himself a Roman Catholic; but since his children could not inherit a capital of forty thousand pounds sterling which he had in England except by declaring themselves Anglicans, she had just come from London, where she had attended to all that.[8] It was at the beginning of the year 1758.[9]

In the year *1753* I fell in love with her eldest daughter[10] at Padua, where I acted in a play with her, and six months later at Venice Madame *XCV* saw fit to exclude me from her society. Her daughter made it possible for me to bear the affront calmly by a charming letter, which I still cherish; besides, being then in love with M. M. and C. C., I easily forgot her. The girl, though only fifteen[11] years old, was a beauty, and to the charms of her figure she added those of a cultivated mind, the spell of which is often more powerful. The Chamberlain to the King of Prussia, Count Algarotti,[12] gave her lessons, and several young patricians hoped to conquer her heart; the one who seemed to have the preference was the eldest son of the Memmo di San Marcuola[13] family. He died four years ago as Procurator of San Marco.

The reader can imagine my surprise when, five years later, I saw the whole family. Miss *XCV* [14] recognizes me instantly, she points me out to her mother, and the latter at once beckons to me with her fan. I went to her box at once.

She receives me by saying that we are no longer in Venice, that she is heartily glad to see me again, and that she hopes I will often come to call on her at the Hôtel de Bretagne[15] in the Rue Saint-André-des-Arts, where she is staying. Her daughter treats me to the same compliment with even greater insistence; she looks a goddess, and it seems to me that after a sleep of five years my love wakes again with an increase in power equal to that which the object before my eyes had gained in the same period of time.

They tell me that they expect to spend six months in Paris before going back to Venice; I reply that I intend to make my residence in Paris, that I have just returned from Holland that day, that I am obliged to spend the next day at Versailles, and that they will see me the day after that at their lodging, eager to offer them any services in my power.

"I have heard," says Miss *XCV*, "that what you have done in Holland must make you dear to France, and I have always hoped to see you; and your prodigious escape

gave us the greatest pleasure, for we were always fond
of you. We learned the details of it from a sixteen-page
letter you wrote to Signor Memmo, which made us
shudder and laugh. As for what you accomplished in
Holland, we heard of it yesterday from Monsieur de la
Pouplinière." [16]

The Farmer-General himself, whom I had first met at
his house in Passy[17] seven years earlier, now entered the
box. After congratulating me briefly, he said that if I
could obtain twenty millions for the East India Company[18] in the same way, he would have me made Farmer-
General. He advised me to get myself naturalized as a
French citizen before it became generally known that I
must be worth at least half a million.

"You cannot have made less."

"The business, Monsieur, will ruin me if I am denied
my brokerage fee."

"You are right to speak out. Everyone is eager to
make your acquaintance, and France is indebted to you,
for you have made securities rise."

It was at supper at Silvia's that my soul reveled in
delight. I was made as much of as if I had been a son
of the house, and on my side I convinced the whole family
that I wanted to be regarded as such. It seemed to me
that I owed all my good fortune to their influence and
their unfailing friendship. I made the mother,[19] the
father, the daughter, and the two sons[20] promise to accept the presents I had for them. Since the richest one
was in my pocket, I presented it to the mother, who immediately gave it to her daughter. It was a pair of earrings which had cost me six thousand florins. Three days
later I gave her a small chest in which she found two
pieces of superb calencar,[21] two of very fine linen, and
trimmings of the Flemish needlepoint known as "English point." I gave Mario, who liked to smoke, a gold
pipe, and my friend [22] a handsome snuffbox. I gave a

watch to the Cadet,[23] of whom I was inordinately fond.
I shall have occasion to speak of this youth, whose qualities made him superior to his station in every respect.
But was I rich enough to give such substantial presents?
No, and I knew it. I made them only because I was
afraid I should not become rich enough. If I had been
sure of it, I would have waited.

I set out for Versailles before dawn. The Duke of
Choiseul received me pen in hand as he had before; his
hair was being dressed. This time he laid down his pen.
After a brief compliment he said that if I felt I was
capable of negotiating a loan of a hundred million florins
at four percent, he would give me a recommendation
which would do me honor. I answered that I might consider it after I learned what recompense for what I had
already done would be given me by way of encourage-
ment.

"Everyone says you have made two hundred thousand
florins."

"Saying it means nothing unless it is proved. I can
claim the brokerage fee."

"True. Go and state your case to the Comptroller-
General."

Monsieur de Boulogne stopped the work he was doing
to receive me graciously, but when I told him he owed
me a hundred thousand florins, he smiled.

"I know," he said, "that you are the holder of bills
of exchange to your order for a hundred thousand écus."

"That is true, but what I own has nothing to do with
what I did. I have proof of it. I refer you to Monsieur
d'Affry. I have an infallible plan for increasing the
King's revenues by *twenty millions* without causing any
complaint among those who will provide them."

"Execute it, and I will have the King himself give
you a pension of a hundred thousand francs and a patent
of nobility if you will become a French citizen."

I went to the private apartments, where Madame la Marquise was having a ballet rehearsed. She greeted me as soon as she saw me and said that I was a clever negotiator whom the gentlemen "down there"[24] had not properly appreciated. She still remembered what I had said to her at Fontainebleau eight years earlier. I replied that all good things came from "up there," and that I hoped to share in them through her kind offices.

Back in Paris I went to the Hôtel de Bourbon to inform my patron of all the results of my journey. He advised me to be patient and to continue to do well; and, when I mentioned that I had seen Madame *XCV* at the theater, he said that La Pouplinière was going to marry her eldest daughter.

The news when I reached my lodging was that my son had left.

"A great lady," said my hostess, "came to call on the Count" (he had immediately been dubbed Count) "and took him away with her."

I pretended to be pleased, and I went to bed. The next morning very early my clerk brought me a letter. It was from the old attorney who was the uncle of the girl whose sponsor I had been when she married Gaetano and whom I had helped to escape from him.[25] He asked me to come and speak with him at the Palais[26] or to tell him where I would be during the day. I went to the Palais.

He told me that his niece had been obliged to take refuge in a convent, where she had instituted proceedings against her husband with the help of a Councilor of the Parlement who was paying all the expenses of the case; but that they absolutely needed me, Count Tiretta, and the servants who had witnessed the scene, to prove the truth of the accusation. I managed all this very easily, and three or four months later the whole affair was ended by a fraudulent bankruptcy[27] on Gaetano's part, which forced him to leave France. I will relate at the proper time and place where I found the wretch three years later. As for his wife, she remained in Paris, happy with her good friend the Councilor, and perhaps she is still living there. I have completely lost sight of her.

Leaving the Palais, I called on Madame XXX, in order to see Tiretta. He was not there. She was still in love with him. I left my address for him, and I went to the Hôtel de Bretagne, in the same street, to make my first call on Madame *XCV*. The woman did not like me, but she received me very cordially. At Paris, and rich, I seemed another person to her. She had with her an old Greek named Zandiri, brother to Signor Bragadin's major-domo, who had just died; I expressed my condolences, and he made no reply. But the whole family avenged me for the man's stupid stiffness. Miss, her sisters, and her two brothers, the elder of whom was fourteen, covered me with caresses. But the levity of the elder brother surprised me. He was impatient to come into his inheritance so that he could devote himself to the wildest profligacy.

Miss *XCV*, as I have described her for my reader, combined with an easy manner a cultivated mind, which she never paraded except when the occasion warranted it and then without the slightest pretension. It was difficult to be near her and not fall in love with her; but, as I came to know some weeks later, being in no degree a flirt, she never allowed the slightest hope to spring up in those who had not had the good fortune to please her. She could be cold without being impolite, and so much the worse for those whose eyes her coldness did not open. During an hour which I spent alone with her she bound me in her chains, I told her so, and she showed that she was pleased. She took the place in my heart which Esther had occupied only a week earlier; but she would not have conquered it if Esther had been in Paris. My attachment to Silvia's daughter was of a kind which did not prevent me from falling in love with another woman. Unless it receives a certain amount of food, a libertine's love very quickly becomes cold, and women know this when they have a little experience. The Balletti girl was a complete novice.

Signor Farsetti,[28] a Venetian nobleman, Commander of the Order of Malta,[29] a man of letters with an interest in the abstruse sciences and a fair poet in Latin verse, arrived at one o'clock. Dinner was about to be served. Madame *XCV* had a place set for him at once; and since I was to dine with Madame d'Urfé I declined the honor. Signor Farsetti, who had known me well in Venice, only gave me a glance. He smiled when Miss praised my courage. She said that I had forced all Venetians to esteem me, and that the French wanted me to become their fellow citizen. He asked me if my position as a collector for the lottery paid me well.

"Enough," I answered, "to keep my clerk happy."

At Madame d'Urfé's I found my supposed son in her arms. She outdid herself in excuses for carrying him off, but I laughingly turned them aside. I told the little man that he must regard Madame as his queen and always open his heart to her. She told me she had made him sleep with her, but that she would have to forgo the pleasure if he would not promise to be better behaved in future. I thought it sublime, and I saw the young man blush. He asked her to tell him how he had offended her.

She said that Saint-Germain would dine with us; she knew that the adept amused me. He came, he sat down at the table—not to eat but to talk, as he always did. He brazenly related incredible stories, which we had to pretend we believed because he said that he had been either an eyewitness or the chief actor in them; but I could not keep from bursting out laughing when he told of something which had happened to him when he dined with the Fathers of the Council of Trent.[30]

Madame was wearing a large armed magnet[31] hanging from her neck. She claimed that at one time or another it would draw lightning down on her and thus she would go to the sun.

"There can be no doubt of it," said the impostor; "but I am the only person on earth who can give magnets a strength a thousand times greater than the usual run of physicists give them."

I said coldly that I would wager twenty thousand écus that he would not even double the strength of the one Madame was wearing. Madame prevented him from accepting the wager, and she told me privately afterward that I would have lost because Saint-Germain was a magician. I said she was right.

A few days later the self-styled magician left for Chambord,[32] one of the royal castles, where the King had given him an apartment and a hundred thousand francs so that he could work without interruption on the dyes which were to make all the cloth manufactories in France prosperous. He had won over the King by installing a laboratory at Trianon for him which often amused him, for he suffered from boredom everywhere except when he was hunting; it was the Marquise who had introduced the adept to him to teach him chemistry; for after he had presented her with the water of youth she believed everything he said. This miraculous water, taken in the quantity he had prescribed for her, did not, the worshiper of truth admitted, have the virtue of restoring youth, for that was impossible, but it had the virtue of preventing old age by keeping the body *in statu quo* for several centuries. She had told the monarch that she really felt she was not aging.

The monarch showed the Duke of Zweibrücken[33] a diamond of the first water weighing twelve carats which

he wore on his finger and which he was convinced he had
made himself, having been initiated into the magisterium[34] by the impostor. He said that he had melted
twenty-four carats of small diamonds which had become one, and that it had later been reduced to twelve
when it was polished on the wheel. Thus convinced of
the adept's knowledge, he had given him the same lodging
at Chambord which he had given the illustrious Maréchal
de Saxe[35] for his lifetime. I heard this story from the
Duke's own lips when I had the honor to sup with him
and the Swedish Count of Lewenhaupt[36] at Metz at the
"King Dagobert" inn.[37]

Before leaving Madame d'Urfé I told her that the
boy might be the person to assure her rebirth, but that
she would spoil everything if she did not wait until he
had reached puberty.

She sent him to board at Viar's, giving him all kinds
of teachers and the name of Count d'Aranda, despite the
fact that he was born in Bayreuth[38] and that his mother
had never had the slightest acquaintance with any Spaniard of that name. I did not go to see him until three
or four months after he was well settled there. I was
always afraid I might be subjected to some affront because of the name the visionary Marquise had given him
without my knowledge.

Tiretta came to see me in a fine carriage. He said
that the lady wanted to marry him, but that he would
never agree even though she had offered him all her
wealth. He could have gone to Treviso with her, paid his
debts, and lived very well there. His destiny prevented
him from following my good advice.

Having made up my mind to take a country house, I
decided on "Little Poland"[39] after looking at several.
It was well furnished, a hundred paces beyond the
Madeleine barrier.[40] The house was on a little hill near
the "Royal Hunt"[41] and behind the Duke of Gramont's[42]

garden. The name the owner had given it was "Airy
Warsaw." [43] It had two gardens, one of which was on
the level of the second floor, three master's apartments,
a stable for twenty horses, baths, a good cellar, and a
large kitchen with all the necessary pots and pans. The
owner of the house was known as the "Butter King," [44]
and this was the name he always signed. Louis XV himself had given it to him one day when he had stopped at
his establishment and found his butter excellent. He
rented me his house for a hundred louis a year and gave
me an excellent female cook, known as "the Pearl," [45]
to whom he consigned all his furniture and the tableware
I should need for six persons, undertaking to furnish
me as much of it as I wanted at one sou per ounce. He
also promised to furnish me all the wines I should order
from him at less than the price in Paris, since he could
obtain them from outside. Everything was cheaper beyond the barriers. He also promised me cheaper fodder
for my horses, and in fact everything, since whatever
entered Paris had to pay and, being there, I was in the
country.

In less than a week I acquired a good coachman, two
carriages, five horses, a groom, and two good footmen
in half-livery. Madame d'Urfé, for whom I gave my first
dinner, was delighted with my house. She took it all as
if it had been done for her, and I let her believe it. I
also let her believe that young Aranda belonged to the
Great Order, [46] that his birth was the result of an operation unknown to the world, that I was only his guardian,
and that he would die without ceasing to live. All this
came out of her own brain, and the best thing I could do
was to agree with her; but she maintained that she knew
nothing except from the revelations of her Genius, who
spoke to her only at night. I escorted her home, and I
left her supremely content.

About this time Camilla[47] sent me the ticket for a

*Alchemists' Laboratory*

*Winter Pleasures on the Amstel*

small *terna* she had won at my office, asking me to come to supper with her and bring the money. It was a thousand écus. At the supper, at which I found all her pretty fellow actresses present with their lovers, I was persuaded to go to the ball at the Opéra,[48] where I had scarcely arrived before I lost all my companions in the crowd. Not being masked, I was attacked by a female black domino,[49] who, telling me in falsetto a quantity of things about myself which were true, made me curious to know who she was. I managed to persuade her to come to a box with me. When she raised her mask I was surprised to see Miss *XCV.* She said she had come to the ball with one of her sisters, the elder of her brothers, and Signor Farsetti, and that she had eluded them to change her domino in a box. She laughed, imagining their uneasiness. She had no idea of relieving them from it until the end of the ball. Finding myself alone with her and in a position to keep her with me all through the ball, I began talking to her of my old flame and of the strength with which it had been rekindled. She received my words kindly; she did not refuse my embraces; and the few obstacles she put in the way of whatever I tried to do assured me that my happiness was only deferred. Delicacy obliged me not to insist, and she showed that she was grateful to me.

I told her I had heard at Versailles that she was to become the wife of Monsieur de la Pouplinière. She answered that people believed it, that her mother wanted it, and that the old Farmer-General expected it, but that she would never consent.

"He guarantees me a dower of a million," she said, "in case I become a widow without children, and his whole estate if I give him a child; but I do not want to make myself miserable with a man whom I dislike when I am no longer mistress of my heart. I love a man in Venice, and my mother knows it; but she insists that the man I love would not be a suitable husband for me. She would rather see me married to Signor Farsetti, who would give up his cross,[50] but I loathe him."

"Has he already spoken?"

"In unmistakable terms, and the indications of my dislike which I constantly give him do not abash him. He is a contemptible visionary, malicious and jealous, who once at table hearing me speak of you as you deserve saw fit to tell my mother she should not receive you."

I offered to serve her unhesitatingly in any way in which she thought I could be of use. She answered with a smile that she would consider herself only too happy if she could count on my entire friendship; and taking fire at that, I said that I had fifty thousand écus at her service and that I was ready to risk the clearest danger to my life in order to win rights over her heart. At this avowal she showed me the fondest gratitude, clasping me in her arms and joining her lips to mine. It would have been base in me to attempt anything further at such a moment. She asked me to come and see her often, assuring me that we would spend hours alone together; it was all that I could want. I promised I would dine with her the next day. So we parted.

After spending an hour in the ballroom, following her everywhere at a distance and congratulating myself on having become so thoroughly her friend, I went to Little Poland. It took me only a quarter of an hour. I was living in the country, and in a quarter of an hour I could be anywhere I pleased in the city. My coachman drove like the wind, my horses being of the kind called *enragés*[51] and not intended to be spared. Such horses, cast-offs from the King's stable, were a luxury. When he drove one of them to death for me I replaced it for two hundred francs. One of the greatest pleasures in Paris is driving fast.

Having promised to dine with Miss, I slept only a few hours. I went out lightly clad, I walked through the Tuileries, crossed the Pont Royal, and appeared before Madame *XCV* covered with snow, which was falling that day in great flakes. She received me with a laugh, saying that her daughter had told her that she had driven me wild at the ball and that I was to dine with her.

"It is Friday," she said, "and you will have to fast, but we have some excellent fish. Meanwhile, go and see my daughter, who is still in bed."

She was sitting up writing, and she put down her pen when she saw me. She said she was only staying in bed because she was lazy and it gave her more freedom. She was going to have some broth, for, not liking fast-day dishes, she did not intend to get up even to go to the table. Unembarrassed by her sister's presence, she took from her portfolio a letter in verse which I had written her when her mother had closed her door to me. She recited it to me from memory, and then was moved to shed a few tears.

"This fatal letter," she said, "which you entitled 'The Phoenix' [52] has decided my destiny and will perhaps be the cause of my death."

I had named it "The Phoenix" because, after lamenting my sad fate, I predicted in the tones of a bard that she would give her heart to a man who would have so many qualities that he could justly be called a phoenix. I devoted a hundred lines to describing such physical and moral qualities as really represented a perfect being worthy to be adored. It was the portrait of a god.

"Well," the tender Miss *XCV* went on, "I fell in love with this imaginary being, and, sure that he must exist, I spent six months looking for him everywhere and stopping when at last I thought I had found him. We loved; I gave him my heart, and we did not separate until I left Venice, four months ago. We stayed in London[53] until the end of the year and we have already been here for six weeks. I have received only one letter from him, but it is not his fault. I am kept under constraint, and I can neither receive letters from him nor write to him.''

This narrative confirmed me in my philosophy. The most decisive actions of our lives arise from very trifling causes. My verse epistle was only a poetical extravaganza, and the being whom I portrayed in it was above humanity; but she thought such a being possible, and she fell in love with him in advance. When she thought she had found him it was not hard for her to find in him all the qualities she wanted him to possess, since it was she herself who gave them to him; and it was all up with her. But for my letter, none of all this would have happened. All things are linked together, and we are the instigators of events in which we are not actors. Hence anything important which happens to us in this world is only what is bound to happen to us. We are but thinking atoms, which move where the wind drives them.

We were summoned to table and we ate a choice dinner with the ocean fish which La Pouplinière had sent. Madame *XCV*, being Greek and extremely superstitious, could not fail to be a bigot. The alliance between God and the devil is infallible in the head of a vain, weak, voluptuous, and timid woman. A priest had told her that converting her husband would assure her of eternal salvation, for in the Scriptures God promised in unmistakable terms *animam pro anima* (''a soul for a soul'')[54] to anyone who converted a heretic. Having converted her husband, she was convinced that she was safe; she had nothing more to do. However, she fasted on Friday, but she was the gainer by it. She liked fish better than meat.

After dinner I went back to Miss's bedside, where she proved to be a match for me until nine o'clock, during which time I was always able to subjugate my desires.

Since I was conceited enough to believe that hers were no less violent than mine, I did not wish to be the weaker.

Not having seen Farsetti, I suspected a break; but I was mistaken. She told me that nothing could persuade the visionary to leave his house on a Friday.

He had seen in his horoscope that he was to be murdered on that day, so his good sense decreed that he should seclude himself. Everyone laughed at him; but he was right nevertheless. He died in his bed four years ago[55] at the ripe age of seventy. He believed he thus proved that a man's destiny depends on good conduct, prudence, and taking precautions to avoid the evils which he has foreseen. The reasoning is excellent—except in the case of the evils foretold in a horoscope if we assume that a horoscope is what the astrologers want us to believe it is; for either the evils foretold can be avoided, and then the horoscope becomes puerile, or it is the voice of destiny, and then they are inevitable. Hence the Chevalier Farsetti was a fool if he thought he had proved anything. He would have proved something to a few limited minds if he had gone out every day and someone had killed him. Pico della Mirandola,[56] who believed in astrology, said: *Astra influunt non cogunt* ("The stars influence, they do not force").[57] I have no doubt of it. But should one have believed in astrology if Signor Farsetti had been murdered on a Friday? Certainly not, even so.

The Count of Égreville had introduced me to his sister the Countess du Rumain,[58] who, having heard of my oracle, had long wanted to meet me. In a few days I gained the friendship of her husband as well and of her young daughters, the eldest of whom, who bore the name Coëtanfao,[59] later became the wife of Monsieur de Polignac.[60] Madame du Rumain was more beautiful than pretty. She was loved for the sweetness of her character, her frankness, and her eagerness to use her influence on behalf of her friends. With her imposing height of five and a half feet, she awed all the Parisian magistrates to whom she applied. At her house I met Madame de Valbelle,[61] Madame de Roncherolles,[62] Princess Chimay,[63] and several other ladies who were the delight of what was called "good society" in Paris. Though Madame du Rumain did not dabble in the abstruse sciences, she needed my oracle even more than Madame d'Urfé did. She was useful to me in a disastrous situation, of which the story follows.

On the next day but one after my long conversation with Miss *XCV*, my valet told me that a young man wished to deliver a letter to me personally. I have him shown in and I ask him who gave him the letter; he answers that I will know when I have read it. He says he has been ordered to wait for my reply. I open it, and I find this:

"At two hours after midnight I need to sleep. What prevents nature from granting me that sad comfort is a burden which weighs on my soul; it is a secret of which I shall feel that I am relieved when it is no longer a secret to you, my only friend at this moment. I am pregnant, and my situation drives me to despair. I bring myself to write you this because I feel that I could never bring myself to tell it to you. A word in reply."

My surprise only allowed me to write her these few words: "I will call on you at eleven o'clock."

A misfortune cannot be called very great unless it turns its victim's brain. Her entrusting such a confidence to writing showed me that poor *XCV*'s wavering reason stood in need of help; and I was very glad that she had thought of me rather than anyone else, even if it meant that I would be ruined with her. Can one think otherwise when one loves? But what imprudence in the step she had taken! One must either speak or remain silent. The feeling which makes the victim of a misfortune prefer

writing to speech can only derive from false shame
(*malus pudor*),[64] which at bottom is nothing but pusil-
lanimity. If I had not been in love with Miss, I should
have found it easier to refuse her my help by letter than
by word of mouth. But I was in love with her. "She
must be counting on that," I said to myself, and the certainty nearly made me cherish her misfortune. If I
could succeed in remedying it, I saw that I was sure of
my reward, of the reward which is—alas!—the only goal
of any man who loves.

I arrived to find her at the door of the hotel.

"You are going out? Where?"

"To mass at the Augustinians." [65]

"Is it a saint's day?"

"No, but my mother insists on my going every day.
Give me your arm. We will talk in the cloister."

Her chambermaid remains in the church, and we go
into the cloister.

"Have you read my letter?"

"Yes. Here it is. I return it to you. Burn it."

"I don't want it. You can burn it yourself. I am four
months[66] gone with child, I am sure of it. I am in despair.
I put myself in your hands. You must procure me an
abortion."

"It is a crime."

"I know that, but it is no worse than killing oneself.
Either an abortion or I will take poison. I have the poison
ready. So, my only friend, you have become the arbiter
of my destiny. Are you displeased that I preferred you
to the Chevalier Farsetti?"

Seeing that I am aghast, she stops, draws her hood forward, and wipes away some tears. My heart bleeds.

"Crime or no crime, my dear Miss, abortion is not in
our power. If the means used to bring it about are mild
their effect is doubtful. If they are violent they threaten
the pregnant woman's life. I will never take the risk of

becoming your murderer; but I will not abandon you. Your honor is as dear to me as your life. Calm yourself, and from this moment imagine that it is I who am in your situation. Be sure that I will find a way out for you and that you will not take poison. Know in the meanwhile that I had no sooner read your letter than my first wholly involuntary reaction was to feel glad that you had chosen me before anyone else in a matter of such importance. You were not wrong. There is not a physician who knows this subject better than I do, and not a man in Paris who loves you better and who is more eager than I am to be useful to you. You shall begin at the latest tomorrow taking the drugs I will bring you, and I warn you that you cannot be too careful about secrecy, for it is a matter of breaking the severest laws. It is an infringement which is punished by death. Have you perhaps already confided in your chambermaid, in one of your sisters?"

"In no one, my dear friend, not even in him who is the cause of my misfortune. I shudder when I think what my mother would say, would do to me if she learned my condition, if she could guess it from watching my figure."

"Your figure is beyond suspicion, it is slim."

"It will become less and less so, and for that reason we must make haste. You shall find me a surgeon who does not know me, and take me to him when I am supposed to be at mass. I will let myself be bled as often as you want."

"I will not take that risk. The surgeon might betray us. I will bleed you myself. It is perfectly easy."

"I am grateful to you. I already seem to feel that you have restored me to life. The favor I ask of you is to take me to a midwife whom I could consult. We can easily go there the first evening there is a ball at the Opéra[67] without letting anyone see us when we leave the ballroom."

"There is no need for that, my dear. It is risky."

"Not at all, for in this vast city there are midwives everywhere, and we cannot possibly be recognized since we can even go masked. Do me this favor. The advice of a midwife can only be useful to me."

I did not have the strength of mind to refuse her the favor; but I made her consent to our waiting for the last ball,[68] where the crowd would make it easier for us to slip away unnoticed. I promised I would go to it in a black domino and wearing a white Venetian mask with a rose painted under my left eye. When she saw me go out she was to follow me and get into the same hackney coach she had seen me enter. All this was done; but we will return to it later.

I dined with her and the family, indifferent to the presence of Farsetti, who dined there too and who had seen me come back from mass with her. We never spoke to each other; but I disdained him.

But here is an enormous mistake[69] which I made, which I have to confess, and for which I have not yet forgiven myself.

Having promised Miss that I would accede to her wish and take her to a midwife, it is certain that if I had been wise myself[70] I ought to have taken her to a respectable woman, for it was only a matter of consulting her on the regimen a pregnant woman should follow and of obtaining some other innocent information. But not a bit of it. I pass through the narrow Rue Saint-Louis on my way to the Tuileries, I see La Montigny[71] going into her house with a pretty woman whom I do not know, I am seized with curiosity, I stop the coach, get out, and go up. After amusing myself for a time, since I am still thinking of Miss *XCV* I ask the procuress to give me the address of a midwife, as I need to consult one on some matter. She directs me to a house in the Marais,[72] the home, she says, of the cleverest of all midwives. She tells me several of her exploits, which show me that she is a criminal; but

no matter, it was enough for me to know that I was not
going to her on any illicit business. So I took down her
address and, since I would have to go there at night, I
went the next day to reconnoiter the door of her house.

Miss at once began taking the drugs which I did not
fail to bring her, all of them potent to weaken and de-
stroy what Love, Nature's master, had created; but seeing no effect from them she could not wait to talk with
the midwife; the night of the last ball arrived, and, as
we had arranged, she recognized me, followed me, entered the same hackney coach, and in less than a quarter
of an hour we got out a hundred paces from the house in
which the infamous creature lived. We see a woman of
fifty,[73] who, showing every sign of being delighted by our
visit, immediately offers us her services.

Miss tells her she thinks she is pregnant and has come
to consult her about what she can do to conceal her pregnancy as much as possible until her time comes. The
hussy replies with a laugh that she can tell her without
beating around the bush that she will be very easy to
abort and that she will accommodate her for fifty louis,
half to be paid at once to buy the necessary drugs and
the other half after she has had a successful miscarriage.

"Since I trust your honesty, you shall trust mine, give
me the twenty-five louis now, and come or send tomorrow
for the drugs and instructions for using them."

She then brusquely pulled up her client's skirt, who
gently asked me not to look at her, and, after feeling her,
lowered the curtain, saying that she could not be further
along than the fourth month. She told us that if her
drugs had no result, she would suggest other procedures,
and that in any case she would return our money.

"I have no doubt of it," I answered; "but be so good
as to tell me what the other procedures are."

"I will teach you how to kill the fetus, which then can
only decamp."

I could have answered her that it was impossible to kill the child without mortally injuring the mother; but I did not want to argue with the infamous creature. I told her that if Madame decided to take her remedies I would come the next morning with the money to buy them. I gave her two louis, and we left.

Miss *XCV* told me she was sure the woman was a scoundrel and that she firmly believed the fetus could not be killed without endangering the mother, and hence she had confidence in no one but me. Saying that she felt cold, she asked me if we had time to make a quick fire at Little Poland, which she wanted to see. This sudden whim surprised and pleased me. On a very dark night she could see nothing of a country house except its interior, but I was far from raising any objection. I thought that the moment of my happiness was at hand.

I change coaches in the Rue de la Ferronnerie,[74] and a quarter of an hour later I am at my door. I give a master's ring, and "the Pearl" comes to open the door saying, as I very well knew, that there was no one at home. I tell her to light a fire and give us something to eat with a bottle of champagne. An omelet.

"Excellent, an omelet," said Miss gaily.

So there we are, in front of the fire, and I with my love in my arms, who seems to enjoy my transports and who does not tell me to restrain myself until she sees I have reason to think I am about to reach the summit of triumph. I have no difficulty in restraining myself, certain that after our little supper she will oppose no obstacle to my victory. Everything promised as much, her manner, her sweetness, her face which shone with gratitude, and her fond and languishing eyes. I was annoyed that she could think I could demand favors as rewards. I was magnanimous enough to want only love.

And now we have finished the bottle, we rise, and, half pleadingly, half using gentle force, I drop onto the

bed, holding her in my arms; but she opposes my intention, first by honeyed words, then by too serious remonstrances, and finally by defending herself. That ends it.
The mere idea of violence revolts me. I begin to plead my
cause, sounding every note. I speak as a lover given hope,
then deceived, then scorned. I say I am disabused, and I
see that she is mortified. I then go down on my knees before her, I ask her to forgive me, and I hear her saying
in the saddest voice that, since she is not mistress of her
heart, she is more to be pitied than I am; then, melting
into tears, she lets her head sink on mine, and our lips
meet. The play is over. The idea of renewing the assault
does not enter my mind except to be disdainfully rejected. After a long silence, of which we were both in
the greatest need, she in order to still the feeling of
shame which overwhelmed her, I to give my reason time
to calm feelings of anger which I thought well justified,
we resumed our disguises and went back to the Opéra.
It was she who, on the way, went so far as to tell me that
she would have to renounce my friendship if I set that
price on it. I answered that feelings of love must yield
to a sense of honor, and that her honor no less than mine
obliged me to be her constant friend, if only to convince
her that she did me an injustice by refusing me favors of
which I was not unworthy, and that I would die before I
would again attempt to gain them.

We parted at the Opéra, where the immense crowd hid
her from my sight in a minute. She told me the next day
that, even so, she had spent the whole night dancing as
hard as she could. She hoped that violent motion might be
the medicine she needed.

I went home in a very bad humor, seeking vainly for
reasons which might justify a refusal I could never have
expected. I could not conclude that Miss's action had been
just and reasonable except by piling sophism on sophism.
Simple common sense was enough to show me that I had

been insulted, despite all imaginable conventions and all the prejudices which custom or education could enforce in civilized society. I thought of the witticism credited to Populia,[75] who had never allowed herself to be unfaithful to her husband except when she was pregnant. *Non tollo vectorem,* she said, *nisi navi plena* (''I do not take a passenger unless the ship is full'').[76] It angered me that I had been shown beyond doubt that I was not loved, and I felt that it would be shameful in me if I continued to love an object which I could no longer hope to possess. I went to sleep resolved to avenge myself and to abandon her to her fate despite the heroism she would credit me with if I acted otherwise. My true honor demanded that I be duped by nothing.

When I woke in the morning I was calm and, consequently, in love. My final resolve was to continue to give her all the help in my power, displaying indifference to what she did not believe she was free to grant me. I knew how difficult it was to play this role well, but I had the courage to play it.

## CHAPTER IX

*I continue my intrigue with the attractive Miss* XCV. *Vain attempts to bring on an abortion. The aroph. Miss runs away and enters a convent.*

I WENT to see her every morning, and since I was really concerned over her condition, she could not take my eagerness to help her out of her difficulty for anything but what it was. No longer seeing me in love with her, she could attribute it only to pure sympathy. So far as I could see, she approved of the change in me, but her approval might be only apparent. I knew that, even if she did not love me, seeing me resign myself so easily must have irritated her. One morning, congratulating me on having got the upper hand of my passion, she added with a laugh that my passion and my desires could not be very strong if I had succeeded in conquering them in less than a week. I answered deprecatingly that I owed my cure to my self-esteem.

"I know," I said, "that I am worthy to be loved, and when I saw that you did not recognize it I became indignant. Do you know the effect of indignation?"

"Very well. It is followed by scorn of the object which has aroused it."

"That is saying too much. Mine was followed by an examination of my conduct and a plan for revenge."

"What kind of revenge?"

"Forcing you to esteem me and at the same time convincing you that I can do without your treasures. I have already become accustomed to seeing them without wanting to possess them."

"And I suppose you think my esteem gives you your revenge; but you are mistaken, for I esteemed you a week ago no less than I do today. I never for a moment believed you capable of abandoning me as punishment for having refused to yield to your ardor, and I congratulate myself on having seen you for what you are."

She then spoke of the opiate which I was having her take and of which she wanted me to increase the dose since she saw no effect from it, but I did not respond; for I knew that taking more than half a dram of the remedy might kill her; nor would I consent to her being bled a third time. Her chambermaid, whom she had just let into the secret, had had her bled by a surgeon who was her lover. I having then told Miss that she should be generous with such people, and she having replied that she had no money, I offered her some. She said she would accept fifty louis, for which she would account to me, and that she needed the amount for her brother Richard.[1] Not having them with me I sent them the next day with a note in which I asked her to turn to no one except myself for anything she needed. But her brother thought I was the man to do him an even more considerable service.

He called on me the next morning to thank me and to beg my help in a serious situation. He showed me a chancre of a very ugly kind, which he had acquired from going all by himself to a place of ill fame. He asked me to speak to his mother and persuade her to have him treated, complaining that Signor Farsetti, after refusing him four louis, had washed his hands of the matter. I did as he asked, but when I told his mother what the trouble was she said it was better to leave him with the chancre he had, which was his third, for she was sure that after he was cured of it he would simply go and get another. I had him cured at my expense; but his mother was right. At the age of fourteen his profligacy knew no bounds.

Having now entered on her sixth month, Miss *XCV* was in despair; she would no longer leave her bed, and she made me miserable. Believing that I was no longer in love with her, she showed me and made me touch her hips and her belly to convince me that she could no longer let anyone see her. I played the role of midwife, displaying complete indifference to her charms and not letting her see a trace of my feeling; but I was at the end of my rope. She talked of taking poison in a tone which made me tremble. I was in the most agonizing of quandaries when Fortune extricated me in a way which proved to be high comedy.

Dining alone with Madame d'Urfé, I asked her if she knew a sure way to bring on an abortion. She answered that Paracelsus's aroph[2] was infallible and not at all difficult, and, seeing that I was interested, she went and fetched a manuscript, which she handed me. It called for preparing an unguent of which the ingredients were powdered saffron, myrrh, and a number of others, and the vehicle honey. The woman who hoped to empty her womb was to put a dose of this opiate on the end of a cylinder of the proper size and insert it into her vagina in such a way as to stimulate the round piece of flesh at the top of her such-and-such. The cylinder must at the same time stimulate the channel leading to the closed door of the little house which sheltered the little enemy whose departure was sought. This procedure, repeated three or four times a day for six or seven days, so weakened the little door that it finally opened and the fetus tumbled out.

Laughing heartily at the prescription, whose absurdity was instantly apparent to common sense, I gave Madame back her precious manuscript and I spent two hours reading the always astonishing Paracelsus and then Boerhaave,[3] who discusses aroph like a reasonable man.

At home by myself the next day and thinking of Miss *XCV*, I decided to communicate this prescription for producing abortion to her, hoping that she might need my help in introducing the cylinder.

Calling about ten o'clock and finding her in bed as usual and depressed because the opiate I was having her take produced no effect, I spoke to her of Paracelsus's aroph as of an infallible topical remedy for weakening the ring of the womb. It was on the spur of the moment that it occurred to me to tell her that the aroph had to be mixed with sperm which had not lost its natural heat for a single instant.

"It is necessary," I said, "for the sperm to touch the ring immediately upon coming out. Repeating the procedure three or four times a day for five or six days, the little door is obliged to open and the fetus to come out perforce of its own weight."

After making certain that she understood the thing thoroughly and showing her the apparently sound physiological reasons for using the remedy, I said that, her lover being absent, she needed to have a friend who would live in the house with her, and whom no one could suspect, to administer the amorous remedy to her three or four times a day. She could not keep from laughing at the idea. She asked me seriously if it was a joke, and I finally saw that she had no more doubts when I offered to bring her the manuscript in which the whole theory of what I had just told her was set forth.

She did not urge me to bring it when I said that the manuscript was in Latin; but I saw that she was persuaded when I told her about the wonders of aroph and what Boerhaave said about it.

"Aroph," I said, "is a great specific for bringing on menstruation."

"And menstruation," she[4] replied, "cannot appear as long as a woman is pregnant, so aroph is an infallible remedy for bringing on an abortion. Do you know how to make it?"

"It is perfectly easy. There are five ingredients, which are powdered and put in honey or butter. It is an unguent which, when it touches the ring, must find it in amorous excitement."

"Then I should think the person who administers it must be in love too."

"Of course, unless he is a being who has so much the nature of a donkey that he does not need to love."

She remained thoughtful for a full quarter of an hour. Though she was very intelligent, the candor of her soul prevented her from suspecting a fraud. Astonished on my side that I had rattled off this nonsense with all the earmarks of truth yet completely on the spur of the moment, I said nothing.

Breaking the silence at last, she said sadly that she could not think of using the remedy, which, however, she considered admirable and natural. She asked me if compounding aroph took a long time, and I answered that it would take only two hours if it was possible to obtain English saffron,[5] which Paracelsus preferred to that from the East.

Her mother, accompanied by the Chevalier Farsetti, came and interrupted our conversation. She asked me to stay for dinner, and I accepted when Miss told me she would dine at the table too. She came to it with the figure of a nymph. I could not believe she was pregnant, much as she had tried to convince me of it. Signor Farsetti sat down beside her, and her mother took a place beside me. Miss, who was thinking of aroph, took it into her head at dessert to ask her table companion, who boasted that he was a great chemist, if he knew of it.

"I even believe," he replied, "that I know it better than anyone."

"What is its use?"

"Your question is too indefinite."

"What does the word 'aroph' mean?"

"It is an Arabic word. You must go to Paracelsus for that."

"It is neither Arabic," I said, "nor of any language. It is a word which hides two others: *aro: aroma; ph: philosophorum.*"

"Is it Paracelsus," Farsetti replied cuttingly, "who made you so learned?"

"No, sir; it was Boerhaave."

"Permit me to laugh, for Boerhaave nowhere says that; but I like a doughty quoter."

"Laugh as much as you please; but here is the touchstone. I never misquote."

So saying, I throw my purse, which is full of louis, on the table. Farsetti says in a scornful tone that he never wagers. Miss laughs and tells him it is the sure way never to lose. I put my purse back in my pocket, and pretending a need, I go out and send my lackey to Madame d'Urfé's to fetch the volume of Boerhaave in which I had read the statement the evening before. I return to the table, and I keep the company amused by my remarks until my lackey brings me the book. I immediately find the place, and I invite Signor Farsetti to see that I had not misquoted. Instead of looking he gets up and leaves. Madame says that he has gone away angry and will not come back; Miss offers to wager that he will come back the next day, and she would have won. After this incident the man became my inveterate enemy, as he always showed me he was when occasion served.

We all went to Passy to a concert given by La Poupli-nière, and we stayed for supper. I found Silvia there, and her daughter, who was sulky with me; she was justified, I could not see her every day, but I did not know what to do about it. The man who kept the company entertained, and who ate nothing, was the adept Saint-Germain. Everything he said was empty boasting, but everything was courteous and witty. I have never in my life known a cleverer and more persuasive impostor.

I spent the whole of the next day at home, answering a great many questions sent me by Esther, but very obscurely in all cases when they touched on business. Aside from my fear of compromising my oracle, I shuddered at the thought that, by misleading her father, I might jeopardize his financial position. He was the most honest millionaire in all Holland. As for Esther, she was now only a fond memory to me.

Miss *XCV* occupied me completely, and despite my seeming indifference I was only too certain that I loved her and that I could not be happy except by becoming her lover with no reservations. But I was miserable when I thought of the situation I should be in when she could no longer hide her big belly from her family. I repented that I had told her about aroph; seeing that she had let three days go by without mentioning it to me, I thought I had aroused her suspicions and that the esteem she had felt for me had changed to scorn. The supposition had humiliated me; I no longer had the courage to call on her, and I do not know if I should have brought myself to do so if she had not written me a note in which she said she had no friend but myself and that she asked no other proof of my friendship except my coming to see her every day, if only for a moment. I took her my answer in person, assuring her that my friendship was constant and that I would never abandon her. I had hoped that she would bring up the subject of aroph, but in vain. At that I concluded that she had not believed any of it and that I could no longer count on it. I asked her if she would like me to invite her mother and the whole family to dinner at my lodging, and she answered that it would please her.

The dinner was very animated. I invited Silvia and her daughter, an Italian musician named Magali,[6] with whom one of Miss's sisters was in love, and La Garde,[7] the basso profundo, who frequented the best society. I had never seen Miss *XCV* gayer than she was that day. When she left me about midnight she told me to come to her early the next day because she had something very important to discuss with me.

Far from failing to appear, I went there at eight o'clock in the morning. She told me she was in despair because La Pouplinière wanted to conclude the marriage and that her mother was pressing her. She was to sign the contract and a tailor was to come and take her measurements to make bodices and all kinds of clothes for her. She said—and she was right—that it was impossible the tailor would not see she was pregnant. She would rather kill herself than either marry when she was pregnant or confess to her mother. I urged it on her that any course was preferable to the dreadful course of suicide, and that in any case it was in her power to get rid of La Pouplinière simply by revealing her condition to him. He would laugh and make the best of it, he would keep her secret and would say no more about marrying her.

"And after that would I be much better off?"

"I undertake to bring your mother round."

"You do not know her. Honor would oblige her to get me out of sight; but she would make me suffer torments to which the most painful death is preferable. But why have you stopped talking about aroph? Is it all a joke?"

"I believe it is a reliable remedy, but what is the use of my talking to you about it? Consider the delicacy which prevents me from doing so. Confide your condition to your lover in Venice, and I undertake to have your letter delivered to him by a trustworthy man in five or six days. If he is not rich I will give you a purse full of gold, so that he can come here immediately and save your honor and your life by administering the aroph to you himself."

"It is an admirable plan and generous on your part; but it is not in the realm of possibilities, and you would agree if you knew all. But suppose that I could bring myself to receive aroph from some man who was not my lover, tell me how I could do it. Even if my lover himself were hidden in Paris he could not spend seven or eight days with me as freely as it seems he would have to do to follow the prescription exactly. So you see there is no use thinking of this remedy any more."

"Then to save your honor you would consent to give yourself to another man?"

"Certainly, if I were sure no one knew about it. But where is such a man to be found? Do you think I could go looking for him, or that it would even be easy to find him?"

Her last words petrified me, for she knew that I loved her. I clearly saw that she wanted me to ask her to make use of my person. Despite my love I could not bring myself to risk a humiliating refusal which would have been an atrocious insult; and besides, I could not believe she was capable of affronting me in this fashion. To force her to speak out, I rose to leave, saying in a sad and pathetic tone that I was more unhappy than she.

She stopped me, asking me how I could say I was more unhappy than she, which left me no alternative to saying, in a rather resentful tone, she had shown me clearly enough that she despised me so greatly that in her present need she would reject my services in favor of those of some unknown man, whom, I added, I had no intention of finding for her. She answered that I was cruel and unjust, that I did not love her to begin with, that I wanted her cruel situation to serve my triumph, which she could only regard as a revenge.

So saying, she turned away to shed tears which touched me; but I let no time pass before I dropped to my knees before her.

"Knowing that I adore you," I said, "how can you suppose that I entertain plans of revenge, and how can you think that I do not feel it when you tell me clearly that, your lover being away, you cannot see what man would help you out of your difficulty?"

"Could I count on you after my refusals?"

"So you think that a true lover could cease to love because of a refusal which may even spring from virtue? Permit me to tell you that at this happy moment I am certain that you love me and that you are sorry I may suppose you would never have made me happy except for the need under which you are laboring."

"You are, my dear friend, the faithful interpreter of my feelings; but it remains to be seen how we can be together with all the freedom we must have."

"I will rack my brains for the answer, and in the meanwhile I will compound the aroph."

Compounding it did not trouble me, for I had already decided that it should be nothing except honey; but I had to spend several uninterrupted nights with her, and that was difficult. I was sorry I had made the stipulation, and I could not think of retracting it. One of her sisters slept in the same room with her, and I could not consider making her spend nights away from the hotel. Chance, as it nearly always did, came to my rescue.

A natural need having made me go up to the fifth floor, I run into the kitchen boy, who tells me not to go to the toilet because someone is there.

"But you have just come out of it."

"Yes, but I only started in."

"Very well, I will wait."

"I beg you not to wait."

"You've been having fun with a girl. I want to see her."

"She won't come out, because you know her. She has locked herself in."

I go to the door and through a crack I see Magdelaine,[8] Miss's chambermaid. I reassure her; I promise her I will be discreet, and I ask her to open the door, my need being urgent. She opens, I give her a louis, and she runs away. After doing my business I go down, and halfway downstairs I find the kitchen boy, who laughs and says I ought to make Magdelaine give him twelve francs.[9] I promise him a louis if he will tell me everything, and he admits that he sees her in the garret, where he spends nights with her, but that the mistress, having put game there three days before, had locked the door. I make him take me there, and I see through the keyhole that the game left room for a mattress, I give the kitchen boy the louis I had promised him, and I go away to ripen my plan. I thought that Miss, if she took Magdelaine into her confidence, could easily come up and spend the night with me in the garret. On the same day I procured a picklock and several skeleton keys, and in a tin box I put several doses of the supposed aroph. I mixed honey with powdered stag's horn.

The next morning I went to the Hôtel de Bretagne, where I immediately had the pleasure of unlocking and locking the garret without needing to use the picklock. I entered Miss's room carrying the key, and in a few words told her my whole plan, showing her the prepared aroph. She said that since she could not leave her room except by passing through the small room in which Magdelaine slept, we should have to let her into our secret and that she left it to me to win her over by the means one

uses with all servants. What troubled us was the kitchen
boy, who, if he managed to find out what was afoot, might
decide to do us harm. On that score I had to consult Magdelaine. I left her,[10] promising that I would act and
would keep her informed of everything through the
chambermaid.

As I went out I told the latter that I would wait for
her in the cloister of the Augustinians, having to talk
with her on an important matter, and she came. After
understanding the whole plan perfectly and assuring me
that her own bed would be in the garret at the appointed
hour, she showed me that we could not do without the
kitchen boy, and that prudence itself obliged us to let
him into the secret. She answered for his fidelity and said
that I should leave her to deal with him. So I gave her the
key and six louis, saying that everything must be ready
for the next day and that she must make arrangements
with Miss. A chambermaid who has a lover is never so
happy as when she is given a role which puts her own
mistress in her power.

The next day at Little Poland the kitchen boy appeared
before me; I was expecting as much. Before he spoke I
told him he must beware of my servants' curiosity and
refrain from coming to my house except when necessary.
He promised he would be cautious, and he told me nothing new; as Magdelaine had assured me, everything
would be in readiness in the garret the next day, as soon
as the whole family had gone to bed. He gave me the key
to the garret, saying that he had obtained another for
himself, and admiring his foresight I gave him six louis,
which had more effect than all my words.

The next morning I saw Miss only for a moment, to
tell her that she would find me in the garret at ten
o'clock, and I was there punctually, sure that no one had
seen me either enter the hotel or go up to the garret. I
was wearing a redingote. I had my box of aroph, a reli-

able flint and steel, and a candle in my pocket. Besides the mattress I found cushions and a good blanket, which was needed since the weather was cold and we had to spend hours there.

At eleven a slight noise causes me a palpitation which always seems a good augury. I go out, I grope my way to Miss and whisper a few words of a sort to reassure us both. Then I show her into our hiding place, shut the door, and barricade it. I quickly light my candle and she appears uneasy; she says that the light may betray us to someone going to the toilet. I reply that we must take the risk, since in the dark she cannot crown me with the aroph in the necessary manner. She agrees, saying that we will blow out the candle immediately afterward. We undress very fast, entirely dispensing with the preliminaries which always precede the performance when love leads up to it. Both of us concentrating on our roles, we play them to perfection. In our utter seriousness we appeared to be a surgeon getting ready to perform an operation and the patient who submits to it. Miss was the operating surgeon. She sets the open box at her right, then lies down on her back, and, spreading her thighs and raising her knees, arches her body; at the same time, by the light of the candle, which I am holding in my left hand, she puts a little crown of aroph on the head of the being who is to convey it to the orifice where the amalgamation is to be accomplished. The astonishing thing is that we neither laughed nor felt any desire to laugh, so engrossed were we in our roles. After the insertion was completed, the timid Miss blew out the candle, but two minutes later she had to let me light it again. The thing had been done to perfection so far as I was concerned, but she did not feel sure about herself. I obligingly said that I did not mind repeating the performance. My formal tone made us both laugh, and she had no difficulty in crowning me again, after seeing that some of the aroph had changed color very slightly from the amalgamation.

This second time the application of the remedy took a quarter of an hour, and she assured me that it had been perfect. I was certain of it. She showed me, with an expression which spoke love and gratitude, that the amalgamation had been twofold, for what she had contributed to it was clearly visible. She said that since our work was not yet over we would do well to sleep.

"You see," I said, "that I am not in need of it," and she surrendered. Another preparation, another combat to the most successful conclusion, which was followed by a longish sleep.

A reflection on our resources which pleased me decided her to husband my strength. We had to preserve ourselves for the nights to come. She went down to her room, and at daybreak I left the hotel with the help of the kitchen boy, who made me slip out by a door I did not know of.

Toward noon I paid Miss a visit. She talked to me reasonably, and she outdid herself in thanks which really exhausted my patience.

"I am amazed," I said, "at your not understanding that your thanks are degrading to me and prove either that you do not love me or that, if you love me, you suppose my love is not equal to yours."

She admitted that I was right, and we became emotional; but we had to save ourselves for the night. My situation was peculiar. Though I loved her I could not be sorry that I had deceived her. It was a slight revenge which I owed to my self-esteem. She on her side said that she was punished for the wrong she had done me when she had refused to yield to my fond entreaties, since I now had a reason to doubt her love. What I really won from her during the nights we spent in vain efforts to bring on an abortion was her promise to think no more of suicide and, whatever the outcome might be, to entrust herself to me and be guided entirely by my advice. She told me several times during our nocturnal dialogues that she felt happy and that she would not cease to feel so even if the aroph should have no effect; but despite this magnanimous sentiment, she continued to hope that it would, and she never stopped applying it to our two selves until the last night of our combats. At our final parting she said that all we had done would seem more apt to engender a superfetation in her organ than to bring it to a repugnance whose consequence would be to make it cast out the fruit of which it was the repository. No one could reason more logically.

Having lost her last hope of bringing on an abortion, and unable to delay any longer in signing the contract of marriage with La Pouplinière and receiving the tailors, she told me she had decided to run away, and she laid it on me to find the means. It became my sole preoccupation. The decision was taken in principle; but I was not willing either to risk being convicted of abducting her or to take her out of the kingdom. Neither of us had ever thought of uniting our destinies by marriage.

With this flea in my ear, I went to the Concert Spirituel [11] at the Tuileries. The piece was an anthem, with words by the Abbé de Voisenon set to music by Mondonville,[12] the proper title of which was "The Israelites on Mount Horeb." [13] It was a new work. It was I who had given the idea for it to the amiable Abbé, who had written it in charming irregular verse. Getting out of my carriage in the Cul-de-sac Dauphin,[14] I see Madame du Rumain getting out of hers alone. She congratulates herself on having met me there; she says she is going to hear the new piece, that she has reserved two seats, and that I would be doing her a favor if I would occupy one of them. Such an invitation being an honor of whose value I was thoroughly aware, I accept. In Paris people do not chatter when they go to a theater to hear music;

so Madame would not have inferred from my silence that I was melancholy; but she guessed it after the concert from my countenance, on which she saw my depression and the sorrow which wrung my soul. She asked me to come and spend an hour at her house to obtain answers to three or four questions which deeply concerned her and to do it quickly because she was going out to supper.

It was all done in half an hour; but the charming woman could not help asking what was the matter with me.

"You are," she said, "quite unlike yourself; you must certainly be fearing some great misfortune; you have some very difficult decision to make. I do not wish to pry into your affairs; but if I can be of use to you at Court, speak, all my influence is at your disposition; you will find me ready to move heaven and earth and even to go to Versailles myself tomorrow morning if the matter is urgent; I have every Minister's ear. Confide your troubles to me, my dear friend, and if I cannot [15] relieve you of them, at least let me share them with you, you can rely on my discretion."

This little discourse seemed to me veritably a voice from Heaven, a command from my Genius to speak freely to this paragon among women who had seen into my soul and who let me know, in unmistakable terms, all the interest she took in me. After looking at her without answering but with eyes in which she could not but see gratitude:

"Yes, Madame," I replied, "I am in the most critical of situations and perhaps on the verge of ruin; but what you have just so openly said to me leads me to hope. I shall now inform you of my painful quandary, entrusting you with a secret which honor makes inviolable; but, certain of your discretion, I do not hesitate to reveal it to you. If you honor me with advice I promise to follow it, and I swear that no one shall ever know I had it from you.''

After this short exordium, which gained me all her attention, I told her the whole story in detail, concealing neither the young lady's name nor any of the circumstances which made it my duty to find some way of saving her. However, I did not tell her the too comical story of the aroph, but I confessed that I had given her drugs to bring on an abortion.

After spending a quarter of an hour in silence she rose, saying that she must now go to Madame de la Marck's,[16] among other things to speak with the Bishop of Montrouge,[17] but that she hoped she could be of use to me.

''Meanwhile,'' she said, ''please come to see me day after tomorrow at eight o'clock, and be so good as not to take any step until we have talked. Good-by.''

She left me with relief in my soul, and I determined to do whatever she told me to do.

The Bishop of Montrouge, to whom she had to speak concerning a matter of which I knew, was the Abbé de Voisenon, who was so called because he went there very often. It was an estate near Paris which belonged to the Duke of La Vallière.[18]

The next day I told Miss *XCV* only that I hoped to bring her good news in two or three days. I did not fail to call on Madame du Rumain on the following day at the appointed hour. The porter told me, with a smile, that I should find the doctor there; but when I appeared he left. It was Herrenschwandt,[19] whom all the pretty women in Paris wanted to have—the same whose role the unfortunate poet Poinsinet[20] took in *The Circle,* a one-act play which had a great success in Paris.

Madame du Rumain began by telling me that she had solved my difficulty and that it was now my part to keep her intervention an inviolable secret.

"Yesterday," she said, "I went to C . . .[21] and I told the Abbess,[22] who is an intimate friend of mine, the whole story. She will receive the young lady into her convent and will give her a lay sister who will serve her in everything, even during her confinement. The young lady is to go alone with a letter which I will give you and which she will send in to her. She will be at once taken in and lodged, she is to receive no visitors and no letters except those which pass through her hands, and she[23] undertakes to send her answers only to me, for you realize she must correspond with no one except you. Hence she will never write to you except through me. You will do likewise, and all the addresses will be left blank. However, I had to tell the Abbess the young lady's name, but I did not tell her yours and she did not ask to know it. Inform her of all this, and when she is ready come and tell me, and I will give you the letter. She must take with her only what she absolutely needs —no diamonds or jewelry of any value. I can also assure you that the Abbess will see her from time to time, and that she will be friendly and will supply her with all sorts of decent books. As for the lay sister who will wait on her, she is not to confide anything to her. Inform her of all this. After she is delivered the young lady will go to confession in preparation for making her Easter communion, and the Abbess will give her a formal certificate which will obviate any difficulties when she appears before her mother, who will be only too glad to see her; and there will be no more question of the marriage, which she will give as the only cause of her running away of her own free will."

After outdoing myself in thanks and praising her prudence, I asked her to give me the letter at once, since there was no time to lose. Here is the short letter which she wrote for me:

"The young lady who brings you this letter, my dear

Abbess, is the one about whom I spoke to you. She wishes
to spend three or four months under your protection in
your convent to recover her peace of mind, perform her
devotions, and be certain that when she returns to her
home there will be no more question of a marriage which
she loathes and which is the cause of her present decision to absent herself from her family for a time.''

She gave it to me unsealed so that Mademoiselle could
read it. The Abbess was a princess; in the extremity of
my gratitude I went down on my knees before the lady,
who was also useful to me later, as I will relate when
the time comes.

Leaving Madame du Rumain's, I went to the Hôtel
de Bretagne, where Miss had only time to tell me that
she was engaged all day and that she would come to
the garret at eleven o'clock, where we should have all
the time we needed to talk. It was charming, for I foresaw that after that day I should not again have an opportunity to hold her in my arms. I spoke to Magdelaine,
who undertook to warn the kitchen boy, and everything
was in readiness.

I repaired to the garret at ten o'clock, and at eleven
I saw Miss, and after giving her the letter to read I
put out the candle and we spent the night like real lovers
without any further thought of aroph.

I repeated exactly to her all the instructions I had
received from the lady, whose name she made no objection to my concealing. I told her that she must leave
the hotel at eight o'clock with her bundle, take a hackney
coach, and go to the Place Maubert,[24] where she would
dismiss it. There she must take another to the Porte
Saint-Antoine,[25] and from there go in yet another to
the convent of which I gave her the name. I begged her
not to forget to burn all the letters she had received from
me and to write to me as often as possible, sealing her
letters, but always leaving the outside blank. I ended by

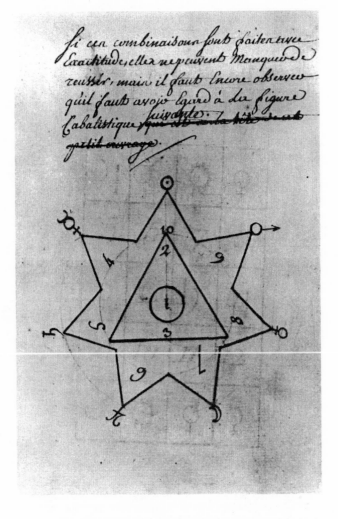

*Casanova's Thoughts on the "Cabalistic Treasure"*

*Wasted Words*

making her accept two hundred louis, urging it upon her
that she might need them though we could not then see
how. She wept when she thought of the dangerous situation in which she was leaving me; but I reassured her
by saying that I had plenty of money and very powerful
protectors. After concerting these measures, we parted.
She promised to set out on the next day but one, and
I promised to go to the hotel on the day after her flight,
pretending to know nothing about it, and to write her
whatever was said.

Her future worried me. She was intelligent; but without experience intelligence often does more harm than
good. I waited in a hackney coach at the corner of a
street, where I saw her arrive, get out at an alley, pay,
and dismiss the coach. A minute later I saw her emerge
with her hood over her head and get into another coach,
which at once drove off. Thus assured that she would
faithfully carry out the rest of my instructions, I went
about my business.

The next morning—it was Quasimodo Sunday[26]—I
felt that I must not fail to go to the Hôtel de Bretagne.
Since I went there every day I could not stop going
without confirming the suspicions of which I must have
become the object. But what a painful task! Obliged to
appear gay and untroubled amid a family whom I was
sure to find distraught and sad!

I went at the hour when the whole family would be
at table, so I walked straight into the dining room. I
enter, smiling and gay as ever, and I take a seat half
behind Madame. I pretend not to have noticed either
her surprise or her flushed face. A minute later I ask
her where Miss is; she looks at me and does not answer.

"Is she ill perhaps?"

"I have no idea."

Her curt tone decides me to appear serious, I assume
a pensive air, and I remain there for a good quarter of

an hour without speaking. I finally break the silence by rising and asking her if I can serve her in any way. She declines very coldly. I leave and go to Miss's room, where I find Magdelaine alone. I ask her, with a wink, where her mistress is, and she begs me to tell her myself if I know.

"Did she go out alone?"

"I have no idea, but they say you know everything. Please leave me."

Pretending to be astonished, I slowly leave the house and get into my carriage, very glad to have got through this burdensome task. I decide that the natural thing for me to do will be not to appear again before the lady, who must know that she has received me very badly, and that, guilty or innocent, I must have been aware of it.

Very early on Tuesday I saw a hackney coach stop at my door and Madame *XCV* and Signor Farsetti get out of it. I go to meet them, I thank them for having come to breakfast with me and ask them to sit down by a good fire. Madame replies that she has not come for breakfast but to talk with me on an urgent matter. She sits down, and Signor Farsetti remains standing. I reply that I am entirely at her service.

"I have come to ask you to restore my daughter to me if she is in your custody, or to tell me where she is, in which case I will attend to it myself."

"Madame, I know nothing of her, and I am amazed that you should suspect me of a crime."

"I do not accuse you of an abduction, I am not here to reproach you with crimes or to threaten you; I have come to ask you to show me your friendship. Help me to recover her this very day; I am sure that you know all; you were her only friend; she spent two or three hours with you every day; it is impossible that she should not have confided everything to you. Take pity on a heartbroken mother. All will be saved, for no one knows anything yet. Her honor will not suffer."

"I understand all that, Madame, but I repeat that I know nothing about her."

She then went down on her knees to me, melting into tears, while Farsetti told her she should be ashamed to humiliate herself before a man of my kind.

"Explain," I said to him, rising, "what you mean by 'my kind.'"

"It is certain that you know everything."

"Only fools are certain. Leave, and wait till I come. You will see me in a quarter of an hour."

I pushed him by the shoulders, and he left, telling Madame to follow him, but she stayed behind to calm me, saying that I must forgive a man who loved her enough to marry her.

"I know that, but your daughter loathes him even more than she does the Farmer-General." [27]

"She is wrong; but there will be no more question of her marrying him. You know everything, for you gave her fifty louis, without which she could not have gone anywhere."

"That is not true."

"It is true. Here is a piece of your letter."

She handed me a scrap of the letter I had written Miss when I sent her the fifty louis which the elder of her two brothers needed. These are the words which could be read:

"I hope that these paltry fifty louis may convince you that I will never spare anything, even my life, to make you sure of my affection."

"Since I am obliged to admit," I said, "that I sent her this money, I will also tell you that I supplied her with it only to pay the debts of your elder son. He received it, and he has thanked me for it."

"My son?"

"Yes, Madame."

"Then I will now make you full atonement."

With that she goes down to the courtyard, where Farsetti was waiting for her, and makes him come upstairs to learn from my own lips that the fifty louis I had sent had been for her son; but he has the impudence to tell me that it was beyond belief. I laugh in his face, and I ask Madame to verify the fact, assuring her that I had always tried to persuade her daughter to marry La Pouplinière.

"How dare you say that," Farsetti interrupts me, "when in your letter you speak of your affection?"

"I admit," I replied, "that I loved her and that, hoping for the honor of cuckolding her husband, I was laying the foundations for it. My love, criminal or not, was the theme of what I said during all the hours I spent with her. If she had confided to me that she wanted to run away, either I would have dissuaded her or I would have gone with her, for I was, as I still am, in love with her. I would never have given her money to go away without me."

"My dear Casanova," Madame then said, "I will believe you are innocent if you will join me in finding her."

"I am perfectly ready, Madame, and I promise to begin making inquiries today."

"When you learn anything, come and tell me."

In accordance with this promise I did not find it hard to call the next morning on Monsieur Chaban, the chief clerk in the police office, and urge him to investigate the girl's flight. I innocently thought that my taking this step would only serve to make me even safer. The man, who was thoroughly imbued with his profession and who had liked me ever since Silvia had introduced me to him at her house five or six years earlier, began to laugh when he learned to what matter I desired him to give his attention. He asked me if I really wanted the English girl's whereabouts discovered. On my side I had no difficulty in seeing that he was only trying to worm information out of me. I had no further doubt of it when, on my way out, I met Signor Farsetti.

I went the next morning to report on my as yet unsuccessful effort to Madame *XCV*. She replied that her own investigation had been more successful than mine, and that if I would go with her to the house in which her daughter then was, she was sure I could persuade her to come home. I answered most calmly that I was ready to go anywhere with her. Taking me at my word, she rose, put on her tippet, and, handing me a card, told me to order my coachman to drive to the address on it.

Cruel moment for me! My palpitating heart seemed to be bursting from my breast. I expected to see the address of the convent where Miss was. I do not know how I should have managed it, but I certainly would not have gone there.

My soul returned to its seat when I read "such-and-such an alley off the Place Maubert."

I give the appropriate order to my coachman; we get out at the alley; and, by exercising great politeness, I give the poor mother the satisfaction of taking her to visit every room, front and back, on every floor. At the end of this strange and useless search I saw that she was unhappy but satisfied and close to begging my pardon. She had learned from the hackney coachman who had driven her daughter that he had let her out at this alley. She told me that the kitchen boy at the hotel had said he had been to my lodging twice with letters, and that Magdelaine said nothing except that she was certain Miss loved me as I loved her.

After taking Madame *XCV* home I called on Countess du Rumain to tell her all that had happened and to write a long letter to the young recluse.

Three or four days later Madame du Rumain gave me the first of her letters, in which she told me of the peace which her soul was enjoying and her extreme gratitude for all that I had done for her. She praised the Abbess and the lay sister and told me the names of the books she had been given, all of them to her taste. She paid six francs a day, and she had given the lay sister four louis, promising her the same amount each month. What she did not like was that the Abbess had asked her never to leave her room.

But what pleased me even more was the letter from the Abbess to the Countess. She spoke in the highest terms of the unfortunate beauty, praising her sweetness, her intelligence, her dignity, and her manners. She promised she would go to see her every day. Madame du Rumain's satisfaction delighted me. I gave her my letter from her to read, and I saw that she was even more content.

The only people who were not contented were Madame *XCV*, Farsetti, and the old Farmer-General, whose disaster was already the talk of reception rooms, the Palais-Royal, and every coffeehouse. I was given a share in it, but I did not care.

As for La Pouplinière, he so far resigned himself that he even made it the subject of a one-act play which he wrote himself and had performed at his little theater[28] in Passy. Such was his character. His device was a cock with the words *Fovet et Favet* ("He forwards and fosters"). Emblem of tolerance, of which, however, he gave a poor exhibition in the famous episode of the fireplace.[29] Three months after "the English girl," as everyone called her, disappeared, he sent one of his cronies to Bordeaux and there married by proxy a very pretty young lady, the daughter of a Capitoul.[30] At the end of two years[31] she gave him a son, who was born six months after his death. The avaricious harridan who was the rich man's heir accused the widow of adultery and had the infant declared illegitimate, to the shame of the Parlement which so adjudged him, and despite the laws of God and man, the entire nobility, and all the intelligent people in France, who had to tolerate the iniquity of this infamous judgment. The scandal was universal, and the innocent widow did not dare to appear anywhere after the incredible loss of a suit which added fresh opprobrium to the same Parlement, which in former times had declared legitimate a child born eleven months after the death of its father, that is of the widow's defunct husband.

A week or ten days after Miss's flight I entirely suspended my visits to her mother; the cold reception I found there decided me to take this course.

## CHAPTER X

*Further incidents. J. J. Rousseau. I establish a business. Castel-Bajac. An action at law is brought against me. Monsieur de Sartine.*

A MONTH later there was no more talk of the matter, I thought it was over, but I was wrong. In the meanwhile I amused myself, and the pleasure I took in spending money lavishly kept me from thinking of the future.

The Abbé de Bernis,[1] on whom I called once a week, told me one day that the Comptroller-General [2] kept asking him for news of me and that I was making a mistake in neglecting him. He advised me to forget my claims and to lay before him the plan for increasing the revenue of the State concerning which I had spoken to him earlier. Since I set great store by the Abbé's advice, for I owed him my fortune, I went to the Comptroller-General and, full of confidence in his good faith, gave him my project. It was for a new law, to be registered by the Parlement, which would oblige every heir to an estate, except estates which passed from father to son, to cede the first year's income from it to the King. All gifts formally made before a notary *inter vivos* ("between living persons") would also be subject to the same law, which could not offend the recipients, for they had only to imagine that the testator had died a year later. The Minister[3] said that my project presented no difficulties; he put it in his secret portfolio and assured me that my fortune was made. A week later he was dismissed, and when I applied to his successor, Silhouette,[4] he coldly told me that he would have me informed if the occasion arose to promulgate the law. The law was instituted in France two years later, and I was laughed at when, saying that I was the originator of it, I asked to what recompense I was entitled.

Not long afterward, the Pope[5] having died, the succession was conferred on the Venetian Rezzonico,[6] who immediately bestowed a cardinalate on my patron De Bernis, whom the King exiled to Soissons two days after he gave him the cardinal's hat;[7] so I was left without a patron, but rich enough not to be troubled by the misfortune. The illustrious Abbé, then at the pinnacle of his fame for having destroyed all Cardinal Richelieu's[8] work by collaborating with Prince Kaunitz to transform the old hatred between the houses of Bourbon and Austria into a flourishing alliance, thus delivering Italy from the miseries of the war of which it became the theater each time there was a break between the two houses, which gained him the first nomination to a cardinalate made by a Pope who, as Bishop of Padua, had come to know all his merits—this noble Abbé, who died last year[9] at Rome, enjoying the particular esteem of Pius VI, was banished from Court for telling the King, who had asked his advice on the subject, that he did not consider the Prince of Soubise[10] the best man to command his armies. As soon as La Pompadour heard it from the King himself, she had power enough to ruin him. Everyone deplored his disgrace, but found comfort for it in verses. A strange nation, which ceases to feel its afflictions as soon as poems or songs make it laugh! In my day the authors of epigrams and songs which attacked the government and the Ministers were put in the Bastille; but that did not prevent the wits from continuing to amuse their particular circles—for in those days the word "club" was unknown—with their satirical jests. A man whose name I have forgotten appropriated the following verses from the younger Crébillon[11] about this time and let himself be sent to the Bastille rather than disavow them. Crébillon told the Duke of Choiseul that he had composed the verses, but that it was possible the prisoner had composed them too. This witticism by the author of *The Sofa*[12] raised a laugh, and nothing was done to him.

> *Grand Dieu! Tout a changé de face.*
> *Jupin opine du bonnet* . . . . . . . *Le Roi*
> *Vénus au conseil a pris place* . . *La Pompadour*
> *Plutus est devenu coquet* . . . . . *M. de Boulogne*
> *Mercure endosse la cuirasse* . . . . *Le Mar. de Richelieu*
> *Et Mars a le petit collet.* . . . . *Le duc de Clermont,*
>                                     *Abbé de*
>                                *St.-Germain-des-Prés.*

("Good God! everything has changed. Jupiter says yes to everyone [the King], Venus has a seat in the Council [La Pompadour], Plutus has become a ladies' man [Monsieur de Boulogne],[13] Mercury has put on armor [Marshal de Richelieu], and Mars wears a clerical collar [the Duke of Clermont, Abbot of Saint-Germain-des-Prés]."[14])

The illustrious Cardinal de Bernis spent ten years in his exile, *procul negotiis* ("far from business")[15] but not happy, as I learned from his own lips fifteen years later at Rome. It is said that there is more pleasure in being a minister than in being a king; but, *caeteris*

*paribus* ("other things being equal"), I find nothing
more idiotic than this dictum, if, as I ought to do, I
consider it in my own case. It amounts to asking if independence is or is not preferable to dependence. The
Cardinal was not recalled to Court, for there is no example of Louis XV's ever recalling a dismissed minister;
but when Rezzonico[16] died he had to go to the conclave
and for the rest of his life he remained the French Ambassador[17] in Rome.

About this time Madame d'Urfé took a fancy to make
the acquaintance of J. J. Rousseau;[18] we went to Montmorency[19] to visit him, taking some music, which he copied wonderfully well. People paid him twice as much as
they would have paid another copyist, but he guaranteed
that there would be no errors. It was the way he made his
living.

We found a man who reasoned well, whose manner was
simple and modest, but who was entirely undistinguished
either in his person or his wit. We did not find what is
called a pleasant man. We thought him rather impolite,
and it took no more for Madame d'Urfé to set him down
as vulgar. We saw a woman[20] of whom we had already
heard. She scarcely looked at us. We went back to Paris
laughing at the philosopher's eccentricity. But here is
a faithful account of a visit paid him by the Prince of
Conti,[21] father of the Prince who was then known as
the Count of La Marche.[22]

The charming Prince goes to Montmorency by himself,
on purpose to spend a pleasant day talking with the philosopher, who was already famous. He finds him in the
park, he accosts him and says he has come to dine and
spend the day with him in unconstrained conversation.

"Your Highness will eat poor fare; I will go and
order another place set."

He goes, he comes back, and after spending two or
three hours walking with the Prince he conducts him to

the room in which they are to dine. The Prince, seeing
three places laid :

"Who," he said, "is the third person with whom you
want me to dine? I thought we should dine alone together."

"The third person, Monseigneur, is another myself.
It is a being who is neither my wife nor my mistress nor
my servant nor my mother nor my daughter; and she
is all those."

"I believe it, my dear friend; but since I came here
only to dine with you, I will leave you to dine with all
those other selves. Good-by." [23]

Such are the absurdities of philosophers when, trying
to be remarkable, they only succeed in being eccentric.
The woman was Mademoiselle Levasseur, whom he had
honored with his name, except for one letter of it, under
the mask of an anagram.[24]

About this same time I was present at the failure of
a French comedy entitled *Aristides' Daughter*.[25] Its author was Madame de Graffigny.[26] That worthy woman
died of grief five days after her play failed. I saw the
Abbé de Voisenon in great distress; it was he who had
encouraged her to have her play presented and who had
perhaps worked on it, as he had on her *Peruvian Letters*
and her *Cénie*.[27] Pope Rezzonico's mother died of joy[28]
at this same time on seeing her son become Pope. Grief
and joy kill more women than they do men. This shows
that women are more sensitive than we are, but also
weaker.

As soon as my supposed son was, according to Madame
d'Urfé, well settled in Viar's boarding school, she insisted that I go with her to visit him. And to tell the
truth, I was surprised.

A prince could not be better lodged, better treated, better dressed, or more respected by everyone in the establishment. She had given him all kinds of teachers, and a

schooled pony so that he could learn equitation. He went
by the name of Count of Aranda. A girl of sixteen or
eighteen and very pretty, the daughter of Viar, proprietor of the school, never left him and announced herself as his young lordship's governess with every sign
of satisfaction. She assured Madame d'Urfé that she
took particular care of him, that when he woke she
brought him his breakfast in bed, then dressed him, and
did not leave him until she had put him to bed. Madame
d'Urfé approved of all her attentions and assured her
she was grateful. The little fellow could say nothing to
me except that I had made his life happy. I decided to
go back by myself one day to sound him out and learn
on what terms he was with the pretty girl.

On the way back I told Madame that 1 was pleased
with everything except the name Aranda, which might
cause difficulties. She replied that the boy had said
enough to show beyond doubt that he really had a right
to bear the name.

"In my desk," she said, "I had a seal with the arms
of that house; as soon as the boy saw them he seized on
the seal and asked me how I happened to have the arms.
I answered that I had them from the Count of Aranda
himself, urging him to tell me how he could prove he
was of the family; but he silenced me by saying that his
birth was a secret he had sworn never to reveal to anyone."

Curious to discover the source of an imposture of which
I should never have believed the young rascal capable,
I went to see him by myself a week later. I found him
with Viar, who, seeing that he addressed me with something very close to humility, must have thought that he
belonged to me. Praising the young Count's talents in
the highest terms, he said that he played the flute excellently, danced and fenced very nimbly, rode very
well, and that no one was better at drawing all the letters

of the alphabet. He then showed me some pens he had cut, with one, three, five, and up to eleven nibs, and urged me to examine him in heraldry, a science so necessary to a nobleman and of which no one had a better knowledge than he.

The boy then blazoned his arms in herald's jargon, which made me laugh for I knew almost none of the terms; but I took pleasure in seeing how skillfully he wrote freehand with his various pens, which simultaneously drew as many straight and curved lines as they had nibs. I told Viar that it was all very gratifying; and very much pleased, he left me alone with him. We went into the garden.

"May I ask," I said, "what this nonsense about your calling yourself Aranda is?"

"It is nonsense, but let it pass, I beg you, for I have to do it to inspire respect here."

"It is a lie which I cannot let pass, for it may have disagreeable consequences which will involve us all. It is an imposture, my friend, of which I did not believe you capable, a feather-brained whim which may become criminal and which I do not know how to make good and save your honor after all you have said to Madame d'Urfé."

I did not end my scolding until I saw him weep and heard him implore me. He said that he would rather endure the mortification of being sent back to his mother than the shame of having to admit to Madame d'Urfé that he had lied and having to give up the name which he had claimed as his own at school. He moved me to pity. I could really do nothing to mend matters short of sending him to live under another name fifty leagues from Paris.

"Tell me," I said, "and mind you tell me the truth, what exactly is the nature of the affection of the pretty young lady who lavishes such attentions on you."

"I think, my dear Papa, that this is a time for the discretion which you and my Mamma have so often recommended to me."

"So that is it! Your objection has told me everything; but there is no place for discretion in a confession."

"Well then, Mademoiselle Viar loves me and gives me proofs of it which leave me in no doubt."

"And you?"

"I love her too; and certainly it can't be wrong for me to return her affection—she's so pretty! and her sweetness and her caresses are such that I could be insensible to them only if I were made of marble or utterly ungrateful. I have told you the truth."

With this avowal, which had already corrupted me, the young man blushed furiously. I was too much interested to change the subject. The charming young girl, in love, demonstrative, holding the little fellow in her arms, making him return her ardors, rose into my mind to beg my indulgence, and she had no difficulty in gaining it. I needed to make him continue his narrative to learn if he had nothing to reproach himself with in the response which it seemed to me he could not but accord to so pretty a girl.

So, assuming that kindly manner in which there is no shadow of reproach:

"Then," I said, "you have become the charming girl's little husband?"

"She tells me so every morning and every evening, and then I enjoy seeing how happy it makes her when I call her my little wife."

"And you are not afraid someone will catch you?"

"That is up to her."

"You are in each other's arms as God made you?"

"Yes, when she comes to put me to bed, but she only stays an hour at most."

"Would you like her to stay longer?"

"Not really, because after I've made love I can't help falling asleep."

"I imagine she is your first mistress in the fine art of love."

"You may be sure of that."

"And if she becomes pregnant?"

"She has assured me it is impossible, and when she told me the reason she convinced me; but in a year or two we both think she would have to fear it."

"Do you think she has had another lover before you?"

"Oh no, I'm sure she hasn't."

This whole dialogue only had the effect of making me irretrievably in love with his young mistress. I left him after asking him at what hour she brought him his breakfast. I could neither disapprove nor put obstacles in the way of the mutual affection of their two young hearts; but I thought the least recompense they owed me for my tolerance was to let me witness their amorous ecstasies at least once.

A Bohemian count, of the Clary[29] family, who had come to me with a letter of introduction from Baron de Bavois,[30] and whom I saw nearly every day, was at that time so filled with the venomous juice which in Italy we call "the French disease" that he needed to go into seclusion for six weeks. I arranged for him to stay at the surgeon Faget's[31] for the sum of fifty louis, which I lent him, since, he said, he was then out of money because of the negligence of his cashier, who lived at Töplitz, to which principality he was the heir. It was untrue. Clary was a handsome man who lied from dark to dawn; but my friendship for him was such that I only pitied him. He lied every time he spoke, and not to deceive but from an unconquerable trait of his character. No man is more unhappy than a liar, especially if he is born a gentleman; and he can only lie if he lacks intelligence since he knows that, once he is discovered to be

a liar, he can only be despised. His lack of intelligence
consists in his believing that he has not been found out
and in imagining that the things he comes out with will
be taken for true if they merely appear probable. He
does not know that despite their probability they do not
have that stamp of truth which is strikingly and instantly
apparent to anyone of intelligence. Yet the liar thinks
he is far more intelligent than those who tell the truth,
which according to him they would not do if they had
the divine faculty of invention. Such a man was the unfortunate Count Clary, of whom I shall speak again and
who came to a bad end. He was very lame; but since it
was due to his hip he carried himself so well when he
walked that I did not observe the very pardonable defect
until three months after I first met him. I saw him limp-
ing as he walked in his room once when he thought he
was alone; when he turned I asked him if he had hurt
himself the day before, and he answered that he had,
blushing to the ears. That time I could not condemn him
for having lied. Walking without a limp was the lie
which cost him the most effort, for on promenades and
when he danced he was bathed in sweat. Being young
and handsome, he did not want anyone to be able to say
he had this defect. He liked gambling when he could
improve upon luck, but in shady company, for among
gentlemen he would not have had the courage to fight
if there was a quarrel; then, too, his manners were not
polished enough for him to figure in good society.

The style in which I lived in Little Poland made it
famous. Everyone talked of the excellent table I kept.
I had fowl fed on rice in a dark room; they were white
as snow, with an exquisite flavor. To the excellence of
the French cuisine I added whatever the other cuisines
of Europe offered to tempt the most refined palates. My
macaroni *al sughillo*,[32] my rice sometimes as pilau,[33]
sometimes *in cagnoni*,[34] my *olla podridas*[35] were the talk

of the town. I matched well-chosen guests with exquisite
suppers, at which my company saw that my pleasure
depended on the pleasure I provided for them. Ladies of
distinction, all of them versed in love, came during the
morning to walk in my garden with unseasoned young
gallants who did not dare open their mouths and whom
I pretended not to see; I gave them fresh eggs and
butter which surpassed even the celebrated butter from
Vambre.[36] These were followed by plenty of Zara maraschino,[37] than which none better was to be had anywhere.
I often lent the unoccupied part of my house to some
bigwig who came there to sup with a woman above suspicion. My house then became a sanctuary impenetrable
even to myself. They knew that nothing escaped me; but
the lady was grateful to me for pretending not to know
her whenever I saw her.

Delighted with this life, and needing an income of a
hundred thousand francs to maintain it, I often tried
to think of some way to make it permanent. A man fer-
tile in schemes whom I met at Calzabigi's seemed sent
by Heaven to provide me with an income even above my
hopes. He talked to me of the extravagant profits made
by silk manufactories, and of those which could be made
by a man who, having the necessary capital, would also
have the courage to establish a manufactory of painted
silks like those from Pekin. He showed me that, with
perfect silks, pure colors, and our designers, who were
better than any in Asia, there was a vast fortune to be
made. He convinced me that, at a price a third less than
was asked for those imported from China, such silks,
which would be even more beautiful, would be preferred
all over Europe, and that despite their being sold so
cheaply the manufacturer would make a profit of a hundred percent. He definitely captured my interest when
he told me that he was himself a designer and painter
and that he was prepared to show me some samples of

his talent. I told him to come and dine with me the next day, bringing his samples, and we would discuss the matter when I had seen them. He came, I looked at them all, and I was amazed. What won me over was the design and the beauty of the colors, of which he had the secret and which would resist rain. The beauty of the foliage in silver and gold surpassed what was admired in silks from China which were sold at very high prices in Paris and everywhere. I saw that the thing would be very easy once the design was applied to the fabrics, since the working girls I would hire and would pay by the day would only have to color it according to instructions and that they would produce as many pieces as I wanted in proportion to their number.

The idea of becoming the head of a manufactory[38] pleased me. I congratulated myself that I would become rich in a manner which would recommend me to the State. However, I decided not to make any move until I had first seen everything clearly, thoroughly investigated receipts and expenditures, and engaged or made sure of trustworthy persons upon whom I could rely, since my own part in the enterprise was to consist in my being furnished the accounts and seeing that everyone did his duty.

I arranged for my man to come and spend a week or so in my house. I wanted him to design and paint under my eyes on fabrics of all colors. He did it very rapidly, and he left me all that he had produced, saying that so far as the lastingness of the colors was concerned I could put the pieces he had painted to any test. I carried the samples in my pockets for five or six days, and I saw that all my good friends were delighted with their beauty and my project. I decided to establish the manufactory; and to that end I consulted my man, who was to be the director.

Having decided to rent a house in the Enclos du

Temple,[39] I went to the Prince of Conti, who, after praising my project warmly, promised me his patronage and
any franchises I might want. In the house which I chose,
the rent for which cost me only a thousand écus a year,
I had a large room in which all my girls were to work,
each at her own frame. I set apart another large room
as a storehouse, and several other apartments on all the
floors as lodgings for the more important employees and
for myself when I wanted to stay there.

I divided my enterprise into thirty shares, of which I
gave five to my painter and designer, keeping the other
twenty-five to distribute proportionally among associates
who would put up the capital. I gave one share to a
doctor who furnished security for the position of storehouse keeper and who came to live in the building with
his whole family, and I hired four lackeys, two maidservants, and a porter. I also had to give another share
to a bookkeeper, who supplied me with two clerks and
also came to live in the building. I did all this in less
than three weeks, keeping several carpenters busy making closets in the storehouse and twenty frames in the
large room. I left it to the director to find twenty girls
to do the painting, whom I would pay every Saturday;
and I put in store three hundred lengths of strong
taffeta, *gros de Tours*,[40] and white, yellow, and green
camlet,[41] to receive the painted designs, the choice of
which I reserved to myself. I paid for everything in cash.

According to a rough calculation made with my director on the basis that sales of our product would not begin until the end of a year, I needed a hundred thousand
écus, which I had. In any case I could sell shares at
twenty thousand francs, but I hoped I should never have
to sell any, for I was aiming at an income of two hundred thousand francs a year.

I saw that the enterprise would ruin me if sales proved
insufficient; but how could I fear that, when I saw the

beauty of my fabrics and heard everyone telling me that I should not sell them so cheaply? In less than a month I spent some sixty thousand francs establishing the firm, and I had undertaken to pay out twelve hundred francs a week. Madame d'Urfé laughed, believing that I was only doing it to put the curious off the scent and ensure my incognito. What pleased me very much, though it should have made me tremble, was the sight of twenty girls, all between the ages of eighteen and twenty-five, all of modest appearance and more than half of them pretty enough, listening attentively to the painter's instructions at their new work. The most expensive among them cost me only twenty-four sous a day, and they were all of good reputation, chosen by the director's wife, who was pious, and to whom I was very pleased to grant this satisfaction, sure that I should have her as my accomplice if I took it into my head to conquer one of the girls. But Manon Balletti shuddered when she saw me the master of this seraglio. She did not hide her displeasure, even though she knew that at nightfall they all went home to eat supper and sleep. But now for what dropped on me from the blue to shatter my peace of mind.

Miss *XCV* had been in the convent for three months and was nearing her time; we wrote to each other twice a week, and I felt perfectly easy about the matter. Monsieur de la Pouplinière having already married, when Miss came out of the convent she would go home, and there would be no more talk.

One day after dining at Madame d'Urfé's I took a stroll in the Tuileries. In the principal walk I see an elderly woman accompanied by a man dressed in black and wearing a sword, who stops and looks at me, then speaks to her. It is perfectly simple; I continue my stroll; but the next time around I see her again, closer to me and standing still to look at me, and I remember having seen the man who was walking with her at a gambling house, and that he bore the Gascon name of Castel-Bajac.[42] On my third time around I recognize the woman as the one to whom I had gone with Miss to consult her about her pregnancy. This convinces me that she has recognized me, but considering it of no significance I leave the garden and go elsewhere.

On the next day but one at eleven o'clock, just as I was getting into my carriage, I see a disreputable-looking man who hands me a paper and tells me to read it. Seeing an incomprehensible scrawl, I ask him to read it himself, and I hear that I am ordered to appear before the Commissary[43] that same day after dinner to answer a complaint lodged against me by the midwife so-and-so. He then leaves.

Unable to imagine what the harridan could be complaining of, and certain that she could not convict me of knowing her, I go to an attorney of my acquaintance and formally empower him to represent me. I inform him that I do not know, and have never known, any midwife in Paris. The attorney went to the Commissary and next day brought me a copy of the complaint.

She alleged that I had come to her on such-and-such a night with a lady five months pregnant, both of us wearing dominoes, which showed that we had come from the ball at the Opéra, and that I had demanded that she give me drugs to bring on an abortion, holding a pistol in my right hand and a roll of fifty louis in my left and ordering her to choose. Fear had made her answer that she did not have the necessary drugs ready, but that she would have them the next evening, whereupon I had left, promising to return. Believing that I would not fail to come, she had the next morning asked Monsieur de Castel-Bajac to hide in the room next to the one in which she would receive me, to protect her against violence, but she had not seen me again. She would not

have put off lodging a complaint if she had known who
I was. On the previous day she had recognized me in the
Tuileries, and Monsieur de Castel-Bajac, who knew me,
having told her my name and address, she had hastened
to accuse me,[44] and she demanded that I be subjected to
the full rigor of the laws. This was the satisfaction
which her outraged honor led her to desire. Castel-
Bajac's name was signed as witness.

My attorney said it was a libel without a shadow of
probability and hence it was my part to see that the
shameless midwife who was proceeding against me should
be punished according to the laws. He said that I should
take the case to the Criminal Lieutenant,[45] and I authorized him to do whatever he thought advisable. Four
days later he came and told me that the magistrate
wanted to speak with me privately at his own house at
three o'clock in the afternoon.

I found a most amiable man. He was Monsieur de
Sartine,[46] whom the King two years later[47] rewarded
by naming him Lieutenant of Police. His former office
was one which he sold, the latter an appointment which
was not for sale. He immediately asked me to sit down.

"Monsieur," he said, "I have asked you to come here
for our mutual advantage, since our interests are inseparable. In the matter of the criminal charge which
has been brought against you, you are right to lodge a
counteraccusation before me if you are innocent; but
first of all you must make your innocence perfectly clear.
I am ready to help you, my position as your judge set
aside; but you must realize that your opponent cannot
be found guilty of libel until convicted of it. I ask you
to give me an extrajudiciary statement. Your case is already of the utmost gravity. It is of such a nature that
despite your innocence you may feel that your honor
demands a certain discretion from you. Your opponents
will not respect your delicacy, and they will press you so

hard that you will find yourself forced either to accept a verdict of guilty if you do not tell all or to fail in what you may consider your honor demands of you in order to prove your innocence. I now make you a confidence completely between ourselves. Know that, within certain limits, honor is so dear to me that I often defend it at the expense of the strict and rigorous rules of criminal justice. Pay me in the same coin; have confidence in me; tell me everything; give me all the information possible, and thus gain my friendship. If you are innocent I risk nothing, for being your friend can never prevent me from being an incorruptible judge; but if you are guilty I am sorry for you. I warn you that I will be just."

After saying everything to him which a due regard for his noble offer prompted, I assured him that since I was not in a situation in which honor demanded discretion of me I had nothing to tell him extrajudicially. The midwife who was accusing me and whom I did not know could only be a criminal who had joined with a man of her own stamp to extort money from me.

"I am willing to believe it," he said; "but if she is a criminal, hear how chance has favored her to make it a long and difficult task for you to prove your innocence. Mademoiselle *XCV* ran away three months ago. You were her intimate friend. No one knows where she is. You are suspected; from the moment she disappeared spies have been paid to follow your every step. The midwife, through the advocate Vauversin,[48] yesterday laid before me an indictment in which it is claimed that the pregnant lady you took to her is the lady who disappeared. The midwife says you were both wearing black dominoes; and it has already been ascertained that you both went to the ball in black dominoes on the night on which the midwife says you went to see her. These are only half-proofs, but they make one tremble."

"What reason have I to tremble?"

"Because a false witness may be paid to swear that he saw you both leave the ball and get into a hackney coach, and a bribed coachman may even swear that he took you to the midwife's house. In that case I should have to begin by ordering your arrest to oblige you to name the person whom you took to the midwife's. You are accused of having subjected her to an abortion and, three months having elapsed, she is thought to be dead."

"I should be found guilty of murder, innocent though I am, and it is you who would sentence me to death. I am sorry for you."

"You are right to be sorry for me; but do not suppose that I would sentence you lightly. Indeed, I am certain that I would never sentence you to death if you are innocent; but you might languish for a long time in prison, innocent though you may be. You see now that this matter has become very serious in twenty-four hours and that in a week it may become terrible. What gained you my interest is the absurdity of the midwife's accusation, which made me laugh; but the rest, which complicates the matter, is grave. I see the likelihood of an abduction; I see love and honor imperiously commanding you to be discreet. I decided to talk with you. Tell me all, and I will spare you all the difficulties which you must expect even though you are innocent. Tell me all, and be sure that the young lady's honor will not suffer. But if you have the misfortune to be guilty of the crimes with which you are charged, I advise you to take measures which it is not for me to suggest to you. I warn you that in three or four days I will have you summoned to the court record office,[49] where you will see me only in my capacity of judge."

Petrified by this harangue, which revealed all the danger of my situation and showed me beyond doubt that I must put the highest value on the worthy man's

offer, I said sadly that, completely innocent though I
was, I must avail myself of his kindness in respect to the
honor of Miss *XCV*, who had committed no crime yet
whom this foul accusation put in danger of seeing her
reputation besmirched.

"I know," I said, "where she is, and I can assure you
that she would never have left her mother if she had not
tried to force her to marry the Farmer-General."

"But he is married;[50] let her return to her home, and
you are safe, unless the midwife persists and proves that
you induced an abortion."

"Alas, Monsieur, there is no question of abortion; but
other reasons prevent her from returning to her family.
I cannot tell you more without a consent which I shall
try to obtain. I can then give you all the information to
which your noble character entitles you. Grant me the
honor of a second hearing in this place day after tomorrow."

"I understand; I will hear you with pleasure, and I
thank you no less than I congratulate you. Good-by."

Seeing that I was on the brink of ruin, I felt that I
was ready to leave the kingdom rather than betray my
unhappy darling's secret. I would gladly have hushed
up the affair with money if I had been in time. It was
obvious that Farsetti had played the principal part, and
that he had never ceased to pursue me and to pay the
spies who followed me everywhere. It was even he who
had set the advocate Vauversin on me. I saw that I must
tell Monsieur de Sartine everything; but I could not do
that until I had obtained Madame du Rumain's permission.

## CHAPTER XI

*I am examined. I give the court record clerk*
*three hundred louis. The midwife and Castel-*
*Bajac are sent to prison. Miss gives birth*
*to a boy and obliges her mother to make*
*me amends. My case is quashed. Miss leaves*
*for Brussels and goes with her mother to*
*Venice, where she becomes a great lady. My*
*working girls. Madame Baret. I am robbed,*
*imprisoned, and set free. I leave for Holland.*
*Helvétius'* Esprit. *Piccolomini.*

I WENT to her the next morning very early. Since
the matter was urgent I had her waked, and I gave her
an account of all the circumstances. She said it was no
time for hesitation, that the Criminal Lieutenant must
be informed in full, and that she would go and speak to
him herself. She immediately wrote him that she would
come to speak with him about an important matter at
three o'clock that afternoon, and he answered that he
would expect her. She went, she told him the whole
story, she said that she[1] was on the eve of being confined and that after her confinement she would go back
to her mother, but without confessing to her that she
had been pregnant. She assured me that I had nothing
more to fear; but that, since the case would continue, I
would be summoned to the court record office on the
next day but one. She advised me to go and see the
record clerk[2] and find some excuse for giving him money.

I was summoned and I appeared. I saw Monsieur de Sartine *sedentem pro tribunali* ("sitting as judge"). At the end of the hearing he said that he was obliged to issue a writ of summons for me. He warned me that I must not leave Paris nor could I marry while it ran, since any criminal prosecution carried with it the suspension of the right to make civil contracts. At my examination I acknowledged that I had gone to the ball wearing a black domino on the night named in the action, but I denied all the rest. In regard to Miss *XCV* I said that neither I nor any member of her family had ever thought that she was pregnant.

Since as a foreigner I had to fear that Vauversin would obtain a writ for my arrest by accusing me of preparing to flee, I made it my excuse to pay a visit to the record clerk and place in his hands, without asking for a receipt, three hundred louis as a guarantee for the court costs if I should have to pay them. He advised me to demand the same guarantee of the midwife, and I instructed my attorney to attend to it; but this is what happened four days later.

As I was taking a walk on the rampart opposite the Rue du Temple[3] a Savoyard approached me and put a note in my hands. I read, and I find that a person who is waiting in an alley fifty paces away wishes to speak with me. I order my carriage, which was following me, to stop, and I go to the alley.

Great was my surprise when I saw Castel-Bajac. He immediately said that he had only a few words to say to me and that we could be sure that no one saw us.

"I have come," he said, "to offer you a sure way of ending a case which must be worrying you and costing you a great deal of money. The midwife is certain that it is you who came to her with a pregnant woman, and she is now sorry to have been the reason for your being accused of abducting her. Give her a hundred louis and she will tell the record clerk she was mistaken. You need not pay the amount until afterward. Come with me to talk with the attorney Vauversin and he will persuade you. I know where he is. Let us go. Follow me at a distance.''

Delighted to see how easily the scoundrels were about to betray themselves and curious to learn how they would go about it, I followed the man to the fourth floor of a house in the Rue aux Ours,[4] where I found the advocate Vauversin. As soon as he saw me he came to the point. He told me that the midwife would appear at my lodging with a witness to tell me to my face that I had been at her house with a pregnant woman, and that she would not recognize me. In his opinion this would be enough to make the Criminal Lieutenant stop all proceedings and would put me in a position to defeat the young lady's mother in court. Considering the scheme well conceived, I told him that I would make myself available at my house in the Enclos du Temple every day until noon. He then said that the midwife needed a hundred louis, and I promised to give them to him whenever she had filed a statement of her mistake at the court record office; and he replied that she would take my word for it but that I must first pay a quarter of the amount, which he was to receive for his expenses and his fee. I stated that I was ready to pay it if he would give me a receipt, and on this question we had a long discussion; but in the end he gave me the receipt with the most complete guilelessness, and I counted him out twenty-five louis. He said that he would secretly advise me how to counter all Madame *XCV*'s proceedings, even though she was his client, since he believed I was innocent. I said I hoped he would continue his good offices, and I went home and wrote an account of the whole incident and immediately sent it to Monsieur de Sartine.

Three days later my valet tells me that a woman is
there with a man and asks to speak with me. I come
out, I ask her what she wants, and she answers that she
wants to speak with Monsieur Casanova.

"I am he."

"Then I have made a mistake."

The man who was with her smiled and they left. On
the same day Madame du Rumain received a letter from
the Abbess in which she announced that her protégée
had been successfully delivered of a fine baby boy, whom
she had already sent to a place where he would be
properly cared for. She said that the new mother would
not leave the convent until six weeks had passed, when
she would go home to her mother with a certificate
which would protect her against any kind of annoyance.

Two or three days later[5] the midwife was sentenced to
prison and put in solitary confinement. Castel-Bajac was
sent to Bicêtre,[6] and Vauversin was stricken from the
list[7] of advocates. Madame *XCV*'s proceedings against
me continued until her daughter reappeared,[8] but always
without effect. Miss *XCV* returned to the Hôtel de
Bretagne toward the end of August,[9] appearing before
her mother with a certificate from the Abbess stating
that she had kept her for four months, during which
time she had never either gone out or received a visitor;
she was returning home now that she need no longer
fear being forced to marry La Pouplinière. She made
her mother go in person to the Criminal Lieutenant
with the same certificate, thereby dropping all proceedings against me. He advised her to maintain a prudent
silence on the matter in future, and to accord me some
reparation because I would have cause to lodge a complaint, which would be even more injurious to her daughter's honor.

Her daughter, though she had no such fear, obliged
her to make me full amends in a written statement,

which I caused to be registered at the record office and
which enabled me to put a formal end to the case. I did
not go to see her again, in order not to encounter Farsetti,
who undertook to conduct Miss to Brussels, since her
honor forbade her to appear in Paris, where everyone
knew her story. She remained in Brussels with Farsetti
and Magdelaine until her mother, with the rest of the
family, rejoined her there to take her to Venice, where
three years later she became a great lady. I saw her
again fifteen years later, widowed and passably happy
in the consideration she enjoyed because of her rank, her
intelligence, and her social virtues; but I never again
indulged in the slightest intimacy with her. Four years
from now the reader will learn where and how I saw
Castel-Bajac again. Toward the end of this same year
1759, before I left for Holland I spent a further sum of
money to obtain the midwife's release from prison.

The life I was leading was that of a happy man; but
I was not happy. The great sums I was spending made
me foresee difficulties. My manufactory would have put
me in a position to maintain it if my sales had not been
halted by the war.[20] I had four hundred pieces of painted
fabrics in my storehouse, and there was no likelihood
of selling them before the peace, and since the so greatly
desired peace was not being made I had to take my
bearings. I wrote to Esther to get her father to let me
have half of my capital, send me a clerk, and go into
equal partnership with me. Monsieur D. O. replied that
if I would transfer the manufactory to Holland he
would see to everything and give me half of the profits.
I loved Paris and I did not consent.

I was spending a great deal at my house in Little
Poland, but the expenditure which was undermining me,
and which no one knew about, was very much greater.
I became interested in all of my working girls in whom
I saw any merit, and, since I did not have the patience

to obtain them cheaply, they had only to seize the opportunity to make me pay a high price for my curiosity. The example of the first one was enough to make them all demand a house and furniture as soon as they saw that they had aroused desires in me. My fancy often lasted only three days, and I always thought the new substitute more worthy of me than her predecessor. I stopped seeing her, but I went on paying her expenses. Madame d'Urfé, believing me wealthy, did not interfere with me; I kept her happy by having my oracle encourage her in her magical operations. Manon Balletti made me miserable with her jealousy and her justified reproaches. She could not understand how I could put off marrying her if I really loved her; she kept saying I was deceiving her. Her mother died of consumption about this time, in her arms and mine. Ten minutes before she expired she commended her daughter to my care. I promised from my soul that I would make her my wife; but Destiny, as is so often said, was against it.

About this same time a serious illness also brought my friend Tiretta's mistress to the grave. Four days before her death she dismissed him in order to devote all her thoughts to her soul, making him a present of a valuable ring and two hundred louis. Tiretta, after asking her to forgive him, packed his things and came to me in Little Poland with the sad news. I put him up at the Enclos du Temple, and four weeks later, approving of his feeling that he should seek his fortune in India, I gave him a letter of introduction to Monsieur D. O. at Amsterdam. In less than two weeks he got him a position as clerk on an East India Company ship which was going to Batavia. He would have become rich if he had behaved himself; he became involved in a conspiracy, he had to flee and underwent great vicissitudes. In 1788 I learned from one of his relatives that he was in Bengal and fairly well-to-do, but that he could not obtain pos-

*The Long-Awaited Hour*

*Jean Jacques Rousseau*

session of his capital in order to return to his native
country and live there happily. I do not know what became of him.

At the beginning of November[11] a household official
at the Court of the Duke of Elbeuf [12] came to my manufactory with his daughter to buy her a dress for her
wedding day. The girl's charming face dazzled me. She
chose a piece of very shiny satin, and I saw her satisfaction and the joy of her soul when she saw that her
father was satisfied with the price; but I could not resist the pain her sorrow caused me when she heard the
clerk tell her father that he must buy the whole length.
It was the rule in my establishment, only the whole
length could be sold. I went to my study to avoid being
forced to make an exception to the rule; and nothing
would have happened if the girl had not asked the director to take her to me. She entered, her eyes swollen
with tears, telling me point-blank that I was rich, I
could buy the whole length myself and let her have the
yards she needed for her dress. I looked at her father,
who appeared to be asking me to forgive her for a boldness which showed that she was still a child. I told him
I liked frankness, and I immediately ordered what she
needed for her dress cut off. She then bewitched me completely by coming and kissing me, while her father,
thinking it a great joke, laughed uproariously. After
paying the price of the material he invited me to the
wedding.

"I am marrying her," he said, "on Sunday; there
will be a supper and dancing, and you will be doing me
honor. My name is Gilbert;[13] I am steward to His Grace
the Duke of Elbeuf, Rue Saint-Nicaise." [14]

I promised him I would go.

I went, but I could neither eat nor dance. Gilbert's
charming daughter kept me as if in ecstasy all the time
I was there, though, in any case, I could never have

adapted myself to the tone of the company. It was a crowd of nothing but household officials with their wives and daughters, I knew no one, no one knew me; I was stupid. In such gatherings the man who is the wittiest often becomes the dullest. Everyone made his joke to the bride, she answered them all, and there were bursts of laughter when they did not understand each other. The bridegroom, thin and downcast, praised his bride for keeping everyone in high spirits. Far from making me jealous of his good luck, the fellow aroused my pity; he was obviously marrying to better himself; I took it into my head to question the bride, and she gave me an opportunity by coming to sit beside me after a con-tradance. She thanked me for what I had done for her, which had enabled her to have the beautiful dress on which everyone was complimenting her.

"But I am sure you can't wait to take it off, for I know what love is."

"It's strange how everyone insists I'm in love, when the fact is I didn't know Monsieur Baret[15] existed until he was introduced to me a week ago."

"And why are you being married in such a hurry?"

"Because my father does everything in a hurry."

"No doubt your husband is rich?"

"No, but he may become so. Day after tomorrow we open a shop for silk stockings at the corner of the Rue Saint-Honoré and the Rue des Prouvaires.[16] I hope you will buy your stockings from us."

"You may be sure of it, and I promise I will be your first customer even if I have to spend the night at the door of your shop."

She laughed, she called her husband, she told him what I had said, and he answered, thanking me, that it would bring him good luck. He assured me that his stockings never became fluffy.

On Tuesday at daybreak I waited in the Rue des

Prouvaires for the shop to open and I went in. The maid asks me what I want and tells me to come back later because her master and mistress are asleep.

"I will wait here. Go get me some coffee."

"I'm not fool enough to leave you alone in my shop."

She was right.

Baret finally comes down, scolds her for not having called him, orders her to go and tell his wife I am there, opens packages, and shows me waistcoats, gloves, pantaloons, until his wife comes down fresh as a rose, white with a whiteness than which it was impossible to see anything more dazzling, asking me to excuse her for being only half dressed and thanking me for having kept my promise.

Madame Baret was of middle stature, seventeen years of age, and, though not a perfect beauty, all that a Raphael [17] could have imagined and executed in the way of prettiness, which has far more power than beauty to fire a heart whose ruling passion is love. Her eyes, her laugh, her always parted lips, the attentiveness with which she listened, her sparkling sweetness, her intense vivacity, the little pride she showed in her charms, the extent of whose power she seemed not to realize at all, kept me in an ecstasy of admiration for this little masterpiece of Nature, which chance or basely interested motives had put in the possession of the poor thin, sickly man before me, concerned with nothing but his stockings, which he valued far more highly than he did the jewel which marriage had given him.

After choosing some twenty-five louis' worth of stockings and waistcoats and enjoying the pleasure I saw displayed on the face of the shop's pretty mistress, I told the maid that I would give her six francs when she brought me the parcel at Little Poland. I left full of love, but without any plan, since I thought the beginning of a marriage presented too many difficulties.

It was on the following Sunday that Baret himself came with my parcel. I gave him six francs, asking him to take them to the maid; he replied that he would not be ashamed to keep them for himself. I gave him a breakfast of fresh eggs and butter, asking him why he had not come with his wife; he answered that she had asked him to bring her, but that he had not dared to for fear of giving offense. I assured him that she would have given me pleasure, for I thought her charming.

"You are very kind."

When I passed her shop in my carriage, which went like the wind, I threw her kisses but did not stop, for I was not in want of stockings and it would have bored me to mingle with the fops whom I always saw at her counter. At the Palais-Royal and the Tuileries everyone was talking of the pretty new shopkeeper, and I was very glad to hear that she was only holding off until she could find a good dupe.

Eight or ten days later, seeing me coming from the direction of the Pont-Neuf,[18] she beckoned to me. I pull the cord,[19] and she asks me to get out. Her husband, after apologizing profusely, says that he wants me to be the first to see some pantaloons in various colors which he has just received. They were the height of fashion in Paris at the time. No well-dressed man would think of going out in the morning except wearing pantaloons. They looked very smart when the young man was well built; but the pantaloons had to be neither too long nor too short, neither too full nor too tight. I tell him to have three or four pairs made to order for me, saying that I am willing to give him the money in advance. He assures me that the ones before me were of all sizes, and he urges me to go upstairs and try them on, asking his wife to go and help me.

The moment was crucial. I go up, she follows me, I ask her to excuse me if I have to take off my nether

garments, she replies that she will imagine she is my
valet and will be glad to do his duties. I immediately
agreed, quickly unbuckling my shoes and yielding to
her ministrations when she insisted on pulling down my
breeches; but I was careful to take them off with due
respect for modesty and to keep on my drawers. It was
now she who took over the whole task of putting pantaloons on me and taking them off again when they did
not fit, always with a modesty equal to that which I
had imposed on myself for the duration of these pleasant
proceedings. She decided that four of them fitted me
perfectly and I did not dare to contradict her. After
giving her the sixteen louis she asked for them, I said
I would be glad if she would kindly bring them to me
at her convenience. She hurried downstairs to solace
her husband and convince him that she was a good
saleswoman. When he saw me appear he said he would
come with his "little wife" to bring me my pantaloons
on the following Sunday; I said it would be a pleasure,
and an even greater one if he would stay for dinner
with me. He answered that since he had important business to transact at two o'clock he could only accept my
invitation if I would permit him to leave to attend it,
assuring me that he would return about five o'clock to
take his wife home. I said that he could easily do so,
since I would not have to go out until six. So the appointment was made, to my great satisfaction.

On Sunday the couple were as good as their word. I
at once ordered my valet to admit no one, and impatient
to see what would happen after dinner I had it served
at noon. The choice dishes and the good wines having
put the couple in high spirits, it was the husband who
suggested to his wife that she should go home alone if
he should happen to be delayed in coming back.

"In that case," I said, "I will see her to your house
at six o'clock after taking a turn on the ramparts."

So it was settled that he would find her at home about nightfall, and he set off very well pleased when he found a hackney coach at my door and I told him it was hired for the rest of the day. So there I am, left alone with the jewel and sure of having her to myself until evening.

He had scarcely gone before I complimented her on the good husband fate had given her.

"With a man of his character you must be happy."

"The word is easily said; but to be happy one must feel it and enjoy peace of mind. My husband's health is so frail that I have to consider him an invalid, and he has debts which oblige us to observe the strictest economy. We came here on foot to save twenty-four sous. The income from our enterprise, which could suffice us if we had no debts, is insufficient. We do not sell enough."

"Yet you have many customers; every time I go by I see your shop full."

"They are not customers but idlers, wastrels, profligates, who bore me with their fawning. They haven't a sou, and we always keep an eye on them for fear they will rob us. If we'd been willing to sell to them on credit we'd have nothing left in our shop. All I can do to get rid of them is to sulk; but it's no use. Nothing discourages them. When my husband is in the shop I leave; but most of the time he's not there. Besides, the scarcity of money results in our selling nothing, and we have to pay our work people every Saturday. We shall have to dismiss them, for we have promissory notes out which fall due soon. We have to pay six hundred francs on Saturday and we have only two hundred."

"I am surprised at your being in such straits so soon after your marriage. Your father must have known the situation, and you certainly brought him a dowry."

"My dowry is six thousand francs and he received four thousand in cash. He used them to open the shop and pay some debts. Our stock is worth three times what we owe; but when there are no sales capital lies idle."

"What you have told me distresses me, and if peace is not concluded I foresee that your situation will become steadily worse and your needs perhaps greater."

"Yes, for when my husband recovers his health we may well have children."

"What! Does his health prevent him from paying you the dues of a husband?"

"Yes, but I do not care."

"I am amazed. It seems to me that a man in your company cannot feel ill unless he is dying."

"He is not dying, but he shows no signs of life."

This sally made it proper for me not only to laugh but to applaud it by embraces which became loving when, mild as a lamb, she offered no resistance. I encouraged her by saying that I could help her in the matter of the promissory note which she had to honor on Saturday, and I took her to a boudoir where nothing necessary for bringing love to its proper conclusion was lacking.

At first she enchanted me by the willingness with which she raised no obstacle either to my caresses or my curiosity; but she surprised me when she took a different attitude from that which should be the forerunner of the supreme enjoyment.

"What!" I said, "could I expect such a refusal at this moment when I believed I saw in your eyes that you shared my desires?"

"My eyes did not deceive you; but what would my husband say if he found me other than what I was yesterday?"

She sees that I am astonished, and she urges me to convince myself.

"Have I a right," she says, "to dispose of a fruit which is the prerogative of marriage before marriage has tasted it at least once?"

"No, my angel, no; I pity you and I adore you; come to my arms and fear nothing. The fruit will be respected, but it is incredible."

We spent three hours in a hundred delicious toyings whose effect was only to increase our ardor, whatever people say to the contrary. A solemn promise to be wholly mine as soon as she could make Baret believe he had recovered his health served as surrogate for all that I could desire. After a stroll on the ramparts I took her home in my carriage, accompanying her to the door and slipping a roll of twenty-five louis into her hands.

In love with her as I thought I had never been in love with any woman, I passed her shop three or four times a day, paying no attention to my coachman's repeated warnings that the long detours were killing my horses. I loved the way she threw kisses and the eagerness with which she watched for the first glimpse of me. We had agreed that she would not beckon me to get out until her husband had put her in a condition to make us happy without any fear. The *fateful* day was not long in arriving. At a sign from her, I stopped. Getting up on the step of my carriage, she told me to wait for her at the door of Saint-Germain-l'Auxerrois.[20] Eager to learn what she had to say, I go there, and a quarter of an hour later I see her with her head hidden in her hood; she gets into my carriage, and saying that she has some errands to do, asks me to take her to the Palais Marchand.[21] I had business; but *amare et sapere vix deo conceditur* ("to love and be wise is scarcely granted to a god").[22] I order my coachman to take me to the Place Dauphine.[23] Good-by to my money! but love commanded me to satisfy her.

At the Palais Marchand she entered every shop into which the pretty proprietress invited her, addressing her as "Princess." Could I object? It was only to look at all the jewelry, the trinkets, the fittings which were rapidly laid before us with honeyed words: "Look at this, my beautiful Princess, look at that. Oh, how it would become you! It is for half-mourning[24] that will be over day after tomorrow." She would look at me then, saying that it certainly was very pretty if only it weren't too expensive; whereupon I, her willing dupe, had to persuade her that if a thing pleased her it could never be too expensive. But while she was choosing gloves and mittens here is what inescapable fate brought to pass so that I should be in a pitiable situation four years later. One thing leads to another in an endless chain.

To my left I notice a girl of twelve or thirteen with a most interesting face in the company of an ugly old woman who was decrying a pair of paste earrings which the girl was holding and admiring; she seemed sad that she could not buy them. I hear her tell the old woman that the earrings would make her happy. The old woman snatches them from her and starts to leave. The shopkeeper tells the girl that she has some which she will let her have more cheaply, and the girl answers that she does not want them. Leaving the shop, she drops a low curtsy to my Princess Baret, who, addressing her as "little Queen," tells her she is as pretty as an angel and kisses her. She asks the old woman who she is, and she answers that she is Mademoiselle de Boulainvilliers,[25] her niece.

"And are you so hardhearted," I say to the old aunt, "that you refuse such a pretty niece these earrings which would make her happy? Will you permit me to present them to her?"

So saying, I hand the earrings to the young lady, who, blushing red as fire, looks at her aunt. The latter gently tells her to accept them and give me a kiss. The shopkeeper says to me that the earrings cost only three louis; at which the scene becomes a comedy, for the aunt angrily tells her she had been going to let her have them for two. The shopkeeper maintains that she had said three. At that the old woman, who was right and who could not bear to let the cheating shopkeeper profit so shamelessly by my politeness, tells the little girl to put down the earrings, and all would have been well; but she spoiled everything by saying that if I would give her niece the three louis she would go and buy earrings twice as pretty in some other shop. As it made no difference to me, though I could not help smiling, I laid the three louis down in front of the young lady, who was still holding the earrings; but the shopkeeper takes them, saying that the bargain had been struck, that the earrings belonged to the young lady and the money to herself. The aunt then called her a cheat, the shopkeeper called her a bawd, passers-by stopped, and foreseeing unpleasantness I gently led out the aunt and the niece, who, delighted to have the pretty earrings, did not care that I had been made to pay a louis too much for them. We will return to the girl at the proper time and place.

I took my Baret, who had made me throw away twenty louis which her husband would have regretted more than I did, back to the church door. She told me on the way that she could come to spend five or six days at Little Poland and that it was her husband himself who would ask me to do them the favor.

"When?"

"No later than tomorrow. Come and buy a few pairs of stockings, I will have a headache, and my husband will talk to you."

I went and, not seeing her, asked him where she was. He said she was sick in bed and that she needed to breathe good country air for a few days. I offered him an apartment at Little Poland, and his face lighted up.

"I will go and ask her to accept," I said; "in the meanwhile, pack me up a dozen pairs of stockings."

I go up, I find her in bed, laughing despite her made-to-order headache. I tell her the thing is done and that she will be told so within a minute. Her husband comes up with my stockings and tells her that I will be kind enough to put her up in my house for a few days; she expresses her gratitude, she is sure she will recover her health by breathing good air, and I ask her to excuse me beforehand if my business prevents me from giving her as much of my company as politeness demands; but that she will lack for nothing and that her husband can come to sup with us every day and leave as early in the morning as he pleases. After thanking me at length, Baret ended by saying that he would have his sister come for all the time that she was to stay at my house. I left, saying that I would give orders that day, and that they would be taken care of whenever they appeared, whether I was at home or not. On the next day but one, coming home at midnight, I learned from my cook that the couple had eaten a good supper and gone to bed. I told her I would have dinner and supper there every day and would be at home to no one.

The next morning when I woke I learned that Baret had left at daybreak, that he had said he would not come back until suppertime, and that his wife was still asleep. I at once paid her my first visit, and after congratulating ourselves again and again on being in unhampered possession of each other, we breakfasted, after which I locked my door and we surrendered to the God of Love.

Surprised to find her just as I had left her the last time I had held her in my arms, I said that I hoped— but she did not let me finish my protest. She said that her husband believed he had done what he had not done, and that it was for us to put him in a position to have no doubt of it in the future. Indeed, it was doing him a necessary service. So Love was the priest at this first sacrifice which my Baret made to Hymen, and I never saw the altar so stained with blood. In her youthful person I observed the greatest satisfaction arising from the proof she was giving me of her courage and from the conviction she was arousing in my inmost being that her passion was of the most genuine kind. I assured her again and again that I would be forever constant to her; and she filled my cup of joy by assuring me that she counted on it. We did not get out of bed except to make our toilets, and we dined together perfectly happy, sure that we would renew our desires only to have the pleasure of quenching them by fresh enjoyments.

"How did you manage," I asked her over dessert, "filled as I know you to be with the fire of Venus, to keep what is due to marriage until you were seventeen?"

"I never loved, that is all. I have been loved, but I could not be persuaded. My father may have believed otherwise when, a month ago, I asked him to get me married quickly."

"Why did you hurry him so?"

"Because I knew that when the Duke of Elbeuf came back from the country he would oblige me to marry a man I loathed and who wanted me at any price."

"Who is this man whom you loathed?"

"One of his pets. A base, infamous swine. The monster! he sleeps with his master who, at the age of eighty-four, insists that he has become a woman and cannot live except with such a husband."

"Is he handsome?"

"Everyone says so, but to me he is revolting."

My charming Baret spent eight days with me, each as happy as the first. I have seldom seen women as pretty as she was, and never any as white. Her dainty breasts, her smooth abdomen, her rounded hips which rose from her flanks to meet her thighs in a curve which no geometrician could ever draw, offered my hungry eyes the beauty which no philosopher has yet been able to

define. I never stopped looking at her except when my
inability to satisfy the desires she aroused in me made
me unhappy. The frieze of the altar on which my flame
had ascended to heaven was a composition into which
nothing entered but little curls of the finest and palest
gold imaginable. In vain did my fingers try to straighten
them; the curls, merely assuming a different form,
showed me that it was impossible. My Baret shared my
intoxication and my ecstasies in a state of perfect calm,
never surrendering to Venus until she felt every element
of her charming person in tumult. She then became like
a dead woman; and she seemed to recover her senses
only to reassure me by demonstrating that she was not.
Two or three days after she went home I gave her two
Mézières[26] notes for five thousand francs each. Her husband was cleared of debt and found himself in a position
to go on with his manufactory, keeping his work people,
and wait for the end of the war.

At the beginning of November I sold ten shares in my
manufactory to Sieur Garnier,[27] of the Rue du Mail,[28]
for fifty thousand francs, giving him one third of the
painted fabrics in my warehouse and accepting a comptroller appointed by him and paid by the company.
Three days after signing the contract I received the
money; but the doctor who was in charge of the warehouse emptied it and made off—a robbery which could
not possibly have been carried out unless he was in con-
nivance with the painter. To make the blow still worse
for me, Garnier had me served with a summons to repay
him the fifty thousand francs. I replied that I owed him
nothing since his comptroller had already taken office;
so the loss must fall equally on all the partners. I was
advised to go to court. Garnier began by declaring the
contract nul and void, even casting a suspicion of fraud
on me. The doctor's surety had disappeared. It had
been from a merchant who had just gone bankrupt.

Garnier obtained an order sequestrating everything in the manufactory and my horses and carriages, which were at Little Poland in the hands of the "Butter King." Beset by such difficulties, I dismissed the working girls and all the employees and servants at my manufactory. Only the painter remained in the building, having nothing to complain of since he had always seen to it that he paid himself his share when fabrics were sold. My attorney was an honest man, but my advocate, who assured me every day that I could not lose my case, was a scoundrel. In the course of the proceedings Garnier sent me an accursed summons ordering me to pay, which I at once took to my advocate, who assured me that he would lodge an appeal the same day and who did nothing of the kind, thus appropriating to himself all the money I had laid out to recover what was mine. The next two summonses were kept from reaching me, and a warrant was issued without my knowledge to arrest me for having failed to appear. I was arrested at eight o'clock in the morning in the Rue Saint-Denis[29] in my own carriage, the chief constable sitting beside me while another, sitting beside my coachman, forced him to drive me to the Fort-l'Évêque.[30]

As soon as I got there the record clerk told me that if I paid fifty thousand francs or gave security, I could go home at once; but having neither the money nor the security ready I remained in prison. When I told the clerk that I had received only one summons he said that it happened only too often but that it was difficult to prove. I demanded that writing materials be brought to the room in which I was put, and I informed my advocate and my attorney and then all my friends, beginning with Madame d'Urfé and ending with my brother, who had just married.[31] My attorney came at once; but my advocate only wrote to me, assuring me that he had lodged the appeal and so, my arrest being

illegal, I could make it cost my opponent dearly but
that I must be patient for a few days and let him act.
Manon Balletti sent me her earrings through her brother;
Madame du Rumain sent me her advocate, who was
known for his honesty, writing me that if I needed five
hundred louis she could send them to me the next day;
my brother did not answer me. Madame d'Urfé answered
that she would expect me for dinner. I thought she had
gone mad. By eleven o'clock my room was full of people.
Baret, who had heard of my arrest, came in tears to offer
me his shop. I was informed that a lady had arrived in
a hackney coach, and not seeing her appear I asked why
she was not allowed to come up. I was told that she had
left after conferring privately with the record clerk.
From the description I was given of her I gathered that
she was Madame d'Urfé.

I was extremely annoyed to be where I was, for it
could not but hurt my reputation all over Paris, aside
from the fact that the discomfort of the prison distressed
me. Since I had thirty thousand francs in ready money
and sixty thousand in jewels, I could have deposited the
amount and left at once, but I could not bring myself
to do so, despite Madame du Rumain's advocate, who
tried to persuade me to get out of prison no matter by
what means. According to him I need only deposit half
the amount, which he would "pin down" at the court
record office until an appeal brought me a verdict which,
he assured me, would be in my favor.

While we were still discussing this the jailer came to
tell me that I was free and that a lady was waiting at
the door for me in her carriage. I sent Leduc (such was
my valet's name) to find out who the lady was, and
when I learned that it was Madame d'Urfé I made my
bow to everyone. It was noon. I had spent four very disagreeable hours[32] in the place.

Madame d'Urfé received me in her berlin with great

dignity. A judge[33] who was with her asked my pardon
in the name of his nation and country, in which foreigners were likely to suffer such indignities. I thanked
Madame in a few words, saying that I was delighted to
be in her debt but that it was Garnier who profited
from her noble generosity. She answered with a smile
that he would not so easily profit from it and that we
would discuss the matter at dinner. She advised me to
go walking in the Tuileries and the Palais-Royal at once,
to convince the public that the rumor of my imprisonment was false. I took her advice, saying that she would
see me again at two o'clock.

After showing myself to good purpose in the two
great promenades, where, pretending not to notice it, I
saw all my acquaintances astonished to see me, I went
and returned her earrings to my dear Manon, who gave
a cry when I appeared. After thanking her and assuring
the whole family that my arrest had been due to a plot
for which I would make all those who had taken a hand
in it pay dearly, I left, promising that I would come to
supper with her, and I went to dine with Madame d'Urfé,
who at once made me laugh by swearing her Genius had
informed her that I had arranged to be arrested on
purpose to get myself talked about, for reasons which I
alone knew. She said that after learning from the record
clerk at the Fort-l'Évêque how matters stood she had
gone home for some municipal obligations[34] she owned
which would have covered a hundred thousand francs
and had deposited them; but that Garnier would have
to deal with her before he got the money if I should be
unable to obtain justice.

She said I ought to begin by attacking my advocate
in criminal court since it was obvious that he had not
lodged my appeal. I left assuring her that she would
recover her security in a few days.

After showing myself in the lobbies of the two theaters

I went to sup with Manon Balletti, who was delighted to have seized the opportunity to give me a proof of her affection. Her joy knew no bounds when I told her I was going to give up my manufactory, for she thought my working girls were the reason why I could not make up my mind to marry her.

I spent the whole of the next day with Madame du Rumain.[35] I felt how deeply I was indebted to her; but she had no such feeling; on the contrary, she thought she could never sufficiently show me her gratitude for the oracles which insured her against ever taking a false step. Despite all the intelligence the lady possessed, she was taken in. I was sorry that I could not open her eyes, and mortified when I considered that I was deceiving her and that but for my deceit she would not feel the regard for me which she showed.

My imprisonment, though it lasted only a few hours, disgusted me with Paris and inspired me with a hatred for all legal proceedings which I still feel. I was involved in two, one against Garnier,[36] the other, in criminal court, against the advocate. My soul was in torment every time I had to curry favor, spend my money on advocates, and waste my hours, which I thought only well used in procuring me pleasures. In this state of turmoil I resolved to assure myself of a regular income sufficient to give me complete peace of mind. I decided to abandon everything, make a second journey to Holland to renew my financial resources, and then return to Paris and invest all the capital I should have accumulated in an annuity for the lifetimes of two persons. The two lifetimes were to be mine and my wife's; and the wife was to be Manon Balletti. I informed her of my plan, and she could not wait to see it executed.

I began by giving up my house[37] in Little Poland, which was to remain mine only to the end of the year; and I withdrew from the Military School the eighty thou-

sand francs which served as the security for my office in
the Rue Saint-Denis. In this way I resigned my paltry
position of collector of the lottery. I gave my office to
my clerk, who had married, and so made him a small
fortune. The man who stood security for him was, as
always, a friend of his wife's; but the poor fellow died
two years later.

Not wanting to leave Madame d'Urfé involved in a
suit against Garnier, I went to Versailles to persuade
the Abbé de Laville, his great friend, to become the
mediator in a compromise. The Abbé, who saw that he
was in the wrong, undertook it, and a few days later
wrote me to go and talk with Garnier himself, assuring
me that I would find him prepared to listen to reason.
He was at Rueil,[38] and I went there. It was a country
house four leagues from Paris which had cost him four
hundred thousand francs. Garnier, who had been Monsieur d'Argenson's cook, had made a fortune in provisions during the last war but one.[39] He lived in opu-
lence, but having the misfortune to be seventy years
old and still to love women he could not be happy. I
found him with three girls, sisters and of good family
as I later learned. They were poor and he kept them. At
table I observed that they showed a certain dignity and
modesty through the humiliation with which poverty afflicts all people of sensibility. Need forced them to pay
court to the old unmarried profligate, with whom they
had perhaps to undergo painful private relations. After
dinner he fell asleep, leaving me to entertain the young
ladies, and when he woke we withdrew to discuss our
business.

When he learned that I was on the verge of leaving,
perhaps never to return to Paris, and that he could not
stop me, he foresaw that the Marquise d'Urfé would use
every legal trick against him to drag the thing out as
long as she pleased and perhaps win the suit. I had to

spend the night there. In the morning he told me, as his last word, that he wanted twenty-five thousand francs or he would litigate until his dying day. I answered that he would find the amount in the hands of Madame d'Urfé's notary after he had released her security at the court record office at the Fort-l'Évêque.

Madame d'Urfé was not persuaded that I had done well to make an arrangement with Garnier until I told her that the Order[40] demanded that I should not leave Paris without first settling all the affairs which could lead to the supposition that I had gone because I could not pay my debts.

I went to take leave of the Duke of Choiseul,[41] who said that he would write Monsieur d'Affry to help me in all my negotiations if I could arrange a loan at five percent, whether from the States-General or from a private company. He said that I could assure everyone that peace would be concluded during the course of the winter and that I could also be sure that he would not let me be denied what was due me when I returned to France. Such were his words to me, and he knew that peace would not be made; but I had no project in mind, and I was sorry I had entrusted Monsieur de Boulogne with my project concerning wills, in which the new Comptroller, Silhouette, showed no interest.

I sold my horses, my carriages, and all my furniture, and I stood security for my brother, who had gone into debt to a tailor, but he was sure that he would soon be able to pay all his debts since he was finishing several pictures for which the people who had ordered them were waiting impatiently.

I left Manon in tears, but I was sure I should make her happy when I returned to Paris.

I set off with one hundred thousand francs in bills of exchange and as much again in jewels, all by myself in my post chaise and preceded by Leduc, who liked to ride at full gallop. He was a Spaniard eighteen years of age whom I cherished because no one dressed my hair better than he. A Swiss lackey, also on horseback, served me as courier. It was December 1st[42] of the year 1759. I had in my carriage Helvétius' *L'Esprit*,[43] which I had not yet found time to read. After reading it I was even more surprised by the sensation it had created than by the Parlement which had condemned it and done everything possible to ruin its author, who was a most agreeable man and far more intelligent than his book. I found nothing new either in the historical part concerning the manners of nations, which was in many places sheer invention, or in the system of ethics founded on reason. It had all been said again and again, and Blaise Pascal[44] had said far more, though more guardedly. If Helvétius wanted to go on living in France he had to retract. He preferred the pleasant life he led there to honor and his own system of philosophy, that is, his own mind. His wife, whose soul was nobler than her husband's, wanted to sell everything they had in France and go to live in Holland rather than submit to the dishonor of a palinode; but her husband thought he should prefer anything to exile. He would perhaps have followed his wife's advice if he could have foreseen that his retraction would make his book a laughingstock. By retracting he appeared to say that he had not known what he was writing, that he had only been joking, that all his arguments were paralogisms. But a number of intelligent minds did not wait until he had contradicted himself to contemn his system. What! because in everything he does man is always the slave of his self-interest, must it follow that any feeling of gratitude becomes absurd and that no act can earn us merit or blame? Are criminals not to be hated and honest men not to be loved? Pitiful philosophy!

It could have been demonstrated to Helvétius that it

is false that in everything we do our own interest is our prime motive and the first to be consulted. Then Helvé- tius did not admit virtue, which is very odd. He was himself highly virtuous. Is it possible that he never saw that he was an honest man? It would be amusing if what made him publish his book was a feeling of modesty. Was he right to make himself contemptible in order to escape the stigma of being proud? Modesty is a virtue only when it is natural; if it is assumed, or practiced because it has been inculcated in school, it is only hy- pocrisy. I never knew a man more naturally modest than the famous D'Alembert.[45]

I spent two days in Brussels, happening to put up at the "Empress"[46] where Miss *XCV* and Farsetti were staying. I pretended not to know her. I went to the Moer- dick[47] and crossed it, leaving my post chaise on the hither side. At The Hague I put up at the "Prince of Orange." The innkeeper persuaded me to eat at the public table when he told me who the company were. He said they were staff officers of the Hanoverian army, English la- dies, and a Prince Piccolomini[48] with his wife. I at once decided to go down to supper.

Unknown to everyone and saying nothing, I attentively examined the face, the manners, and the bearing of the supposed Italian Princess, who was pretty enough, and more especially of her husband, whom I thought I knew. I learned at table that the famous Saint-Germain was staying at the same inn.

Just as I was going to bed Prince Piccolomini enters my room and embraces me as an old acquaintance.

"One glance that you gave me," he said, "showed me that you recognized me immediately. I recognized you instantly too, despite the sixteen years which have passed since we last met in Vicenza.[49] Tomorrow you may tell everyone that we have recognized each other; that I am not a prince, but Count Piccolomini, and here is my passport from the King of Naples, which I beg you to read.''

He had not let me say a word, and I could not place him. I read the passport and I find ''Ruggero di Rocco, Count Piccolomini.'' I then recollect a Rocco Ruggeri who taught fencing in Vicenza, I look at him, and I remember him. I congratulate him on no longer practicing the profession. He answers that, his father still being alive at that time and not giving him anything to live on, he practiced the profession to keep from starving, concealing his name and rank. After his death he had gone to take over his inheritance and at Rome had married the beautiful lady I had seen. He ended by inviting me to come to his room after dinner, where I would find pleasant company and a faro bank which he kept. He said frankly that if I liked he would take me into partnership with him and that I would not lose by it. I promised to pay him a visit.

After visiting the Jew Boas and politely refusing the lodging he offered me I made my bow to Count d'Affry, who, after the death of Her Highness the Princess of Orange, Regent of the Netherlands, had assumed the rank of Ambassador.[50] He received me very well, saying that if I had come back hoping to enter into some transaction which would be profitable to France, I was wasting my time. He said that the action of the Comptroller-General Silhouette[51] had lowered the credit of the nation to such a degree that its bankruptcy was expected. He was very sorry about it. Though he kept saying that payments were only suspended for a year and that it made no difference, he was wasting his breath; everyone was indignant.

After thus bemoaning his situation, he asked me if I knew a certain Count of Saint-Germain who had recently[52] arrived at The Hague, whom he had never seen, and who said that the King had authorized him to borrow a hundred millions.

''When people come to ask me about him,'' he said, ''I

can only answer that I do not know him, for I am afraid
I may compromise myself. You cannot but see that such
an answer from me must only hamper his negotiations,
but it is his own fault. Why did he not bring me a letter
from the Duke of Choiseul or from Madame la Marquise?
I believe the man is an impostor, but I shall have information about him in a week or ten days."

I then told him everything that was known about this
strange and extraordinary man, and he was surprised
to learn that the King had given him an apartment at
Chambord; but when I told him that he possessed the
secret of making diamonds he laughed and said he no
longer doubted he could find the hundred millions. He
invited me to dinner the next day.

I had scarcely got back to the inn before I sent in my
name to the Count of Saint-Germain, who had two
Haiduks[53] at his door. He received me by saying that I
had forestalled him.

"I imagine," he said, "that you have come here to do
something for our Court; but you will find it difficult,
for the Exchange is scandalized by the action that idiot
Silhouette has just taken. However, that will not prevent
me from finding a hundred millions; I gave my word for
it to Louis XV, whom I may call my friend, and in three
or four weeks my mission will be accomplished."

"Monsieur d'Affry will help you to succeed."

"I do not need him. I shall not even go to see him, for
he might boast that he had helped me."

"You go to the Court, I presume, and the Duke of
Brunswick[54] could be useful to you."

"He is of no interest to me. I do not care to make his
acquaintance. I need only to go to Amsterdam. My own
credit is enough. I love the King of France, for there is
not a better man than he in the whole kingdom."

"Then come down to dinner at the common table, you
will find people of distinction."

"You know I do not eat; besides, I never sit down at

a table where I may find people with whom I am not acquainted.''

''Then good-by, My Lord, we shall meet again in Amsterdam.''

I went down to the public room, where, while waiting for dinner to be served, I chatted with the officers who were present. When I was asked if I knew Prince Piccolomini I replied that I had recognized him after supper and that he was a count, not a prince.

He came down with his wife, who spoke only Italian. I paid her my respects, and we sat down to dinner.

CHAPTER I

1. *Valdobbiádene:* In the southern foothills of the Alps, about 12 miles south of Feltre and on the opposite side of the Piave Valley.
2. *State Inquisitor:* Lorenzo Grimani (1689 - after 1780), Venetian patrician, several times Senator, State Inquisitor from Oct. 1, 1756.
3. *Saepe . . . impellens:* "Which often forbids, seldom prompts"—Cicero, *De Divinatione,* 1, 54. (Cf. Vol. 1, p. 158.)
4. *Vitturi:* Probably the then Mayor of Treviso, Bartolomeo Vitturi (1719-1773), Venetian patrician.
5. *Thirteen:* At this season, about 7:00 A.M.
6. *Marcantonio Grimani:* Nephew of Lorenzo Grimani (see note 2), later Procuratore di San Marco, married Maria Pisani in 1746.
7. *Lire:* The Venetian lira; a zecchino contained 22 lire.
8. *The river:* The river Piave, which C. must have crossed south of Feltre.
9. *Rombenchi:* Gabriele Rombenchi was then the Spanish and Neapolitan Consul in Venice.
10. *Capuchin:* One of the three principal branches of the Franciscan Order; the monastery mentioned by C. cannot be certainly identified; so too C.'s route from Treviso through Valdobbiádene to Borgo di Valsugana is difficult to follow in detail, since his statements, especially in regard to the length of his alleged day's journeys on foot, are exaggerated.
11. *Twenty-two o'clock:* At this season about 4:00 P.M.
12. *Zecchino:* A gold coin minted in Venice from the thirteenth century (cf. note 7).
13. *La Scala:* Venetian border post between Feltre and Valsugana.
14. *Borgo di Valsugana:* Principal town of the upper Brenta

Valley (Val Sugana); it belonged to the bishopric of Trento.

15. *Pergine:* Some six miles south of Trento, near the Lago di Caldonazzo.

16. *Count d'Alberg:* The reference may be to Baron de Dalberg, a French Freemason.

17. *Mench:* Probably the proprietor of the business house of G. A. Menz in Bolzano, which also acted as a bank.

18. *Arrived in Munich:* C. here added and then crossed out "about the middle of the month."

19. *The "Stag":* The inn "Zum Goldenen Hirschen" was located at 18 Theatinerstrasse from 1728 to 1861. Its guest book for 1756 does not include the names of C. and the Venetians he mentions.

20. *Countess Coronini:* Maria Theresia, Countess Coronini-Cronberg (died 1761), lady-in-waiting at the Bavarian Court and later at the Court of Emperor Charles VII (cf. Vol. 4, Chap. II).

21. *Santa Giustina:* Old church and convent of the Augustinian nuns in Venice; the convent was secularized in 1810.

22. *Elector:* Maximilian III Joseph von Wittelsbach (1727-1777), son of Emperor Charles VII, Elector from 1745.

23. *Somaschians:* There is no record of a Somaschian establishment in Munich.

24. *Confessor:* Father Daniel Stadler, S.J. (1705-1764); he was the Elector's tutor and later his confessor.

25. *The Empress:* Empress Maria Amalia died Dec. 11, 1756.

26. *Hot stove:* The fear of being buried alive was common in 18th-century Munich. The dead were left on a bier as long as possible; and in winter a stove was kept burning close by.

27. *Michele dall'Agata:* Venetian dancer and ballet master (1722-1794); he was active in Munich from 1752 to 1756.

28. *Gardela:* Ursula Maria Gardela, also Gardella (1730-1793 or '94), daughter of a Venetian gondolier; she was a dancer (cf. Vol. 1, Chap. VI).

29. *Malipiero:* Alvise Gasparo Malipiero (1664-1745), Venetian patrician and Senator.

30. *Teresa:* Teresa Imer (1723-1797), celebrated Italian actress and theater director. For the episode to which C. here refers, see Vol. 1, Chap. VI.

31. *St. Moritz:* Former collegiate church in Augsburg, built in the 11th century, restored in the 15th and 18th centuries, partly destroyed in 1944; now a parish church.

32. *Darmstadt:* Joseph, Landgrave of Hesse-Darmstadt (1699-1768), Prince-Bishop from 1740. C., who was never at home in German, writes "d'Armestat."

33. *Madame Rivière:* She was the widow of a Polish official. C. doubtless met her and her children during his first stay in Paris, though this is the first time he mentions her in his memoirs.

34. *The elder:* Marie Rivière (born ca. 1740), studied ballet in Paris ca. 1750 and appeared as a dancer first in Dresden from 1753 and in Paris from 1757. Her projected marriage to the actor Désormes did not take place; instead, she accepted an engagement to dance in Parma and there she became mistress of the Regent.

35. *Brothers:* Marin Balbi (1719-1783), Venetian patrician and monk of the Somaschian Order, had five brothers.

36. *The Republic:* The Republic of Venice.

37. *Messer Grande:* Title of the Venetian Chief of Police (also Missier Grande or Capitan Grande).

38. *"The Four":* Name of a group of four prison cells at the disposition only of the Venetian State Inquisitors (cf. Vol. 4, Chap. XIII, n. 6).

39. *Rezzonico:* Carlo Rezzonico (1693-1769), from 1758 Pope as Clement XIII.

40. *The "Spirit":* Auberge de l'Esprit. Its existence is first recorded in 1306. Rousseau stayed there in 1765, and Goethe and Herder in 1770. It was torn down in the 1930's.

41. *Balletti:* The Balletti family then lived in the Rue du Petit Lion Saint-Sauveur, near the Comédie Italienne.

42. *Fifteen years old:* Maria Magdalena, known as Manon, Balletti (1740-1776), was baptized on April 4, 1740; so C. makes her too young by two years.

43. *In the same street:* In the house of a wigmaker named Quinson.

44. *Hôtel de Bourbon:* C. sometimes writes Hôtel, sometimes Palais, de Bourbon. He refers to the old Palais Bourbon, built in 1722, which was replaced by a new building in 1772 (now the Chamber of Deputies).

45. *Head:* Although De Bernis was appointed a minister on Jan. 2, 1757, he did not take the oath as Secretary of State for Foreign Affairs until June 29th of that year.

46. *Pont Royal:* Built 1685-1689 from plans by Mansart, it connects the Tuileries with the Quai d'Orsay. Hackney coaches waited near the end of the bridge on the left bank of the Seine to be hired for the journey to Versailles.

47. *"Chamber pot": Pot de chambre,* a type of hackney coach then much in use.

48. *Cantillana:* Don José Baeza y Vicentello, Count of Cantillana (1714-1770), Spanish (not Neapolitan) Ambassador in Venice 1738-1740, then in Turin, and from 1753 in Paris.

49. *Assassin:* Robert François Damiens (1715-1757); the attempted assassination took place on Jan. 5, 1757, about 6:00 P.M.

50. *Martinière:* Germain Pichault de la Martinière (1697-1783), first surgeon to Louis XV from 1747.


CHAPTER II

1. *Écu:* Silver coin of two denominations; the *gros écu* was worth six francs, the *petit écu* three.

2. *She:* C. first wrote "Mathilde," then crossed it out and substituted the pronoun (cf. Vol. 4, Chap. XII, n. 6).

3. *Louis:* Gold coin, first minted ca. 1640. Value: 24 francs.

4. *Erizzo:* Niccolò Erizzo (1722-1806), Venetian patrician, Ambassador of the Republic in Paris from 1754 to 1760, later in Vienna; Procurator from 1761.

5. *Madame la Marquise:* The Marquise de Pompadour (cf. Vol. 3, Chap. IX, n. 30).

6. *Choiseul:* Étienne François, Count of Stainville (1719-1785), from 1758 Duke of Choiseul, French Ambassador in Rome from 1753 to 1757, in Vienna from 1757 to 1758, Minister of Foreign Affairs from 1758 to 1761 and from 1766 to 1770; Minister of Marine from 1761 to 1766, Minister of War from 1761 to 1770.

7. *Boulogne:* Jean de Boulogne, also Boullogne, Count of Nogent (1690-1769), Comptroller-General from 1757 to 1759.

The office of Comptroller-General (Contrôleur général) had existed from 1547; but it was not made a ministerial post until 1661. From then on the Comptroller-General was at the head of the entire administration in the departments of agriculture, commerce, finance, and domestic affairs.

8. *My first visit:* Choiseul later asserted that he had never met C. personally. Perhaps he did not remember him or thought it best to disavow his acquaintance; in any case he provided C. with a letter of recommendation.

9. *Under the Leads: I Piombi,* prison so named from its situation under the lead roof of the Doge's Palace. For C.'s confinement there and his escape, see Vol. 4, Chaps. XII ff.

10. *Chancellery:* The Cancelleria Ducale (Doge's Chancellery), through which C. passed when he made his escape from the Leads (see Vol. 4, Chap. XVI).

11. *Pâris-Duverney:* Joseph de Pâris-Duverney (1684-1770); son of a tavernkeeper, he made a fortune from provisioning the army, was ennobled ca. 1720, from 1751 First Intendant of the École Militaire; intimate friend of De Bernis.

12. *Military School:* The École Militaire Royale, on the Champ de Mars, was founded in 1751; it was open to sons of the nobility between the ages of eight and eleven, who were educated there for four years. Upon completing their studies they were commissioned second lieutenant (*sous-lieutenant*) or cornet (*cornette*).

13. *Plaisance:* Name of the château which Pâris-Duverney had built at Neuilly-Plaisance, east of Paris.

14. *Pâris de Montmartel:* Jean Pâris de Montmartel, Count of Sampigny (1690-1760), Councilor of State, banker to the Court, and Comptroller-General.

15. *Le Normand:* Charles François Paul Le Normand de Tournehem, Farmer-General; about 1720 he was the lover of Louise Madeleine Poisson, the mother of Jeanne Antoinette Poisson, later Marquise de Pompadour.

16. *Law:* John Law of Lauriston (1671-1729), Scottish financier; in 1715 he was granted a patent to establish an issuing bank in France. His "system" was based on issuing notes secured by the French colonial possessions in North America. Under his direction the Compagnie d'Occident, which he

founded in 1717 (later the Compagnie des Indes), issued stock which soon became the object of frenzied speculation. His excessive issuing of stock and bank notes brought on an inflation in 1720 and then a desperate economic crisis in France. Law had to leave the country and died in poverty in Venice.

17. *Minister of Foreign Affairs:* C. first wrote "de l'abbé de Bernis," then canceled it and substituted "M. de R. S.," which he finally replaced by "ministre des Affaires étrangères." This indicates that, when he was writing this chapter, C. was at pains to conceal De Bernis's name. It further indicates that the existing version of his relationship with M. M. and De Bernis, in which the name of the latter is given in full, did not receive its final form until after De Bernis's death in 1794.

18. *Intendant of Finances:* In 18th-century France there were usually six Intendants des Finances; they divided the various aspects of the financial administration among them, under the direction of the Finance Minister.

19. *Harpocrates:* Greek form of the name of an Egyptian god, the son of Isis and the dying Osiris; his images show him holding one finger to his mouth, so he was (probably erroneously) later taken to be the God of Silence.

20. *Fontenelle:* Bernard Le Bovier de Fontenelle (1657-1757), celebrated French writer, a forerunner of the Enlightenment.

21. *Soubise:* Charles de Rohan, Prince of Soubise (1715-1787), Marshal of France. The Franco-Austrian army under his command was defeated by Frederick the Great at Rossbach, Thuringia, in 1757, early in the Seven Years' War (1756-1763). A protégé of the Marquise de Pompadour, he was appointed to the supreme command of the French army on Feb. 5, 1758.

22. *Calzabigi:* Giovanni Antonio Calzabigi (born ca. 1714), Secretary to the Ambassador from the Kingdom of the Two Sicilies in Paris from 1750; co-organizer of the Loterie de l'École Militaire (C.'s lottery) in 1757, financial adviser in Berlin ca. 1760.

23. *Lottery:* C. refers to a "lottery." Lotteries in various forms had long been known in France. But C. applies the

term to the so-called *lotto genovese*, the basic conception
of which is very similar to that of the modern "numbers
game." This form of lottery goes back to the election of the
Great Council in the Republic of Genoa; ninety names
were written on slips and placed in an urn, from which
five were drawn; the citizens bet on the results. The *lotto*
with ninety numbers was officially instituted in Genoa in
1620. Players could stake on one, two, three, four, or five
numbers. A combination of two numbers was termed an
*ambo*, of three a *terno*, of four a *quaterna*, of five a *cinquina*.

24. *Insurance companies:* There were already insurance companies in the 18th century, but they only covered marine
risks.

25. *Castelletto:* Schedule of the players' ventures in public
lotteries.

26. *Council:* The Council (Conseil) of the École Militaire
then consisted of the Minister of War, the First Intendant,
the Commander-in-Chief of the army, and the Intendant
Pâris-Duverney.

27. *Quaterna . . . cinquina:* Combinations of four or five
numbers staked on in a lottery and coming out in the same
drawing (cf. note 23, above, and Vol. 3, Chap. VI, n. 32).
The winner of a *quaterna* received 60,000 times his stake,
the winner of a *cinquina* received an astronomical sum.
According to A. Zottoli (*G. Casanova*, Rome, 1945, I, 57 ff.)
C.'s calculations here contain many errors.

28. *Terno:* Combination of three numbers staked on in a
lottery and coming out at the same drawing (cf. note 23,
above, and Vol. 3, Chap. VI, n. 32). The winner of a *terno*
received 4800 times his stake.

29. *Courteuil:* Jacques Dominique de Barberie, Marquis de
Courteuil (1697-1768), statesman, Intendant of Finances
from 1752.

30. *My brother:* Ranieri Calzabigi (1714-1795), co-organizer
of the École Militaire lottery in 1757, later held a government financial post in Vienna; he was also a writer and
composed the libretti for his friend Gluck's *Orfeo ed Euridice*
(1762) and *Alceste* (1767).

31. *L'Hôpital:* Paul François de Galucci, Sieur de l'Hôpital

(1697-1776), French Ambassador Extraordinary in Naples from 1740 to 1750 and in St. Petersburg from 1756 to 1761.

32. *Till the Greek Kalends:* I.e., "indefinitely," "for ever and ever." (Unlike the Romans, the Greeks did not reckon by kalends.)

33. *La Générale La Mothe:* Calzabigi's wife Simone was the widow of General Antoine Duru de La Mothe (died 1735). She had inherited from him the privilege of being the sole distributor of "gouttes d'or," a medicine highly esteemed at the time.

34. *Baroness Blanche:* Baroness Anne Pétronille Thérèse Blanche (ca. 1714-1763).

35. *De Vaux:* Louis Basile de Bernage, Sieur de Vaux, Baroness Blanche's lover from 1746.

36. *La Présidente:* Since many French ladies of some distinction used this title at the period, it is impossible to determine to which of them C. here refers.

37. *Madame Razzetti:* Wife of A. Razzetti, musical director of the Royal Theater in Turin (1743-1751), later violinist at the Paris Opéra.

38. *Fondpertuis:* Papillon de Fondpertuis, Intendant and Farmer-General from 1762. C. confuses him with his relative Denis Pierre Jean, Marquis de Papillon de la Ferté (1727-1794), also a Master of the Revels, who was Madame Razzetti's lover.

39. *Master of the Revels: Intendant des Menus Plaisirs du Roi.* This official disbursed the funds set aside for concerts, balls, entertainments, theatrical performances, and the like.

40. *Private apartments:* The *petits appartements* in the Palace of Versailles were the living quarters of the royal family. Louis XV's suite of rooms was connected by a staircase with the suite occupied by the Marquise de Pompadour.

41. *Laville:* Jean Ignace de Laville (ca. 1690-1774), abbé and diplomat; Secretary for Foreign Affairs.

42. *Up there:* The Marquise alludes to the exchange between herself and C. at their first meeting (cf. Vol. 3, Chap. IX). "Those gentlemen" are the Venetian State Inquisitors.

43. *D'Alembert:* Jean Le Rond d'Alembert (1717-1783), famous mathematician and philosopher and a co-editor of the *Encyclopédie* (cf. Vol. 2, Chap. X, n. 10).

*Gynecological Chair and Obstetrical Instruments*

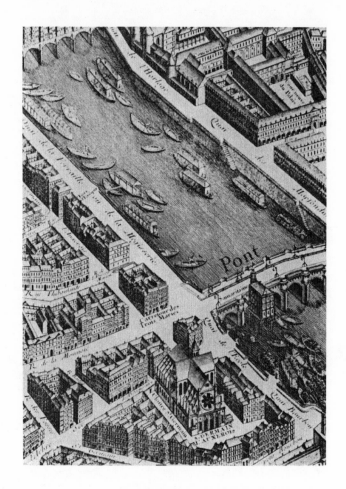

*Fort-l'Évêque, Paris*

44. *Franc:* Silver coin first minted in 1575; later, money of account which, by the 18th century, had become a synonym for the livre; value, 20 sous.
45. *I opened the sixth:* C.'s name does not appear in the extant list of lottery collectors for 1758, presumably because he used the title of Director; he is listed late in 1758 and in 1759 as the manager of an office in the Rue Saint-Martin.
46. *La Cattolica:* Giuseppe Agostino Bonanno Filingieri e del Bosco, Principe di Roccafiorita e della Cattolica (died 1779), Spanish Grandee, Neapolitan Ambassador Extraordinary in Madrid from 1761 to 1770.
47. *First drawing:* It did not take place until April 18, 1758; C. is here anticipating events.
48. *Ambi:* The player of an *ambo* staked on two numbers. If he won he received 240 times his stake (cf. note 23 to this chapter).
49. *Madame Silvestre:* Antonia de Silvestre (1683 - after 1757), wife of the painter Louis de Silvestre (1675-1760), who was Director of the Dresden Academy from 1727 to 1748 and from 1752 Director of the Académie Royale de Peinture, Sculpture et Gravure in Paris.
50. *The celebrated gallery:* The Dresden Gallery, founded in 1722.
51. *He was received:* Francesco Casanova was admitted to the Académie in Aug. 1761 but was not made a full member until May 1763.


CHAPTER III

1. *Signora Manzoni:* Catterina Manzoni, née Capozzi (1706-1787), married to the Venetian notary Giovanni Maria Manzoni (1702-1786) in 1729; a staunch friend of C.'s, in whom she took a motherly interest during his early days in Venice (cf. especially Vol. 1, Chaps. IV and VI).
2. *Tiretta:* Count Edoardo Tiretta (1734 - ca. 1809), fled from Treviso to Paris in 1757; he later became Governor of Bengal.
3. *Pawn office: Monte di Pietà.* The one in Treviso (which belonged to the Republic of Venice) was managed by a

278 *History of My Life*

number of "Conservatori del Monte." (Cf. Vol. 2, Chap. VIII, n. 26.)

4. *Mine:* His father, Count Ghirardo Tiretta, had died in 1752.

5. *In mourning:* Many Parisians wore mourning as an expression of grief for the attempted assassination of the King.

6. *Lacoste:* Jean Emmanuel de Lacoste, also La Coste (ca. 1709 - after 1761), member of the Celestine Order, released from his vows ca. 1750; confidential agent of the Farmer-General Le Riche de la Pouplinière; sentenced to the Bastille and then to the galleys in 1760.

7. *Hôtel de Koelen:* No such establishment has been found in contemporary sources.

8. *Madame Lambertini:* Angelica Lambertini, also Lamberti (1714 - after 1759), of Modena; widow of Nicolas Jouvenel, also known as Marquis de Jouvenel (died 1749); she was notorious in Paris for her dissolute life and was sentenced to prison in 1759. She was not related to Pope Benedict XIV, whose civil name was Prospero Lambertini.

9. *Trévoux:* City on the Saône, about 15 miles north of Lyons. However, the lottery swindle was based on the so-called "Loterie de Gemont" (Gmund in Swabia).

10. *Lenoir:* He was an official in the municipal administration of Paris and had been Madame Lambertini's lover since 1753.

11. *Tax farming administration:* Farming out the collection of the royal revenues, especially taxes, to private individuals was a common practice under the Old Régime. Until 1726 different portions of the tax revenue were allotted to different tax farmers. In that year the collection of all taxes was consolidated under a Fermier Général, whose office was in the Hôtel des Fermes in Paris.

12. *A stout woman:* This person, to whom C. afterward always refers as "Madame XXX," has not yet been identified. Certain scenes in which C. makes her figure resemble episodes in Restif de la Bretonne's novel *Monsieur Nicolas* (first published 1794-1797). Though it cannot be proved, C. may well have borrowed from Restif.

13. *A niece:* C. calls her "Mademoiselle de la M—re" in the sequel. She has not yet been identified.

14. *Brelan:* French card game for from two to six players, played with 36 cards.

15. *Melun:* Town on the Seine, about 28 miles southeast of Paris.

16. *Parlement of Rouen:* The Parlements were the highest judicial courts in France under the Old Régime. In addition to the Paris Parlement, there were provincial Parlements, among which that of Rouen was not only one of the largest but was famous for its frequent opposition to the Crown.

17. *Noble:* As a member of the Parlement of Rouen, Mademoiselle de la M—re's father belonged to the so-called "noblesse de robe" ("nobility of the law"). Even this lesser nobility regarded marriage with a merchant as a misalliance.

18. *La Grève:* The Place de la Grève (now Place de l'Hôtel de Ville) was frequently the scene of executions.

19. *On the spot:* C. writes *sonica*, to which the editor adds "Sic!" But it is a perfectly good French word, still included in mid-19th-century dictionaries and usually glossed "in the nick of time." It may have that meaning here, for it is not beyond C.'s frequent looseness to be jumping from the scene he is recounting to the general consideration that it is almost too late to be securing places for an execution which is to be performed within a few days.

20. *Piquet à écrire:* It differed from the usual game of piquet by its method of scoring.

21. *"Comet":* A complicated card game, first introduced during the reign of Louis XV. (C. has said earlier that Mademoiselle de la M—re knew *no* card games.)

22. *Berryer:* Nicolas René Berryer de Renonville (1703-1762); Lieutenant-General of Police 1747, Minister of Marine 1758; protégé of the Marquise de Pompadour.

23. *Vae victis . . . :* Livy V, 48, where it is attributed to Brennus, leader of the Gauls, after his victory over the Romans ca. 390 B.C.

24. *Saxon porcelain:* From the manufactory at Meissen, the first of the kind in Europe, founded in 1710.

25. *March 28th:* Though the negotiations for the lottery were begun on Jan. 5, 1757, it was not authorized until Oct. 15th of that year and the offices were not opened until Feb. 1758.

Hence Damiens's execution took place before the establishment and the first drawing of the lottery. Cf. note 47 to
the preceding chapter.

26. *Horrible spectacle:* Damiens was sentenced to have his
flesh torn off with pincers and then to be quartered alive.

27. *Massacred:* The reference shows that this part of C.'s
memoirs was written or revised after 1793.

28. *Rue Saint-André-des-Arts:* In the 6th Arrondissement, near
the Seine.

29. *Hôtel de Buci:* A well-known restaurant at the time, in the
Rue de Buci in the 6th Arrondissement.

30. *Petits-paquets:* Also called *tiercets;* one of the many card
games of the period.

31. *Desforges:* Not certainly identified. He may be either (1)
the Abbé Jacques Desforges, a canon of Chartres, who was
sentenced to the Bastille in 1758 for publishing a tract ad-
vocating marriage for the clergy, or (2) the poet Paul
Maillard Des Forges (1699-1772), but the latter is not
known to have been an abbé.

32. *Bishop of Auxerre:* Jacques Marie de Caritat de Condorcet
(1703-1783), Bishop of Auxerre from 1754, opponent of
Jansenism, uncle of the celebrated philosopher Antoine
Nicolas de Condorcet.

33. *Jansenist:* Jansenism was a 17th-century reformist move-
ment within the Roman Catholic Church. By the 18th
century the word had come to mean a moral rigorist in
general. (Cf. Vol. 4, Chap. VI, n. 9.)

34. *Comédie Française:* From 1689 to 1770 in the Rue des
Fossés-Saint-Germain (now Rue de l'Ancienne Comédie),
in the 6th Arrondissement.

35. *As the King of Prussia said:* The King's use of an accusative
after the preposition *de* is an egregious error in Latin. No
such rebuke as the one attributed to D'Alembert in C.'s note
is found in his extant letters to Frederick the Great.

36. *Spanish Embassy:* In the Rue Guénégaud, in the 6th
Arrondissement.

37. *La Villette:* Formerly a village northeast of Paris; now
part of the 19th Arrondissement.

38. *Comédie Italienne:* The company played in the Hôtel de

Bourgogne, at the corner of the Rue Mauconseil and the
Rue Française, near the Church of Saint-Eustache.

39. *Clément:* Charles François Clément (ca. 1720 - after 1790),
French composer and harpsichordist.

40. *Béguines:* There had been no convents of Béguines in
France since Louis XI forbade the order in the 15th century.
C. here uses the term pejoratively.

41. *La Quinault:* Jeanne Françoise Quinault (1699-1783), celebrated actress at the Comédie Française from 1718 to 1741;
or perhaps her elder sister Mademoiselle Marie Anne Quinault (1695-1791), the Regent's mistress from 1715 to 1723.

42. *Madame Favart:* Marie Justine Favart, née Duronceray,
known as "La Chantilly" (1727-1792), dancer, first appeared
in Paris in 1745.

43. *Voisenon:* Claude Henri de Fusée de Voisenon (1708-1775),
French poet and writer of light fiction, friend of Voltaire.

44. *Mademoiselle Amelin:* Ca. 1715 - after 1766, married her
lover the police officer De Chalabre in 1766; she had borne
him two children.

45. *Paton:* Probably a certain Pattoni, a well-known professional gambler of the period, from Piedmont.

46. *Kornmann:* Jean Kornmann (died 1770), of Strassburg,
banker and marriage broker.

47. *Rue des Greniers-Saint-Lazare:* In the 3rd Arrondissement.

CHAPTER IV

1. *At The Hague:* The Abbé de Laville had worked closely with
the French Ambassador in The Hague, the Marquis de
Fénelon, at various times between 1735 and 1745 and
had represented him during his absences. In 1746 he was
appointed Secretary to the Minister of Foreign Affairs. He
was made a bishop four days before his death (1774).

2. *Garnier:* Jean Garnier was in D'Argenson's service for many
years, he made a fortune in army provisions, and in 1749
was appointed Major-domo to the Queen. C. had met his
son during his first stay in Paris (cf. Vol. 3, Chap. XI).

3. *D'Argenson:* Marc Pierre de Voyer de Paulmy, Count of

Weil-d'Argenson (1696-1764), from 1720 Lieutenant-General of Police, from 1742 Minister of War; he was exiled in 1757.

4. *Galiani:* Fernando Galiani (1728-1787), of Naples, served as his country's Embassy Secretary in Paris from 1759 to 1769; writer and political economist, a leading figure in the Enlightenment; his correspondence (written in French), especially his letters to Madame d'Épinay, constitutes a notable contribution to French literature. Since Galiani did not arrive in Paris until June 1759, C. could not have met him before his journey to Dunkirk in 1757.

5. *Henriade:* Epic poem by Voltaire, in which he celebrates Henri IV as a champion of religious freedom (first published at Rouen in 1723; second, enlarged edition, London 1728). In his treatise on the Neapolitan dialect (*Sul dialetto napoletano*) the Abbé Galiani mentions a translation of the *Iliad* into Neapolitan by Niccolò Capasso; no copy of it is extant.

6. *May:* Contemporary sources show that C.'s journey to Dunkirk did not take place until Aug. 1757.

7. *First Gentleman of the Bedchamber:* The office of Gentilhomme de la Chambre du Roi was created by François I in 1545. From the reign of Louis XIV four such officers were appointed at once and served in succession. They worked in close collaboration with the Intendant des Menus Plaisirs (cf. note 39 to Chap. II of this volume).

8. Cf. Horace, *Satires*, I, 9, 57: *muneribus servos corrumpam* ("I will corrupt the servants with gifts").

9. *Gesvres:* François Jacques Potier, Duke of Gesvres (1692-1757), was Intendant des Menus Plaisirs from 1743 to 1746 and later a Gentleman of the Bedchamber and Governor of Paris.

10. *Île de France:* One of the former French provinces, with Paris as its capital; divided among several of the modern Départements in the reorganization of 1791.

11. *Saint-Ouen:* Then a village, now one of the northern suburbs of Paris.

12. *Conciergerie:* A *conciergerie* was properly the residence of a bailiff; here doubtless some official building part of which was used as an inn.

13. *Du Bareil:* Jacques Charles Prévot, Marquis du Bareil (died 1762), Field Marshal 1748, Vice-Admiral 1753.
14. Italian proverb already quoted by C. in Vol. 1, Chap. VI.
15. *Aire:* Some 40 miles south of Dunkirk, in the old county of Artois.
16. *Commandant:* The Commandant of Aire from 1755 to 1765 was Mathurin de Laval (died 1786).
17. *The war:* The Seven Years' War, then in its second year.
18. *Twenty-four-sou piece:* In addition to the franc of 20 sous, there were silver coins with values of 12, 15, 24, and 30 sous.
19. *Saint-Omer:* Some 30 miles south of Dunkirk, between Lille and Calais.
20. *Intendant:* The Intendant of Amiens from 1754 to 1760 was Étienne Maynon d'Invau.
21. *Prosecutor:* Procureur, former judicial official who managed the causes of others in court. It was an important office, so the man who accepted money for helping C. was probably only a prosecutor's clerk.
22. *Catalan laws:* Probably an allusion to the severe supplements to the laws promulgated by Antoine Raymond de Sartine, Count of Alby (1729-1801), born in Barcelona, whose father had been Intendant of Catalonia. As they were not published in Spain until 1759 (*Apuntamientos sobre las leyes de Partida*), C. can hardly have known of them in 1757.
23. *Commissary of War:* Commissaire de Guerre, title of an official with supervisory powers over army personnel and equipment.
24. *La Bretonnière:* Though several persons bearing this name appear in the personnel records of the War Ministry for the period, none of them is listed as a Commissaire de Guerre. Hence no identification is possible.
25. *Hôtel de Saxe:* Name of an inn. The Rue Colombier (C. writes "du Colombier") is in the 6th Arrondissement.
26. *Britard:* C. probably means Auguste Louis Simon Brissard, who was Farmer-General from 1754 to 1763.
27. *Crémille:* Louis Hyacinthe Boyer de Crémille (1700-1768), was Minister of War (not of Marine) from 1757 to 1762.

CHAPTER V

1. *Camilla:* Giacoma Antonia Veronese, called Camilla (1735-1768), Italian actress and dancer; she first appeared at the Comédie Italienne in 1744 (cf. Vol. 3, Chap. XI).

2. *Barrière Blanche:* One of the sixty customs barriers at which duties were levied on certain goods entering Paris. The Barrière Blanche ("White Barrier"), on the right bank of the Seine, took its name from the white cross on an inn sign.

3. *Égreville:* Nicolas Rouault, Count of Égreville (born 1731).

4. *Gamaches:* Charles Joachim Rouault, Marquis de Gamaches (1729-1773).

5. *Countess du Rumain:* Constance Simone du Rumain, née Rouault de Gamaches (1725-1781).

6. *La Tour d'Auvergne:* Nicolas François Julie La Tour d'Apchier, Count of La Tour d'Auvergne (born 1720).

7. *Rue Taranne:* Originally Rue de la Courtille, later Rue Taranne, near the Church of Saint-Germain-des-Prés (6th Arrondissement); it no longer exists.

8. *Princess of Anhalt:* Johanna Elisabeth, Princess of Anhalt-Zerbst (1712-1760), lived in Paris from July 1758 under the name of Countess of Oldenbourg. C. again anticipates events here.

9. *Line:* One-twelfth of an inch.

10. *Talisman of Solomon:* More usually "Seal of Solomon," was the five-pointed star, which in Western cabalism was held to protect against evil demons.

11. *Marquise d'Urfé:* Jeanne, Marquise d'Urfé, née Camus de Pontcarré, married in 1724 to Louis Christophe de Larochefoucauld de Lascaris, Marquis d'Urfé et de Langeac, Count of Sommerive (1704-1734).

12. *Anne d'Urfé:* Anne de Lascaris d'Urfé (1555-1621), French poet; he divorced his wife about 1598 and became a priest. C., however, is probably thinking of his younger brother, Honoré de Lascaris d'Urfé (1568-1625), author of the pastoral novel *L'Astrée* (5 vols., 1607-1627), which was widely read both in France and abroad.

13. *Duchess of Lauraguais:* Diane Adélaïde, Duchess of Lauraguais (ca. 1713-1769).

14. *Duchess of Orléans:* Louise Henriette, née Princess of
Bourbon-Conti (1726-1759), married in 1743 to Louis
Philippe, Duke of Chartres, who became Duke of Orléans
in 1752 (cf. Vol. 3, Chap. XI).

15. *Madame de Boufflers:* Marie Louise, Marquise de Boufflers-
Rouverel, from 1749 lady-in-waiting to the Duchess of
Chartres and Orléans.

16. *Madame du Blot:* Niece of Madame de Mauconseil, became
a lady-in-waiting to the Duchess of Chartres and Orléans in
1749.

17. *Melfort:* André Louis Hector, Count of Drummond-Mel-
fort (1722-1788), of Scottish extraction; officer in the French
army and Freemason.

18. *Quai des Théatins:* Now the Quai Voltaire (renamed in
1791). The Hôtel de Bouillon is no. 17 on the present Quai
Malaquais.

19. *Regency:* On the death of Louis XIV in 1715 the Duke of
Orléans became Regent until Louis XV came of age in 1723.
The period of the Regency brought a relaxation in the for-
mality of court etiquette.

20. *Turenne:* Godefroy Charles Henri La Tour d'Auvergne,
Prince de Turenne (1727-1791), from 1772 Duke of Bouillon;
the Count of La Tour d'Auvergne's cousin.

21. *Great Work:* The *opus alchemicum* was the highest goal
of alchemy, the transmutation of all metals into gold.

22. *Her library:* The d'Urfé library was famous for its richness;
it was sold in 1770 and later came into the possession of the
Bibliothèque Nationale and the Bibliothèque de l'Arsenal.

23. *The great d'Urfé:* Claude d'Urfé, Baron of Châteauneuf
(1501-1558), Steward of the King's Household, French
Envoy to the Council of Trent in 1547.

24. *Renée of Savoy:* She was married to Jacques I d'Urfé
(not to Claude d'Urfé) in 1554.

25. *Paracelsus:* Philippus Aureolus Theophrastus Paracelsus
(1493-1541), his real name Theophrastus Bombastus von
Hohenheim, of Einsiedeln (Switzerland); famous physician
and philosopher, founder of hermetic medicine.

26. *The universal medicine:* The "panacea" of the alchemists, from the mythical Panakeia, daughter of Aesculapius, who was credited with the ability to cure all diseases; also known as *aurum potabile.*

27. *Steganography:* Cryptography.

28. *Powder of projection:* According to alchemical doctrine, a powder which, scattered over molten metals, turned them into gold.

29. *Tree of Diana:* An artificial form of vegetation produced by the mixture of two metals with a solvent such as nitric acid. The most suitable metals are silver and lead.

30. *Talliamed:* Benoît Maillet (1656-1738), author of *Talliamed ou entretiens d'un philosophe indien avec un missionaire* ("Talliamed or conversations between an Indian philosopher and a missionary"), Amsterdam, 1748.

31. *Le Maserier:* Jean Baptiste Le Maserier (1697-1760), abbé and writer; edited *Talliamed* (cf. note 30), adding a biography of Maillet.

32. *Regent:* See note 19, above. The Regent was an ardent disciple of alchemy.

33. *Égérie:* Egeria, a fountain nymph; in Roman mythology she was credited with advising King Numa Pompilius, hence her name came to be applied to any woman who acted as an adviser.

34. *Raymond Lully:* Ramón Lull (1235-1316), Catalan mystic, writer, philosopher, and missionary. The authenticity of the alchemical works ascribed to him is doubtful.

35. *Arnold of Villanova:* Provençal or Catalan physician and alchemist (ca. 1235-1313). The authenticity of his alchemical writings has been questioned.

36. *Roger Bacon:* English Franciscan and scholar (ca. 1214-1294); composed numerous works in philosophy, theology, and natural history; known as "Doctor Mirabilis."

37. *Geber:* Europeanized name of the Arabian or Persian physician and natural historian Jabir ibn Hayyan (8th century); in the Middle Ages he was considered the foremost authority on alchemy.

38. *Platina del Pinto:* The Rio Pinto is a river in Peru. Platinum, which was brought to Europe in 1743 (see the next

note), was at first supposed to be a kind of silver; its true nature was not ascertained until 1752.

39. *Wood:* Charles Wood found platinum in 1741 and brought the new metal to London for the first time in 1743.

40. *Aqua regia:* A mixture of nitric acid and hydrochloric acid.

41. *Burning glass:* Convex mirror used to concentrate the sun's rays on a particular point.

42. *Athanor:* A self-feeding furnace, made of bricks or clay, used by alchemists. Openings in its sides allowed the heat to be used for various purposes.

43. *"Lepers":* Alchemical term for the six baser metals: silver, mercury, lead, copper, iron, and zinc.

44. *Fixed salt:* According to the alchemical doctrine of Paracelsus, there were three basic substances: salt, sulphur, and mercury. Urine was often used as a salt.

45. *Pentacle:* A five- or six-pointed star. Here the five-pointed star (see note 10 to this chapter).

46. *Planetary Geniuses:* The cabala, which took over the Ptolemaic system of the universe, assigned a genius to each of the planets: Aratron to Saturn, Bethor to Jupiter, Phal to Mars, Och to the Sun, Hagith (or Hagioh) to Venus, Ophiel to Mercury, Phul to the Moon.

47. *Agrippa:* Cornelius Heinrich Agrippa von Nettesheim (1486-1535), German physician, philosopher, and astrologer; his works on magic, especially his *De occulta philosophia*, were considered authoritative by the alchemists.

48. *Count of Trèves:* Presumably Abraham B. Gershon, French cabalist of Jewish descent, born in Trèves, and known in the second half of the 18th century as the author of several occult treatises. He was not a count.

49. *Polyphilus:* Francesco Colonna's allegorical romance, the *Hypnerotomachia Polyphili*, written ca. 1467, was published at Venice in 1499 in an illustrated edition which is considered one of the masterpieces of Renaissance printing.

50. *Ineffable names:* The names of the angels of the seven planetary heavens.

51. *The planetary hours:* In astrology each hour has a cabalistic name and is governed by a particular planet and its angel.

52. *Anael:* The angel Anael governs Friday under the rule of the planet Venus, whose Genius is Hagith (or Hagioh).

53. *Zoroaster:* The reformer of the ancient Persian religion was later held to be the inventor of magic.

54. *Artephius:* Latinized name of a Jewish or Arabian philosopher who lived ca. 1130. His treatise on the philosopher's stone was translated into French by Pierre Arnauld in 1612.

55. *Sandivonius:* Latinized name of a 17th-century German physician.

56. *Brothers of the Rosy Cross:* Secret associations which began to spring up in Europe in the 17th century and in the 18th were identified especially with alchemy (cf. Vol. 3, Chap. VI, n. 9).

57. Cf. Genesis 24, 9: "And the servant put his hand under the thigh of Abraham his master and sware to him. . . ." (The Vulgate text is more specific: *sub femere* ["under his upper thigh"].)

58. *Word:* The meaning is "male semen" (cf. Vol. 8, Chap. IV).

59. *Electrum:* Alchemical term for an alloy composed of three parts of gold and one part of silver.

60. *Gerin:* Neither this person nor the Macartney (C. writes "Macartnei") named in the next sentence has been identified.

61. Esprit des Lois: By Charles de Secondat, Baron de Montesquieu (1689-1755), first printed in 1748; one of the most important works of political philosophy produced in the 18th century.

62. *D'Arzigny:* Probably Joseph Charles Luc Costin Camus, Count of Arginy (died 1779), high-ranking cavalry officer.

63. *Charon:* No councilor of this name has been identified. C. may be referring to Élie Bochart de Saron, who was a councilor.

64. *Great Chamber:* The Grand' Chambre was the highest chamber in each Parlement; it dealt with judicial cases involving great noblemen, cases of lèse-majesté, and the like.

65. *Madame du Châtelet:* The Marquise Adélaïde Marie Thérèse du Châtelet-Fresnières, née d'Urfé (1717 - after 1776); she accused her mother, Madame d'Urfé, of unlawfully withholding large sums of money from her; her mother succeeded in having her placed under guardianship and disinherited her.

66. *Had bought it:* High offices, including judgeships, were freely bought and sold at the period. C.'s play here on "*faire* raison" ("do justice"), where the second *faire* becomes "fabricate," seems impossible to translate.

67. *Viarmes:* Nicolas Élie Pierre Camus de Viarmes, Councilor in the Rouen Parlement from 1752.

68. *Remonstrances au Roi:* The French Parlements had gained the right to refuse to regard the King's edicts as law until after they were registered by the Paris Parlement; the same was true of the provincial Parlements in respect to the edicts of provincial governors. Registration could be refused; in such cases the King made his appearance and held a so-called *lit de justice* (from the throne under a baldachin) to compel registration. Not content with merely refusing, the Parlements also set forth their objections in the so-called "remonstrances." The King could also reject these in a *lit de justice;* however, the possibility of making remonstrances gave the Parlements considerable influence on public opinion.

69. *Madame de Gergy:* Anne Languet, Countess of Gergy, widow of the Count of Gergy (died 1734), who had been French Ambassador in Venice from 1723 to 1731.

70. *Saint-Germain:* Also Count Tzarogy, Prince Racoczy, General Soltikoff, Marquis of Montferrat, etc. (ca. 1696-1784), adventurer extraordinary, whose real origin is unknown. In his *Soliloque d'un penseur* (Prague, 1784) C. maintains that Saint-Germain was none other than an Italian fiddler named Catalani.

71. *"Elemental spirits":* The doctrine of the cabala assigns particular spirits to each of the four elements: gnomes to earth, undines to water, sylphs to air, salamanders to fire.

72. *Paralis:* This name first appears in Vol. 2, Chap. VIII, where it designates the guardian angel of C. and his three patrician friends, Bragadin, Dandolo, and Barbaro; he later makes it the name of his own Genius.

CHAPTER VI

1. *Pontcarré . . . Viarmes:* Geoffroy Macé Camus de Pontcarré, Councilor from 1753, and Jean Baptiste Élie Camus de Viarmes (1702 - after 1764).

2. *Provost of the Merchants:* The merchants of Paris had a provostal court of their own made up of the Provost of the Merchants, four municipal magistrates, a royal advocate, a city advocate, and a substitute. Monsieur de Viarmes held the office of Provost from 1758 to 1764.

3. *I have mentioned:* Cf. Chap. V, n. 67.

4. *Was never present:* Cf. Chap. V, n. 65.

5. *We:* I.e., C. and Madame d'Urfé.

6. *An estate:* Madame d'Urfé owned estates in Forez in the upper Loire Valley and the château of Pontcarré near Paris.

7. *Livre:* Livre is synonymous with franc.

8. *Hypostasis:* Union of the divine and human natures in one person.

9. *Salamander:* One of the four kinds of elemental spirits of the cabala, associated with fire.

10. *Word:* See note 58 to the preceding chapter.

11. *Academy:* The Académie Royale de Peinture, de Sculpture et de Gravure. For C.'s brother's admission to it, see Chap. II, n. 51.

12. *Married a dancer:* Francesco Casanova's marriage to Jeanne Jolivet, who had danced in the ballet of the Comédie Italienne under the name of Mademoiselle d'Alancour from 1759, did not take place until June 1762.

13. *Bursar . . . benefices:* Louis Pierre Sébastien Marchal de Saincy was "économe général du clergé" from 1750 to 1762.

14. *Holland:* The name was applied to the seven United Provinces of the Netherlands from the 17th century.

15. *Duke of Choiseul:* Étienne François, Count of Stainville (1719-1785), was made Duke of Choiseul in 1758 (cf. Chap. II, n. 6).

16. *D'Affry:* Louis Auguste, Count d'Affry (1710-1793), of Swiss extraction, from 1755 French Envoy, from 1759 French Ambassador, in The Hague.

17. *Invalides:* The Hôtel Royal des Invalides (7th Arrondissement) was built as a home for retired and invalid soldiers under Louis XIV from 1670 to 1674.

18. *About to be made:* The peace treaty which ended the Seven Years' War was not signed until 1763.

19. *Berkenrode:* Mattheus (Matthys) Lestevenon, Heer van Berkenrode en Strijen (1715-1797), was Ambassador of

the United Netherlands in Paris from 1749 to 1792.

20. *Landelle:* He was the proprietor of a then well-known restaurant, the Hôtel de Buci, in the street of the same name (6th Arrondissement).

21. *Ex-Jansenist:* Madame XXX. "Jansenist" was applied in the 18th century to persons of rigorous morals (cf. Vol. 4, Chap. VI, n. 9, and Vol. 5, Chap. III, n. 33).

22. *Quai de Gesvres:* Street along the Seine opposite the Île de la Cité near the Hôtel de Ville (4th Arrondissement).

23. *Gothenburg:* The Swedish East India Company, founded in 1731, had its main office at Gothenburg until 1814.

24. *Tourton & Baur:* The banking firm of Tourton & Baur, founded by the Swiss Christophe Jean Baur in 1740, had its office from 1754 in a building on the Place des Victoires (on the boundary between the 1st and 2nd Arrondissements).

25. *Florin:* The guilder (or florin) had been minted in the United Netherlands from 1679 and remained current until 1838. One guilder (florin) = 20 stuivers.

26. *Boas:* Tobias Boas, banker at The Hague.

27. *Jacht:* Dutch, "light sailing vessel."

28. *"English Parliament":* The famous inn "Het Parlament van Engeland" was closed in 1795 and reopened in 1814 under the name "Wapen van Engeland"; it was near the "Korte Poten," in the center of the city.

29. *Kauderbach:* Johann Heinrich Kauderbach (1707-1785), Saxon diplomat and writer, lived in The Hague from 1730; after serving as Corresponding Minister, then as Resident, he was appointed Ambassador from the Elector of Saxony in 1750.

30. *Feast of the Maccabees:* The Jewish festival of Hanukkah, celebrated for a week beginning on Dec. 25th.

31. *Ducats:* The ducat of the Netherlands was a gold coin which had been minted from 1586. For its value, see the following note.

32. *Stuivers:* A ducat was worth 3 guilders, 9 stuivers; it was roughly equivalent to 10 francs. C.'s figures are inaccurate (cf. note 34).

33. *Bank of Amsterdam:* Founded in 1609, it was the oldest bank in northern Europe.

34. *Livres tournois:* The French franc (or livre) was minted

from the 13th century in the city of Tours (whence the name), and later by the royal mint in Paris; from 1667 it became a standard coin throughout France. C.'s figures (400,-000 Netherlands ducats = 4 million livres tournois or francs) show that he was correctly informed as to the value of the ducat (cf. note 32).

35. *Pels:* The banking firm of Andries Pels & Zoonen in Amsterdam, founded by Andries Pels (1655-1731). In 1758 the director of the firm was Henrick Bicker (1722-1783), whom C. erroneously calls "Pels."

36. *Swedish Ambassador:* Joachim Frederik Preis (1666-1759), Swedish Resident from 1719, Swedish Ambassador in The Hague from 1725.

37. *D. O.:* Together with canceled versions such as "Op" or "O. p.," C.'s "D. O." undoubtedly designates the Hope family. The reference is probably to Thomas Hope (1704-1779), of Scottish descent but born at Amsterdam, who founded a bank there ca. 1726. C. at first writes "Mr. D. O.," but soon gives it up for the usual French "M." (for Monsieur). Perhaps Hope, though born in Holland, was thought of as an Englishman. Cf. C.'s use of "Miss" for Giustiniana Wynne, whose father was English, in Chap. VIII of this volume.

38. *St. John's Day:* St. John the Baptist was the original patron saint of Freemasonry; his feast was celebrated on June 24th. Later the Apostle John was also made a patron of the lodges; his feast day was Dec. 27th. The anniversary of the founding of the Grand Lodge of Holland was celebrated on the same day.

39. *Count de Tott:* Baron (not Count) de Tott, of Hungarian descent but born in France; officer in the French army; brother of François, Baron de Tott (1733-1793), who in 1755 went to Constantinople in the suite of the French Ambassador Vergennes and was made French Consul in the Crimea in 1763.

40. *Mother:* The Regent Anne, daughter of King George II of England and widow of the Stathouder William IV of Orange, who died in 1751. She ruled for her son William V (1748-1806). She died on Jan. 12, 1759, after a long illness.

41. *Stathouder:* The Republic of the United Provinces (from

1581) declared its independence in the Peace of Westphalia
(1648). Sovereignty resided in the Estates (Staaten) of the
provinces and the Estates General; executive power in the
Stathouder, of the House of Orange.

42. *Sinzendorf:* Philipp Joseph, Count Sinzendorf (1726-1788),
Austrian diplomat; he spent two weeks in The Hague at the
end of Dec. 1758.

43. *The Porte:* The official designation of the government of
the Turkish Empire was "the Sublime Porte," from the gate
of the Sultan's palace. There was no accredited representative
of Turkey in The Hague at the time; perhaps C. met some
high Turkish dignitary who was there unofficially.

44. *Bonneval:* Count Claude Alexandre Bonneval (1675-1747),
commander in the French and Austrian armies; about 1730
he entered the service of Turkey and became a Moham-
medan (cf. especially Vol. 2, Chap. IV).

45. *Iphigenia:* The reference is to *Iphigénie en Aulide,* by
Racine (1639-1699).

46. *"Prince of Orange":* No inn by this name is documented in
The Hague; however, there was an inn named "De Prins
van Oranje" in the Keizerstraat in Scheveningen, to which
C. probably refers.

47. *Greek philosopher:* Diogenes Laërtius (VII, 185) relates
concerning the Greek philosopher Chrysippus (282-209 B C.)
that he gave his donkey, which had eaten some figs which
belonged to him, undiluted wine and died laughing at the
spectacle of the drunken donkey.

48. *Special rights:* In the 18th century in most European
countries there were strict regulations intended to assure post
coaches of precedence under all circumstances.

49. *"Star of the East":* In Dutch, "De Ster van Osten"; a
letter from Manon Balletti to C. dated Dec. 9, 1758, is addressed to him at the "Rondeel," which was one of the oldest
and best hostelries in Amsterdam. C. may have changed his
lodging or may have confused the names.

50. *Cape wine:* Wine was already brought to Europe from
South Africa in the 18th century, especially from the Cape
of Good Hope.

51. *Esther:* Fictitious name, probably Lucia Hope (1741-1765),

possibly the daughter of Zachary Hope (1711-1770), brother of Thomas Hope (cf. note 37 to this chapter). If this is so, she was not Thomas Hope's daughter but his niece; in 1764 she married Adolf Jan Heshuysen (born 1736), partner in a banking firm in Haarlem and Amsterdam.

52. *Teresa Imer:* Italian singer (1723-1797), married to the dancer Angelo Pompeati in 1745 (cf. especially Vol. 1, Chap. VI, and Vol. 3, Chap. XIII).

53. *The Margrave:* Friedrich von Bayreuth (1711-1763), Margrave from 1735.

54. *M. M.:* Here again "M. M." replaces a canceled "Mathilde." (For C. C. cf. Vol. 3, Chaps. XIII-XVI; for M. M., Vol. 4, Chaps. I-X.)

55. This recitative has not been identified. A possible alternative translation is: "You have come to your end . . ."

56. *A widow:* Teresa Imer had separated from her husband in 1754, but he was still alive.

57. *Eau de Luz:* There was an "eau de Luz," a mineral water from the spring of Saint-Sauveur, near Luz in the Pyrenees. However, C. probably means "eau de Luce," a kind of smelling salts.

58. *Sophie:* Teresa Imer had three children: a son Joseph (born 1746), a daughter Wilhelmine Frederike (born 1753), and a third child the date of whose birth is not known. Possibly the last is the Sophie to whom C. here refers.

59. *Montperny:* Théodore Camille, Marquis de Montperny (died 1753), from 1746 Gentleman of the Bedchamber at the Margrave's Court in Bayreuth.

60. *Prince Charles of Lorraine:* Karl Alexander, Prinz von Lothringen (1712-1780), brother of Emperor Franz I; Austrian Field Marshal, 1746; Governor of the Austrian Netherlands (Flanders, Brabant, Hennegau, Namur, and Luxemburg), 1748-1756.

61. *In Vienna:* Angelo Francesco Pompeati did not commit suicide in Vienna until 1768.

62. *Exchange:* The splendid building of the Amsterdam Exchange (De Beurs), dedicated in 1611, housed the most important institution of the kind in 18th-century Europe; the great hall could hold 6000 people.

63. *Daler:* The Swedish daler was a silver coin minted from the beginning of the 16th century. 1 daler = 4 marks = 32 oere.

64. *Five percent:* C. writes "cinq pour cent" though he has previously spoken of fifteen percent and calculates with the latter figure.

65. *Zaandam:* C. writes "Cerdam" and "Serdam." Town some six miles northwest of Amsterdam, formerly a favorite residence of rich Netherlanders.


## CHAPTER VII

1. *Medea:* Medea appears with her two children, whom she is about to kill, in the climactic scene of Euripides' tragedy of the same name.

2. *V. D. R.:* Perhaps Pieter Meermann, son of Jan Meermann, who was Burgomaster of Rotterdam in 1758.

3. *Princess Galitzin:* Ekaterina, Princess Galitzin, also Golitsyn (1719-1761), daughter of Antioch Dmitrovich, Prince Kantemir; married to Dmitri Mikhailovich Galitzin, who was Russian Ambassador in Paris in 1761.

4. *Louis:* A louis was worth 24 francs.

5. *Agio:* Premium.

6. *"Second Bible":* There were three inns in Amsterdam all named "Byble" and all in the same street (Warmaesstraat); they were distinguished from one another as "First," "Second," and "Third."

7. *Rigerboos:* Jan Cornelis Rigerboos, obviously a close friend of Teresa Imer. It is possible that his name was really Jan Rijgerboos Cornelis, and that Teresa Imer took the name "Cornelys" when she went to London (cf. Vol. 9, Chaps. VII and VIII).

8. *States-General:* The parliament of the seven United Provinces was called "De Staten Generaal"; it was made up of sixty members and met in The Hague.

9. *Musicau:* Apparently C.'s attempt to spell Dutch *musiek-huis*, a tavern where there was music and dancing. They were plentiful in Amsterdam in the 18th century.

10. *Contrada:* The six *sestieri* (municipal districts) of Venice were divided into *contrade*.

11. *Lucia:* Daughter of the caretaker on the Count of Montereale's estate at Pasiano (cf. Vol. 1, Chaps. IV and V).

12. *Reischach:* Judas Thaddaeus, Freiherr von Reischach (1696-1782), Austrian diplomat.

13. *Pesselier:* Charles Étienne Pesselier (1712-1763), French financier.

14. *Pounds sterling:* According to C.'s later figures, the pound sterling was then worth 11 guilders.

15. *French East India Company:* The Compagnie des Indes Orientales, founded by Richelieu in 1642, was merged in 1719 with Law's newly created Compagnie des Indes, but continued to exist under its original name after Law's bankruptcy. The Dutch East India Company, founded in 1602, was very powerful in the 17th century, but then lost ground to the competition of English influence in India and was dissolved in 1795.

16. *Texel:* Dutch island in the North Sea, at the entrance to the former Zuider Zee.

17. *Carnival:* In all probability C. was not in Holland during the Carnival either in 1758 or 1759, but had already returned to Paris in January. But it is possible that in Amsterdam Carnival was considered to begin as early as January.

18. *One hundred thousand florins:* This and the following amount add up to the ten percent which O. D. had promised C. as his share of the profit from the supposedly lost ship.

19. *Pâris de Montmartel:* Jean Pâris de Montmartel (1690-1760), Comptroller-General and banker to the French Court, brother of Joseph de Pâris-Duverney, Intendant of the École Militaire (cf. this volume, Chaps. II and III).

20. *Masulipatam:* A fine cotton fabric, from the State of Masulipatam in southern India.

21. Seneca, *Epistles,* CVII.

22. *10th of February:* C.'s dates for his stay in Holland are not reliable; he probably means Jan. 10, 1759.

23. *Rue Montorgueil:* These streets are in the 1st and 2nd Arrondissements.

## CHAPTER VIII

1. *My patron:* In Dec. 1758 De Bernis was disgraced and from then on lived at his château of Vic-sur-Aisne, near Soissons. Hence C. cannot have visited him at his official quarters in the Hôtel de Bourbon in Jan. 1759.
2. *Venetian Ambassador:* Niccolò Erizzo (1722-1806) was the Venetian Ambassador in Paris from 1754 to 1760 (cf. note 4 to Chap. II of this volume).
3. *Gentleman-in-ordinary:* Appointment to this office was accompanied by the issuance of a patent of nobility. The document which made Voltaire "Monsieur de Voltaire" is dated June 8, 1758.
4. *Viar:* Probably a certain Viard who appears in contemporary documents as a *permissionnaire*, that is, a teacher who was licensed to board up to twenty pupils and who also taught them.
5. *Was playing:* Rosa Giovanna Balletti, called Silvia, died on Sept. 18, 1758, hence before C.'s first journey to Holland.
6. *Madame* XCV: Lady Anna Wynne, née Gazzini (1713 - after 1780); born on the island of Leukas in the Ionian Sea, she married Sir Richard Wynne, whose mistress she had been, in 1739, and after his death in 1751 made several journeys between Venice and London in order to have her children brought up as Roman Catholics but at the same time to assure them of receiving their inheritance in England.
7. *Four girls:* Of her four daughters, Anna Amalia had already died (1748-1750); C. presumably counts in Toinon, a French girl who lived in the household as the friend and confidante of the eldest daughter.
8. *Attended to all that:* In England Lady Wynne and her children had been obliged to renounce Roman Catholicism in order to obtain possession of the inheritance.
9. *1758:* Perhaps an error on C.'s part, since the events he relates took place at the beginning of 1759. Or perhaps he is reckoning in the Venetian manner, *more Veneto*, as he often

does in the memoirs. In Venice the new year began on March 1, so that January and February still belonged to the previous year.

10. *Eldest daughter:* Giustiniana Franca Antonia Wynne (1737-1791) was married in 1761 to Philip Joseph, Count Orsini-Rosenberg, the Austrian Ambassador in Venice. C. has already mentioned her and her mother at the end of Chapter IX, Volume 3, where he gives their right names. The events which follow obviously decided him to conceal the name; what led him to choose the letters *XCV* remains a mystery.

11. *Fifteen:* Giustiniana was already sixteen in 1753.

12. *Algarotti:* Francesco, Count Algarotti (1712-1764), a prominent figure of the Enlightenment both in his poetry and in his prose works, was made an honorary member of the Berlin Academy of Sciences and a Gentleman of the Bedchamber to Frederick the Great in 1747.

13. *Memmo di San Marcuola:* Probably Andrea Memmo (1729-1793), Venetian patrician, diplomat, and Senator, who married Elisabetta Piovene in 1769 and became Procurator in 1785. Different branches of a Venetian patrician family added to their names a determinative drawn from the name of the parish in which they lived. The Church of San Marcuola is on the Grand Canal near the Palazzo Vendramin.

14. *Miss XCV:* According to English usage, Giustiniana Wynne, as the eldest daughter, was addressed or referred to simply as Miss Wynne, her younger sisters by their Christian names, as Miss Mary, and so on. C.'s later use of "Miss" standing alone, like French "Mademoiselle," is of course completely unidiomatic.

15. *Hôtel de Bretagne:* This was a very modest hostelry in in the Rue Saint-André-des-Arts (6th Arrondissement). In the extant letters of Giustiniana Wynne there is mention only of the Hôtel de Hollande, which was in the same street and of a better class.

16. *Pouplinière:* Alexandre Jean Joseph Le Riche de la Pouplinière, also Popelinière (1692-1762), Farmer-General from 1718.

17. *Passy:* Le Riche de la Pouplinière's château was in what was then the village of Passy, now the Rue Raynouard (16th Arrondissement).

18. *East India Company:* Cf. note 15 to the preceding chapter.
19. *The mother:* Since Silvia had died in Sept. 1758, C. may be confusing the events of his return from Holland with those of his earlier return from Dunkirk in 1757. His asking if he was rich enough to give such presents points to the same supposition, for he was certainly rich enough on his return from Holland.
20. *Two sons:* Silvia had three sons; however, her second son, Luigi Giuseppe, had been a ballet master in Stuttgart from Sept. 1757, and her youngest son, Guglielmo Luigi (born 1736), died before 1757.
21. *Calencar:* A colored fabric from India.
22. *My friend:* Antonio Stefano Balletti (1724-1789), dancer and actor, C.'s intimate friend.
23. *The Cadet:* Luigi Giuseppe Balletti (born 1730), from 1751 dancer at the Comédie Italienne, from 1757 ballet master in Stuttgart (cf. note 20), whose nickname in the family was "the Cadet."
24. *"Down there":* Allusion to the Venetian State Inquisitors (cf. note 42 to Chap. II of this volume).
25. *Escape from him:* Cf. Chap. VI of this volume.
26. *Palais:* The old Palais de Justice on the Île de la Cité, the earliest portions of which were built in the 11th century, was originally the residence of the French Kings; at the beginning of the 15th century Charles VI ceded it to the Parlement. In the 18th century it was a favorite meeting place, since it contained many shops.
27. *Bankruptcy:* Gaetano did not declare a fraudulent bankruptcy until Oct. 1760; he left Paris on Oct. 29th of that year.
28. *Farsetti:* Tommaso Giuseppe Farsetti (ca. 1720-1792), Venetian patrician, poet, translator, and bibliophile. His Latin poems were published at Paris in 1755 and at Parma in 1776.
29. *Order of Malta:* Originally the Order of the Hospital of St. John of Jerusalem (Ordo militiae Sancti Joannis Baptistae hospitalis Hierosolymitani), the earliest knightly monastic order, it was founded as a charitable institution during the Crusades but soon added military service to its charitable activity. In the 14th century the Order conquered the island of Rhodes, only to lose it to the Turks in 1523. In 1530

Emperor Charles V gave it the island of Malta; it then assumed the name Knights of Malta. Its headquarters are now in Rome.

30. *Council of Trent:* This Council, which ushered in the Counter-Reformation, was held from 1545 to 1563.

31. *Armed magnet:* To conserve its magnetism the poles of a magnet were connected by a piece of soft iron.

32. *Chambord:* Magnificent Renaissance château, built by order of François I from 1523 to 1533. It is in Touraine, south of the Loire and not far from Blois.

33. *Zweibrücken:* Christian IV, Duke of Zweibrücken (1722-1775).

34. *Magisterium:* Term for the higher secrets of alchemy; probably goes back to the hermetic philosopher Artephius (12th century) and his treatise on the philosopher's stone.

35. *Maréchal de Saxe:* Moritz (French, Maurice), Count of Saxony (1696-1750); entered the French service in 1720, made Marshal of France in 1744, became a French citizen in 1746.

36. *Lewenhaupt:* Adam, Count of Lewenhaupt (died 1775) (C. writes "Levenhoop"), of Swedish origin, entered the French service in 1713, made a Field Marshal in 1762.

37. *"King Dagobert" inn:* In the 18th century the Auberge du Roi Dagobert was a famous hostelry in the present Rue Tête d'Or; it was demolished early in the 19th century.

38. *Bayreuth:* Giuseppe Pompeati (1746 - ca. 1797) was born in Vienna, not in Bayreuth.

39. *"Little Poland":* La Petite Pologne was properly a group of houses outside of the then city limits, probably near the Barrière de la Pologne, one of the city's customs barriers; the houses were near the present Gare Saint-Lazare. C. here and later also uses it as the name of his house itself.

40. *Madeleine barrier:* This barrier, which was probably identical with the Barrière de la Pologne, existed from 1720 to 1787 as one of the sixty barriers at which duties on certain articles brought into Paris were levied.

41. *"Royal Hunt":* Probably the name of one of the inns which abounded in the district.

42. *Gramont:* Antoine Antonin, Duke of Gramont (1722-1799); the garden of his country house was between the present

Rue de Clichy and Rue Saint-Lazare (9th Arrondissement).

43. *"Airy Warsaw":* The name of C.'s country house was *Cracovie* (not *Varsovie*) *en bel air.*

44. *"Butter King":* Marin Le Roy (died 1764), dealer in vegetables and butter; he lived on Place Vendôme and owned several houses and a shop in Little Poland.

45. *"The Pearl":* La Perle; her name was Madame Saint-Jean, as appears from a letter of Manon Balletti's.

46. *Great Order:* The Rosicrucian Order, of which in Chap. V C. has implied to Madame d'Urfé that he is himself a member. (Cf. note 56 to that chapter and Vol. 6, Chap. V, p. 106.)

47. *Camilla:* See note 1 to Chap. V of this volume.

48. *Ball at the Opéra:* The Académie Royale de Musique (the Opéra) had the privilege of giving public balls. The balls took place every Sunday between St. Martin's Day and Advent, and twice a week during the Carnival.

49. *Domino:* A masquerade costume consisting of a robe with a hood and including a half mask. The term is also used (as here) to designate a person wearing a domino.

50. *Cross:* The cross of the Order of Malta. As Commander of the Order, Farsetti was forbidden to marry.

51. *Enragés:* Fast, mettlesome horses which were fed only on hay; they could be hired in Paris to make the journey to Versailles as quickly as possible.

52. *"The Phoenix":* Sacred bird of Egyptian and later Greek mythology. In Roman times the myth acquired a new meaning: the phoenix burns itself and is reborn from its ashes.

53. *In London:* On their way from Venice Lady Wynne and her family stayed in Paris from Nov. 1758 to July 1759, then went to London via Brussels. So Giustiniana was certainly not in London in 1758.

54. Cf. Leviticus XXIV, 18. (The Authorized Version gives "life for life.")

55. *Four years ago:* Farsetti died in 1793; hence C. revised his manuscript in 1797.

56. *Mirandola:* Giovanni Pico della Mirandola (1463-1494), Italian humanist and philosopher, member of Lorenzo de' Medici's circle; he sought to achieve a synthesis of Christian, Greek, and Jewish religious thought.

57. In later astronomical works Pico della Mirandola is named

as the originator of this formula, among others by Kepler.

58. *Countess du Rumain:* Constance Simone Flore Gabrielle du Rumain (1725-1781), married in 1746 to Charles Yves Levicomte du Rumain, Marquis of Coëtanfao, Count of Penhouët.

59. *Coëtanfao:* Constance Gabrielle Bonne du Rumain (1747-1783); as the eldest daughter of Count du Rumain, who lived almost exclusively on his estate of Coëtanfao in Brittany, she seems to have used this name because she had a right to the title of Marquise de Coëtanfao.

60. *Polignac:* Marie Louis Alexandre, Marquis de Polignac (died 1768), married Constance Gabrielle du Rumain (see note 59 above) in 1767.

61. *Madame de Valbelle:* Marguerite Delfine, Marquise de Valbelle.

62. *Madame de Roncherolles:* Louise Françoise Gabrielle, Marquise de Roncherolles (died 1773).

63. *Princess Chimay:* Gabrielle, Princess of Chimay, also Chimai, married to Thomas Alexandre Marc de Hennin-Liétard, Prince Chimay; she was notorious between 1760 and 1764 for her many love affairs.

64. Horace, *Epistles*, I, 16, 24.

65. *The Augustinians:* The church and monastery of the "Grands Augustins" were on the left bank of the Seine in the present 6th Arrondissement; the name "Quai des Grands Augustins" alone survives. The church was demolished in 1797 and the monastery divided up.

66. *Four months:* According to the testimony of the midwife in court (cf. Chap. IX), Giustiniana was already seven months pregnant in Feb. 1759. Her child was born at the beginning of May.

67. *Ball at the Opéra:* Cf. note 48 to this chapter.

68. *The last ball:* In 1759 the last ball at the Opéra was held on Feb. 27th; according to the midwife's testimony the consultation took place between Feb. 9th and 12th; according to the testimony of Castel-Bajac, on Feb. 19th or 20th.

69. *Enormous mistake:* C. writes "une faute *madornale*," using an Italian word for "enormous," "outrageous," and the like.

70. *Wise myself:* The French for "midwife" is *sage-femme*

(literally, "wise woman"); C.'s play on "wise woman" and "wise myself" cannot be rendered in English.

71. *La Montigny:* By her real name Dupuis, she was first a prostitute and then became the owner of several bordellos, among others the Hôtel Montigny.

72. *The Marais:* Originally a swamp (hence the name), the Marais was built up and was considered a fashionable residential district in the 18th century (now in the 4th Arrondissement). The midwife Reine Demay did not live there but in the Rue des Cordeliers, now the Rue de l'École de Médecine (6th Arrondissement).

73. *Woman of fifty:* According to the trial documents the midwife was only 30 or 33 years of age.

74. *Rue de la Ferronnerie:* Between the Halles Centrales and the Seine (1st Arrondissement).

75. *Populia:* A Roman woman who is mentioned by Macrobius and of whom nothing more is known.

76. Macrobius, *Saturnalia,* II, 5, 9. Macrobius attributes it not to Populia but to Julia, the daughter of Augustus.

CHAPTER IX

1. *Richard:* Richard William Wynne (1744-1799), later lived in England and was rector of Ayot St. Lawrence (Hertford-shire).

2. *Aroph:* A highly esteemed medicament in earlier medicine, several times mentioned by Paracelsus; no less than eighteen formulas for it have survived.

3. *Boerhaave:* Hermann Boerhaave (1668-1738), famous Dutch physician, professor at the University of Leiden; he discusses aroph in his *Elementa Chemiae* (1732).

4. *She:* The printed text gives *il,* which must be either a typographical error or a slip of C.'s.

5. *English saffron:* Despite Paracelsus's injunction, English saffron was generally considered inferior to saffron from the East. In medicine saffron was believed to promote menstruation.

6. *Magali:* Domenico Magali, also Magalli, Italian singer; he appeared in Venice from 1749 and continued to sing in London until 1760.

7. *La Garde:* Died after 1780; French court musician, from 1757 music teacher to the "Enfants de France" (the children and grandchildren of the reigning King). He had a fine bass voice.

8. *Magdelaine:* Nothing is known of her except what C. recounts. His spelling her name with a "g" suggests that she may have been English.

9. *Twelve francs:* I.e., half of the louis which C. had given Magdelaine.

10. *Her:* I.e, Miss *XCV*.

11. *Concert Spirituel:* On holy days, when the theaters were closed, concerts of religious music had been given in the Salle des Cent Suisses in the Tuileries Palace since 1729.

12. *Mondonville:* Jean Joseph Cassanea de Mondonville (1711-1772), French composer.

13. *"The Israelites on Mount Horeb":* Oratorio with words by Voisenon; it was first performed in 1758, a year before the time of which C. is writing. Another oratorio by the same author, "Les Fureurs de Saul," was performed on April 3, 1759.

14. *Dauphin:* Perhaps the present Passage Dauphine, in the 6th Arrondissement.

15. *Cannot:* The text has *ne veux pas* ("am not willing to"), which would seem to be a slip for *ne peux pas*.

16. *Madame de la Marck:* Marie Antoinette Françoise, Countess of La Marck (born 1719), née Countess of Noailles, married to the Count of La Marck in 1744.

17. *Montrouge:* Suburb of Paris, directly south of the Porte d'Orléans. C. explains the "Bishop" three paragraphs further on.

18. *La Vallière:* Louis César de la Baume Le Blanc, Duke of La Vallière (1708-1780), Grand Falconer to the King and Governor of the province of Le Bourbonnais.

19. *Herrenschwandt:* Johann Friedrich Herrenschwandt (1715-1798), of Swiss descent, celebrated physician of the period, from 1750 physician in ordinary to the Duke of Orléans.

20. *Poinsinet:* Antoine Alexandre Henri Poinsinet de Noirville

(1735-1769), French dramatist; he was himself the author of *The Circle* (*Le Cercle ou la soirée à la mode*).

21. *C . . .:* Conflans-l'Archevêque, also Conflans-les-Carrières, village at the junction of the Marne with the Seine, now part of greater Paris; the nuns of the convent were Benedictines.

22. *The Abbess:* Henriette Marguerite de Mérinville (born ca. 1709); she was Abbess of the Prieuré de Notre-Dame de la Conception O.S.B., in Conflans-l'Archevêque.

23. *Her . . . she:* The Abbess.

24. *Place Maubert:* Off the Boulevard Saint-Germain, in the 5th Arrondissement.

25. *Porte Saint-Antoine:* It was in the present Place de la Bastille.

26. *Quasimodo Sunday:* In 1759 it fell on April 22nd. Giustiniana Wynne's letters show that she left home on April 5th.

27. *The Farmer-General:* When she ran away, Giustiniana Wynne left two letters, one to her mother and the other to La Pouplinière; in both of them she said she was running away to avoid marrying the Farmer-General.

28. *His little theater:* The plays which La Pouplinière wrote to be performed in his private theater at Passy were not published, and the manuscripts of them have not survived.

29. *Episode of the fireplace:* The Duke of Richelieu rented an apartment in the house next to La Pouplinière's and had a passageway built connecting it with Madame de la Pouplinière's bedroom, so that he could visit his mistress freely. The passageway came out in the fireplace of her room. (Cf. Vol. 3, Chap. XI, n. 26.

30. *Capitoul:* C. is mistaken in regard to the city, which was not Bordeaux but Toulouse. La Pouplinière married Marie Thérèse de Mondran, whose grandfather had been appointed a "capitoul," on July 31, 1759. This title of the highest municipal magistrates of Toulouse goes back to Latin *capitulum*.

31. *At the end of two years:* The child, Alexandre Louis Gabriel de la Pouplinière, was born on May 28, 1763, hence almost four years after the marriage took place and not quite six months after his father's death.

CHAPTER X

1. *Bernis:* The Abbé de Bernis had been made a cardinal on Sept. 11, 1758; in Dec. 1758 he had fallen into disgrace and since then had lived at his château of Vic-sur-Aisne, near Soissons.

2. *The Comptroller-General:* Until March the office was held by De Boulogne; from March 4 to Nov. 21, 1759, by De Silhouette (cf. note 4).

3. *The Minister:* De Boulogne. As Comptroller-General he was not a minister though his power as head of the entire administration equaled that of a minister.

4. *Silhouette:* Étienne de Silhouette (1709-1767), Comptroller-General of Finances from March to Nov. 1759.

5. *The Pope:* Benedict XIV had died on May 3, 1758. His successor Clement XIII was elected on July 7, 1758. C. makes a number of chronological errors in this and the following chapter.

6. *Rezzonico:* Carlo Rezzonico (1693-1769), made a cardinal in 1743; Pope under the name of Clement XIII from 1758.

7. *Gave him the cardinal's hat:* The ceremony took place on Nov. 30, 1758; the King's letter containing the order for De Bernis's exile is dated Dec. 13, 1758.

8. *Richelieu:* Armand Jean du Plessis, Duke of Richelieu (1585-1642), Cardinal from 1622, chief Minister to King Louis XIII (1610-1643) from 1624, one of the most important French statesmen. He established the centralism of the French State and, in foreign policy, achieved the supremacy of France in Europe at the expense of the Hapsburg dynasty.

9. *Last year:* De Bernis died at Rome on Nov. 1, 1794.

10. *Soubise:* Charles de Rohan, Prince of Soubise (1715-1787); for his career, see note 21 to Chap. II of this volume.

11. *The younger Crébillon:* Claude Prosper Jolyot de Crébillon (1707-1777), known as Crébillon le jeune or Crébillon fils; author of novels and tales, many of which are erotic in subject. His father, a well-known dramatic poet of the

period, was C.'s French teacher in 1753 (cf. Vol. 3, Chap.
VIII).

12. *The Sofa: Le Sopha,* novel by the younger Crébillon.

13. *De Boulogne:* He was Comptroller-General.

14. *Clermont . . . :* Louis de Bourbon-Condé, though a priest,
had received a dispensation from the Pope to bear arms;
however, as a general he lost the Battle of Krefeld in 1758.

15. Horace, *Epodes,* 2, 1. Horace makes it one of the ingredients
of happiness, hence C.'s "but not happy."

16. *Rezzonico:* Pope Clement XIII (Carlo Rezzonico) died
in 1769.

17. *Remained the French Ambassador:* De Bernis was the
French Ambassador in Rome from 1769 to 1791. He did not
die until 1794.

18. *J. J. Rousseau:* Jean Jacques Rousseau (1712-1778).

19. *Montmorency:* From 1756 to 1762 Rousseau lived at
Montmorency, north of Paris, from May to Aug. 1759 as
the guest of the Maréchal de Luxembourg in the latter's
château there.

20. *A woman:* Marie Thérèse Levasseur (1721-1801), of
Orléans, housemaid; Rousseau's mistress, whom he married
in 1768.

21. *Prince of Conti:* Louis François, Prince of Bourbon-Conti
(1717-1776), French general and statesman.

22. *Count of La Marche:* Louis François Joseph, Prince of
Bourbon-Conti, Count of La Marche (1734-1814).

23. *Good-by:* The historicity of this anecdote has been con-
tested.

24. *Anagram:* Taking "u" and "v" as interchangeable,
"Levasseur" contains all the letters of "Rousseau" except
the "o."

25. *Aristides' Daughter: La fille d'Aristide,* by Madame de
Graffigny, was first performed on April 29, 1758. She did not
die until Dec. 13th of that year (see the following note).

26. *Madame de Graffigny:* Married to François Huguet de
Graffigny, Chamberlain to the Duke of Lorraine; she was
Helvétius' aunt (1695-1758).

27. *Peruvian Letters . . . Cénie:* Madame de Graffigny's *Lettres péruviennes,* modeled after Montesquieu's famous *Lettres*

*persanes,* was published in 1747. Her *Cénie* was first performed in 1750.

28. *Died of joy:* Vittoria Rezzonico, mother of Pope Clement XIII, died on June 29, 1758, at Padua; her son became Pope on July 6 of that year.

29. *Clary:* Probably Franz Wenzel, Count of Clary (1708 - after 1766). His family held the fief of Töplitz in Bohemia.

30. *Bavois:* Louis, Baron de Bavois (1729-1772), served in the Venetian army from 1752; friend of C.'s (cf. especially Vol. 3, Chaps. V and VI).

31. *Faget:* Jean Faget (ca. 1700-1762), well-known Parisian physician.

32. *Al sughillo:* "With sauce"; in C.'s day macaroni (Italian, *maccherone*) also meant what are now called *gnocchi* (a kind of dumpling).

33. *Pilau:* Oriental preparation of rice with meat, fowl, or fish, and spices.

34. *In cagnoni: Riso in cagnoni* roughly corresponds to the modern Milanese *risotto.*

35. *Olla podrida:* A Spanish dish, a stew of various kinds of meat, with vegetables and spices.

36. *Butter from Vambre:* Butters produced in various parts of France have long been celebrated. However, no *beurre de Vambre* is recorded. Perhaps the name was that of some then well-known farm near Paris.

37. *Zara maraschino:* Maraschino from the city of Zara (now Zadar) in Dalmatia was particularly esteemed in the 18th century.

38. *A manufactory:* Contemporary sources mention a manufactory of Chinese and painted silk in the Enclos du Temple (today No. 18 Rue Dupetit-Thouars, in the 3rd Arrondissement). But C.'s name does not appear among the partners. However, it is known that a foreigner by the name of Scotti established a manufactory for printed silk in 1758, which was soon closed. Here, too, C.'s name does not appear. But since he had relatives in Parma named Scotti, it is possible that he used their name. The assumption is supported by the fact that the court records show that Garnier sued a certain "Scotti" (see Chap. XI of this volume).

39. *Enclos du Temple:* It formerly belonged to the Order of

the Temple; the shopkeepers who lived there were exempt from certain taxes and enjoyed other privileges. In C.'s time the Enclos belonged to the Prince of Bourbon-Conti as Grand Prior of the order in France.

40. *Gros de Tours:* A silk fabric from Tours, popular in France from the 17th century.

41. *Camlet:* A fabric of wool, sometimes camel's hair intermixed with silk or other threads.

42. *Castel-Bajac:* Louis, Marquis de Castel-Bajac; his estate was near Toulouse (Gascony).

43. *Commissary:* In Paris in the 18th century there were forty-eight Police Commissaries, two or three for each of the twenty divisions of the city.

44. *Accuse me:* The midwife's deposition is dated March 16, 1759.

45. *Criminal Lieutenant:* Lieutenant criminel; in collaboration with seven judges he conducted criminal cases. From the 16th century the office could be bought.

46. *Sartine:* Antoine Raymond Jean de Sartine, also Sartines, Count of Alby (1729-1801), Criminal Lieutenant from 1755, Lieutenant-General of Police from 1759, appointed Minister of Marine in 1774.

47. *Two years later:* The appointment was made in Nov. 1759.

48. *Vauversin:* Jean de Vauversin (died 1775), advocate from 1744.

49. *Court record office: Greffe,* the office in which all the documents in a case were deposited.

50. *Is married:* La Pouplinière married Marie Thérèse de Mondran, of Toulouse, on July 31, 1759 (cf. Chap. IX of this volume).

## CHAPTER XI

1. *She:* I.e., Miss *XCV.*

2. *Record clerk:* The clerk in charge of the *greffe* (see note 49 to the preceding chapter).

3. *Rue du Temple:* In the 2nd and 3rd Arrondissements.

4. *Rue aux Ours:* In the 3rd Arrondissement.

5. *Two or three days later:* The midwife, Reine Demay, was

arrested on April 20, 1759, imprisoned in the Grand Châtelet, but freed as early as May 4, 1759.

6. *Bicêtre:* Château on the southern outskirts of Paris; under Louis XIII a hospital for wounded soldiers, from the time of Louis XIV also a prison.

7. *Stricken from the list:* Vauversin was still an advocate in 1775; perhaps he was forbidden to exercise his profession for a certain period.

8. *Until her daughter reappeared:* Lady Wynne's suit against C. was still being prosecuted when he left Paris in the fall of 1759.

9. *End of August:* Giustiniana Wynne left the convent at the end of June and left Paris for Brussels on July 18, 1759.

10. *The war:* The Seven Years' War (1756-1763).

11. *Beginning of November:* In all probability C. had already left Paris by the end of Sept. 1759.

12. *Elbeuf:* Emmanuel Maurice de Lorraine, Prince of Elbeuf (1677-1763); he was an archaeologist and discovered the ruins of Herculaneum.

13. *Gilbert:* Presumably a name invented by C.; so, too, Baret.

14. *Rue Saint-Nicaise:* It was near the Palais-Royal; it no longer exists.

15. *Baret:* Cf. note 13.

16. *Rue . . . des Prouvaires:* In the 1st Arrondissement, near the central market (Les Halles).

17. *Raphael:* Raffaello Santi (1483-1520), famous Italian painter of the High Renaissance.

18. *The Pont-Neuf:* The oldest stone bridge in Paris, connecting the two banks of the Seine across the northwest end of the Île de la Cité; it was begun in 1578 under Henri III and completed in 1603.

19. *Pull the cord:* The door of a carriage could be opened from inside by pulling a cord provided for the purpose.

20. *Saint-Germain-l'Auxerrois:* Because of its nearness to the Louvre, it was long the court church; begun in 606 and frequently restored.

21. *Palais Marchand:* Alternative name for the old Palais de Justice, in which there were many shops (cf. note 26 to Chap. VIII of this volume).

22. Ascribed to Publilius Syrus. Publilius (first century A.D.), of Syria, freedman and author of short comic dialogues (mimes). Aphorisms were selected from these, perhaps by Seneca; the selection was enlarged in the Middle Ages by aphorisms from other sources and contains some 700 items.

23. *Place Dauphine:* On the Île de la Seine, west of the Palais de Justice.

24. *Half-mourning:* The reference appears to be to the mourning which C. has described the Parisians as wearing in sorrow for the attempted assassination of the King (cf. note 5 to Chap. III of this volume).

25. *Mademoiselle de Boulainvilliers:* Marie Anne Geneviève Augspurgher, also Auspurgher (ca. 1746 - after 1777), known as "La Charpillon"; lived as a child in Paris under the name of Mademoiselle de Boulainvilliers. She was probably the illegitimate daughter of the Marquis Anne Gabriel Henri Bernard de Rieux Boulainvilliers (1724-1798), who was Provost of the Merchants (cf. Chap. VI, n. 2) from 1766; she was later a celebrated courtesan in London (cf. Vol. 9, especially Chaps. XI and XII).

26. *Mézières:* There was a farmer-general by this name from 1756 to 1784. In the 18th century the French Treasury, always short of money, issued notes against taxes which were signed by the tax farmers and which it took care to keep in good standing.

27. *Garnier:* Jean Garnier (cf. Chap. IV, n. 2).

28. *Rue du Mail:* In the 2nd Arrondissement, near the Bourse.

29. *Rue Saint-Denis:* In the 1st and 2nd Arrondissements. C. could not be arrested in the Enclos du Temple, where he had his manufactory, because the district enjoyed immunity. His arrest took place on Aug. 23, 1759, on a charge of forging bills of exchange.

30. *Fort-l'Évêque:* Properly "For-l'Évêque" (from Latin *forum* in the sense of "court"). Originally the seat of the episcopal court in Paris; after the episcopal jurisdiction was abolished in 1674 it became a state prison for debtors and actors. The building was torn down in 1783.

31. *Just married:* Francesco Casanova did not marry Marie Jeanne Jolivet until June 1762.

32. *Four . . . hours:* C. was not released until Aug. 25, 1759,
    so he spent two days in prison.

33. *Judge: Un président à mortier;* title of one of the nine
    judges of the Great Chamber of the Parlement; the symbol
    of their office was a black satin cap in the shape of a mortar.

34. *Municipal obligations:* Text: *octrois . . . sur l'Hôtel de
    Ville;* Paris levied duties (*octrois*) on certain imported arti-
    cles; the right to collect them could be bought.

35. *Madame du Rumain:* It has been suggested that this is a
    slip of C.'s for "Madame d'Urfé." The present translator
    disagrees and has adhered to C.'s text.

36. *Garnier:* The principal plaintiffs in the action against C. in
    the matter of the forged bills of exchange were a certain
    Oberty and a certain Louis Petitain. C. has obviously altered
    the facts to suit his purposes.

37. *Giving up my house:* C. had sent Manon Balletti to live in
    his country house; she remained there until the end of Oct.
    1759.

38. *Rueil:* On the Seine near Saint-Germain-en-Laye; now part
    of greater Paris.

39. *The last war but one:* The War of the Austrian Succession
    (1740-1748).

40. *The Order:* The Rosicrucian Order, to which C. implied to
    Madame d'Urfé that he belonged at their first meeting (cf.
    note 56 to Chap. V; also note 46 to Chap. VIII).

41. *Choiseul:* The Duke of Choiseul (cf. this volume, Chap.
    II, n. 8) had been appointed Minister of Foreign Affairs in
    Nov. 1758, after De Bernis was banished.

42. *December 1st:* The case against C. ended with his being
    found guilty of forgery on Dec. 22, 1759, but he was already
    in Holland. He must have left Paris very hurriedly. Giustini-
    ana Wynne was informed of his departure by Nov. 3, 1759.

43. *Helvétius' L'Esprit:* Claude Adrien Helvétius (1715-1771),
    Farmer-General and author, married to Anne Catherine de
    Ligneville-d'Autricourt in 1751. A leading figure of the En-
    lightenment, in his chief work, *De l'Esprit* ("On Intel-
    ligence"), he carried the concepts of hedonism and sensualism
    to their logical consequences. Published in 1758, the book was
    soon put on the Index and condemned by the Sorbonne and

the French censorship; Helvétius publicly repudiated it in 1759, perhaps out of consideration for the Royal Censor Tercier, who had approved the manuscript for publication.

44. *Pascal:* Blaise Pascal (1623-1662), famous French philosopher and mathematician.

45. *D'Alembert:* See note 43 to Chap. II of this volume.

46. *The "Empress":* The hostelry had existed since 1691 under the name "De Keiserin," later "À l'Impératrice"; it was in the Rue des Carrières (Kantersteen), later Rue de l'Impératrice; it no longer exists.

47. *Moerdick:* Properly the name of a village on the shore of the Maas, across which travelers were ferried to Holland; C. mistakenly uses it for the mouth of the Maas itself.

48. *Prince Piccolomini:* Ruggieri Rocco called himself Count Piccolomini; according to information supplied to the Venetian State Inquisitors by the spy Manuzzi, he came from Naples; he was a professional gambler and fencing teacher.

49. *Sixteen years . . . Vicenza:* Accordingly C. met him in Vicenza in 1743; but he says nothing of it in his memoirs, though he does mention staying in Vicenza in 1753.

50. *Ambassador:* The Regent Anne died on Jan. 12, 1759. D'Affry was appointed Ambassador in the course of the month.

51. *Silhouette:* Silhouette had ordered all silver articles delivered to the Royal Mint; it was rumored that he intended to issue paper currency. Appointed Comptroller-General of Finances on March 4, 1759, he was dismissed from the office on Nov. 21st of the same year.

52. *Recently:* In all probability Saint-Germain did not reach Holland until the beginning of Feb. 1760 and fled from there on April 17th. Hence C., who left Amsterdam in mid-Feb., can only have met him there during the first days of Feb. 1760.

53. *Haiduk:* Also Heyduck (from the Hungarian *hajdu*), originally one of a class of mercenery foot soldiers, later a domestic in the house of a nobleman.

54. *Brunswick:* Ludwig Ernst, Duke of Brunswick (Braunschweig) (1718-1788), General in the service of the Emperor, from 1749 Dutch Field Marshal, guardian of the children of the deceased Regent Anne.

HISTORY OF MY LIFE

*Volume 6*

# CONTENTS

## *Volume 6*

# Contents

# LIST OF PLATES

## *Volume 6*

# VOLUME 6

## CHAPTER I

THE ADVENTURESS was Roman, still young, tall, well built, with black eyes and a dazzlingly white complexion—but of the artificial whiteness one sees at Rome on the faces of nearly all loose women and which is so distasteful to delicate perceptions which love natural beauty. She had attractive manners and an appearance of intelligence, but it was only an appearance. Since she spoke only Italian no one but an English officer named Walpole[1] talked with her. Despite his never addressing a word to me, I felt drawn to him; and it was not an effect of sympathy, for if I had been blind or deaf Sir Walpole would have left me completely indifferent.

Signora Piccolomini irked me; but after dinner I went up to her room with the entire company. The Count sat down to a game of whist and Walpole played primero[2] with the Countess, who cheated him. He stopped after losing some fifty ducats, and the lady asked him to take her to the theater.[3] She left her husband playing whist. I went too.

In the parterre I found Count Tott,[4] brother of the Count Tott whose stay in Constantinople made him famous. He told me he had left France because he had fought with a man who had rallied him on not being present at the Battle of Minden,[5] having purposely put off rejoining his corps. He proved his courage by giving him a wound with his sword. He said he had no money, and I opened my purse to him; he opened his to me five years later at Petersburg. Having seen me speak to the Italian Countess, he said that her husband was a cheat; I did not answer.

After the play I go back to the inn. The waiter tells me that Prince Piccolomini has left in a hurry with his valet and a small trunk. A moment later his wife appears, her maid whispers something to her, and she says that her husband has left because he has fought a duel and that it often happened to him. She invited me to supper with Walpole, and she ate with a very good appetite.

At dessert an Englishman who had made one at the whist table with Piccolomini came upstairs and told Walpole that the Italian Count, caught cheating, had given the lie to their fellow Englishman, who had accused him, and they had gone out together. An hour later the Englishman had come back to the "English Parliament," where he was lodging, wounded in the forearm and shoulder. It was a trifling affair. I went to bed.

The next day after dining with Count d'Affry[6] I return to the inn and I receive a letter from Count Piccolomini, dispatched by express messenger and contain-

ing an enclosure addressed to his wife. He asked me to
bring her to him in Amsterdam at the "City of Lyons," [7]
where he was lodging, after giving her his letter. He
wanted to know how the Englishman he had wounded
was doing.

The favor he asked of me almost made me laugh, for I
had no inclination to grant it. I took her letter to the
Signora, who was sitting up in bed playing cards with
Walpole. She has scarcely read it before she tells me she
cannot leave until the following day, and she specifies an
hour. I reply that business prevents me from having the
honor of serving her, and Walpole, informed of the matter, offers to take advantage of my refusal. She accepts,
and they arrange to leave after dinner the next day in
time to spend the night at Leiden. The plan was carried
out as made; but now for my turn.

The day after they left I sit down at table with all the
others and with two Frenchmen who have just arrived.
After taking their soup one of the two Frenchmen says
that the "famous" Casanova must be in Holland. The
other replies that he would be very happy to find him
and call him to account in no uncertain terms. As I am
sure that I have never had anything to do with the man,
the blood instantly rushes to my head, but I control myself. I ask him quietly if he knows Casanova.

"I have good reason to know him," he replies in the
self-satisfied tone which is always offensive.

"You do not know him," I say sharply, "for I am he."

Not in the least disconcerted, and even with a certain
insolence, he says that I am mistaken if I think I am the
only man in the world named·Casanova.

His answer put me in the wrong, and I was left with no
reply but determined that, at the right time and place,
I would take him by the collar and force him to show me
the other Casanova who might possibly be in Holland and
whom he wanted to call to account. Meanwhile I bit my

lips and bore with patience the sorry figure I must be cutting in the eyes of the officers who, having heard the tone of the short dialogue, might well suspect me of cowardice. Meanwhile the impudent fellow, making the worst of my situation and the best of his victory, which gave him the upper hand of me at least on the score of wit, talked away about anything and everything. He went so far as to ask me from what country I came, and I thought it proper to reply that I was a Venetian.

"Then you are a good friend to France, for your republic is under French protection."

I was in too bad a humor to laugh. I told him, in the tone one uses to make someone understand that he arouses one's contempt, that my republic was not, and had never needed to be, under the protection of France or of any other sovereign nation during the thirteen centuries of its existence.

"And will you now," I said, "to excuse your ignorance, tell me that there are two republics of Venice in the world?"

At that a general burst of laughter restored me to life and seemed to impose silence on the insolent fool; but his evil demon started him talking again at dessert. The conversation turned to the Earl of Albemarle.[8] The Englishmen present, praising him, said that if he had lived France and England would not then be at war. Another praised Lolotte,[9] his mistress. I said that I had met her at the Duchess of Fulvy's,[10] and that no woman had ever better deserved to become the Countess of Hérouville. The Count of Hérouville,[11] Lieutenant-General and man of letters, had just married her. But I had scarcely concluded her eulogy before the Frenchman looks at me with a laugh and says he once spent a night with her at La Pâris's.[12] It was then that I could not keep from raising my plate with four fingers and showing him the under side of it. He got up and, going to the

fireplace, stood with his back to it. He had his sword and
the sword knot which indicated that he was an officer.
The conversation turned to other matters. Two minutes
later we all got up from table. Everyone left except my
man, who had told his crony that they would meet at the
theater. Being now certain that the fool would follow me,
I left the inn and walked in the direction of Scheveningen. I saw him follow me at forty paces' distance and
come toward me when he saw me stop and stand in the
wood waiting for him.

At ten paces from me he unsheathed, and I did not need
to fall back in order to have time to do the same. It was
he who fell back when he felt the point of my sword in
his chest from my straight lunge, which has never failed
me, without my needing to fence at all. He said when I
came up to him, lowering my sword, that we would meet
again in Amsterdam if I was going there. I did not see
him again until six years later in Warsaw, where I took
up a collection for him. His name was Varnier. I do not
know if he was the Varnier[13] who was President of the
National Convention[14] under Robespierre.

When I returned to the inn after the play I was told
that he had left for Rotterdam with his crony after
spending an hour in his room with a surgeon. At supper
no one said anything about the matter to me nor did I
speak of it. Only an English lady said that a man of
honor could not sit down at a common table without feeling called upon to fight, prudent though he might be.

Having nothing to do at The Hague, I left the next
morning an hour before dawn in order to reach
Amsterdam that evening. At noon I encountered Sir
James Walpole at an inn, where he told me he had left
Amsterdam on the previous day an hour after restoring
the chaste wife to the arms of her scoundrelly husband.
He had satisfied his passing fancy and he wanted no
more of her.

I reached Amsterdam about midnight and found very good lodgings at the "Second Bible." [15] My impatience to see Esther kept me from sleeping well. Her nearness revived all my old flame.

At ten o'clock I called on Monsieur D. O., who received me with demonstrations of the greatest friendship, lamenting that I had not come to stay with him. When he learned that I had given up my manufactory he said that since I could not decide to transfer it to Holland I had done well, for it would have ruined me. After complaining of the bad faith of France, the cause of his being involved in several bankruptcies, he told me to go and see Esther.

She received me by giving a cry and running into my arms. I found her two inches taller and her figure proportionately fuller. No sooner had we sat down than the first thing she wanted to do was to convince me that she had become as well versed in the cabala as I was. She said that it made her life happy, that through it she had become mistress of her father's will, and so she was sure he would never marry her except to a man of her own choice.

"Your father," I said, "must suppose that I taught it to you."

"So he does; and he told me one day that he forgives me anything I may have sacrificed to you to win the great secret. But I told him the truth, I stole it from you, and, like you, I have become the surprising divinity who answers; for I am sure that your answers come from nowhere but your own mind."

"How could I have said where the portfolio was and that the ship was not lost?"

"It was you who threw the portfolio there after finding it, and as for the ship, you took a chance. Admit that, since you are honest by nature, you must have been very uneasy. But I shall never be so bold. When my

father gives me questions of that sort I answer very
obscurely. I do not want him to lose the confidence he has
in my oracle, still less would I want to become the cause
of some misfortune which would affect me too nearly.''

''If the deception makes you happy I cannot but leave
you to practice it. But permit me to feel the utmost
admiration for your talent. You are unique.''

''I am not interested in your admiration, I want a
sincere avowal.''

''I cannot be more sincere than I am.''

At that the charming girl became serious. Determined
not to lose the advantage I had over her, I thought of
predicting something to her which could be known only to
God, or of guessing what she thought. I was absolutely
determined to keep the upper hand of her. We went down
to dinner; but a sad and silent Esther greatly troubled
me.

There was a fourth person at the table, and I concluded that he was in love. He kept his eyes on her constantly. We did not speak of the cabala until after he had
left us. He was her father's favorite secretary, with whom
he would have liked to see her in love; but he was not fit
for the role.

''Is it possible,'' Monsieur D. O. asked me, ''that my
daughter has learned to draw answers from your oracle
without your having taught her?''

''I did not believe it possible until today, but she has
just convinced me that I was wrong. I can now teach it
to no one else, on pain of losing it myself. Such was the
oath I made to the wise man who taught me the calculation. Your daughter, not having taken the same oath,
can freely communicate her knowledge to anyone she
pleases.''

With great quickness of mind she replied that the
oracle itself, when she had asked it if she could communicate the method of calculating it to anyone else, had

answered that if she revealed its secret without its permission she would no longer find truth in its replies. I saw her soul, and I rejoiced to see that she had become calm. Whether I had been lying or not, she owed me gratitude. I had upheld her to her father; but she saw that I had done it only out of politeness, and she wanted me to admit as much when I was alone with her.

The worthy man had the curiosity to ask us both the same question, to see if one would answer white and the other black. Esther saying that she was curious too, he wrote the same question on two sheets of paper. She went to her room to obtain her answer and I obtained mine where I was. She came back with hers before mine was finished. Monsieur D. O. asked if he would do well to get rid of all the French securities he had, at no matter what loss. Esther's oracle answered that, on the contrary, he should try to acquire more of them cheaply, for France would never go bankrupt. Mine answered that if he sold he would be sorry, for a new Comptroller-General[16] would pay everyone the following year. After embracing us both the worthy man left, saying that the agreement between our answers would make him richer by at least half a million in the course of the year, though at the risking of losing three. His daughter looked alarmed; but he embraced her again, saying that it would be only a quarter of what he owned.

Esther, left alone with me, was very much pleased by the compliments I offered her on her excellent answer, which was appropriate yet at the same time daring, for she would not be as well informed as I was concerning French affairs.

"I thank you," she said, "for upholding me. But admit that, to please me, you lied like a trooper."

"Of course, for I see that you are happy; and I will even tell you that you need know no more about it."

"Say that I *cannot* know more. Admit that is true."

"I will admit it to ease your mind."

"You are a cruel man. You answered that there will be a new Comptroller-General in France. By that you risk compromising the oracle; I should never dare to. My dear oracle! I am too fond of it to expose it to such a disgrace."

"It proves that I am not the author of it; but I would wager that Silhouette will be dismissed, now that the oracle has told me so."

"My dear friend, your stubbornness makes me miserable. I cannot be satisfied until I am sure that I possess the cabala as you do, neither more nor less, and now you can no longer tell me that you make it up in your head. You must convince me of the contrary."

"I will consider it, if it will please you."

And so I spent the whole day with the girl, who had everything to make her the happiest of mortals and who would have made me happy if, not loving my freedom[17] above everything else, I could have considered settling in Holland.

The next morning my evil genius made me go to the "City of Lyons"; it was the inn at which Piccolomini was staying. I found him with his wife and a collection of scoundrels who, as soon as they heard my name, all flocked around me. There was a Chevalier Saby,[18] who was wearing the uniform of a major in the service of the King of Poland and whom I had met in Dresden. There was a Baron Wiedau,[19] from Bohemia, who at once told me that his friend the Count of Saint-Germain had arrived[20] at the "Star of the East" and had immediately asked where I was staying. There was a gaunt bravo who was introduced to me as the Chevalier de la Perrine and whom I at once recognized as the Talvis[21] who had broken the Prince-Bishop's bank at Pressburg and had lent me a hundred louis. There was another Italian, who looked like a tinsmith, who was named Neri, and who

told me he had seen me at a *musicau* a year earlier.[22] I
remembered that I saw the unfortunate Lucia there. With
all these sharpers there was also the pretended wife of
the Chevalier Saby; she was a rather pretty Saxon
woman who was paying court to the Countess Piccolomini, speaking very broken Italian. The first thing I did
was to return, with polite thanks, a hundred louis in cash
to La Perrine, who insolently remarked that he now remembered having lent me a hundred louis in Pressburg,
but that my returning them had not made him forget
what was really of consequence.

"You owe me a revenge," he said, "sword in hand.
Here is the scar of the pink you gave me seven years
ago." [23]

With that he opens his ruffle and shows the company
a small scar. The scene had struck the whole room dumb;
the hundred louis, the scar, the demand for revenge, all
seemed equally extraordinary. I told the Gascon that in
Holland I gave no revenges, for I had business, but that
I would defend myself wherever I should be attacked
and in the meanwhile I warned him that I always went
armed with pistols. He replied that he wanted his revenge
sword in hand, but that he would give me time to finish
my business.

Piccolomini, who already had designs on the hundred
louis, immediately made a bank at faro. If I had been wise
I would not have played; but the desire to recover the
hundred louis I had just paid out prompted me to take a
*livret*.[24] Before supper I lost a hundred ducats and
after supper I won them back in counters. When I asked
to be paid so that I could go to bed, Piccolomini gave
me a bill of exchange on the Bank of Amsterdam drawn
by a firm in Middelburg.[25] I did not want to take it; but
I thought I must yield when he said he would negotiate
it for me in the morning. I left the gang of thieves, refusing La Perrine, who had lost the hundred louis, the

loan of another hundred which he insisted I owed him
in requital. In his ill humor he said insulting things to
me; but I bore it and went off to bed, thoroughly resolved
not to return to such a den of cutthroats.

However, the next morning I go out, intending to get
the value of the bill of exchange from Piccolomini. I
first go into a coffeehouse for breakfast, and there find
Rigerboos, Teresa's friend, whom my reader may remember.[26] After an embrace and some talk of "our lady"
(as he always called her), who was in London and
making a fortune there, I showed him my bill of exchange, telling him how it had come into my possession.
He looks at it and says it is forged, that it is a copy of
the genuine one, which had been paid the day before.
Seeing that I am loath to believe it, he takes me with him
to the merchant, who shows me the original which he had
paid to a person he did not know. I ask Rigerboos to come
with me to call on Piccolomini, who would perhaps cash
it for me even so, and, if not, he would be a witness to
whatever might take place.

We go there. Piccolomini, after greeting us politely,
tells me to give him the bill of exchange. which he will
at once send to the merchant to be cashed. Rigerboos
speaks up and tells him that the merchant on whom it
was drawn will not pay it since he has paid it already,
and that the bill he had given me was only a copy of
the original. He pretends to be astonished, he says it is
unbelievable, but that he will look into the matter.

"You shall look into it," I said, "at your convenience;
but in the meanwhile give me five hundred florins."

He says that I know him, that I can wait, that he
guarantees the bill, he raises his voice, his wife comes
and joins in, and then his valet, who is a ruffian. Rigerboos takes me by the arm, leads me outside, and takes me
to see a very fine-looking man who was the equivalent of
a police lieutenant. After hearing the whole story he asks

me to leave the bill with him and to tell him where I
shall be dining. I name Monsieur D. O. and that is
enough. We leave, I thank Monsieur Rigerboos, and I go
to see Esther.

She receives me with some concern, reproaching me
for not having put in an appearance the day before. It
flatters me. She was charming. I say that I have to be
careful not to see her every day, for her eyes search my
soul. After saying that she does not believe a word of it
she asks if I have thought of a way to convince her. She
says that if it is true that my cabala is an intelligence
which has nothing to do with hers, I could make the
cabala itself tell me how to go about enlightening her.
I pretend to find her expedient a good one, and I promise
to ask the question for her. Her father arrived from the
Exchange and we sat down at table. We had come to
dessert when a police officer arrived bringing me five
hundred florins from the Magistrate, for which I gave
him a receipt. After he left I told Monsieur D. O. the
whole story, and the beautiful Esther reproached me for
preferring bad company to hers. She asked me to go
with her to a Dutch comedy, at which I was bored because she gave it her entire attention. Back at her house
she told me the whole plot of the play, then we ate
supper, and nothing was said of the cabala. I promised
her and Monsieur D. O. that I would come to dine with
them every day or would let them know when I could
not.

The next morning at eight o'clock I saw Count Piccolomini before me in my room; his not having had himself announced made me suspicious. I quickly rang, and
my Spaniard came up. He asked me to send him away
because we needed to talk privately. I said that he did
not understand Italian and that I had good reason to
keep him there; but my valet understood everything.

"Yesterday about noon," he said, "two men entered

my room accompanied by the innkeeper, for not knowing French they needed an interpreter. One of them
asked me if I would or would not instantly pay five
hundred florins which I owed you because of a forged
bill of exchange which I had given you and which he
had with him. He said that I must answer yes or no on
the spot without arguing, for such was the order they
had received from the Police Magistrate. Thus badgered,
I decided to pay and did so; but I was very much surprised when the same man told me through the interpreter that he would not give me back the bill until I
had stated from whom I had received it, since it was
forged and the laws governing commerce demanded that
the forger be found. I replied that I did not know the
person who had given it to me. I said that I had been
amusing myself in my room with a small bank at faro
when a man had come in and begun playing on the security of the note and had left after losing it. After he
had gone I learned that he had come alone and that
none of the persons present knew him. The other man
had the interpreter tell me that I should take measures
to find the man, for otherwise the law would hold me
to be the forger and would proceed against me. After
signifying all this to me they left with the bill. My wife
went after dinner to the Police Magistrate to remonstrate
with him, and he heard her out after sending for an
interpreter. The answer he gave her was that it was his
duty to discover the person guilty of forgery, that law
and order demanded it, to say nothing of the honor of
Monsieur Casanova, who might be suspected of being the
forger, and that the merchant himself could proceed
against me in an effort to find out who had forged his
signature. You see my situation. Everything depends
on you; you have received your money, get me out of
this difficulty. You have friends, use your influence, and
no more will be heard of the matter.''

I answered that I did not see what I could do, and I ended by advising him to sacrifice the scoundrel who had given him the forged bill or to disappear. He left, saying I would be sorry.

My Spaniard told me he had heard threats and that I should be on my guard; but I ordered him to hold his tongue, I dressed, and I went to Esther's, where I was faced with trying once more to convince her that my oracle was divine.

She gave me a question in which she challenged the oracle to reveal something which could be known only to herself. It was no time to take chances. Really at a loss, I said that the oracle might reveal some secret which she would later regret my having learned. She replied that she had nothing to fear, and that it was no use for me to think up excuses. Here is the bright idea which finally came into my mind.

In the middle of the little dimple at the bottom of her chin Esther had a pretty black mark, very small but slightly rounded and garnished with four or five slender very short black hairs. This little mark, which we Italians call *neo*,[27] added a charm to her pretty face. Knowing as I did that all marks of this kind which are seen on anyone's face or neck or hands or arms are duplicated on the part of the body corresponding to the visible part, I was certain that Esther must have exactly the same kind of mark as the one on her chin in a place which, modest as she was, she could never have let anyone see, and that she might not even know herself that she had it. Strong in this certainty, I decided to astonish her by answering a question of the kind in exactly these words: "Beautiful and discreet Esther, no one knows that you have a mark exactly like the one at the bottom of your chin on the most secret place in your body consecrated only to love."

Esther did not need a translation, for as the numbers

came from my pen she read them as if they had been letters. She said calmly and serenely that, since I did not need to know what the answer said, I would be doing her a favor if I left it to her.

"Gladly. I even promise you I will never be curious about it. I am satisfied if you are convinced."

"I shall be convinced when I find that what it says is true."

"Do you think I do not know the thing the answer says?"

"I shall be sure you do not know it when I find that what it says is true; but if it is true the oracle will be justified. The thing is so secret that I do not even know it myself. There is no occasion for your knowing it. It is a trifle which cannot interest you, but enough to convince me that the oracle is animated by an intelligence which has nothing to do with your mind."

Unfeigned feeling, driving out deceit, softened me to the point of shedding some tears, which Esther could only interpret to my advantage. They came from my remorse. I loved her, nevertheless I deceived her; but, admitting my guilt, I could only like myself the less, and that avenged her.

Yet I was not entirely sure that what my oracle had told Esther would convince her of its divinity. She could not but be convinced for the moment; but she might cease to be so if she ever learned that the correspondence between marks on the human body was natural and necessary, and with that her conviction would not only disappear but be replaced by contempt. This fear put me in agony, for love loses heart as soon as it discovers that the object it loves is unworthy of its esteem.

After dinner I took leave of her to call on Rigerboos and thank him for what he had done for me with the Police Magistrate. As for Piccolomini's threat, he advised me to go armed with pistols against anything that

might happen to me and to fear nothing in Holland. He
said he was about to leave for Batavia on a ship of which
he owned the entire cargo and was putting all his money
into it, that in the ruinous state of his affairs it was the
only resource left to him. He was making the voyage
without insuring the ship, which would double his profit.
If it was captured or shipwrecked he would perish too;
so he could lose nothing. He laughed as he told me all
this, but he could not talk in such a fashion unless he
was in despair. My dear old friend Teresa Trenti[28] had
contributed in no small measure to his ruin. She was in
London, where, according to what she wrote us, she was
doing well. Instead of Trenti she now called herself
Cornelys. This was Rigerboos's name,[29] though I had not
known it until then. We spent an hour writing to that
most unusual woman, a man whom Rigerboos was commending to her good offices being about to leave for
London. After that we went sleighing at top speed on
the frozen Amstel. This amusement, so much enjoyed
by the Dutch and in my opinion so boring, cost a ducat
an hour. After that we went to eat oysters, and then
we stopped in at *musicaus,* one after another, with no
idea of indulging in debauchery; but this is what happened. It was decreed that every time I preferred certain
diversions to Esther's society some misfortune would
befall me.

As we entered one *musicau* Rigerboos inadvertently
called me by my name; at the same moment I saw one
of the strumpets who are always to be found in these
filthy bordellos come up and look at me closely, and despite the dim light which lit the stinking room I at once
recognized Lucia, whom I had also seen in another place
of the same kind a year earlier[30] and who had not recognized me. I turned away, but it was no use; she came
closer, spoke to me sadly, reminded me who she was, saying that she was as happy to see me in such a flourishing

condition as I must be sad to see what she had become. I condoled with her, and I called to my friend and invited him to go to a room upstairs with me, where the girl would entertain us by telling her story. Lucia had not become actually ugly, but something worse—repulsive. In the nineteen years which had passed since I saw her at Pasiano every kind of debauchery had made her so. She told a very short story at great length. The courier L'Aigle[31] had taken her to lie in at Trieste, where he had remained for five or six months afterward, living on her. A ship's captain who had fallen in love with her persuaded the courier, who passed for her husband, to take her with him to Zante,[32] where he was going for merchandise. At Zante the courier had enlisted and four years later had deserted, leaving her stranded; she stayed there five or six more years, living on what her charms brought her. She had left Zante with a very pretty girl with whom an English naval officer had fallen in love and had gone to England, which she had left two or three years later for Holland, where I saw her. Aside from her mother tongue she had a smattering of Greek, English, French, and Dutch. She emptied two bottles during the hour she spent telling us her sad story, she told us she lived on what some pretty girls she was keeping earned, they being obliged to give her half. Her beauty having vanished, her only resource had been to become a bawd; it was the classic ending; but poor Lucia was only thirty-three; however, she looked fifty, and a woman's age is exactly the age she looks.

Rigerboos asked her if the girls who lived with her were at the *musicau,* and she answered that they were not and that they would never come there, for they were young ladies of good birth who lived with their uncle, who was a Venetian gentleman. At that I burst out laughing. Lucia said that she was only telling me what they had told her and that if we wanted to see them

they were only fifty paces away in a house she rented;
we could go there without apprehension, for their uncle
slept in another part of the city. He only came to dinner
to learn what acquaintances they had made and to collect
the money they had earned. Rigerboos declared that we
must go to see them, and being very curious to speak
with some noble Venetian ladies, I told Lucia to take
us there. I knew very well that they could only be
whores, that their uncle must be a complete rascal, but
there was nothing for it but to go.

I see two quite pretty girls. Lucia announces me as
a Venetian; at which they are beside themselves with
surprise and delighted to see someone with whom they
can talk. I know at once from their dialect that they
are Paduans, I tell them so, they admit it; I ask them
their uncle's name, and they say there are good reasons
why they cannot tell me. Rigerboos says that we can do
without knowing and takes the one he finds most to his
taste. Lucia orders up oysters, ham, a quantity of bottles,
and retires to her room. I did not feel like playing the
fool; but Rigerboos wants to laugh and be rowdy; they
try to play the prude, he banters them, I follow his lead,
they decide to give in, and after putting them in a state
of nature we proceed, often changing partners, to do
to them whatever animality suggests to those who go to
such places only for something to laugh at. After three
or four hours we pay and leave. I privately give poor
Lucia six ducats. The girls got four ducats each, which
in Holland is very good pay. We leave and go to our
lodgings to sleep.

The next morning I wake up very late and in a bad
humor, partly from the debauch of the previous night,
which always leaves the soul sad—*adfigit humo* ("fastens
to earth")[33]—partly because of Esther, who must have
been expecting me. I was to go there for dinner, it was
a regular arrangement, but I shall not want for excuses;

I ring for Leduc to dress me. He goes down to fetch my coffee. I see La Perrine come in, with the so-called Wiedau whom I had seen at Piccolomini's and who said he was a friend of the Count of Saint-Germain, the adept. I was sitting on the bed putting on my stockings. I had three fine rooms, but they were at the back of the house, where, if I had made an outcry, no one would have heard me; I had a bell near the fireplace, which was at the other end of the room; it would be at least a quarter of an hour before Leduc came back with my coffee, I saw almost nothing for it but to let myself be murdered. It was Wiedau who began, telling me that to get out of his difficulty Count Piccolomini had accused them of having given him the bill of exchange in question, and that he had warned them he had done so.

"Our safety demands that we leave at once, and we have no money; we are desperate. Give us only four hundred florins immediately, that will be enough—but immediately and without arguing. Otherwise we will make our escape on foot; but not until we have taken what we see over there; and this is what will persuade you." So saying each of the two robbers draws two pistols from his pockets.

"Violence," I said, "is not necessary. Here you are— and I wish you a good journey."

I take from my breeches pocket a roll of a hundred ducats, I say I do not care about the extra hundred and twenty florins, and I advise them to go before my valet comes up. Wiedau takes it, his hand shaking, puts it in his pocket without even opening it, and La Perrine, always the Gascon,[34] comes over to me and, praising me for my magnanimity, embraces me. After which the two scoundrels make for the door and leave. I consider myself very fortunate to have escaped from the danger so cheaply. I ring repeatedly, not to have them followed but to be dressed quickly, letting my toilet go by the board and stopping neither to inform Leduc of the incident nor to complain to the host of what has happened to me in his inn. After ordering Leduc to go to Monsieur D. O.'s and present my apologies for being unable to dine with him, I go to the Police Magistrate, for whom I have to wait two hours. After hearing my story the worthy man said he would do everything in his power to have the robbers arrested, but that he feared it was too late. I told him that Piccolomini had come to see me, and after giving him a full account of all that he had wanted me to do, I told him he had threatened that I would be sorry. He assured me he would see to it. After that I went home, with a very bitter taste in my mouth, to make my toilet and catch my breath. A lemonade without sugar made me vomit a great deal of bile. I went to Monsieur D. O.'s about nightfall and found Esther serious and looking a little offended; but she changed her attitude when she saw that I looked discomposed.

"Tell me, quick—quick—" she said, "if you have been ill, and I shall feel relieved."

"Yes, my dear, and worse than ill; but now I am perfectly well; you will see it at supper, for I have eaten nothing since dinner yesterday."

It was true; I had eaten only some oysters with the Paduan hussies. The charming Esther invited me to embrace her, and unworthy though I was, I assured her of my affection.

"The news I can tell you," she said, "is that I am sure you are not the author of your oracle, or at least that, like me, you are so only when you wish to be. The answer it gave me is correct, and correct to the point of being divine. It told me something that no one could know, since I did not know it myself. You cannot imagine how surprised I was when I discovered this truth. You are in possession of a treasure; your oracle is infallible; but if it is infallible, it must never lie about anything; it tells me that you love me, and that makes me rejoice, for you are the man of my heart; but I need a proof of your love which, if it is true that you love me, you cannot refuse me. Here, read your answer, I am sure you do not know what it says. Afterward I will tell you what you must do to make Esther perfectly happy.''

I read, pretending that I am reading it for the first time. I kiss the words of the oracle which said that I loved her, I express my delight that the answer has convinced her so easily, then I ask her to forgive me if I cannot believe that such a thing was unknown to her. She replies, blushing slightly, that I would not think it impossible if it was allowable for her to convince me. Then, coming to the proof she demanded to assure her that I loved her, she said I must tell her my secret.

''You love me,'' she said, ''and you cannot object to making a girl happy who will very soon be your wife and whose master you will become. My father will consent. When I am your wife I will do whatever you ask; we will even go to live somewhere else if you wish; but all this will never happen until you have taught me how to obtain an answer without first going to the trouble of making it up in my own head.''

I took her beautiful hands and, kissing them, I said that she knew I was bound to keep my promise to a girl in Paris who certainly could not be compared to her, but that, even so, I was no less obliged to keep it. Alas! Could I give her a better excuse, since I could not teach her a different method of consulting the oracle than the one she used?

Two or three days later an officer was announced to me by a name which I did not know; I sent him word that I was occupied and, my valet being out, I locked my door. After all that had happened to me I had determined to receive no one. The police had failed to catch up with the two robbers who had tried to murder me,

and Piccolomini had vanished; but there were still members of their gang in Amsterdam.

An hour later Leduc comes back and hands me a letter
written in bad Italian, which had been given him by an
officer who was waiting for the answer. I saw that it was
signed by the same name which I did not know. He
wrote that we were acquainted, but that he could only
tell me his name in private and that he had come to see
me only for my own good.

I told Leduc to show him in and to remain in my room.
I see a man of my stature, forty years of age, wearing a
military uniform, and with the look of a gallows bird.

He begins by telling me that we had met in Cerigo
sixteen or seventeen years earlier.[35] I then remember that
I had gone ashore there for a short time when I was accompanying the Bailo[36] to Constantinople, and that the
man must be one of the two poor wretches to whom I
had given alms. I asked him if it was he who had told
me he was the son of a Count Pocchini,[37] of Padua, who
was not a Count, and he congratulated me on my good
memory. I ask him what he has to say to me, and he
answers that he cannot speak in my servant's presence.
I tell him to speak in Italian, and I order Leduc to wait
in the antechamber.

He then tells me that he has learned I had visited his
nieces, that I had treated them like whores, and so he
insists that I give him satisfaction. Weary of being pes-
tered, I run for my pistols and, aiming one of them at
him, I order him to leave. Leduc comes running, and
the scoundrel makes off, saying that he will find me
somewhere.

Ashamed to go and complain to the Police Magistrate,
to whom I should have had to tell the whole scandalous
story, I merely reported the matter to my friend Rigerboos, leaving it to him. The result of his intervention
was that the police ordered Lucia to get rid of the two

Countesses. Lucia herself came the next morning to tell me, with tears in her eyes, the story of the police action, which reduced her to destitution again. I gave her six sequins and she left in better spirits. I asked her not to come to visit me again. Everything I did away from Esther turned out disastrously for me.

It was the perfidious Major Saby who, three days later, came to tell me to be on my guard because a Venetian officer who claimed that I had dishonored him was saying everywhere that since he had vainly asked me to give him satisfaction he had the right to murder me. He said he was desperate, that he wanted to leave, and that he had no money.

When I think of all the annoyances to which I was subjected during the short time of my second stay in Amsterdam, when I could have been living there perfectly happily, I conclude that we are always the first cause of our misfortunes.

"I advise you," Saby went on, "to give the wretch fifty florins and so rid yourself of an enemy."

I agreed, and I gave them to him at noon in a coffee-house which the Major named to me. My reader will see where I met him again four months later.

Monsieur D. O. invited me to sup with him at the Burgomaster's Lodge. It was a great favor, for, contrary to all the usual rules of Freemasonry, no one was admitted there except the twenty-four members who composed it. They were the richest millionaires on the Exchange. He said that he had announced my coming, and that in compliment to me the Lodge would be opened in French. I made such a good impression that I was declared a supernumerary for as long as I should stay in Amsterdam. Monsieur D. O. told me the next day that I had supped with a company which could command three hundred millions.

The next day Monsieur D. O. asked me to do him the

favor of obtaining the answer to a question which, saving his daughter's presence, her oracle had answered too obscurely. Esther urged me to comply. He asked the oracle: Was the man who was trying to persuade him and his associates to enter into a transaction of the utmost consequence really a friend of the King of France?

I instantly see that the man can be no one except the Count of Saint-Germain. Monsieur D. O. was not aware that I knew him. I could not help remembering what Count d'Affry had told me. Here was the opportunity to add luster to my oracle and give my charming Esther something to think about.

After framing the question in a pyramid and writing above the four keys the letters O S A D, all only to impress her the more, I extract the answer, beginning with the fourth key, D. Here it is:

"The friend disavows. The order is signed. It is granted. It is refused. Everything disappears. Delay."

I immediately pretend to find my answer very obscure. Esther, surprised, concludes that it says a great deal in a strange style. Monsieur D. O. says that it is clear to him, and he calls the oracle "divine."

"The word 'delay,' " he says, "is directed to me. You are both clever, you and my daughter, at obtaining oracles, but in interpreting them I am cleverer than you. I shall stop everything. The project is to pay out a hundred millions against the pledge of the French crown diamonds. It is a transaction which the King wants to complete without his ministers' having a hand in it or even knowing of it. So I beg you to mention it to no one."

As soon as Esther was alone with me she said that for once she was certain that this last answer did not come out of my head, and she begged me to tell her what the four letters meant and why I usually omitted them. I replied that I omitted them because experience had taught me that they were not necessary, but that since writing them was enjoined as part of constructing the pyramid I added them when I thought there was a special need for it.

"What do the four letters mean?"

"They are the initials of the ineffable names of the four cardinal intelligences of the earth. It is forbidden to utter them, but anyone who wishes to receive the oracle must know them."

"Ah, my dear friend, do not deceive me, for I believe everything, and since my good faith is divine, it is murder to abuse it. Then you would have to tell me the four ineffable names if you should teach me the cabala?"

"Certainly. And I cannot reveal them except to the person whom I make my heir. Breaking that command is punished by forgetting. Admit, beautiful Esther, that the threat must make me afraid."

"I admit it. Alas for me! Your heir will be your Manon."

"No. She does not have a mind capable of this art."

"Yet you must decide on someone, for you are mortal. My father will give you half of his fortune without obliging you to marry me."

"Alas! What have you said? As if the condition that I must marry you could be irksome to me!"

Three or four days later at ten o'clock in the morning Monsieur D. O. comes hurrying into Esther's room where she was working with me at learning how to operate the oracle by all the four keys and to double, triple, and quadruple it at will. Surprised by his excitement, we rise, he embraces us again and again, he tells us to embrace each other.

"What is this, my adorable Papa?"

He makes us sit down on either side of him and he reads us a letter he has just received from Monsieur Calkoen,[38] one of the secretaries to Their High Power.[39]

The letter said in substance that the French Ambassador, in the name of the King his master, had demanded that the States-General deliver over the pretended Count of Saint-Germain and that he had been answered that the person so named would be delivered to His Most Christian Majesty[40] as soon as he was found. In consequence of this promise, the letter went on, it having been discovered that the person sought was lodging at the "Star of the East," officers had been sent to the inn to take him into custody, but they had not found him. The innkeeper said that the Count had left at nightfall, taking the road to Nijmegen. He was being pursued, but there was no hope of catching up with him. *It was not known* how he had managed to discover that the order had been given and thus escape his doom.

*"It is not known,"* said Monsieur D. O. with a laugh, "but everybody knows it. Monsieur Calkoen himself must have informed this friend of the King of France that a search would be made for him at midnight and that he would be seized if he let himself be found. He was not such a fool. The government will tell the Ambassador it is very sorry His Excellency delayed too long before asking for the person; and the answer will be no surprise to him, for it is the one which is always given in such cases. All the words of the oracle have been verified. We were on the verge of paying him the one hundred thousand florins which he required at once. The pledge was the finest of the crown diamonds, which remains in our hands, but which we will return to him as soon as he appears to claim it, unless the Ambassador demands it. I have never seen a finer stone. You now see the nature of the great debt I owe to your oracle. I am going at once to the Exchange, where the whole Company will express its gratitude to me. After dinner I will entreat you to ask whether we should declare that we have this fine diamond or had better remain silent."

After this magnanimous discourse he again embraced us and then left.

"Now is the time," said Esther, "when you could give me the greatest proof of friendship you can give me, which will cost you nothing and will fill my cup with honor and happiness."

"Command me, my angel, how could I refuse you what will cost me nothing?"

"After dinner my father will want to know if the return of the diamond will be demanded, or if the Company would do better to announce that it is in their custody before they are summoned to produce it. Tell him to apply to me for the answer, and offer to ask the question yourself as well, if my answer is obscure. Put the question now, and I will answer in exactly your words. My father will love me all the better."

"Oh, my dear Esther! Would that I could do far more to assure you of my friendship! Come, let us begin at once."

I insist that she frame the question herself, that she put the four puissant letters in their place with her own hand, and I make her begin her answer by using the divine key. Then, after performing the additions and subtractions which I suggest, she is amazed to obtain the following answer: "The Company would do better to say nothing, for all Europe would laugh at it. The supposed diamond is only paste."

I thought the charming girl would go mad for joy. She was choking with laughter.

"What an answer!" she said. "The diamond is false. How stupid of them to let themselves be taken in! And it is from my oracle that my dear papa will learn this! And it is you who give me such a present! It will be verified at once, and finding that the stone is false, the grave and reverend Company will be under the greatest

obligation to my father, for actually it is on the verge of
dishonor. Can you leave me the pyramid?''

''I leave it with you very gladly, but it will not help
you to learn more than you already know.''

The scene became comic after dinner when the worthy
Monsieur D. O. learned from his daughter's oracle that
the stone was false. He burst into incredulous exclama-
tions. He thought it unbelievable; and he asked me to
put the same question, and when he saw the same answer
come out, though in different words, he left to have the
diamond submitted to every test and to advise silence
when the truth was discovered. But his advice proved
useless. Everyone heard the story, and people said, as
they were bound to say, though it was not true, that the
Company had fallen into the snare and given the impostor the hundred thousand florins he had demanded.

Esther was very proud; but her longing to possess the
science of the oracle as she was convinced I possessed it
became extreme. Word arrived that Saint-Germain had
gone to Emden and then to England. I shall return to
him at the proper place. But now for the blow which
fell on me out of the blue on Christmas Day[41] and which
nearly killed me.

I received a large package from Paris with a letter
from Manon which read as follows:

''Be reasonable and receive the news I send you calmly.
This package contains all your letters and your portrait.
Return my portrait to me, and if you still have my letters burn them. I count on your honor. Think of me no
more. On my side I will do all that lies in my power to
forget you. Tomorrow[42] at this hour I shall be the wife
of Monsieur Blondel,[43] Architect to the King and member of his Academy.[44] You will greatly oblige me if,
when you return to Paris, you will pretend not to know
me wherever you may meet with me.''

Her letter left me in consternation after depriving me

of thought for two full hours. I sent word to Monsieur
D. O. that as I was not well I would stay in my room all
day. I open the packet and, looking at my portrait, I
think I behold a prodigy. My countenance, which had
been cheerful before, now seems threatening and angry.
I began writing to the faithless girl, each time tearing
up my letter as soon as I had finished it. At ten o'clock
I took a bowl of soup, then I went back to bed; but I
could not sleep. Countless plans, no sooner formed than
rejected. I decided to go to Paris and kill this Blondel
whom I did not know and who had dared to marry a
girl who belonged to me and whom everyone believed to
be my wife. I raged at her father and at her brother,
who had not written the news to me. The next morning
I sent word to Monsieur D. O. that I was still ill. I spent
the whole day now writing, now reading over the faithless girl's letters. My empty stomach sent vapors to my
brain which prostrated me; when I recovered I raved,
talking to myself in fits of rage which lacerated my soul.

At three o'clock Monsieur D. O. came to urge me to
go with him to The Hague, where on the next day, which
was St. John's Day,[15] all the notable Freemasons of
Holland were to assemble; but he did not insist when
he saw the state I was in.

"What is the trouble with you?"

"A great grief; I beg you not to ask me more."

He left in distress, asking me to see his daughter. I
saw her appear before me the next morning with her
governess. Astonished to see me so undone, she wanted
to know what the grief was which my mind could not
conquer. I asked her to sit down and not to insist on my
talking of it, assuring her that her mere presence was
enough to keep my sorrow from increasing.

"As long as we talk of other things, my dear friend,
I will not think of the misfortune which crushes my
soul."

"Get dressed and come and spend the day with me."

"Since Christmas Eve I have lived on nothing but chocolate and a few bowls of broth. I am very weak."

At that I saw alarm on her charming countenance.

A moment later she wrote a few lines and handed them to me to read. She said that if a large sum of money, aside from the amount her father owed me, could lighten my grief, she could be my doctor. I answered, after kissing her hand, that what I lacked was not money but a mind strong enough to make a decision. She then said that I should turn to my oracle, and I could not help laughing.

"How can you laugh at it?" she said, with admirable logic. "It seems to me that the cure for your sorrow must be perfectly well known to it."

"I laughed, my angel, because, oddly enough, it was in my mind to tell you that it was you who should consult your oracle. I will tell you that I do not consult mine because I am afraid it will suggest a remedy which I should like even less than the sorrow which afflicts me."

"You could always refuse to employ it."

"If I did that I should fail in the respect which I owe the intelligence."

I saw that my answer overwhelmed her. A moment later she asked me if I would like to have her stay with me all day. I answered that if she would stay for dinner I would get up, I would have three places set at a small table, and I would certainly eat. I saw that she was pleased and happy; she said she would prepare salt cod [46] at the table just as I liked it, and cutlets and oysters. After telling her governess to send their sedan chair home, she went to the hostess's room to order a choice dinner and the stove and the alcohol she needed to cook her little ragouts on the table.

Such was Esther. She was a treasure who was willing to be mine, but on condition that I give her my treasure, which I could not give her. Feeling cheered by the idea that I was to spend the whole day with her, I became certain I could begin to forget Manon. I used the time to get out of bed. When she came back she was delighted to see me up. She begged me with the most enchanting cajoleries to have my hair done and to dress as if I were going to a ball. Her sudden whim made me laugh. She said it would amuse us. I called Leduc and, telling him that I was going to a ball, ordered him to fetch a suitable coat from my trunk, and when he asked me which one Esther said she would choose it. Leduc opened the trunk and, leaving her to her own devices, came to shave me and dress my hair. Happy in her role, Esther made her governess help her lay out on the bed a ruffled shirt and the coat she liked best among my stock. I took a second bowl of broth, of which I felt the need, and I foresaw that I should spend a pleasant day. I began to think that I did not hate Manon but felt contempt for her; analyzing this new feeling gave me hope and renewed my old courage.

I was by the fire letting Leduc dress my hair and enjoying the pleasure which Esther, whom I could not see, was taking in her occupation, when I see her before me, sad and uncertain, holding the letter in which Manon gave me my dismissal.

"Am I to blame," she said timidly, "if I have discovered the cause of your grief?"

"No, my dear. Pity me and let us say no more about it."

"Then may I read them all?"

"All, if you like. You will only pity me the more."

All of the faithless girl's letters and all mine were arranged by date on the night table. Esther fell to reading. As soon as I was dressed and we were alone, for her governess was making lace and never joined in our conversation, Esther said that nothing she had read had ever interested her as much as these letters.

"These accursed letters," I replied, "will be the death

of me. After dinner you shall help me burn them all, even the one which orders me to burn them.''

''Give them to me instead; they shall never leave my hands.''

''I will bring them to you tomorrow.''

There were more than two hundred [47] of them, and the shortest were four pages long. Delighted to have been given them, she said she would gather them together at once and take them home that evening. She asked me if I would send her back her portrait, and I answered that I did not know what to do with it.

''Send it back to her,'' said Esther indignantly; ''I am sure your oracle will give you the same advice. Where is it? May I see it?''

I had her portrait inside a gold snuffbox which I had never shown her for fear that, finding Manon was the prettier, she would suppose I was only showing it to her from a vanity which could not but be injurious to me. I quickly opened my jewel case and handed her the snuffbox. Any other woman but Esther would have found Manon ugly or at least thought she must pretend to find her so; but Esther praised her to me, saying only that the girl's base soul did not deserve to have such a pretty body.

She then wanted to see all the portraits I had, which Signora Manzoni had sent me from Venice, as my reader may remember. There were some nudes, but Esther did not play the prude. O-Morphi [48] delighted her, and she thought her history, which I told her in full, most curious. The portrait of M. M. as a nun and then stark naked made her laugh; she wanted to know the story, but I excused myself. We sat down to dinner and spent two hours over it. Passing very rapidly from death to life, I dined with the greatest possible appetite; Esther kept congratulating herself on having had the skill to be my doctor. Before we rose from the table I promised her I

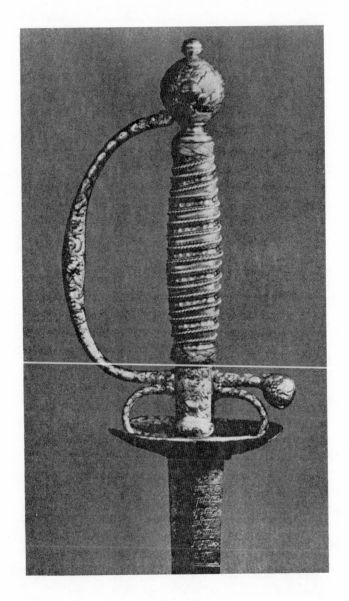

*Hilt of French Dress Sword*

*Girl Examining Her Treasure*

would send Manon's portrait to her husband the next day, and Esther at once approved of my resolve; but an hour later she put a question to the oracle, writing O S A D above the keys and asking if I ought to send her portrait back to the jilt. She calculated, she computed, she added, all the while telling me, though with a smile, that she was certainly not making up the answer, and she extracted the command that I should return the portrait, but to herself, and not commit the base act of sending it to her husband.

I praised her, I embraced her again and again, I told her I would obey the oracle's command, and I ended by congratulating her on no longer needing me to teach her the science, since she was already in full possession of it. At that Esther laughed and, fearing that I really believed it, was at pains to assure me of the contrary. It is in such toying that love delights and in a very little time grows gigantic.

"Should I be too curious," she said, "if I asked you where your portrait is? She says in her letter that she is sending it back to you."

"In my anger I threw it I don't know where. You must realize that such an object, so scorned, can give me no pleasure."

"Let us look for it, my dear friend, I should like to see it."

We found it at once beside some books I had on my bureau. Esther, in astonishment, says that it is a speaking likeness; I think I may go so far as to offer it to her, declaring, however, that it is unworthy of such an honor; and she accepts it with demonstrations of the most vehement gratitude. I spent one of those days with her which we may call happy, if we make happiness consist in a reciprocal and tranquil satisfaction, with none of the violence of aroused passion. She left at ten o'clock, after I promised her I would spend all the next day with her.

After nine hours of the kind of sleep which amazes us when we wake because we seem not to have slept at all, I called on Esther, who was still sleeping but whom her governess insisted on waking. She received me sitting up in bed, all smiles, and pointing to my correspondence, over which she had spent the greater part of the night. She let me kiss her rose and lily face, preventing my hands from touching her alabaster bosom, a third of which dazzled me, but not keeping my eyes from gazing on its beauty. I sat down by her knees, praising her charms and her intelligence, both of a quality to cast a thousand Manons into oblivion. She asked me if her whole body was beautiful, and I answered that, not having become her husband, I had no idea, and she smiled and praised my discretion.

"However," I said, "I learned from her nurse that her figure was perfect and that no blemish broke either the whiteness or the smoothness of her hidden parts."

"You must have a different idea of me," said Esther.

"Yes, my angel, for the oracle let me into a great secret; but that does not keep me from believing you are perfectly beautiful everywhere. If I were your husband I could easily refrain from touching you there."

"Then you think," she said blushing and a little aggrieved, "that by touching me there you would feel something which might lessen your desires?"

At this thrust, which unmasked me completely, I felt overwhelmed with shame of the most painful kind. I begged her to forgive me, and the force of feeling made me shed a few tears on her beautiful hands, to which she responded in kind. Both of us burning with the same fire, we would have seized the occasion to yield to our desires if prudence had permitted. We enjoyed only a sweet ecstasy followed by a calm which made us reflect on the sweet enjoyments which it was in our power to procure. Three hours passed very quickly. She told me to go into her sitting room so that she could dress. We dined with the secretary, whom she did not like and who could not but be very jealous of my good fortune.

We spent the rest of the day together in the confidences which are exchanged when the first foundations of the most intimate tenderness are laid between two persons of different sex who feel that they are born for each other. We were still on fire; but in her sitting room Esther was not as free as in her bedchamber. I went home to my lodging well satisfied with my position. I thought I saw that she might decide to become my wife without demanding that I teach her what I could not teach. I regretted that I had not left her to believe her mastery was as great as mine, and I felt that it was no longer possible for me to show her that I had deceived her and still obtain her forgiveness. Yet only Esther could make me forget Manon, whom I already began to think unworthy of all that I had meant to do for her.

Monsieur D. O. having returned, I went to dine with him. He had been glad to learn that his daughter had cured me by spending a whole day with me. When we were alone he told us he had learned at The Hague that the Count of Saint-Germain had the secret of making diamonds which differed from real ones only in weight, which, however, was no bar to his acquiring great wealth through this art alone. I should have made him laugh heartily if I could have told him all I knew about the man.

The next day I took Esther to the concert. She said that on the following day she would not leave her room and that we could talk about our marriage. It was the last day of the year 1759.[49]

## CHAPTER II

*I enlighten Esther. I leave for Germany. My
adventure near Cologne. The Burgomaster's
wife; I conquer her. Ball at Bonn. Welcome
from the Elector of Cologne. Luncheon at
Brühl. First intimacy. I sup uninvited at General Kettler's. I am happy. My departure
from Cologne. La Toscani. The jewel. My arrival at Stuttgart.*

January 1, 1760.

THIS MEETING with Esther could not but have
consequences. Love had summoned me to it, and Honor
must be of the party. I went, determined not to deceive
the angelic girl and certain that I would not fail in my
resolve. I found her in bed. She said she would stay there
all day and that we would work. Her governess brought
us a small table, and she placed before me several questions, all intended to convince me that, before becoming
her husband, I should impart my science to her. They
were all of a tenor which would oblige the intelligence
either to command or forbid me to satisfy her. I could
do neither, for a prohibition might have irked her to the
point of losing any inclination to grant me her favors. I
got out of it by equivocal answers until Monsieur D. O.
came to summon me to dinner. He allowed his daughter
to remain in bed, but on condition that she would spend

the rest of the day without working, for intellectual effort could only increase her headache. She promised, and I was greatly relieved.

Leaving the table, I returned to her room and found her asleep. I felt I should respect her slumbers; but when she woke, reading the heroid [1] of Eloise and Abelard set us on fire. The conversation turning to the secret which the oracle had revealed to her and which could be known only to herself, she allowed my hand to search for it, and when she saw me doubtful because it could not be felt she made up her mind to expose it to view. It was no bigger than a millet seed. She let me kiss it until I lost my breath.

After spending two hours in amorous toyings without ever coming to the great act, which she was right to refuse me, I resolved to tell her the truth, although I saw that after two confessed false confidences the third might well revolt her.

Esther, who was infinitely intelligent and whom I could never have deceived if she had been less so, heard me without surprise, without interrupting me, and without the slightest trace of anger. At the end of my confession she replied that, being sure that I loved her and finding this last confidence obviously false, she was convinced that my reason for not teaching her to operate the cabala was that it did not lie in my power, and hence she would no longer urge me to do what I could not or would not.

"And so," she said, "let us be good friends until death and say no more on the subject. I forgive you, and I am sorry for you if love deprived you of the courage to be sincere. You have convinced me of your science only too well. That is over and done with. You could never have known a thing which concerned only me, and which I myself did not know."

"My dear, don't let your logic run away with you.

You did not know you had the mark, and I knew you had it.''

''You knew it? How did you find out? It is incredible.''

''I will tell you all.''

I thereupon expounded to her the whole theory of the correspondence between the signs on the human body, ending by astonishing and convincing her when I said I was certain that her governess, who had a large mole on her right cheek, must have one like it on her left thigh.

''I will find out,'' she said; ''but I am surprised that you alone possess this knowledge.''

''The thing is well known, my charming friend, to everyone acquainted with anatomy, physiology, and even astrology, a chimerical science when it is carried to the point of finding the causes of all our actions in the stars.''

''Then tomorrow, tomorrow and no later, bring me books in which I can find out many such things. I cannot wait to become learned and able to astonish the ignorant with my numerical cabala, for any science without charlatanry never impresses them. I will devote myself to study. Let us love each other, my dear friend, until death. We need not marry to do that.''

I returned to my inn well satisfied and as if relieved of a great burden. The next day I brought her all the books I could find which were sure to entertain her. There were good ones and bad, but I warned her of that. My *Conics*[2] pleased her because she saw that it bore the stamp of truth. Wanting to shine with the help of the oracle, she needed to become a good natural scientist, and I set her on the right road. I then decided to make a little journey in Germany before returning to Paris; and she approved my plan, very glad when I assured her that I would see her again before the end of the year. But though I did not see her again I cannot reproach myself with having deceived her, for everything that happened to me prevented me from keeping my promise.

I wrote to Monsieur d'Affry, asking him to send me a passport which I needed because I wanted to make a trip through the Empire, where the French and all the then belligerent powers were campaigning.[3] He replied very politely that I did not need one, but that if I insisted he would send it to me. His letter was enough. I put it in my portfolio, and at Cologne it gave me more standing than a passport.

I transferred to Monsieur D. O. all the money I had in the hands of several bankers. He gave me a circular letter of credit drawn on ten or twelve of the most prominent firms in Germany. So I left in my post chaise, for which I had sent to Moerdijk, with nearly a hundred thousand Dutch florins at my disposal, with plenty of valuable jewels and rings, and richly turned out in every respect. I sent back to Paris a Swiss lackey with whom I had started out, keeping only Leduc, who sat behind.

Such is the whole story of my second short stay in Holland, where I accomplished nothing to better my fortune. I had troubles there, but when I remember them I conclude that love made up to me for everything.

I stopped at Utrecht for only a day to see the estate[4] belonging to the Herrnhuters;[5] and on the next day but one I reached Cologne at noon; but half an hour before I arrived there five deserters, three on my right and two on my left, aimed at me, demanding my purse. My postilion, threatened with death by a pistol in my hand, gave his horse both spurs, and the murderers fired their muskets at me, but they harmed only my carriage. They did not have the sense to fire at the postilion. If I had carried two purses, as the English do, the lighter one being intended for bold robbers, I should have thrown it to the wretches; but since I had only one, and it very well stocked, I risked my life to save it. My Spaniard was amazed that the balls, which he had heard whistling past his head, had not touched him. At Cologne the

French were in winter quarters.[6] I found lodgings at the "Sign of the Sun."[7] Entering the public room, I saw the Count of Lastic,[8] Madame d'Urfé's nephew, who after making me all the usual offers took me to see Monsieur de Torcy,[9] who was the Commandant. Instead of a passport I showed him Monsieur d'Affry's letter, and no more was needed. When I told him what had just befallen me he congratulated me on my good luck, but he blamed me in no uncertain terms for the display I had made of my courage. He said that if I was in no hurry to leave I should perhaps see them hanged; but I wanted to leave the next day.

I had to dine with Monsieur de Lastic and Monsieur de Flavacourt,[10] who together persuaded me to go to the theater.[11] So I had to dress, for I was sure to be introduced to ladies and I wanted to make an impression.

Having taken a place on the stage[12] and seen a pretty woman turn her lorgnette on me, I asked Monsieur de Lastic to introduce me, and between the first and second acts he took me to her box, where he began by naming me to Count von Kettler,[13] Lieutenant-General in the Austrian service who was attached to the French army, as the French Monsieur de Montazet[14] was to the Austrian. Immediately afterward he introduced me to the lady, who at once struck me. She first asked me questions about Paris, then about Brussels, where she had been brought up, though she did not seem to listen to my answers. My laces, my watch charms, my rings, distracted her attention.

Changing the subject, as if she had suddenly remembered it was her duty to inquire, she asked me if I would spend some days in Cologne, and she pretended to be hurt when I answered that I expected to dine in Bonn the next day. General Kettler then rose, saying that *he was sure the beautiful lady could persuade me to put off my departure;* and he went out with Lastic, leaving me alone with the interesting beauty. She was the wife of

Burgomaster $X$,[15] and Count Kettler was always with her.

"Is he wrong," she said invitingly, "to be certain I have that power?"

"I do not think so, but he might be wrong in thinking that you would wish to use it."

"Excellent. Then we must trap him, if only to punish him for his indiscretion. Stay."

This unfamiliar language left me gaping. I had to recollect myself. Could I expect such terminology in Cologne? I thought "indiscretion" sublime, "punishment" perfectly apt, "trap" delicious, and the idea of my being the instrument of the trapping struck me as divine. It would have been stupid to inquire further. Assuming a submissive and grateful air, I indicated my obedience by bending over her hand and kissing it.

"Then you will stay, and it is very kind of you, for if you left tomorrow it would seem that you had come here only to affront us. The General is giving a ball tomorrow, and you shall dance with us."

"Dare I flatter myself, Madame, that I shall not share the honor of escorting you in all the contradances with anyone else?"

"I will dance with someone else only when you are tired."

"That is, when I drop dead."

"But where did you get that pomade which perfumes the air? You were on the stage and I smelled it."

"It comes from Florence, and if it goes to your head I will at once have my hair dressed again."

"Good Heavens, that would be murder! Such a pomade would make me completely happy."

"And you will make me so if you will permit me to send you twelve jars of it tomorrow."

The General's return prevented her from answering. I rose to leave.

"I am sure," he said, "that you have put off your departure. Madame has made you promise to sup and dance at my house tomorrow. Has she not?"

"She has led me to hope, General, that you would do me so much honor, and that I shall have the honor of dancing the contradances with her. How could I leave after that?"

"You are right. I will expect you."

I left the box in love and already happy in imagination, and went back to the stage, where the scent of my pomade won me compliments from all the young officers. It was a present from Esther, and this was the first time I had used it. The box contained twenty-four jars; I took out twelve and sent it to her at nine o'clock the next morning, wrapped in waxed cloth and sealed, and addressed to her as if it came from a merchant.

I spent the morning having a hired servant show me the wonders of Cologne, all of them heroi-comic. I laughed when I saw the statue of the steed Bayard,[16] which Ariosto has made so famous, ridden by the four sons of "Aymon."[17] He was Duke Amone, father of the invincible Bradamante and the fortunate Ricciardetto.

All the guests at Monsieur de Castries's,[18] where I dined, were surprised that General Kettler had himself invited me to his ball, since he was extremely jealous of his lady, who only put up with him to feed her vanity. He was advanced in years, with a repulsive face and no qualities of mind which gave him any claim to inspire love. However, he had to resign himself to my sitting beside her at his supper and spending the whole night either talking or dancing with her. I returned to my lodging so much in love that I gave up all thought of leaving. In a moment of fervor I made bold to tell her that if she would promise me a meeting alone I would stay in Cologne for the whole Carnival.[19]

"And if after I promised," she answered, "I failed you, what would you say?"

"I would lament my fate in solitude and say that you had been unable to keep your word."

"You are kind. Stay with us."

On the next day but one after the ball I made her my first visit and she introduced her husband, a fine man who was neither young[20] nor handsome but most obliging. An hour later, hearing the General's carriage stop at her door, she said that if he asked me if I was planning to attend the Elector's[21] ball at Bonn I must answer that I would certainly be there. Five or six minutes later I slipped away.

I knew nothing about the ball, but I at once made inquiries. The entire nobility of Cologne were invited to it, and, since it was a masked ball,[22] anyone could attend it. I decided to go, but as incognito as possible, even if the General did not ask me the question. It seemed to me that, by advising me how to answer him, Madame $X$ had ordered me to go. I could put no other interpretation on it. I was certain that she would be present, and I hoped. The woman's mind was of the subtlest. Nevertheless, to everyone who asked me if I was going to the ball, I answered that I had reasons for not attending it; and to the General himself I said that I would not go when he asked me, in Madame $X$'s presence, if I would be there. I said that my health did not permit me that pleasure. He replied that all pleasures were to be eschewed when they might injure one's health.

The day on which the ball was to be given I left at nightfall alone in a post carriage with my strongbox and two dominoes and wearing a coat which no one had seen on me. At Bonn I engaged a room, where I masked and left the second domino and my strongbox. I locked it and went to the Court in a sedan chair. Unknown to everyone, I saw all the ladies of Cologne, and the beautiful $X$ with her face unmasked sitting at a faro bank punting by ducats. I see with pleasure that the banker

is Count Verità,[23] of Verona, who had made my acquaintance in Bavaria. He was in the Elector's service.
His small bank contained only five or six hundred ducats,
and the punters, both men and women, were some ten or
twelve. I stand beside Madame, and the banker gives me
a *livret* and offers me the cards to cut. I decline, and
Madame *X* cuts.

I begin punting, staking ten ducats on one card, it
loses four times running, and the same thing happens to
me at the next deal. At the third deal no one will cut.
The banker turns to the General, who was not playing,
and he cuts. I take it for a good omen, I stake fifty
ducats, and I get the *paroli*.[24] At the next deal I broke
the bank. Everyone was curious, I saw that I was followed, nevertheless I managed to escape. I had my sedan
chair carry me to my room, where I changed dominoes
and left my money; I went back to the ball, where I saw
a new banker and a great deal of gold; but having decided to play no more I had no money. Everyone was
wanting to discover who the masker was who had broken
the bank. I prowl everywhere; I see Madame *X* conversing with Count Verità, who is sitting beside her, I approach, and I hear them speaking of me; he was saying
that the Elector wanted to know who the masker was
who had broken the bank, and that General Kettler had
informed him that it might be a Venetian who had arrived in Cologne a week or ten days earlier. She said I
had told her I was not well enough to go to the ball.
The Count said that he knew me, that if I was in Bonn
the Elector would learn of it, and that I would not leave
before he had spoken with me. Hearing all this, I foresaw that I could easily be discovered after the ball; but
I defied him to do it as long as I was there. But I did
the wrong thing. A contradance was being formed, I
took a fancy to dance, not foreseeing that I should have
to remove my mask. This proved to be the case when it

was too late for me to retreat. When Madame $X$ saw me she said she had been mistaken and had wagered that I was a masker who had broken Count Verità's bank. I replied that I had only just arrived.

But at the end of the contradance, when Count Verità saw me, he said that since I was at the ball he was sure I was the person who had broken his bank; I kept denying it, and after eating something at the buffet I went on dancing. Two hours later Count Verità told me with a laugh that I had gone to change my domino and where my room was.

"The Elector," he said, "has learned the whole story, and to punish you for your trickery he commands me to tell you that you shall not leave tomorrow."

"Will he have me arrested?"

"Why shouldn't he, if you refuse to dine with him tomorrow?"

"I will obey. Where is he? Present me at once."

"He has left; but come to me tomorrow at noon."

When he presented me the prince was standing among five or six courtiers, and I had an awkward moment, for, never having seen him, I was looking for a person in ecclesiastical dress and did not find him. It was he himself who ended my embarrassment by saying to me in the Venetian dialect that he was robed as the Grand Master of the Teutonic Order.[25] I nevertheless made him the customary slight genuflection, and when I started to kiss his hand he withdrew it and clasped mine. He said that when he was in Venice I was under the Leads, that his nephew the Elector of Bavaria[26] had told him that when I escaped I had stopped in Munich, and that he would not have let me go if, instead of to Munich, I had gone to Cologne. He said he hoped that after dinner I would tell him the story of my escape, and that I would stay for supper and a little masquerade which we would find amusing. I promised to tell him the whole story of my escape if he had the patience to listen, for it took two hours to tell it, and I then made him laugh by repeating my brief dialogue with the Duke of Choiseul [27] on the subject.

During dinner the prince continued to speak to me in Venetian; he said the most obliging things. He was gay, and with the health he appeared to enjoy no one would have foreseen that his life was to be short. He died a year later.

As soon as he rose from the table he asked me to tell the whole story of my escape, which kept the whole distinguished company interested for two hours. My reader knows the story; but in written form it is nowhere near as interesting as it is when I tell it.

The Elector's little ball was most pleasant. It was a masquerade. We had all dressed as peasants[28] in a private wardrobe of the prince's, where the ladies went to dress in one room while the men dressed in another. Since the Elector himself was dressed as a peasant, anyone who should have refused to wear a similar disguise would only have made himself ridiculous. General Kettler looked a real peasant; Madame $X$ was delicious. Nothing was danced but contradances and ballets in the style of several German provinces,[29] which were most unusual. There were only three or four women of the recognized nobility; the rest, some pretty, others less so, were private acquaintances of the Elector, who was all his life a great lover of the fair sex. Two of these women[30] danced the furlana,[31] and the Elector took the greatest pleasure in making me dance it. It is a Venetian dance which has not its equal for violence in all Europe; it is danced by couples and, there being two women, they almost killed me. Completely out of breath after twelve or thirteen, I begged for mercy. In a dance whose name I have forgotten the men kissed the peasant girls they caught; I did not beat about the bush: I kept catching Madame $X$,

and the peasant-Elector kept saying "Bravo, bravo."
Poor Kettler was furious.

She found an opportunity to tell me that all the ladies
from Cologne would leave the next day at noon, and
that it would be to my credit if I would invite them all
to luncheon at Brühl,[32] sending them two or three[33]
notes in which I should write the names of the men by
whom they were escorted.

"Put yourself in Count Verità's hands," she said,
"and he will see to it; just tell him that you want to do
the same thing the Prince of Zweibrücken[34] did two
years ago; but lose no time. Count on twenty people,
and set the hour. Above all make sure that the notes are
distributed at nine o'clock in the morning."

Delighted with the power which the charming woman
believed she could exercise over me, I instantly decided
to obey her. Brühl, luncheon, twenty people, like the
Duke of Zweibrücken, one o'clock, Count Verità—I was
as well informed as if she had spent an hour instructing
me.

I leave at once, still dressed as a peasant; I ask a page
to show me to Count Verità's rooms. He laughs to see
how I am dressed, I tell him my plan in a few words, I
ask his help as if my business were a most urgent matter
of state.

"What you want," he said, "is perfectly easy. It will
cost me no more than the trouble of writing a note to
the steward in charge there and sending it to him at
once. Simply tell me how much you wish to spend."

"As much as possible," I said.

"You mean as little."

"No, as much, for I wish to entertain splendidly."

"All the same you must name an amount, for I know
the man."

"Tell him two hundred ducats."

"That is enough. The Duke of Zweibrücken spent no more."

He writes the note, he sends it, assuring me that all will be attended to. I leave him, thinking of the notes. I speak to a bright-looking Italian page. I tell him I will pay a ducat to a valet who will give me the names of the ladies from Cologne who had come to Bonn and of the gentlemen who had accompanied them. A half hour later I received word that all was done. Before going to bed I myself wrote eighteen notes, and the next morning sealed and sent them to their addresses by a hired servant for whom the innkeeper vouched.

At nine o'clock I went to take leave of Count Verità, who gave me, on the Elector's behalf, a gold box adorned with a portrait-medallion of him robed as Grand Master of the Teutonic Order. I was very sensible of this mark of condescension; I wanted to go and thank His Highness, but the Count said I might wait until I passed through Bonn on my way to Frankfort.

The hour for my luncheon was set at one o'clock, but at noon I was already at Brühl. It is a pleasure house belonging to the Elector, the beauty of which lies in the taste of its furnishings. It was a copy of Trianon.[35] In a spacious room I saw a table set for twenty-four persons; there were silver-gilt forks and spoons, porcelain plates, and, on the buffet, a profusion of silverware and large silver-gilt dishes. On two other tables at the other end of the room I saw bottles filled with the most celebrated wines of all Europe and an assortment of all kinds of sweets. When I told the steward that it was I who was giving the luncheon, he said that I would be well satisfied and that he had been there since six o'clock in the morning. He said that the cold collation would be limited to twenty-four dishes; but that I should have twenty-four plates of English oysters and a dessert which would cover the entire table. Seeing a large number of servants, I said they were not needed; but he said they were, for the guests' own servants would not come in. He said I should not be concerned, because they were informed of it.

I received all my guests at the doors of their carriages, confining my compliments to begging pardon for the boldness which had procured me the honor of their company. At one o'clock the luncheon was served, and I saw joy in Madame *X*'s lovely eyes when she saw the same lavishness which the Elector would have displayed. She was not unaware that everyone knew it was all done for her, but she was delighted to see that I paid no more attention to her than I did to the others. There were twenty-four places set, and though I had sent out only eighteen notes the places were all taken. Hence there were six people who had come without being invited. This pleased me. I refused to sit down; I served the ladies, darting from one to another and eating what they gave me where I stood.

The English oysters ended only with the emptying of the twentieth bottle of champagne. When the luncheon itself began, the company was already tipsy. Composed, as it should be, only of entrées, it was the choicest of repasts. Not a single drop of water was drunk, for neither Rhine wine nor Tokay will tolerate it. Before the dessert was served an immense dish containing a ragout of truffles was set on the table. It was emptied in accordance with my advice to wash it down with maraschino.

"It is like water," said the ladies, and they drank it as if it really were water. The dessert was magnificent. The portraits of all the sovereigns of Europe appeared on it, the guests complimented the steward, who was there, and he, bridling with vanity, said it was all pocketable, whereupon everyone pocketed some. Then the General made a very stupid remark, which the company howled down by a general burst of laughter.

"I am sure," he said, "that this is a trick the Elector has played on us. His Highness has wished to remain incognito, and Monsieur Casanova has perfectly served the prince's design."

After the great burst of laughter, which gave me time to think:

"If, General," I said modestly, "the Elector had given me such an order I should have obeyed it; but it would have been a humiliation. His Highness has seen fit to do me a far greater honor, and here it is."

So saying, I handed him the snuffbox, which then made the round of the table two or three times.

My guests rose, and everyone was astonished to have spent three hours at table. After all the usual compliments the distinguished company set off for Cologne in order to be there in time for the play. Very well pleased with my brilliant entertainment, I left the worthy steward twenty ducats for the servants. He asked me to write Count Verità that I was satisfied.

I reached Cologne in time to go to the curtain raiser. Having no carriage, I went to the theater in a sedan chair. Seeing Madame *X* with Monsieur de Lastic, I went to her box. She at once said mournfully that the General had felt so ill that he had been obliged to go to bed. A moment later Monsieur de Lastic left us alone, whereupon the charming woman paid me compliments which were worth a hundred of my luncheons. She said that the General had drunk too much Tokay and that he was a filthy beast who had said it was well known who I was and that it was entirely improper to treat me like a prince. She had replied that, on the contrary, I had treated them like princes of whom I was the very humble servant. At that he had insulted her.

"Tell him to go to the devil," I said.

"It is too late. A woman whom you do not know would capture him; I would pretend indifference, but I should not like it."

"I understand very well. Why am I not a great prince! In the meanwhile I must tell you that I am far more ill than Kettler. I am at death's door."

"You are joking, I suppose."

"I am speaking seriously. Those kisses at the Elector's ball gave me a taste of a strange nectar. If you do not take pity on me I shall leave here unhappy for the rest of my life."

"Put off leaving. Forget about Stuttgart. I think of you; and it is not my fault. Believe me, I have no wish to deceive you."

"This evening, for example, if you did not have the General's carriage and I had mine I could see you home with perfect propriety."

"Do not worry! Haven't you yours?"

"No."

"In that case it is I who must take you home; but, my dear friend, it must come about perfectly naturally. You will give me your arm to my carriage, I will ask you where yours is, and when I hear you say you haven't one I will tell you to get in and I will drop you at your inn. It will only be ten minutes; but until we can do better it is something."

I answered only with my eyes, for joy overwhelmed my soul. After the play up comes her footman to tell her the carriage is at the door. We go down, she asks me the question we have agreed upon, and when she hears that I have no carriage, she does better. She tells me that she is going to the General's to ask after his health, and that if I wish to go there she can take me to my inn afterward.

Her quickness of mind was divine. We had to cross the whole, ill-paved city twice. It was a closed carriage. We did what we could, but almost nothing. The moon was ahead of us, and the beastly coachman kept looking around. It gave me the horrors. The sentinel told the coachman that His Excellency could see no one. She orders him to drive to my inn, and now we had the moon behind. We did a little better, but badly, nothing was right. The scoundrel never drove so fast in his life. However, when I got out I gave him a ducat. I went to bed, mortally in love, and in a sense worse off than before. Madame *X* had convinced me that making me happy made her happy. I decided to stay on in Cologne until the General was gone.

The next day at noon I went to the General's to have my name entered;[36] but he was receiving visitors. I was shown in. Madame *X* was there. I pay the General the appropriate compliment, and he responds only with a cold bow. There were many officers standing about, so four minutes later I slipped away. He stayed at home for three days, and Madame *X* never went to the theater.

On the last day of the Carnival the General invited a large company[37] to supper, and after supper there was to be dancing. I go as usual to make my bow to Madame *X* in her box, I am left alone with her, she asks me if the General has invited me to supper, I answer no, and she replies in a peremptory and indignant tone that I must go even so.

"You have spoken without thinking," I said gently, "I will obey you in anything except that."

"I know all that you can say. You must go. I shall consider myself insulted if you are not at the supper. You can never give me a greater proof of your affection and esteem."

"Say no more. I will go. But tell me if you realize that your fatal command puts my life in danger, for I am not the man to pretend indifference if the brute insults me."

"I am well aware of that; I love your honor at least as much as I do your life. Nothing will happen to you, I answer for it, leave it all to me. You must go. Promise me this instant that you will, for I have made up my mind. If you will not go, I will not go either; but after that we shall not see each other again."

"I will go. Let us say no more about it."

Monsieur de Castries entered just then, and I went back to the stage. Foreseeing the worst of insults, which was bound to have fatal consequences, I spent two hours in hell. Yet I prepared to be on my good behavior. I went to the General's immediately after the play; only five or six people were present. I go up to a canoness who was fond of Italian poetry, and our conversation becomes engrossing; within half an hour the room was full; the last to arrive was Madame *X* with the General. Occupied with the lady, I remain where I am, so he does not see me. Madame *X*'s cajoleries left him no time to look over the company. He goes elsewhere. A quarter of an hour later the Canoness is summoned to supper, she takes my arm, in a moment I am sitting at the table beside her, and in another moment all the places are occupied. But a foreigner who must have been invited remains standing. The General exclaims that it is impossible, and while he waits for a place to be set for him he passes his guests in review, and since I am not looking at him he names me and says:

*"Monsieur, I did not invite you."*

I reply, firmly but respectfully:

*"That is true, General, but since I am sure it can only have been an oversight, I have come nevertheless to pay Your Excellency my respects."*

After answering in these words, I continued talking to the Canoness without looking at anyone. Nobody spoke until after three or four minutes of the bleakest silence. The Canoness then said some amusing things, which I relayed to the other guests, and suddenly the whole table was gay.

The General sulked, which was by no means all the same to me. I was determined to put him in a good humor, and I watched for the opportunity. It came at the second course. Monsieur de Castries praised the Dauphine,[38] the conversation moved on to her brother

the Count of Lausitz,[39] to her other brother the Duke of
Kurland,[40] and then to the former Duke Biron,[41] who
was in Siberia, and to his personal qualities. One of the
guests said that his only merit was to have pleased the
Empress Anna;[42] I begged to differ.

"His great merit is to have faithfully served the last
Duke Kettler,[43] who, but for the courage of the now unfortunate man, would have lost all his field equipment
in the war then ending. It was Duke Kettler himself
who, with a heroism worthy of history, sent him to the
Court of Petersburg, and Biron never asked for the
dukedom. He only wanted to enforce his claim to the
countship of Wartenberg,[44] recognizing the rights of the
younger branch of the house of Kettler, which would be
reigning today but for the whim of the Czarina, who
insisted on making her favorite Duke."

"I have never met anyone better informed," said the
General, looking at me, "and but for that whim I should
be reigning today."

After this modest statement he burst out laughing
and sent me a bottle of Rhine wine with a label bearing
the date 1748. From then on he talked with no one but
me, and we rose from the table good friends. There was
dancing all night; the Canoness was my partner. I
danced only one minuet with Madame *X.* Toward the
end of the ball he asked me if I was leaving soon, a
question which no one of any intelligence asks. I replied that I should not leave until after the review.

I went to bed well satisfied that I had given Madame
*X* such a proof of my love that it would be hard to imagine a stronger, but thanking Fortune that the reply
which my good Genius had suggested to me had reduced
the brute to reason, for God knows what I would have
done if he had dared order me to leave his table. The first
time we met again she told me that she had shuddered
when she heard him tell me he had not invited me.

"It is certain," she said, "that he would have said more to you if your proud excuse had not petrified him, and in the contrary case I had made up my mind what I should do."

"What?"

"I would have risen and we would have left together; Monsieur de Castries has told me that he would have done likewise, and I believe that all the ladies you invited to Brühl would have followed our example."

"But even that would not have ended the matter, for I would have demanded satisfaction."

"I understand that, and I ask you to forgive me for having exposed you to the danger; but on my side I shall never forget it until I have completely convinced you of my gratitude."

Hearing three or four days later that she was ill, I went to see her at eleven o'clock in the morning, so that I should not find the General there. She received me in her husband's room; he at once asked me if I had come to dine with them, and I answered yes. I enjoyed the dinner more than I did the supper at the General's two days after I arrived in Cologne. The Burgomaster was one of those men who preferred peace in his household above all things, and his wife ought to have loved him, for he was not among those who say: *Displiceas aliis, sic ego tutus ero* ("Be unpleasing to other men, and I shall be safe").[45]

Before dinner she showed me the whole house:

"This is our bedroom, and this is a little room in which I sometimes sleep alone when propriety demands it; and this is a public church, which we can consider our chapel,[46] for from these two grated windows we see the mass. We attend it only on feast days, making our way down this small staircase, at the foot of which there is a door, of which this is the key."

It was the second Saturday in Lent; we ate a very

good fast-day dinner; but the food was what interested me least. What made my amorous soul completely happy was the charming woman, whom, at the age of twenty-five, I saw adored by her whole family. She had a sister-in-law and several children—the progeny of a brother of her husband's—whose guardian he was. I left early to write to Esther, whom my new passion was leading me to neglect.

The next day, wearing early-morning dress, I went to hear mass at Madame $X$'s little church. It was a Sunday. I saw her come out of the little door under the grated windows. She was followed by her nieces, and her lovely head was swathed in the hood of her cloak. The door was so far recessed into the wall that it could not be seen. The devil, who, as everyone knows, sets more snares in church than anywhere else, instantly inspired me with the happy plan of spending whole nights in her arms, going up to her room through this auspicious door.

I told her my plan the next day at the theater. She laughed. She said she had thought of it too and that she would give me a note with the necessary directions, wrapped up in the gazette, as soon as possible. We could not talk. A lady from Aix-la-Chapelle who had come to spend a few days in Cologne occupied her entire attention, and the box was full of visitors.

She publicly gave me the gazette the next day, saying that she had found nothing of interest in it. Here is a copy of the letter I found enclosed:

"The happy plan which love has conceived is not susceptible to difficulties but it is to uncertainties. The wife sleeps in the little room only when the husband requests her to permit this separation; and then it may continue for three or four days. She thinks that the reason for the request will soon arrive, but long familiarity makes it impossible for her to impose upon him. Hence it will be necessary to wait. The woman in love will see to informing the lover. The method will be to

hide in the church, and there can be no thought of corrupting the man who opens it and locks it up. Though
poor he is too stupid to corrupt. He would betray the
secret. The only way is to hide in the church and be
locked in. He locks it at noon on week days and in the
evening on feast days, and he opens his church at dawn
every day. When the time comes the door will be shut
in such a way that, to open it, the lover will only need to
give it a little push. Since the little room is separated
from the bedroom only by a very thin partition, he is
warned that he must never blow his nose and that he
must not catch a cold, for it would be disastrous if he
happened to cough. The lover's getting away will present
no difficulty. He will go down to the church and he will
leave it as soon as he finds it opened. Since the beadle
will not have seen him when he locked up, it is against
all probability that he will see him when he opens it.''

Her letter put my soul in ecstasy. I kissed it countless
times. The next morning I went and examined the whole
inside of the church; this was the most important thing
to do. There was a pulpit, in which the man would not
have seen me; but the steps to it were in the sacristy,
which was kept locked. I decided on one of the two con-
fessionals, which had half doors in front. By lying down
where the confessor put his feet, I might well not be
seen; but the space was so small that I thought it could
not possibly contain me with the half door closed. I
waited until about noon, and I got into it when I saw
there was no one left in the church. I fitted, but so poorly
that I would be seen by any person who came near. In
all undertakings of this kind one accomplishes nothing
if one does not count on Fortune. Resolved to entrust
myself to her sway, I went home fairly well satisfied. I
wrote my goddess an account of all I had done, wrapping
my narrative in the same gazette and handing it to her
at the theater, where I saw her every day.

A week or ten days later she asked the General in my presence if he had any errand for her husband, who was to leave for Aix-la-Chapelle the next day at noon and would return in three days.

It was all I needed to know. A glance she gave me told me that I was to take advantage of her announcement. What joy! And all the greater because I had a slight cold. The next day was a feast day, which was even more to the good; I would not hide in the confessional until evening and so should avoid the fatigue of spending the whole day in the church.

I went there at four o'clock and crouched in the darker confessional, commending myself to God. At five o'clock the man with the keys, after making a round of the church which was only perfunctory, left and locked the door. I came out and sat down on a bench, from which, seeing her outline through the grating, I was sure that she had seen me. She closed the blind.

A quarter of an hour later I went to the door, pushed, and it opened. I closed it and, groping my way, sat down on the lowest stairs. There I spent five hours, which, as I was expecting my happiness, I should not have found trying if the rats which kept coming and going close by had not constantly preyed on my mind. Accursed beast, which I have never been able to ignore, even as I have never succeeded in overcoming the unbearable nausea it causes me! Yet it is only ugly and stinking.

At ten o'clock she came, carrying a candle, to rescue me from the anguish in which I lived only for her. The reader can imagine the reciprocal delights of that happy night in general, but he cannot guess its details. She said she had got together a little supper for me; but I had no appetite except that which her charms aroused; besides, I had dined at four o'clock. We spent seven hours in intoxication, often interrupting them by amorous talk only to renew our delights.

*Le bellezze d'Olimpia eran di quelle*
*Che son più rare; e non la fronte sola*
*Gli occhi, le guancie, e le chiome avea belle,*
*La bocca, il naso, gli omeri, e la gola;*
*Ma discendendo giù da le mammelle,*
*Le parti che solea coprir la stola*
*Fur di tanta eccellenza, che ante porse*
*A quante ne avea il mondo potean forse.*

*Vinceano di candor le nevi intatte*
*Et eran più che avorio a toccar molli:*
*Le poppe ritondette parean latte*
*Che fuor de giunchi allora allora tolli:*
*Spazio fra lor tal discendea, qual fatte*
*Esser veggiam fra piccolini colli*
*L'ombrose valli in sua stagion amene*
*Che'l verno abbia di neve allora piene.*

*I rilevati fianchi, e le bell'anche,*
*E netto più che specchio il ventre piano*
*Parean fatte, e quelle cosce bianche*
*Da Fidia a torno, o da più dotta mano.*
*Di quelle parte debbovi dir anche etc. etc.*

("Olympia's beauties were of the rarest; not
her forehead alone but her eyes, her cheeks,
her hair were beautiful, and her mouth, her
nose, her shoulders, and her throat; but, to
descend from her breasts, the parts which
her dress usually covered were of such excellence that they might well have been rated
above all the excellencies the world had to
show. They vanquished untouched snow in
whiteness and were softer to the touch than
ivory: her little rounded breasts were like
curds just taken from their reed basket; a
space ran down between them such as we see
the shady valleys between little hills to be
in their pleasant season but which winter had
then filled with snow. Her molded flanks, her

beautiful hips, and her flat stomach, more
shining than a mirror, seemed shaped, with
her white thighs, by Phidias or some more
skillful hand. Of those parts I must further
tell you," etc. etc.) [47]

Madame $X$ had a husband who needed nothing but his
own constitution and the affection he felt for her to do
his duty to her every night without fail. Whether by way
of regimen or from scrupulosity, he did not claim his
rights during the critical days of each moon, and to insure himself against temptation he banished his dear
wife from his side; but during the happy night we spent
together she was not in a state that called for separation.
We both owed our unexpected happiness to the excellent man's lucky journey. I parted from her exhausted
but not satiated. Clasping her in my arms, I assured
her that she would find me no less eager the next time
we could meet. I returned to the confessional, where the
light of the dawning day should make it easier for me to
hide from the eyes of the man with the keys. As soon as
I saw the door open I went home to bed. I did not go
out until time for the theater, where I should again see
the charming object of which love had granted me possession.

It was not until two weeks later that, getting into her
carriage, she told me she would sleep in the little room
the next night. It was a weekday. Since the church was
open only in the morning I went there at eleven o'clock
after eating a good breakfast. I slipped into the confessional as easily as I had the first time, and the beadle
locked up his church about noon.

The thought that I had to spend ten hours either in the
church or in the darkness at the foot of the stairs in company with the rats was not pleasant, but Love makes waiting precious to the lover who is sure that Love will keep
his word.

At one o'clock I saw a sheet of paper fall to the pavement under the grated window. With my heart pounding, I go and pick it up, and I find these words:

"The door is unlocked. I think you will be better off there than in the church. You will find a small dinner, a night lamp, and books. You will be uncomfortably seated, but I could do nothing about that. These ten hours will be less long to you than to me, you may be sure. I told the General I was ill. So you can imagine there is no chance of my going out today. May God keep you from coughing, especially tonight, for a man's cough is entirely different from a woman's."

Love! Charming god who thinks of everything! I do not hesitate for an instant. I go in, and on part of three steps I see napkins, tableware, tasty little dishes, bottles, glasses, a portable stove, and a bottle of alcohol. I see ground coffee and lemons, sugar and rum, in case I should feel like making punch. Also some amusing books. What surprises me is that Madame *X* had been able to do it all without anyone in the household being the wiser.

The charm of the preparations lay in their seeming rather intended to keep a man entertained than to feed him. I spent three hours reading, then three hours eating, making tea, and then punch. After that I went to sleep; and my angel came to wake me at ten o'clock. But this second night was less animated than the first; there were fewer possibilities because of the darkness and more constraint because of the nearness of her husband, whom the slightest noise would have wakened. We spent three or four hours in the arms of sleep.

This was the last night we spent together. The General went to Westphalia,[48] and she had to go to the country. I promised her I would come back to Cologne the following year; but several misfortunes kept me from doing so. I took leave of everyone, and I left regretted.

My stay of two and a half months[49] in that city did not lighten my purse, despite the fact that every time I was persuaded to play for money I lost. The game at

Bonn more than paid my expenses with something over. The banker Frantz[50] complained that I had drawn nothing from him. I would not have behaved so well had I not had a tender attachment, which made it necessary for me to convince everyone who was watching me that I deserved to be treated well.

I left at the middle of March and stopped at Bonn to make my bow to the Elector. His Highness was not there. I dined with Count Verità and the Abbé Scampar,[51] who was His Highness's favorite. An unofficial letter which the Count gave me for a Canoness whom he praised and who was to be at Coblenz was my reason for stopping there; but instead of the Canoness, who had gone to Mannheim, I found at my inn a woman of the theater named Toscani,[52] who was on her way back to Stuttgart with her very young and charming daughter. She had come from Paris, where she had spent a year having her taught serious dancing by the celebrated Vestris.[53] Delighted to see me again, the girl immediately showed me a spaniel which I had given her a year earlier. The little creature was her delight. The girl, who was a veritable jewel, easily persuaded me to take a trip to Stuttgart, where, in any case, I could not but enjoy all possible pleasures. Her mother was eager to see what the Duke[54] would think of her daughter, whom she had destined from childhood to the lust of a prince who, though he then had an official mistress, wanted also to have all his ballerinas in whom he saw anything of interest. La Toscani assured me at supper that her little girl was a virgin, and she swore that the Duke should not have her until he had dismissed his reigning mistress and given her the same position. The reigning mistress was the dancer Gardela,[55] the same daughter of a Venetian gondolier of whom I spoke in my first volume and the same wife of Michele dall'Agata whom I encountered in Munich when I escaped from the Leads.

Neither the Toscani girl nor her mother was offended by my curiosity as to the purity of the jewel reserved for the Duke of Württemberg, and their vanity was concerned to convince me they were telling the truth. It was a pastime which engaged me for two full hours the next day with the two adorable creatures, for nothing in the world would have persuaded the mother to leave me alone with her treasure, of which I might boldly defraud her. But far from objecting to her presence, I showed her that she was dear to me. She laughed, and admired my honorably extinguishing in herself all the fire which her daughter kindled in my soul with her charms, from which I never turned my eyes. Though still young, the mother did not seem to mind my needing the spectacle in order to play the role of lover to her successfully. She seemed to consider her daughter, whom she adored, a part of herself; but she was sure that she was playing the leading role. She was wrong, and I asked nothing better. Her daughter would not have needed her mother to set me on fire; but without the presence of the former the latter would have found me ice.

So I decided to go to Stuttgart to see La Binetti,[56] who was forever talking about me as of some miracle of nature. La Binetti was the daughter of the Venetian gondolier Ramon, and I had had a hand in getting her launched the same year in which Signora Valmarana[57] had married her off to the French dancer Binet, who had Italianized his name. At Stuttgart I was to renew my acquaintance with La Gardela, the younger Balletti,[58] of whom I was very fond, the Vulcani girl [59] whom he had married, and several other old friends who were to make the short time I was prepared to spend in that city a veritable paradise. At the last post station I renounced the precious company of La Toscani. I went to lodge at the "Bear," [60] to which the postilion took me. In the next volume[61] the reader will see what kind of mishaps befell me in that city.

*1760. La Gardela as reigning mistress. Portrait of the Duke of Württemberg. My dinner at La Gardela's and its consequences. Unlucky encounter. I gamble, I lose four thousand louis. Lawsuit. Successful flight. My arrival in Zurich. Church consecrated by Jesus Christ in person.*

AT THIS period the most brilliant Court in all Europe was that of the Duke of Württemberg. He maintained it through the large subsidies which France paid him for the use of ten thousand men. It was a fine army, which all through the war had distinguished itself only by its mistakes.

The great expenditures in which the Duke indulged went for munificent salaries, superb buildings, hunting establishments, and all sorts of whims; but what cost him fabulous sums was the theater. He had actors and singers for French plays and comic operas, he had Italian *opera seria* and *opera buffa,* and ten couples of Italian dancers,[1] every one of whom had been the leading dancer in some famous Italian theater. The composer of his ballets was Noverre,[2] who often used a corps of a hundred; he had a machinist to make settings which tempted the audience to believe in magic. All his ballerinas were pretty, and they all boasted that they had at

*The Prince Elector Clement Augustus at a Masked Ball*

*Isabella of Italian Comedy*

least once made their amorous sovereign happy. The
leading ballerina was a Venetian, the daughter of the
gondolier Gardelo, the very girl whom the Venetian Senator Malipiero, who was the first person to give me a
good education, brought up for the theater by paying a
dancing master to teach her. The reader may remember
that on my escape from the Leads I encountered her at
Munich, married to the dancer Michele dall'Agata. The
Duke of Württemberg, having fallen in love with her, applied for her to her husband, who considered himself
fortunate to be able to surrender her to him; but a year
later,[3] loving her no longer, he gave her the title of
Madame and retired her with a pension. By thus elevat-
ing her he made all the other ballerinas jealous; for,
believing that they were more worthy to become his
mistresses than one who, after all, held only the title and
the honors, they did all they could to topple her. But
La Gardela knew how to maintain her position. Far from
boring the Duke by reproaching him with his infidelities,
she congratulated him on them. Since she did not love
him she felt far happier in his neglect than she would
have been if she had been obliged to put up with him as a
lover. Her overpowering ambition was satisfied by the
honors which he accorded her. She enjoyed seeing all the
ballerinas who aspired to please the Duke solicit her good
offices; she received them amiably and encouraged them
to win the sovereign's love, while he, considering
such tolerance in the favorite admirable and heroic, felt
obliged to do everything possible to convince her of his
undivided esteem. In public he paid her all the honors
which, according to etiquette, he could legitimately have
paid only to a princess.

What I clearly realized in a few days was that whatever the prince did was done only to get himself talked
about. He wanted it said that no living prince was more
intelligent or more talented than he, or more accom-

plished in the art of inventing pleasures and enjoying
them, or better fitted to reign, or possessed of a better constitution for coping with all the pleasures of the table,
of Bacchus, and of Venus, without ever infringing on the
time he needed to rule his State and manage its departments, of which he insisted on being head. To have
leisure for all this he had decided to cheat nature out of
the time he needed for sleep. He thought it was within
his power, and he dismissed in disgrace any valet who
could not get him out of bed after three or four hours of
sleep to which he had been obliged to succumb. The valet
whose task it was to wake him was authorized to do whatever he pleased with his sovereign person to deliver it
from the poppies of Morpheus. He shook him, he made
him swallow quantities of coffee, he even put him in a cold
bath. When His Most Serene Highness was at last awake
he assembled his ministers to deal with current business;
then he gave audience to all comers, who for the most
part were thick-headed, ignorant, obstinate peasants with
grievances, who thought they need only speak with their
sovereign for a moment to have him right their wrongs
on the spot. But nothing was more comical than these
audiences which the Duke granted to his poorer subjects.
He became furious trying to make them listen to reason,
and they left his presence in terror and despair. He acted
differently with pretty peasant girls. He examined their
grievances in private, and though he granted them nothing they went away satisfied.

Since the French subsidies were not enough for his immense expenditures he loaded his subjects with taxes,
which became so intolerable that a few years later they
appealed to the Diet of Wetzlar,[4] which forced him to
change his methods. His dearest notion was to rule, following in the footsteps of the King of Prussia, who always
laughed at him. His Highness had married the daughter
of the Margrave of Bayreuth,[5] who was the most beautiful

and accomplished princess in all Germany. About this
time she took refuge with her father, unable to bear a
cutting affront[6] to which her undeserving husband subjected her. Those who said that she left him because she
could not bear his infidelities were misinformed.

After putting up at the "Bear" and dining alone, I
dress, I go to the Italian *opera seria,* with which the Duke
provided the public gratis in the fine theater he had built.
He was in the circle in front of the orchestra, surrounded
by his court. I take my place alone in a box on the first
tier, delighted that I could listen undistracted to the
music of the famous Jomelli,[7] who was in the Duke's
service. An aria sung by a celebrated castrato[8] having
greatly pleased me, I clap. A moment later a man comes
and speaks to me rudely in German. I reply with the four
words of German I know, which mean, "I do not understand German." He leaves and another comes and tells
me in French that, since the sovereign is present, it is
forbidden to clap.

"Very well. I will come when the sovereign is not
present, for when an aria pleases me I cannot help clapping."

After giving this answer I send for my carriage, but
the same officer appears and says that the Duke wishes to
speak with me. So I go to the circle with him.

"You are Monsieur Casanova?"

"Yes, Monseigneur."

"Where have you come from?"

"From Cologne."

"Is this the first time you have been in Stuttgart?"

"Yes, Monseigneur."

"Do you expect to stay here long?"

"Five or six days, if Your Highness permits."

"As long as you please, and you will also be permitted
to clap."

At the following aria the Duke clapped, and everyone

did the same; but since I had not liked the aria I remained still. After the ballet the Duke went to call on his pensioned favorite, where I saw him kiss her hand, then leave.

An officer who did not know that I was acquainted with her told me that she was "Madame," and that since I had had the honor to speak with the prince I could also have that of going to kiss her hand in her box. I took it into my head to reply that I thought I need not do so because she was a relative of mine. An arrant lie, which could only do me harm. I see that he is surprised; he leaves me and goes to my relative's box and informs her of my sudden appearance. She turns to look at me and beckons me with her fan. I go, laughing to myself over the stupid role I am about to play. I have no sooner entered her box than she gives me her hand, which I kiss, addressing her as "cousin." She asks me if I had told the Duke I was her cousin, I answer no; but she undertakes to do it and invites me to dine with her the next day.

At the end of the opera she leaves, and I go to pay my respects to the ballerinas while they undress. When she catches sight of me La Binetti, whom I had known the longest, appears to be overcome with joy and invites me to eat at her table every day. The violinist Kurz,[9] who had been with me in the orchestra at San Samuele,[10] introduces his marvelously pretty daughter[11] to me, saying peremptorily that the Duke should never have her; but he soon afterward had her and was loved by her; she gave him two children; she could well have made him constant, for she was intelligent as well as beautiful; but at that time the Duke had a need to be inconstant. After Kurz's daughter I saw the youthful Vulcani girl, whom I had known at Dresden and who surprised me by introducing her husband, who flung himself on my neck. It was the younger Balletti, brother of my jilt,[12] a lad full of talent and intelligence whom I loved to distraction.[13]

All these acquaintances were gathered around me when
the officer to whom I had said I was related to La Gardela
came up and told the company the whole story; but La
Binetti said to him in so many words that it was not true
and laughed in my face when I told her she could not
know enough about it to contradict me. She too being
the daughter of a gondolier, La Binetti thought I should
have given her the preference over the other, and perhaps
she was right.

The next day I dined very gaily with the favorite despite her telling me that, not having seen the Duke, she
did not know how he would take it. Her mother considered our joke of calling cousins unworthy of her approval.
She told me that her relatives had never been actors; I
asked her if her sister was still alive, and she was very
much put out by my question. Her sister was a fat, blind
slut who begged for alms on a bridge in Venice.

After spending the whole day pleasurably in the company of the favorite, who was the oldest of all my
acquaintances of this kind, I took my departure, assuring her that I would come to breakfast with her the next
morning; but as I left the house her mustached porter
most ungraciously paid me a compliment in the worst
taste. He ordered me, without telling me at whose bidding, not to set foot in the house again. Thus brought to
recognize what a stupid thing I had done, I returned to
my inn in a very bad humor. If I had not promised La
Binetti that I would dine with her the next day, I should
have decamped immediately and thus have avoided all
the unpleasant things which happened to me in that city
by my own fault.

La Binetti lived in the house of her lover, who was the
Viennese Envoy.[14] The house formed part of the rampart, so that by climbing through her windows one was
outside of the town. If I had been capable of falling in
love at the time, all my old fondness would have

reawakened, for her attractions were enchanting. The
Viennese Envoy was tolerant, and her husband was a real
beast who frequented houses of ill fame. We dined very
gaily, and having nothing further to do in Württemberg,
I decided to leave on the next day but one, for on the
following day I was to go to see Ludwigsburg with La
Toscani and her daughter. The engagement had already
been made, and we were to meet at five o'clock in the
morning; but here is what happened to me when I left La
Binetti's house toward nightfall.

Three engaging-looking officers whose acquaintance I
had made at a coffeehouse come up to me, and we take a
few turns together. They tell me they have got up a
party with light women, and that if I wish they will be
happy to have me join them. I say that, not speaking
German, I should be bored; they reply that the women
they are to meet are Italian; and they persuade me.

Toward dusk we return to the city and go to the fourth
floor of a disreputable-looking house where in a dirty
room I find the two supposititious nieces of Pocchini, and
a moment later I see Pocchini himself,[15] coming to embrace me with great effrontery and calling me his best
friend. The caresses to which the girls treat me confirm
our old acquaintance, and the whole situation decides me
to dissimulate.

The officers begin raising a row, I do not follow their
example; but that does not abash them. I repent too late
of having agreed to go there with men whom I did not
know, but the thing was done. All the misfortunes which
befell me in Stuttgart arose entirely from my own bad
conduct.

A pothouse supper is served, I do not eat, but not to
appear impolite I drink two or three glasses of Hungarian wine. Cards are brought, one of the officers makes
a bank, I punt, with my head spinning; I lose fifty or
sixty louis which I have with me. I refuse to play any

more; but the noble officers cannot bear that I should leave regretting that I supped with them. They persuade me to make a bank of a hundred louis, and they give me counters for the amount. I lose; I replenish the bank, and I lose it, then I increase it and keep increasing it, always losing, and at midnight they say "Enough." We reckon up all the counters, and I am found to owe them something like four thousand louis. My head was spinning so fast that they had to send for a sedan chair to take me back to my inn. As he undresses me my valet says I have neither my watches nor a gold snuffbox. I do not forget to tell him to wake me at four o'clock, and I fall asleep.

He wakes me punctually. I am astonished to find in my pockets about a hundred louis, though I perfectly recollect the large sum I had lost on my word; but I put off thinking about it, together with my watches and my snuffbox, until another time. I take another snuffbox, I go to La Toscani's, we go to Ludwigsburg, I am shown everything, we dine very well, and we return to Stuttgart. I was in such a good humor that no one in the party could have imagined the considerable misfortune which had befallen me the night before.

The first thing my Spaniard told me was that no one in the house where I had supped knew anything about either my watches or my snuffbox; and the second was that three officers had come to call on me at nine in the morning and had told him they would come to breakfast with me the next day. They did so punctually.

"Gentlemen," I said, "I have lost an amount which I cannot pay, and which I should certainly not have lost were it not for the poison you made me swallow in your Hungarian wine. In the bordello to which you took me I was robbed of valuables worth three hundred louis; but I will complain of it to no one. If I had been sensible nothing would have happened to me."

They began protesting loudly. They talked to me in accordance with the role which a show of honor obliged them to play; but all their words were useless, for I had already decided that I would pay nothing. At the height of our dispute, in come Balletti, La Toscani, and the dancer Binetti, who heard what the whole dispute was about. They left after breakfasting; and one of the three officers then proposed the following compromise:

They would take at their actual value everything I had in the way of gold jewelry and diamonds, and if these did not suffice to make up the amount I owed they would accept a written undertaking from me to pay them at a specified time.

I replied that I could not pay them at all, whereupon they began to threaten. I said, with perfect self-possession, that they had only two ways to make me pay. One would be to bring suit against me, and in that case I would procure an advocate to defend me. The other, which I proposed with all due modesty, was to let them take it out on my body in all honor and in complete secrecy, one at a time and sword in hand. As usual, and as I might have expected, they replied that they would do me the honor of killing me after I had paid them. They went off cursing and assuring me that I would be sorry.

I left and went to La Toscani's, where I spent the whole day with a gaiety which, situated as I was, seemed madness; but such was the power of her daughter's charms, and I needed to be gay.

La Toscani, however, who had witnessed the rage of the three intrepid gamblers, convinced me that I should be the first to take legal action against them, for if I let them get the start of me they might gain a great advantage; so she sent for an advocate, who, after hearing the facts, said that I should go directly to the sovereign. They had taken me to a house of ill fame; they had made me drink doctored wine which had deprived me of my reasoning powers, they had gambled, and gambling was forbidden, they had won an enormous amount from me, and in the brothel I had been robbed of my possessions, which, being drunk, I had realized only when I got back to my inn. The facts spoke for themselves. To the sovereign, to the sovereign, to the sovereign!

The next morning I decide I will do it; and, since he hears everyone, I think I need not write; I go to Court to talk with him. At twenty paces from the palace door I encounter two of my gentlemen, who swagger up to me and say that I must think about paying them; I start to go on without answering; I feel my left arm caught, and by a perfectly natural impulse I angrily draw my sword, the officer of the guard comes running, I cry out that I am being stopped from laying a justified complaint before the sovereign. The officer hears from the sentry and from all the crowd around me that I had drawn my sword only in self-defense, he decides that no one can keep me from going up.

I go up; I am allowed to proceed to the last anteroom, I demand a hearing, I am assured that I will receive it, the officer who had caught me by the arm comes up, he tells what story he pleases in German to the officer who is serving as chamberlain and who apparently belonged to the gang; and an hour passes and I am not granted an audience. Finally the same officer who had assured me the sovereign would give me a hearing comes and tells me that the sovereign already knows everything, that I may go home, take no steps, and be sure that I will receive justice.

So I leave the palace, intending to go to my inn; but I run into the dancer Binetti, who, having heard the whole story, persuades me to come and dine at his house, where the Viennese Envoy would take me under his protection to safeguard me from the violence these scoundrels might attempt to do me, despite what the fellow in the Duke's antechamber had said. I go; La Binetti, blazing up over my wrongs, goes to inform the Envoy, who, after hearing the whole story from me, says that the Duke might well know nothing about it, so I should write a brief account of the occurrence and send it to him. In this way, according to the Envoy, I should be certain to receive justice.

I quickly write down the ugly story, and the Envoy assures me that it will be in the prince's hands in less than an hour. At dinner La Binetti gives me the most unequivocal assurances that the Viennese Envoy will be my protector, and we spend the day in good spirits; but toward nightfall my Spaniard comes to tell me that if I go to the inn I shall certainly be arrested, for an officer who had gone to my room and not found me there had stationed himself at the street door; he had been there for two hours and had posted two soldiers at the foot of the stairs. La Binetti does not want me to go to the inn; she makes me stay at her house, and my valet leaves, coming back with everything I need to undress and spend the night under the roof of my good friend, where I had no violence to fear. The Envoy comes home at midnight, he makes no objection to La Binetti's having given me a refuge, he says that the sovereign has undoubtedly read my petition.[16] So I go to bed quite easy, and three days pass without my seeing any result from my petition or hearing anyone say a word about my case. La Binetti would never let me go out.

On the fourth day, when I was consulting the whole household on what I should do, the Envoy received a letter from the Secretary of State[17] asking him, at the sovereign's behest, to dismiss me from his house, since I had a suit pending with some of His Highness's officers and my being in his house prevented justice from taking its course and deciding in favor of one party or the other in the matter to be examined. In this letter, which I read, the Secretary assured the Envoy that strict justice would be done me. So I had to accede to going back to my inn. This made La Binetti so furious that she called the Envoy names, at which he merely laughed and said he could not keep me in defiance of the Duke.

After dinner, when I was on the verge of going to see my advocate, a bailiff brings me a summons, which my host translates for me. I was to go at once to I forget what notary, who was to receive and record my deposition. I went with the summons server, and I spent two hours with the man, who wrote down in German all that I told him in Latin. He told me to sign, but I protested that I could not sign a document whose contents I did not know, and at that point we had a long argument, but I remained unshaken. He became angry, saying that I could not cast doubt on the good faith of a notary; I replied that in that case he could do without my signature, and, leaving him, I went on to see my advocate, who told me that I had been right not to sign, that he would come to me at my inn the next morning to receive my power of attorney, and that thereafter my business would be his.

Relieved by the man's apparent honesty, I went back to the inn to eat supper and sleep tranquilly; but the next morning my valet came in with an officer who told me quite politely in good French that I must not be surprised to find myself under arrest in my room with a sentry at my door, for, I being a foreigner, my opponent had the right to make sure that I would not flee while the preliminary investigation was being made. He asked for my sword, which to my great regret I was obliged to give him. It was steel, worth fifty louis, and had been a present to me from Madame d'Urfé. I at once sent word of my arrest to my advocate, who assured me that it would continue for only a very few days. Having to stay in my room, I began to receive visits from dancers male and female, who were the only honest people I knew. Poisoned by a glass of wine, cheated, robbed, I was now deprived of my freedom and in fear of being sentenced to pay a hundred thousand francs, to procure which I should have to let myself be stripped to my shirt, since no one knew what I had in my portfolio. My mind was as if numbed by such tyranny; I had written to "Madame" Gardela, and had received no answer. La Binetti, La Toscani, and Balletti dining or supping with me were my only consolation. The swindling officers had all come to talk with me one after the other, each trying to make me give him money without the knowledge of the others and each promising to get me out of my difficulty. Each in turn would have been satisfied with three or four hundred louis; but even if I had given it to one of them I had no assurance that the other two would not return to the charge. I told them in turn that they bored me and that I would take it as a favor if they would no longer trouble themselves to visit me.

On the fifth day of my arrest the Duke of Württemberg left Stuttgart for Frankfort, and on the same day La Binetti came to say that the Viennese Envoy had told her to inform me that the sovereign had promised the officers he would not intervene in the matter, hence he thought I was in danger of becoming the victim of an iniquitous judgment. So he advised me to try to extricate myself by sacrificing everything I had in gold and diamonds in exchange for a formal release from my pretended creditors. La Binetti did not share his opinion, but she felt it her duty to convey what the Envoy had ordered her to communicate to me.

I could not bring myself to give up my rings and empty my strongbox, in which I had watches, snuffboxes, other kinds of boxes, cases, and portraits to the value of more than forty thousand francs; but it was my advocate himself who made me resolve on vigorous action when, talking with me privately, he said without beating around the bush that if I could not manage to settle the matter by paying, I should begin to think of taking to my heels, for otherwise I was lost. "The police judge," he said, "will give a summary judgment, for you, as a foreigner, will not be allowed to delay your case by the ordinary legal maneuvering. You would have to begin by furnishing bail. Witnesses have been found in this city to testify that you are a professional gambler, that it was you who lured the officers to the lodging of your countryman Pocchini, that it is not true that they got you drunk, and not true that your watches and snuffbox were stolen. It is averred that they will be found in your luggage when the court orders all your effects inventoried. Look for that to happen tomorrow or the day after, and beware of doubting any part of what I have told you. Officers of the court will come here and empty your two trunks, your strongbox, and your pockets, everything will be listed and everything put up for auction the same day; and if the money realized is not enough to pay your debt and the court costs and the costs of your arrest, you will be *enrolled, Sir*, as a common soldier in the troops of His Most Serene Highness. I myself heard the officer who is your largest creditor say with a laugh that the four louis you will be given as enlistment money will be counted in, and that the Duke will be delighted to have acquired a very fine man."

The advocate took his departure, leaving me petrified. His discourse threw me into such a spasm that in less than an hour I thought all the fluids in my body were seeking an outlet from their several seats. I! Stripped to my shirt and made a soldier! I! It shall not be! Let us find some way to gain time!

I at once wrote to the officer who was my principal creditor that I would settle; but only with all three of them together in the presence of a notary and witnesses to legalize their release and so make it possible for me to leave at once. It was unlikely that one of them would not be on guard duty the next morning, but I hoped I should gain at least a day; meanwhile I trusted that God in his mercy would send me some ideas.

I wrote a letter[18] to the presiding police magistrate, addressing him as "Monseigneur" and begging for his powerful protection. I said that, having decided to sell my belongings to put an end to the actions at law with which my creditors were seeking to overwhelm me, I begged him to suspend the proceedings, the costs of which I would pay. In addition I asked him to send me a trustworthy man to appraise my possessions as soon as I informed him that I had come to an agreement with the officers who were my creditors, with whom I begged him to intervene on my behalf. It was my valet who delivered the two letters to their respective addresses.

After dinner the officer, who had received my letter and who was demanding two thousand louis, came to my room. He found me in bed, I told him I thought I had fever, and it was with pleasure that I heard him condole with me. He said that he had just been talking with the presiding police magistrate, who had given him my letter to read.

"Your decision to make a settlement," he said, "is the right course; but there is no need for the three of us to be together. I shall have full powers from my two friends, which the notary will accept."

"Sir, all I ask is to see you together, and I do not think you can refuse me that satisfaction."

"You shall have it; but if you are in a hurry I warn you that you cannot have us together until Monday, for one of us is on guard duty for the next four days."

"I will wait until Monday; but give me your word of honor that all legal proceedings will be stopped until then."

"I give it, and here is my hand. In return I ask you for a small favor. I have taken a fancy to your post chaise. I ask you to let me have it for what it cost you."

"Gladly."

"Call the innkeeper and tell him it is my property."

"Certainly."

He summons the innkeeper; I tell him that my chaise is the gentleman's property, and he replies that I can do what I like with it when I have paid him, and so saying he goes. The officer laughs, he says he is sure he will have the chaise, he thanks me, and he leaves.

Two hours later an honest-looking man who spoke good Italian comes to bring me word from the chief of police that my creditors will meet together on the coming Monday, and that it is he who will appraise my belongings. He advises me to stipulate in the settlement that my effects are not to be put up for auction and that my creditors will abide by the values he sets on them. He promises that I will be satisfied. After replying that I will make him a present of a hundred louis, I rise and ask him to look at everything in my two trunks and at my jewels.

After examining everything and saying that my laces alone were worth twenty thousand francs, he assures me that I have more than the value of a hundred thousand francs and that he will privately tell my creditors something very different.

"Counting on that," he said, "try to bring them down to accepting half of what you owe them, and you will leave with half of your effects."

"In that case you shall have fifty louis, and in the meanwhile here are six."

"I accept them. Rely on my friendship. Everyone in Stuttgart is aware that your creditors are scoundrels; and the Duke knows them; but he thinks it proper to pretend he is unaware of their machinations."

After these two successes I breathed again. Having

five days before me, I must use them to make sure of escaping with all of my possessions except my carriage. It was difficult, but not as difficult as escaping from the Leads. So I must not be found wanting either in boldness or in plans. I sent word to La Toscani, Balletti, and the dancer Binetti, inviting them to supper. I needed to discuss the thing with people who had nothing to fear from the wrath of my three persecutors.

After a good supper I give my three friends a full account of my situation and tell them my decision to escape without losing any of my belongings.

Binetti speaks first. He says that if I can get out of the inn and go to his house I can get out through one of the windows, that I shall then be in the open country a hundred paces from the highroad, whence I can travel by post beyond the Duke's State. Balletti looks out the window of my room, which gave onto the street, and decides that I cannot get out by it because of the wooden roof of a shop. I agree with him, and I say I will find some other way to get out of the inn and that what troubles me is my luggage. La Toscani says I must abandon my trunks and send everything I have to her, and that she will undertake to send me everything wherever I decide to stop.

"I will carry it all away," she says, "little by little, under my petticoats."

Balletti tells her his wife will help her, and we finish laying our plan. I promise Binetti that I will be at his house at midnight on Sunday, even if I have to kill the sentry who was always at the door of my room except at night. The sentry locked me in, went off to bed, and came back the next morning. Balletti vouches for a faithful servant of his and undertakes to have him on the highroad in a post carriage which will be waiting for me. La Toscani adds that all my possessions can be loaded onto the same carriage in other trunks. She at once began carrying off two suits, putting them under her skirt. During the following days three women helped me to such effect that by midnight on Saturday my trunks were empty and so was my strongbox, everything valuable in which I put into my pockets.

On Sunday La Toscani brought me the keys to two trunks into which she had put all my clothes, and Balletti came to assure me for the first time that a post carriage would be on the highroad at my orders under the care of his servant. Unquestionably certain of all this, I contrived my escape from the inn as follows:

The soldier who walked back and forth at the door of my room was in the habit of leaving as soon as he saw that I was in bed. He wished me good night, locked the door, put the key in his pocket, and went. He returned in the morning, but he did not open my door until I called. Then my valet came in.

The soldier on duty was also in the habit of eating what I sent him from my own supper on a small table outside. So these are the instructions I gave my Spaniard:

"After supping," I said, "instead of going to bed I will make ready to leave my room, and I will leave it as soon as I see no more light outside. Once out of the room I will go down the stairs and I shall have no trouble leaving the inn. I will go straight to Binetti's and from there I will get out of the city and I will go to Fürstenberg[19] and wait for you there. Nobody can keep you from leaving tomorrow or the next day. So as soon as you see that I am ready in my room, you must put out the candle which will be on the table where the sentry will be eating supper; you can easily put it out as you snuff it. You will take it to my room to light it again; and I will seize the moment of darkness to leave. When you have lit the candle again you will go back to the soldier and finish the bottle of wine. When you tell him

I have gone to bed he will come to bid me good night as usual, he will lock me in, and leave with you. There is no likelihood that he will come in and speak to me when he sees me in bed.''

To deceive the soldier I put a wig-block in a nightcap on the bolster and propped up the covers in such a way that anyone would be deceived. And it all went off very well, as I learned from Leduc three days later, in full detail.

While Leduc was drinking with the sentry I stood with my pelisse over my naked body, a hunting knife in my belt because I no longer had a sword, and two pistols in my pockets.

As soon as the darkness outside assured me that the candle had been extinguished, I left the room, went downstairs, and left by the inn door without meeting anyone. It was a quarter before midnight. I hurry along to Binetti's house; by the moonlight I see his wife waiting for me at a window. She comes and opens the door for me, I go upstairs with her, and, not losing an instant, she takes me to the window by which I am to get out; Balletti's wife was there to help let me down, and her husband was in mud up to his knees to catch me. I began by throwing my pelisse down to him.

The two charming women put a rope around my chest under the arms and, holding its two ends, gradually let them out in time with my very smooth, easy, and completely safe descent. Never was man better served. Balletti caught me in his arms, gave me my pelisse, then told me to follow him.

Defying sloughs into which we sank up to our knees and making our way through holes worn by dogs wherever hedges obstructed our path or over stiles to keep cattle out, we reached the highroad very tired, though it was only three or four hundred paces from the rampart. We covered the same distance to reach the carriage, which stood waiting for me at an isolated pothouse. Balletti's manservant was sitting in it. He got out at once, saying that the postilion had just gone into the pothouse and would come back when he had drunk a mug of beer. I at once took his place, and after tipping him well I told his master to go back with him and leave me to deal with all the rest.

It was April 2nd [20] in the year 1760, my birthday, which all my life has been noteworthy for some incident.

Two minutes later the postilion comes out of the pothouse and asks me if we shall have long to wait, believing that he is speaking to the same person with whom he had set out from Cannstatt. I do not enlighten him, I tell him to go to Tübingen without stopping to change horses at Waldenbuch,[21] and he obeys me; but I laughed to see the face he made when he saw me at Tübingen. Balletti's valet was very young and decidedly short; when he told me I was not the person with whom he had set off, I replied that he must be drunk, and, satisfied with the two florins I tipped him, he did not retort. I left at once, and I did not stop until I reached Fürstenberg, where I was safe.

After supping well and sleeping even better, I wrote the same letter to each of the three officers. I challenged all three of them to a duel, telling them bluntly that if they did not come I would never utter their names again without adding that they were the lowest of the low. I promised to wait for them for three days from the time I was writing, hoping to kill all three of them and thus become famous throughout Europe. I also wrote to La Toscani, to Balletti, and to La Binetti, asking them to look after my valet.

The officers did not come, but during the three days the innkeeper's daughters made the time pass as pleasantly as I could wish.

On the fourth day at noon I saw Leduc ride up at full

gallop with his portmanteau roped to his saddle. The
first thing he said was that I ought to go to Switzerland,
for the whole city of Stuttgart knew I was there and I
had reason to fear that the three officers might take their
revenge by having me murdered. After I let him know
that I did not want his advice, he told me the whole
story of what happened after my escape. Here it is, just
as he related it.

"After you left," he said, "I went to bed. The next
morning at nine o'clock the sentry came to walk up and
down by your door, and at ten the three officers arrived.
When I told them you were still asleep they left, telling
me to fetch them from the coffeehouse as soon as your
room was unlocked; but not seeing me they came back
about noon and ordered the sentry to open your door.
I enjoyed the next scene.

"They think they see you asleep, they wish you good
morning, go to your bed, shake you, the straw gives way,
the wig-block falls, and seeing them dumfounded I cannot hold back my laughter. 'So you're laughing, you dog.
You shall tell us where your master has gone.'

"The words being accompanied by a cut from a cane
I reply with a curse that they have only to ask the sentry.
The sentry says you can only have got out through the
window, but the corporal is summoned, and the innocent
soldier is arrested just the same. The innkeeper comes
up at the noise, he opens the trunks, and, seeing they
are empty, he says your post chaise will pay him; and
ignores the officer who protests that you had given it
to him.

"Another officer appears and, after hearing the story,
he decides you can only have got out through the window,
so he orders the soldier released; for me, however, they
had only the foulest injustice. As I went on saying that
I did not know where you had gone and that I couldn't
help having laughed, they saw fit to put me in prison.

They said I would be kept there until I told where you were, or, if not you, at least your possessions.

"The next day one of the officers came and told me I would be sent to the galleys if I persisted in holding my tongue. I replied that, on the word of a Spaniard, I knew nothing about it; but that even if I did know I would never tell, for in honor I could not become a spy on my own master. At that the gentleman ordered a turnkey to give me a lashing, and after the ceremony I was set free. I went to bed at the inn, and the next morning all Stuttgart knew that you were here, where you had challenged the officers to come and fight. They are not such fools, people say, as to do that; but Madame Binetti ordered me to tell you to leave here, because they might have you murdered. The innkeeper sold your post chaise and your trunks to the Viennese Envoy, who, they say, arranged for you to get out by the windows of the apartment which he rents to La Binetti. I took the post without anyone trying to stop me, and here I am."

Three hours after he arrived I took the post to Schaffhausen and from there I went to Zurich with hired horses, because in Switzerland there is no post.[22] I put up very comfortably at the "Sword."[23]

Alone after supper in the wealthiest city in Switzerland, into which I had, as it were, dropped from the clouds, for I was there without the least premeditation, I give myself up to reflections on my present situation and my past life. I recall the good and the bad which has befallen me and I examine my conduct. I find that I have drawn upon myself all the evils from which I have suffered and that I have abused all the favors Fortune had done me. Still under the impression of the disaster which I have just barely avoided, I shudder and decide to stop being Fortune's plaything and put myself beyond her reach. Being possessed of a hundred [24] thousand écus, I determine to invest it in a way to secure me a permanent income subject to no fluctuation. Perfect peace is the greatest good of all.

Thus deliberating I go to bed, and pleasant dreams make me happy in peaceful solitudes, in abundance, and in tranquillity. I seemed, in a beautiful countryside which belonged to me, to enjoy a freedom which is sought in vain in society. I was dreaming, but even while I dreamed I told myself that I was not dreaming. A sudden awakening at daybreak gives me the lie; I feel angry, and, determined to realize my dream, I get up, I dress, and get out, not caring where I am going.

An hour after leaving the city I am among a number of mountains; I should have thought I had lost my way if I had not continued to see ruts which assured me that the road would lead me to some hospitable place. Every quarter of an hour I came upon peasants; but I took pleasure in not asking them for any directions. After walking slowly for six hours I suddenly found myself in a great plain between four mountains. To my left I have a beautiful distant view of a large church attached to a building of symmetrical design which invites passing travelers to direct their steps thither. As I approach I see that it can only be a convent or a monastery, and I feel glad that I am in a Catholic canton.

I enter the church, I see that it is resplendent with marble and altar ornaments, and after hearing the last mass I go into the sacristy, where I see Benedictine monks. One of them, whom I judged by the cross he wore to be the Abbot, asks me if I wish to see all the things worth seeing in the sanctuary, which I can do without going outside the altar rail; I reply that it will be an honor and a pleasure, and he comes himself, with two other monks, to show me extremely rich ornaments, chasubles covered with large pearls, and sacred vessels covered with diamonds and other precious stones.

Having a very poor knowledge of German and none

at all of the Swiss dialect, which is to German as Genoese is to Italian, I ask the Abbot in Latin if the church has been long built, and he tells me its history in detail, ending by informing me that it is the only church[25] which was consecrated by Jesus Christ in person. He notices my astonishment, and to convince me that he has told the pure and simple truth he takes me into the church and shows me on the surface of the marble five concavities which the fingers of Jesus Christ had left in it when he consecrated the church. He had left these impressions[26] so that unbelievers could not doubt the miracle and to save the Father Superior the trouble of sending for the diocesan Bishop to consecrate it. The same Father Superior had learned the aforesaid truth by divine revelation in a dream which told him distinctly to think no more of it because the church was *divinitus consecrata* ("consecrated by God"), in proof of which he would see the five concavities in such and such a place in the church. The Father Superior went there, saw them, and thanked God.

## CHAPTER IV

*I resolve to become a monk. I make my confession. Delay of two weeks. Giustiniani, the apostate Capuchin. I change my mind; what leads me to do so. Escapade at the inn. Dinner with the Abbot.*

---

THE ABBOT, delighted by the obedient attention with which I had listened to his nonsense, asked me where I was lodging, and I replied "Nowhere," because when I had arrived from Zurich on foot I had simply entered his church. He then joins his hands and lifts them to heaven, as if to thank God for so touching my heart that I have gone on a pilgrimage to carry my sins there, for, to tell the truth, I have always looked like a great sinner. He said that, it being noon, he would consider it an honor if I would go and dine with him, and I accepted. I did not yet know where I was, and I did not want to ask, well satisfied to let it be believed I had come there on a pilgrimage expressly to expiate my crimes. On the way he said that his monks were fasting but that I could eat meat with him since he had obtained a dispensation from Benedict XIV which allowed him to eat meat every day with three guests. I replied that I should be glad to share the privilege. As soon as we entered his apartment he showed me the dispensation, framed under glass and hanging on the tapestried wall opposite the table, where it could be read by the curious and the scrupulous. Since there were only two places, a servant in livery quickly set another. He immediately introduced me to the third at table, saying that he was his Chancellor.[1]

"I am obliged," he said with the greatest modesty, "to have a chancellery, since, as Abbot of Our Lady of Einsiedeln, I am also a prince[2] of the Holy Roman Empire."

I breathed again. At last I knew where I was, and I felt very glad, for I had both read and heard of Our Lady of the Hermits. It was the cisalpine Loreto.[3] At table the Prince-Abbot took it upon himself to ask me from what country I came, if I was married, and if I intended to make a tour of Switzerland, offering me letters of introduction for wherever I wished to go. I replied that I was Venetian and unmarried and that I would accept the letters with which he was so kind as to honor me when I had told him who I was in a conference I hoped to have with him, in which I would acquaint him with all matters which concerned my conscience.

It was thus that I bound myself to confess to him, without the idea having entered my head the moment before. It was my foible. I thought I was simply doing what God willed whenever I carried out some unpremeditated idea which came into my head from nowhere. After I had thus to all intents and purposes told him that he was to be my confessor, he treated me to discourses full of unction, which did not bore me during a very choice dinner, including, among other things, woodcock and snipe.

"What, most reverend Father! Game of this sort at this season?"[4]

"It is a secret, Monsieur, which I will be glad to tell

you. I keep it for six months in such a way that the air cannot spoil it.''

The Prince-Abbot was an accomplished epicure as well as a fine judge of wine, though he affected sobriety. His Rhine wine was exquisite. A salmon trout was served, he smiled, he told me in Ciceronian Latin that there would be pride in refusing to eat it because it was fish, and he supported his sophism with great skill. He watched me attentively; his examination of my dress relieved him of any fear that I would ask him for money, and I saw that it gave him confidence. After dinner he dismissed the Chancellor, showed me all over the monastery, and finally took me to the library, where I saw a portrait of the Elector of Cologne[5] as Elector-Bishop. I said it was a good likeness except that the painter had made him less handsome than he was, and I immediately showed him his portrait in my fine snuffbox, which I had never taken from my pocket during our dinner. He laughingly praised His Electoral Highness's whim of having himself painted as Grand Master and admired the beauty of the snuffbox, meanwhile conceiving a higher and higher idea of me. But the library[6] would have made me protest aloud if I had been alone. It consisted entirely of folios. The most modern among them were a century old, and all these bulky books treated of nothing but religion: Bibles, commentators, the Fathers, several legists[7] in German, annals, and Hoffmann's great dictionary.[8]

"But your monks," I said, "must have books on the physical sciences, history, and travel in their rooms."

"No," he said, "they are honest fellows whose only concern is to do their duty and live in peace."

It was then that I first felt a desire to become a monk, but I did not tell him so. I simply asked him to take me to his study, where I would make him a general confession of my manifold sins, so that on the next day, ab-

solved from all my crimes, I could receive the Holy
Eucharist from him, and he at once conducted me to a
small pavilion, where he would not let me kneel. He made
me sit down facing him, and in less than three hours
I told him a quantity of stories which were scandalous
enough but devoid of literary grace since I had to use
the style of a penitent, though when I recounted my
follies I could not find it in my heart to condemn them.
Nevertheless he at least did not doubt my attrition;[9] he
said that contrition would come when, by a regular
course of conduct, I had regained grace; for according
to him, and even more according to me, without grace
it was impossible to feel contrition. So, after uttering the
words which have power to absolve the whole human
race, he advised me to retire to a room which he appointed for me, to spend the rest of the day in prayer,
and to go to bed early after supping, if it was my habit
to sup. He said that I should communicate the next day
at the first mass, and we parted.

Alone in my room, I pursued the idea which had come
to me before I confessed. I thought I saw that I was
really in the place where I could live happily until my
final hour, escaping once and for all from the sway of
Fortune. I believed it depended only upon me, for I
felt certain that the Abbot would not refuse me the
habit of his order, provided I gave him, for example,
ten thousand écus to furnish me an income which would
go to the monastery after my death. To be happy I
thought I needed only a library, and I was sure I should
be allowed to make it of what books I pleased, provided
I presented it to the monastery, only reserving to myself
free use of it during my lifetime. As for the society of
the monks, the discord and the petty spites which I knew
to be inseparable from their nature, I was sure that I
would not be troubled in that way, since, wanting nothing and having no ambition which could arouse their

jealousy, I had nothing to fear. I foresaw that I might repent, and I shuddered with horror; but I was pleased to think I could circumvent even that. When I asked for the habit of St. Benedict I would ask for a delay of ten years before I decided to make my profession. In any case I was resolved not to aspire to any office or any monastic dignity; I wanted only to enjoy my peace and all the decent freedom which I could claim without giving rise to the slightest scandal. To induce the Abbot to grant me the ten years' novitiate I intended to ask of him, I would make it a condition that I would forfeit the ten thousand écus I would have given him in advance if I decided to renounce the habit. I put my whole plan in writing, I slept on it, and the next morning after receiving the Holy Sacrament I presented it to the Abbot, who was expecting me to take a cup of chocolate with him.

He read it before we breakfasted, he said nothing, and, having read it again while walking up and down, he said he would answer me in the afternoon.

After dinner the worthy Abbot told me that his carriage was ready to take me to Zurich, where he asked me to wait two weeks for his answer. He promised to bring it to me himself and gave me two sealed letters, begging me not to fail to deliver them in person.

"Most reverend Father, I am infinitely obliged to Your Highness, I will deliver your letters, I will wait for you at the 'Sword,' and I hope you will grant my dearest wish."

I took his hand, which he modestly allowed me to kiss.

When my Spaniard saw me he gave a laugh which told me what he was thinking.

"What are you laughing at?"

"I am laughing at your having found something to amuse you for two days when you have scarcely arrived."

"Tell the innkeeper that I want a carriage at my disposal every day for two weeks and a good hire manservant."

The innkeeper, whose name was Ott[10] and who had the title of Captain, came in person to tell me that in Zurich there were only open carriages; I made the best of it, and he vouched to me for the honesty of the hire manservant. The next day I took my letters to their addresses; they were to Monsieur Orelli[11] and Monsieur Pestalozzi,[12] neither of whom was at home. They both came to call on me in the afternoon, they invited me to dinner, each fixing a day, and asked me at once to go with them to the municipal concert, since it was the only entertainment in the city, though restricted to subscribing citizens and to foreigners who paid an écu, but they said I must go as a citizen and they outdid each other in praise of the Abbot of Einsiedeln.

The concert, which was only instrumental, bored me. The men were all on one side, where I sat between my two sponsors; the women were all on the other, which annoyed me, for despite my recent conversion I saw three or four whom I thought attractive, who kept looking at me, and with whom I would gladly have flirted. At the end of the concert the departure of the audience broke up the division, and the two citizens introduced their wives and daughters to me; the two daughters were actually the most charming girls in Zurich. The ceremonies in the street were very short, so, after thanking the gentlemen, I went back to my inn. The next day I ate family dinner with Monsieur Orelli, where I duly praised his daughter's merits but without indicating by the slightest of the usual little liberties that I might have taken a fancy to her. The next day at Monsieur Pestalozzi's I played exactly the same role, despite the fact that the young lady could very easily have inspired me to gallantry. To my great astonishment I was perfectly discreet, and within four days everyone in Zurich knew that my behavior was exemplary. I noticed in the public promenades that people looked at me with respect, which was something entirely new to me. I became more and more persuaded that my idea of becoming a monk was a genuine vocation. I felt bored, but I saw that such a sudden change in my way of life could not but produce that effect. My boredom would vanish when I had become accustomed to being good. I spent three hours each morning with a language teacher who instructed me in German; he was Italian, a native of Genoa, his name was Giustiniani,[13] he had been a Capuchin, and despair had driven him to apostasy. The poor man, to whom I gave an écu of six francs[14] every day, considered me an angel, an instrument of Providence, and in the folly of my supposed vocation I took him for a devil straight from Hell, for he seized every moment when I interrupted his interminable lesson to denigrate all religious communities to me, and the ones which presented the best appearance were, according to him, the most corrupting since they were the most attractive. He solemnly termed all monks the vilest scum of the human race.

"But," I said to him one day, "Our Lady of Einsiedeln, for example? You will admit—"

"What! It is a gang of eighty lazy, ignorant, vicious hypocrites, real swine who—"

"But His Most Reverend Highness the Abbot?"

"An upstart peasant, who plays the prince and is conceited enough to think he is one."

"But so he is."

"Nonsense—it is a mask; I consider him nothing but a clown."

"What has he done to you?"

"Nothing. He is a monk."

"He is my friend."

"If that is so, forgive me for what I said."

Yet Giustiniani was undermining me. At six in the afternoon on the fourteenth day of my supposed conversion, the day before that on which the Abbot had promised to visit me, I was at my window which gave

on the bridge and from which I saw both the people
passing by and everyone who arrived at my inn by carriage. I see a four-horse carriage arrive at a fast trot, it
stops at the entrance, the waiter goes to open the carriage door, for there was no footman up behind, and I
see four well-dressed women get out. I see nothing unusual in the first three, but the fourth, who was dressed
*en amazone*[15] as the expression went, strikes me. A young
brunette, with very large, black, prominent eyes under
two fearless brows, with a lily complexion and cheeks
of roses, wearing a blue satin bonnet from which dangled
a silver tassel which hung over one ear—she is a talisman
which stupefies me. I lean over the window sill to gain
ten inches, and she raises her charming head as if I had
called to her. My strange posture makes her look at me
attentively for half a minute—too much for a modest
woman. She enters, I run to the window of my anteroom,
which gave on the corridor, and I see her coming quickly
up to overtake her companions, who had already gone
by. When she is opposite my window she happens to
turn her head, and, seeing me standing there, she falls
back half a step, crying out as if she had seen a ghost,
but she recovers in an instant, bursts out laughing, and
runs into the room in which her three friends were.

Defend yourselves, mortals, against such an encounter,
if you have the strength. Persist, if you can, fanatics, in
the mad idea of burying yourselves in a monastery after
seeing what I saw then in Zurich on the twenty-third
day of April. I sank onto my bed to calm myself. Five
or six minutes later I go back to the window on the
corridor, and seeing the waiter leaving the room of the
new arrivals I tell him I will sup downstairs at the common table.

"If you want to sup there to see those ladies, it is no
use. They will sup in their room at eight o'clock so that
they can leave tomorrow at daybreak."

"Where are they going?"

"To Einsiedeln to perform their devotions. They are all Catholics."

"Where are they from?"

"From Soleure."

"What are their names?"

"I have no idea."

I lie down on my bed again, I consider going to Einsiedeln. But what will I do there? They are going to confess, to receive communion, to talk with God, with the saints, with the monks; what sort of figure shall I cut? Then, too, I may meet the Abbot on the road, in which case, no matter what the cost, I shall have to retrace my steps. I dismiss the idea; but I see that if I had such a friend as I wished I had, I would set up an ambuscade and carry off the Amazon, than which nothing would have been easier for they were unaccompanied. I consider going and boldly asking them for supper, but I am afraid the other pious pilgrims will refuse me; I thought the Amazon could only be pious for form's sake, since her physiognomy was eloquent, and it had been long since any woman's physiognomy had been able to deceive me.

But suddenly the happiest idea comes into my agitated mind. I go to my window on the corridor and stay there until the waiter passes; I call him into my room, give him a louis, and tell him he must instantly lend me a green apron like his own, for I want to serve the ladies at table.

"What are you laughing at?"

"I am laughing at your notion. I will fetch you the apron. The prettiest of the ladies asked me who you are."

"Possibly, for she saw me as she went by, but she will not recognize me. What did you tell her?"

"Only that you are an Italian."

"Remember to hold your tongue."

*Gossip in the Boudoir*

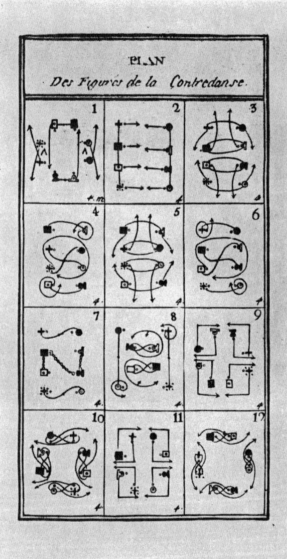

*Figures of Contradance "La nouvelle de Lille"*

"I asked your Spaniard to come and serve at supper, for I am all alone and I have the table downstairs."

"He is not to come into the room while I am playing my role, for the idiot couldn't help laughing, and everything would be ruined. Call him. He shall take care of going to the kitchen and bringing me the dishes outside."

The waiter comes back up with the apron and Leduc. I tell him perfectly gravely what I want him to do; he laughs like an idiot but promises he will obey me. So I have them bring me the carving knife, I do up my hair in a cadogan,[16] I put the apron over a scarlet waistcoat laced with gold, I examine myself in the mirror, and I find I have the look of baseness and false modesty demanded by the part I am to play. I am in raptures. They come from Soleure. They speak French.[17] Leduc comes to tell me that the waiter is ready to bring up the supper. I enter their room and, looking at the table, say:

"You will be served at once, Mesdames."

"Then be quick about it," said the ugliest, "we have to get up before daylight."

I arrange the chairs, and out of the corner of my eye I see the beauty, who has not moved, I give her a lightning glance, I see that she is startled. I go to meet the waiter, I help him set the dish on the table, and the waiter leaves, saying:

"*Stay here, you,* I have to serve downstairs."

I take a plate and set it before the one who has wounded me; I did not look at her, but I saw her perfectly, in fact I saw nothing else. She was astonished; the others did not even notice me. I hurry to change her plate, then I quickly change the others; they all help themselves to the soup, and in the meanwhile I carve a capon *au gros sel* [18] in their presence with marvelous skill.

"That," said my charmer, "is a waiter who serves well. Have you been long in service here, my lad?"

"Only a few weeks, Madame. You are too kind."

I had hidden my cuffs, which were of needlepoint, under the sleeves of my vest and had buttoned it at the wrists; but, the frill beginning to show a little at the opening, she said to me:

"Wait, wait."

"What do you wish, Madame?"

"Let me look. This is magnificent lace."

"Yes, Madame, so I have been told; but it is old. An Italian nobleman who stopped here gave it to me."

So saying, I let her pull out the whole cuff; which she did slowly and not looking at me, yet putting me very much at my ease so that I could enjoy her charming face to the full. What a delicious moment! I knew she had recognized me, and, seeing that she was keeping my secret, how I grieved at the thought that I could only carry my masquerade just so far. One of her friends finally made her stop examining my cuff by saying:

"What curiosity! One would think you had never seen lace."

My heroine blushed. Supper over, they each went into a corner to undress while I cleared the table; but the beauty sat down to write. I was very nearly conceited enough to think she was writing to me. After carrying everything away, I remained at the door.

"What are you waiting for?" she asked me.

"You are wearing boots, Madame. Unless you mean to go to bed with them on."

"Right you are. I am sorry I have to put you to so much trouble."

"Isn't that what I'm for, Madame?"

I having gone down on my knees, she surrendered her legs to me and went on writing; I unlaced her boots, I took them off, then I unbuckled the kneeband of her breeches so that I could take off her stockings and have the pleasure of seeing and touching her calves, but she stopped writing and said:

"That's enough, that's enough, I wasn't aware you were going to so much trouble. We shall see each other again tomorrow evening."

"Then you will be supping here, Mesdames?"

"Certainly."

I left, taking her boots with me and asking her if she wanted me to lock the room or to leave the key inside.

"Leave it inside, my lad, I will lock the door myself."

I went away, and she immediately locked herself in. My Spaniard at once relieved me of the boots and, laughing like a maniac, says she has caught me.

"What do you mean?"

"I saw everything. You played your part like an angel, and I'm sure that tomorrow morning she'll tip you a louis, but if you don't give it to me I will tell everything."

"There, you scoundrel, take it in advance, and bring me supper."

Such were the pleasures of my life, which I can no longer obtain; but I have the pleasure of enjoying them again by recalling them. Yet there are monsters who preach repentance, and stupid philosophers who say they are only vanities.

I slept with the Amazon in imagination, a factitious satisfaction but unalloyed; and I was at her door the next morning, carrying her cleaned boots, just when the coachman came to tell them to get up. I asked them for form's sake if they wanted breakfast, and they laughed and said they had no appetite. I went out to let them dress; but the door being open, my eyes breakfasted on an alabaster breast. She summoned me and asked where her boots were, and I begged her to let me lace them. As she already had her stockings on and was wearing velvet breeches, she acted as if she were a man—and besides, what is a waiter? So much the worse for him if he dares to hope that anything substantial will follow some trifle

he is granted. He will be punished, for he will never be
bold enough to press on. Today in my old age I have some
privileges of that sort, and I enjoy them, despising myself but also despising the women who grant them to me.

After she left I went back to bed, and on waking I
learned that the Abbot was in Zurich. Monsieur Ott told
me an hour later that he would dine with me alone in
my room. I said that it was my part to pay and that he
was to treat us like princes.

The worthy prelate entered my room at noon and congratulated me on the good reputation I had gained in
Zurich, from which he concluded that my vocation was
still in force.

"Here," he said, "is a distich which you shall put
over the door of your apartment:

> *Inveni portum. Spes et fortuna valete;*
> *Nil mihi vobiscum est: ludite nunc alios."*

> ("I have reached port. Hope and For-
> tune, farewell; I have nothing to do with
> you: henceforth make others your play-
> things.")[19]

"It is a translation," I said, "of two lines of Greek
by Euripides;[20] but they can serve some other time, for
since yesterday I have changed my mind."

He congratulated me, saying that he hoped all my desires would be fulfilled and assuring me confidentially
that it was easier to earn salvation by remaining in the
world than by retiring to a monastery. This language
did not seem to me that of a hypocrite but that of an
honest and sensible man. After dinner I expressed all
possible gratitude to him, I accompanied him to the door
of his carriage, and I saw him set off well content. I
at once went to the window of my room which overlooked the bridge, there to wait for the angel who had
come from Soleure expressly to deliver me from the

temptation of becoming a monk. The most beautiful of
castles in Spain delighted me until the arrival of her carriage. It arrives at six o'clock, I hide, but in a position
to watch the ladies alight. I see them, and I am annoyed
that all four of them look at the window at which the
beauty had seen me on the previous day. Their curiosity,
which could not exist unless the beauty had revealed the
whole secret, showed me that she had told all, and I was
nonplused. I was stripped not only of the hope of carrying the charming adventure further but also of my confidence that I could play my role well; I foresaw that I
might well lose my stage presence, become annoyed, and
be hissed; these ideas spoiled everything; I was instantly
determined not to play a farce for them in which I could
only laugh out of the wrong side of my mouth. If I had
interested the Amazon as she had interested me, she
would not have given the game away; she had told them
all; so she did not intend to carry the thing further, or
else she lacked the intelligence to see that her indiscretion
stopped me in my tracks, for two of the three others
actually repelled me, and if a woman whom I find pleasing sets me up a woman whom I find repulsive pulls me
down. Foreseeing all sorts of tiresome consequences if I
did not appear at the table, I went out. I ran into
Giustiniani, and when I told him I felt very much like
spending a couple of hours with some young and mercenary beauty, he took me to a door where he said I
would find what I wanted on the third floor if I whispered
his name to the old woman I would see there. He did not
dare come with me, because someone might find it out
and cause him trouble in a city where the police were
very strict in that department. He even told me I ought
not to enter the house until I was sure I would not be
seen, and I waited until dusk. I went there; I ate poorly
but had a sufficiently amusing time with two young
working girls until midnight. My generosity, which was

a thing unknown in that country, won me the friendship
of the old woman, who promised me treasures of the
same sort if I continued to come to her house, taking
every care not to be seen.

Upon my return Leduc told me I had done well to slip
away, for the whole inn had learned of my masquerade,
and everyone, including Monsieur Ott, would have had
great sport lurking outside of the room to see me play
the role of waiter, which, as I could not but have noticed
them, would have made me very angry.

"It was I," he said, "who took your place. The lady's
name is V. . . .[21] I never saw anything so appetizing."

"Did she ask where the other waiter was?"

"No. But the others asked me, several times."

"And Madame de V . . . never said anything?"

"Not once. She was gloomy, even to the point of pretending not to be interested in you when I told her that
the waiter who had served them yesterday had not come
because he was ill."

"Why did you say I was ill?"

"I had to say something."

"Did you unlace her boots?"

"She wouldn't let me."

"Who told you her name?"

"Their coachman. She's just been married [22] to an old
man."

I retired to bed, and early the next morning I went to
the window to watch them get into their carriage; but I
stayed behind the curtain. Madame was the last, and, for
an excuse to look up, she asked if it was raining and took
off her satin bonnet. I quickly took off my nightcap, and
she saluted me with a most gracious smile.

## CHAPTER V

*I leave Zurich. Comic incident at Baden. So-*
*leure. Monsieur de Chavigny. Monsieur and*
*Madame . . . . I act in a play. I feign illness*
*to forward my good fortune.*

---

MONSIEUR OTT came to my room to introduce his two young sons[1] to me; they were with their tutor, who brought them up like princes. In Switzerland an innkeeper is often a man who keeps a fine house and presides over a table at which he thinks it no disgrace to take money from those who come there to dine. He is right; he sits at the head of it only to see that each of his guests is properly served. If he has a son he does not let him sit at the table but makes him serve at it. In Schaffhausen the son of the innkeeper, a captain in the Imperial army, stood behind my chair to change my plate while his father dined with all the guests. He would not have done it elsewhere; but in his father's house he considered it an honor; and he was right. Such is the opinion of the Swiss, which some superficial minds see fit to ridicule. However, it is true that the Swiss, like the Dutch, fleece foreigners when they can; but the fools

*105*

who let themselves be fleeced deserve it; terms must be settled in advance. It was thus that, in Basel, I protected myself against Imhof [2] who was notorious for fleecing his patrons at the "Three Kings."

My host congratulated me on my waiter's disguise; he said he was sorry he could not have seen me, and he praised me for not having repeated the masquerade at the second supper. After thanking me for the honor I had done his establishment he asked me also to grant him that of dining at his table at least once before I left. I promised I would dine at it that very day.

Determined to go to Soleure to court the beautiful Amazon, I obtained a letter of credit on Geneva. I wrote Madame d'Urfé to send me a strong letter for Monsieur de Chavigny, [3] the French Ambassador, whose countenance I told her I greatly needed for the interests of our Order, [4] and to dispatch it to me as quickly as possible in care of the post at Soleure. I wrote several other letters, among them one to the Duke of Württemberg which must have left a bitter taste in his mouth.

At my host's table at the inn I found staff officers, good fare, and a magnificent dessert of confectionery. After dinner I lost a hundred louis at *passe-dix*, [5] and the same sum the next day at the house of a rather wealthy young man who invited me to dinner. His name was Escher. [6]

On four of my days in Zurich I amused myself at the house of the woman to whom Giustiniani had sent me— but not at all successfully, for the girls she got for me only spoke a thick Swiss dialect. Without words the pleasure of love is lessened by at least two thirds. In Switzerland I made the same odd observation which I made in Genoa. Both the Swiss and the Genoese, who speak very badly, write very well.

I had scarcely left Zurich before I had to stop at Baden [7] to get a carriage I had bought repaired. It is the city in which the deputies from the cantons hold their general assembly. I put off my departure in order to dine with a Polish lady who was going to Einsiedeln, but after dinner I had an amusing adventure. At her own urging I danced with the innkeeper's daughter; it was a Sunday. The innkeeper comes out, his daughter runs away, and the scoundrel declares I must pay a fine of one louis; and he shows me a placard which I cannot read. I refuse to pay; I appeal to the judge of the place, he goes off, acquiescing. A quarter of an hour later he summons me to a room in his inn, where I see him with a wig and a gavel; he tells me he is the judge. He writes, he confirms my sentence, and I have to give him another écu because he has written. I said that if his daughter had not tempted me into it I would not have danced, whereupon he pays a louis for his daughter. I had to laugh. I left the next morning very early.

At Lucerne I saw the Papal Nuncio,[8] who invited me to dinner, and at Fribourg[9] Count d'Affry's wife,[10] who was young and giddy; but now for what I saw eight or ten leagues before arriving at Soleure.

At nightfall I was taking a walk with the surgeon of the village. A hundred paces from me I see a man climbing up the outside of a house, reaching a window, and going in.[11] I point him out to the surgeon, he laughs and tells me it is a peasant lad going to spend the night alone with his fiancée.

"He spends the whole night with her," he said, "and he leaves in the morning more in love than ever because she has not granted him the final favors. If she did, he might not marry her, and she would find it very hard to get a new lover."

At the post station in Soleure[12] I found a letter from Madame d'Urfé enclosing one from the Duke of Choiseul addressed to Monsieur de Chavigny, Ambassador. It was sealed, but the name of the minister who had written it

was on the outside. I hire a carriage by the day, I dress
as I would for Versailles, I go to the door of the Ambassador's residence, he is not receiving, and I leave the
letter for him. It was a feast day, I go to the last mass,
where I do not see the beautiful lady, and after taking a
little stroll I return to my inn. An officer was waiting
for me with an invitation from the Ambassador to dine
"at the Court." [13]

Madame d'Urfé wrote me in her letter that she had
gone straight to Versailles and that she was sure the
Duchess of Gramont[14] had persuaded the minister to
write a most efficacious letter for me. I was very glad,
for I intended to play the role of an important personage. The Marquis de Chavigny had been the French Ambassador in Venice thirty years[15] before this time; I
knew a great deal about him and I could scarcely wait
to make his acquaintance.

I go at the appointed hour, I am not announced, as
soon as the double doors are opened for me I see the
handsome old man come to meet me, and I hear him
address me in the most obliging and courtly terms. He
introduces all his entourage to me; then, pretending to
have misread my name, he takes from his pocket the
Duke of Choiseul's letter and reads aloud the passage
in which he asks him to show me every consideration.
He makes me sit down at his right on a sofa, and he
asks me only such questions as oblige me to say that I
am traveling simply for pleasure, that the Swiss nation
is in several respects superior to all others, and that this
moment is the happiest of my life since it has procured
me the honor of his acquaintance.

Dinner is served, and His Excellency gives me the
place beside him and on his right. There were fifteen or
sixteen places at the table, and each guest was served
by a footman in the Ambassador's livery. The conversation turning that way, I said to him that he was still
spoken of in Venice with the fondest admiration.

"I shall always remember," he said, "the kindnesses which were shown me during my whole term as Ambassador; but be so good as to name those who still speak of me. They must be very old."

It was just what I wanted. Signor Malipiero had informed me of events during the Regency[16] which had gained him great credit; and Signor Bragadin had told me about his love affair with the celebrated Stringhetta.[17]

His cook was excellent; but the pleasure of talking to him led me to neglect that of eating. I saw him redden in his delight; he said to me as we rose from the table that he had never dined with greater pleasure at Soleure and that my recalling his Venetian gallantries to him had made him young again. He embraced me and asked me to spend all my time at his house, day and night, as long as I remained in Soleure. In his turn he talked much of Venice; after praising its system of government he said there was not a city in the world where one could eat better fare, even on fast days, only provided one made sure to procure good oil and foreign wine. About five o'clock he invited me to take a drive with him in a vis-à-vis,[18] getting into it first so that I should have to take the forward-facing seat.

We got out at a pretty country house, where we were served ices. On the way back to the city he said that he entertained a large company every evening, both men and women, and he hoped that, so far as it lay in his power, I would not be bored. I could scarcely wait to see the company; I thought it impossible that I should not see Madame . . . among them.

People began to arrive. Many of the women were ugly, some passable, and none pretty. Card games were arranged, and I was put at a table with a young blonde and an ancient dame who pretended to wit. Bored and not once opening my mouth, I lost five or six hundred counters. When the time came to pay, the old hand told me they came to three louis.

"Three louis?" I said.

"Yes, Monsieur. Two sous a counter. Did you think we were playing for coppers?" [19]

"On the contrary, Madame. I thought it was for twenty sous,[20] since I never play for less."

She left my boast unanswered, but she blushed.

After walking around the room and not seeing the beauty I hoped to find, I prepared to leave. The Ambassador had retired. I see two ladies talking together and looking at me; I recognize them as the ones I had seen at Zurich with Madame . . . ; I avoid them, and leave.

The next morning one of the Ambassador's household officials comes to tell me that His Excellency is coming and has sent me word so that he will be certain to find me. I said I would wait for him. I tried to think how I could get information about Madame . . . from him, but he saved me the trouble.

A quarter of an hour later I receive the worthy nobleman as it becomes me to do. After some desultory talk he smiled and said he was about to tell me the most unlikely thing imaginable, but he informed me in advance that he did not believe a word of it. After this preamble he said that two ladies who had seen me at the reception, and whose names he told me, had come to his room after I left to warn him to beware, because I was the waiter at the inn at Zurich.

"You waited on them at table ten days ago when they were on their way to perform their devotions at Our Lady of the Hermits—they are sure of it; and they say that yesterday, on the other side of the Aar, they met your fellow waiter, who had apparently run away with you, God knows why. They said that as soon as you realized last evening that they recognized you, you slipped away. I laughed and answered that I would be sure they were mistaken even if you had not brought me a letter from the Duke of Choiseul, and that I would have them to dinner with you today. I said that you might well have disguised yourself as a waiter in the hope of obtaining the favors of one of their party. They said the supposition was ridiculous, that you were nothing but a potboy with a knack for carving a capon and a deft hand at changing everyone's plate; and that they are ready to compliment you on your talents if I will permit it. I replied that they would make you laugh and me too. If there is any truth in this tale be so good as to tell me all the circumstances."

"Every one, and gladly. But we must observe a certain discretion, for it is a comedy which might be injurious to a person whom I would rather die than harm."

"So the story is true? You make me most curious."

"True and not true. I hope that Your Excellency does not believe I am the waiter at the 'Sword.' "

"No. I should never believe that. You played the part."

"Precisely. Did they tell you there were four of them?"

"I know that. There was the beauty too; and now I see the whole thing. You are quite right, discretion is essential, for her reputation is spotless."

"That I did not know. What happened is perfectly innocent, but it might be told with additions which could injure the honor of that charming woman, whose merits filled me with admiration."

I then told him the whole story, ending by saying that I had come to Soleure only to make her acquaintance and, if possible, to court her.

"If it is not possible," I said, "I will leave in three or four days, but not before seeing the two blabbers covered with ridicule, for they must know very well that the waiter was only a mask. They cannot pretend not to know it, except for the express purpose of putting an affront on me and injuring Madame, who was very ill advised to let them into the secret."

"Softly, softly! So many things at once! Let me embrace you. Your story really delights me. Leave it to me. You shall not go away, my dear friend; you shall court Madame. Permit me to laugh. I have been young, and a pair of beautiful eyes has often made me disguise myself too. Today at table with those two mischief-makers you shall prick their bubble, but good-naturedly. The thing is so innocent that even Monsieur . . . will laugh over it. His wife cannot but know that you love her, I presume?''

''She must have seen into my soul even though I did no more than take off her boots.''

''Funnier and funnier.''

He went away laughing, and at the door of his carriage he embraced me for the third time. Certain, as I could not but be, that Madame . . . had told her three companions everything she knew before returning to Zurich, the . . . joke[21] with which the two harridans had gone to the Ambassador struck me as both malicious and perfidious; but my heart's interests obliged me to let their calumny pass as wit.

At half past one I enter the Embassy and after making my most humble bow to the Ambassador I see the two ladies. I ask the one who looked the more malicious, who limped, and whose name was F., if she recognizes me.

''Then you admit you are the waiter at the inn in Zurich.''

''Yes, Madame. I was for an hour, to have the honor of seeing you close by; and you punished me by never addressing a word to me; I hope I shall not be so unfortunate here, and that you will permit me to pay court to you.''

''This is amazing. You played the waiter so well that no one could have guessed you were playing a part. We shall now see if you play your present role as skillfully; and if you will come to call on me I shall be honored.''

After this compliment the whole company learned the

story; and just then Madame . . . arrives with her husband. She sees me and instantly says to him:

"There's the waiter at Zurich."

The worthy man thanks me most politely for having done his wife the honor of taking off her boots. I see that she has told him everything and I am glad. Monsieur de Chavigny seated her on his right, and my place at the table proved to be between the two women who had calumniated me.

Though they both repelled me, I flirted with them, having the firmness scarcely ever to look at Madame . . . , who was even more beautiful than she had been in riding clothes. Her husband did not seem either jealous or as old as I had supposed. The Ambassador invited them both to his ball, and he asked her to play the heroine in *L'Écossaise*[22] again, so that I could tell the Duke of Choiseul I had been well entertained at Soleure. She replied that there were two actors missing; he offered to play Lord Monrose and I instantly said I would play Murray. The arrangement infuriating my table companion F., for it left her to play the hateful role of Lady Alton, she let fly a shaft at me.

"Why isn't there a waiter's part in the play?" she said. "You would act it wonderfully well."

"But you," I replied, "will teach me to act the part of Murray still better."

The Ambassador settled on a day five or six days later, and the next morning I was sent my short part. The ball having been announced as in my honor, I returned to my inn for another suit, and I reappeared in the ballroom dressed with the utmost elegance.

I opened the ball, dancing the minuet with a woman who must have had precedence over all the others, then I danced with them all; but the wily Ambassador arranged for me to dance the contradances with Ma-

dame . . . , and no one could object. He said that Lord
Murray must dance with no one but Lindane.

At the first pause in the contradance I told her that
I had come to Soleure only for her, that but for her I
should never have been seen as a waiter, and that hence
I hoped she would permit me to pay court to her.
She said that there were reasons which forbade her to
receive visits from me, but that opportunities to see each
other could not fail to arise if I did not leave at once
and would refrain from showing her certain attentions
which must give rise to talk. Love, readiness, and prudence together could not have made me a more satisfying answer. I promised her all the discretion she could
ask. On the instant my love became of heroic mold and
thoroughly determined to make secrecy its law.

Having declared that I was a novice in the art of the
theater, I asked Madame F. to instruct me. I went to
her in the morning, but she thought it was only an excuse. By going, I was paying court to Madame . . . ,
who was perfectly aware of my motive for acting as I
did. She[23] was a widow between thirty and forty years
of age, with a malicious temperament, a yellowish complexion, and an awkward walk, because she tried to conceal the fact that she was lame. She was forever talking,
and, since she tried to display a wit which she did not
possess, she bored me. Nevertheless I had to pretend I
was in love with her. She made me laugh one day when
she said she would never have thought I was timid by
nature after seeing me play the role of waiter so well
at Zurich. I asked her what made her suppose me timid,
and she did not answer. I had made up my mind to
break with her after we had acted *L'Écossaise.*

Our first performance was attended by all the best
people in the city. Madame F. was delighted to inspire
loathing in her role, being sure that her own person had
no part in producing the effect. Monsieur de Chavigny

drew tears. People said he had played his part better
than Voltaire[24] did. But my blood froze when in the third
scene of the fifth act Lindane said to me: "What! You!
You dare to love me!" [25] She uttered the seven words so
strangely, in a tone of such deliberate scorn, even stepping momentarily out of her part, that the whole audience applauded wildly. The applause nettled and disconcerted me, for I thought her manner had trespassed
on my honor. When silence was restored and I, as my role
prescribed, had to answer her with, "Yes, I adore you,
and I must," [26] I brought out the words in a tone so
moving that the applause redoubled: *Bis, bis* from four
hundred voices forced me to repeat them.

But despite the applause we decided at supper that
we did not know our parts well enough. Monsieur de
Chavigny said that the second performance would be
put off until the next day but one and that on the
morrow we would hold a private rehearsal at his country
house, where we would dine. We congratulated each
other on our acting. Madame F. said that I had played
my role well, but that I had done even better as the
waiter, and the laugh was on her side; but I had it on
mine when I replied that she had played Lady Alton
excellently, but that it could hardly be otherwise since
it required no effort on her part.

Monsieur de Chavigny told Madame . . . that those
in the audience who had applauded her for the passage
in which she expressed amazement that I should love her
had been wrong, since by putting scorn into the words
she had stepped out of her part, for Lindane could not
but have a high regard for Murray.

The Ambassador came next day to fetch me in his
carriage, saying that there was no need for me to use
mine. All the actors were assembled at his country house.
He at once said to Monsieur . . . that he believed he
had settled his business and that they would talk about

it after they had dined and rehearsed the play. We sat down at table; and afterward we got through the whole rehearsal without once needing to be prompted. Toward nightfall he told the company that he expected them all for supper at Soleure, and everyone left except Monsieur . . . , with whom he had business to discuss. I had no carriage. At the moment of departure I had a most pleasant surprise:

"Ride in my carriage with me," said the Ambassador to Monsieur . . . , "and we will discuss our business. Monsieur de Seingalt[27] will have the honor of escorting your lady in yours."

I at once give my hand to that miracle of nature, who gets in with an air of the greatest indifference, warmly pressing my hand. So there we are, sitting face to face.

A half hour went by like a minute; but we did not waste it talking. Our mouths joined and did not separate until we were ten paces from the door of the Embassy. She got out first. Her flushed face terrifies me. It not being her natural color, we would reveal our crime to every eye in the room. Her honor did not permit me to expose her in such a state to the scrutiny of Madame F., who would have felt even more triumphant than humiliated by a discovery of such consequence.

It was Love who made me think of a unique expedient, and Fortune, who often favored me, who saw to it that I had in my pocket a small box containing a sternutative.[28] I urged her to take a pinch of it at once, and I did the same. The excessive dose began to produce its effect halfway up the stairs, and we continued to sneeze for a good quarter of an hour; the blame for her tattletale redness was put entirely on her sneezes. When they stopped she said she no longer had a headache but that in future she would beware of taking such a violent remedy. I saw Madame F. lost in thought, but she dared say nothing.

This foretaste of my good fortune decided me to stay in Soleure for as long as it might take me to crown my happiness. I immediately determined to rent a country house. Any man in my situation and endowed with a heart would have made the same resolve. I saw before me a perfect beauty whom I adored, whose heart I was certain I possessed, and whom I had barely touched; I had money, and I was my own master. I thought it far more reasonable than my notion of becoming a monk at Einsiedeln. I was so full of my happiness, present and to come, that I dismissed all thought of "what people would say." I left everyone at the table and sought out the Ambassador a minute after he withdrew. As a man of the world, I could not conscientiously deny the lovable old man his right to a confidence which he had so signally deserved.

As soon as we were alone he asked me if I had profited by the favor he had done me. After kissing his noble countenance several times I told him all in these five words: "I can hope for everything." But when he heard the story of the sternutative the compliments he lavished on me were endless, for the lady's greatly changed physiognomy could have raised the suspicion of a struggle. After my narrative, which made him laugh heartily, I told him that, being under the necessity of crowning my happiness and at the same time sparing the lady's honor, and having nothing better to do, I wanted to rent a country house in which I would calmly wait for Fortune to favor me. I said that I looked to his good offices to obtain me a furnished house, a carriage at my disposal, two manservants, a good cook, and a housekeeper-chambermaid who would attend to my linen. He said that he would look into it. The next day our play went very well, and on the day after he imparted his plan to me as follows:

"I see, my dear friend, that in this intrigue your

happiness depends upon your satisfying your passion
without in any way injuring Madame . . .'s good name.
I am even sure you will leave at once without having obtained anything if your departure is necessary to her
peace of mind. This will show you that I am just the
man to advise you. If you really want not to be found
out, you must refrain from the taking of the least step
which could make anyone who does not believe that there
is such a thing as an action without meaning suspect
the truth. Even the most speculative mind cannot take
the brief interview which I arranged for you yesterday
to be anything but the effect of the purest chance, and
the incident of the sternutative foils the deductions of
the most penetrating malice, for a lover who wants to
make the most of an occasion favorable to his passion
does not begin by bringing on convulsions in his beauty's
head when a fortunate chance has placed her in his
power, and no one can guess that a sternutative was
used to hide a reddened face, for it is not often that
consummation produces that effect and that a lover fore-
sees it to the point of carrying such a stimulant in his
pocket. So what has already happened is not enough to
reveal your secret. Monsieur . . . himself, who, though
he does not want to show jealousy, is nevertheless jealous
of his wife, cannot have seen anything out of the way
in my having him drive back to Soleure with me, for it
is beyond all likelihood that I should wish to be your
Mercury, while naturally and in accordance with the
rules of the most ordinary politeness, which he has never
refused to honor, his dear wife was the person who, on
the return journey here, should occupy the place in my
vis-à-vis which I kindly let him occupy himself, because
of the interest I took in his important business.

"After this long exordium, which I have delivered in
the style of a secretary of state speaking in council, let
us come to the conclusion. Two things are necessary to

set you on the road to fruition. The first, which concerns you, is to contrive to make Monsieur . . . your friend without ever giving him cause to suspect that you have designs on his wife. The second, which concerns the lady, is to do nothing which can be observed without making the reason for it known to everyone. So I say to you that you shall not take this country house until, between us, we have hit upon a perfectly plausible reason of a nature to throw dust in the eyes of speculation. I thought of such a reason yesterday when I was considering your case.

"You must pretend to be ill, and think of an illness of which what you say to him will leave the doctor in no doubt. Fortunately I know a doctor whose passion is prescribing country air, with baths of his own composition, for almost every disease. He is to come here one of these days to take my pulse. You shall summon him to your inn for a consultation and give him two louis; I am certain he will at least prescribe the country for you and will tell the whole town that he will surely cure you. Such is Herrenschwandt's[29] way, though he is a learned man."

"What! Is he here? He is a friend of mine. I met him in Paris at Madame du Rumain's."

"This is his brother.[30] Think up an illness which is fashionable and won't disgrace you. We will find the house afterward, and I will give you a young man who will cook excellent dishes for you."

Choosing an illness cost me some thought. I gave Madame . . . an outline of my plan in the wings, and she approved of it. I begged her to find some way by which we could write to each other, and she said she would try. She said that her husband had the highest opinion of me, and that he had seen nothing wrong in my having been in her coupé with her. She asked me if Monsieur de Chavigny had taken her husband with him because it had happened that way or on purpose, and I answered: "On purpose." She raised her beautiful eyes to heaven and bit her lip.

"Are you sorry, my charmer?"

"Alas! . . . no."

Three or four days later the doctor came to see the last performance of *L'Écossaise* and dine at the Ambassador's. He having complimented me at dessert on my look of good health, I said that looks were deceptive and I asked him for a consultation. Delighted that he had been mistaken, he promised me an hour the next day at my inn. He came, and I told him what God put into my mouth.

"I suffer every night," I said, "from amorous dreams which wear me out."

"I know the complaint, Monsieur, and I will cure you of it by two remedies. The first, which you may not much like, is to go and spend six weeks in the country, where you will not see objects which, by stimulating the seventh pair of nerves, bring on the lumbar discharge which must also make you very melancholy when you wake."

"So it does."

"Oh, I know that! The second remedy consists in cold baths, which will keep you amused."

"Are they far from here?"

"They are wherever you please, because I will write you a prescription for them at once. The apothecary will make them up for you."

After writing his prescription and accepting my two louis he left, and before noon the whole town had heard of my illness and my decision to make a stay in the country. Monsieur de Chavigny joked about it at table, telling Herrenschwandt he should forbid me to receive calls from ladies. Monsieur F.[31] said I should be forbidden certain miniatures of which my jewel box was full. Monsieur . . . , who was an anatomist, pronounced the doctor's reasoning splendid. I publicly asked the Ambassador to be so good as to find me a country house, and a cook because I liked to eat well.

Tired of playing a false role which I considered no longer necessary, I stopped calling on Madame F. She took it upon herself to reproach me in no uncertain terms for my inconstancy, saying that I had hoodwinked her. She said she knew all, and she threatened vengeance. I replied that she had nothing to avenge herself for, since I had never wronged her, but that if she was planning to have me murdered I would demand guards. She replied that she was not Italian.

Delighted to have got rid of the viper, I could now turn all my thoughts to Madame . . . . Monsieur de Chavigny, active as ever on my behalf, made Monsieur . . . believe that I was just the person to persuade the Duke of Choiseul, Colonel-General of the Swiss Guards,[32] to pardon a cousin[33] of his who had killed his man in a duel at La Muette.[34] He had told him I could do anything through the Duchess of Gramont; and, informing me of all this, he asked me if I would undertake to apply for the pardon and if I thought I might be successful. It was the sure way to gain Monsieur . . .'s entire friendship. I replied that I could not be certain I would succeed, but that I would gladly undertake it.

He then arranged to have the whole case explained to me in his presence by Monsieur M . . . , who brought all the documents stating the circumstances of the *factum,* which was perfectly simple, to my inn.

I spent most of the night writing a letter intended to persuade first the Duchess of Gramont and then the Duke her father;[35] and I wrote to Madame d'Urfé that the well-being of the Rosicrucian Order depended upon the King's pardoning the officer, who had been obliged to leave the kingdom because of the duel.

The next morning I took the Ambassador the letter

which was to be seen by the Duke. He judged it excellent and told me to go and show it to Monsieur . . . , whom I found in his nightcap. Full of gratitude for the interest I was taking in his concerns, he thanked me effusively. He said that his wife was still in bed and asked me to wait and breakfast with her, but I asked him to make her my excuses, for since the post left at noon I had little time.

So I went back to my inn, where I sealed my letters and sent them to the post; then I went and dined alone with the Ambassador, who was expecting me.

After praising my prudence in refusing to wait until Madame . . . was up and assuring me that her husband must have become my bosom friend, he showed me a letter from Voltaire thanking him for having played the role of Monrose in *L'Écossaise,* and another from the Marquis de Chauvelin,[36] who was then staying with Voltaire at "Les Délices." [37] He promised to visit him before leaving for Turin, where he was to be Ambassador.

After dinner I went back to my room to dress, for there was to be a reception and supper at "the Court" that day. Such was the name given to the residence of the French Ambassador in Switzerland.

## CHAPTER VI

*My country house. Madame Dubois. Base trick*
*which the lame harridan plays on me. My*
*grievous misfortunes.*

---

AS I enter the drawing room I see Madame . . . in a
corner, poring over a letter. I go to her and apologize
for not having waited to breakfast with her; she replies
that I did right and adds that if I have not yet taken the
country house I need I can do her a favor by deciding on
the one her husband will propose to me, probably during
supper that evening.

She could say no more, for she was summoned to take a
hand at quadrille.[1] I excused myself from playing. At
table everyone talked to me about my health and the
baths I was to take in a country house I intended to rent.
As his wife had forewarned me, Monsieur . . . told me
about one near the Aar which was charming.

"But," he said, "it has to be rented for at least six
months."

I replied that, provided I liked it and should be free to

leave when I pleased, I would pay for the six months in advance.

"It has a reception room than which there is none finer in the whole canton."

"So much the better; I'll give a ball in it. Let us go to see it tomorrow morning at the latest. I will come to your house for you at eight o'clock."

"I look forward to it."

Before going to bed I ordered a four-horse berlin, and at eight o'clock I found Monsieur . . . ready. He said that he had tried to persuade his wife to come with us, but that she was a slug-a-bed. In less than an hour we reached the fine house,[2] and I thought it marvelous. There were master's rooms enough to lodge twenty. In addition to the reception room, which I admired, there was a retiring room hung with choice engravings. A large garden, a fine orchard, waterworks and fountains, and excellent facilities for baths in the main building. After approving of everything we went back to Soleure. I asked Monsieur . . . to make all the arrangements so that I could move in the next day. I saw his wife, who appeared delighted when her husband told her I had liked the house. I said I hoped they would often do me the honor of dining there, and Monsieur . . . gave me his word for it. After paying him the hundred louis which were the rent for six months, I embraced him and went, as always, to dine with the Ambassador.

I at once said that in deference to the suggestion his wife had made to me beforehand I had rented the house Monsieur . . . had proposed, and he thought well of it.

"But," he said, "do you really mean to give a ball there?"

"Certainly I do, provided my money can buy me everything I need."

"You'll have no difficulty about that, for you can turn to me for anything your money won't buy you. I see you want to be lavish. In the meanwhile you shall have two menservants, the housekeeper, and the cook; my major-domo will pay them and you can reimburse him; he is honest. I'll come to eat with you from time to time, and I shall listen with pleasure to the delightful story of your current intrigue. I think most highly of the young woman; her conduct is beyond her years, and the proofs of love she gives you must make you respect her. Does she know that I know everything?"

"She knows no more than that Your Excellency knows we love each other, and she takes no exception to that, for she is certain of your discretion."

"She is a charming woman."

An apothecary to whom the doctor sent me left the same day to compound the baths which were to cure me of a disease I did not have; and two days later I went myself, after ordering Leduc to follow with all my luggage. But I was not a little surprised when, on entering the apartment I was to occupy, I saw a young woman, or perhaps a girl, with an extremely pretty face approach me and start to kiss my hand. I draw it back, and my astonished look makes her blush.

"Do you belong to the household, Mademoiselle?"

"His Excellency the Ambassador's major-domo engaged me to serve you as housekeeper."

"Pardon my surprise. Let us go to my bedroom."

As soon as I am alone I tell her to sit down beside me on the couch. She replies in the gentlest and most modest fashion that she could not accept such an honor.

"As you will; but I hope you will make no objection to eating with me when I ask you to, for it bores me to eat alone."

"I will obey you."

"Where is your room?"

"There. It was the major-domo who showed it to me; but it is for you to give what orders you please."

The room was behind the alcove which contained my bed. I go into it with her, and I see dresses on a sofa; next to it a boudoir with all the usual array of petticoats, bonnets, shoes, and slippers, and a fine open trunk in which I see an abundance of linen. I look at her, I try to penetrate her serious manner, I approve of her reserve, but I think I had better subject her to some close questioning, for she was too interesting and too well dressed to be a mere chambermaid. I presume it is a trick Monsieur de Chavigny has played on me, for such a girl, whose age could not be more than twenty-four or twenty-six and who possessed the wardrobe I saw, seemed to me more fit to be the mistress of a man like myself than his housekeeper. I ask her if she knows the Ambassador and what wages she is to have, and she answers that she knows the Ambassador only by sight and that the major-domo had told her she would be paid two louis a month besides meals in her room. She said she was from Lyons, a widow, and that her name was Dubois.

I leave her, unable to decide what will happen, for the more I looked at her and talked with her, the more interesting I found her. I go to the kitchen, and I see a young man kneading dough. His name was Durosier. I had known his brother when he was in the service of the French Ambassador[3] in Venice. He said my supper would be ready at nine o'clock.

"I never eat alone."

"I know that."

"How much are you paid a month?"

"Four louis."

I see two likely-looking, well-dressed menservants. One of them says he will bring me what wine I order. I go to the small bathhouse, where I find the apothecary's apprentice preparing the bath I am to take on the morrow and every day.

After spending an hour in the garden I go to the care-

taker's, where I see a numerous family, among them some
not unpromising daughters. I spend two hours talking
with them, delighted that everyone speaks French. As I
wanted to see the whole of my house, the caretaker's wife
took me everywhere. I returned to my apartment, where
I found Leduc unpacking my luggage. After telling him
to give my linen to Madame Dubois, I went to write. It
was a pretty study, facing north, with one window. A
ravishing view semed made to inspire the soul of a poet
with the most felicitous ideas engendered by the freshness
of the air and the palpable silence which soothes the ear
in a smiling countryside. I felt that, to enjoy the sim-
plicity of certain pleasures, a man must be in love and
fortunate in love. I congratulated myself.

I hear a knock. I see my beautiful housekeeper, who,
with a smile quite unlike the one worn by a person who is
about to complain, asks me to tell my valet to treat her
politely.

"How has he been rude to you?"

"Perhaps not at all by his lights. He wanted to kiss me,
I refused, and he, thinking it was his right, became a
trifle insolent."

"In what way?"

"He laughed at me. Excuse me, Monsieur, if I resented
it. I don't like being sneered at."

"You are right, my dear helpmate. Sneering always
comes from either stupidity or malice. Leduc shall be
told at once that he is to respect you. You shall sup with
me."

Leduc coming to ask me some question half an hour
later, I told him he must treat Madame Dubois with
respect.

"She's a prude—she wouldn't let me kiss her."

"As for you, you're a blackguard."

"Is she your chambermaid or your mistress?"

"Perhaps she is my wife."

"Well and good. I will go and amuse myself at the caretaker's."

I was well satisfied with my little supper and with an excellent Neuchâtel [4] wine. My housekeeper was accustomed to wine from "La Côte," [5] which was delicious too. In short, I was well pleased with the cook, with my housekeeper's modesty, and with my Spaniard, who changed her plate for her without putting on airs. After ordering my bath for six o'clock in the morning I told my servants to retire. Thus left alone at table with the too beautiful woman, I asked her to tell me her story.

"My story is very short. I was born in Lyons. My father and mother brought me to Lausanne with them, or so they have told me, for I do not remember it myself. I know I was fourteen when my father, who was coachman to Madame d'Hermenches, [6] died. The lady took me into her household, and three or four years later I entered the service of Lady Montagu [7] as a chambermaid, and her old footman Dubois married me. Three years later I was left a widow at Windsor, where he died. The air of England threatening me with consumption, I asked my generous mistress to let me leave her service, which she granted me, paying for my traveling expenses and giving me some valuable presents. I went back to my mother's house in Lausanne, where I entered the service of an English lady who was very fond of me and who would have taken me to Italy if she had not become suspicious of the young Duke of Roxburghe, [8] who showed signs of being in love with me. She loved him, and she thought I was secretly her rival. She was wrong. She gave me a quantity of presents and sent me back to my mother's, where I have lived for two years by the work of my hands. Monsieur Lebel, [9] major-domo to the Ambassador, asked me four days ago if I wished to enter the service of an Italian nobleman as housekeeper and told me the conditions. I accepted, since I have always had a great desire to see Italy ; that desire was the reason for my folly ; and here I am.''

''What folly ?''

''Coming to you without knowing you beforehand.''

''Then you would not have come if you had known me beforehand ?''

''Certainly not, for I shall no longer be able to find service with a woman. Do you think you are the kind of man to have a housekeeper like me without people's saying that you have me for something else ?''

''I expect as much, for you are very pretty and I scarcely look a milksop ; but I do not care.''

''I wouldn't care either, if my station in life allowed me to defy certain prejudices.''

''Which is to say, my beauty, that you would like to go back to Lausanne.''

''Not now, for that would be unjust to you. People might believe you had offended me by being too free, and you yourself might reach a wrong conclusion about me.''

''What conclusion, if you please ?''

''You would conclude that I want to make an impression on you.''

''That might be, for your sudden and unreasonable departure would annoy me greatly. Even so, I am sorry for you. Thinking as you do, you can neither want to stay with me nor leave. Yet you must decide one way or the other.''

''I have already decided. I shall stay, and I am almost certain that I shall not regret it.''

''I like your hope ; but there is one difficulty.''

''Will you be so good as to explain ?''

''I must, my dear Dubois. I cannot abide either melancholy or certain scruples.''

''You will never find me melancholy ; but please let us come to an understanding on the article of scruples. What do you mean by scruples ?''

"I like that. In common usage the word 'scruple' means a superstitious malice which sees vice in an act which may be innocent."

"If an act leaves me in doubt I am not inclined to put a bad construction on it. My duty only bids me watch over myself."

"You have read a good deal, I should think."

"It's the one thing I do, really, for otherwise I'd be bored."

"Then you have books?"

"Many. Do you understand English?"

"Not a word."

"I'm sorry, for they would entertain you."

"I don't like romances."

"No more do I. I like that. What, may I ask, made you decide so quickly that I am romantic?"

"And I like that! Your outburst delights me, and I am glad I have got you to laugh at last."

"Excuse me if I laugh, because—"

"Because me no becauses. Laugh in season and out of season; you'll never find a better way to handle me. I should say you've hired yourself out to me too cheaply."

"I have to laugh again, for it lies with you to increase my wages."

I rose from the table very much surprised by this young woman, who seemed in a fair way to find the chink in my armor. She could reason; and in this first dialogue she had already drained my resources. Young, beautiful, elegantly dressed, and intelligent—where she would lead me I could not guess. I was eager to talk with Monsieur Lebel, who had procured me such a piece of household furniture.

After clearing the table and taking everything into her room, she came to ask me if I used curl papers under my nightcap. It was Leduc's province; but I gladly gave her the preference. She managed it very well.

*Waldeck, Summer Residence of the French Ambassador in Switzerland*

*Woman Triumphant*

"I foresee," I said, "that you will serve me as you did Lady Montagu."

"Not quite; but since you do not like melancholy, I must ask you a favor."

"Ask it, my dear."

"I would rather not wait on you in your bath."

"May I die if the thought has entered my head. It would be a scandal. Leduc shall do it."

"Then pray forgive me, and I make bold to ask you another favor."

"Tell me freely whatever it is you want."

"May I have one of the caretaker's daughters sleep with me?"

"If it had ever occurred to me I swear I would have asked you to do just that. Is she in your room?"

"No."

"Go and fetch her."

"I'll do it tomorrow, for if I went now people would start inventing reasons. Thank you."

"You are prudent, my dear. And be sure I will never stand in the way of your being so."

She helped me to undress, and she must have found me perfectly modest; but thinking of my behavior before I fell asleep I saw that it did not spring from virtue. My heart was Madame . . .'s, and the widow Dubois had rather overawed me; perhaps I was her dupe, but I did not dwell on the thought.

In the morning I rang for Leduc, who told me he had not expected to have the honor. I called him a fool. After taking a cold bath I went back to bed, ordering him to bring two cups of chocolate. My helpmate entered, in a very fetching dishabille and all smiles.

"You are in good spirits, my beautiful housekeeper."

"In good spirits because I am very glad to be with you, I slept well, I've been for a walk, and in my room there's a very pretty girl, who will sleep with me."

"Call her in."

I laughed when I saw a girl as ugly as she seemed to be shy. I told her she would drink chocolate with me every morning, and she showed that she was pleased, saying that she liked it very much. In the afternoon Monsieur de Chavigny came and spent three hours with me, and he was satisfied with the whole house but greatly surprised by the housekeeper Lebel had provided for me. He had said nothing to him about her. He thought it was the perfect cure for the love which Madame . . . had inspired in me. I assured him that he was wrong. He addressed her with the utmost politeness.

No later than the next day, just as I was about to sit down at table with my helpmate, a carriage enters my courtyard and I see Madame F. get out of it. I am surprised and annoyed, but I could not avoid going to meet her.

"I did not expect you would honor me with a visit, Madame."

"I came to ask you to do me a favor, after we have dined."

"Then come at once, for the soup is on the table. Permit me to present Madame Dubois. Madame de F.," I say to the latter, "will dine with us."

My helpmate did the honors of the table, playing the role of hostess like an angel, and Madame F., despite her pride, put on no airs. I did not speak twenty words during the whole dinner nor bestow any attentions on the madwoman, for I was impatient to learn what kind of favor she wanted to ask of me.

As soon as the widow Dubois left us, she told me bluntly that she had come to ask me to let her have two rooms for three or four weeks. Greatly surprised by her effrontery, I reply that I cannot grant her the favor.

"You will grant it, for the whole town knows that I have come here to ask it."

"And the whole town will know that I have refused you. I want to be alone and entirely free; any company at all would be burdensome."

"I will not burden you in any way; you need not even know that I am in your house. I shall not consider it impolite if you do not inquire after my health, and I will not inquire after yours even if you fall ill. I will have my maid cook for me in the small kitchen, and I will not walk in the garden when I know you are there. The apartment for which I ask you is the two last rooms on the second floor, which I can enter and leave by the small stairway without being seen and without seeing anyone. Now tell me if, in strict politeness, you can refuse me the favor."

"If you knew even the rudiments of politeness you would not ask it of me, and you would not insist after hearing me refuse you."

She does not answer, and I stride up and down the room like a maniac. I consider having her put out the door. I think I have the right to treat her as insane, then I reflect that she has relatives, and that she herself, treated without any consideration, will become my enemy and perhaps take some horrible revenge. Finally I think that Madame . . . would disapprove any violent means I might resolve upon to get rid of the viper.

"Very well, Madame," I say, "you shall have the apartment, and an hour after you enter it I will go back to Soleure."

"Then I accept the apartment, and I will move into it day after tomorrow, and I do not believe you will be so foolish as to go back to Soleure on that account. You would set the whole town laughing."

So saying, she rose and left. I let her go without stirring from where I was; but a moment later I repented of having yielded, for her errand and her effrontery were equally beyond all bounds. I called myself stupid, a coward, a fool. I ought not to have taken the thing seriously, I should have laughed at it, made a mock of her, told her clearly that she was mad and forced her to leave, calling in the caretaker's whole family and my servants as witnesses. When I told the widow Dubois what had happened she was amazed. She said behavior of that sort was incredible, and that my giving in to such high-handed proceedings was equally so, unless I had very strong reasons for what I had done.

Seeing that her reasoning was sound, and not wanting to tell her anything, I took the course of saying no more to her on the subject. I went for a walk until suppertime, and I remained at table with her until midnight, finding her ever pleasanter company, full of intelligence and most amusing in all the little stories she told me about herself. Her mind was extremely unprejudiced, but she maintained that if she did not follow the principles of what are called prudence and honor she would be made unhappy. So her good behavior resulted rather from her philosophy than from her virtue; but if she had not been virtuous she would not have had the firmness to practice her philosophy.

I considered my encounter with the F. woman so extraordinary that I could not keep from going the next morning early to regale Monsieur de Chavigny with it. I told my helpmate that she might dine without waiting for me if she did not see me back by the usual hour.

The Ambassador had been informed that Madame F. was coming to see me, but he burst out laughing when I told him how she had succeeded.

"Your Excellency finds it comic, but not I."

"So I see; but, believe me, you must pretend to laugh at it too. Act at all times as if you did not know she was in your house, and she will be sufficiently punished. People will say she is in love with you and that you will have none of her. I advise you to go and tell the whole

story to Monsieur . . . and invite yourself to stay for
dinner with him. I have talked with Lebel about your
beautiful housekeeper. He meant no harm. Having gone
to Lausanne an hour after I charged him to find you a
respectable chambermaid, he remembered it, spoke of
you to La Dubois, and the thing was done. It is a lucky
find for you, because when you fall in love she won't
keep you languishing."

"I don't know, for she has principles."

"I am sure you will not be taken in by them. I will
come to you for dinner tomorrow and will enjoy hearing
her talk."

"Your Excellency will afford me the greatest pleasure."

Monsieur . . . greeted me warmly and at once congratulated me on the admirable conquest[10] which was
sure to make my stay in the country a pleasure. Though
she suspected the truth, his wife congratulated me too;
but I saw that they were both astounded when I told
them the whole story in detail. Monsieur . . . said that
if the woman really became a burden to me I need only
ask the government to serve her with an immediate order
never to set foot in my house again. I replied that I did
not want to employ that resource, since, in addition to
being dishonorable to her, it would prove me a weakling,
for everyone must know that I was master in my own
house and that she could never come to lodge there
without my consent. His wife said thoughtfully that I
had done well to let her have the apartment and that
she would go to call on her, for she had herself told her
she would have an apartment in my house the next day.
I said no more about it, and, invited to take potluck with
them for dinner, I stayed. Since I had shown Madame
. . . nothing but ordinary politeness, her husband could
have no suspicion that we were in communication. She
seized an opportunity to tell me that I had done well to

let the spiteful woman have the apartment and that I
could invite her husband to come and spend two or three
days with me after Monsieur de Chauvelin, who was expected, had gone. She also said that the wife of the caretaker of my house was her nurse, and that she would
write me through her when the need arose.

After calling on two Italian Jesuits who were passing
through Soleure and inviting them to dinner the next
day, I went home. My helpmate kept me entertained
until midnight with philosophical problems. She was
devoted to Locke.[11] She said that the faculty of thought
was not a proof of the spirituality of our soul, since God
could give the property of thought to matter. I laughed
heartily when she said there was a difference between
thinking and reasoning.

"I think," I said, "that you would be reasoning well
if you let yourself be persuaded to go to bed with me,
and you think you are reasoning very well in refusing."

"Believe me," she answered, "that between a man's
reason and a woman's there is the same difference that
there is between the two sexes."

We were drinking our chocolate at nine o'clock the
next morning when Madame F. arrived. I did not even
go to the window. She dismissed her carriage and went
to her apartment with her chambermaid. Having sent
Leduc to Soleure to wait for letters for me, I asked my
helpmate to dress my hair, saying that we should have
the Ambassador and two Italian Jesuits for dinner. I
had already told my cook to prepare good fast-day and
meat dishes, it being a Friday. I saw that she was delighted, and she dressed my hair perfectly. After shav-
ing, I offered her my first salutation of the day, and she
accepted it with good grace, though she refused me her
beautiful lips. It was the first time I kissed her cheeks.
Such was the footing on which we lived together. We
loved each other, and we were virtuous; but she must

have suffered less than I did because of the coquetry which is only too natural to the fair sex and often stronger than love.

Monsieur de Chavigny arrived at eleven o'clock. I had not invited the Jesuits to dinner before consulting him, and I had sent my carriage for them; while waiting we went for a stroll. He asked my housekeeper to join us as soon as she had seen to all her domestic duties. He was one of those men whom France, when she was a monarchy, kept to send, at the proper time and as circumstances demanded, to win over the powers she wished to have embrace her interests. Such was Monsieur de l'Hospital,[12] who was able to gain the heart of Elisabeth Petrovna,[13] such the[14] Duke of Nivernais,[15] who did as he pleased with the Court of St. James's[16] in 1762, such were a number of others whom I knew. Walking in my garden, the Marquis de Chavigny found in my housekeeper all the qualities necessary to make a young man happy; and she enchanted him completely at table, where she overwhelmed the two Jesuits with sallies informed by a humor which was never unkind. After spending the whole day with the greatest enjoyment, he went back to Soleure, asking me to dine with him as soon as he sent me word that Monsieur de Chauvelin had arrived.

That agreeable man, whose acquaintance I had made at the Duke of Choiseul's in Versailles,[17] arrived two days later. He at once recognized me and introduced his charming wife,[18] who did not know me. Since chance put me at the table beside Madame . . . , I was in such high spirits that I said most amusing things. Monsieur de Chauvelin said that he knew some very pleasant stories about me.

"But," replied Monsieur de Chavigny, "you do not know the Zurich story"; and he told it to him.

Monsieur de Chauvelin said to Madame . . . that, to have the honor of serving her, he would have turned

coachman, but Monsieur . . . replied that I was far
more squeamish, for the lady who had made such an impression on me was staying as my guest in a house I had
rented in the country.

"We will pay you a visit," Monsieur de Chauvelin
said to me.

"Yes," Monsieur de Chavigny answered, "we will all
go together."

And he instantly asks me to lend him my beautiful
reception room to give a ball in no later than the following Sunday.

It was thus that the old courtier kept me from undertaking to give the ball myself. It was a piece of bragga-
docio which would have done me harm. I should have in-
fringed on the right, which was the Ambassador's alone,
to entertain these illustrious foreigners during the five
or six days they were planning to spend in Soleure; and,
besides being a blunder, it would have let me in for a
great deal of expense.

In connection with the plays which were acted at
Monsieur Voltaire's, the conversation turned to *L'Écossaise,* and my table companion was praised, and blushed,
and became as beautiful as a star. The Ambassador invited us all to his ball the next day. I returned home
madly in love with the charming woman whom Heaven
had destined from birth to cause me the greatest grief
I have ever suffered in my life. I leave my reader to
judge.

My helpmate had gone to bed when I returned, and
I was glad of it, for Madame . . .'s eyes had not left me
a grain of reason. She found me sad the next morning,
and she rallied me on it with wit tempered by kindness.
While we are breakfasting Madame F.'s chambermaid
suddenly appears and hands me a note. I tell her I will
send an answer. I unseal it and I find:

"The Ambassador has sent me an invitation to his

ball. I have replied that I did not feel well, but that if I felt better by evening I would go. I think that since I am in your house, I should go with you or not at all. So if you do not wish to do me the favor of escorting me, I beg you to do me that of saying I am ill. Excuse me if I have thought I might break our agreement in this one instance, for it is a case of at least making a show of good manners in public.''

Furious, I take a pen and write:

"You have seized, Madame, on a good subterfuge. It will be announced that you are ill, for I beg to forgo the honor of escorting you, on the principle of enjoying complete freedom.''

My housekeeper laughed at the note the lady had written me and declared that she had deserved my reply. I sealed it and sent it to her. I spent a very pleasant night at the ball, for I talked a great deal with the object of my passion. She laughed at my answer to Madame F.'s note, but she disapproved of it— "for," she said, "the poison of anger will circulate through her veins, and God knows what ravages it will make when it bursts out.''

I spent the next two days at home, and very early on Sunday the Ambassador's servants came to bring everything needed for the ball and the supper, and to make all the arrangements for the orchestra and for lighting the whole house. The major-domo came to make his bow to me while I was at table. I had him sit down, and I thanked him for the fine present he had made me by giving me such a pleasant housekeeper. He was a handsome man, no longer young, honest, witty, and with his trade at his fingertips.

"Which of you two," he asked us, "is the worse fooled?''

"Neither of us," said the widow Dubois, "for we are equally satisfied with each other.''

The first to arrive, about nightfall, was Madame . . . , with her husband. She spoke very politely to my help-mate, without showing the least surprise when I said she was my housekeeper. She said it was my bounden duty to take her to see Madame F., and I had to obey. She received us with every appearance of good will, and she went out for a stroll with us, escorted by Monsieur . . . . After a turn around the garden Madame . . . told me to take her to her nurse.

"But who is your nurse?"

"The caretaker's wife," Monsieur . . . answered; "we will wait for you in Madame's apartment."

"Tell me something," she said on the way. "Your housekeeper certainly sleeps with you."

"No, I swear it. I can love no one but you."

"If that is the case you ought not to keep her, for no one can believe it."

"I do not care, so long as it is not you who believes me to be in love with her."

"I will believe nothing but what you tell me. She is very pretty."

We call on the caretaker's wife, who, addressing her as "daughter," gives her countless caresses; then she goes off to make us a lemonade. Left alone with her, I could do no more than give her fiery kisses, which rivaled hers. She had on only a very light petticoat under a taffeta dress. God, what charms! I am sure that her excellent nurse would not have come back so soon if she could have guessed how much we needed her to delay. But not a bit of it. Never were two glasses so quickly filled with lemonade!

"It was all made, was it?"

"No, Monseigneur; but I am quick."

The innocence of the question and the answer made my beautiful angel burst out laughing. On the way back to Madame F.'s she said that since time was always against us we must wait to seize it until her husband de-

cided to spend three or four days with me. I had already
invited him, and he had promised to come.

Madame F. set preserves before us and praised them,
especially a quince marmalade which she begged us to
taste. We excused ourselves, and Madame . . . trod on
my foot. She told me afterward that she was suspected
of having poisoned her husband.

The ball was magnificent, as was the supper at two
tables, each laid for thirty, in addition to the buffet at
which more than a hundred people ate. I danced only
one minuet with Madame de Chauvelin, having spent
almost the whole night talking with her husband, who
was highly intelligent. I presented him with my translation of his short poem on the Seven Deadly Sins,[19] which
greatly pleased him. When I promised to visit him in
Turin he asked me if I would bring my housekeeper with
me, and, on my answering no, he said I was making a
mistake. Everyone thought her charming. She was urged
to dance, but in vain; she told me afterward that if she
had accepted, all the women would have hated her. She
danced very well.

Monsieur de Chauvelin left on Tuesday, and at the
end of the week I received a letter from Madame d'Urfé
telling me she had spent two days at Versailles pursuing
the matter in which I was interested. She sent me a
copy of the pardon signed by the King in favor of
Monsieur . . .'s cousin. She said that the minister had
already sent it to his regiment, thus restoring the culprit
to the rank he had held before the duel.

Scarcely have I received her letter before I order my
horses harnessed to take me to Monsieur de Chavigny
with the news. My soul was flooded with joy, and I did
not hide it from the Ambassador, who congratulated me
in the most flattering terms, for through my intervention
Monsieur . . . had obtained, without spending a copper,
what he would have paid very dearly for if he had been
obliged to buy it. To make the thing appear even more

important, I asked the Ambassador to tell the news to Monsieur . . . himself. He instantly sent him a note asking him to come at once.

The Ambassador received him by handing him a copy of the pardon, at the same time saying that he was indebted for it entirely to me. The worthy man, beside himself with contentment, asked me how much he owed me.

"Nothing except your friendship; but if you wish to give me a token of it, come and spend a few days with me, for I am dying of boredom. The thing you asked me to do for you must have been very easy, for you see how quickly you have been satisfied."

"Very easy? I have been working for a year, moving heaven and earth, and not succeeding; and in two weeks you have accomplished everything. My life is at your disposal."

"Embrace me, and come to see me. I consider myself the happiest of mortals when I can oblige such men as you."

"I must be off now to tell my wife, who will jump for joy."

"Yes, go to her," said the Ambassador, "and come to dinner tomorrow with just the four of us."

The Marquis de Chavigny, an old courtier and a man of intelligence, made some reflections on the court of a monarch, where nothing was easy or difficult in itself, for the one was constantly becoming the other. He knew Madame d'Urfé from having courted her when the Regent loved her in secret. It was he who had nicknamed her Égérie[20] because she said she learned everything from a Genius who was with her every night she slept alone. He then talked to me of Monsieur . . . , who must have conceived the greatest friendship for me. He was persuaded that the sure way to reach a woman who had a jealous husband was to conquer the husband, because friendship by its very nature excluded jealousy.

The next day at the dinner for four, Madame . . . , in her husband's presence, showed me a friendliness equal to his, and they promised to come and spend three days with me during the following week.

I saw them arrive one afternoon without having sent me word. When I saw her chambermaid get out of the carriage too, my heart leaped for joy; however, its transports were moderated by two unpleasant announcements: the first, conveyed to me by Monsieur . . . , was that he must return to Soleure on the fourth day; the second, conveyed by Madame . . . , was that Madame F. must constantly be of the company. I at once took them to the apartment which I had chosen for them and which was the most suitable for my plans. It was on the ground floor on the opposite side of the house from mine. The bedroom had an alcove with two beds separated by a partition in which there was a communicating door. It was entered through two anterooms, the door to the first of which gave on the garden. I had the key for all these doors. The chambermaid was to sleep in the room above their bedroom.

Obedient to my goddess's decree, we called on Madame F., who received us very cordially, but who, on the excuse of leaving us free, declined to spend all of the three days in our company. However, she saw fit to yield when I told her that our agreement should be in force only when I was alone. My housekeeper supped in her room without my having had to tell her to do so, and the ladies did not ask about her. After supper I escorted Madame and Monsieur to their apartment, after which I could not avoid escorting Madame F. to hers; but I excused myself from being present at her evening toilet, despite her urging. When I wished her good night she said with a knowing look that after I had behaved so well I deserved to attain what I desired. I made no answer.

The next day toward nightfall I told Madame . . .

that, having all the keys, I could enter her room and her bed at any hour. She replied that she expected to have her husband with her, for he had treated her to the flatteries he always bestowed on her when he had that in mind; but that it could be the next night, for he had never yet wanted to amuse himself two days in succession.

Toward noon we saw Monsieur de Chavigny arrive. A fifth place was quickly laid; but he protested loudly when he learned that my housekeeper was to dine alone in her room. The ladies said he was right, and we all went to make her lay by her needlework. She was the soul of our dinner; she kept us wonderfully entertained with amusing stories about Lady Montagu. When no one was within earshot Madame . . . told me it was impossible that I did not love her. After saying that I would show her otherwise I asked her to confirm her permission for me to spend two hours in her arms.

"No, my dear, for he told me this morning that the moon changes today at noon."

"Then he has to have permission from the moon to discharge his duty to you?"

"Exactly. According to his astrology, it is the way to preserve his health and to have a boy by the will of Heaven, for if Heaven does not take a hand I see no likelihood of it."

I could only laugh and resign myself to waiting for the next day. When we were taking our stroll she said that the sacrifice to the moon had been made, and that to be perfectly safe and free from any fear she would persuade him to make an extra one, after which he would fall asleep. So, she added, I could come an hour after midnight.

Sure that my happiness was imminent, I surrender to the joy which such a certainty inspires in a lover who has long been in a state of desire. It was the only night in which I could hope, for Monsieur . . . had decided to sleep in Soleure the next day; I could not expect a second night which might have been more animated than the first.

After supper I escort the ladies to their apartments, then retire to my room and tell my helpmate to go to bed, since I have much writing to do.

Five minutes before one o'clock I leave my room, and, the night being dark, I grope my way around half the house. I go to open the door of the apartment in which my angel was; but I find it open, and it does not occur to me to ask why. I open the door of the second antechamber, and I feel a grip. The hand she puts over my mouth tells me I must not speak. We let ourselves fall on the wide couch, and I instantly attain the height of my desires. It was the summer solstice. Having but two hours before me, I did not lose a minute; I used them in giving reiterated proofs of the fire which was devouring me to the divine woman I was sure I held in my arms. I thought that her decision not to wait for me in her bed had been supremely farsighted, since the sound of our kisses might have waked her husband. Her furies, which seemed to exceed mine, raised my soul to heaven, and I felt certain that of all my conquests this was the first in which I could rightly take pride.

The clock tells me I must leave; I get up after giving her the sweetest of kisses, and I return to my room, where I surrender to sleep in perfect contentment. I wake at nine o'clock, and I see Monsieur . . . , who with the greatest satisfaction shows me a letter he had just received from his cousin, telling him his good news. He asks me to come and take chocolate in his room, since his wife is still at her toilet. I quickly put on a dressing gown, and, just as I am starting off with Monsieur . . . , in comes Madame F., who thanks me in a tone of great glee and tells me she is going back to her house in Soleure.

"Wait a quarter of an hour, we are to breakfast with Madame . . . ."

"No, I have just wished her good morning, and I am off. Good-by."

"Good-by, Madame."

No sooner has she left than Monsieur . . . asks me if she has gone mad. There was reason to think so, for, having been treated with perfect politeness, she ought at least to have waited until evening and left with Monsieur and Madame.

We went to take breakfast and indulge in commentaries on her sudden departure. Then we set out to stroll in the garden, where we found my housekeeper, whom Monsieur . . . approached. I thought Madame seemed a trifle depressed, so I ask her if she slept well.

"I did not go to sleep until four o'clock, after sitting up waiting for you in vain. What mishap kept you from coming?"

This question, which I could not possibly expect, freezes my blood. I look at her, I do not answer, I cannot shake off my surprise. It leaves me only when I am horror-struck, guessing that the woman I had held in my arms was F. I instantly withdraw behind the hedge to recover from an agitation which no one can rightly conceive. I felt that I was dying. To keep from falling I leaned my head against a tree. The first idea which came to me, but which I instantly dismissed, was that Madame . . . meant to disavow our meeting; any woman who gives herself to a man in a dark place has the right to deny it, and it may be impossible to convict her of lying; but I knew Madame . . . too well to suppose her capable of such perfidy, of a baseness inconceivable to any woman on earth except those veritable monsters who are the horror and shame of the human race. At the same moment I saw that if she had told me she had waited in vain merely to enjoy my surprise, she would have been lacking in delicacy, for in a matter of this sort the slightest doubt is already a degradation. So I saw the truth. F. had supplanted her. How had she managed it? How had she known? It was something to be reasoned out, and reasoning does not follow from an idea which oppresses the mind until the oppression has lost the greater part of its power. So I am left with the horrible certainty that I have spent two hours in the company of a monster from hell, and the thought which kills me is that I cannot deny having felt happy. That is what I cannot forgive myself, for the difference between the one woman and the other was immense and subject to the infallible tribunal of all my senses; however, sight and hearing could not enter in. But that is not enough for me to forgive myself. Touch alone should have sufficed me. I cursed Love, Nature, and my own cowardly weakness in consenting to receive into my house the monster who had dishonored my angel and made me despise myself. At that moment I sentenced myself to death, but fully determined, before I ceased to live, to tear to pieces with my own hands the Megaera[21] who had made me the most wretched of men.

While I am plunged in this Styx[22] Monsieur . . . appears, asking me if I feel ill, and is horrified to see my pallor; he says that his wife had been uneasy over it; I reply that I had left her because of a slight attack of dizziness, and that I already felt well again. We rejoin them. My helpmate gives me *eau des Carmes*[23] and says playfully that what had affected me so strongly was Madame F.'s departure.

When I was again with Madame . . . and at a distance from her husband, who was talking with the widow Dubois, I said that what had troubled me was that what she had said was certainly a joke.

"I was not joking, my dear; so tell me why you did not come last night."

At this answer I thought I should drop dead. I could not bring myself to tell her the reality, and I did not know what I should invent to justify myself for not having gone to her bed as we had agreed. Somber and speechless, I was in this state of irresolution when Dubois's little maid came to give her a letter which Madame F. had sent by express messenger. She opens it and gives me the enclosure, which was addressed to me. I put it in my pocket, saying that I will read it at my convenience, they do not urge me, they laugh. Monsieur . . . says it is love; I let him chatter on, I gain control of myself; dinner is announced, we go; I cannot eat, but it is laid to my indisposition. I could not wait to read the letter, but I had to find the time. After we get up from table I say that I feel better, and I take coffee.

Instead of getting up the usual game of piquet, Madame . . . says that it is cool in the covered walk and we should take advantage of it. I give her my arm, her husband gives his to the widow Dubois, and we go.

As soon as she was certain they could not hear what she had to tell me, she began as follows:

"I am sure you spent the night with that evil woman, and I may, though I don't know how, be compromised. Tell me all, my dear, this is my first intrigue; but if I am to learn from it I must know everything. I am sure that you loved me; alas, do not leave me now to believe that you have become my enemy!"

"Good heavens! I your enemy!"

"Then tell me the whole truth, and above all before you read the letter you have received. I implore you in Love's name to hide nothing from me."

"Here is the whole story in a few words. I enter your apartment at midnight, and in the second anteroom I feel a grip, a hand over my mouth tells me not to speak, I clasp you in my arms, and we fall on the couch together. Do you understand that I must be certain it is you, that I cannot possibly doubt it? So, never saying a word to you, and never hearing you speak to me, I spent the two most delicious hours I have spent in all my life; accursed two hours, the memory of which will make this world hell to me until my last breath. At a quarter past three o'clock I left you. You know all the rest."

"Who can have told the monster that you would come to my room at one o'clock?"

"I have no idea."

"Admit that, among the three of us, I am the most to be pitied and perhaps the only one who is unhappy."

"In God's name never believe that, for I am planning to go and stab her and then kill myself."

"And in the scandal which will follow, to leave me the most unfortunate of all women. Let us be calm. Give me the letter she wrote you. I will read it among the trees, you shall read it afterward. If they saw us reading it we should have to let them read it too."

I give it to her, and return to Monsieur . . . , whom my helpmate was convulsing with laughter. After our dialogue I felt a little more sane. The assurance with which she had insisted on my giving her the monster's letter had pleased me. I was curious about it, yet I felt loath to read it. It could only enrage me, and I feared the effects of a righteous anger.

Madame . . . rejoined us, and after we had separated again she handed me the letter, telling me to read it alone and in a calm frame of mind. She asked me to give her my word of honor that I would do nothing in the matter without first consulting her, sending her word of all my ideas through the caretaker's wife. She said we need not fear that F. would tell what had happened, since she would be the first to publish her own shame, and that our best course was to dissimulate. She made me still more curious to read the letter by saying that the harpy gave me a warning which I must not ignore.

What pierced my soul during my angel's very sensible discourse was her tears, which streamed from her eyes without any distortion of her beautiful face. She tried to moderate my all too visible distress by mingling smiles with her tears; but I saw only too well what was taking place in her noble and generous soul not to understand the pitiable state of her heart from her certainty that the vile F. knew beyond peradventure that there was an illicit understanding between us. It was this which made my despair unbounded.

She left at seven o'clock with her husband, whom I thanked in words so unfeigned that he could not doubt that they sprang from the purest friendship, and really I was not deceiving him. What natural sentiment can prevent a man who loves a woman from feeling the most sincere and affectionate friendship for her husband, if she has one? Many laws only serve to increase prejudices. I embraced him, and when I started to kiss Madame's hand he generously asked me to do her the same honor. I went to my room impatient to read the letter from the harpy who had made me the most wretched of men. Here it is, in a faithful copy, except for a few expressions which I have corrected:

"I left your house, Monsieur, sufficiently content, not because I had spent two hours with you, for you are not different from other men and in any case my whim was only something to amuse me, but because I have avenged myself for the public marks of contempt which you have shown me, for I have forgiven you the private ones. I have avenged myself on your scheming by unmasking your designs and the hypocrisy of your . . . , who in future can no longer look down on me with the show of superiority which she borrowed from her pretended virtue. I have avenged myself by making her wait up for you all last night, as she must have done, and by the comic dialogue between you this morning in which you

must have let her know that I had appropriated what
was intended for her, and by your no longer being able to
believe her a miracle of nature, for if you took me for
her I cannot be in any way different from her, and hence
you must be cured of the mad passion which possessed
you and made you adore her in preference to all other
women. If I have opened your eyes you are indebted to
me for a good deed; but I dispense you from any gratitude, and I even permit you to hate me, provided your
hatred leaves me in peace, for if in future I consider your
behavior insulting I am capable of coming out with the
whole story, having nothing to fear on my account, for
I am a widow, my own mistress, and in a position to
laugh at what anyone may say about me. I need no one.
Your . . . , on the other hand, is obliged to keep up a
front. But here is a warning I give you, to convince you
that I am kind.

"Know, Monsieur, that for ten years I have had a
slight indisposition which I have never been able to cure.
You did enough last night to contract it; I advise you
to take remedies at once. I warn you, so that you will be
careful not to transmit it to your beauty, who in her
ignorance might give it to her husband, and to others,
which would make her miserable, and I should be sorry,
for she has never harmed me or wronged me. Since I
thought it impossible that the two of you would not
cuckold the dear man, I came to stay in your house only
to convince myself by clear evidence that my conclusion
was not unfounded. I carried out my plan without needing anyone's help. After spending two whole nights in
vain on the couch which you well know, I resolved to
spend a third there too, and it crowned my enterprise
with success. No one in the house ever saw me, and my
chambermaid herself does not know the purpose of my
nocturnal wanderings. Hence it lies with you to bury the
episode in silence, and I advise you to do so.

"P.S.—If you need a doctor, impress discretion upon him, for it is known in Soleure that I suffer from this little ailment, and people might say you got it from me. That would be insulting."

The calculated insolence of this letter struck me as so out of all proportion that it almost made me laugh. I knew perfectly well that F. could only hate me, after the way in which I had treated her; but I should never have believed that she could carry her revenge to such lengths. She had given me her disease; I could not yet see the symptoms, but I had no doubt of it; the misery of having to cure it already possessed me. I had to give up my love affair, and even go away to be cured to avoid the gossip of malicious tongues. The prudent decision I reached in two hours of dark meditation was to say nothing, but with the firm determination to have my revenge the moment an opportunity arose.

Having eaten nothing at dinner, I really needed to sup well and get a sound sleep. I sat down at table with my helpmate, whom, in the sorrow of my soul, I never once looked in the face all through supper.

## CHAPTER VII

*The preceding chapter continued. I leave Soleure.*

---

BUT AS soon as the servants had gone and we were left sitting face to face, the young widow, who was beginning to love me because I made her happy, took it upon herself to make me talk.

"Your sadness," she said, "is not like you, and it frightens me. It might relieve you to confide your concerns to me. I ask it only because you interest me; I might be able to help you. Be sure of my discretion. To encourage you to speak freely and to have some confidence in me, I can tell you everything I now know about you without having made any inquiries or used any of the other means by which an indiscreet curiosity could pry into what it is not for me to know."

"Very well, my dear. Your frankness pleases me; I see that you are my friend, and I am grateful to you for it. So begin by telling me frankly all that you know about the things which are troubling me at this moment."

"Gladly. You and Madame . . . are lovers. Madame F., who was here, and whom you treated very badly, played some spiteful trick on you, which, I think, very nearly resulted in a misunderstanding between you and Madame . . . ; then she left your house with a rudeness which nothing can condone. This upsets you. You fear there will be further consequences; you are painfully aware that you must decide on a course; your heart and your mind are at odds, passion and sentiment war in you. I'm not sure. I am only guessing. What I am sure of is that yesterday you looked happy, and today I feel you are to be pitied, and I feel it because the friendship you have inspired in me could not be greater. I outdid myself today keeping Monsieur . . . amused, I tried my best to entertain him, so that he would leave you free to talk with his wife, who seems to me well worthy to possess your heart."

"All that you have said is true; your friendship is precious to me, and I value your intelligence. Madame F. is a monster who has made me wretched in order to avenge herself for my scorn; and I cannot take any revenge on her. Honor forbids me to tell you more; besides, neither you nor anyone else can possibly give me advice which could lift the burden of my grief from me. I may well die of it, my dear; but meanwhile I beg you to remain my friend and always to talk to me with the same sincerity. I will always listen to you attentively. This is the way in which you can be useful to me, and I shall be grateful to you for it."

I spent a cruel night, which has always been a most unusual thing for a man of my temperament. Righteous anger alone, mother of the desire for revenge, has always sufficed to keep me awake, and sometimes, too, the announcement of a great happiness which I did not expect. Intense satisfaction deprives me of the comfort of sleep, and of appetite as well. Otherwise, even in the greatest anguish of mind, I have always eaten well and slept still better; in consequence, I have always extricated myself from situations to which, but for that, I should have succumbed. I rang for Leduc very early; the little girl came to tell me Leduc was ill and that Madame Dubois would bring me my chocolate.

She came, and she said I looked like a corpse and that I had done well to forgo my baths. No sooner had I drunk my chocolate than I vomited it up, for the first time in my life. It was my helpmate who had made it for me; otherwise I should have believed that F. had poisoned me. A minute later I vomited all that I had eaten for supper and, with great effort, a bitter, green, viscous phlegm which convinced me that the poison I had vomited had been administered by black rage, which, when it is strong enough, kills the man who denies it the revenge it demands. It was demanding F.'s life, and, but for the chocolate which drove it out, it would have killed me. Exhausted by my efforts, I saw my helpmate crying.

"Why are you crying?"

"I don't know what you may think."

"Be easy, my dear. I think that my condition is gaining me the continuance of your friendship. Leave me, for now I hope to sleep."

And in fact I woke restored to life. I was happy to find that I had slept for seven hours. I ring, my helpmate comes in and tells me that the surgeon from the next village wants to speak with me. She had come in very sad; suddenly I see her become cheerful, I ask her the reason, and she says that she sees me brought back to life. I tell her we will dine after I have heard what the surgeon has to say. He comes in and, after looking all around the room, whispers in my ear that my valet has the pox. I burst out laughing, for I expected something terrible.

"My dear friend, take care of him and spare no expense; I will recompense you generously; but next time don't put such a long face on your confidences. How old are you?"

"Eighty in a few days."

"God preserve you!"

As I feared that I was in the same condition, I felt sorry for my poor Spaniard, who, after all, was having the accursed plague for the first time, whereas I was at something like my twentieth.[1] It is true that I was fourteen years older than he.

My helpmate, coming back to dress me, asks me to tell her what the old fellow had said to make me laugh so hard.

"Gladly; but first tell me if you know the meaning of the word 'pox.'"

"I do. One of Lady Montagu's couriers died of it."

"Excellent; but pretend you don't know. Leduc has it."

"Poor fellow! And is that what made you laugh?"

"It was because the surgeon made such a mystery of it."

After combing my hair she said that she, too, had a great confidence to make to me, after which I must either forgive her or dismiss her on the spot.

"More trouble! What the devil have you done? Out with it!"

"I robbed you."

"What! When? How? Can you give it back? I didn't think you were a thief. I never forgive thieves, or liars either."

"How hasty you are! Yet I am sure you will forgive me, for I robbed you only half an hour ago, and I will restore it to you this minute."

"If it was only half an hour ago, you deserve a plenary indulgence, my dear; now give me back what you have no right to keep."

"Here it is."

"F.'s letter? Have you read it?"

"Of course. That was my theft."

"Then you have stolen my secret, and the theft is of the gravest because you can't restore what you took. O my dear Dubois, you have committed a great crime."

"I know it. Such a theft cannot be made good; but I can assure you that what I took shall remain in me as if I had utterly forgotten it. You must forgive me, quickly, quickly."

"Quickly, quickly! You are a strange creature. Quickly, quickly, then, I forgive you, and I embrace you; but in future refrain not only from reading but even from touching my papers. I have secrets[2] which I am not free to divulge. So forget the horrors you have read."

"Listen, please. Permit me not to forget them, and you may be the gainer. Let us discuss this terrible business. It made my hair stand on end. The monster has dealt your soul a mortal blow and your body another, and the foul creature has got Madame . . .'s honor in her keeping. This, my dear master, I think her greatest crime; for, despite the affront, your love will survive, and the disease the harridan has given you will go away; but Madame . . .'s honor, if the foul creature does what she threatens to do, is lost forever. So do not order me to forget, but on the contrary let us discuss the situation and try to find a remedy. Believe me, I am worthy of your trust and I am sure that before long I shall win all your esteem."

I thought I was dreaming when I heard a young woman of her station in life talk to me more sensibly than Minerva did to Telemachus.[3] It took no more than what she had just said to gain her not only the esteem for which she hoped but my respect as well.

"Yes, my dear friend," I said, "let us consider how

to deliver Madame . . . from the danger which threatens
her, and I am grateful to you for believing that it is not
impossible. Let us think of it and talk of it day and
night. Continue to love her, and forgive her for her first
misstep, guard her honor, and pity my state; be my true
friend, cease to use the odious title of 'master,' and replace it by that of 'friend'; I shall be that to you so
long as I live, I swear it. Your wise words have won my
heart; come to my arms."

"No, no, there's no need for that; we are young and
we could only too easily be led into offending. To be
happy I want only your friendship, but I do not want it
for nothing. I want to deserve it by convincing proofs
which I shall give you of mine. I will go and order dinner
served, and I hope you will feel perfectly well after
it."

So much discretion astonished me. It might be assumed; for after all to counterfeit it the widow Dubois
had only to know its principles; but that was not what
troubled me. I foresaw that I should fall in love with her
and risk becoming the dupe of her morality, which her
self-esteem would never let her abandon even if she fell
in love with me in the full sense of the word. So I decided
to leave my budding love unfed. Leaving it forever in
infancy could not but make it die of boredom. Boredom
kills the young. At least such was my hope. I forgot that
it is impossible to feel nothing but friendship for a
woman whom one thinks pretty, whom one sees constantly, and whom one suspects of being in love. Friendship at its apogee becomes love, and, relieving itself by
the same sweet mechanism which love needs to make itself happy, it rejoices to have become stronger after the
fond act. This is what befell the fond Anacreon[4] with
Smerdis, Cleobulus, and Bathyllus.[5] A Platonist[6] who
maintains that one can be merely the friend of a pleasing
young woman with whom one lives is a visionary. My

housekeeper was too attractive and too intelligent; it was impossible that I should not fall in love with her.

We did not begin to talk until we had eaten a good dinner, for there is nothing more imprudent and dangerous than talking in the presence of servants, who are always malicious or ignorant, who misunderstand, who add and subtract, and who think they are privileged to reveal their masters' secrets without being taken to task for it because they know them without having been entrusted with them.

My helpmate began by asking me if I was sufficiently convinced of Leduc's loyalty.

"He is, my dear, a rascal at times, a great libertine, brave, even daring, quick-witted and ignorant, a brazen liar whom no one but myself can shake. With all his faults the scoundrel has one great good quality—whatever orders I give him he carries out blindly, braving any danger to which his obedience may expose him; he defies not only the cudgel but even the gallows if he sees it only in the distance. When I am traveling and it becomes necessary to know if I can risk fording a river in my carriage, he undresses without a word from me and sounds the bottom swimming."

"That will do. He is all you need. I announce to you, my dear friend—for so you will have me call you—that Madame . . . has nothing more to fear. Do as I tell you, and if Madame F. will not behave herself she will be the only one to be dishonored. But without Leduc we can do nothing. However, we must first learn the whole story of his pox, for there are several things which could thwart my plan. So go at once and find out from him yourself, and above all learn if he has told the servants about his misfortune. After you have learned everything, order him to keep the strictest silence concerning your interest in his illness."

Not racking my brains to guess her plan, I immediately

go up to Leduc's quarters. I find him alone and in bed, I sit quietly down beside him and promise to get him cured provided he will tell me, without deviating from truth in anything, every least circumstance of the disease he had caught. He said that on the day he had gone to Soleure to fetch my letters he had dismounted halfway along the road to drink a glass of milk at a dairy where he had found an accommodating peasant girl who in only a quarter of an hour had bestowed on him what he instantly showed me. What was keeping him in bed was a great swelling of one testicle.

"Have you confessed this to anyone?"

"To no one, for I should be laughed at. Only the surgeon knows of my illness; but he doesn't know whom I caught it from. He told me he would rid me of the swelling at once, and that I can wait on you at table tomorrow."

"Very good. Continue to say nothing."

As soon as I repeated all this to my Minerva, she asked me these questions:

"Tell me if Madame F. can really swear that she spent those two hours on the couch with you."

"No, for she neither saw me nor heard me speak."

"Good. Then answer her infamous letter at once, saying that she has ✠ed because you never left your room, and that you are going to make all necessary inquiries in your household to learn who the poor wretch is whom she infected without knowing him. Write, and send her the letter this instant; and in an hour and a half you shall send her a second letter, which I will now write and you shall copy."

"My charming friend, I see your ingenious plan; but I gave Madame . . . my word of honor that I would take no steps in the matter without telling her beforehand."

"Then there's nothing for it but to break your word of honor. It is love which keeps you from going as far as I do; but everything hinges on speed and on the time between the first letter and the second. Do it, my dear friend, and you shall know the rest when you read the letter I am going to write. Write the first one now.''

What made me act was nothing short of an enchantment, which I cherished. Here is a copy of the letter I wrote in the firm persuasion that my helpmate's plan was unparalleled:

''The shamelessness of your letter is as surprising as the three nights you spent convincing yourself that your vile suspicion had a foundation. Know, monster from hell, that I did not leave my room, so you spent the two hours with God alone knows whom; but I may find out, and I will inform you. Give thanks to Heaven that I did not unseal your infamous letter until Monsieur and Madame . . . had gone. I received it in their presence, but scorning the hand which had written it I put it in my pocket, and neither of them asked about it. If they had read it I would certainly have pursued you and killed you with my own hands, woman unworthy of life. I am perfectly well, but I have no intention of convincing you of it to prove that it was not I who enjoyed your carcass.''

After showing it to the widow Dubois, who approved of it, I sent it to the wretch who had made me wretched. An hour and a half later I sent her this one, which I simply copied without adding a word to it:

''A quarter of an hour after I wrote to you the surgeon came to tell me that my valet needed his services because of a discharge he had recently contracted and symptoms which showed that he had absorbed the venomous poison of the pox. I ordered him to take care of him; and later I went alone to see the patient, who, not without some reluctance, confessed to me that it was from you he had received the fine gift. He told me that, having seen you enter Madame . . .'s apartment alone and in the dark after he put me to bed, he became curious to

see what you were doing there, for if you had wished to
call on the lady herself, who at that hour must be in
bed, you would not have gone in by the door onto the
garden. After waiting an hour to see if you would come
out, he decided to go in too when he saw that you had
left the door ajar. He swore to me that he did not go in
with any idea of enjoying your charms, which I had no
difficulty in believing, but to see if it was not some other
man on whom that good fortune was being bestowed.
He assured me that he nearly shouted for help when you
seized him, putting one hand over his mouth, but that
he changed his mind when he found himself pulled down
on the couch and covered with kisses. He said that, feeling certain that you took him for someone else, he had
done his duty by you for two hours on end in a manner
which should have earned him a very different reward
from the one you gave him, whose dismal symptoms he
saw the next day. He left you, still without having
spoken, at the first ray of dawn, fearing he would be
recognized. Nothing could be easier than that you should
have taken him for me, and I congratulate you on having enjoyed in imagination a pleasure which, being what
you are, you would certainly never have obtained in
reality. I warn you that the poor fellow is determined
to pay you a visit, and that I cannot stop him; so be
gentle with him, for he might tell the story, and you
must realize the consequences of that. He will himself
acquaint you with his demands, and I advise you to grant
them.''

I sent it to her, and an hour later I received her answer
to the first letter, which, having contained only ten or
twelve lines, was not long. She said that my scheme was
ingenious, but that it would get me nothing, since she
was sure of the facts. She defied me to visit her within a
few days to convince her that the state of my health
was different from hers.

At supper my helpmate told me stories meant to cheer

*Gracious Service*

*Bathhouse on La Matte, Bern*

me up, but I was too gloomy to respond to them. We were now to take the third step which was to crown our work and drive the shameless F. to the wall; and since I had written the two letters in obedience to her instructions, I saw that I must obey her to the end. It was she who told me what orders I was to give Leduc when I summoned him to my room in the morning. She wanted to have the satisfaction of hiding in the alcove behind the curtains so that she could herself hear me tell him what to do.

So, having summoned him, I asked him if he was fit to ride to Soleure on an errand which was of the utmost importance to me.

"Yes, Monsieur; but the surgeon insists that I begin taking baths tomorrow."

"So you may. You will leave at once for Madame F.'s in Soleure, you will not have yourself announced as coming from me because she must not know that I have sent you to her. Say that you need to speak with her. If she will not receive you, wait in the street; but I think she will receive you, and even without witnesses. You will tell her that she has given you the pox without your asking her for it, and that you insist on her giving you the money you need to regain your health. You will tell her that she kept you at work for two hours in the dark without recognizing you, and that but for the nasty present she gave you, you would never have spoken; but that, finding yourself in the state which you will show her, she should not blame you for having come to her. If she resists, threaten to take her to court. That is all. You will come back without losing a minute to tell me what she answers you."

"But if she has me thrown out of the window, I shan't be back very soon."

"You need have no fear of that; I give you my word for it."

"It is a strange errand."

"You are the only person in the world who can carry it off."

"I am ready; but there are a few questions I need to ask. Has the lady really got the pox?"

"Yes."

"I'm sorry for her. But how am I to tell her she gave it to me when I've never talked with her?"

"Talking isn't the way it's given, you nincompoop. You spent two hours with her in the dark and without talking; she will learn that she gave it to you when she thought she was giving it to someone else."

"Now I begin to see it. But if we were in the dark, how can I know it was she I was with?"

"You saw her go in; but you can be sure she will not ask you any questions."

"I will be off at once. I'm more curious than you are to hear what she'll answer me. But here is something else I need to know. She may try to haggle over the money she is to give me for a cure; and in that case please tell me if I shall be content with a hundred écus."

"That's too much in Switzerland; fifty are enough."

"It's not much for two hours' work."

"I'll give you another fifty."

"That sounds more like it; I am off, and I think I understand everything. I won't say so, but I'll wager it's you to whom she gave the present, that you are ashamed of it and want to deny it."

"Possibly. Keep your mouth shut and go."

"Do you know, my friend, that he is a clown in a thousand?" said my helpmate, coming out of the alcove. "I almost burst out laughing when he told you he wouldn't be back soon if she had him thrown out of the window. I am sure he will do the thing marvelously well, and by the time he gets to Soleure she will already have sent off her answer to the second letter. I'm very curious to see it."

"You are the author of this farce, my dear; it is sublime, plotted in masterly fashion. One would not attribute it to a young woman with no experience in intrigues."

"Yet it is my first, and I hope it will succeed."

"If only she doesn't challenge me to show her that I am well."

"But you feel well so far, I think."

"Very well."

"It would be a good joke, if it weren't true that she must at least have the whites." [7]

"In that case I should have no fears for my health; but what would happen to Leduc? I cannot wait to see the end of the play, for the peace of my mind."

"You shall write it, and send it to Madame . . . ."

"There's no doubt of that. You understand I must say I am the author; but I will not cheat you out of the reward your work deserves."

"The reward I want is for you to have no more secrets from me."

"That's odd. How can you be so interested in my concerns? I cannot see you as naturally curious."

"That is an ugly fault. You will only make me curious when I see that you are sad. Your considerate behavior toward me is the reason I am fond of you."

"I am really touched, my dear. In future I promise I will confide to you anything that can keep you from being uneasy."

"Oh, how happy I shall be!"

An hour after Leduc left, a man arrived on foot and gave me a letter from F. and a package, saying that he was to wait for the answer. I told him to wait outside. My helpmate being present, I asked her to read the letter and myself went to the window. My heart was pounding. She called me when she had read it and said that all was well. Here is the letter:

"Whether all that you tell me is true or is an invention of your scheming mind—of which, unfortunately for you, all Europe is informed—I accept as true what I cannot deny has the appearance of truth. I am in despair that I have harmed an innocent person, and I willingly pay the penalty. I beg you to give him the twenty-five louis which I send you; but will you be generous enough to use all your authority as his master to bind him to the strictest silence? I hope so, for, knowing me as you do, you must fear my vengeance. Consider that if the story of this farce comes out I can easily put it in a light which will cause you distress and open the eyes of the honest man whom you are deceiving; for I will never let it drop. As it is my wish that we do not meet again, I have found an excuse to visit my relatives in Lucerne tomorrow. Write me if you receive this letter."

"I am sorry," I said to my helpmate, "that I made Leduc go, for she is a violent woman and something regrettable may happen."

"Nothing will happen. Send back her money at once. She will give it to him in person, and your revenge will be complete. She can have no more doubts. You will know all when he comes back in two or three hours. Everything has gone perfectly, and the honor of the charming and noble woman whom you love is completely safe. You have now only the unpleasant certainty that you bear the wretched creature's disease in your blood; but I think it is no great matter and can easily be cured, for persistent whites cannot be called the pox, and indeed it is not often, as I learned in London, that the whites are transmitted. We can also be very glad that she leaves tomorrow for Lucerne. Laugh, my dear friend, I beg you, for our play is still a comedy."

"Alas, it is a tragedy. I know the human heart; Madame . . . can no longer love me."

"It is true that some change—but this is not the time

to think of that. Quick, answer her in a few lines and send her back the twenty-five louis."

Here is my brief answer:

"Your base suspicion, your horrible plan for revenge, and the shameless letter you wrote me are the reasons for your present repentance. Our messengers crossed, and it is not my fault. I send back your twenty-five louis. I could not stop Leduc from going to see you; but you can easily appease him. I wish you a good journey, and I promise to avoid any chance of seeing you. Learn, wicked woman, that the world is not entirely peopled by monsters who set traps for the honor of those who hold honor dear. If at Lucerne you see the Papal Nuncio,[8] mention me to him and you will learn what opinion Europe holds of my mind. I can assure you that my valet has told no one the story of his present indisposition, and that he will continue not to tell it if you have received him well. Good-by, Madame."

After having the widow Dubois read my letter, of which she approved, I sent it off with the money.

"The play is not yet over; we still have three scenes: the Spaniard's return, the appearance of your painful symptoms, and Madame . . .'s astonishment when she learns the whole story."

But two hours pass, then three and four, then the whole day, and Leduc does not appear, and I am thrown into real anxiety, although the widow Dubois, never yielding an inch, kept saying he could only be so late because he had not found F. at home. There are characters incapable of foreseeing disaster. Such was I until the age of thirty when I was imprisoned under the Leads. Now that I am entering my dotage everything I foresee is black. I see it in a wedding to which I am invited, and at the coronation[9] of Leopold II, I said: *Nolo coronari* ("I do not want to be crowned"). Accursed old age, fit

to inhabit hell, where others have already placed it:
*tristisque senectus* ("wretched old age").[10]

At half past nine, by the light of the moon, my helpmate saw Leduc riding up at a walk. I had no candle,
she stationed herself in the alcove. He came in, saying
that he was dying of hunger.

"I waited for her," he said, "until half past six, and,
when she saw me at the foot of the stairs, she said she
had nothing to say to me. I replied that it was I who
had something to say to her, and she stopped to read a
letter which I saw was in your handwriting, and she put a
package in her pocket. I followed her into her room,
where, finding no one present, I told her she had given
me the pox and that I asked her to pay the doctor for
me. I was getting ready to show her proof, but, looking
away, she asked me if I had been waiting for her long;
and when I replied that I had been in her courtyard
from eleven o'clock, she went out, and, having learned
from the servant whom it seems she sent here the hour at
which he had got back, she returned and, closing the
door, gave me this package, saying that I would find
twenty-five louis in it to cure me if I was sick and adding
that if I loved my life I must refrain from talking to
anyone at all on the subject. I left, and here I am. Is
the package mine?"

"Yes. Go to bed."

My helpmate then came out in triumph, and we embraced. The next morning I saw the first symptom of my
wretched disease; but three or four days later I saw that
it amounted to very little. A week later, after taking
only *eau de nitre*,[11] I was entirely rid of it—quite unlike
Leduc, who was in a very bad state.

I spent the whole morning of the next day writing to
Madame . . . , telling her in great detail all that I had
done despite the promise I had made her. I sent her
copies of all the letters, and everything necessary to

prove to her that F. had left for Lucerne convinced that her revenge had been entirely imaginary. I ended my twelve-page letter by confessing that I had just found I was ill but assuring her that in two or three weeks I should be completely well. I gave my letter to the caretaker's wife with the greatest secrecy, and on the next day but one I received eight or ten lines from her telling me that I would see her during the week with her husband and Monsieur de Chavigny.

Alas for me! I had to renounce any idea of love; but the widow Dubois, my only companion, who, Leduc being ill, spent every hour of the day with me, was beginning to preoccupy me too greatly. The more I abstained from attempting anything, the more I fell in love with her, and it was in vain I told myself that by dint of seeing her constantly and letting nothing come of it I should at last become indifferent to her. I had presented her with a ring, saying that I would give her a hundred louis for it if she ever wanted to sell it, and she assured me that she would not dream of selling it until she was in need after I had dismissed her. The idea of dismissing her seemed nonsense. She was unspoiled, sincere, amusing, with a natural intelligence which enabled her to reason in the soundest manner. She had never loved, and she had married an old man only to please Lady Montagu.

She wrote to no one but her mother, and I read her letters to please her. Having asked her one day to show me the replies, I could not help laughing when she said she did not answer her because she had never learned to write.

"I thought she was dead," she said, "when I came back from England, and it made me very happy when I reached Lausanne and found her in perfect health."

"Who escorted you?"

"No one."

"It is unbelievable. Young, with the figure you have, well dressed, thrown in the company of so many different kinds of people, young men, libertines, for they are everywhere—how were you able to defend yourself?"

"Defend myself? I never needed to. The great secret is never to look at anyone, to pretend not to hear, not to answer, and to lodge alone in a room, or with the hostess when one happens on a decent inn."

She had not had an adventure in all her life, she had never strayed from her duty. She had never had the misfortune—so she put it—to fall in love. She kept me amused from morning to night without a sign of prudery, and we often addressed each other as *"tu."* She talked to me admiringly of Madame . . .'s charms, and she listened with the utmost interest when I recounted my vicissitudes in love, and when I came to certain descriptions and she saw that I was concealing some too piquant circumstances, she urged me to tell her everything plainly with a charm so potent that I had to satisfy her. When my overfaithful descriptions were too much for her, she burst out laughing, got up, and after putting her hand over my mouth to keep me from going on, she ran away to her room, where she locked herself in to prevent me, she said, from coming to ask her for what at those moments she was only too desirous of granting me; but she did not tell me all this till we were in Bern. Our great friendship had reached its most dangerous period just when F. tainted me.

After supper on the day preceding the one on which Monsieur de Chavigny unexpectedly came to dine at my house with Madame . . . and her husband,[12] my helpmate asked me if I had been in love in Holland. I thereupon told her what had happened to me with Esther; but when I came to my examining her *labia minora* to find the little mark which she alone knew, my charming housekeeper ran to me to stop my mouth, shaking with laughter and falling into my arms. At that I could not refrain from searching her so-and-so for some mark, and in her spasms of laughter she could offer me very little resistance. Not being able to proceed to the great con- clusion because of my health, I begged her to help me to a crisis which had become a necessity for me, at the same time doing her the same sweet service. It lasted scarcely a minute, and our curious eyes took their amorous but inactive share in it. After it was over she said, laughing but at the same time serious:

"My dear friend, we love each other, and if we are not careful we shall not long confine ourselves to mere trifling."

So saying, she rose, gave a sigh, and after wishing me good night went off to sleep with the little girl. It was the first time that we let our senses carry us away. I went to bed knowing that I was in love and foreseeing all that was bound to happen to me with this young woman, who had already gained a very strong hold on my heart.

We were pleasantly surprised the next morning to see Monsieur de Chavigny with Monsieur and Madame . . . . We strolled until dinnertime, then sat down at table with my dear Dubois, by whom I thought my two male guests were enchanted. Strolling after dinner, they never left her side; and for my part I had all the time I needed to repeat to Madame . . . the whole story I had written her, though I did not tell her it was Dubois who de- served the credit, for it would have mortified her to learn that her weakness was known to her.

Madame . . . told me that she had taken the greatest pleasure in reading the whole account simply because F. could no longer believe she had spent the two hours with me.

"But how," she asked, "were you able to spend two hours in that woman's company without knowing, even despite the dark, that it was not I? I am humiliated that the difference between her and me had no effect on you. She is shorter than I am, much thinner, and what amazes me is that her breath is foul. Yet you were deprived only of sight, and everything escaped you. It is unbelievable.''

''I was intoxicated with love, my dear; then, too, the eyes of my soul saw only you.''

''I understand the power of imagination, but imagination should have lost all its power in the absence of one thing which you knew beforehand you would find in me.''

''You are right; it is your beautiful bosom, and when I think today that all I had in my hands was two flabby bladders I want to kill myself.''

''You were aware of it, and it did not disgust you?''

''Sure that I was in your arms, how could I find anything in you disgusting? Even the roughness of the skin and the too commodious retiring room did not have the power to make me doubt or to lessen my ardor.''

''What are you saying! Loathsome woman! Foul, stinking sewer! I cannot get over it. Could you forgive all that in me?''

''Since I believed I was with you, everything could not but seem divine.''

''Not at all. Finding me such, you should have thrown me on the floor, even beaten me.''

''Ah, my love! How unjust you are now!''

''That may well be, my dear, I am so angry with the monster that I do not know what I am saying. But now that she has given herself to a servant, and after the mortifying visit she could not refuse, she must be dying of shame and anger. What amazes me is her believing him, for he is four inches shorter than you; and can she really believe that a valet could do the thing as you must have done it to her? I am sure that she is in love with him even now. Twenty-five louis! It's obvious. He would have been satisfied with ten. How lucky that the fellow was so conveniently ill! But did you have to tell him everything?''

''How can you think so! I let him suppose she had arranged to meet me in the anteroom and that I really spent two hours with her. Reasoning from what I ordered him to do, he saw that, in my disgust at knowing I was infected, and being in a position to deny the whole thing, I had hit on a plan which would punish her, avenge me, and keep her from ever boasting that she had possessed me.''

''It's a delightful comedy. The fellow's impudence is astonishing and his boldness even more so, for F. could have lied about being ill, and then you see what a risk he took.''

''It occurred to me, and it gave me some qualms, for I was perfectly well.''

''But now you are under treatment, and I am the cause of it. I am in despair.''

''My illness, my angel, is trifling. It is a discharge resembling the one called the whites. I drink nothing but *eau de nitre;* I shall be well in a week or ten days, and I hope—''

''Ah, my dear!''

''What?''

''Let us think of it no more, I implore you.''

''That is a revulsion which may be very natural when love is not strong. Alas for me!''

''No—I love you, and you would be unjust if you ceased to love me. Let us be fond friends and no longer think of giving each other proofs of it which might be fatal to us.''

''Accursed and infamous F.!''

''She has gone, and in two weeks we, too, will leave for Basel, where we shall remain until the end of November.''

''The die is cast, and I see that I must submit to your decision, or rather, to my destiny, for everything that has happened to me since I came to Switzerland has been disastrous. What consoles me is that I have been able to save your honor.''

''You have won my husband's esteem, we shall always be true friends.''

''If you must leave I see that I had better leave before you. That will make the horrible F. even more convinced that our friendship was not illicit.''

''You think like an angel, and convince me more and more that you love me. Where will you go?''

''To Italy, but first I shall stop in Bern and then in Geneva.''

''So you will not come to Basel, and I am glad, because people would talk. But, if you can, look happy during the few days you are to be here, for sadness does not become you.''

We rejoined the Ambassador and Monsieur . . . , whom the widow Dubois's talk had not left time to think of us. I reproached her for being so chary of her wit when she was with me, and Monsieur de Chavigny told us he thought we were in love; whereupon she took him up, and I continued to walk with Madame . . . .

''That woman,'' she said, ''is a masterpiece. Tell me the truth, and before you leave I will show you my gratitude in a way which will please you.''

''What do you wish to know?''

''You love her and she loves you.''

''I think so, but until now—''

''I do not want to know more, for if it is not yet done it will be done, and that comes to the same thing. If you had told me you did not love each other I should not have believed you, because it is impossible for a man of your age to live with such a woman and not love her. Extremely pretty, very intelligent, gay, with a ready tongue—she has everything to enchant, and I am sure you will find it hard to part from her. Lebel has done her a bad turn, for her reputation was excellent; but now she will not find employment with decent people."

"I shall take her to Bern with me."

"An excellent idea."

Just as they were leaving I said that I would come to Soleure to bid them good-by, since I had decided to leave for Bern in a few days. Reduced to giving up all thought of Madame . . . , I went to bed without supping, and my helpmate felt she should respect my grief.

Two or three days later I received a note from Madame . . . telling me to come to her house at ten the next day and ask to stay for dinner. I obeyed her exactly. Monsieur . . . said he would be delighted, but that he had to go to the country and could not be sure he would be back until one o'clock. He added that if I wished I could keep his wife company until he returned, and as she was at her embroidery frame with a girl I accepted on condition that she would not let me interrupt her work.

But toward noon the girl went away, and, left alone, we went to enjoy the fresh air on a terrace adjoining the house where there was an arbor from which, sitting at the back of it, we could see all the carriages that entered the street.

"Why," I instantly said, "did you not procure me this happiness when I was in perfect health?"

"Because then my husband believed you had only played the waiter for my sake and that I must dislike you; but your behavior has made him perfectly easy, to say nothing of your housekeeper, with whom he believes you are in love and whom he loves so much himself that I think he would gladly change places with you for a few days at least. Would you consent to the exchange?"

Having only an hour before me, and it no doubt the last in which I could convince her of the constancy of my love, I threw myself at her feet, and she put no obstacles in the way of my desires, which to my great regret had to be held in check, never going beyond the limits prescribed by the consideration I owed her blooming health. In what she allowed me to do, her greatest pleasure must certainly have consisted in convincing me how wrong I had been to be happy with F.

We ran to the other end of the arbor and into the open when we saw Monsieur . . .'s carriage enter the street. It was there that the worthy man found us, excusing himself for having been gone so long.

At table he talked to me almost constantly about the widow Dubois, and he did not seem satisfied until I told him I intended to take her to her mother's arms in Lausanne. I bade them farewell at five o'clock in order to call on Monsieur de Chavigny, to whom I told the whole story of my cruel adventure. I should have thought it a crime not to tell the lovable old man the whole of the charming comedy which he had done so much to set in motion.

Admiring the widow Dubois's quick intelligence—for I concealed nothing from him—he assured me that, old as he was, he would consider himself happy if he could have such a woman with him. He was very much pleased when I confided to him that I was in love with her. He said that without going from house to house I could take my leave of all the good society in Soleure by attending his evening assembly, not even staying for supper if I did not want to get home too late; and that is what I did. I saw my beauty, expecting that in all probability it would be for the last time; but I was mistaken. I saw her ten years later; and in the proper place my reader shall learn where, how, and on what occasion. I accompanied the Ambassador to his room, thanking him as he deserved and asking him for a letter to Bern, where I planned to spend some two weeks, and at the same time I asked him to send me his major-domo so that I could settle our accounts. He promised to have him bring me a letter for Monsieur de Muralt,[13] Avoyer of Thun.

Back at my lodging and sad at my imminent departure from a city where I had enjoyed only trifling gains in comparison with the real losses I had suffered there, I quietly thanked my helpmate for her kindness in waiting up for me, and I bade her good night, informing her that we would leave for Bern in three days and asking her to pack my trunks.

"Then you are taking me with you?" she said.

"Yes—that is, if you are interested enough in me to be glad you are coming."

"I am very glad; and the more so because I see that you are sad and in a way ill, whereas you were healthy and very gay when I entered your service. If I had to leave you I think the only thing that would make up to me for it would be to see you happy."

Just then the old surgeon came to tell me that Leduc was so ill that he could not get out of bed.

"I will have him treated at Bern. Tell him we shall leave day after tomorrow in time to dine there."

"Though it is only seven leagues he cannot make the journey, for he has lost the use of all his limbs."

I go to see him, and, as the surgeon had said, I find him unable to move. He had the use of nothing but his lips to speak and his eyes to see.

"Otherwise I feel perfectly well," he said.

"I believe you; but I want to dine at Bern tomorrow, and you cannot move."

"Have me carried, and find someone to cure me there."

"Very well; I will have you carried in a litter on two poles."

I ordered a manservant to look after him and to arrange everything necessary to get him to Bern at the "Falcon" inn,[14] hiring the two horses needed to carry the litter.

At noon I saw Lebel, who gave me the letter to Monsieur de Muralt which the Ambassador had written for me. He presented his account already receipted, and I paid him with the greatest pleasure, having found him honest in everything. I had him dine with me and the widow Dubois, and I was glad I had done so, for he amused us greatly. She held his attention from the beginning to the end of dinner; he told me that it was only now that he could say he had become acquainted with her, for at Lausanne he had spoken with her only two or three times, and formally. Getting up from table, he asked me to allow him to write to her, and it was she who gave him no time to retract and held him to his promise.

Lebel was a pleasant man, not yet fifty, and with a thoroughly honest face. When he left he embraced her in the French fashion, without asking my permission, and she submitted with good grace.

She said after he left that since his acquaintance could only be useful to her she was delighted that they were to correspond.

We spent the next day getting everything ready for our short journey. I saw Leduc set off in the litter to spend the night four leagues from Soleure. The next day at four o'clock in the morning, after liberally tipping the caretaker's family, the cook, and the lackey I was leaving behind, I set off in my carriage with my dear helpmate, and at eleven o'clock I arrived in Bern, putting up at the "Falcon," where Leduc had arrived two hours before me. After coming to an agreement with the host—for I knew very well what sort of men Swiss inn-keepers were—I ordered the manservant I had kept, and who was from Bern, to take good care of Leduc and put him in the hands of the best-known doctor for the pox in the city. After dining with my helpmate in her room—for I had a room of my own—I delivered my letter to Monsieur de Muralt's porter, then went for a walk wherever chance should direct me.

## CHAPTER VIII

*Bern. La Matte. Madame de la Saône. Sara.*
*My departure. Arrival at Basel.*

ARRIVED AT a high point in the city from which
I saw the wide countryside and a small river,[1] I went
down at least a hundred steps and stopped upon seeing
thirty or forty cabins which could only be booths for
people wanting to take baths.[2] An honest-looking man
asked me if I wished to bathe, and I having answered
that I did he opened a cabin, and any quantity of bath
girls came running up to me. The man said that each of
them hoped for the honor of attending me in the bath,
and that I was free to choose the one I wanted. He said
that a petit écu would pay for the bath, the girl, and my
breakfast as well. Like the Grand Turk, I throw my
handkerchief to the one who most attracts me, and I go in.

She fastens the door inside, she changes my shoes for
slippers, and, frowning and never looking me in the
face, she puts a cotton cap on my front hair and my
pigtail, and she undresses me: when she sees I am in

the bath she undresses too and gets in, without asking my leave; and she begins rubbing me everywhere except on the place which, seeing that I kept my hand over it, she guessed I did not want her to touch. When I felt I had been rubbed enough I ask her for coffee. She gets out of the bath, rings, and opens the door. Then she gets back into the bath, as free in her movements as if she had been dressed.

A minute later an old woman brings us coffee, then leaves, and my bath girl gets out again to fasten the door, then returns to where she was.

I had already seen, though without letting my eyes linger on her, that the girl had all the beauties which an ardent lover imagines the object of his passion to possess. True enough, I felt that her hands were not soft, so contact might well prove her skin not to be so either, nor did I see on her face the look of distinction which we term nobility, or the smile with which good breeding prophesies sweetness, or the subtle glances which suggest things unspoken, or the pleasing expressions of reserve, respect, timidity, and modesty. Except for all that, my Swiss girl at the age of eighteen had everything to delight a man who was in good health and no enemy to nature; nevertheless she did not tempt me.

"What is this?" I said to myself. "The girl is beautiful, her eyes are large, her teeth white, the rose of her complexion bespeaks her good health, and she affects me not at all? I see her stark naked, and she does not arouse the slightest emotion in me? Why? It can only be because she has nothing of what coquetry borrows to inspire love. It follows that we love the false and the artificial, and the true no longer seduces us unless it is heralded by a vain show. If in our acquired habit of going clothed and not stark naked the face which one shows to everyone is what matters least, why should we make the face the most important thing of all? Why is it what makes

us fall in love? Why do we decide upon its sole testimony
if a woman is beautiful or not, and why are we even
able to forgive her if the parts she does not show us are
the very opposite of what her pretty face has led us
to assume? Would it not be more natural and reasonable,
would it not be better, to go always with the face covered
and the rest stark naked, and fall in love with an object in that way, asking nothing else to crown our flame
but a countenance corresponding to the charms which
would already have made us fall in love? It would certainly be better, for then we would fall in love only
with perfect beauty, and we could easily forgive it when,
the mask removed, we found an ugly face where we had
imagined a beautiful one. It would follow that only
ugly women could never resolve to uncover their faces,
and that the only ones who would consent would be
the beauties; but the ugly ones at least would not make us
sigh for fruition; they would grant us everything to
avoid being forced to unmask, and they would only bring
themselves to that when, by the enjoyment of their real
charms, they had convinced us that we could easily do
without the beauty of a face. Besides, it is obvious and
indisputable that inconstancy in love exists only because
of the diversity of faces. If faces were not seen, a man
would always remain the constant lover of the first
woman who had pleased him.''

Getting out of the bath, I handed her the towels, and
when I was sufficiently dried I sat down and she put on
my shirt, then, just as she was, dressed my hair. Meanwhile I put on my nether garments, and, after buckling
my shoes, she dressed in a minute, the air having already
dried her. As I left I gave her a petit écu and then six
francs for herself; but she returns them with a scornful
look and leaves. This gesture sent me back to my inn
mortified, for she was not a girl to be slighted, and she
thought I had slighted her.

After supper I could not refrain from telling my helpmate the whole story, to which she listened with great attention, adding her own commentary. She said she certainly was not pretty, for I could not have resisted the desires she would have inspired in me, and that she would very much like to see her. I offered to take her there, and she said she would enjoy it, but that she would have to dress as a man. So saying, she rises, and a quarter of an hour later I see her before me, wearing a well-fitting coat of Leduc's but without breeches, for she had not been able to put them on. I told her to take her choice among mine; and we put off the expedition until the next morning.

At six o'clock I saw her before me completely dressed and with a blue redingote which disguised her perfectly. I dressed quickly and, not bothering to eat breakfast, we went to La Matte. This is the name of the place. Animated by her pleasure in the outing, my good housekeeper was radiant. It was impossible that anyone should see her and not know that her clothing was not that of her sex, so she kept herself as closely wrapped in her redingote as she could.

We had scarcely got down the steps when the same man appears and asks us if we want a bath for four, and we enter the cabin. The girls appear, I show my helpmate the pretty one who had not seduced me, and she takes her; I take another, tall and well built and with a proud look, and we lock the door. I quickly let my girl put a cap over my hair, I undress and get into the bath, and my new attendant does likewise. My helpmate was taking her time; the newness of the thing astonished her, she seemed to regret having undertaken it, she laughed to see me there in the hands of the big Swiss girl, who was rubbing me all over, and she could not bring herself to take off her shift; but finally one shame prevailed over the other, and she got into the bath, as if only the force of circumstances had compelled her to show me all her beauties; but she had to let me wait on her, though without excusing the other girl from coming in and doing her duty.

The two girls, who had more than once taken part in similar diversions, prepared to entertain us with a spectacle which I knew very well but which was completely new to my helpmate. They began doing to each other the same thing they saw me doing with the widow Dubois. She watched them, in great astonishment at the fury with which the girl I had taken played the man's role to the other. I was somewhat surprised myself, despite the furies which M. M. and C. C. had displayed before my eyes six years earlier, and than which it was impossible to imagine anything finer. I should never have believed that anything could distract me when I was for the first time holding in my arms a woman I loved and who possessed to perfection everything which could engage my senses; but the strange combat in which the two young Maenads were embroiled occupied her too. She told me that the supposed girl I had taken was a boy despite her bosom, and that she had just seen it. T turn, and the girl herself, seeing my interest, displays a clitoris, but enormous and stiff. I tell my amazed helpmate what it is, she replies that it cannot possibly be that, I make her touch and examine it, and she has to give in. It looked like a thick, nailless finger, but it was flexible; the wench, who coveted my beautiful housekeeper, told her that it was stiff enough for her to put it into her if she would permit, but she refused, and it would not have amused me. We told her to continue her endeavors with her friend, and we laughed a great deal, for the congress of the two young girls, though comic, yet excited us to the height of voluptuousness. It was too much for my helpmate, she surrendered completely to nature, even anticipating me in all that I could desire. It was a celebration which continued for two hours and which sent us back to our inn thoroughly satisfied. I gave the girls, who had entertained us very well, two louis; but not with any intention of going back there. We had no need of that to go on exchanging proofs of our love. My helpmate became my mistress, and a perfect mistress she was, making me completely happy, even as I made her, during all the time I spent in Bern. Since I was already completely cured, no unfortunate consequences marred our mutual satisfaction. If pleasures are transitory, so too are pains, and when, in a season of enjoyment, we remember the pains which preceded it, we love them, *et haec aliquando meminisse juvabit* ("and one day it will be pleasant to remember even these things").[3]

At ten o'clock the Avoyer of Thun was announced. Dressed in black and in the French fashion, grave, gentle, mannerly, and well on in years, he pleased me. He was one of the wise heads in the government. He insisted on reading me the letter Monsieur de Chavigny had written him; I said that if it had been unsealed I would not have delivered it. He invited me to dinner the next day in mixed company and to a stag supper on the day after. I left with him, and we went to the library,[4] where I met Monsieur Felix,[5] an unfrocked monk, who was rather facile than erudite, and a promising young scholar named Schmid,[6] already well known in the republic of letters. A man learned in natural history[7] who had the names of ten thousand different shells by heart bored me because I knew nothing of his science. Among other things he told me that the Aar, the famous river of the canton, had gold in its sands; I said that all large rivers had it, and he seemed not to agree with me.

I dined at Monsieur de Muralt's with the four or five Bernese women who enjoyed the highest reputation, and I thought they deserved it, especially a Madame de Sacconay,[8] who was most agreeable and very well educated. I would have paid court to her if I had stayed longer in the capital of Switzerland—if Switzerland could have a capital.

The Bernese ladies dress well, though not elaborately, since luxury is forbidden by law; their manner is easy, and they speak excellent French.[9] They enjoy the greatest freedom, and they do not abuse it, despite the gallantry which is the life of social occasions, for decency is everywhere observed. I noticed that husbands are not jealous there, but they insist that their wives shall always be at home by nine o'clock for family supper. During the three weeks[10] I spent in the city a woman eighty-five years of age interested me by her knowledge of chemistry. She had been the intimate friend of the famous Boerhaave.[11] She showed me a sheet of gold which he had made in her presence and which before being transmuted was copper. She assured me that he possessed the stone,[12] but she said it had the power to prolong life only a few years beyond a century. According to her, Boerhaave had not known how to use it. He had died of a cancer between the heart and the lungs before reaching the perfect maturity which Hippocrates[13] sets at the age of seventy. The four millions which he left his daughter showed that he possessed the art of making gold. She said he had given her a manuscript which contained the whole process, but that she found it obscure.

"Publish it."

"God forfend!"

"Then burn it."

"I haven't the heart."

About six o'clock Monsieur de Muralt came to take me to see some military maneuvers which the citizens of Bern, all of whom are soldiers, were performing outside the city. I asked him the meaning of a bear[14] at the gate, and he said that in German Bern meant "bear," and so it was the symbol of the canton, which was sec-

ond [15] in rank though the largest if not the richest. It
was a peninsula formed by the Aar, whose source was
near that of the Rhine.[16] He talked to me about the power
of his canton, its lordships and bailiwicks, and he explained what an Avoyer was; then he launched into political institutions, describing the different systems of
government which made up the Helvetian body politic.

"I can well understand," I said, "that since the cantons number thirteen, each of them can have a different
government."

"There is even a canton," he said, "which has four." [17]

But what I greatly enjoyed was the supper with
fourteen or fifteen men, all of them senators. No high
spirits, no frivolous talk, no literature; but civil law,
the interests of the State, commerce, economy, speculation, love of country, and the duty to value liberty
above life. But toward the end of supper all these rigid
aristocrats began to expand, *sollicitam explicuere frontem*
("to smooth the care-wrinkled brow"),[18] an inevitable
effect of drink. They pitied me. They praised sobriety,
but they thought I carried mine too far. However, they
did not force me to drink, as the Russians and the
Swedes do, and often the Poles.

At midnight the gathering broke up. It was an unheard-of hour in Switzerland. They thanked me and
sincerely asked me to count on their friendship. One of
them who, before he had become tipsy, had condemned
the Republic of Venice for banishing the Grisons[19] became sufficiently enlightened by wine to ask me to excuse
him. He said that every government could not but understand its own interests better than all the foreigners who
criticized what it did.

Entering my room, I found my helpmate in my bed; I
was delighted. I gave her countless caresses which must
have convinced her of my affection and my gratitude.
Why should we restrain ourselves? We were bound to

consider ourselves husband and wife, and I could not foresee that the day would come on which we would part. When people love each other, that seems impossible.

I received a letter from Madame d'Urfé, asking me to offer my services to Madame de la Saône,[20] the wife of a Lieutenant-General of her acquaintance, who had left for Bern in the hope of curing a skin disease which disfigured her. The lady had already arrived with strong recommendations to all the leading families in the city. She gave a supper every day, having an excellent cook, and invited only men. She had announced that she would return no one's visits. I went at once to make my bow to her; but what a sad sight!

I see a woman dressed with the utmost elegance, who, when I appear, rises from the sofa on which she was voluptuously seated and, after dropping me a pretty curtsy, resumes her place, asking me to sit down beside her. She sees my surprise and confusion; but, pretending to notice nothing, she treats me to the usual amiabilities. This is how she looked:

She was very well dressed, and her hands and her arms, which she displayed to just above the elbow, could not be more beautiful. Under a transparent fichu one saw a white, youthful bosom down to its rosy buds. Her face was frightful; it aroused pity only after it had inspired horror. It was a blackish crust, as dreadful as it was disgusting—a hundred thousand pimples making up a mask which extended from the top of her neck to the top of her forehead and from ear to ear. Her nose was invisible. In short, all that one saw of her face was two fine eyes and a lipless mouth which she kept half open to show two incomparable rows of teeth and to talk in a delightful style seasoned with witticisms and jests in the best taste. She could not laugh, for the pain caused by the contraction of the muscles would have made her cry; but she seemed content to see her listeners laugh.

Despite her pitiful condition her mind was vivacious and well furnished, her bearing and her manners those of the Parisian nobility. She was thirty[21] years of age, and she had left three young and very pretty children behind in Paris. Her house was in the Rue Neuve des Petits-Champs,[22] and her husband was a very handsome man; he adored her and had never left her bed. All the soldiers in the world could not have had his courage; but he must certainly have refrained from kissing her, for the mere thought of it made one shudder. An overflow of milk had reduced her to this appalling condition after her first childbed [23] ten years earlier. The Paris Faculty[24] had labored in vain to rid her face of the monstrous infection, and she had come to Bern to put herself in the hands of a famous doctor who had undertaken to cure her and whom she was not to pay until he had kept his promise. This is the language of all empirical physicians, and it has no meaning except what the guilelessness of the patient gives it. Sometimes they cure him; but even if they do not, they manage to make him pay by the simple process of proving to him that if he was not cured it was his own fault.

But at the height of my conversation with her, in comes the doctor. She had begun taking his remedy. It was drops he compounded from a preparation of mercury. She told him that the itching which tormented her and which forced her to scratch seemed to have grown worse; he said that she would not be rid of it until the end of the cure, which would take three months.

"As long as I scratch," she replied, "I shall be in the same state, and the cure will be endless."

He beat about the bush. I left, and she invited me to supper every day. I went that evening, and I saw her eat everything with appetite and drink good wine. The doctor had forbidden her nothing. I foresaw—and I was right—that she would never be cured. She was in high spirits, and her talk kept the whole company amused. I understood very well that one could become accustomed to seeing her and not feel repelled. When I told my helpmate the whole story she said that despite her ugliness the lady might make men fall in love with her by her character, and I could only admit it.

Three or four days after this supper a handsome youth of eighteen or twenty, in a bookseller's shop to which I had gone to read the gazette, politely told me that Madame de la Saône was sorry not to have had the pleasure of seeing me again since I had supped with her.

"So you know the lady?

"Did you not see me at supper there?"

"Yes, now I recall you."

"I keep her supplied with books, for I am a bookseller, I sup there every evening, and what is more I breakfast alone with her every morning before she gets out of bed."

"I congratulate you. I would wager that you are in love with her."

"You mean that for a jest. The lady is more worthy of love than you suppose."

"I am not jesting. I agree with you: even so, I would wager you would not be brave enough to enjoy her final favors if she offered them to you."

"You would lose."

"Very well, let us wager; but how will you convince me?"

"Let us wager a louis; but be discreet. Come to supper there this evening. I will tell you something."

"You shall see me there, and the wager stands."

When I told my helpmate of my wager she became very curious to know what the upshot would be and how the young man would go about convincing me, and she begged me to tell her after he had done so. I promised her I would.

That evening Madame de la Saône reproached me most

politely, and I found her supper as pleasant as the one before. The young man was present; but since Madame never once addressed him no one paid any attention to him.

After supper he saw me to the "Falcon," and on the way he told me I had only to say the word and I could see him in amorous combat with the lady if I would go there at eight o'clock the next morning.

"Her chambermaid," he said, "will tell you that she is receiving no one; but she will not stop you from going into the anteroom when you say you will wait. The anteroom has a door, glazed to the top from half way up, through which one would see the lady in bed if a curtain over the glass on the inside did not prevent it. I will draw the curtain back, leaving a small space uncovered, so that you will see everything. When I have done my business I will leave; she will ring, and then you can have yourself announced. At noon, if you will allow me, I will come to the 'Falcon' with books for you, and if your conscience tells you that you have lost the wager, you shall pay me."

I said I would not fail to be there, and I ordered the books he was to bring me.

Curious to see a feat so extraordinary—though I did not consider it impossible—I go at the appointed hour, the lady is not receiving, but the chambermaid makes no objection to my waiting until she is up. I enter the anteroom, I see the small piece of uncurtained glass, I put my eye to it, and I see the indiscreet young man at the side of the bed, holding his conquest in his arms. A bonnet covered her head so that no part of her lamentable face could be seen.

As soon as the hero became aware that I was where I could see him he did not keep me waiting. He rose and exposed to my sight not only his beauty's treasures but his own. Short, but of gigantic proportions where the lady wanted it, he seemed to be displaying the fact to arouse my jealousy and humiliate me, and perhaps to conquer me too. As for his victim, he showed her to me in front view, back view, and every possible profile in five or six different postures, which he employed with her-culean vigor in the act of love, the disfigured woman responding with all her strength. I saw a body than which Phidias[25] could not have carved one more beautiful and a whiteness more perfect than that of the finest marble from Paros.[26] I was so excited by them that I fled. I went to the "Falcon," where, if my helpmate had not hastened to give me the palliative which I needed, I should instantly have had to go to La Matte for it. After I told her the whole story she became even more curious to make the acquaintance of its hero.

He came at noon, bringing the books I had ordered, for which I paid him, giving him an extra louis, which he took with a laugh and a look which said that I should be very glad to have paid the wager. He was right. After looking at him with great attention, my helpmate asked him if he knew her, and he said no.

"I saw you as a child," she said; "you are the son of Monsieur Mingard,[27] the minister of the Gospel. You must have been about ten years old when I saw you in Lausanne."

"It is possible, Madame."

"So you did not want to become a minister?"

"No, Madame. I felt too strongly drawn to love to choose that profession."

"You were right, for ministers must be discreet, and discretion is a hindrance."

At this thrust, which my housekeeper launched at him in pure high spirits, the poor fool blushed, but we did not let him lose heart. I asked him to dine with us, and though he never mentioned Madame de la Saône, he told us not only many of his own successes in love but also all the amorous adventures which gossip ascribed to the ladies of Bern or slander invented for them.

After he left, my helpmate, who had come to the same conclusion as myself, said that a young man of his character was worth seeing only once. I saw to it that he did not call on us again. I was later told that Madame de la Saône sent him to Paris and made him rich. I shall say no more of him or of the lady, to whose house I did not go again, except once to bid her good-by when I left Bern.

I lived happily with my dear mistress, who kept telling me that she was happy. No fear, no concern for the future troubled her fair soul; she was sure, as I was, that we would never part, and she constantly told me that she would forgive me all my infidelities provided I never failed to confess them to her frankly. She had the character I needed in a woman to live at peace and content; but I was not born to enjoy so great a happiness.

After two or three weeks of our stay in Bern my helpmate received a letter from Soleure. It was from Lebel. Having seen her read it carefully, I asked her what news it contained. At that she tells me to read it, and sits down in front of me to see into my soul.

The major-domo, wasting no words, asked her if she would become his wife. He said that he had put off proposing it to her until he had set his affairs in order and made sure that he could marry her even if the Ambassador should refuse his permission. He said that he had enough to live well on in B. without having to remain in service, but that he would not have needed to take these precautions since he had just talked with the Ambassador and had received his full consent. So he asked her to answer him at once, telling him, first, if she accepted him and, second, if she would prefer going to live with him in B., where she would be absolute mistress in her own house, or would rather remain in Soleure at the Ambassador's as his wife, which could only increase their capital. He ended by saying that whatever she brought him would be hers, and that he would guarantee the whole of it to her, up to a hundred thousand francs. That would be the amount of her dowry. He did not say a word about me.

"It is for you, my dear, to do whatever you wish; but I cannot imagine your leaving me and not making me the unhappiest of men."

"And I shall be the unhappiest of women the instant I am not with you, for, provided you love me, I do not care at all if you make me your wife."

"Very good. So what will you answer him?"

"You shall see my letter tomorrow. I will tell him politely but frankly that I am in love with you and happy, and, since that is the case, I cannot possibly accept the excellent match which Fortune offers me in him. I will even say that if I were wise I see I could not refuse his hand, but that, being madly in love, I can only obey the God of Love."

"I think your letter is excellently put, for to refuse such an offer you can have no other valid reason than the one you give him; besides, it would be absurd to try to make anyone believe we are not in love with each other, for it is only too obviously true. Nevertheless, my angel, his letter saddens me."

"But why, my dear friend?"

"Because I haven't a hundred thousand francs ready to give you this instant."

"Oh, my friend! I care nothing for that. You are certainly not a man to become poor; but even if you did, I feel that you would make me happy by sharing your poverty with me."

At this point we exchanged the usual tokens of love which happy lovers give each other in such situations, but in the effusion of our feeling a tinge of sorrow darkened our souls. Languishing love seems to double in strength, but this is not true. Love is a little wanton which wants to be fed on smiles and play; a different diet sends it into a consumption.

The next day she wrote to Lebel as she had instantly decided to do upon receiving the too serious news; and at the same time I thought it my part to write Monsieur de Chavigny a letter into which love, sentiment, and philosophy entered in equal measure. I asked him to give me his best advice on the matter, not hiding it from him that I was in love but that, being at the same time a man of honor, I found it as painful to resolve to tear out my own heart as to raise an obstacle to the widow Dubois's permanent happiness.

My letter pleased her greatly, for she would be glad to know what the Ambassador thought about the matter. Having received letters of introduction for Lausanne— from Madame d'Urfé to the Marquis Gentil de Langal- lerie,[28] and from the Baron de Bavois,[29] then colonel and proprietor of the Bala Regiment, to his uncle and aunt— I decided to spend two weeks there. My helpmate was delighted at the prospect. When one loves, one believes that the object of one's love is worthy of it, and that everyone must be jealous of the happiness he sees in an- other.

A Monsieur de M. F.,[30] a member of the Council of Two Hundred,[31] whom I had met at one of Madame de la Saône's suppers, had become my friend. He having come to see me, I had introduced my helpmate to him, he treated her as if she were my wife, he had introduced his own wife to her on the promenade, and he had come to supper with us, bringing her and their elder daughter, whose name was Sara,[32] who was thirteen years old, dark and decidedly pretty, and who, having a very keen mind, made us laugh with guileless remarks of whose effect she was perfectly conscious. In short, her great art lay en- tirely in making people believe she was ingenuous, and her father and mother really believed she was.

*Pretended Innocence*

*Holograph of a Letter from Bernard de Muralt
to Albrecht von Haller*

The girl had announced that she was in love with my helpmate; she lavished all sorts of caresses on her; she often came to us in the morning asking for breakfast, and when she found us in bed she called my helpmate her wife, and made her laugh by putting her hand under the covers, tickling her, and saying, with kisses, that she was her little husband and she wanted to give her a child. My helpmate laughed.

One morning, joining in the laughter, I said that she made me jealous, that I thought she was really a little man, and that I wanted to see if I was wrong. So saying, I lay hold of her; and the sly minx, protesting that I was wrong but offering very little resistance, left my hand perfectly free to convince me that she was a little girl. I then let her go, aware that she had trapped me, for such an investigation on my part was exactly what she wanted, and my helpmate told me so; but as I did not care one way or the other I did not believe her.

The next time, coming in just as I was getting up, and still pretending to be in love with my helpmate, she said that, since I had assured myself she was not a man, I could not object to her lying down in my place. My helpmate, who was in the mood for a laugh, tells her it is an excellent idea, and little Sara, jumping for joy, takes off her dress, unlaces her petticoat, and springs on top of her. At this point the spectacle began to interest me. I went and locked the door. My helpmate letting her do as she wished, the little jade, who was stark naked and who had uncovered all the other's beauties, took so many positions to accomplish her purpose that I began to feel a desire to show her how the thing was done. She looked on with rapt attention until the end, evincing great surprise.

"Do it to her again," she said.

"I can't," I replied, "for, as you see, I am dead."

Pretending innocence, she undertakes to bring me back to life, and she succeeds; whereupon my helpmate told her that since the credit for having revived me was hers, it was for her to do what would make me die again. She said she was very willing, but that she didn't have room enough to lodge me, and, so saying, she took a position which showed me she was speaking the truth and that it would not be her fault if I could not do it to her.

Assuming in my turn the innocent and serious air of a man who is willing to grant a favor, I contented the minx, who showed no sign from which we could swear she had not done the thing before. No exhibition of pain, no blood to indicate a rupture; but I had sufficient reason to assure my helpmate that Sara had never known another man.

Her expressions of gratitude made us laugh, together with her adjurations to say nothing to Mamma or Papa, for they would scold her just as they had scolded her the year before when she had got her ears pierced without their permission.

Sara knew that we were not taken in by her feigned naïveté, but she pretended not to know it in order to gain her ends. Then who had taught her the art? No one. Natural intelligence, less rare in childhood than in youth, but always rare. Her mother said that her naïveté was the dawning of intelligence, but her father took it for stupidity. If she had been stupid, our laughter would have disconcerted her and she would not have gone on. I never saw her so happy as when her father deplored her stupidity; she pretended to be astonished, and, to repair one deliberate blunder, she came out with a worse one. She plied us in turn with questions to which, since we could not answer them, we were reduced to replying only with laughter, for they always arose from the most logical reasoning. Sara could have pursued the argument and proved to us that the stupidity was on our side, but that would have betrayed her duplicity.

Lebel did not answer the widow Dubois, but the Ambassador wrote me a four-page letter in which, like the wise man he was, he showed me that if I were as old

as he, and also in a position to make my housekeeper
happy after my death, I should never let her go, especially since she was of the same mind as I, but that being
young, and not intending to marry her, I should not only
consent to a marriage which would undoubtedly make
her happy but do my best to persuade her to enter into
it, and the more so because, with the experience I had,
I must foresee that I would one day repent of having let
the present opportunity escape, for, in his view, it was
impossible that, with the lapse of time, my love would
not become pure friendship; in which case he left me to
see for myself that, when I should need new loves, the
widow Dubois, as merely my friend, could not but restrict
my freedom and hence condemn me to repentance, which
always makes a man unhappy. As if for form's sake he
said that when Lebel had told him of his plan, far from
withholding his consent he had encouraged him, for my
housekeeper, in the four or five times he had seen her, had
completely gained his good will, hence he would be very
glad to see her so well situated in his house, where, without in the least offending against propriety, he could enjoy the charms of her intelligence without having any designs on those others of which, at his age, he could not
think. He ended his eloquent letter by saying that Lebel
had not fallen in love with Madame Dubois like a young
man but after due reflection and that hence he would not
hurry her. She would learn this from the answer he was
now writing her. A marriage should never be entered into
except composedly.

My helpmate, after reading his letter attentively,
handed it back to me with an air of indifference.

"So what do you think now, my dear?"

"That I should do as the Ambassador says. If he considers that we need be in no hurry, that is all we want. So
let us think no more of it and love each other. His letter
is wisdom itself; yet I must tell you I cannot imagine our

becoming indifferent to each other, though I know it can happen.''

''Not indifferent, you are wrong there.''

''I mean good friends.''

''But friendship, my dear, is never indifferent. All that is true is that love may cease to play any part. We know that, because it has been so ever since the human race has existed. So the Ambassador is right. Repentance may come to torture our souls when we no longer love each other. So let us get married tomorrow, and thus punish the vices of human nature.''

''We will get married too, but by the same token let us not be in a hurry.''

My helpmate received Lebel's letter on the next day but one. She thought it as reasonable as the Ambassador's; but we had already decided to give the matter no more thought. We resolved to leave Bern for Lausanne, where the people to whom I had letters of introduction were expecting me, and which offered much more in the way of amusements than Bern.

In bed and in each other's arms, my helpmate and I made an arrangement which we agreed was very promising and very wise. Lausanne was a small city, where she was sure I would be made much of and where for at least two weeks I would have only time to pay calls and attend the dinners and suppers which would be given for me every day. All the nobility knew her, and the Duke of Roxburghe,[33] who had been in love with her, was still there. Her appearance with me would be the daily gossip of every gathering, which in the end would be extremely annoying to us both. In addition, there was her mother, who would certainly not find fault with her but who in her heart would not be too happy to see her serving as housekeeper to a man whose mistress common sense alone would show everyone she must be.

After all these reflections we decided that she would go to her mother's at Lausanne by herself, and that two or three days later I would go to stay there, also alone, for as long as I pleased, though of course I could see her every day at her mother's. As soon as I left Lausanne and arrived in Geneva she would join me, and from there we would travel together wherever I wished so long as we loved each other.

It was on the next day but one after we made this arrangement that she set out, in fairly good spirits, for, being sure of my constancy, she was congratulating herself on doing a very wise thing; but she left me sad. Farewell visits occupied me for two days; and since I wanted to make the acquaintance of the celebrated Haller[34] before I left Switzerland, Monsieur de Muralt, the Avoyer, gave me a letter for him, to my great satisfaction. He was Bailiff of Roche.[35]

When I went to take leave of Madame de la Saône I found her in bed and was obliged to spend a quarter of an hour alone with her. Talking, as was to be expected, of nothing but her ailment, she brought the conversation around to the point where morality and propriety allowed her to show me that the sacred fire[36] which disfigured her face respected her entire body. I was no longer in such admiration of Mingard's bravery, for she would have found me prepared to do as much to her. Nothing could possibly be prettier, and it was easy to look only there. Exhibiting herself so readily, the poor woman avenged herself for the wrong nature did her by making her face hideous, and at the same time her sense of politeness may have made her think it her duty thus to reward a man well-bred enough to summon the strength to converse with her. I am sure that if she had had a pretty face she would have been very chary of all the rest of herself.

On the last day I dined at M. F.'s, where the charming Sara took me to task for having sent my "wife" off ahead of me. We shall see how I met her again in London three years later.

Leduc was still taking the cure and very weak; but I

insisted on his leaving with me, for I had a great deal of luggage and I could trust no one else.

It was thus that I departed from Bern, which left so happy an impression on my memory that I am cheered every time I recollect it.

Having to consult the physician Herrenschwandt[37] on behalf of Madame d'Urfé, I stopped at Murten where he lived. He kept me for dinner to convince me of the excellence of the fish from the lake there; but on returning to the inn[38] I decided to spend the night because of a curiosity which my reader will kindly forgive me.

Dr. Herrenschwandt, after accepting two bright louis for his consultation on the tapeworm, putting it in writing for me, invited me to take a walk with him along the highroad to Avenches[39] as far as a chapel filled with bones of the dead.

"The bones," he told me, "are those of a party of Burgundians whom the Swiss killed in the famous battle." [40]

I read the Latin inscription, I laugh, and then I tell him in all seriousness that since it contained an insulting jest it became farcical and that the gravity of an inscription did not permit a wise nation to set those who read it laughing. The Swiss doctor would not agree. Here is the inscription: *Deo. Opt. Max. Caroli inclyti, et fortissimi Burgundiae ducis exercitus Muratum obsidens, ab Helvetiis caesus, hoc sui monumentum reliquit anno 1476* ("To All-Good and Omnipotent God. The army of the famous and most valiant Charles, Duke of Burgundy, which, besieging Murten, was massacred by the Swiss, left this monument to itself in the year 1476").[41]

My notion of Murten until that moment was exalted. Its fame for seven centuries, three great sieges[42] sustained and repulsed—I expected to see something, and I saw nothing.

"Murten, I take it," said I to the physician, "must have been razed, destroyed, for—"

"Not at all, it is just what it has always been."

The man who wishes to be well informed will be wise to read, and then to travel to correct what he has learned. To know wrongly is worse than to know nothing. Montaigne[43] says that one must know rightly. But now for my adventure at the inn.

A girl in the household who spoke Romansh[44] struck me as something very much out of the ordinary, she looked like the stocking-seller[45] I had had in Little Poland; she made a great impression on me. Her name was Raton. I offer her six francs for her favors; but she refuses, saying that she is a decent girl. I order horses put to my carriage. When she sees me ready to leave she says, in a manner at once smiling and shy, that she needs two louis, and that if I will give them to her and not leave until the next day she will come and spend the night in my bed.

"I will stay, but remember to be kind."

"You will be satisfied."

When everyone had gone to bed she came with a trace of perturbation which was just the thing to increase my ardor. Having a call of nature, I ask her where the place is, and she points it out to me at the edge of the lake. I take the candle, go there, and, doing my business, read the nonsense which one always sees in such places, to right and left. Here is what I read to my right: "August 10, 1760. A week ago Raton gave me a ropy clap which is killing me."

I do not suppose there are two Ratons; I thank God, I am tempted to believe in miracles. I return to my room in seeming good humor, and I find Raton already in bed. So much the better. Thanking her for having taken off her shift, which she had thrown between the bed and the wall, I pick it up, and she takes fright. She tells me it is soiled by something perfectly natural; but I see how the case really stands. I reproach her, she does not answer, she dresses, weeping, and makes off.

Thus did I escape. But for a call of nature and the scribbled "to whom it may concern," I should have been doomed, for I would never have thought of examining a girl whose complexion was all lilies and roses.

The next day I went to Roche, to make the acquaintance of the celebrated Haller.

## CHAPTER IX

*Monsieur Haller. My stay in Lausanne. Lord Roxburghe. Mademoiselle de Sacconay. Dissertation on beauty. A girl theologian.*

I SAW a stout man six feet tall, with a fine face, who, after reading Monsieur de Muralt's letter, did me all the honors of his house and opened his precious store of knowledge in the sciences to me, answering my questions accurately and above all with a modesty which could not but strike me as exaggerated, for even as he taught me he did his best to seem a schoolboy; by the same token, when he asked me scientific questions I found in them all that I needed in order not to answer them wrongly. He was a great physiologist, a doctor, an anatomist who, like Morgagni,[1] whom he called his master, had made new discoveries in the microcosm. During the time I stayed in his house he showed me a great many letters from him and from Pontedera,[2] who was professor of botany in the same university, for Haller was also a very learned botanist. Hearing me speak of these great men, whose milk I had sucked,[3] he mildly complained of Pontedera, whose letters were almost indecipherable,[4] besides being composed in very obscure Latin. A member of the Berlin Academy wrote him that the King of Prussia, after reading his letter, had given up the idea of suppressing the Latin language entirely. "A sovereign," Haller wrote him in his letter, "who should succeed in proscribing the tongue of Cicero and Horace from the republic of letters would raise an imperishable monument to his own ignorance. If men of letters should have a common language in which to communicate their knowledge to one another, the most suitable of all the dead languages is certainly Latin, for the reigns of Greek and Arabic have ended."

Haller was a great Pindaric[5] poet and a competent statesman who deserved well of his country; he told me that the only way to give precepts was to prove their validity by example. Being a good citizen, he could not fail to be an excellent husband and father; and such I saw that he was. He had a wife whom he had married some time after losing his first[6] and whose beautiful countenance testified to her sound intelligence, and a pretty daughter[7] eighteen years of age, who scarcely spoke at table except sometimes in low tones to a young man who was seated beside her. After dinner, when I was alone with my host, I asked him who the young man was whom I had seen seated beside his daughter.

"He is her tutor."

"Such a tutor and such a pupil might well fall in love with each other."

"Yes, please God."

This Socratic answer showed me the stupid impertinence of my remark. I open an octavo volume of his works[8] and I read: *Ultrum memoria post mortem dubito* ("I doubt if memory subsists after death").

"Then you do not believe," I said, "that the memory is an essential part of the soul?"

The philosopher was forced to tergiversate, for he had

reasons not to render his orthodoxy open to doubt. At table I asked him if Monsieur de Voltaire often came to visit him. He smiled and repeated these lines from the great poet of reason: *Vetabo qui Cereris sacrum vulgarit arcanae sub iisdem sit trabibus* ("I will deny my roof to him who has revealed the rites of mystic Ceres").[9] After this answer I did not again mention religion to him during the three days I spent in his house. When I told him that I was eagerly looking forward to making the acquaintance of the famous Voltaire he replied without a trace of bitterness that I was justified in wanting to make his acquaintance but that a number of people had found him, despite the law of physics, "greater at a distance than nearby." *

I found Monsieur Haller's table very well supplied, but himself very abstemious. He drank only water and at dessert a small glass of liqueur drowned in a large glass of water. He talked to me at length of Boerhaave, whose favorite pupil [11] he had been. He said that, after Hippocrates, Boerhaave had been the greatest of all physicians and a greater chemist than Hippocrates and than all those who had existed after him.

"Then why did he not reach a ripe age?"

"Because *contra vim mortis nullum est medicamen in hortis* ('against the power of death there is no medicine in herb gardens');[12] but if Boerhaave had not been a born doctor he would have died before the age of fourteen from a malignant ulcer which no doctor could cure. He cured it by rubbing himself with his own urine in which he dissolved common salt."

"Madame[13] told me that he had the philosopher's stone."[14]

"So it is said, but I do not believe it."

---

* *De loin c'est quelque chose, et de près ce n'est rien* (La Fontaine).[10] (C.'s note.)

"Do you think it is possible to make the stone?"

"I have been working for thirty years to show that it is impossible, and I cannot convince myself of it. One cannot be a good chemist and not admit that the Great Work is a possibility within the laws of physics."

When I took my leave he asked me to write him my opinion of the great Voltaire, and this was the beginning of our correspondence in French. I have twenty-two letters[15] from him, the last of them dated six months before he, too, died prematurely.[16] The older I grow, the more I regret my papers. They are the real treasure which attaches me to life and makes me hate death.

At Bern I had read J. J. Rousseau's *Héloïse*,[17] and I wanted to hear what Monsieur Haller would say about it. He told me that the little he had read of the novel, to satisfy his friend, had been enough for him to judge the whole work.

"It is," he said, "the worst of all novels because it is the most eloquent. You will see the Pays de Vaud.[18] It is beautiful country, but do not expect to see the originals of the brilliant portrayals Rousseau paints for you. Rousseau believed that it is permissible to lie in a novel. Your Petrarch[19] did not lie. I have his Latin works, which no one reads any more because his Latinity is awkward, but their neglect is unjustified. Petrarch was a man of learning, and no impostor in his love of his noble Laura,[20] whom he loved just as any other man loves a woman with whom he is enamored. If Laura had not made Petrarch happy, he would not have sung her praises."

It was thus that Monsieur Haller talked to me of Petrarch, dismissing the subject of Rousseau, even whose eloquence he disliked because he made it brilliant only by the use of antithesis and paradox. The stout Swiss was a learned man of the highest order, but in the most unostentatious way possible, showing it neither in the bosom of his family nor when he was with people who can find entertainment without recourse to scientific discussions. He accommodated himself to whatever company he was in, he was pleasant, and he offended no one. But what did he have to make everyone like him? I do not know. It is easier to say what he did not have than what he had. He did not have any of the faults to which wits, as they are called, and men of learning are prone.

His virtues were austere, but he took care not to display their austerity. He certainly despised the ignorant who, instead of remaining within the limits which their intellectual poverty prescribes, rattle on about everything under the sun and even try to turn the laugh against those who know something; but his contempt for them was never shown. He knew too well that ignorance scorned turns to hatred; and he did not want to be hated. Monsieur Haller was a learned man who did not leave his intelligence to be guessed at, for he showed it, but who did not want to take advantage of the reputation he enjoyed; he spoke well, he said things worth hearing without preventing anyone in the company from doing likewise. He never talked of his works, and when someone mentioned them to him he changed the subject; and when he was of a different opinion he contradicted his opponent only with reluctance.

No sooner had I reached Lausanne than, thinking I could preserve my incognito, I naturally gave the preference to my heart. I went to see the widow Dubois, without having to ask anyone where she lived, so well had she described for me the streets through which I had to pass to reach her house. I found her with her mother; but my surprise was extreme when I saw Lebel. She did not leave me time to show it. After giving a cry she sprang into my arms, and her mother welcomed me as politeness prescribed. I asked Lebel how the Ambassador was and how long he had been in Lausanne.

Assuming a cordial tone, the worthy man replied that the Ambassador was very well and that he himself had arrived in Lausanne that morning on business and, coming to see Madame Dubois's mother after dining, he had been very much surprised to find her daughter here.

"You know," he said to me, "what my intentions are; I must leave tomorrow; and when you have made up your mind, if you will write to me I will come for her and take her to Soleure, where I will marry her."

To this no less clear than honorable avowal I replied that I would never oppose the will of my dear helpmate; and she on her side said that she would never make up her mind to leave me until I dismissed her. Finding our answers too vague, he frankly told me that he must have a definite and final answer, whereupon, intending to reject his proposal in its entirety, I said I would write to him fully in ten or twelve days. He left for Soleure the next morning.

After he was gone my dear one's mother, whose native shrewdness served her for intelligence, talked sense to us in the style our state of mind compelled her to use, for, in love as we were, we could not resolve to part. Meanwhile, I settled it with my helpmate that she would wait for me every day until midnight, and that we would come to a decision, as I had promised Lebel we would do. She had her own room and a very comfortable bed, and she gave me a good enough supper. In the morning we were very much in love and not at all inclined to think about Lebel's proposal. However, we had a little discussion.

My reader may remember that my helpmate had promised to forgive me all my infidelities on condition that I would confess them to her frankly. I had none to confess, but at supper I told her the story of Raton.

"We must both consider ourselves very fortunate," she said, "because if you hadn't by chance needed to go to the place where you found the salutary warning, you would have lost your health, and since the disease would not have declared itself at once, you would have infected me with it.''

''It is possible, and I should be in despair.''

''I know that; and all the sadder because I would not complain of it.''

''I see only one way to avoid such a misfortune. When I have been unfaithful to you I will punish myself by abstaining from giving you proofs of my love.''

''That would be to punish *me*. If you really loved me you would find a better remedy, I think.''

''What remedy?''

''Not being unfaithful to me.''

''You are right. Please forgive me, and I will use it in future.''

''I think you will find it hard.''

The author of such dialogues is Love; but Love gains nothing by composing them.

The next morning at my inn, when I had dressed and was preparing to take my letters to the persons to whom they were addressed, I saw the Baron de Bercher, uncle of my friend Bavois.[21]

''I know,'' he said, ''that my nephew owes his good fortune to you, that he is esteemed, that he will be made a general at the next promotion, and my whole family will be most happy, as I am, to make your acquaintance. I come to offer you my services, and I invite you to dine at my house today and after that to come there when you have nothing better to do; but at the same time I beg you to say nothing to anyone about the reprehensible step he took in becoming a Catholic, for it is a thing which, in the view of this country, is dishonorable to him, and the dishonor is of a kind which reflects on all his relatives.''

I promised never to mention this episode in his life when I talked of him, and to go and eat family dinner

with him at once. All the persons to whom I had letters
impressed me as respectable, well-bred, most polite, and
very talented. I thought Madame Gentil de Langallerie
the most attractive among the ladies; but I did not have
time to pay more particular court to one than to another.
Dinners, suppers, and balls every day, at all of which
politeness demanded my attendance, were a restraint on
me almost beyond endurance. I spent two weeks in that
small city, where I was never free precisely because all
its inhabitants make a great point of enjoying freedom.
I could not go to spend the night with my helpmate
except once; I could not wait to be off with her to Geneva,
where everyone wanted to give me letters to Monsieur de
Voltaire; who nevertheless, I was told, was detested there
because of his caustic turn of mind.

"What, Mesdames! Is not Monsieur de Voltaire good-
natured, amiable, cheerful, and affable with you, who
were kind enough to act in his plays[22] with him?"

"No, Monsieur. When he had us rehearse our parts he
scolded us; we never said anything as he wanted it, we
did not pronounce one word correctly; he criticized our
voices, our manner, and it was even worse when we performed the play. What an uproar over an added or
omitted syllable which had ruined one of his lines! He
terrified us. One of us had laughed in the wrong place;
another, in *Alzire*,[23] had only pretended to cry."

"Did he want you to cry in good earnest?"

"In good earnest; he wanted us to shed real tears; he
maintained that an actor could not make his audience
cry unless he really cried himself."

"There I think he was right; but a sensible author
knows better than to be so strict with amateurs. Such
things can only be demanded of professional actors; but
every author has the same failing. He never thinks the
actor has given his words the force needed to convey their
real meaning."

"One day, thoroughly sick of his outbursts, I said it was not my fault if his words did not have the force they ought to have."

"I am certain he only laughed."

"Laugh? Say sneer! He is insolent, cruel, and, in short, unbearable."

"But you overlooked all his faults, I am sure."

"Don't be too sure of that, for we drove him away."

"Drove him away?"

"Precisely; he suddenly gave up the houses[24] he had rented and went to live where you will find him, and he never comes here any more, even when he is invited, for after all we admire his genius and we only made him angry in order to avenge ourselves and teach him to behave. Get him to talk about Lausanne, and you'll hear what he'll say about us, though laughingly, for that is his way."

I several times encountered Lord Roxburghe,[25] who had vainly loved my helpmate. He was a handsome young man, whose equal for taciturnity I have never met. I was immediately told that he was witty, well educated, and did not suffer from melancholy; in society, at assemblies and balls and dinners, his manners consisted only in bows; when he was addressed he replied very laconically in good French, but with a shyness which showed that questions made him uncomfortable. Dining at his house, I asked him something concerning his country which required five or six sentences, and he answered very well, but blushing. The famous Fox,[26] who was also at the dinner and who was then twenty years of age, made him laugh, but speaking to him in English. I saw the Duke again at Turin eight months later, in love with Madame Martin,[27] the wife of a banker, who knew how to loosen his tongue.

In the same city[28] I saw a girl eleven or twelve years old[29] whose beauty struck me. She was the daughter of

Madame de Sacconay, whose acquaintance I had made in Bern. I do not know what destiny had in store for the girl, who made the strongest impression on me to no purpose.

Nothing on earth has ever had such domination over me as a beautiful woman's face, even if she is only a child. Beauty, I have been told, has that power. I agree, for what attracts me certainly seems to me beautiful; but is it really beautiful? I must doubt it, because what seems to me beautiful does not always have the general consensus in its favor. Hence perfect beauty does not exist or does not have such power in itself. All those who have discussed beauty have tergiversated; they should have kept to the name the Greeks and Romans gave it: Form. Hence beauty is nothing but form par excellence. What is not beautiful does not possess a form; and this *deformis* was the opposite of *pulchrum* or *formosum*. We do well to seek the definition of things, but when we have it in their names why need we look for it elsewhere? If the word "form," *forma,* is Latin, let us look at its accepted meaning in Latin, not in French—which, however, often says *déforme*[30] instead of *laid* ("ugly"), apparently unaware that its opposite must be a word which indicates the existence of form, which can only be beauty. We should note that *informe* in French as well as Latin means "without shape." It is a body which has no definite appearance.

So what has always exercised an absolute sway over me is the living beauty of a woman, but that beauty as it exists in her face. That is where the spell resides, and this is so true that the Sphinxes we see at Rome and Versailles almost make us fall in love with their bodies though they are deformed in the fullest sense of the word. Looking at their faces, we come to consider their deformity beautiful. But what is this beauty? We simply do not know; and when we try to reduce it to laws, or to state those laws, we tergiversate like Socrates.[31] All that I know is that the surface which enchants me, which transports me, which makes me fall in love, is what is called beauty. It is an object of sight, for which I speak. If my sight could speak it would speak of beauty to better purpose than I.

No painter outdid Raphael in the beauty of the figures produced by his brush; but if someone had asked Raphael what that beauty was, whose laws he knew so well, he would have replied that he had no idea, that he knew it by heart and believed that he had produced it when he saw it before his eyes. ''This figures pleases me,'' he must have said, ''hence it is beautiful.'' He must have thanked God for having been born with an admirable sense of beauty. But *omne pulchrum difficile* (''whatever is beautiful is difficult''). The only admired painters were those who excelled in the beautiful; their number is small. If we are willing to dispense a painter from giving his works the quality of beauty any man can become a painter, for nothing is easier than to produce ugliness. The painter who is not ordained to be such by God himself cannot but produce it. We may note how rare it is to find a good painter among those who have devoted themselves to portrait painting. It is the most material branch of their art. They are of three kinds. There are those who make ugly likenesses; if you ask me, they should be paid with cudgels, for they are impertinent and they never admit that they have made the sitter uglier, or less beautiful. The second kind, who must be allowed a certain merit, are those whose likenesses are perfect and even astonishing, for the portrait seems to speak.

But few, indeed very few, are those who catch likenesses perfectly and at the same time add an imperceptible touch of beauty to the faces they have portrayed on their canvases. Painters of this kind deserve the fortunes they have made. Such was Nattier,[32] of Paris, whom I knew at the age of eighty[33] in the fiftieth year of this century. He painted the portrait of an ugly woman; she perfectly resembled the face Nattier had given her on his canvas, nevertheless in the portrait everyone thought her beautiful. Yet, examining the portrait, it was impossible to find anything changed. All that had been added or taken away was imperceptible.

"What is the source of this magic?" I asked Nattier one day when he had just painted the ugly Mesdames de France[34] and made them as beautiful as stars.

"It proves the divinity of beauty, which everyone adores, though no one knows in what it consists; and it also shows how imperceptible is the difference between the beauty and the ugliness of a countenance, which nevertheless seems so great to those who have no knowledge of our art."

The Greek painters were pleased to make Venus, the goddess of beauty, squint. The commentators may say what they like. The painters were wrong. Two squinting eyes can be beautiful; but if they squint I am sorry for it and I find them less beautiful.

On the ninth day of my stay in Lausanne I supped and spent the night with my helpmate, and in the morning, drinking coffee with her and her mother, I told her that it would soon be time to say good-by. Her mother said that, in all honesty, I ought to undeceive Lebel before I left, and she showed me a letter from the worthy man which she had received the day before. He asked her to urge it upon me that if I could not make up my mind to resign her daughter to him before I left Lausanne I would find it even harder to do so when I had gone elsewhere and she had perhaps given me a living pledge of her affection which would increase my attachment to its mother. He said that he certainly had no idea of going back on his word, but that he would consider himself all the happier if he could say he had received the woman he had married from the hands of her mother.

The good mother left us, weeping, and I remained with my dear mistress, discussing this most important matter. It was she who had the courage to tell me that I must instantly write Lebel either to stop thinking about her or to come and take her away at once.

"If I write him to stop thinking about you, I must marry you."

"No."

After uttering which "no," she left me alone. Only a quarter of an hour's thought was enough to make me write Lebel a short letter in which I told him that the widow Dubois, being her own mistress, had decided to give him her hand, and that I could only consent and congratulate him on his good fortune. In consequence I asked him to set out from Soleure at once in order to receive her from her mother's hands in my presence.

I then went to her mother's room, handing the letter to her daughter and saying that if she approved of it she had only to add her signature to mine. After reading and rereading it, her mother weeping all the while, she fixed her beautiful eyes on my face for a moment, then signed. At that I told the mother to find a trustworthy man to take the letter to Soleure at once. The man came and at once set off with my letter.

"We shall see each other again," I said to my helpmate, embracing her, "as soon as Lebel arrives."

I returned to my inn and, to wrestle with my grief, I shut myself in my room, giving orders to say that I was indisposed.

Toward evening four days later Lebel appeared before me and, after embracing me, left, saying that he would wait for me at his fiancée's. I begged him to excuse me, saying that I would dine with him at her house the next day. I made all my arrangements for leaving after din-

ner, and the next morning said good-by to everyone.
Toward noon Lebel came for me.

Our dinner was not melancholy, but neither was it
cheerful. When I was about to leave I asked my ex-help-
mate to give me back the ring I had let her have in exchange for a hundred louis, as we had agreed; and she
took them very sadly.

"I wouldn't have given it back," she said, "for I am
not in need of money."

"In that case," I said, "I give it back to you, but
promise me you will never sell it, and keep the hundred
louis as well, an inadequate recompense for the services
you have rendered me."

She gave me the gold wedding ring from her first
marriage, and she left me, unable to hold back her tears.
After wiping mine away:

"You are," I said to Lebel, "about to take possession
of a treasure which I cannot commend to you too highly.
It will not be long before you know all its value. She
will love you alone; she will take care of your household; she will never have a secret from you; she will
amuse you with her wit and easily drive away the slightest shadow of ill humor which may visit you."

When I went to her mother's room with him to take a
final leave, she asked me to put off my departure until
I had supped with her once again, and I replied that,
the horses being harnessed and at my door, the delay
would cause talk; but I promised to wait for her, with
her husband and her mother, at an inn which was two
leagues[35] away on the road to Geneva, where we could
stay as long as we pleased, and Lebel was delighted with
the little excursion.

Everything being ready when I got back to the inn, I
set out at once and stopped at the appointed place,
where I immediately ordered supper for four. I saw them
arrive an hour later. The unconstrained and happy air

of the new bride surprised me, and especially the composure with which she came and embraced me. She made me feel awkward, she had better sense than I had. However, I had the strength to fall in with her frame of mind; it seemed impossible that she had loved me and that she could thus change in one jump from love to pure friendship; nevertheless I make up my mind to imitate her and I do not refuse to exchange the outward marks which are permitted to friendship and which are supposed not to arouse sensations which go beyond its limits.

During supper I thought I saw that Lebel was more delighted by his luck in obtaining such a woman than by the right he had acquired to possess her in order to satisfy a strong passion he had conceived for her beforehand. I could not be jealous of a man whose sentiments were such. I also saw that my helpmate's high spirits came only from her wish to communicate them to me and thus make her future husband certain that she would not fail him in anything. She must also have felt very well satisfied to have attained a regular and stable position in life, safe from the whims of Fortune.

These reflections at the end of supper, which lasted two hours, put me in the same frame of mind as my late helpmate. I was content to regard her as a treasure which had belonged to me and which, after making me happy, was going to make another man so with my full consent. I felt that I was giving my helpmate the reward she deserved, as a generous Mussulman gives freedom to a cherished slave in recompense for loyalty. I looked at her, I laughed at her jokes, and the memory of the pleasures I had enjoyed in her company stood me in stead of their present reality, without any bitterness and without any regret that I had deprived myself of the right to renew them. I even thought I felt sorry when, looking at Lebel, he did not seem to me a man to replace me. She, divining my thought, told me with her eyes that she did not care.

After supper, Lebel having said that they must really go back to Lausanne so that he could be at Soleure on the next day but one, I embraced him, asking him to remain my friend until death. While he was preparing to enter the carriage with her mother, my helpmate, going down the stairs with me, told me with her usual frankness that she would not be happy until the wound was entirely healed.

"Lebel," she said, "can gain no more than my esteem and my friendship, but that will not prevent me from being his alone. Be certain that I have loved no one but you, and that you are the only man who has taught me the power of the senses and the impossibility of resisting it when nothing stands in its way. When we meet again, as you lead me to hope, we shall be ready to be perfect friends and very glad that we decided on the step we have just taken; and as for you, I am sure that in a short time a new object, whether more or less worthy to fill my place, will end your grief. I do not know if I am pregnant, but if I am you will be satisfied with the care I will give your child, whom you shall take from my custody when you please. Yesterday we made an arrangement in that respect which will leave us in no doubt when I am brought to bed. We agreed that we will marry as soon as we reach Soleure; but we will not consummate the marriage until two months from then; thus we will be sure that my child is yours if I bear it before April; and we will gladly let the world believe that it is the legitimate fruit of our marriage. It is he who conceived this wise plan, which will bring peace to our house and free my husband's mind from the least doubt in the more than perplexed question of the power of the blood, in which he believes no more than I do; but my husband will love our child as if he were its father, and if you write to me I will answer, sending you news of my pregnancy and our household. If I have the happiness to give you a child, whether a girl or a boy, it will be a memento which I will cherish far more dearly than your ring. But we are in tears, and Lebel is looking at us and laughing.''

I could only answer by clasping her in my arms, and I consigned her to her husband's in the carriage, he saying that our long conversation had given him the greatest pleasure. They set off, and the chambermaids, thoroughly tired of standing there with candles in their hands, were very glad of it. I went off to bed.

The next morning when I got up, a pastor of the Geneva church having asked me if I would be so good as to give him a seat in my carriage, I granted his request. We had only ten leagues to travel, but since I wanted to eat something at noon I let him make the arrangements.

A man of eloquence and a professional theologian, he kept me amused all the way to Geneva by the ease with which he answered every question, even the thorniest, which I could put to him on the subject of religion. There were no mysteries for him, everything was reason; I never encountered a priest to whom Christianity came as easily as it did to this worthy man, whose life, as I learned at Geneva, was of the purest; but I came to the conclusion that his way of being a Christian was not peculiar to him, his doctrine being that of his entire church. When I undertook to convince him that he was a Calvinist only in name since he did not believe that Jesus Christ was of the same substance as God the Father, he replied that Calvin[36] had never claimed to be infallible, like our Pope; I said that neither did we believe the Pope infallible except when he laid down the law *ex cathedra,* and, quoting the Gospels, I struck him dumb. I made him blush when I reproached him with Calvin's having

believed that the Pope was the Antichrist of the Apoc-
alypse. He replied that the error could not be eradi-
cated in Geneva unless the government ordered the ef-
facement of an inscription on the church, which everyone
read and in which the head of the Roman Church was so
designated.[37] He said that the populace was ignorant
and stupid everywhere, but that he had a niece who, at
the age of twenty, did not think like the populace.

"I hope," he said, "to make you acquainted with her.
She is a theologian and pretty."

"I shall see her with pleasure, Monsieur, but God
keep me from arguing with her."

"She will force you to argue, and you will be very
glad of it, I promise you."

I asked him for his address, but instead of giving it to
me he said he would come to my inn himself to take me
to his house. I put up at the "Scales," [38] and was very
well lodged. It was August 20, 1760.[39]

Going to the window, I happen to look at the panes
and I see, written with the point of a diamond: "You
will forget Henriette too." Instantly remembering the
moment when she had written the words for me thirteen
years[40] earlier, I felt my hair stand on end. We had
stayed in that very room when she parted from me to
return to France. I flung myself into a chair to indulge
in all my reflections. Ah, my dear Henriette! Noble and
fond Henriette whom I had so greatly loved, where are
you? I had never heard or asked news of her from anyone. Comparing myself with myself, I decided that I
was less worthy to possess her than I had been then. I
could still love, but I found in myself neither the delicacy
which was then mine, nor the exalted feelings which
justify the errors of the senses, nor considerateness, nor
a certain probity; and, what horrified me, I did not have
the same vigor. Yet it seemed that the mere memory of
Henriette restored it to me completely. Abandoned by
my helpmate, as I had just been, I felt a rush of such

strong enthusiasm that I would have gone to see her[41] on the instant if I had known where to find her, though her prohibitions were still in my memory.

Early the next morning I went to the banker Tronchin, who had all my money. After showing me my account he gave me, at my request, a letter of credit on Marseilles, Genoa, Florence, and Rome. In cash I took only twelve thousand francs. I had fifty thousand French écus[42] at my disposal. After taking my letters to their addresses I returned to the "Scales," impatient to see Monsieur de Voltaire.

I found the pastor in my room. He invited me to dinner, saying that I would find Monsieur Villars Chandieu[43] there, who after dinner would take me to Monsieur de Voltaire's, where I had been expected for several days. So after making a brief toilet I went to the pastor's house, where I found the whole company interesting, but especially his young niece,[44] the theologian, whom her uncle did not bring into the conversation until dessert:

"How did you entertain yourself this morning, my dear niece?"

"I read St. Augustine, but finding that I disagreed with him in the sixteenth section I dropped him; and I believe I have refuted him in a few words."

"On what point?"

"He says that the Virgin Mary conceived Jesus through the ears.[45] This is absurd for three reasons. First, because God, not being matter, did not need an opening to enter the body of the Virgin. Second, because the aural passages have no connection with the womb. Third, because, having conceived through the ears, she ought also to have given birth through the same channel; and in that case you," she said, looking at me, "would be right to believe her a virgin during and after her childbearing."

The surprise of all the guests was equal to mine, but

we had to forbear. The divine spirit of theology can rise above any carnal sensation, at least it must be credited with possessing that great privilege. The erudite niece did not think she was abusing it, and in any case she was sure of forgiveness. It was to me that she turned for an answer.

"I should be of your opinion, Mademoiselle, if I were a theologian and, as such, allowed myself to examine miracles in the light of reason; but since I am not, allow me, at the same time that I admire you, to condemn St. Augustine for having tried to analyze the power of the Annunciation. What seems to me certain is that if the Virgin had been deaf the incarnation could not have taken place. It is also true anatomically that since the three pairs of nerves which actuate the sense of hearing do not send any branch to the womb it is impossible to conceive how the thing can have been accomplished; but it is a miracle."

She answered me very charmingly that it was I who had spoken like a great theologian, and her uncle thanked me for having given his niece a good lesson. The company made her talk on various subjects, but she did not shine. Her forte was the New Testament. I shall have occasion to speak of her when I go back to Geneva.

We went to Monsieur de Voltaire's, who was just getting up from table. He was surrounded by gentlemen and ladies, so my presentation became a solemn occasion. This solemnity was very far from predisposing Voltaire and the company in my favor.

## CHAPTER X

*Monsieur de Voltaire; my discussions with the great man. A scene at his house in connection with Ariosto. The Duke of Villars. The Syndic and his three beautiful girls. Argument at Voltaire's. Aix-en-Savoie. The Marquis Desarmoises.*

"THIS," I said to him, "is the happiest moment of my life. At last I see my master; it is twenty years, Monsieur, since I became your pupil."

"Honor me with another twenty, and then promise to bring me my wages."

"I promise; but, on your side, promise to wait for me."

"I give you my word for it, and only death—not I— will break my word."

A general laugh greeted this first Voltairean sally. It was in the nature of things. The function of such laughter is to encourage one disputant, always at the expense of the other; and he to whom the laughers give their suffrage is always sure to win; they constitute a claque which operates in good society too. I expected as much, but I hoped that my turn would come to let fly at him.

Two newly arrived Englishmen are introduced. He rises, saying:

*"These gentlemen are English. I wish I were."*

A poor compliment, for it forced them to answer that they wished they were French, and perhaps they did not want to lie, or they should be ashamed to tell the truth. A man of honor, I think, has the right to put his own country above all others.

No sooner has he sat down again than he returns to me, saying politely, but still with a laugh, that as a Venetian I must certainly know Count Algarotti.[1]

"I know him, but not by virtue of being a Venetian, for seven eighths of my dear fellow countrymen are unaware that he exists."

"I should have said 'as a man of letters.' "

"I know him from having spent two months with him at Padua[2] seven years ago; and I admired him principally because I discovered that he admired you."

"We are good friends; but to deserve the esteem of all who know him he does not need to admire anyone."

"If he had not begun by admiring, he would not have achieved fame. Admiring Newton, he succeeded in making it possible for ladies[3] to talk about light."

"Did he really succeed?"

"Not as well as Monsieur de Fontenelle in his *Pluralité des mondes*;[4] but he can be said to have succeeded."

"That is true. If you see him in Bologna, be so good as to tell him that I am awaiting his letters on Russia.[5] He can send them to me in care of the banker Bianchi in Milan. I am told that Italians do not like his Italian."

"I can well believe it: his style, in all his Italian writings, is his alone; it is infected with gallicisms; we think it pitiful."

"But do not French turns of expression make your language more beautiful?"

"They make it intolerable, just as a French stuffed

with Italian expressions would be, even if it were written
by you.''

"You are right, one must write purely. Livy has been
taken to task; his Latin has been said to be tainted with
Patavinity.'' [6]

"The Abate Lazzarini[7] told me, when I was beginning
to write, that he preferred Livy to Sallust.'' [8]

"The Abate Lazzarini, author of the tragedy *Ulisse il
giovane*? [9] You must have been very young, and I wish
I had known him; but I knew the Abate Conti,[10] who
had been Newton's friend and whose four tragedies cover
the whole of Roman history.''

"I, too, knew and admired him. When I was with those
great men, I congratulated myself on being young; today, here with you, I feel as if I dated from day before
yesterday, but it does not humiliate me; I wish I were
the youngest member of the human family.''

"You would be better off than if you were the oldest.
May I ask to what branch of literature you have devoted
yourself?''

"To none; but perhaps the time will come. In the
meanwhile I read as much as I can, and I indulge myself in studying humanity by traveling.''

"That is the way to know it, but the book is too big.
The easier method is to read history.''

"History lies; one is not certain of the facts; it is
boring; and studying the world on the run amuses me.
Horace, whom I know by heart, is my guidebook, and I
find him everywhere.''

"Algarotti knows all of him by heart too. You are
certainly fond of poetry?''

"It is my passion.''

"Have you written many sonnets?''

"Ten or twelve which I like, and two or three thousand which I may not even have reread.''

"The Italians are mad about sonnets.''

"Yes—provided one can call it madness to wish to bestow on a given thought a harmonious measure capable of putting it in the best light. The sonnet is difficult, Monsieur de Voltaire, for we may neither extend the thought for the sake of the fourteen lines nor shorten it."

"It is the bed of the tyrant Procrustes.[11] That is why you have so few good ones. We have not one,[12] but that is the fault of our language."

"And of the French genius, too, I believe, which supposes that expanding a thought makes it lose all its brilliance and force."

"And you are not of that opinion?"

"I beg your pardon, it is a matter of the nature of the thought. A witticism, for example, is not enough for a sonnet."

"Which Italian poet do you love best?"

"Ariosto; and I cannot say that I love him better than the rest, for he is the only one I love. Yet I have read them all. When, fifteen years ago, I read your strictures on him,[13] I at once said that you would retract when you had read him."

"I am grateful to you for thinking I had not read him. I had read him; but, being young, having an inadequate knowledge of your language, and being prejudiced by the Italian writers who worship your Tasso, I unfortunately published an opinion which I sincerely thought was my own. It was not. I worship your Ariosto."

"I breathe again. So have an excommunication pronounced on the book in which you ridiculed him."

"All my books are excommunicated already; but I will now give you good proof of my retraction."

It was then that Voltaire astonished me. He recited by heart the two great passages in the thirty-fourth and thirty-fifth cantos of the divine poet in which he tells of Astolpho's conversation with St. John the Apostle,[14] never skipping a line, never pronouncing a word except

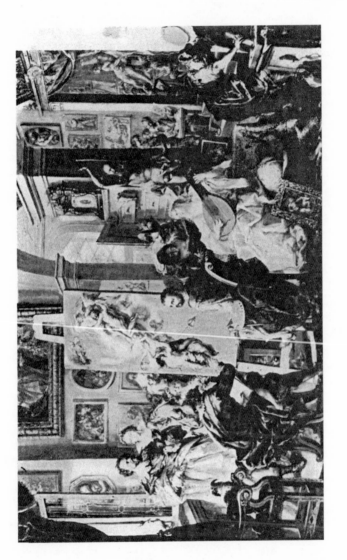

*Studio of a Rococo Painter*

*Voltaire Arguing*

in accordance with strict prosody; he pointed out their beauties to me, with reflections which only a truly great man could make. One could have expected nothing more from the greatest of all the Italian commentators. I listened to him without breathing, without once blinking my eyes, hoping in vain to catch him in a mistake; turning to the company, I said that I was overwhelmed with astonishment, and that I would inform all Italy of my wonder and the reason for it.

"All Europe," he replied, "shall be informed by me of the most humble amends which I owe to the greatest genius she has produced."

Insatiable for praise, the next day he gave me his translation of Ariosto's stanza: *Quindi avvien che tra principi e signori.*[15] Here it is:

> *Les papes, les césars apaisant leur querelle*
> *Jurent sur l'Évangile une paix éternelle;*
> *Vous les voyez demain l'un de l'autre ennemis;*
> *C'était pour se tromper qu'ils s'étaient réunis:*
> *Nul serment n'est gardé, nul accord n'est sincère;*
> *Quand la bouche a parlé, le coeur dit le contraire.*
> *Du ciel qu'ils attestaient ils bravaient le courroux,*
> *L'intérêt est le dieu qui les gouverne tous.*

("Popes and monarchs, ending their division, swear eternal peace on the Gospels; tomorrow you see them enemies; it was to deceive each other that they had assembled: no oath is kept, no agreement is sincere; when the mouth has spoken, the heart says the opposite. They dared the wrath of the heaven which they called to witness; interest is the god which governs them all.")

At the end of Monsieur de Voltaire's recitation, which brought him the applause of all present, though not one of them understood Italian, Madame Denis,[16] his niece, asked me if the famous passage her uncle had declaimed was one of the finest in the great poet.

"Yes, Madame, but not the very finest."

"Then judgment has been handed down as to the very finest?"

"Certainly—otherwise Signor Lodovico would not have received his apotheosis."

"I did not know he had been beatified."

At that all the laughers, with Voltaire at their head, were on Madame Denis's side—I alone excepted, who remained perfectly serious. Voltaire, nettled by my gravity:

"I know," he said, "why you do not laugh. You claim that it is by virtue of a superhuman passage that he was called 'divine.' "

"Precisely."

"What passage is it?"

"The last thirty-six stanzas of the twenty-third canto, which give a technical description of the way Orlando went mad. Since the beginning of the world no one has known how a person goes mad except Ariosto, who was able to write it, and who toward the end of his life went mad too.[17] Those stanzas, I am certain, have made you shudder; they inspire horror."

"I remember them; they make love terrible. I cannot wait to read them again."

"Perhaps Monsieur will be so kind as to recite them to us," said Madame Denis, with a sly glance at her uncle.

"Why not, Madame, if you will have the goodness to listen."

"Then you have taken the trouble to learn them by heart?"

"As I have read Ariosto through two or three times a year ever since I was fifteen years old, he has fixed himself in my memory from beginning to end with no effort on my part and, as it were, despite me, except for his genealogies and his historical passages, which tire the mind without touching the heart. Only Horace has remained imprinted entire in my soul, despite the often too prosaic verses in his Epistles.''

''We can allow you Horace,'' added Voltaire; ''but Ariosto is a great deal, for it is a matter of forty-six long cantos.''

''Say fifty-one.'' [18]

Voltaire remained silent.

''Come, come,'' said Madame Denis, ''let us have the thirty-six stanzas which make one shudder and which earned their author the appellation of 'divine.' ''

I thereupon recited them, but not in the style of declamation which we use in Italy. To please, Ariosto has no need to be thrown into relief by a monotonous singsong on the part of the person who delivers him. The French are right in finding this singsong intolerable. I recited them as if they were prose, animating them by voice, eyes, and the varying intonation necessary to express feeling. My audience saw and felt feeling expressed. They saw and felt the effort I made to hold back my tears, and they wept; but when I came to the stanza:

> *Poichè allargare il freno al dolor puote*
> *Che resta solo senza altrui rispetto*
> *Giù dagli occhi rigando per le gote*
> *Sparge un fiume di lacrime sul petto*

> ("Because he who is alone, with no one
> to consider, may give the reins to his
> grief, from his eyes he pours a stream of
> tears which flow down his cheeks to his
> breast"),[19]

my tears burst from my eyes so impetuously and abundantly that everyone present shed tears too, Madame Denis shuddered, and Voltaire ran to embrace me; but he could not interrupt me, for Orlando, to go completely mad, had to discover that he was in the same bed as that in which Angelica had lately lain in the arms of the too fortunate Medoro,[20] which happened in the following stanza. My plaintive and mournful tone gave place to the tone of terror inspired by the madness whose prodigious force drove him to ravages such as only an earthquake or lightning could cause. At the end of my recitation I somberly received the congratulations of the entire company. Voltaire exclaimed:

"It is what I have always said: to draw tears, one must weep oneself; but to weep, one must feel, and then the tears come from the soul."

He embraced me, he thanked me, and he promised to recite the same stanzas to me the next day and to weep as I had done. He kept his word.

Pursuing the subject of Ariosto, Madame Denis said it was astonishing that Rome had not put him on the Index. Voltaire replied that, on the contrary, Leo X [21] had issued a bull excommunicating all who dared to condemn him. The two great families of Este and Medici[22] found it to their interest to support him:

"But for that," he added, "the one line on Constantine's donation of Rome[23] to Sylvester,[24] which says that it *puzza forte* ('stinks strongly'),[25] would have been enough to bring an interdict on the poem."

I said that, begging his pardon, the line which had caused even more of an outcry was the one in which Ariosto throws doubt on the resurrection of the whole human race at the end of the world.

"Speaking of the hermit who tried to prevent Rodomonte from capturing Isabella, Zerbino's[26] widow," I said, "Ariosto describes the African as tiring of his preaching, seizing him, and throwing him so far that he breaks him to pieces against a rock, where he is instantly killed and remains in a sleep such

> *Che al novissimo dì forse fia desto.*
>
> ('That he perhaps may wake on the
> last day.')

"That *forse* ('perhaps'), which the poet inserted only as a rhetorical ornament, caused an outcry which would have made the poet laugh heartily."

"It is a pity," said Madame Denis, "that Ariosto did not abstain from his hyperboles."

"Be quiet, my niece; they are all deliberate and all of the greatest beauty."

We talked on other subjects, all of them literary, and the conversation finally turned to *L'Écossaise,* which had been acted at Soleure. The whole story was known. Voltaire told me that if I would act in his house he would write Monsieur de Chavigny to persuade Madame . . . to come and act Lindane and that he would take the part of Monrose. I declined, telling him that Madame . . . was at Basel and that in any case I had to leave the following day. At that he protested vehemently, roused the whole company against me, and maintained that my visit became an insult if I did not stay for at least a week. I replied that, having come to Geneva only for him, I had nothing else to do there.

"Did you come here to talk to me or to hear me talk?"

"Principally to hear you talk."

"Then stay here three days at least, come to dine with me every day, and we will talk."

I said I would do so, and then took my leave to go to my inn, for I had a great deal of writing to do.

A Syndic[27] of the city, whom I will not name and who had spent the day at Voltaire's, came a quarter of an hour later, asking me to let him sup with me.

"I was present," he said, "at your argument with the great man, though I said nothing. I hope I may have you to myself for an hour."

I embraced him and, asking him to excuse me for receiving him in my nightcap, said that he could spend the whole night with me if he wished.

The amiable man spent two hours with me, never speaking of literature, but he had no need of that to please me. He was a great disciple of Epicurus and Socrates; capping anecdotes, outdoing each other in laughter, and talk about every kind of pleasure to be procured in Geneva kept us occupied until midnight. When he left, he invited me to sup with him the following evening, assuring me that our supper would be amusing. I promised to wait for him at my inn. He asked me not to mention our engagement to anyone.

The next morning young Fox came to my room with the two Englishmen whom I had seen at Monsieur de Voltaire's. They proposed a game of quinze[28] with stakes of two louis, and, having lost fifty louis in less than an hour, I stopped. We made a tour of Geneva and at dinnertime went to "Les Délices." [29] The Duke of Villars[30] had just arrived there to consult Tronchin,[31] who had kept him alive by his art for ten years.

During dinner I said nothing; but afterward Voltaire made me talk about the Venetian government, knowing that I must bear it a grudge. I disappointed his expectation; I attempted to prove that there is no country on earth in which one can enjoy greater freedom. Seeing that the subject was not to my liking, he took me out to his garden, which he told me he had created. The principal walk ended at a stream; he said it was the Rhone, which he was sending to France. He made me admire the fine view of Geneva and the Dent Blanche,[32] which is the highest of the Alps.

Deliberately turning the conversation to Italian literature, he began talking away on the subject with great wit and erudition, but always ending with an erroneous judgment. I did not contradict him. He spoke of Homer, Dante, and Petrarch, and everyone knows what he thought of those great geniuses. His inability to refrain from writing what he thought harmed him. I only said that if these authors had not deserved the esteem of all who studied them they would not have been given the high place they held.

The Duke of Villars and the famous physician Tronchin joined us. Tronchin—tall, well built, handsome, polished, eloquent though not talkative, a learned natural scientist, a wit, a physician, favorite pupil [33] of Boerhaave, and without either the jargon or the charlatanism of the pillars of the Faculty—captivated me. His principal medicine was only diet; but to prescribe it he had to be a great philosopher. It was he who cured a consumptive of venereal disease by the mercury which he gave him in the milk of a she-ass which he had subjected to thirty rubbings by the strong arms of three or four porters. I write this because I have been told it, but I find it hard to believe.

The person of the Duke of Villars caught all my attention. Examining his bearing and his face, I thought I saw a woman of seventy[34] dressed as a man, thin, emaciated, weak, but who in her youth might have been beautiful. His blotched cheeks were covered with rouge, his lips with carmine, his eyebrows were blackened, his teeth were false, as was the hair which was glued to his head by quantities of pomade scented with ambergris, and in his top buttonhole was a large bouquet which came up to his chin. He affected grace in his gestures, and he spoke in a soft voice which made it difficult to understand what he said. Withal he was very polite, affable, and mannered in the style of the Regency.[35] I have been told that when he was young he loved women, but that in his old age he assumed the modest role of wife to three or four handsome minions, each of whom in turn enjoyed the honor of sleeping with him. The Duke was the Governor of Provence. His whole back was gangrened, and according to the laws of nature he should have died ten years earlier; but Tronchin kept him alive by diet, feeding the sores, which

if they had not been fed would have died and taken the
Duke with them. This is truly to live by art.

I went with Voltaire to his bedroom, where he changed
his wig and the bonnet he wore over it to keep from catching cold. On a large table I saw the *Summa*[36] of St.
Thomas and some Italian poets, among them the *Secchia
rapita* of Tassoni.[37]

"It is," he said, "the only tragicomic poem which
Italy possesses. Tassoni was a monk, a wit, and a learned
genius as a poet."

"The rest perhaps—but not learned, for, ridiculing the
Copernican system, he says that, following it, one could
not arrive at the theory either of lunations or of
eclipses."

"Where does he say anything so stupid?"

"In his *discorsi academici*."[38]

"I haven't them, but I will get them."

He wrote down the title.

"But Tassoni," he went on, "criticized your Petrarch[39] very well."

"And thereby disgraced his taste and his reading, as
did Muratori."[40]

"Here he is. Admit that his erudition is immense."

*"Est ubi peccat"* ("He is sometimes wrong").[41]

He opened a door, and I saw an archive of nearly a
hundred bulky packages.

"That," he said, "is my correspondence. You see
nearly fifty thousand [42] letters, which I have answered."

"Have you copies of your answers?"

"Of most of them. It is the duty of a valet whom I
keep for no other purpose."

"I know printers who would give a great deal of money
to possess themselves of this treasure."

"Beware of printers when you are ready to give something to the public, if you have not already begun."

"I will begin when I am old."

And in this connection I quoted a macaronic verse of Merlin Cocai.[43]

"What is that?"

"It is a verse from a famous poem[44] in twenty-four cantos."

"Famous?"

"And what is more, worthy to be; but to appreciate it one must know the Mantuan dialect."

"I shall understand it. Have it sent me."

"I will present it to you tomorrow."

"I shall be obliged to you."

We were fetched from there, and we spent two hours in conversation with the company, in which the great, brilliant poet kept everyone amused, always applauded though satirical and often caustic, but always laughing and never failing to raise a laugh. He maintained a princely establishment, and only at his house did one find choice fare. He was then sixty-six years of age and had an income of a hundred and twenty thousand livres. They who said and say that he became rich only by cheating the booksellers are mistaken. On the contrary, the booksellers cheated him badly, except the Cramers,[45] whose fortune he made. He gave them all his works for nothing, and thus it was that they circulated so widely. At the time I was there he gave them *La Princesse de Babylone*,[46] a charming tale which he wrote in three days.

My Epicurean Syndic came to the "Scales" for me as he had promised. He took me to a house on the right-hand side of the next street, which runs uphill. He presented me to three young ladies,[47] two of them sisters, and all made for love though one could not call them beautiful. An easy and gracious welcome, intelligent faces, and a promise of gaiety which was not disappointed. The half hour before supper was spent in decent but unrestrained conversation; during supper, however, the Syndic having set the tone, I foresaw what would happen after supper.

The day being hot, on the pretext of cooling ourselves, and being sure that no one would come to interrupt us, we were soon very nearly in the state of nature. I should have given offense if I had not followed the example of the four others. What an orgy! We rose to such a pitch of gaiety that, having recited Grécourt's[48] *Y grec*, I took it upon myself to demonstrate to the three girls in turn why the decree *Gaudeant bene nati* ("Let the well-born rejoice") had been promulgated. I saw the Syndic pluming himself on the present of my person which he had made to the three girls, who, from what I saw, must have fared very poorly with him, whose concupiscence affected only his head. It was their sense of obligation which an hour after midnight made them give me an ejaculation I really needed. I repeatedly kissed the six fair hands which humbled themselves to the task, which is always humiliating to any woman made for love, but which could not be so in the farce we had played, for having had the kindness to spare them, I had, with the help of the voluptuous Syndic, done them the same service. They thanked me endlessly, and I saw that they were in raptures when the Syndic invited me for the next day.

But it was I who thanked him again and again when he saw me to my inn. He told me that he alone had been responsible for bringing up the three girls, and that I was the first man whose acquaintance he had allowed them. He begged me to continue to be on my guard against making them pregnant, for it would be a fatal misfortune for them in a city as captiously strict on the point as Geneva.

The next day I wrote Monsieur de Voltaire an epistle in blank verse, which cost me more trouble than if I had rhymed it. I sent it to him with Teofilo Folengo's[49] poem; and I made a great mistake in sending it, for I should have known he would not like it. I then went to Mr. Fox's, where the two Englishmen offered me my re-

venge. I lost a hundred louis. After dinner they left for
Lausanne.

Having learned from the Syndic himself that his three
girls were not rich, I went to a jeweler to have six doblones de a ocho[50] melted, ordering him to make me three
balls of two ounces each immediately. I knew how I could
go about giving them to the girls without humiliating
them.

At noon I went to Monsieur de Voltaire's, who was not
visible, but Madame Denis made up to me for it. She had
a sound intelligence, excellent taste, learning without pretension, and a great dislike for the King of Prussia. She
asked me for news of my beautiful housekeeper, and she
was very glad to hear that the Ambassador's major-domo
had married her. She asked me to tell her how I had escaped from the Leads, and I promised to satisfy her request some other day.

Monsieur de Voltaire did not come to the table. He did
not appear until about five o'clock, carrying a letter.

"Do you know," he asked me, "the Marchese Albergati Capacelli,[51] Senator of Bologna, and Count Paradisi?"[52]

"I do not know Paradisi, but I know Signor Albergati
by sight and reputation; he is not a Senator but a
'Forty,'[53] born in Bologna, where the Forty are fifty."

"Heaven preserve us! What a riddle!"

"Do you know him?"

"No; but he sends me Goldoni's[54] plays, Bologna
sausages, the translation of my *Tancrède*,[55] and he is
coming to see me."

"He will not come, he is not so foolish."

"What do you mean by that? Though it is true that
coming to see me is foolish."

"I am talking about Albergati. He knows he would be
the loser by it, for he enjoys the idea you may have of
him. He is sure that if he comes to visit you, you will see

his nothingness or his whole bag of tricks, and good-by illusion! In other respects he is a worthy gentleman with an income of six thousand zecchini and theatromania.[56] He is a good actor and the author[57] of prose comedies which are not funny.''

"You paint a pretty picture of him. But how can he be both forty and fifty?''

"As noon at Basel is eleven o'clock." [58]

"I understand—just as your Council of Ten numbers seventeen." [59]

"Even so. But the accursed Forty of Bologna are another matter.''

"Why accursed?''

"Because they are not answerable to the Exchequer, and so they commit all the crimes they please and go to reside outside the State, where they still live on their revenues.''

"That's a blessing, not a curse; but let us continue. No doubt the Marchese Albergati is a man of letters.''

"He writes well, for he knows his language; but he bores his reader because he enjoys the sound of his own voice and he is diffuse. And he has nothing in his head.''

"He is an actor, you said.''

"Excellent when he plays something of his own, especially in the part of the lover.''

"Is he handsome?''

"On the stage, but not in ordinary life. His face has no expression.''

"But his plays are liked?''

"Not at all. They would be booed if people understood them.''

"And what do you say of Goldoni?''

"He is our Molière.''

"Why does he call himself poet to the Duke of Parma?'' [60]

"To give himself a title, for the Duke knows nothing

about it. He also calls himself an advocate,[61] but he is one only *in posse*. He is a good writer of comedies, and that is all. I am his friend, and everyone in Venice knows it. In society he does not shine, he is as insipid and sweet as marshmallow.''

''So someone wrote me. He is poor, and he wants to leave Venice. The owners of the theaters where his plays are performed must not like that.''

''There was talk of giving him a pension; but the decision went against it. It was thought that if he had a pension he would stop working.''

''Cuma[62] refused Homer a pension for fear that all blind people would demand one.''

We spent the day very pleasantly. He thanked me for the *Macaronicon*[63] and promised to read it. He introduced a Jesuit[64] whom he had in his service, saying that his name was Adam but that he was not the first of men; and I was told that, amusing himself playing backgammon with him, when he lost he often threw the dice and the dicebox in his face.

I was scarcely back at my inn in the evening before I received my three gold balls, and a moment later I saw my dear Syndic, who took me to his orgy.

On the way he discussed the sense of modesty which prevents our displaying the parts which from childhood we have been taught to keep covered. He said that modesty of this kind could often derive from a virtue; but that the virtue was weaker than the force of education, since it could not resist an attack when the aggressor knew what he was about. The easiest strategy, in his opinion, was not to admit its existence, to show that one had no regard for it and ridicule it; the thing to do was to surprise it by setting the example, leaping the barriers of shame, and victory was certain; the boldness of the attacker made the modesty of the person attacked vanish instantly.

"Clement of Alexandria," [65] he said, "a man of learning and a philosopher, said that the modesty which seems so firmly rooted in women's minds was really only in their underclothes, because as soon as they were persuaded to take those off not a shadow of it remained."

We found the three young ladies, lightly clad in linen dresses, sitting on a large sofa, and we sat down in front of them on armless chairs. The half hour before supper was devoted to charming badinage like that of the evening before and to quantities of kisses. It was after supper that the combat began.

As soon as we were sure that the maid would not come to interrupt us again, we made ourselves comfortable. The Syndic began by taking from his pocket a package of English coveralls, praising that admirable defense against a misfortune which could give rise to dread repentance. They knew of it, and they seemed satisfied, laughing at the shape which the inflated instrument took before their eyes, when I said that I certainly loved their honor even more than their beauty, but that I could never consent to seek happiness with them by wrapping myself in a piece of dead skin.

"Here," I say, taking from my pocket the three gold balls, "is what will safeguard you against any untoward consequences. After fifteen years' experience I am in a position to assure you that with these balls you have nothing to fear and that in future you will not need these miserable sheaths. Honor me with your complete confidence in this respect, and accept this small present from a Venetian who adores you."

"We are grateful to you," says the elder of the sisters; "but how does one use this pretty ball to avert a disastrous big belly?"

"All that is necessary is for the ball to be in the cabinet of love during the combat. It is an antipathic virtue in the metal which prevents pregnancy."

"But," remarks the cousin,[66] "the little ball may easily slip out of the place before the action is over."

"Not at all, when one knows how to go about it. There is a posture which will prevent the ball from coming out by its own weight."

"Show us," says the Syndic, taking up a candle to light me when I put the ball in place.

The charming cousin had said too much to withdraw and refuse the proof which her cousins wanted. I placed her at the foot of the bed in such a way that it was impossible for the ball, which I inserted, to fall out; but it fell out after the act, and she saw that I had cheated her, but she pretended not to notice it. She picked up the ball, and she challenged the two sisters to do as much. They underwent the operation with every sign of interest.

The Syndic, having no faith in the virtue of the ball, would not trust it. He limited his pleasure to looking on, and he had no reason to complain. After half an hour's respite I began the ceremonies again without the balls, assuring them that they ran no risk, and I kept my word.

When I left, I saw the three girls overwhelmed; they felt they had contracted obligations to me and had given me nothing. Bestowing countless caresses on the Syndic, they asked him how he had guessed that I was the man who deserved to be let into their great secret.

As we were leaving, the Syndic urged the three girls to ask me to stay another day in Geneva for their sake, and I assented. He was to be occupied the next day. For my part I really needed a day's rest. He saw me to my inn, treating me to the most flattering compliments.

After sleeping soundly for ten hours I felt fit to go and enjoy Monsieur de Voltaire's charming company; but the great man was pleased on that day to indulge in raillery, ill-humored jests, and sarcasm. He knew that I was to leave the next day.

He began at table by saying that he thanked me for

my present of Merlin Cocai, certainly made with good intentions, but that he did not thank me for the praise I had
bestowed on the poem, since I had been the cause of his
wasting four hours reading nonsense. My hair stood on
end, but I controlled myself. I replied quite calmly that
on another occasion he might find it worthy of the greater
praise which he himself could bestow. I cited several ex-
amples of the inadequacy of a first reading.

"True enough—but as for your Merlin, I leave him to
you. I have put him beside Chapelain's[67] *La Pucelle.*"

"Which pleases all competent critics, despite its versi-
fication. It is a good poem, and Chapelain was a poet; his
genius has not escaped me."

My statement could not but offend him, and I should
have known it after he told me that he would put the
*Macaronicon* I had given him beside *La Pucelle.* I knew,
too, that a filthy poem by the same name, which was
widely circulated, was supposed to be by him; but since
he disavowed it[68] I thought he would conceal the pain
which my frankness must have caused him; but not a bit
of it—he contradicted me sharply and I became no less
sharp. I told him that Chapelain had the merit of making
his subject agreeable without currying the favor of his
readers by filth and impiety.

"Such," I said, "is the opinion of my master Monsieur
de Crébillon." [69]

"You cite a great judge. But in what is my confrère
Crébillon your master?"

"He taught me to speak French in less than two years.
To show him my gratitude I translated his *Rhadamiste*[70]
into Italian Alexandrine verse. I am the first Italian who
dared to adapt that meter to our language."

"The first, if you will pardon me, was my friend Pier
Jacopo Martelli." [71]

"Pardon *me.*"

"Why, I have his works,[72] printed at Bologna, in my
room."

"You can only have read verses of fourteen syllables[73] without alternating masculine and feminine rhyme. Yet he believed he was imitating Alexandrines, and his preface made me laugh. Perhaps you did not read it."

"Monsieur, I have a passion for reading prefaces. Martelli proves that to Italian ears his verses sound the same as Alexandrines do to the French."

"He is egregiously wrong, and I ask you to be the judge. Your masculine verse has only twelve syllables and your feminine thirteen; all Martelli's verses have fourteen, except those which end in a long syllable, which at the end of a verse always counts as two. Observe that Martelli's first hemistich is always and forever of seven syllables, whereas in the French Alexandrine it is forever and always of six. Either your friend Pier Jacopo was deaf or he had a bad ear."

"Then in the theory of your verse you follow all our rules?"

"All of them, despite the difficulty; for nearly all our words end in a short syllable."

"And how was your new meter received?"

"It was not liked, because no one knew the way to recite my verses; but when I delivered them myself in our literary circles I triumphed."

"Do you remember a passage from your *Rhadamiste*?"

"As many as you please."

I then recited to him the same scene which I had recited to Crébillon in blank verse ten years earlier, and he seemed impressed. He said that the difficulty was not perceptible, and it was the greatest compliment he could pay me. In his turn he recited a passage from his *Tancrède*, which I believe he had not then published and which was later rightly judged a masterpiece.

We should have ended on good terms, but a line of Horace which I quoted to applaud one of his ideas led him to say that Horace was a great master of the drama because of his precepts, which would never grow stale.

"You break only one of them," I said, "but you break it like a great man."

"Which one?"

"You do not write *contentus paucis lectoribus* ('satisfied with a few readers')." [74]

"If Horace had had to fight superstition he would have written for everyone, as I do."

"You might, it seems to me, spare yourself the trouble of fighting it, for you will never succeed in destroying it, and even if you did, pray tell me with what you would fill its place."

*"I like that! When I deliver the human race from a ferocious monster which devours it, can I be asked what I will put in its place?"*

"It does not devour it; on the contrary, it is necessary to its existence."

"Loving the human race, I should wish to see it happy as I am, free; and superstition cannot be combined with freedom. What makes you think that servitude can make a people happy?"

"Then you would wish to see sovereignty in the people?"

"God forbid! One alone must govern."

"Then superstition is necessary, for without it the people will never obey the monarch."

"No monarch—for the name makes me see despotism, which I must hate as I do servitude."

"Then what would you have? If you want the ruler to be one man, I can only consider him a monarch."

"I want him to command a free people, then he will be its leader, and he cannot be called a monarch, for he can never be arbitrary."

"Addison[75] tells you that such a monarch, such a leader, is not among possible beings. I am for Hobbes.[76] Between two evils, one must choose the lesser. A people without superstition would be philosophical and philosophers will never obey. The people can be happy only if they are cursed, downtrodden, kept in chains.''

''If you have read me you will have found the proofs by which I demonstrate that superstition is the enemy of kings.''

''If I have read you! I have read and reread you—and especially when I am not of your opinion. Your first passion is love of humanity. *Est ubi peccas* ('You are sometimes wrong').[77] That love blinds you. Love humanity, but you can only love it as it is. It is incapable of the benefits you would lavish upon it; and, giving them, you would only make it more unhappy and more wicked. Leave it the monster which devours it; the monster is dear to it. I never laughed so much as when I saw Don Quixote[78] having a very hard time defending himself from the galley slaves to whom he had just magnanimously given their freedom.''

''Are you Venetians free?''

''As free as it is possible to be under an aristocratic government. The freedom we have is not as great as that which the English enjoy, but we are content. My imprisonment, for example, was an outright act of despotism; but knowing that I had myself abused my freedom, at certain moments I considered that they had been right to imprison me without the usual formalities.''

''At that rate no one is free in Venice.''

''Possibly; but grant that, to be free, it is enough to believe that one is so.''

''I will not so easily grant it. Even the aristocrats who are members of the government are not free—for example, they cannot travel without permission.''

''It is a law to which they deliberately subjected themselves in order to preserve their power. Would you say that a Bernese is not free because he is subject to the sumptuary laws?[79] It is he himself who is the lawmaker.''

It was to change the subject that he asked me where I had come from.

"From Roche. I should have been very sorry to leave Switzerland without seeing the famous Haller. I am paying homage to my learned contemporaries—and you will be the savory at the end of the feast."

"You must have enjoyed Monsieur Haller."

"I spent three excellent days with him."

"I congratulate you. One should go down on one's knees to that great man."

"I think so too; you do him justice, and for his sake I regret that he is not so fair to you."

"So! Then possibly we are both mistaken."

At this answer, whose whole merit is in its quickness, all the company applauded.

There was no more talk of literature, and I played a silent part until, Monsieur de Voltaire having withdrawn, I went up to Madame Denis and asked her if she had any commissions for me in Rome.

I left rather well pleased that on this last day I had reduced the gladiator to reason. But I was left with a grudge against him which for ten years made me criticize everything I read, old or new, which the great man had given or was giving the public. I repent of it now, despite the fact that when I read what I published against him[80] I find that my censures were based on sound reasoning. I should have kept quiet, respected him, and doubted my own judgments. I should have reflected that but for the raillery with which he offended me on the third day I should have thought him sublime in everything. This reflection alone should have kept me silent, but an angry man always believes he is right. Reading me, posterity will number me among the Zoiluses,[81] and the very humble amends I make him today will perhaps not be read.

I spent part of the night and the next day writing

down the three conversations I had with him, which I have now copied in abridged form. Toward nightfall the Syndic came for me, and we went to sup with his three young ladies.

In the five hours we spent there we indulged in all the extravagances I could invent. When I left, I promised to see them again on my return from Rome, and I kept my word. I departed from Geneva the next day after dining with my dear Syndic, who went with me as far as Annecy,[82] where I spent the night. The next day I dined at Aix-en-Savoie,[83] intending to spend the night at Chambéry;[84] but fate was against it.

Aix-en-Savoie is an ugly place where there are mineral waters and, at the end of summer, some people of fashion. I did not know it. I was dining quietly and in haste, intending to leave at once for Chambéry, when I see a company of gay and fashionable-looking people, both men and women, come in and prepare to sit down at the table. I watch them from where I sit, acknowledging their salutations with a bow. From their conversation I learn that they are all there to take the waters. A man of imposing appearance approaches me politely and asks if I am going to Turin; I reply that I am going to Marseilles.

Dinner is served, and they all sit down. I see attractive women and men of a stamp to be their husbands or their lovers. I decide that the place offers possibilities for amusement. They were all speaking French or Piedmontese, and they seemed to be people who did not stand on formality. I foresee that if I am asked I shall easily be persuaded to spend the night there.

Having finished dinner when they had not yet come to the roast, and my coachman not being able to leave for an hour, I go up to a pretty woman and congratulate her on the good which the waters of Aix must be doing her, since the appetite with which she was eating aroused it in anyone who watched her. She imperiously challenges me to prove that I am speaking the truth by sitting down beside her, and at the same time she offers me the slice of roast which she had been served. The chair being empty, I accept her challenge, and I eat as if I had not dined.

I then hear a voice saying: "It is the Abbé's place," and another voice answers: "He left half an hour ago." "Why did he go?" asks a third person; "he was to be here a week longer." Voices are lowered, the conversation is continued in whispers, but the departure of some abbé being of no interest to me I continue to eat, confining my attention to the lady, who serves me the best bits. I tell Leduc, who was behind my chair, to have champagne brought for me; the lady is fond of it and drinks with me; and the whole table orders champagne. I see that she is animated, I flirt with her; and I ask her if she is always so strict in holding all the men who offer her homage to their word. She replies that not all of them are worth the trouble. Pretty and witty—I try to think of a pretext for putting off my departure, and chance gives it to me.

"For once," says a lady to the beauty who was drinking with me, "an empty place proves to be just the thing."

"Very much so, for my neighbor was boring me."

"Did he have no appetite?" I ask her.

"Bah! gamesters have none except for money."

"Usually; but you have unusual powers, for I have never in my life dined twice."

"It was because you were challenged. I am sure you will not sup."

"Let us wager that I sup."

"We will wager the supper, but I want to see it."

"Done."

The whole table applauds; the lady blushes with pleasure, and I order Leduc to tell the coachman that I will not leave until the next day.

"It is my part," says the lady, "to order the supper."

"Yes, for it is you who will pay for it. My duty, in a wager of this kind, is to keep up with you. If I eat as much as you do, I have won."

At the end of dinner the man of imposing appearance called for cards and made a small bank at faro. I expected as much. He spread before him twenty-five Piedmontese pistoles,[85] and some silver money to amuse the ladies. The bank amounted to about forty louis. Remaining simply a spectator for the first deal, I saw that the banker was playing in a manner to do him credit.

While he was shuffling for the second deal the beautiful lady asked me why I was not playing. I whispered to her that she had made me lose my appetite for money; she smiled. Thinking that after this declaration I was bound to play, I took forty louis from my purse and lost them in two deals. I got up, answering the banker's condolences by saying that I never risked more than the amount in the bank. One of the company then asked me if I knew an Abbé Gilbert;[86] I answered that I had known a man of that name in Paris who came from Lyons and who owed me his ears, so I would cut them off wherever I met him. The questioner did not reply, and the company remained silent, pretending to notice nothing. I saw that the Abbé Gilbert must be the man whose place I had occupied. Having seen me arrive, he had taken flight. At my house in Little Poland I had entrusted him with a ring which had cost me five thousand florins in Holland, and he had decamped the next day.

Everyone having left the room, I ask Leduc if I am well lodged. He takes me to see a large unfurnished room in an old house a hundred paces from the inn, all the other rooms in which were occupied. The innkeeper told me he had no other room and that he would have a bed, chairs, and tables brought at once. I had to make the best of it. I told Leduc that he would sleep in my room, and to have all my luggage taken there immediately.

"What do you make of the Abbé Gilbert?" he said. "I

did not recognize him till just as he was setting out, and I thought for a moment of taking him by the collar."

"It is a thought which you should have executed."

"Some other time."

Leaving the room, I see a man approaching me who congratulates himself on being my neighbor and offers to accompany me if I am going to see the fountain.[87] I thank him and accept. He was a tall, thin, blond man who at the age of fifty still had his hair, who must once have been handsome, and whose excessive affability should have made me suspect him; but I needed someone to chat with. On our way to the fountain he gave me an account of the people with whom I had dined. He began by telling me that the waters of Aix were good, but that no one in the company I had seen was there to take them.

"I am the only one," he said, "who is obliged to take them, for I am consumptive; I grow thinner every day, and if I do not find an effectual remedy I cannot live long."

"Then all these gentlemen have come here only to amuse themselves?"

"To gamble. They are all Piedmontese or Savoyards. As I come from Lorraine, I am the only Frenchman. My father, who is eighty years of age, is the Marquis Desarmoises.[88] He lives to infuriate me, for because of a marriage I contracted without his consent he disinherited me; but since I am the only son I shall have everything when he dies, if I outlive him. I have a house in Lyons; but I never never go there because of my elder daughter, with whom I have the misfortune to be in love. My wife prevents me from making her listen to reason."

"That is odd. Otherwise you think she would take pity on her amorous father?"

"She might, for she is a good, obedient girl."

## CHAPTER XI

*My adventures at Aix-en-Savoie. My second*
*M. M. Madame Z.*

---

WALKING TOWARD the fountain in the company
of a man who, having no acquaintance with me, was telling me these things in perfect good faith and with not
the slightest fear of horrifying me and making me think
him a criminal of the deepest dye, I reflected that, supposing me to be the same sort of person as himself, he
could only think he was doing me great honor. But,
wanting to know him still better:

"Despite the Marquis your father's severity," I said,
"you no doubt live very well."

"Very badly. I have a pension from the Department of
Foreign Affairs as a retired courier. I let my wife have
it to live on, and for my part I manage by traveling. I
play backgammon very well, and all gambling games; by
winning more than I lose, I live."

"Is what you have just told me known to all the company here?"

"To them all. Why should I hide it? I am a man of honor and I have a dangerous sword."

"I do not doubt it. Do you allow Mademoiselle Desarmoises to have a lover? If she is pretty—"

"Extremely pretty; I should not object; but my wife is pious. If you go to Lyons I will give you a letter to her."

"Thank you, but I am going to Italy. May I ask you who the gentleman is who made bank?"

"He is the famous Pancalieri, Marquis de Prié[1] since the death of his father, whom, since you are a Venetian, you must have known as Ambassador. The gentleman who asked you if you knew the Abbé Gilbert is the Chevalier $Z$,[2] husband of the lady with whom you are to sup. The others are all Piedmontese or Savoyard Counts or Marquises; two or three are sons of merchants, and the women are all related to one another or mistresses of some man in the company. They are all professional gamesters and very sharp; when a stranger passes through here, if he plays he can hardly escape them, for they are all in it together. They think they have you hooked; beware."

Toward nightfall we returned to the inn, where we found all the gamesters at various gambling games. My new friend played draughts with a Count Scarnafigi.[3] Since I had refused all invitations to play, the husband of my beauty offered to play faro with me, each dealing in turn, for forty zecchini. I had just lost that amount when supper was served. The lady found me no less gay on that account, and she paid the wager very honorably. During supper her glances, the source of which I knew, showed me only too clearly that she intended to dupe me, so I thought I was out of danger on the article of love; but I should have feared Fortune, who always favors bankers at faro and who had already given me a scratch. I should have left, but I did not have the strength of mind. All I could do was to promise myself I would be extremely careful, and since I had plenty of money at my disposal in good paper, and a sufficiency in cash, I should not have found a course of prudent play difficult.

Immediately after supper the Marquis de Prié made a bank which, adding up the gold and the silver, might be worth three hundred zecchini. This contemptible sum showed me that I could lose much and win little, for it was obvious that he would have made me a bank of a thousand zecchini if he had them. So I placed fifty lisbonini[4] before me, modestly saying that when I had lost them I would go to bed. Halfway through the third deal I broke the bank. The Marquis said he would put up another two hundred louis; I replied that I wanted to leave at dawn, and I withdrew.

Just as I was getting into bed Desarmoises came and asked me to let him have twelve louis, assuring me that he would repay them. I give them to him instantly and, after embracing me warmly, he said that Madame *Z* had undertaken to keep me in Aix for at least another day. I laughed. I ask Leduc if the coachman has been notified, and he replies that he will be at my door at five o'clock in the morning. Desarmoises leaves, saying that he would wager I will not leave. I go to bed, scoffing at his idea, and fall asleep.

The next day at dawn the coachman comes to tell me that, one of his horses being sick, he cannot leave. I see that Desarmoises has spoken the truth, but I laugh. I order the coachman out of my room, and I send Leduc to ask the innkeeper for post horses. The innkeeper comes and tells me he has no horses, and that to procure some would take all morning. The Marquis de Prié, having left an hour after midnight, had emptied his stable. So I tell him I will dine at Aix, but that I count on his promise and so will leave at two o'clock.

I go out to visit the fountain and, stopping at the stable, I see one of my coachman's horses lying down and the man himself crying. I believe there is no trickery, and I console him by paying him, saying that I have no further need for him. I go to the fountain. And now, my dear reader, for something straight out of a romance, but which is nevertheless true. If you think it fictitious, you are wrong.

Twenty paces before I reach the waters I see two nuns coming from that direction, both veiled, one whose figure leads me to conclude that she is young, the other obviously old. The thing which strikes me is their habit, for it is the same as that of my dear M. M., whom I had last seen on July 24, 1755. That had been five years ago. Their sudden appearance did not suffice to make me believe the nun I saw was M. M., but it was enough to make me curious. They were walking toward the fields, I turn back to intercept them, to see them face to face, and to show myself. But I tremble when I see the younger one, who was walking ahead of the older, raise her veil; I see M. M. I could not possibly doubt it, I had too much cause to know her. I walk toward her, she quickly lowers her veil, and she takes another path, obviously to avoid me. I instantly fall in with whatever reasons she may have, and I turn back, but without losing sight of her; I follow her at a distance to see where she will stop. Five hundred paces farther on I see her enter a solitary peasant's house. It is enough. I go back to the fountain to learn what I can.

"The charming and unfortunate M. M.," I said to myself on the way, "has fled from her convent, desperate, perhaps mad, for why did she not discard the habit of her order? Perhaps she has come to take the waters here with permission from Rome, and that is why she has a nun with her and must wear her habit. But such a long journey can only have been made on some false pretext. Can she have yielded to some inclination, of which the fatal result has been pregnancy? She may be in difficulties, and now she is glad to have found me. She will have found me ready to do anything for her she may want, and my constant friendship will convince her that I was not unworthy to possess her heart."

So musing, I come to the waters, where I see the whole company from the inn. They all say they are delighted that I have not gone. I ask the Chevalier *Z* after his wife, he replies that she is fond of lying in bed, and that I would do well to go and make her get up. I take leave of them to go to her, and the local doctor comes up to me and says the waters of Aix will make me twice as healthy. I ask him point-blank if he is the doctor of a pretty nun I had seen. He replies that she takes the waters but talks to no one.

"Where is she from?"

"Nobody knows; she is lodging in a peasant's house."

I leave the doctor, and nothing can stop me from going to talk with the peasant who is lodging her; but when I am a hundred paces from the house I see a peasant woman coming to meet me. She says that her ladyship the nun asks me to come back at nine o'clock, that the lay sister will be asleep then, and she can talk with me. I assure her that I will not fail to come, and I give her a louis.

I go back to the inn, certain that I will talk with the adorable M. M. at nine o'clock. I ask where Madame *Z*'s room is, and, entering without knocking, I say that her husband has sent me to make her get up.

"I thought you had left."

"I shall leave at two o'clock."

I find the young woman even more appetizing in bed than at the table. I help her put on a corset, and I become ardent; but she overawes me. I sit down at her feet, I talk to her of the sudden blow which her beauty has dealt my soul, and of my unhappiness at having to leave without giving her adequate proof of my ardor; she laughs and answers that I am my own master and can stay if I will.

"Encourage me to hope for your favors, and I will put off leaving until tomorrow."

"You are in too much of a hurry, and I beg you to calm yourself."

Making the best of the little she let me do, though pretending, of course, to yield to force, I had to put myself to rights on the appearance of her husband, who, however, made some noise before coming in. It was she who told him that she had persuaded me to defer my departure until the next day. He congratulated her, and, saying that he owes me a revenge, he produces cards and sits down on the other side of his wife, making her serve as our table. I stop when a servant comes to announce dinner. Madame says that, not having time to dress, she will dine in bed; her husband says we will dine with her, and I agree. He goes to order dinner, and, on the strength of having lost another eighteen or twenty louis, I tell her clearly that I will leave after dinner if she will not promise to be kind to me in the course of the day. She replies that she will expect me for breakfast the next morning at nine, and that we will be alone. She gives me a more than trifling down payment, and I promise to stay.

We dine with her, sitting beside her bed; I send Leduc to tell the innkeeper that I will not leave until the next day after dinner, and I see both husband and wife well pleased. Madame wishes to get up, I leave her, promising to return in an hour to play hundred-point piquet with her. I go to my room for money, and I find Desarmoises, who assures me that the coachman had been paid two louis to substitute a sick horse for his own. I laugh and say that I cannot win on one side without losing on the other, that I am in love with Madame *Z*, and that I will put off my departure until she has satisfied me.

I went back to her room and played piquet at a louis a hundred with her until eight o'clock. I then excused myself on the pretext of a bad headache, paying her ten or twelve louis and reminding her that she was to wait for me in bed and give me breakfast at nine o'clock. I left her surrounded by people.

By the light of the moon I walked alone to the house where I was to talk with M. M., impatient to know the outcome of my visit, on which my destiny might depend. Suspecting the possibility of a trap, I had a pair of unfailing pistols in my pocket and my sword under my arm. At twenty paces from the house I see the peasant woman, who says that, since the nun cannot come downstairs, I must be prepared to climb up to her room, entering through the window. She takes me behind the house and shows me a ladder leaning against the window by which I am to go in. Seeing no light, I would have decided not to go; but hearing "Come and fear nothing" spoken to me by M. M. herself from the window, which in any case was not too high, I have no more doubts, I climb up, I enter, and I clasp her in my arms, covering her face with kisses. I ask her in Venetian why she has no candle, and I beg her to satisfy my impatience at once by telling me the whole story of what seemed to me a miracle.

But never in my life have I been so surprised as when I heard a voice which was not M. M.'s reply, not in Venetian but in French, that I did not need a candle to tell her what Monsieur de Cou. . .[5] had decided to do to extricate her from her fatal situation.

"I do not know Monsieur de Cou. . . ; you are not the nun I saw this morning. You are not a Venetian."

"Alas for me! I have made a mistake; but I am the nun you saw this morning. I am French; I implore you in God's name to be discreet, and to go, for I have nothing to say to you. Speak in a whisper, for if my lay sister, who is asleep, should wake up I am ruined."

"Have no doubt of my discretion. What deceived me was a striking resemblance. If you had not shown me your face I should not have come here; forgive me the auda-

cious caresses my love bestowed on you, thinking you
another.''

"You have amazed me. Would that I were the nun in
whom you are interested! I am in the most terrible of
quandaries.''

"If ten louis, Madame, can be of service to you I beg
you to accept them.''

"Thank you, but I have no need of money. Permit me
also to return the louis you sent me.''

"I gave it to the peasant woman, and you surprise me
more and more. What is your calamity, which money cannot cure?''

"It may be that God has sent you to help me. Perhaps
you will give me good advice. So listen to me, just for a
quarter of an hour.''

"Yes, and with the greatest interest. Let us sit down.''

"Alas, there is neither chair nor bed here.''

"Then speak.''

"I am from Grenoble. I was forced to take the veil at
Chambéry. Two years later Monsieur de Cou. . . so far
led me astray that I received him in my arms in the convent garden, which he entered by climbing the wall.
Finding that I was pregnant, I told him so. The idea that
I should bear the child in my convent being horrible, for
they would have locked me in a cell to die, he thought of
getting me out by the order of a doctor, who would
threaten me with death if I did not come here to take
these incomparable waters to cure me of the disease which
the same doctor would say I have. The doctor was found,
and Princess XXX,[6] who is always at Chambéry, let into
the secret, persuaded the Bishop[7] to grant me three
months' leave and to obtain the Abbess's consent to it.
Having made my arrangements, I thought I should be
leaving at the end of my seventh month; but apparently
I was mistaken, for the three months are almost over and
I am still pregnant. I absolutely must go back to the con-

*Playing Piquet*

*Peasant House*

vent, and you will understand that I cannot bring myself to it. The lay sister whom the Abbess put to watch over me is the cruelest of women. She has orders not to let me speak to anyone and to keep me from showing myself. It was she who ordered me to turn back when she saw you change your direction to meet me. I raised my veil to let you see that I was she whom I believed you were seeking; luckily she did not notice it. The viper wants me to go back to the convent in three days on the ground that my sickness, which she believes to be dropsy, is incurable. She would not let me talk with the doctor, whom I might have won over by telling him the truth. I long for death. I am twenty-one years old.''

''Do not weep so. But how could you have given birth here without your lay sister being aware of it?''

''The peasant woman who lets me this lodging, and in whom I confided, assured me that as soon as I felt the first pains a soporific which she bought in Annecy would put her to sleep. It is from the effect of the same drug that she is asleep now in the room under this garret.''

''Why was I not let in by the door?''

''To hide you from the peasant woman's brother; he is malicious too.''

''But what reason did you have to believe Monsieur de Cou. . . had sent me?''

''Because ten or twelve days ago I wrote him and described my distress so vividly that I think it impossible he will not find some way to rescue me. I thought he had sent you.''

''Are you sure your letter reached him?''

''The peasant woman herself put it in the post at Annecy.''

''You should have written to the Princess.''

''I did not dare.''

''I will go to the Princess myself, or to Monsieur de Cou. . . , or anywhere, even to the Bishop to get you an extension, for you cannot go back to the convent in your present condition. Decide, for I can do nothing without your consent. Do you want to come with me? I will bring you clothes tomorrow and take you to Italy, and I will look after you as long as you live.''

Instead of an answer I hear only the sad sound of her sobs. Not knowing what more to say, I promised I would come back the next day to learn what decision she had taken, for she had to decide on one course or another. I went down by the same ladder, and, giving the peasant woman another louis, I told her I would come back the next day but that she must arrange to let me in by the door and must double the dose of opium she had given the lay sister.

I went home to bed, all in all very glad that I had been wrong in my idea that the nun might be my dear M. M.; but having seen such a likeness I was extremely curious to see her more closely. I was sure she would grant me the favor the next day. I laughed over the kisses I had given her. An unspoken presentiment told me that I would be of use to her. I felt that, when the worst came to the worst, I could not abandon her; and I congratulated myself when I saw that, to do a good deed, I did not need to be led into it by my senses, for as soon as I learned that it was not on M. M. that I had lavished my kisses I felt that they had been thrown away. It did not even occur to me to embrace her when I left.

Desarmoises told me in the morning that, not seeing me at supper, the whole company had racked their brains trying to guess where I might be. Madame *Z* had praised me in the highest terms, heroically withstanding the raillery of the two other ladies and boasting that she could keep me in Aix as long as she should stay there.

I had really become curious about her, and I should have been sorry to leave the place without having had her in due form at least once.

I enter her room at nine o'clock and find her dressed. I protest, she says it should make no difference to me, I sulk, and I take chocolate with her in silence. She offers me my revenge at hundred-point piquet, but I decline and get up to leave. She asks me to escort her to the fountain, and I reply that if she takes me for a child she is wrong, that I do not care to pretend I am pleased with her when I am not, and that she can get anyone she likes to escort her to the fountain.

"Good-by, Madame."

So saying, I went downstairs, not listening to what she was saying to keep me with her. At the inn door I told the innkeeper I would leave without fail at three o'clock, and, being at her window, she heard me. I went straight to the fountain, where the Chevalier Z asked me how his wife was; I told him I had left her in her room in good health. We saw her arrive a half hour later with a stranger who had just arrived and whom a Monsieur de Saint-Maurice greeted warmly. Madame Z calmly left him and took my arm. After complaining of my behavior she said that she had wanted to put me to a test and that if I loved her I should defer my departure again and come to breakfast with her the next morning at eight o'clock. I replied, quietly but seriously, that I would think it over. I maintained the same attitude all through dinner, having said two or three times that I would certainly leave at three o'clock; but needing to find some excuse for not leaving, since I had promised to visit the nun, I let myself be persuaded to make a bank at faro.

So I went to fetch all the gold I had, and I saw the whole company as surprised as they were pleased when I placed before me some four hundred louis in Spanish and French gold coins and fifteen or twenty in silver. I announced that I would stop at eight o'clock. The new arrival laughed and said that perhaps the bank might not last that long. It was three o'clock. I asked Desarmoises to serve as my croupier; and I began dealing, with all the slowness demanded by the presence of eighteen or twenty punters and my knowledge that they were all professional gamblers. At each deal I opened a fresh pack of cards.

About five o'clock, my bank being the loser, a carriage arrives. We are told that it is three Englishmen coming from Geneva and changing horses to go on to Chambéry. A moment later I see them enter and I greet them. It was Mr. Fox and his two friends who had played quinze with me. My croupier gives them each a *livret*,[8] they accept with pleasure, and room is made for them. Each of them punts at ten louis, stakes on two and three cards, makes *paroli, sept et le va,* and the *quinze*[9] as well; I saw that my bank was in danger of being broken, and, putting a good face[10] on it, I encouraged them. God being neutral, they could only lose; and he was neutral. At the third deal all their purses were empty. Their horses were harnessed.

While I was shuffling, the youngest of them takes a bill of exchange from his portfolio and, after showing it to his two friends, asks me if I will accept it on a card without knowing how much it is for.

"Yes," I replied, "if you will tell me on whom it is drawn and provided that the amount is not more than my bank."

After thinking for a little and looking at the bank, he said that his bill of exchange was not as much as my bank and that it was a sight bill on Zappata at Turin. I accept. He cuts, and puts his bill on the ace. The two others say they are in for a half share. The ace never turning up, I am left with twelve cards, and I calmly tell the Englishman that he is at liberty to withdraw. He refuses. I deal two hands; the ace does not appear; I had eight cards; there were four aces, and my last card was not an ace.

"My Lord," I said, "the odds are two to one that the ace is here; I am willing to let you off, withdraw."

"You are too generous," he answered; "deal."

The ace appeared and not in a doublet; I at once put the bill of exchange in my pocket without unfolding it, and the Englishmen left, laughing and thanking me. A minute later Fox came back and, roaring with laughter, asked me to lend him fifty louis. I instantly gave them to him with the greatest pleasure. He returned them to me in London three years later.

The whole company was curious to know the value of the bill of exchange, but I wanted to have the pleasure of satisfying no one's curiosity. Being curious myself, I found when I was alone that it was for eight thousand Piedmontese lire.[11]

After the Englishmen departed, Fortune decided to favor my bank. I stopped about eight o'clock, there being no one left except the ladies, who had won. All the men had lost. I won over a thousand louis, and Desarmoises received twenty-five, for which he was grateful. After stopping in my room to lock up my money, I went to see the nun.

The good peasant woman let me in by the door, saying that everyone was asleep and that she had not needed to double the dose to put the lay sister to sleep for she had never waked. What was this! I go up to the garret, and by the light of a candle I see my nun with her face covered by a veil. The peasant woman had put a long sack filled with straw against the wall; it served us as a seat, and a bottle on the floor served as the candlestick for the candle which gave us light.

"What decision have you reached, Madame?"

"None, for something has happened which has us in despair. My lay sister has been asleep for twenty-eight hours."

"She will die in convulsions or of apoplexy tonight,

if you do not call a doctor who can perhaps summon her back to life with castoreum."[12]

"We have thought of that, but we do not dare. You see what the consequences would be. Whether he cures her or not, he will say we gave her the poison."

"God in heaven! I pity you. Even if you call the doctor now, I fear it is too late and you would call him to no purpose. Considering everything, you must bow to the decrees of Providence and let her die. The harm is done, and I know no remedy for it."

"We must at least think of her salvation and call a priest."

"A priest is certain to be ignorant and, wanting to appear the opposite, will tell everything. No priest, Madame; you shall have him sent for when she is dead; you will give him something to drink, and he, far from thinking that you could have poisoned her, will be concerned only to soothe your tears."

"Then must we let her die?"

"No. We must leave her to nature."

"If she dies I will send a messenger to the Abbess, who will send me another lay sister."

"And you will gain at least a week; and meanwhile you will perhaps bear your child; so you see that your happiness may depend on this misfortune. Do not weep, Madame; let us bow to the will of God; permit the peasant woman to come here, for I must impress the importance of silence on her and the absolute need for the utmost prudence in the matter, which may be the ruin of us all, for if it were discovered that I came here I should be thought the poisoner."

Summoned, the peasant woman comes up, and she understands everything. She realizes her own danger and promises me that she will not go for the priest until she sees that the lay sister is dead. I make her accept ten louis, to use as she sees best in the atrocious situation in which we all found ourselves. Seeing herself rich, she kisses my hands, she weeps, she kneels and promises to do whatever I tell her. She goes downstairs again.

The nun, sinking into somber reflections, weeps all the more; and, considering herself guilty of the murder, she thinks she sees Hell open, anguish chokes her, and she falls in a faint at the other end of the sack. Not knowing what to do for her, I run to the stairs and call the peasant woman, who comes up, then goes down again for vinegar. Having no alcoholic essence, I raise her veil and put a pinch of errhine into her nose, and I laugh, remembering how seasonably I had given a pinch of it to Madame . . . at Soleure.[13] The peasant woman comes back with vinegar, and, the errhine beginning to act, the nun sneezes; but I am as if petrified when, turning, she lets me see her face. I see M. M.'s, and such a perfect likeness that I cannot think I am deceived. I stand there motionless, letting the woman take off her coif to rub her temples with the vinegar she has brought. What recalls me from my amazement is her black hair and, a moment later, her eyes of the same color, which the strong sternutative had made her open. I am then convinced that she is not M. M., whose eyes were blue, but I fall madly in love with her. I take her in my arms, and the woman, seeing that she has revived, departs. I cover her with kisses, and she cannot defend herself because of her sneezing. She begs me in Jesus' name to respect her and let her put on her veil again, saying that otherwise she will incur excommunication, but her fear of excommunication at such a moment makes me laugh. She assures me that the Abbess had threatened her with it if she let a man see her.

I then left her to the peasant woman's ministrations, fearing that the effort of sneezing might bring on her delivery. I promised to see her again the next day at the same hour, and she implored me not to abandon her.

Such as I am, it was impossible for me to abandon

her; but it was no longer to my credit; I had fallen in love with this new, black-eyed M. M. I was determined to do everything for her, and certainly not to let her go back to the convent in her condition. I felt that in saving her I was carrying out a command from God. God had willed that I should take her for M. M. God had made me win a great deal of money. God had provided Madame Z so that the curious could not guess the real reason for my deferred departure. What have I not attributed to God in the course of my life! Yet the rabble of philosophers have always accused me of atheism.

The next morning about eight o'clock I found Madame Z in bed and still asleep. Her chambermaid asked me to go in on tiptoe, and shut the door. Twenty years had passed since a Venetian woman whose sleep I had respected had laughed at me when she woke and would have nothing more to do with me. Madame Z tried to pretend she was a very sound sleeper, but she had to show me unmistakable signs of life when she felt too filled with it herself, and laughter succeeded the act. She said that her husband had gone to Geneva to buy her a repeating watch[14] and that he would not be back until the next day.

"You can," she said, "spend the night with me."

"Night, Madame, is for sleep. If you are not expecting anyone I will spend the whole morning with you."

"Very well. No one will come here."

She then put my hair in a cap of her husband's, and we were instantly in each other's arms. I found her as amorous as I could wish, and she was convinced that I was her match in every respect. We spent four splendid hours, often cheating each other but only to give us something to laugh at. After the last combat she asked me, in recompense for her love, to spend three more days at Aix.

"I promise, my beautiful Z, to remain here as long as

you will give me such proofs of friendship as you have given me this morning.''

"Then let us get up and go downstairs for dinner.''

"Downstairs? If you could see your eyes!"

"Let them guess. The two Countesses will die of mortification. I want everyone to be certain that you are staying on only for my sake.''

"I am not worth the trouble, my angel, but I will be glad to oblige you, even if I lose all my money in these three days.''

"I should be sorry for that; but if you do not punt you will not lose, even though you let the ladies rob you.''

"Believe me, I let myself be robbed only by ladies. You, too, took me for some *parolis de campagne*." [15]

"True, but not as often as the Countesses; and I regret it, for they may think you love them. After you left, the Marquis de Saint-Maurice said you should never have offered to let the Englishman withdraw on eight cards, for if he had won he might have thought you knew it.''

"Tell Monsieur de Saint-Maurice that a man of honor is incapable of harboring such a suspicion, and that in any case, since I knew the young nobleman's character, I was morally certain that he would not accept my offer.''

When we went down to dinner everyone applauded. The beautiful *Z* acted as if I were at her beck and call, and I assumed the utmost modesty. After dinner no one dared invite me to make a bank; they were all out of money. They got up a game of trente et quarante,[16] which went on all day. I lost only some twenty louis. Toward dusk I slipped away, and, after going up to tell Leduc that he was never to leave my room while I was in Aix, I started toward the house where the unfortunate nun must be impatient to see me appear; but despite the darkness I think I see that I am being followed. I stop, the people behind me overtake me and go on. Two minutes later I start off again, and I see the same pair, whom I would never have overtaken if they had not slowed their pace. Since it could still be natural, I leave the road, though not so as to lose my way, sure that I can return to it when I no longer have reason to think I am followed. But my suspicion becomes certainty when at some distance I see two phantoms; I stop under a tree and fire one of my pistols into the air. A minute later, seeing no one, I proceed to the peasant's house, after returning to the fountain to make sure I should not miss the road.

I go up to the usual place, and by the light of two candles on a small table I see the nun in bed.

"Are you ill, Madame?"

"I am well, thank God, after giving birth to a boy at two o'clock this morning, whom my kind hostess has taken God knows where. The Holy Virgin has answered my prayers. I had only one violent pain, and a quarter of an hour later I was sneezing again. Tell me if you are a man or an angel, for I fear to sin by worshiping you."

"You give me news which fills me with joy. And your lay sister?"

"She is still breathing, but we have no hope that she can escape death. Her face is distorted. We have committed a great crime."

"God will forgive you. Adore Eternal Providence."

"The peasant woman is sure you are an angel. It is your powder which brought on my confinement. I shall never forget you, even though I do not know who you are."

The woman comes up, and, after congratulating her on ministering so well to the nun in childbed, I again exhort her to make much of the priest she will summon when the lay sister has breathed her last, to prevent him from suspecting the cause of her death. She assures me that all will be well, that no one knew either that the lay sister had been ill or why Madame had stayed in bed. She said that she had herself taken the infant to Annecy, and that she had bought everything which could be needed in her house as things now stood. She said that her brother had gone away the night before and would not be back for a week, and so we had nothing more to fear. I gave her another ten louis, asking her to buy a few pieces of furniture and to have something ready for me to eat the next day; she said she still had a good deal of money, but when she heard me reply that all the money she had left was for her I thought she would go mad with gratitude. Seeing that my presence embarrassed the new mother, I left, promising that I would come to see her the next day.

I could not wait to be well out of this perilous situation, but I could not cry victory until the lay sister was buried. I trembled, for the priest, unless he was an idiot, must see beyond doubt that the dead woman had died from poison.

The next morning I found the Chevalier *Z* in his room with his wife, both engaged in examining the handsome watch he had bought for her. He congratulated her in my presence on having been able to keep me in Aix. He was one of those men who would rather be known as a cuckold than as a fool. I left him in order to accompany his wife to the waters, and on the way she told me she would be alone the next morning and that she would not again be curious about my eight o'clock walk.

"So it was you who had me followed?"

"Yes, I, just as a joke, for there are nothing but mountains in that direction; but I did not think you were so ill-natured. Luckily your shot missed."

"My dear, I fired into the air, for fear is enough to teach curiosity a lesson."

"So they won't follow you another time."

"And if they do, I may let them, for my walk is innocent. I am always back in my room by ten o'clock."

We were still at table when we saw a berlin drawn by six horses arrive, bringing the Marquis de Prié, a Chevalier of the Order of St. Louis,[17] and two charming ladies, one of whom, Madame Z told me, was the Marquis's mistress. Four places are immediately laid, everyone sits down again, and while waiting to be served the Marquis is told the whole story of the bank I had made and the arrival of the Englishmen. The Marquis congratulates me, saying he would never have expected to find me still at Aix, and Madame Z says that I would have left if she had not prevented me. Accustomed to her tactlessness, I admit it. He says he will make a small bank for me after dinner, and I answer that I will play against it. He made it a hundred louis, and I played, losing that amount in two deals, after which I rose and went to my room to answer several letters. At nightfall I went to see the nun.

"The lay sister is dead, Monsieur; she will be buried tomorrow, the day we were to return to our convent. Here is the letter I am writing the Abbess. She will send me another lay sister, unless she orders me to return to the convent with this peasant woman."

"What did the priest say?"

"He said she died of a lethargy arising from her brain which had liquefied, which must have brought on an apoplectic stroke. I would like to have fifteen masses said for her—may I?"

"You shall do as you wish."

I at once instructed the peasant woman to have them said at Annecy and to tell the priest only that he was to offer them according to the intention of the person who sent him the payment for them. She promised she would do so. She said that the dead woman was hideous, and that she had put two guards to watch her so that the witches would not come in the form of cats and steal one of her limbs.

"Tell me from whom you bought the laudanum."

"The woman who sold it to me is a very respectable midwife. We needed it to put poor Madame to sleep when the birth pangs took her."

"When you left the child at the hospital did anyone recognize you?"

"Have no fear. I put it in the wheel [18] when nobody saw me, with a note saying that it had not been baptized. The burial costs six francs, which the priest will be glad to pay, for, God forgive her, we found two louis on her. Madame said to let the priest keep the rest to say masses for her."

"Couldn't she have two louis with a clear conscience?"

"Madame says not."

She then told me that they had only two Savoyan soldi [19] a day, and that they could not have a copper without the Abbess's knowledge, on pain of excommunication.

"But now," she said, "I live like a princess, as you shall see at supper. Though this good woman knows that the money you gave her is hers, she keeps lavishing it on me. I can't stop her."

At that I encourage her to spend, giving her another ten louis. She said that she would buy some cows, and that I had made the fortune of her house.

Left alone with her, and her charming face, which reminded me only too much of M. M.'s, making me ardent, I talked to her about her seducer, saying that I was astonished he had not given her the help she needed in the cruel situation to which he had brought her. She replied that she could not have accepted even the smallest sum of money because of her vows of poverty and obedience, and that she would give the Abbess a louis she had left from the charity the Bishop had procured for her,

and that as for her forsaken condition at the fatal moment when she had met me, she could only conclude that
he had certainly not received her letter.

"Is he rich and handsome?"

"Rich, but extremely ugly, a hunchback and fifty years
old."

"Then how could you fall in love with him?"

"I was not in love. He roused my pity. He wanted to
kill himself. I was afraid. I went to the garden on the
night he swore he would be there, only to beg him to
leave it; and he left, but after having satisfied his wanton desire."

"So he forced you?"

"No, he could not have done that. He wept, and he
begged me so hard that I let him on condition that he
would not come to the garden again."

"Weren't you afraid of becoming pregnant?"

"I don't understand it at all, since I have always believed that for a girl to become pregnant she had to do
it with a man at least three times."

"Unlucky ignorance! So he did not keep asking you
for further meetings in the garden?"

"I refused, because our confessor made me promise,
if I wanted absolution, that I would not see him again."

"Did you tell your confessor who your seducer was?"

"Of course not. That would have been to commit another sin."

"Did you tell your confessor that you were pregnant?"

"Not that either, but he must have supposed it. He
is a saint, who may have prayed to God for me; and my
meeting you is perhaps the fruit of his prayers."

I remained silent for a quarter of an hour, absorbed
in deep reflection. All the girl's misfortunes had come
from her candor, her innocence, and a mistaken feeling
of pity which led her to grant a monster who was in

love with her something which she regarded very lightly because she had never been in love. She was religious, but, her religion being merely a habit, it was very weak. With her, religion was a matter of calculation. She loathed sin because she had to purge herself of it by confession on pain of eternal damnation, and she did not want to be damned. She had plenty of common sense, and too little intelligence because she had never been taught by experience. Considering all this, I foresaw that she would be very reluctant to grant me what she had freely given to Monsieur de Cou. . . ; she had repented too sorely to run the same risk with another man.

The peasant woman came up, laid two places on a small table, and brought us supper. Everything was new— linen, plates, glasses, knives, spoons—and everything very clean. The wines were very good and the dishes exquisite because nothing was elaborate. Game, roast, delicious fish, and excellent cheeses. I spent an hour and a half eating, drinking, and talking. The nun ate almost nothing, but that did not keep me from emptying two bottles. I was on fire. The peasant woman, delighted with my praise, promises me the same sort of fare every night, she clears everything away, and goes downstairs. Again alone with a woman whose face was an enchantment and who filled me with desires which, after the appetizing supper, I could not restrain, I talk to her of her health and of the discomfort from which she must be suffering after childbirth. She said that she felt perfectly well and that she could go to Chambéry on foot.

"The only thing," she said, "which troubles me a little is my breasts; but the peasant woman assures me that by day after tomorrow the milk will recede and they will return to their natural condition."

"Will you allow me to examine them?"

"Look."

Naked in her bed, she pulls down her shift, and, think-

ing she is only being obedient and polite, even afraid
that she is committing the sin of pride or is wronging me
by supposing that my thoughts are anything but decent,
she lets me look at the whole of her charming bosom and
touch it all over and all round. Taking care not to alarm
her candor, I control myself, I ask her without any show
of excitement how she feels a little lower down, and,
as I put the question, I extend one hand, but she stops
it from reaching its goal, saying that she still feels a
little uncomfortable. I beg her pardon; I tell her I hope
to find her perfectly well the next day; I say that the
beauty of her bosom only increases the interest she has
inspired in me, and I give her a tender kiss, which she
thinks it her duty to meet with one of her own. I feel
carried away, and, convinced that I must either risk
losing all her confidence or go at once, I leave her, calling
her by the sweet name of "my dear daughter."

I arrived at my inn soaking wet, for it was raining.
The next morning I rose late. I put in my pocket the two
portraits I had of M. M. in her habit and stark naked,
intending to astonish the nun. I went to Madame *Z*'s
room, and, not finding her there, went on to the fountain,
where she reproached me. After dinner the Marquis de
Prié made the bank; however, finding only a hundred
louis in it, I saw that he hoped to win much but was
willing to risk only a little. Nevertheless I took a hundred
louis from my purse. He said that, if I wanted amusement, I should not stake on only one card. I replied that
I would put a louis on each of the thirteen. He laughed
and said I would lose.

But as it turned out, in less than three hours I won
eighty louis. At every deal I won a *quinze et le va* and
sometimes two. I left, as I did every day, at nightfall,
and I found the invalid charming. She said she had a
slight fever which, according to the peasant woman, she
was bound to have, and that she would be well the next

day and would get up. When I put out my hand to raise her coverlet she kissed it, saying that she was very glad to give me that token of her daughterly fondness. She was twenty-one years of age and I thirty-five. My affection for her was much stronger than a father's. I said that the confidence she showed me by receiving me undressed in her bed increased the fatherly fondness I felt for her, and that she would see me melancholy if on the next day I found her wearing her habit.

"Then you will find me in bed," she replied, "and willingly, for in the hot weather we are having my woolen habit stifles me. I thought that being all dressed, as decency demands, I might please you better; but I am content if you do not mind."

The peasant woman came up and gave her a letter from the Abbess which her nephew had that moment brought for her from Chambéry. She told her that she would send her two lay sisters who would bring her back to the convent and that, since she had recovered her health, she could make the short journey on foot and thus save the money for a better use; but she added that since the Bishop was in the country and she needed his permission the lay sisters could not set out for a week or ten days. She ordered her, on pain of excommunication, never to leave her room in the meanwhile and to speak to no man, not even to the owner of the house in which she was staying, who must have a wife. She ended by saying that she would have a mass sung for the repose of the deceased lay sister's soul.

The peasant woman asked me to face the window, since Madame needed to do something. After that I sat down close beside her on her bed again.

"Tell me, Madame," I said, "if during this week or ten days I may come to pay you my respects without offending your conscience, for I am a man. I have stayed here only for you, who have inspired the greatest interest in me; but if you are reluctant to receive me because of this strange excommunication, speak, and I will leave tomorrow."

"Monsieur, it is an excommunication which I have already incurred; but I hope that God will not confirm it, since instead of making me wretched it has made me happy, and I tell you frankly that your visits are now the joy of my life, and I consider myself doubly happy if you like coming to see me. But I wish you to tell me, if you can do so without indiscretion, for whom you took me the first time you came to me in the dark, for you cannot imagine my surprise nor the fear I felt. I had no notion of kisses like those with which you covered my face, but which could not make my excommunication worse because I did not consent to them; and you have told me yourself that you thought you were giving them to another woman."

"Madame, I will satisfy your curiosity. I can do so now I know you are aware that we are human, that the flesh is weak, and that it drives the strongest souls to commit sins despite reason. You shall now hear all the vicissitudes which marked the two years of a love affair with the most beautiful and most intelligent, if not the most prudent, of all the nuns in my country."

"Monsieur, tell me all; having fallen into the same fault, I should be unjust and inhuman if I were scandalized by any detail, for you certainly could not have done more with the nun than Cou. . . did with me."

"No, Madame. I was lucky. I did not give her a child; but if I had I would have carried her off and taken her to Rome where the Holy Father, seeing us at his feet, would have released her from her vows; and my dear M. M. would now be my wife."

"Good God! M. M. is my name."

This coincidence, which was really nothing, amazed us both. Strange, fickle chance, which nevertheless acts powerfully on predisposed minds and produces important consequences! After remaining silent for a few minutes I told her all that had befallen me with M. M., concealing nothing. At my vivid descriptions of our amorous combats I saw that she was often excited, and when at the end of my story I heard her ask if she really was so much like her that I took her for M. M., I drew her portrait as a nun from my portfolio and placed it in her hands.

"It is my portrait," she said, "except for the eyes and the eyebrows. It is my habit! It is wonderful. What a combination of circumstances! I owe all my happiness to this likeness. Thank God you do not love me as you loved this dear sister who has my face and even my name. Here are the two M. M.s. Inscrutable Divine Providence! All thy ways are adorable. We are but weak, ignorant, proud mortals."

The peasant woman came to serve us a supper even more appetizing than the one of the previous evening, but the invalid ate only a bowl of soup. She promised me she would sup heartily the next night.

An hour which I spent with her after the peasant woman had cleared away made her certain that I felt for her only a father's fondness. Of her own free will she showed me her bosom, which had not yet returned to its normal state, and let me touch it all over, never even thinking that it could arouse the slightest emotion in me, and she took all the kisses which I bestowed on her beautiful lips and her beautiful eyes for demonstrations of the most innocent friendship. She laughed and said she thanked God her eyes were not blue. When I reached the point at which I could no longer control myself I left her and went back to my room to go to bed. Leduc gave me a note from Madame *Z* in which she said we would see each other at the fountain because she had been invited to breakfast with the Marquis's mistress.

At the fountain she told me that the whole company

maintained that, staking on thirteen cards, I was bound to lose, for it was false that in each deal there was a card which won four times, but that the Marquis had said that, even so, he would no longer allow me to stake in that way and that his mistress had undertaken to make me play as usual. I thanked her.

Back at my inn I lost fifty louis playing quinze with the Marquis before dinner, and afterward I let myself be persuaded to make a bank. So I went to my room for five hundred louis; then I install myself at the big table, prepared to defy Fortune. I took Desarmoises as my croupier, announcing that I would honor only cards on which money had been placed, and that I would stop at half past seven o'clock. As it happens, I am seated between the two most beautiful of the ladies, and in addition to the five hundred louis which I take from my purse I call for a hundred écus de six francs to amuse the ladies. But now for what happened.

Seeing only opened packs of cards before me, I demand fresh ones. The major-domo tells me he has sent a man to Chambéry to buy a hundred packs and that he must be back soon.

"Meanwhile," he says, "you can deal with these packs. They are as good as new."

"I don't want them as good as new, but new. I have principles, my friend, which all Hell cannot make me abandon. While I wait for your man I will simply look on. I am sorry I must wait to offer my services to these beautiful ladies."

No one dared say a word to me. I left my seat and gathered up my money. The Marquis de Prié made the bank, and played in a way to do him credit. I remained beside Madame *Z*, who made me her partner and the next day gave me five or six louis. The man who was to come back from Chambéry did not arrive until midnight. I considered I had escaped by the skin of my teeth, for in that part of the world there are people with amazingly sharp eyes. I went and put my money back in my strongbox, then went to see the nun, who was in bed.

"How are you, Madame?"

"Say 'my daughter,' for I wish you were my father so that I could embrace you without any fear."

"Well then, my dear daughter, fear nothing and open your arms to me."

"Yes, let us embrace."

"My infants are prettier than they were yesterday. Let them feed me."

"What madness! Dear Papa, I believe you are drinking your poor daughter's milk."

"It is sweet, my dear friend, and the little I have swallowed is balm to my soul. You cannot be sorry you have granted me this pleasure, for nothing is more innocent."

"No, of course I'm not sorry, for you gave me pleasure too. Instead of calling you Papa I'll call you my baby."

"How I love the good humor I find you in tonight!"

"It's because you have made me happy. I have no more fears. Peace has returned to my soul. The peasant woman told me that in a few days I'll be just as I was before I knew Cou. . . ."

"Not quite, my angel, for your belly, for example—"

"Be still. There's nothing to tell by, I'm amazed myself."

"Let me look."

"Oh, no, please, please! But you may touch it. Is it true?"

"Quite true."

"Oh, my friend! Don't touch that."

"Why not? You can't be different from my old M. M., who cannot be more than thirty now. I will show you a full-length portrait of her, she is stark naked."

"Have you it here? I'd like to see it."

I thereupon take it from my portfolio, and I see that she is in raptures. She kisses it. She asks me if it was all painted from nature, and she sees her own likeness more strikingly in the portrait of my M. M. nude than in the one where she had on her habit.

"But," she said, "it was you who ordered the painter to give her such long hair."

"Certainly not. In our country nuns are only obliged not to let men see their long hair."

"In our country too. They cut it, and then we let it grow again."

"Then you have long hair?"

"As long as hers; but you won't like it because it is black."

"What are you saying? I prefer dark hair to blond. In God's name, let me see it."

"You ask me in God's name to commit a sin, for I incur another excommunication; but I can refuse you nothing. I will show it to you after supper, for I don't want to scandalize the peasant woman."

"You are right. I think you are the most lovable of all beings, and I shall die of grief when you leave this happy cottage to return to your prison."

"I must go there to do penance for all my sins."

How happy I was! I felt sure that I would obtain everything after supper. When the woman appeared I gave her another ten louis. From her amazement I saw that she might think I was out of my mind. I told her I was very rich and that I wanted to convince her I did not think myself rich enough to reward her properly for her motherly care of the nun. She wept for gratitude. She gave us an exquisite supper, at which the invalid thought she could be guided by her appetite; but my state of contentment prevented me from following her example; I could not wait to see the beautiful black hair of this victim of her own goodness of heart. At that moment it was this appetite which dominated me and which left no room for another.

As soon as the woman left us alone together, she took off her coif, and at that I really believed I was seeing M. M. with black hair. She amused herself making it fall over her shoulders like the hair in the portrait I showed her, and she enjoyed hearing me say what was incontestable truth: the contrast provided by her hair and her black eyes made her appear whiter than M. M. It was not true. They were two whites which were equally dazzling but which differed in their tint; it was a difference perceptible only to the eyes of a lover. However, the living object triumphed over the painted image.

"You are whiter," I said, "more beautiful, and more dazzling because of the contrast between black and white; but I think my first M. M. was more loving."

"She may have been so, but not more tender-hearted."

"Her amorous desires must have been more intense than yours."

"I can believe it, for I have never loved."

"That is surprising. But nature and the impulse of the senses—"

"That is an inclination, my dear friend, which we easily satisfy in the convent; we accuse ourselves to our confessor, for we know it is a sin; but he treats it as childish trifling, for he absolves us without giving us any penance; he is a wise old priest, learned and austere in his life; we shall be very sorry when he dies."

"But when you are dallying with another nun like yourself do you not feel that you would love her better if at that moment she could become a man?"

"You make me laugh. It is true that if my little friend became a man I should not be sorry; but you may be sure that we really do not spend our time hoping for such a miracle."

"It can only be because of a lack in your temperament. M. M. was your superior in that way; she preferred me to C. C.; but you would not prefer me to your little friend at the convent."

"Certainly not, for with you I should be breaking my vow, and I should risk consequences which even now make me tremble every time I think of them."

"Then you do not love me?"

"How dare you say that! I love you so much that I am sorry you are not a woman."

"I love you too, but your wish makes me laugh. I would not become a woman to please you, and the more so because, as a woman, I am sure I should not think you so beautiful. Sit up, my accommodating friend, and let me see how your beautiful hair covers half of your beautiful body."

"Gladly. Must I take down my shift?"

"Of course. How beautiful you are! Let me suck the last sweet drops of your milk."

After granting me this delight, gazing at me with a look of the most perfect willingness and letting me clasp her in my arms, unaware, or pretending to be unaware, of the intensity of the pleasure I must be feeling, she said that if friendship was permitted such satisfactions it was preferable to love, for never in her life had her soul known a purer joy than I had given her by clinging to her breasts, as I had done.

"Let me," she said, "do the same to you."

"Here I am, my angel, but I have nothing there."

"Never mind. We'll do it for fun."

After she had satisfied herself we spent a quarter of an hour exchanging kisses. I could bear no more.

"Tell me the truth," I said. "In the fury of these kisses, in these transports which we are pleased to call childish, do you not feel a much greater desire?"

"I will confess that I feel it, but it is sinful; and certain as I am that you feel it too, we must end this dangerous trifling. Our friendship, my dear baby, has become love. Has it not?"

"Yes, love, and love which cannot be conquered. Let us yield to it."

"On the contrary, my dear friend, let us stop now. In future let us be prudent and not again risk becoming its victims. If you love me, you must think as I do."

So saying, she gathered up her hair, and, after putting it under her cap, I helped her to pull up her shift, the coarse linen of which struck me as unworthy of her soft skin; I told her so, and she replied that she was used to it, so it did not hurt her at all. My soul was in the greatest consternation, for the pain my restraint caused me seemed infinitely greater than the pleasure I should have gained from complete fruition; but I had to be certain I should not find the slightest resistance, and I was not certain of it. A folded rose petal spoiled the pleasure of the famous Smindyrides,[20] who loved a soft bed. So I preferred to bear my pain and leave, rather than risk finding the rose petal which troubled the voluptuous Sybarite. I left irretrievably in love. I returned to my lodging at two o'clock in the morning, and I slept until noon.

Leduc gave me a note he should have given me before I went to bed. He had forgotten it. Madame Z said that she would expect me at nine o'clock and would be alone; that she was giving a supper, to which she was sure I would come, and that she would leave afterward; she hoped that I would leave too, or that I would at least accompany her as far as Chambéry.

Though I still loved her, all the three points she made in her letter set me laughing. It was too late for me to breakfast with her. I could not accept her invitation to supper because of my nun, whom at that moment I would not have left for the greatest conquest; nor could I undertake to accompany her as far as Chambéry, for it might well happen that I could not leave M. M.

I found her in her room a minute before she went down to dinner. She was furious. She had expected me for breakfast. I told her I had received her note an hour earlier; and she went down without giving me time to tell her I could not promise either to sup with her or to have the honor of escorting her to Chambéry. At table she was sulky with me, and after dinner the Marquis de Prié told me he had new cards and that the whole company wanted to see me deal. There were ladies and gentlemen who had arrived from Geneva that morning; I went for money and made them a bank of five hundred louis. At seven o'clock I had lost more than half that amount, but I stopped nevertheless, putting what was left in my pocket. After giving Madame *Z* a melancholy glance, I went to my room to put away my money, then went to the cottage, where I saw my angel in a big brand-new bed, and a pretty Roman bed [21] for me beside the big one. I laughed at the discrepancy between all this furniture and the dirty garret we were in. Instead of a compliment I gave the peasant woman fifty louis, saying that they were for the rest of the time M. M. would be staying with her, but that she must spend no more on furniture.

Such is, I believe, the character of most gamblers. I should perhaps not have given her such a sum if I had won a thousand louis. I had lost three hundred, and I felt as if I had won the two hundred which were left. I gave her the fifty as if I were paying them on a winning card. I have always loved to spend, but I have never known myself to throw away money except in the course of play. I took the greatest pleasure in giving money which cost me nothing to a person who would set the greatest store by it. My soul was flooded with joy when I saw gratitude and admiration on the noble countenance of my new M. M.

"You must," she said, "be immensely rich."

"Make no mistake. I love you very passionately, that is all. Unable to give you anything directly because of your vow, I lavish what I possess on this good woman so that she will have more and more reason to make you happy during the few days you are yet to stay in her house. But by indirection it will, I hope, make you love me more and more."

"I cannot love you more. I am never unhappy now except when I remember that I must return to the convent."

"You told me yesterday that the thought made you happy."

"And it is just since yesterday that I have become a different woman. I spent a most dreadful night. I could never fall asleep without finding myself in your arms, always waking with a start just as I was about to commit the greatest of sins."

"You did not struggle so hard before committing it with a man whom you did not love."

"That is true, but it is precisely because I was not in love with him that I did not think I was committing a sin. Can you understand that, my dear friend?"

"It is a metaphysics conceived by your pure, divine, and innocent soul, and I understand it perfectly."

"Thank you. You fill me with contentment and gratitude. I rejoice when I think that you are not in a state of mind like mine. I am now sure that I shall gain the victory."

"I will not oppose you, though it distresses me."

"Why?"

"Because you will believe you must refuse me caresses which, though of no consequence, made my life happy."

"I have thought of that."

"You are crying?"

"Yes, and what is more, I love these tears. I have two favors I must ask of you."

"Ask, and be sure they will be granted."

CHAPTER I

1. *Walpole:* C. later refers to him as Sir James Walpole. It has been suggested that he was a relative of Sir Robert Walpole and of Horace Walpole, fourth Earl of Oxford (1717-1797), but the identification is uncertain.

2. *Primero:* A card game widely played in the eighteenth century.

3. *The theater:* C. probably refers to the Comédie Française, which in the eighteenth century performed at The Hague in a former mall in Casuariestraat.

4. *Count Tott:* Brother of Baron (not Count) François de Tott (1733-1793), born in France of Hungarian parents; in 1755 he went to Constantinople in the suite of the French Ambassador Vergennes and in 1767 was appointed French Consul in the Crimea.

5. *Battle of Minden:* Prince Ferdinand of Braunschweig defeated the French in a battle near Minden on Aug. 1, 1759 (Seven Years' War).

6. *D'Affry:* Louis Auguste, Count d'Affry (1710-1793), French Ambassador in The Hague from 1759.

7. *"City of Lyons":* "De Stad Lyon," an inn situated in a quarter of the city which had an unsavory reputation even down to recent times.

8. *Albemarle:* William Anne Keppel, Earl of Albemarle (1702-1754), was English Ambassador in Paris from 1749 until his death on Dec. 22, 1754.

9. *Lolotte:* Louise Gaucher, known as Lolotte (died 1765), actress and mistress of Albemarle and other prominent men; in 1757 she married Antoine de Ricouart, Count of Hérouville.

10. *Duchess of Fulvy:* Probably Hélène Louise Henriette Orry de Fulvy (died 1768), married until 1751 to the Intendant

of Finances Jean Henri Louis Orry de Fulvy; she was not
a duchess.

11. *Hérouville:* Antoine de Ricouart, Count d'Hérouville de
Claye (1713-1782), French officer and writer.

12. *La Pâris:* Justine Pâris, by her real name Bienfait (ca.
1705 - after 1755), conducted a well-known brothel in the
Rue de Bagneux until 1750 and then established the Hôtel
du Roule, which in 1751 became the property of a Madame
Carlier (cf. Vol. 3, Chap. IX).

13. *Varnier:* C. presumably means Marc Guillaume Albert
Vadier (1736-1828), a deputy in the National Convention
(see the following note) and a member of the Committee of
General Security.

14. *National Convention:* In Sept. 1792 the Assemblée Nationale was replaced by the Convention Nationale, which
abolished the monarchy and proclaimed the republic on Sept.
22, 1792.

15. *"Second Bible":* Cf. Vol. 5, Chap. VII, n. 6.

16. *A new Comptroller-General:* The Comptroller-General of
Finances, Étienne de Silhouette (1709-1767), had already
been replaced on Nov. 21, 1759, by Henri Bertin d'Andilly
(1719-1793), who held the office until Dec. 1763. Hence C.'s
dates are inaccurate.

17. *My freedom:* C. first wrote *Manon et toute l'Europe*
("Manon and the whole of Europe"), then substituted *liberté*.

18. *Saby:* Antoine Saby (ca. 1716 - after 1778), French adventurer and professional gambler.

19. *Wiedau:* Johann Carl, Freiherr von Wiedau (died after
1776), officer and adventurer.

20. *Had arrived:* It was not until the beginning of Feb. 1760
that Saint-Germain reached The Hague and Amsterdam,
where he was received into the house of the brothers Thomas
(Monsieur D. O.) and Adrian Hope. C.'s account of the
episode of the diamond undoubtedly differs greatly from the
facts.

21. *Talvis:* Michel Louis Gatien, Vicomte de Talvis (also
Tailvis, Taillevis, Taibris) de la Perrine, French officer, adventurer, and professional gambler (cf. Vol. 3, Chap. XII).

22. *A year earlier:* C. first wrote *deux ans*, then crossed it out

and substituted *un an*. He thus correctly gives the date of his first stay in Holland as the winter of 1758-1759. For *musicau* and the episode referred to, see Vol. 5, Chap. VII, and *ibid.*, n. 9.

23. *Seven years ago:* Here, similarly, C. substituted *sept* for *huit*. The incident took place during C.'s first stay in Paris in the fall of 1752.

24. *Livret:* In basset and faro, the 13 cards given to each punter (cf. Vol. 3, Chap. I, n. 18).

25. *Middelburg:* Town on the island of Walcheren at the mouth of the River Scheldt.

26. *Whom the reader may remember:* Jan Cornelis Rigerboos and Teresa Imer-Pompeati (cf. Vol. 5, Chap. VII).

27. *Neo:* Mole.

28. *Teresa Trenti:* Teresa Imer (1723-1797), Italian singer, married the dancer Angelo Pompeati in 1745; from 1756 to 1758 she was a theater director in Holland under the name of Teresa Trenti.

29. *Rigerboos's name:* Teresa Imer went to London and there in 1760 opened Carlisle House, at which various kinds of entertainment were provided, under the name of "Mrs. Cornelys" (cf. Vol. 1, Chap. IV, n. 6).

30. *A year earlier:* Cf. Vol. 5, Chap. VII.

31. *L'Aigle:* Cf. Vol. 1, Chap. V.

32. *Zante:* Zakynthos, island in the Ionian Sea; it belonged to Venice at the time.

33. Horace, *Satires,* II, 2, 79: *Atque adfigit humo divinae particulum aurae* ("And fastens to earth a particle of the divine spirit").

34. *The Gascon:* Gascons were held to be both braggarts and given to theatrical gestures.

35. *Sixteen or seventeen years earlier:* C.'s meeting with Pocchini took place in 1741 (cf. Vol. 2, Chap. IV).

36. *Bailo:* Title of the Venetian Ambassador to Constantinople (cf. Vol. 2, Chap. III).

37. *Son of a Count Pocchini:* Antonio Pocchino (1705-1783), adventurer, descended from a noble Paduan family; he was banished to Cerigo in 1741, reappeared in Padua in 1746, and from then on led a wandering life.

38. *Calkoen:* Either Cornelis Calkoen (1696-1764), or his brother Jan (1694-1768), or their nephew Abraham (1729-1796); all three were Dutch diplomats and high government officials.

39. *Their High Power:* In the original *L. H. P.* for "Leur Haute Puissance," corresponding to the Dutch "Hunne Hoogmogenden," designation for the States-General (cf. Vol. 5, Chap. VII, n. 8).

40. *His Most Christian Majesty:* A title of the French King.

41. *Christmas Day:* C. is in error. The last of Manon Balletti's letters to him, preserved at Dux, is dated Feb. 7, 1760. The letter in which she announced her marriage to him is not extant; but it cannot have been written before the middle of Feb. 1760.

42. *Tomorrow:* Manon Balletti did not marry Jacques François Blondel until July 29, 1760; the reference may be to their engagement.

43. *Blondel:* Jacques François Blondel (1705-1774), French architect, from 1755 member of the Académie Royale d'Architecture.

44. *Academy:* Cf. note 43; it was founded by Colbert in 1671, and had its seat in the Louvre from 1692 to 1793, when it was abolished.

45. *St. John's Day:* Dec. 27 (cf. Vol. 5, Chap. VI, n. 38).

46. *Salt cod:* C. writes *cabillao*, apparently a cross between French *cabillaud* and Spanish-Portuguese *bacalao, bacalhao* or Italian *bacallao*.

47. *Two hundred:* Only 42 letters from Manon Balletti to C. were preserved at Dux, and none of those which he wrote to her.

48. *O-Morphi:* See Vol. 3, Chap. XI.

49. *Last day of the year 1759:* The events recounted probably took place in Feb. 1760. Possibly C. is again using the Venetian reckoning, according to which the new year began on March 1.

CHAPTER II

1. *Heroid:* A letter in verse which the poet puts into the mouth of some famous character of history or legend. Ovid origi-

nated the genre with his *Heroides*. Alexander Pope had revived it in 1717 with his "Eloisa to Abelard," the translation
of which by Charles Pierre Colardeau (published in 1738)
made the heroid fashionable in France.

2. *Conics:* C. writes *conis;* no doubt the *Comics* of the Greek
mathematician Apollonius of Perga (3rd century B.C.), Com-
mandino's Latin translation of which, *Apollonii Pergaei Coni-
corum Libri quatuor* (Venice, 1566), was widely used in
Europe as a textbook.

3. *Campaigning:* In the Seven Years' War.

4. *Estate:* Zeyst, near Utrecht.

5. *Herrnhuters:* A Protestant sect which derived from the Mo-
ravian Brotherhood; some disciples of this religious society
founded the new village of Herrnhut on the property of
Count Zinzendorf in Berthelsdorf.

6. *Winter quarters:* During the winter of 1759-60 Cologne
served as the winter quarters of the French army under the
command of the Duke of Broglie.

7. *"Sign of the Sun":* No inn by this name appears to have
existed in Cologne; the records show that C. stayed at the
"Gasthaus zum Heiligen Geist."

8. *Lastic:* The Marquis (not Count) François de Lastic, French
Field Marshal.

9. *Torcy:* Paul François de Torcy (ca. 1690-1761), French
Field Marshal from 1757.

10. *Flavacourt:* François Marie de Fouilleux, Marquis de
Flavacourt (died 1763), French Field Marshal.

11. *Theater:* The French company played in a wooden booth
on the Heumarkt (Haymarket).

12. *On the stage:* 18th-century theaters still provided seats on
the stage; they were preferred by the nobility.

13. *Kettler:* Friedrich Wilhelm, Count von Kettler (ca. 1718-
1783), of the Westphalian nobility, General in the Austrian
service; during the Seven Years' War he was Austrian Military Attaché to the French.

14. *Montazet:* Antoine Marie de Malvin, Count of Montazet
(ca. 1711-1768), Lieutenant-General from 1760; during the
Seven Years' War he was French Military Attaché in Austria.

15. *Burgomaster X:* At this period Cologne regularly had six
Burgomasters—two (elected annually) who performed the

duties of the office, and the four who had held office during the two previous years. The reference is undoubtedly to Franz Jakob Gabriel von Groote, Herr auf Kendenich, Thurn, Wolfskeel und Dransdorf (1721-1792), Burgomaster of Cologne from 1756 to 1789; he had married Maria Ursula Columba, née Zum Pütz, in 1749.

16. *Bayard:* The steed ridden by Rinaldo, son of Amone (see the following note), in Ariosto's *Orlando furioso*—which accounts for C.'s interest. C. cannot have seen a statue of Bayard, but presumably saw a painting of the fabulous steed in the convent church of St. Reinhold (Regnauld), on the Marsilstein, which was demolished in 1854.

17. *The four sons of "Aymon":* Aymon (Amone), legendary Count of Dordogne, fought against Charlemagne with his 4 sons. Their adventures were sung in the chanson de geste *Renaut de Montauban* (12th century); it inspired the French romance *Les Quatre fils Aymon* (1495), which was imitated in many languages and probably served as the source for Ariosto's Amone, Rinaldo, Ricciardetto, and other characters in the *Orlando furioso*.

18. *Castries:* Charles Eugène Gabriel de La Croix, Marquis de Castries (1727-1801), from 1758 French Lieutenant-General.

19. *Carnival:* In 1760 the Carnival ended on Feb. 19th. C. did not reach Cologne until the beginning of February; so he must here mean only what remained of the Carnival season.

20. *Young:* Von Groote was only 4 years older than C.

21. *Elector:* The Elector Clemens August von Wittelsbach (1723-1761).

22. *Masked ball:* Doubtless the ball on Shrove Tuesday, at which the nobility were required to appear masked but the burghers unmasked. The Elector's balls were given in the theater of the palace (later the University Library). When C. was in Cologne Beethoven's father and grandfather were players in the Electoral orchestra.

23. *Verità:* Count Marco Verità, Marchese di Fubine (ca. 1705-1775), of Verona; in the Elector's service from 1744.

24. *Paroli:* The original stake doubled.

25. *Grand Master of the Teutonic Order:* The Elector had held this office from 1732. His knowledge of Venetian probably

went back to his stay in Venice during his pilgrimage to Loreto and Rome in 1755.

26. *Elector of Bavaria:* Maximilian III Joseph von Wittelsbach (1745-1777).

27. *Dialogue with the Duke of Choiseul:* See Vol. 5, Chap. II.

28. *Dressed as peasants:* Doubtless for a so-called "peasant wedding," a favorite type of costume ball; it probably took place on Ash Wednesday. The Elector had a large stock of masquerade costumes in his castle at Bonn.

29. *In the style of several German provinces:* Probably the ländler, a dance rather like the waltz, which was a novelty at the time.

30. *Two of these women:* No doubt 2 Italian ballerinas from the Elector's ballet company.

31. *Furlana:* A dance from the northern Italian province of Friuli (cf. Vol. 2, Chap. 4, n. 36).

32. *Brühl:* At Brühl, between Cologne and Bonn, the Elector owned the palace of Augustusburg and the small hunting lodge of Falkenlust, built in 1737 by the elder François Cuvilliés. C.'s luncheon doubtless took place in one of the numerous pavilions in the palace grounds.

33. *Two or three:* C. later says that he sent out 18 invitations. The discrepancy remains unresolved.

34. *Zweibrücken:* Friedrich Michael, Count Palatine of Zweibrücken-Birkenfeld (1724-1767), French Field Marshal, later Imperial Field Marshal General.

35. *Trianon:* The Grand Trianon and the Petit Trianon in the park of Versailles, built respectively by Louis XIV and Louis XV, may have been the models for the Augustusburg palace at Brühl (built from 1725, with a celebrated staircase by Balthasar Neumann).

36. *Name entered:* I.e., in the list of those who had called to inquire after the General's health.

37. *Invited a large company:* Presumably on the occasion of the Elector's creating him a Knight of the Order of St. Michael.

38. *The Dauphine:* Marie Josèphe (1731-1767), daughter of King Augustus III of Poland, second wife of the Dauphin Louis (1729-1765), and mother of Louis XVI.

39. *Lausitz:* Franz Xaver, Prince of Saxony, Count von der Lausitz (1730-1806), second son of King Augustus III of Poland.

40. *Kurland:* Karl Christian Joseph, Duke of Kurland, third son of King Augustus III of Poland.

41. *Biron:* Ernst Johann Biron (1690-1772), Duke of Kurland from 1737, favorite of the Czarina Anna Ivanovna; exiled to Siberia from 1740 to 1762.

42. *The Empress Anna:* Anna Ivanovna (1693-1740), Czarina from 1730, niece of Peter the Great, married Friedrich Wilhelm Kettler, Duke of Kurland (died 1711), in 1710.

43. *The last Duke Kettler:* Ferdinand Kettler (1655-1737), Duke of Kurland from 1711, died without issue. The story C. tells concerns Prince Alexander Kettler and Karl von Bühren, father of Biron (cf. note 41 and the following note).

44. *Claim to the countship of Wartenberg:* Ernst Johann Biron became an imperial Count in 1733 and in 1734 received the *Freie Standesherrschaft* of Wartenberg in Silesia.

45. Tibullus, IV, 13, 6.

46. *Our chapel:* The Church of "Maria im Tempel" was directly beside the Von Grootes' house, but had no entrance to it. Presumably C. refers to the "Elendskirche" on the Katherinengraben, which was connected with the two houses on either side of it; the beadle lived in one of them, the other belonged to the Von Groote family.

47. Ariosto, *Orlando furioso*, XI, 67-69.

48. *Went to Westphalia:* Count Kettler went to Paris in the middle of March 1760, but perhaps to Westphalia before that. In Paris he informed Choiseul of a "terrible conspiracy" hatched by C. Choiseul evinced no concern. It is possible that C. was traveling on a secret mission.

49. *Two and a half months:* C. must have reached Cologne at the beginning of Feb. and have left it at the end of March.

50. *Frantz:* Johann M. Frantz (died 1771), of Augsburg, banker in Cologne.

51. *Scampar:* Friedrich Ludwig von Scampar (died 1783), Prior of the Church of St. Kunibert in Cologne, Archdeacon of Deutz and Duisburg, Canon of the Church of the Holy Apostles in Cologne.

52. *Toscani:* Isabella Toscani (died 1778), wife of the Italian actor Giovanni Battista Toscani and mother of Luisa Toscani.

53. *Vestris:* Gaetano Apollino Baldassare Vestris, also Vestri (1729-1808), of Florence, famous dancer; he lived in Paris from 1748 to 1781.

54. *The Duke:* Karl Eugen, Duke of Württemberg (1728-1793).

55. *Gardela:* Ursula Maria Gardela (1730-1793 or '94), daughter of the Venetian gondolier Antonio Gardela; dancer (cf. Vol. 1, Chap. VI); married Michele dall'Agata, of Venice, ballet master.

56. *La Binetti:* Anna Binetti (died after 1784), daughter of a Venetian gondolier named Ramon; Italian dancer, married the French dancer Georges Binet in 1751 (cf. Vol. 2, Chap. VIII).

57. *Signora Valmarana:* Cecilia Valmarana, née Priuli, Venetian patrician.

58. *The younger Balletti:* Luigi Giuseppe Balletti (1730 - before 1788), from 1757 ballet master in Stuttgart.

59. *The Vulcani girl:* Italian actress, daughter of a certain Bernardo Vulcani.

60. *The "Bear":* It was partly destroyed in 1791, rebuilt, and reopened as "Das Grünes Haus" ("The Green House"); it survived until the last war.

61. *Next volume:* I.e., according to C.'s original division of the manuscript.

CHAPTER III

1. *Plays . . . Italian dancers:* The new opera house was built in 1750 under Duke Karl Eugen and rebuilt even more magnificently in 1758; the French actors appeared there from 1757, the ballet from 1758, the *opera buffa* not until 1766.

2. *Noverre:* Jean Georges Noverre (1727-1810), from 1747 ballet master in various European cities; he was in Stuttgart from 1760 to 1767.

3. *A year later:* Duke Karl Eugen brought Ursula Maria

Gardela to Stuttgart in 1757, but the year of which C. is writing is 1760.

4. *Diet of Wetzlar:* The Reichskammergericht, the supreme tribunal of the Holy Roman Empire, which had its seat in Wetzlar from 1693 to 1806.

5. *Daughter of the Margrave of Bayreuth:* Elisabeth Friederike Sophie, Princess of Ansbach-Bayreuth (1732-1780), daughter of the Margrave Friedrich of Bayreuth, married Duke Karl Eugen in 1748 but left him in 1754.

6. *A cutting affront:* The Duke had banished his wife's favorite waiting woman from the Court; like any other subject, the Duchess asked for an audience, which he refused her.

7. *Jomelli:* Niccolò Jomelli (1714-1774), Italian composer, in the service of the Duke of Württemberg from 1754 to 1769.

8. *A celebrated castrato:* The castrati singing at Stuttgart in 1760 were Francesco Bozzi, Ferdinando Mazzanti, and Francesco Guerrieri.

9. *Kurz:* Andreas Georg Johann Maria Kurz (1718 - after 1774), German violinist, at the Court of the Duke of Württemberg from 1753 to 1774.

10. *San Samuele:* Theater in Venice (cf. Vol. 2, Chap. VI).

11. *His . . . daughter:* Katharina Kurz, daughter of Andreas Kurz (cf. note 9), celebrated dancer; she made her debut in Stuttgart and appeared in Venice from 1773 to 1790.

12. *My jilt:* I.e., Manon Balletti, who had abruptly ended her relationship with C. (cf. the previous chapter).

13. *Loved to distraction:* C. speaks no less warmly of Luigi Giuseppe Balletti in Vol. 5, Chap. VIII.

14. *Viennese Envoy:* Meinhard Friedrich Ried (Rüdt), Freiherr von Collenberg, was the Imperial Ambassador in Stuttgart from 1758 to 1761.

15. *Nieces . . . Pocchini:* Cf. Chap. I of this volume and, for Pocchini's biography, note 37 to the same chapter.

16. *Petition:* C.'s petition could have no effect, since the Duke himself empowered his adjutants to operate gambling houses.

17. *Secretary of State:* Friedrich Samuel Montmartin (1713-1773), who was appointed to the post in 1758.

18. *I wrote a letter:* Documents discovered in Stuttgart show that C. was in fact arrested and fled from the "Zum Bären"

inn. On April 9, 1760, his valet presented a petition asking to be freed from prison; the document is signed "De Julliers," whereas C. always calls him "Leduc."

19. *Fürstenberg:* Then the seat of the Margravate; later incorporated into the Grand Duchy of Baden.

20. *April 2nd:* In 1760 April 2nd was a Wednesday, not a Monday.

21. *Waldenbuch:* Village between Stuttgart and Tübingen.

22. *No post:* Regular post stations providing a change of horses were not established in Switzerland until 1830; however, stagecoaches were in operation on some highways.

23. *The "Sword":* This famous hostelry had existed from the 15th century; among others, Mozart and Goethe stayed there.

24. *A hundred:* C. first wrote "ninety," then crossed it out. A document preserved at Dux shows that on April 24, 1760, C. pawned clothing and jewelry for 80 louis d'or. This suggests that his statements concerning his wealth may have been exaggerated. However, it is possible that, to facilitate his escape, he got rid of certain articles which he had been seen wearing. There may even be some secret mission behind C.'s journey (cf. note 48 to Chap. II of this volume). The document mentioned is the first to show the name "Chevalier de Seingalt."

25. *The only church:* C. refers to the monastery of Einsiedeln in the canton of Schwyz, founded in the 10th century. The celebrated church was built from 1719 to 1735 after plans by K. Moosbrugger. C.'s account or his recollection of his walk can scarcely be accurate, since Einsiedeln is some 25 miles from Zurich.

26. *These impressions:* Many 18th-century accounts of travel mention the impressions and the legend connected with them.

CHAPTER IV

1. *Chancellor:* The rank of chancellor was the highest secular office in the monastery of Einsiedeln; it was held from 1755 to 1763 by Thomas Fassbind, of Schwyz.

2. *Prince:* The Abbots of Einsiedeln were created Princes of

the Holy Roman Empire by the Emperor Rudolf in 1274. However, they had neither a seat nor a voice in the Diet. The Prince-Abbot of Einsiedeln at the time of C.'s visit was Nikolaus II (Sebastian) Imfeld (1694-1773), who had held the office from 1734.

3. *Loreto:* Celebrated place of pilgrimage in central Italy, south of Ancona.

4. *At this season:* C.'s question makes no sense, since woodcock are hunted at any time in the spring and fall.

5. *Elector of Cologne:* The Elector Clemens August (cf. Chap. II of this volume). The portrait C. mentions is no longer at Einsiedeln.

6. *The library:* The library at Einsiedeln was and still is famous for its wealth of incunabula and ancient manuscripts.

7. *Legists:* Expounders of Roman civil law.

8. *Hoffmann's . . . dictionary:* Johann Jakob Hoffmann's historical and chronological dictionary, published in 4 volumes at Basel in 1668, was still a standard reference work.

9. *Attrition:* Theologically, repentance for sin arising only from fear of punishment (in contradistinction to *contrition,* repentance for sin because it is displeasing to God).

10. *Ott:* Matthias Ott (died 1766); proprietor of the "Zum Schwert" inn at Zurich. The construction of C.'s sentence shows that he was amused by the coincidence in sound between the innkeeper's name, which he spells "Ote," and the French for his profession, *"hôte."*

11. *Orelli:* Hans Heinrich von Orelli (1715-1785); he became Burgomaster of Zurich in 1778; in 1760 he held two lesser municipal offices.

12. *Pestalozzi:* Presumably Jakob Pestalozzi (1711-1787), who served as a municipal councillor from 1767. C. writes "Pestaluci."

13. *Giustiniani:* Probably Giuseppe Benedetto Giustiniani, earlier a monk in the Benedictine monastery of Monte Cassino; he composed verse panegyrics on the Empress Maria Theresa and on Frederick the Great, who both rewarded him. However, C. says he was a Capuchin.

14. *Écu of six francs:* See Vol. 5, Chap. II, n. 1.

15. *En amazone:* That is, wearing a riding habit; from Ama-

zon, one of the race of female warriors famous in Greek legend.

16. *Cadogan:* A knot or loop of ribbon in which the hair is tied back from the head; menservants were usually required to wear their hair thus at the period.

17. *They speak French:* Soleure (German, Solothurn), where the French Ambassador resided, was strongly under French influence at the time.

18. *Au gros sel:* Served in the broth in which it was cooked and sprinkled with coarse salt.

19. Several Latin translations of this originally Greek distich exist. It is carved on one of the pillars of Petrarch's tomb at Arquà.

20. *Euripides:* The lines are not by Euripides but by some unknown Greek poet.

21. *V . . . :* C. first wrote and then crossed out "de Rol." The woman in question was the Baroness Marie Anne Louise (Ludovika) Roll von Emmenholtz (died 1825).

22. *Married:* According to the parish register she married a relative of the same name, Baron Urs Victor Joseph Roll von Emmenholtz (1711-1786), but not until July 29, 1769. It is possible that the year was incorrectly entered in the register and that the date was 1759. C. subsequently calls her only "Madame . . ." and her husband only "M." In the translation these forms have been regularized as "Madame . . ." and "Monsieur . . ." throughout.


CHAPTER V

1. *Two . . . sons:* Of these, only one is documented: Anton Ott (1748-1800), who inherited the inn from his father.

2. *Imhof:* Johann Christoph Imhof, proprietor of the "Zu den Drei Königen" inn in Basel from 1739 to 1765.

3. *Chavigny:* Anne Théodore Chavignard, Chevalier de Chavigny, Baron of Usson and Count of Toulongeon (1689-1771), French diplomat, Ambassador in Switzerland from 1753 to 1762. From 1522 the French Ambassador in Switzerland always resided in Soleure (Solothurn).

4. *Our Order:* The Rosicrucian Brotherhood (cf. Vol. 5, Chap. XI, n. 40).

5. *Passe-dix:* Game played with 3 dice; the winner must lead by more than 10 points.

6. *Escher:* J. Escher, merchant at Berg, near Zurich. The document mentioned in note 24 to Chap. III of this volume is signed by him.

7. *Baden:* Watering place on the Limmat in the canton of Aargau, some 15 miles northwest of Zurich.

8. *Papal Nuncio:* Lucerne was the seat of the nunciature for the Catholic cantons; from Nov. 1759 to Aug. 1760 the office of *administratore* was held by Niccolò Cassoni. He was succeeded as Nuncio by Niccolò Oddi, who had previously held the same office in Cologne.

9. *Fribourg:* German, Freiburg; town southwest of Bern, on the linguistic frontier between German and French Switzerland. C.'s accounts of his travels are puzzling; from Zurich by way of Baden, Lucerne, and Fribourg to Soleure is four times as long a journey as from Zurich to Soleure direct. Perhaps he confused the dates, for on his later journey to Lausanne he necessarily passed through Fribourg.

10. *Count d'Affry's wife:* Presumably the Countess Marie Elisabeth d'Affry, née von Alt (died 1778), wife of the French Ambassador in The Hague. She came from a noble family of the canton of Fribourg; D'Affry owned the château of Saint-Barthélémy there and died there in 1793.

11. *A man . . . going in:* This ancient wooing custom, called *Kiltgang* in Switzerland and *Fensterln* in Bavaria, is still practiced.

12. *Post . . . in Soleure:* The then celebrated Auberge de la Couronne was also the post station in Soleure.

13. *"The Court":* In the 16th century part of the Franciscan monastery in Soleure was rebuilt as the residence of the French Ambassador and was thereafter known as "Maison de France" or "Cour des Ambassadeurs."

14. *Duchess of Gramont:* The Duchess Béatrix de Gramont (1730-1794) was the sister of the Duke of Choiseul.

15. *Thirty years:* C. is in error: the Marquis de Chavigny was French Ambassador in Venice from 1750 to 1751; however,

he had traveled in Italy on diplomatic missions (Genoa, Modena, Naples, Florence) from 1719 to 1722, that is, some 40 years before C. made his acquaintance in Soleure.

16. *The Regency:* The Duke of Orléans was Regent from the death of Louis XIV in 1715 until the minority of the Dauphin (later Louis XV) ended in 1723.

17. *Stringhetta:* Name of a Venetian courtesan celebrated ca. 1730.

18. *Vis-à-vis:* A light carriage with 2 facing seats.

19. *Coppers:* Text: *liards.* The liard was a copper coin worth one fourth of a sou.

20. *Twenty sous:* 20 sous are equivalent to one franc or livre.

21. *The . . . joke:* The marks of elision presumably stand for some unprintable adjective.

22. *L'Écossaise:* Voltaire's comedy *Le Café ou l'Écossaise* was published in April 1760 as a translation from the English of a "M. Hume." Voltaire at first denied being the author of it. The first performance in Paris was given on July 26, 1760. The heroine of the play is the beautiful Scottish girl Lindane, who is beloved by Murray; Monrose is her father; and Lady Alton appears as an intriguing and jealous woman who tries to win Murray.

23. *She:* I.e., Madame F.

24. *Voltaire:* Voltaire was enamored of the theater, often produced plays in his house, and acted in them himself.

25. *L'Écossaise,* Act 5, Scene 3. C. misquotes slightly.

26. *Ibid.* C. again misquotes slightly.

27. *De Seingalt:* C. first wrote "de Casanova," crossed it out, and substituted "de Seingalt." This is the first time he gives himself this name in his memoirs.

28. *Sternutative:* A substance which provokes sneezing.

29. *Herrenschwandt:* Johann Friedrich von Herrenschwandt (1715-1798), physician to the Swiss Guards Regiment in Paris, physician in ordinary to the King.

30. *His brother:* Only one brother of Herrenschwandt's is known, and he was a celebrated economist. Possibly he had another brother who practiced medicine in Soleure.

31. *Monsieur F.:* Text: *M. F.* Probably a slip of C.'s for "Mme F." Madame F. was a widow.

32. *Swiss Guards:* A select corps which formed part of the King's household troops. It goes back to the Swiss mercenaries hired by Louis XI and his successors. The post of Colonel-général des Suisses et Grisons, created in 1571, was of great importance. Choiseul was not appointed to it until Feb. 24, 1762.

33. *A cousin:* François Joseph Roll von Emmenholtz, officer in the French service from 1759.

34. *La Muette:* Royal hunting lodge in Passy (now the 16th Arrondissement of Paris). The last traces of it vanished in 1926.

35. *The Duke her father:* Probably an error on C.'s part. The Duke of Choiseul, to whom as minister the appeal was made, was the Duchess of Gramont's brother, not her father.

36. *Chauvelin:* François Claude, Marquis de Chauvelin (1716-1773), French commander; Ambassador in Genoa (1747-1753) and Turin (1754-1765); friend of Louis XV and Voltaire.

37. *"Les Délices":* In 1755 Voltaire bought a property near Geneva, changing its name from "Saint Jean" to "Les Délices"; it is now within the Geneva city limits and is the seat of the Musée Voltaire. In the same year he rented a country house in Montrion, near Lausanne, but in 1757 also took a house in Lausanne itself. Finally, in 1758, he bought the small château of Ferney, north of Geneva, and from then on lived now at one of these properties, now at another, but most frequently at "Les Délices." In 1760 he gave them all up except Ferney, which remained his permanent residence until his death.

CHAPTER VI

1. *Quadrille:* An old card game for 4 persons, played with the 40 cards remaining after the eights, nines, and tens are discarded.

2. *Fine house:* Until recently it was assumed that this was the château of Waldeck, built in the 16th century by Jean Victor de Besenval de Brunnstatt. But since that property served in the 18th century as the summer residence of the

French Ambassador, the assumption must be abandoned. Presumably the house was the château of Rienberg, which belonged to the Roll family and was demolished in 1798; C.'s description of the building and grounds supports this assumption.

3. *In the service of the French Ambassador:* In Vol. 4, Chaps. III and IV, C. says that De Bernis had a French cook, but does not name him.

4. *Neuchâtel:* Town at the north end of the Lac de Neuchâtel (Neuenburger See), with many vineyards in the vicinity.

5. *"La Côte":* The shore of the Lac de Neuchâtel which lies in the canton of Vaud; it is still famous for its wines.

6. *Madame d'Hermenches:* Louise d'Hermenches, Baroness de Constant de Rebecque (died 1772); her husband, David Louis d'Hermenches, whom she married in 1754, was a friend of Voltaire's.

7. *Lady Montagu:* C. writes "Miladi Montaigu"; probably Elizabeth Montagu, née Robinson (1720-1800), English woman of letters, who, however, did not have a title; it is also possible that C. means Lady Mary Wortley Montagu (1689-1762), though she lived in Italy until 1761.

8. *Roxburghe:* C. writes "de Rosburi"; probably John Ker, Duke of Roxburghe (1740-1804).

9. *Lebel:* Obviously an invented name, as is "Madame Dubois"; the manuscript shows that C. started to write a different name here, then decided on "Lebel" (which in other places he writes "Le-bel").

10. *Admirable conquest:* Ironically, of Madame F.

11. *Locke:* C. writes "Loke"; John Locke (1632-1704), English philosopher.

12. *L'Hospital:* Paul François Galucci de l'Hospital, Marquis de Châteauneuf-sur-Cher (1697-1776), from 1741 to 1762 French Envoy Extraordinary to the Court of the Czarina (see the next note).

13. *Elisabeth Petrovna:* Daughter (1709-1762) of Peter the Great, Czarina from 1741.

14. *The:* The text has *"du,"* which is either a typographical error or shows that C. changed his construction in the middle of the sentence.

15. *Nivernais:* Louis Jules Henri Barton Mancini-Mazarini, Duke of Nivernais and Donziois (1716-1798), French diplomat; he was Envoy Extraordinary to the English Court during the negotiations for the peace treaty (Sept. 15, 1762 - May 11, 1763) which ended the Seven Years' War.

16. *Court of St. James's:* A frequent designation for the English Court (from St. James's palace).

17. *Whose acquaintance I had made . . . in Versailles:* C. probably met the Marquis de Chauvelin (cf. note 36 to Chap. V of this volume) on one of the latter's periodical trips from Turin when he was serving as Ambassador there.

18. *His charming wife:* Agnèse Thérèse, née Mazzade, Marquise de Chauvelin (born ca. 1741).

19. *Poem on the Seven Deadly Sins:* Published in 1758, and attributed to the Abbé Philippe de Chauvelin (ca. 1716-1770), brother of the Marquis. C.'s translation of it into the Venetian dialect (*I sette Capitali, canzone*) was preserved among his papers at Dux. According to other sources the Marquis himself was the author of the poem, which he composed at the Prince de Conti's estate of L'Isle-Adam when he was there alone with 7 beautiful women.

20. *Égérie:* Cf. Vol. 5, Chap. V, n. 33.

21. *Megaera:* Name of one of the three Furies.

22. *Styx:* A river in Hades; its water was held to be poisonous.

23. *Eau des Carmes: Aqua carmelitarum,* melissa cordial, whose manufacture was formerly the secret of the Carmelite nuns. Highly reputed as a medicament in the 18th century.

## CHAPTER VII

1. *Twentieth:* To this date (1760) in his memoirs C. has recorded 8 such infections.

2. *Secrets:* Possibly a reference to C.'s being a Freemason or to his activities as a secret agent.

3. *Minerva . . . Telemachus:* In the *Odyssey* Pallas Athena (in Roman mythology, Minerva) frequently gives Odysseus' son Telemachus good advice. But rather than the *Odyssey,* C. very probably had in mind Fénelon's celebrated didactic novel *Les Aventures de Télémaque* (first published in 1690).

4. *Anacreon:* Greek poet from Teos in Ionia (5th century B.C.), whose principal subjects were wine and love.
5. *Smerdis, Cleobulus, . . . Bathyllus:* Three youths whose beauty Anacreon praises.
6. *A Platonist:* C. doubtless refers to the Renaissance interpreters of the Platonic dialogues, who made an oversimplified distinction between sensual and so-called "Platonic" love.
7. *The whites:* Leukorrhea.
8. *Nuncio:* Cf. note 8 to Chap. V of this volume.
9. *Coronation:* Leopold II was crowned Emperor at Prague on Sept. 6, 1791.
10. Vergil, *Georgics,* III, 67.
11. *Eau de nitre:* A solution of saltpeter.
12. *Dine at my house with Madame . . . and her husband:* The text has *dîner chez moi la . . . et son mari,* which makes no sense; the "with" of the translation is a conjecture based on C.'s account of the incident earlier in this chapter.
13. *Muralt:* Bernard de Muralt (1709-1780), from 1760 Avoyer of Thun, a district of the canton of Bern; the title of "Avoyer" (the word has the same root as "advocate") was given to the highest magistrates of some Swiss cantons. The castle of Thun was the official residence of the Burgomaster of Bern.
14. *"Falcon" inn:* Well-known hostelry in the Judengasse (now Rue de la Préfecture). A letter from Muralt to Haller shows that C. lodged at the "Crown" ("La Couronne"). (See the Appendix.) Neither hostelry exists today.

CHAPTER VIII

1. *River:* Bern is situated on a sort of peninsula in a deep valley cut by the Aar.
2. *Baths:* The "de la Matte" or "Lammat" baths in the lower town were also houses of prostitution. The street is still named "An der Matte."
3. *Aeneid,* I, 203; the original reads *olim* instead of C.'s *aliquando.*
4. *Library:* The municipal and university library of Bern is

still in the same building in Kesslergasse; it was earlier a Franciscan monastery.

5. *Felix:* Fortunato Bartolomeo Felix, or de Felice (1723-1789), of Italian descent; first a Catholic priest, in 1755 he fled from a monastery to which he had been confined; he later turned Protestant and became a celebrated publisher in Switzerland (Yverdon).

6. *Schmid:* Friedrich Samuel Schmid (1737-1796), Swiss antiquarian, in the service of the Margrave Karl Friedrich von Baden-Durlach.

7. *A man learned in natural history:* Probably Élie Bertrand (1713-1797), natural historian and theologian; he was pastor of the French church in Bern from 1744 to 1765.

8. *Madame de Sacconay:* Rose Marie de Sacconay, née Wurstemberger, married to Charles Frédéric de Sacconay (1714-1778), Swiss statesman and commander.

9. *Dress well . . . speak . . . French:* French is still learned in Bern as a matter of course. The laws of the time forbade the inhabitants of Bern to wear gold or silver embroidery, precious stones, lace, or costly furs.

10. *Three weeks:* Bernard de Muralt's letter to Haller of June 21, 1760, implies that C. spent about 2 months in Bern. If this is so, he cannot have stayed in Soleure as long as he says he did.

11. *Boerhaave:* See Vol. 5, Chap. IX, n. 3.

12. *The stone:* The philosopher's stone.

13. *Hippocrates:* Celebrated Greek physician (460 - ca. 370 B.C.).

14. *Bear:* The arms of the city of Bern display a bear.

15. *Second:* In 1760 the Swiss Confederation was made up of 13 cantons, among which an imperial decree of 1361 had made Zurich the first; Bern came second, though its territory was far larger, covering about one third of Switzerland.

16. *Near that of the Rhine:* The sources of the Aar and the Rhine are some 20 miles apart as the crow flies.

17. *Four:* The administration of certain cantons was then divided among several different political bodies (Neuchâtel, for example).

18. Horace, *Carm.*, III, 29, 16.

19. *Grisons:* The group of immigrants from the canton of Grisons (most of them artisans) were not officially banished from Venice until 1766, but after the expiration of the treaty of alliance and friendship in 1706 difficulties had been made for them, principally at the instigation of the guilds.

20. *Madame de la Saône:* Marie Anne, Marquise de la Saône, also Sône (ca. 1723-1772); married in 1745 to Aymar Félicien de Boffin, Marquis de la Saône (died after 1772).

21. *Thirty:* She was born at the latest in 1723, so at the time she met C. she was at least 37 years old.

22. *Rue Neuve des Petits-Champs:* Former continuation of the present Rue des Petits-Champs (1st Arrondissement); it no longer exists.

23. *Milk . . . first childbed:* She bore her first child in 1746. The belief that her milk could enter the bloodstream and cause numerous diseases in a young mother was widely held, though it is medically untenable.

24. *Paris Faculty:* The Medical Faculty of the University of Paris.

25. *Phidias:* The most famous of Greek sculptors (5th century B.C.).

26. *Paros:* The famous marble quarries of Greek antiquity were on the island of Paros in the Aegean Sea.

27. *Mingard:* Jean Pierre Daniel Mingard, Protestant pastor in Lausanne. The son here mentioned could be either Jean Isaac Samuel (1739-1777) or Jean François Abraham (born 1737).

28. *Langallerie:* The Marquis Gentil de Langallerie (died 1773). He was the illegitimate son of the Landgrave Wilhelm VIII of Hesse and the Marquise de Langallerie; he lived in the villa "Mon Repos" near Lausanne.

29. *Bavois:* David de Saussure, Baron de Bercher et de Bavois (1700-1767), of Swiss descent, was first an officer in the French army, then one of the 4 colonels of the militia of Bern.

30. *Monsieur de M. F.:* Louis de Muralt-Favre (1716-1789), cousin of Bernard de Muralt; Swiss diplomat and high government official; married Sara Favre in 1745.

31. *Council of Two Hundred:* The so-called "Great Council" of Geneva had 200 members; it was founded in 1526 and survived as a governing body until 1798.

32. *Sara:* Anna Sara de Muralt-Favre was not born until 1750. The reference is probably to her older sister Marguerite.

33. *Roxburghe:* See note 8 to Chap. VI of this volume.

34. *Haller:* Albrecht von Haller (1708-1777), Swiss physician, botanist, and poet, professor at the University of Göttingen from 1736 to 1753, ennobled in 1749 by the Emperor Franz I. In addition to important works in natural history he composed a volume of poems, *Versuch schweizerischer Gedichte*, which included his well-known didactic poem on the Alps.

35. *Roche:* In the upper valley of the Rhone, some 7 miles south of Montreux.

36. *Sacred fire:* St. Anthony's fire—erysipelas.

37. *Herrenschwandt:* See note 29 to Chap. V of this volume; he lived in the château of Greng, near Murten.

38. *The inn:* Probably the "Zum schwarzen Adler," which still exists; it is on the principal street, near the city gate.

39. *Avenches:* Some 7 miles from Murten, on the road to Lausanne.

40. *The famous battle:* At the Battle of Murten the Confederation defeated the troops of Charles the Bold of Burgundy on June 22, 1476.

41. *. . . Anno 1476:* C.'s laughter seems to be due to the fact that the word *sui*, the genitive of the third person reflexive pronoun, can be taken as the dative singular of *sus, suis*, "hog," in which case the latter part of the inscription would mean "left this monument to a hog." The ossuary was rebuilt as a chapel in 1755; in 1798 it was destroyed by a Burgundian regiment. In 1822 the Confederation erected a memorial obelisk.

42. *Three great sieges:* Murten was besieged and destroyed for the first time in 1033-34. In the 14th century the fortified town was the headquarters of the Bernese troops fighting against Fribourg. In 1476 it was besieged by Charles the Bold.

43. *Montaigne:* The reference is probably to Montaigne, *Essais*, I, 25 ("On Pedants").

44. *Romansh:* The language of the Grisons. Ladin, a Romansh

dialect, was made the fourth official language of Switzerland in 1938.

45. *Stocking-seller:* Madame Baret (cf. Vol. 5, Chap. XI).

## CHAPTER IX

1. *Morgagni:* Giovanni Battista Morgagni (1682-1771), professor at the University of Padua; the founder of pathological anatomy.
2. *Pontedera:* Giuliano Pontedera (1688-1757), professor at the University of Padua. Only 3 of his letters to Haller have survived.
3. *Whose milk I had sucked:* C. doubtless attended lectures by Morgagni and Pontedera when he was a student in Padua (1738-1741).
4. *Almost indecipherable:* His surviving letters to Haller are perfectly legible.
5. *Pindaric:* In the manner of the Greek poet Pindar (521-441 B.C.), whose odes were imitated in the modern languages from the 16th century. C. alludes to Haller's poem *Die Alpen* ("The Alps").
6. *After losing his first:* Haller married three times: first Marianne Wyss (died 1736), then in 1738 Elisabeth Bühner (died 1739), and in 1741 Sophie Amalie Charlotte Teichmeyer, daughter of a doctor in Jena.
7. *A pretty daughter:* Haller had several daughters, among them two whose birth dates come closest to fitting C.'s "eighteen years of age": Friederike Amalia Katharina (born 1742) and Charlotte (born 1743).
8. *His works:* No collected edition of Haller's works was ever published. Perhaps C. saw the *Sammlung kleiner Schriften,* published at Bern in 1756.
9. Horace, *Carmina,* III, 2, 26-28.
10. "From a distance it is something, near by it is nothing."— La Fontaine, *Fables,* IV, 10.
11. *Favorite pupil:* Haller studied medicine under the famous physician Hermann Boerhaave (1668-1738) at the University of Leiden from 1725 to 1726.
12. From the article on death entitled "Medicinae limites"

("The Limits of Medicine") in *Flos Medicinae Scholae Salerni*, X, II, 2.

13. *Madame:* C. follows this with neither name nor initial, but the reference must be to the unnamed 85-year-old lady who had known Boerhaave and whose reminiscences of him C. records in the previous chapter of this volume.

14. *Philosopher's stone:* C. writes "pierre *philosophorum*."

15. *Twenty-two letters:* No letters either from or to Haller have been found among C.'s papers.

16. *Died prematurely:* Haller died in 1777 at the age of 70.

17. *Héloïse: Julie, ou la Nouvelle Héloïse* was not published until early in 1761. Perhaps Haller had access to a copy of the manuscript, which was completed in Jan. 1760. Or perhaps C. took Haller's critique from a letter written later and inserted it here.

18. *Pays de Vaud:* The present canton of Vaud (German Waadt); it embraces the territory north and east of Lake Geneva.

19. *Petrarch:* Francesco Petrarca (1304-1374), Italian poet, scholar, and humanist. His Latin works have been unjustly neglected in favor of his poems in Italian.

20. *Laura:* Many of Petrarch's Italian poems celebrate his love of a beautiful "Laura"; she may have been Laure de Noves, who was married to Hugues de Sade, of Avignon, in 1325 and died in 1348.

21. *Bercher . . . Bavois:* David de Saussure, Baron de Bercher et de Bavois (1700-1767), was the uncle of Louis, Baron de Bavois, who had been serving as an officer in the Venetian army from 1752 (cf. especially Vol. 3, Chaps. V and VI).

22. *Act in his plays:* Voltaire often had his plays acted by members of Bernese society at one of his own houses or at "Mon Repos," the villa of his friend the Marquis de Langallerie.

23. *Alzire:* Tragedy by Voltaire, first performed in 1736.

24. *Gave up the houses:* Voltaire gave up his houses in Montrion and Lausanne in 1760 and thereafter lived at Ferney, some 7 miles north of Geneva and on French soil (cf. note 37 to Chap. V of this volume).

25. *Lord Roxburghe:* C. writes "le lord de Rosburi"; see note 8 to Chap. VI of this volume.

26. *The famous Fox:* This cannot be the celebrated Charles James Fox (1749-1806), who was only 11 years of age in 1760. C. must refer to his elder brother, Stephen Fox (1744 - ca. 1775).

27. *Madame Martin:* Wife of Pierre Henri Martin, banker in Turin; he married her in 1758, when he was already an old man; she was much his junior.

28. *Same city:* I.e., Lausanne.

29. *A girl eleven or twelve years old:* Probably Louise Elisabeth de Sacconay (born 1744).

30. *Déforme:* No such adjective exists in French, which, however, does have the adjective *informe* and the past participle *déformé.*

31. *Socrates:* Socrates's supposed opinions concerning beauty are set forth in Plato's *Phaedrus.*

32. *Nattier:* Jean Marc Nattier (1685-1766), French portrait painter.

33. *Eighty:* C. is in error, for Nattier was only 65 years of age in 1750.

34. *Mesdames de France:* Title of the daughters of the French King (cf. Vol. 3, Chap. IX, n. 44).

35. *Two leagues:* C.'s "league" is approximately 2½ miles.

36. *Calvin:* Jean Calvin (1509-1564), founder of the reformed church in France and Switzerland; from 1535 he lived and worked in Geneva, where he enforced a very strict code of morals.

37. *So designated:* The inscription was on a bronze tablet affixed not to the church but to the town hall of Geneva; it begins: *"Quum anno 1535 profligata romani antichristi tirannide . . ."* It was removed under the French rule in 1798 and not again affixed to a wall of the Cathedral of St. Peter until 1900.

38. *The "Scales":* The *"Zur Waage"* inn (*"À la balance"*) was opened in 1726 and was considered the best in Geneva; it was located in the present Rue du Rhône.

39. *August 20, 1760:* The date is improbable. In a letter dated July 7, 1760, Voltaire already referred to a person who must certainly be C. In addition, on June 25, 1760, C. wrote Muralt from Lausanne that he stayed there only 2 weeks. It would seem that he made 2 stays in Geneva.

40. *Thirteen years:* The parting took place in the winter of 1749-50 (cf. Vol. 3, Chap. V).

41. *Her:* I.e., Henriette.

42. *French écus:* The *gros écu,* which was worth 6 francs.

43. *Villars Chandieu:* Charles Barthélémy de Villars Chandieu (1735-1773), married Louise Elisabeth de Sacconay (cf. note 28 to this chapter) in 1762.

44. *His young niece:* Probably the orphaned Anne Marie May (born 1731), who later married a certain Gabriel von Wattenwyl.

45. *Through the ears:* This notion is attributable to some of his interpreters rather than to Augustine himself.

CHAPTER X

1. *Algarotti:* Francesco Algarotti (1712-1764), given the title of Count by Frederick the Great in 1740; born in Venice, he was a well-known writer and critic of the Enlightenment (cf. note 3).

2. *Padua:* Algarotti left the Prussian Court in 1753 and thereafter lived in Mirabello, near Padua.

3. *Ladies:* Algarotti's best-known work was *Il Newtonianismo per le dame ovvero Dialoghi sopra la luce ed i colori* ("Newtonianism for ladies, or Dialogues on light and colors"); following the example of Fontenelle, to whom the book was dedicated, it attempted to make scientific knowledge accessible to non-specialists. It was first printed at Naples in 1737.

4. *Pluralité des mondes:* Fontenelle's *Entretiens sur la pluralité des mondes* ("Conversations on the Plurality of Worlds") (Paris, 1686) was the first attempt in modern times to put scientific material into literary form and so give it a general audience.

5. *His letters on Russia:* The reference is to Algarotti's *Viaggi in Russia* ("Travels in Russia"), which was published at Venice in 1760. The second edition (Paris, 1763) was entitled *Saggio di Lettere sulla Russia.* Voltaire was then composing his history of Russia in the time of Peter the Great (*Histoire de l'Empire de Russie sous Pierre-le-Grand*).

6. *Livy . . . Patavinity:* Titus Livius (59 B.C. - A.D. 17), famous Roman historian; he came from Padua (Latin, Patavium), whence "Patavinity," the dialect of that city.

7. *Lazzarini:* Domenico Lazzarini (1668-1734), Professor of Greek and Latin at the University of Padua.

8. *Sallust:* Gaius Sallustius Crispus (86 - ca. 35 B.C.), Roman historian.

9. *Ulisse il giovane:* "The Young Ulysses," written in 1720; C. was 9 years old when he first went to Padua in April 1734; Lazzarini died in July of the same year.

10. *Conti:* Antonio Schinella Conti (1677-1749), Italian poet. He had met Newton in London in 1715; his four tragedies, *Giunio Bruto, Marco Bruto, Giulio Cesare,* and *Druso,* were posthumously published in 1 volume (Florence, 1751).

11. *Procrustes:* Legendary highwayman of Attica, who bound his victims on an iron bed and either stretched or cut off their legs to make them fit it; whence the metaphorical expression "the bed of Procrustes."

12. *Have not one:* This dictum of Voltaire's only shows that he was as little appreciative as most of his contemporaries of French Renaissance poetry.

13. *Your strictures on him:* In his *Essai sur la poésie épique* (1726) Voltaire had placed Tasso far above Ariosto.

14. *Astolpho . . . St. John the Apostle:* In Ariosto's *Orlando furioso* Astolpho makes a fantastic journey to the moon to recover the mad Orlando's wits. In the course of it he meets St. John the Apostle. C. refers to Canto XXXIV, 61 ff., and Canto XXXV, 3 ff., of the *Orlando furioso.*

15. *Orlando furioso,* XLIV, 2. Voltaire included his translation, with minor changes, in the article "Épopée" in his *Dictionnaire philosophique* (1764). There he also praises Ariosto in the highest terms (cf. note 13 to this chapter).

16. *Madame Denis:* Louise Denis, née Mignot (1712-1790), Voltaire's niece; after her husband's death in 1744 she lived with Voltaire, who made her his sole heir; her second marriage (1780) was to a Commissary of War named Duvivier.

17. *Went mad too:* Ariosto did not go mad; C. may be momentarily confusing him with Tasso, who did.

18. *Fifty-one:* The first edition of the *Orlando furioso* (1516)

contains 40 cantos; the final edition (1532) contains 46. The edition of 1545, brought out by Ariosto's son Virgilio, added 5 cantos of an epic similar in form and theme, which Ariosto had begun late in his life. So C. is justified in his "fifty-one."

19. *Orlando furioso*, XXIII, 122, 1-4.

20. *Angelica . . . Medoro:* Characters in the *Orlando furioso*. Orlando, who is passionately in love with Angelica, the daughter of an Oriental king and magician, discovers that she had given her love to the simple shepherd Medoro.

21. *Leo X:* Giovanni de' Medici (1475-1521), as Pope Leo X (from 1513), the great patron of the poets and artists of the Italian Renaissance.

22. *Este . . . Medici:* The Medici family in Florence and the Este family in Ferrara were the greatest fosterers of the arts in the Italy of the 15th and 16th centuries. Ariosto lived at the Este Court, as did Tasso later.

23. *Donation of Rome:* The so-called Donation of Constantine, a forged document of the 8th century, declares that the Emperor Constantine the Great, under whose rule Christianity was made the state religion of the Roman Empire, had conferred imperial rank and temporal rule over Rome and Italy on Pope Sylvester I.

24. *Sylvester:* St. Sylvester, Pope from 314 to 355.

25. *Orlando furioso*, XXXIV, 80, 6, where the original reads: *or putia forte*. The fact that the "Donation of Constantine" was a forgery was discovered by the Italian humanist Lorenzo Valla (1406-1457); hence Ariosto's *or* ("now").

26. *The hermit . . . Zerbino:* Characters in the *Orlando furioso*. "The African" is Rodomonte. The death of the hermit is described in XXIX, 6-7, whereas the line C. proceeds to quote is from the episode of Orlando killing the shepherds (XXIV, 6, 4).

27. *Syndic:* Title of the four highest officers of the commune of Geneva. Here perhaps Michel Lullin de Châteauvieux (born 1695), who, as "Seigneur scolarque," controlled the publication of books and in that capacity frequently had dealings with Voltaire.

28. *Quinze:* A card game in which the player who ends with 15 points or the closest approximation to it is the winner.

29. *"Les Délices":* Name of Voltaire's house near Geneva (cf. note 37 to Chap. V of this volume).

30. *Villars:* Honoré Armand, Duke of Villars (1702-1770), French general and Governor of Provence; from 1734 member of the Académie Française.

31. *Tronchin:* Théodore Tronchin (1709-1781), celebrated Swiss physician; connected with the well-known banking family of the same name.

32. *Dent Blanche:* Mont Blanc.

33. *Pupil:* Tronchin entered the University of Leiden in 1728 and obtained his doctorate there in 1730.

34. *Seventy:* Villars was 58 years of age in 1760.

35. *Regency:* The period of the Regency (1715-1723) was characterized by a relaxation in manners after the formal etiquette of the Court of Louis XIV.

36. *Summa:* The *Summa theologiae* of Thomas Aquinas (1226-1274), the great monument of Scholasticism.

37. *Tassoni:* Alessandro Tassoni (1565-1635), Italian poet, famous especially for his heroi-comic epic *La Secchia rapita*, which narrates the bitter struggle between the cities of Modena and Bologna over a stolen pail.

38. *Discorsi academici:* C. doubtless means Tassoni's *Dieci libri di pensieri diversi* (1620), in which he attacks the Copernican system.

39. *Criticized . . . Petrarch:* In his *Considerazioni sopra le rime del Petrarca* (1609) Tassoni launches his satiric barbs at Petrarch's innumerable imitators rather than at Petrarch himself.

40. *Muratori:* Lodovico Antonio Muratori (1672-1750), Italian historian and literary critic. He also attacked Petrarchism.

41. Horace, *Epistles*, II, 1, 63.

42. *Fifty thousand:* Voltaire's extant letters number 20,054.

43. *Merlin Cocai:* Pseudonym of Teofilo Folengo (1496[?]-1544); cf. Vol. 1, Chap. VIII, n. 4. He was a native of Mantua.

44. *A famous poem: Il Baldus*, a comic epic in macaronic Latin, of which there were 4 revisions, published in 1517, 1521, 1540, and 1552, respectively.

45. *Cramers:* The brothers Gabriel Cramer (1723-1793) and Philibert Cramer (1727-1779), printers and publishers in

Geneva. From 1756 to 1775 they published nearly all of
Voltaire's writings. Voltaire released all his author's rights
to them in exchange for an unlimited number of author's
copies.

46. *La Princesse de Babylone:* It was first published in 1768;
hence C.'s statement is erroneous.

47. *Three young ladies:* Perhaps Pernette Elisabeth de Fernex
(born 1730), her sister Marie (born 1732), and their cousin
Jeanne Christine (born 1735); they belonged to an im-
poverished noble family, whose name was derived from the
estate of Fernex (Ferney), which Voltaire acquired in 1758.

48. *Grécourt:* Jean Baptiste Joseph Villaret de Grécourt
(1683-1743), Canon of Tours and poet. His licentious *Y grec*
("The Letter Y") reads in part:

> *Marc une béquille avait*
> *Faite en fourche, et de manière*
> *Qu'à la fois elle trouvait*
> *L'oeillet et la boutonnière.*
> *D'une indulgence plénière*
> *Il crut devoir se munir,*
> *Et courut, pour l'obtenir,*
> *Conter le cas au Saint-Père*
> *Qui s'écria: "Vierge Mère*
> *Que ne suis-je ainsi bâti!*
> *Va, mon fils, baise, prospère,*
> *Gaudeant bene nati!"*

49. *Teofilo Folengo:* Real name of the author of *Il Baldus* (cf.
notes 43 and 44 to this chapter).

50. *Doblones de a ocho:* Spanish gold coins of the weight and
value of 8 gold scudi.

51. *Capacelli:* The Marchese Francesco Albergati Capacelli
(1728-1804), Bolognese Senator, author of comedies.

52. *Paradisi:* Count Agostini Paradisi (1736-1783), Italian
scholar and poet.

53. *"Forty":* The Senate of Bologna was called the "Quaranta"
("Forty"), despite the fact that it numbered 50; the name
was also applied to its members.

54. *Goldoni:* Carlo Goldoni (1707-1793), famous Italian writer of comedies; friend of the Marchese Albergati Capacelli.

55. *Tancrède:* Voltaire's tragedy of this name was first produced in his house in 1759 and at the Comédie Française the next year.

56. *Theatromania:* Albergati had a private theater built in his villa at Zola Predosa, some 5 miles west of Bologna.

57. *Author:* In 1760 Albergati had only translated French comedies and tragedies. The first of his own comedies was not published until 1768.

58. *Noon . . . eleven o'clock:* Until 1791 the clocks of Basel were set an hour fast. All the various explanations of the fact appear to be apocryphal.

59. *Council of Ten . . . seventeen:* The Venetian Council of Ten included, in addition to its 10 official members, the Doge and his 6 councillors, making 17 in all.

60. *Poet to the Duke of Parma:* In 1756 the Duke of Parma commissioned Goldoni to write plays for the Court theater and gave him this title and a yearly pension of 700 francs.

61. *Advocate:* Goldoni had studied law in Pavia and Modena, became a Doctor utriusque iuris in 1731, and practiced as an advocate in Venice and Pisa (1733).

62. *Cuma:* Otherwise Cyme, an important port on the coast of Asia Minor; it was one of the 7 cities which claimed in antiquity to be the birthplace of Homer. C., who writes "Cume," perhaps confuses it with Cumae in Italy.

63. *Macaronicon:* Alternative title of Teofilo Folengo's *Il Baldus.*

64. *A Jesuit:* Antoine Adam, S.J. (1705 - after 1786); he was Voltaire's almoner from ca. 1764 to 1776.

65. *Clement of Alexandria:* Titus Flavius Clemens (2nd-3rd century), Father of the Church; he discusses modesty in Books II and III of his *Paidagogos.*

66. *The cousin:* C. first wrote *la cadette* ("the youngest"); the change substantiates the identifications proposed in note 47 to this chapter.

67. *Chapelain:* Jean Chapelain (1595-1674), French poet and literary critic, first Secretary of the Académie Française.

His epic poem *La Pucelle* ("The Maid"—i.e., Joan of Arc) was begun in 1630; the first 12 cantos were published in 1656.

68. *He disavowed it:* Voltaire finished his burlesque epic on Joan of Arc, *La Pucelle*, in 1739, but did not then dare to publish it. Though manuscript copies circulated in both Paris and Geneva, Voltaire denied his authorship of it. The first unauthorized editions began to appear from 1755 in Frankfurt, Geneva, London, and Paris. The first authorized edition was published by Cramer at Geneva in 1762. The work was condemned to be publicly burned in Paris in 1757.

69. *Crébillon:* Prosper Jolyot de Crébillon (1674-1762), French dramatist, Royal Censor from 1735 (cf. Vol. 3, Chap. VIII).

70. *Rhadamiste:* Crébillon's tragedy *Rhadamiste et Zénobie* (cf. Vol. 3, Chap. VIII).

71. *Martelli:* Pier Jacopo Martelli (1665-1727), Italian poet; he was the first to introduce an approximation of the French Alexandrine verse into Italian (see note 73, below).

72. *Works:* Pier Jacopo Martelli, *Opere,* 7 vols., Bologna, 1729-1733.

73. *Fourteen syllables:* The French Alexandrine has 12 syllables (not counting the allowable unaccented syllable after the caesura and the obligatory unaccented syllable in the rhyme words of every second pair of lines). Martelli's equivalent contains, according to Italian metrical reckoning, 14 syllables —the so-called *verso martelliano* (cf. Vol. 4, Chap. VIII, n. 23).

74. Horace, *Satires,* I, 10, 74.

75. *Addison:* Joseph Addison (1672-1719), part author of the celebrated *Spectator* papers. He supported liberal ideas in his tragedy *Cato* (1713).

76. *Hobbes:* Thomas Hobbes (1588-1679), English philosopher. He defended absolute monarchy in his *Leviathan* (1651).

77. Altered from Horace, *Epistles,* II, 1, 63 (cf. note 41, above). Instead of *Est* the text here has *Et,* presumably a typographical error.

78. *Don Quixote:* The reference is to Miguel de Cervantes Saavedra (1547-1616), *El ingenioso Hidalgo Don Quijote de la Mancha,* Pt. I, Chap. XXII.

79. *Sumptuary laws:* Cf. note 9 to Chap. VIII.

80. *What I published against him:* Principally in C.'s *Scrutinio del libro "Éloges de M. de Voltaire"* (Venice, 1779).

81. *Zoilus:* Greek rhetorician from Amphipolis in Macedonia, probably flourished in the 3rd century B.C.; he was famous for his carping and malicious criticism of Homer.

82. *Annecy:* Town in Haute-Savoie (France), at the northwestern end of the lake of the same name, about 22 miles south of Geneva.

83. *Aix-en-Savoie:* Now Aix-les-Bains, watering place on the Lac du Bourget, with warm springs, some 20 miles from Annecy.

84. *Chambéry:* Capital of the old Duchy of Savoy, some 8 miles south of Aix-les-Bains.

85. *Pistoles:* The Piedmontese pistole, also pistola di Savoia or doppia di Piemonte, was a gold coin worth 24 Piedmontese lire.

86. *Gilbert:* He is not mentioned earlier in C.'s memoirs.

87. *The fountain:* The two thermal springs at Aix-les-Bains are on the hill to the east of the town. In 1760 they still flowed from caves hewn into the rock; the great pumproom was not built until 1782.

88. *Desarmoises:* There was a Charles des Armoises, Marquis d'Annoy, but he died childless in 1778; probably the reference is to Antoine Bernard Desarmoises (died ca. 1762).

CHAPTER XI

1. *Prié:* Giovanni Antonio I Turinetti, Marquis de Prié (Priero) et Pancalieri (1687-1753), Austrian statesman; from 1747 to 1753 Austrian Ambassador in Venice. His son Giovanni Antonio II Turinetti, Marquis de Prié et Pancalieri (1717-1781), was a then well-known gambler and libertine.

2. *The Chevalier Z:* Laforgue expanded this to "Zeroli," but the ms. gives only "Z."

3. *Scarnafigi:* C. writes *"un comte de Scarnafisch":* probably Giuseppe, Count of Ponte de Scarnafigi (died 1788), Sardinian Ambassador in Lisbon, London, Vienna, and Paris.

4. *Lisbonini:* Italian designation for the Portuguese dobra, a gold coin minted from 1722; value 4 escudos.

5. *Cou. . . :* C. here writes "Cou" but makes it "Cou. . ." later.

6. *Princess XXX:* The municipal archives of Chambéry have yielded no information concerning a princess who resided there at this time.

7. *The Bishop:* In 1760 Chambéry was not yet the seat of a bishopric (which it became in 1802) but was under the jurisdiction of the Bishop of Grenoble, as was the convent.

8. *Livret:* See note 24 to Chap. I of this volume.

9. *Sept et le va . . . quinze:* In faro *sept et le va* and *quinze et le va* signify respectively 7 and 15 times the original stake.

10. *A good face:* The text has *contenant,* presumably for *contenance.*

11. *Piedmontese lire:* The lira Savoiarda, a gold coin minted from 1561 and worth 20 soldi; the soldo was worth 12 denari.

12. *Castoreum:* A secretion of the beaver, used in medicine as a stimulant and antispasmodic.

13. *A pinch . . . to Madame . . . at Soleure:* See Chapter V of this volume.

14. *Repeating watch:* Watchmaking was already the principal industry in Savoy.

15. *Parolis de campagne:* The term means the original stake doubled.

16. *Trente et quarante:* A card game.

17. *Chevalier of . . . St. Louis:* The Order of St. Louis was established by Louis XIV in 1693 as a distinction for deserving officers.

18. *The wheel:* A sort of turntable in the walls of hospitals and conventual establishments; unwanted infants were left on it to be brought up as foundlings.

19. *Savoyan soldi:* The soldo di Savoia, a copper coin minted from 1561 and worth 12 denari.

20. *Smindyrides:* A citizen of Sybaris famous, even in that city of luxurious living, for his effeminacy.

21. *Roman bed:* A favorite article of furniture at the time, a sort of couch on which one ate in a semi-reclining position, after the Roman fashion.

# APPENDIX

## Bernard de Muralt's Letter to Albrecht von Haller*

Most honored sir and my very dear friend,

We have had staying here at the Crown for a couple of months a foreigner named Chevalier de Seingalt who was well recommended to me by the Marquis de Gentil on the strength of recommendations in his favor which he received from a lady of consequence in Paris. He left here day before yesterday for Lausanne, where he will stay for some time, and whence he proposes to visit you, being curious (1) to see you and (2) [to see] the saltworks. He asked me for a letter of recommendation to you, dear sir and friend, which I was prevented from writing before he left and which, in any case, I preferred to send you by post. This foreigner is worth your seeing and you will find him a really curious and interesting specimen. He is an enigma which we have not been able to decipher here, nor could we make out what manner of man he is. He does not know as much as you do, but he knows a great deal. He talks on all subjects with great spirit, and appears to have seen and read a prodigious amount. He is said to know all the oriental languages, of which I am not competent to judge. He had no direct letter of recommendation to anyone here. It appears that he did not wish

---

* *The first page of the original letter is reproduced facing page 195.*

to be known. He received a great many letters by post every day, wrote all morning, and told me that his correspondence was entirely concerned with matters of general interest, a system of accounting and a well-known formula for saltpeter.

He speaks French like an Italian, having been brought up in Italy. He told me the story of his life, too long for me to repeat it to you. He will tell it to you whenever you wish. He told me that he is a free man, a citizen of the world, that he obeyed the laws of all the sovereigns under whom he lived. He led an extremely well-regulated life here. His predominant interest, from what he told me, is natural history and chemistry. My cousin De Muralt, the adept, who was greatly attached to him and who has also given him a letter to you, supposes that he is the Count of Saint-Germain. He gave me proofs of his knowledge of the cabala which are astonishing if they are genuine and which would make him almost a sorcerer, but here I cite you my author; in short, he is a most singular personage. His clothes and appointments are of the best. After you, he intends to go and politely point out to Monsieur de Voltaire a large number of errors in his books. I do not know if so charitable a man will be to Voltaire's taste. When you have seen him do me the favor of telling me what you think of him. But, what will interest me more, please give me news of your doings and your health. . . .

                                        B. de Muralt

Bern, June 21, 1760